Check for abbreviations that should be spelled out
Use adverb form to modify verbs and other modifiers (524, 526)
Check agreement of subject and verb, pronoun and antecedent (499, 512)
Check for omission or misuse of apostrophe (567)
Check for words that should be capitalized (571–572)
Strengthen sequence of ideas; show relevance of detail (47, 387–398, 402–404)
Expression is too colloquial for its context (425)
Use semicolon or period between independent clauses (587)
Check for awkward, inaccurate, inappropriate wording (409, 424–427, 434–445)
Define or explain abstract and technical terms (151 ff)
Develop your point more fully—support, explain, illustrate (393–403)
Check dictionary for syllabication of the word (554)
Rewrite the sentence to indicate what the modifier modifies (529)
Check for unemphatic, anticlimactic diction or organization (398, 464)
Do not puctuate as a sentence—lacks an independent clause (580)
Put items joined by "and," "but," "or" in same grammatical category (541–542)
Check standing of debatable usage in glossary (620 ff)
Check for unsatisfactory forms or constructions (486 ff)
Check for unidiomatic, un-English expression (415)
Rewrite the sentence to make it clearer or more natural (468–472, 474)
Check for faulty or unnecessary capitalization (571–572)
Examine for logical weaknesses (181 ff)
Shift modifier into more appropriate position or rewrite sentence (528)
Check for omission or misuse of punctuation (577 ff)
Break up into paragraphs that reflect organization (387 ff)
Avoid confusing or unnecessary paragraph break (387 ff)
Check reference of pronouns (512–515)
Avoid unnecessary or awkward repetition (474)
Check faulty predication, incomplete or mixed construction (531–539)
Check for inadequate or inappropriate subordination (457–458, 471–472)
Check for shift in time or use of pronouns, shift to passive (544–547)
Expression is too slangy for its context (426)
Check for spelling errors (557 ff)
Use appropriate tense of verb (506–508, 544)
Strengthen transition from point to point (47–56, 389)
Remove deadwood (435, 468)
Correct obvious error
Correct obvious omission
Use punctuation mark indicated (see reference chart, 578)

THIRD EDITION

Words and Ideas

Hans P. Guth

California State University,
San Jose

THIRD EDITION

Words and Ideas

Note: In this 1972 printing of Words and Ideas, *third edition, footnote and bibliography style has been brought into harmony with recommendations in* The MLA Style Sheet, *second edition (1970).*

Hans P. Guth, *Words and Ideas*, Third Edition.

L. C. Cat. Card No.: 69–18083

Printed in the United States of America

4 5 6 7 8 9 10 – 74

ACKNOWLEDGMENTS

I am indebted to the following for permission to reprint copyrighted material:

George Allen & Unwin Ltd. for permission to use a passage from Bertrand Russell, *Mysticism and Logic.*

The American Historical Association for permission to use a passage from Carl L. Becker, "Everyman His Own Historian," *The American Historical Review*, January 1932.

The American Scholar for permission to use passages from articles by Neal W. Klausner, Joseph Wood Krutch, Donald J. Lloyd, and Philip M. Wagner.

Maxwell Anderson for permission to use a passage from his article "It Comes with the Set," *New York Herald Tribune*, September 6, 1957.

Appleton-Century-Crofts, Inc., for permission to use a passage from *A History of the English Language*, second edition, by Albert C. Baugh. Copyright © 1957, Appleton-Century-Crofts, Inc.

The Atlantic Monthly for permission to use passages from articles by Laird Bell, Saul Bellow, Paul Brooks, Curtis Cate, John K. Galbraith, Erle Stanley Gardner, Oscar Handlin, Gerald W. Johnson, Alfred Kazin, Walter Lippmann, T. S. Matthews, Charles W. Morton, Vance Packard, Leslie C. Stevens, Joseph Wechsberg, and Edward Weeks.

Bantam Books, Inc., for permission to use a passage from Clancy Carlile, "The Animal Fair," *New Campus Writing No. 2*, published by Bantam Books, Inc.

Beacon Press for permission to use a passage from "Notes of a Native Son," by James Baldwin, reprinted by permission of the Beacon Press, © 1955 by James Baldwin.

Columbia University Press for permission to use a passage from Gilbert Highet, *Man's Unconquerable Mind*, Columbia University Press, 1954.

Commentary for permission to use a passage from an article by David Daiches (*Commentary*, April 1957).

Commonweal for permission to use a passage from an article by Gunnar D. Kumlien.

James B. Conant for permission to use a passage from *The American High School Today*.

John Crosby for permission to use a passage from his article "Seven Deadly Sins of the Air," *Life*.

Dodd, Mead & Company, Inc., for permission to use a passage from Stephen Leacock, *Last Leaves*, copyright 1945 by Dodd, Mead & Company, Inc.

John Dos Passos for permission to use a passage from *The 42nd Parallel*.

Doubleday & Company, Inc., for permission to use passages from *The Summing Up* by W. Somerset Maugham, copyright 1938 by W. Somerset Maugham; from "Whistling Dick's Christmas Stocking" in *Roads of Destiny* by O. Henry; and from "The Meadow Mouse" by Theodore Roethke, from *The Collected Poems of Theodore Roethke*, copyright © 1963 by Beatrice Roethke as Administratrix of the Estate of Theodore Roethke, all reprinted by permission of Doubleday & Company, Inc.

E. P. Dutton & Co., Inc., for permission to use a passage from *Education and Freedom* by H. G. Rickover.

Clifton Fadiman for use of a passage reprinted by special permission from *Holiday*, copyright © 1957 by The Curtis Publishing Company.

Fortune for permission to use passages from articles by Adlai E. Stevenson (October 1955) and William H. Whyte (November 1950).

Harcourt, Brace & World, Inc., for permission to use passages from S. I. Hayakawa, *Language in Thought and Action* (Harcourt, Brace & World); from Laurence Perrine, *Sound and Sense* (Harcourt, Brace & World); from *All the King's Men* by Robert Penn Warren, copyright 1946 by Harcourt, Brace & World, Inc., and reprinted with their permission; from *To the Lighthouse* by Virginia Woolf, copyright 1927 by Harcourt, Brace & World, Inc., renewed by Leonard Woolf, reprinted by permission of the publishers; and from Alfred Kazin, *A Walker in the City* (Harcourt, Brace & World, Inc.).

Harper & Row, Publishers, Inc., for permission to use passages from J. B. Priestley, *Rain upon Godshill* and *Margin Released;* from E. B. White, *One Man's Meat;* and from articles by James Baldwin, Bruce Bliven, Heywood Broun, Robert Brustein, Miriam Chapin, John Fischer, John W. Gardner, Robert L. Heilbroner, Jane Jacobs, Marion K. Sanders, C. P. Snow, Dr. Ian Stevenson, Philip M. Wagner, and William S. White.

The New York Times and Sean O'Casey for permission to use a passage from *The New York Times Book Review*.

Oxford University Press, Inc., for permission to use a passage from Rachel L. Carson, *The Sea Around Us*.

Prentice-Hall, Inc., for permission to use a passage from Monroe C. Beardsley, *Thinking Straight: Principles of Reasoning for Readers and Writers*, 2nd ed. © 1956. By permission of Prentice-Hall, Inc., Englewood Cliffs, N. J.

Queen's Quarterly for permission to use a passage from an article by K. W. Maurer.

Random House, Inc., for permission to use a passage from Jonathan Norton Leonard, *Flight into Space*, copyright 1953 by Jonathan Norton Leonard; and for permission to reproduce entries taken from *The Random House Dictionary of the English Language* (© Copyright 1966) and reprinted by permission of Random House, Inc.

The Reporter for permission to use passages from articles by Robert Bendiner, Marya Mannes, and William Lee Miller; and additional passages from articles by Michael Harrington, Lois Phillips Hudson, Ken Macrorie, Marya Mannes, William Lee Miller, George Steiner, copyright 1962 and 1963 by The Reporter Magazine Company.

Virginia Rice for permission to use passages from Paul Horgan, "Pages from a Rio Grande Notebook," *The New York Times Book Review*, copyright © 1955 by Paul Horgan.

Saturday Review for permission to use passages from articles by Frederick Lewis Allen, John Mason Brown, Henry Steele Commager, Elmer Davis, John Van Druten, James A. Michener, Ashley Montague, Edith M. Stern, and William H. Whyte, Jr.; and additional passages from articles by Malcolm Cowley, James K. Feibleman, Claude M. Fuess, Arthur Mayer, Liston Pope, Bertrand Russell, Hartzell Spence, Albert Szent-Gyorgyi, Harold Taylor, and Richard L. Tobin.

Charles Scribner's Sons for use of passages from Eugene Field, *The House;* and from "The Golden Honeymoon" by Ring Lardner, copyright 1922, 1950 by Ellis A. Lardner (*How to Write Short Stories*), reprinted by permission of the publishers, Charles Scribner's Sons.

Simon and Schuster for permission to use a passage from Ben Hecht, *A Child of the Century*, Simon and Schuster, Publishers; and from Clifton Fadiman, ed., *I Believe*.

The Society of Authors for permission to use a passage from Bernard Shaw, *Man and Superman*.

Edward J. Steichen for permission to use a passage from an article in *Holiday*.

Time for use of passages reprinted courtesy of *Time*, copyright Time Inc. 1958.

Karen Traficante for permission to reprint the essay "In Defense of *The*

American Dream" from the magazine *Orbit*, published at Illinois State University.

University of Oklahoma Press for use of a passage reprinted from *Is the Common Man Too Common?* by Joseph Wood Krutch and others, copyright 1954 by University of Oklahoma Press and used by permission.

The Viking Press, Inc., for permission to use passages from Harrison Brown, *The Challenge of Man's Future;* Carl Van Doren, *Three Worlds;* John Steinbeck, *The Grapes of Wrath;* and Lionel Trilling, *The Liberal Imagination.*

Willis Kingsley Wing for use of a passage from Sloan Wilson, "It's Time to Close Our Carnival," reprinted by permission of Willis Kingsley Wing, copyright © 1958 by Sloan Wilson.

The World Publishing Company for permission to reproduce entries from *Webster's New World Dictionary of the American Language*, College Edition, copyright 1958 by The World Publishing Company.

Yale University Press for permission to quote from Charles S. Brooks, *Chimney-Pot Papers;* and from David Riesman, *The Lonely Crowd.*

PREFACE

To the Teacher

Words and Ideas, Third Edition, derives from the following convictions about English composition as a subject:

- *Good writing can be taught* — not once and for all, but in the kind of course that offers frequent opportunities for writing and that enables the student to develop his skill and confidence through gradually more challenging assignments.

- *The emphasis in a writing course should be on positive procedures for generating good prose.* No writer can be effective whose overriding concern is the mere avoidance of error. The student will respect a writing course that confronts him with genuine writing problems, gives him realistic advice on how to proceed, and makes possible the sense of satisfaction that derives from meaningful work well done.

- *The best teacher of writing is not the subject-matter specialist but the teacher of English.* Ideally, every college teacher would teach effective communication. But in practice, the student acquires a respect for language, and a sense of its power and resources, from teachers whose first love is language and literature.

- *In the ideal English program, composition and literature are organically related.* A good composition course recognizes the creative and imaginative elements in expository prose. A good literature course provides ample opportunity for written expression, and develops the student's command of the written word.

- *Freshman English is not a mere service course but an essential part of a college education.* Students today are everywhere dissatisfied with courses that serve only a remote ulterior purpose, that are merely an introduction to an increasingly more narrow and irresponsible specialism. They ask for courses that have meaning and relevance in their own right.

A Rationale for a Composition Course

There are many kinds of materials that can prove useful in a composition course; and there are many ways of organizing a program of instruction in writing. But to be effective, such a program must in some way reflect the teacher's understanding of the *process* of composition. It must reflect his sense of how a writer works. Rhetoric is the study of how good prose is produced. To be meaningful, rhetoric cannot be a "rhetoric of parts," offering finger exercises in limited aspects of composition. It must be a "rhetoric of the whole," which never loses sight of the central question: "What does it take to produce a piece of writing that is worth writing and worth reading?"

The rhetoric of *Words and Ideas* starts with a definition of the finished product that the writing process aims at: "The Whole Theme" (Chapter One). It then builds a writing program that explores four essential relationships: (1) the writer and his experience; (2) writing and thinking; (3) the writer and his audience; (4) the writer and his reading.

- *Writing from Observation and Experience.* As in its previous edition, *Words and Ideas* stresses the need for developing the student's powers of observation. It stresses the preliminary stage of gathering the material and mobilizing the resources without which writing remains an empty exercise. Chapters Two through Four ("Observation and Description," "Personal Experience," and "Opinion") all encourage the student to draw on his own observation and experience for the material that will give his writing authentic substance, for the evidence on which to base (and with which to support) responsible opinions. Increasingly, textbooks and programs in composition are beginning to share this emphasis on the "prewriting" stage.

- *Writing and Thinking.* The next two chapters of the rhetoric focus on the kind of thinking that must go on in the student's mind if he is going to give shape and structure to his materials. Chapter Five ("Definition") stresses the relationship between thinking and language; Chapter Six ("Logic") stresses the relationship between thinking and organization. In a meaningful rhetoric, logic cannot be in a final chapter, added as an afterthought. The student's ability to think his material through is central to his performance as a writer. If he cannot think clearly, he cannot write well. The art of writing well is the art of making up one's mind. In *Words and Ideas*, the core of the rhetoric is devoted to the kinds of thinking that go into formulating responsible opinions and presenting them in clearly organized writing.

• *The Writer and His Audience.* The next two chapters relate the student's writing to the demands and expectations of the reader. Chapter Seven ("Persuasion") explores the tension between the writer's loyalty to his subject and his need for the reader's attention and assent. Chapter Eight ("Tone and Style") concentrates on effectiveness of style. It develops the student's sense of what makes reading apt, striking, and a pleasure to read.

• *The Writer and His Reading.* The remaining two chapters of the rhetoric focus on writing that draws on the work of other writers. Chapter Nine ("The Research Paper") focuses on the student's basic task: to sift, and to integrate into his own writing, material from different printed sources. Chapter Ten ("Writing About Literature") stresses the student's close reading of imaginative literature, and aims at helping him develop and structure his active response.

How to Use This Book

The Third Edition of *Words and Ideas* has been reorganized to bring it into closer harmony with prevailing course patterns, while at the same time keeping it flexible enough to make it adaptable to varying needs of students and preferences of instructors:

(1) The book now starts with a new chapter on the whole theme, surveying the whole writing process and stressing basic patterns of organization.

(2) After the initial survey, Chapters Two through Ten provide the basic framework for a course that explores major rhetorical principles by showing them at work in different kinds of writing. In order, these chapters provide a *cumulative program* in which each theme that the student is asked to write is treated as a purposeful whole.

(3) In many programs, Chapter Eight ("Tone and Style"), Chapter Nine ("The Research Paper"), and Chapter Ten ("Writing About Literature") will prove most appropriate to the second half of a two-quarter or two-semester course.

(4) Several of the handbook chapters serve the double purpose of reference and classroom instruction. Many instructors will early in the course assign all or part of the chapter on diction, which as a whole provides a more than usually comprehensive introduction to the resources of the dictionary. Some instructors find it useful to teach the chapter on the paragraph before they go on to the whole theme, but most teachers probably will find this chapter, with its emphasis on form, more useful after the student has first studied materials like Chapters One through Four, with their emphasis on substance and purpose. For similar reasons, the chapter on sentence style may prove most useful late in the first-semester course — perhaps in conjunction with the chapter on persuasion, where emphasis is on the effect writing has on the reader.

(5) The sections of the handbook dealing with punctuation, grammatical usage, and the like, are designed primarily for convenient reference. Even these, however, are written so as to provide at the same time coherent instruction and exercise materials for the student needing help with mechanics.

Changes in the Third Edition

In writing the Third Edition of *Words and Ideas,* I have aimed at relating the freshman course organically to the world of today's teachers and students; making the book as *useful* as possible to the teacher; making the book reflect the changes in the composition course that have taken place during the last ten years; bringing in new models and exercises from the best current professional and student writing.

Specific changes are as follows:

Three new chapters: The new Chapter One, "The Whole Theme," takes the student step by step through the whole process of composition. The emphasis is on four basic kinds of themes: process, thesis and support, classification, comparison and contrast. This chapter incorporates the material on outlining, and on introductions and conclusions, formerly contained in the handbook chapter on organization.

The new Chapter Ten, "Writing About Literature," places the emphasis on *kinds of critical papers* most frequently assigned in a composition or introduction to literature class: explication, studying a character, the central symbol, tracing the theme, defining a critical term, comparison and contrast. The chapter provides many sample outlines and models for student papers.

The new Chapter Nineteen, "Practical Prose Forms," covers the summary, the business letter, and the essay exam.

Stronger positive emphasis: While continuing to alert students to familiar pitfalls, the new *Words and Ideas* gives stronger emphasis to the means by which *good writing is produced.* Throughout the rhetoric, the emphasis is on direct application to student writing. In each of the chapters devoted to description, personal experience, definition, logic, and persuasion, a new or expanded section describes typical kinds of papers, gives advice on how to structure a typical student theme, and provides sample outlines and models.

A leaner style: Most of the rhetoric has been *completely re-written,* and much of the handbook trimmed down, for a leaner, more vigorous style. There is less exhortation, more demonstration. Major principles stand out more clearly for emphasis. Logical sequence of materials is easier to grasp at a glance for purposeful study and efficient reference.

New material: New *exercise material* illustrates a greater diversity of concerns and is drawn from a wider range of both professional and student writing. *Writing samples* include new selections from Mary McCarthy, John Updike, James Baldwin, Edward Albee, Marshall McLuhan. New sources range from the *National Review* to underground student newspapers. The new student research paper, "The Furor over Ibsen," is a lively inquiry into a controversy with intriguing contemporary parallels.

In working on this new edition, I have learned from teachers, students, and former students now turned teacher. I have profited from many detailed reviews and personal conferences with teachers from different parts of the country. Among those who have furnished me with new materials and new ideas, I want to thank especially Palmer Czamanske, Valparaiso University; Wallace Graves, San Fernando Valley State College; John Nichol, University of Southern California; Naomi Clark, Gwendolyn Large, and Mary Sapsis of San Jose State College. I am indebted to the following for invigorating criticism and pointed advice: John A. Barsness, Boise College; Jack D. Campbell, Oklahoma State University; Earl J. Dias, Southeastern

Massachusetts Technological Institute; O. B. Emerson, University of Alabama; Robert Eschbacher, Seton Hall University; William Gillis, Bradley University; George D. Gleason, Southwest Missouri State College; William Jordan, Chicago City Junior College; Faye Kelly, American University; M. L. Mackenzie, University of British Columbia; George Mather, Chicago City Junior College; Thomas G. McGuire, Los Angeles Valley College; Howard K. Moore, Lowell Technological Institute; James W. Peck, University of Alabama; Lester E. Pope, Shoreline College; Jane Raymond, West Valley College; Ian Ross, University of British Columbia; Audrey J. Roth, Miami-Dade Junior College; Amalie R. Shannon, Lehigh University; Robert K. Stone, University of Wisconsin at Milwaukee; Fred Tarpley, East Texas State University; A. M. Tibbetts, University of Illinois; Herbert H. Umbach, Valparaiso University; J. Sherwood Weber, Pratt Institute; Arthur N. Wilkins, Metropolitan Junior College.

Finally, I want to express my debt to three men who, by their dedication to the good cause, have over the years kept alive my conviction that English composition is a course well worth working for: Ronald Freeman of UCLA, Wallace Douglas of Northwestern University, and Ken Macrorie of Western Michigan University.

H. Guth

BIBLIOGRAPHY

The following books develop in detail various topics discussed more briefly in this text:

Baugh, Albert C. *A History of the English Language.* 2nd ed. New York: Appleton-Century-Crofts, Inc., 1957. Widely used as a textbook in courses on the history of the language. Traces the history of English grammar, influences on the English vocabulary, changing attitudes toward language.

Beardsley, Monroe C. *Thinking Straight: Principles of Reasoning for Readers and Writers,* 3rd ed. Englewood Cliffs, N. J.: Prentice-Hall, Inc., 1966. A thorough and systematic introduction to applied logic, with special attention to the problems encountered by the critical reader. Succeeds where many books fail: in making the study of logic intelligible and relevant. Especially good on the relationship between thought and language.

Brooks, Cleanth, and Robert Penn Warren. *Modern Rhetoric,* 2nd ed. New York: Harcourt, Brace & World, Inc., 1958. Contains a detailed and well-illustrated discussion of the traditional four forms of discourse: exposition, argument, description, and narration.

Bryant, Margaret M., ed. *Current American Usage.* New York: Funk & Wagnalls Company, Inc., 1962. Completed with the cooperation of eminent linguistic authorities, this book contains a full discussion of disputed points of usage. Rulings are based on the principle that "any expression is standard English if it is used by many cultivated people to communicate in speech or writing." Includes a short bibliography of published studies for each item listed.

Evans, Bergen, and Cornelia Evans. *A Dictionary of Contemporary American Usage.* New York: Random House, Inc., 1957. Discusses many debatable terms and expressions, examining historical data, implications, and overtones that are beyond the scope of an unspecialized dictionary. Often decides questions of debated usage in favor of expressions that, though common in speech and writing, are considered objectionable by conservative readers.

Fowler, W. H. *A Dictionary of Modern English Usage,* 2nd ed. revised by Sir Ernest Gowers. New York: Oxford University Press, 1965. A recent updating of a famous book that vigorously championed an intelligent, discriminating conservatism in matters of usage. Although based primarily on British usage, Fowler's preferences and dislikes are shared by many of his American readers.

Hayakawa, S. I. *Language in Thought and Action,* 2nd ed. New York: Harcourt, Brace & World, Inc., 1964. Based on the author's widely read *Language in Action.* A popular introduction to semantics, the study of the relationship between words and things, and words and ideas. Excellent on the purposes of language, and on the role of language in society.

Laird, Charlton, and Robert M. Gorrell. *English as Language: Backgrounds, Development, Usage.* New York: Harcourt, Brace & World, Inc., 1961. An excellent collection of resource materials for a serious study of the problem of usage, with materials on the history of lexicography.

Pyles, Thomas. *The Origin and Development of the English Language.* New York: Harcourt, Brace & World, Inc., 1964. Traces the history of writing, of our sound system, and of our grammar from the point of view of the modern linguist.

Roberts, Paul. *English Sentences.* New York: Harcourt, Brace & World, Inc., 1962. A school grammar incorporating material from both structural and transformational grammar. An excellent introduction to the concerns and procedures of modern grammarians.

Thomas, Owen. *Transformational Grammar and the Teacher of English.* New York: Holt, Rinehart and Winston, Inc., 1965. Relates the theory and practice of modern transformational grammar to the concerns of teachers and students of English. An admirable attempt to make revolutionary new developments in linguistics intelligible to those whose concern is with understanding and using English.

Wells, Walter. *Communications in Business.* Belmont, California: Wadsworth Publishing Company, Inc., 1968. A lively, well-illustrated introduction to effective business English. Good on the major kinds of business letters; excellent pointed advice on how to achieve a vigorous, effective style.

CONTENTS

A Concise Handbook

CHAPTER SIXTEEN / Punctuation 575
Outline 576

INTRODUCTION

This is a book about writing. Its aim is to help you write expository prose — ordinary nonfiction prose, conveying facts, opinions, ideas. This kind of prose does much of the world's work — in instructions, letters of application, business memos, textbooks, technical reports. It also provides the language of the public dialogue, of our social and political relations — in campaign literature, articles on foreign policy, newspaper editorials, letters to the editor. It finally provides a medium for self-expression and reflection — in personal letters, autobiography, statements of personal philosophy or religious belief.

Teachers and editors do not always agree on how good writing is produced and how it can best be taught. But they do agree remarkably on the qualities they look for in first-rate work. Here are the most widely recognized virtues of competent expository prose:

- Good writing is *authentic*. It proceeds from accurate observation and careful study of evidence. It does not merely repeat second-hand ideas.

- Good writing is *thoughtful*. It reflects the author's desire to think things through, to do justice to a topic.

- Good writing is *organized*. It shows the writer's ability to marshal his ideas: to select what is important and to present it in plausible order.

- Good writing is *effective*. It shows that the writer is aware of his audience, that he respects its standards, expectations, or needs.

- Good writing is *well written*. It shows the author's respect for language, his sense of its power, richness, and variety. Good writing is a pleasure to read.

1

Kinds of Writing

Some basic principles apply to most of the writing that you will encounter. What you learn about gathering and organizing material during one project will help you with the next. What you learn about how to reach your reader while doing one assignment will benefit you also later. But different kinds of writing have purposes and problems of their own. An honest study of writing cannot provide ready-made formulas fit for all occasions. It *can* help you develop confidence by having you tackle a variety of assignments, increasing in difficulty and calling for somewhat different skills.

Though kinds of writing overlap, here are some familiar types that you will be able to identify:

Technical Writing   It is not enough for an engineer to develop a new process or a new mechanism. He must know how to explain it to others. Technical exposition requires a writer to clarify things first in his own mind and then to present them to his reader in such a way that he will say: "Yes, I see. Yes, I understand." Technical writing is *objective;* the writer's personality, his likes and dislikes, do not enter into it.

News Reporting   The ideal journalist finds the facts, seizes on what is significant, and presents the results without fear or favor. Like the technical writer, he keeps his eye on the *object* — what is there, what is happening, how something works.

Imaginative Description   The nature writer makes us share in the sights and sounds of the natural world in which we live. An account of travel makes us visualize objects, people, and scenes. Imaginative description is not a bare-fact kind of writing. It brings in the personal reactions of the observer. His feelings — of joy, surprise, loneliness — color what he describes.

Autobiography   Autobiography tells the story of events that have special meaning for the writer. He tries to re-create the authentic feeling of first-hand experience. At the same time, he tries to make his readers see the pattern in the weave, the figure in the carpet. In autobiography, the writer takes stock of what has made him what he is.

Informed Opinion   When we read an editorial, or a column by a well-known commentator, we are in effect turning to an experienced observer and asking: "What do you make of it?" We expect him to *interpret:* to point to cause and effect, trace parallels, spell out implications for future action.

Argument   Argument is objective and *methodical*. It takes us from known facts or shared assumptions step by logical step to conclusions. It appeals to the reader's willingness to think the matter through on its merits. We are likely to encounter systematic argument in an economist's analysis of the causes of inflation, in a philosopher's examination of logical proofs for the existence of God.

Persuasion   Persuasion is the purpose of the advertisement, the political pamphlet, or the religious tract. The persuasive writer wants his audience to change its mind, or its ways. He keeps his eye firmly on his *readers*, employing a strategy that will do justice to their background, preferences, and dislikes. Persuasion is successful when the reader says, "You are right. I'll go and do as you say."

Satire   The satirist uses his *wit* as a means of persuasion. He has a sharp eye for the ridiculous and quickly seizes on the absurdities and contradictions of his opponents. He mimics people who are pompous and exposes those who are hypocrites. His weapons range from good-natured irony to sarcasm and inspired invective.

Scholarship   Scholarly research draws on previously published sources. It requires the writer to sift evidence and to hunt down missing links. In a research report or a scholarly article, we expect not superficial first impressions but conclusions carefully worked out and solidly supported.

Literary Criticism   In a book review or a critical article, the author tells us what he makes of a poem, a short story, a novel, or a play. The critic's job is partly *interpretation* — to help the public understand a new and difficult work, to call the attention of a casual reader to what he may have missed. But another part of the critic's task is *evaluation* — to champion what he considers valuable or promising, to expose what he considers shoddy.

A Writing Program

The first part of this book, "A College Rhetoric," presents a writing program designed to help you improve systematically your command of written English. The program is focused on kinds of expository writing most relevant for the typical college student and most clearly intended for the general reader. (Thus, there is no direct treatment of technical writing or news reporting, which call for specialized training offered in separate courses.) This part of the book is designed as *a practitioner's rhetoric* — a guide addressed to the central question, "How does a competent writer actually put together a piece of writing that will be worth reading?"

The first chapter of the book surveys the whole writing process. Chapters 2 through 10, the remaining chapters of the rhetoric, show the principles of good prose at work in different kinds of writing. Each of these chapters describes typical kinds of papers, gives advice on how to structure a typical student theme, and provides sample outlines and models. Each chapter serves a double function: It helps you deal with the particular problems of a kind of writing—description, autobiography, definition, persuasion. At the same time, it shows you what a particular kind of writing can best teach you about writing in general.

Here is what the different chapters of the rhetoric contribute to the writing program:

Chapter One, "The Whole Theme," takes you step by step through the *whole process of composition*. It examines the major stages in writing a theme: exploring the subject, bringing it into focus, working out a plan of organization that does justice to the material, and presenting the results effectively to the reader. The emphasis is on four basic kinds of themes: process, thesis and support, classification, comparison and contrast.

The next three chapters—"Observation and Description," "Personal Experience," and "Opinion"—help you to *mobilize your own resources*. They treat writing as the process of working up authentic materials from your own observation, experience, and reading. They encourage you to give substance to your writing by drawing on what *you* know, what *you* have seen and felt.

Chapters Five and Six, "Definition" and "Logic," focus on the relationship between *writing and thinking*. When are words "mere words," and when do they convey clear and distinct ideas? When does a paper carry us along through a series of necessary logical steps, and when do we balk at the jumps we are asked to take? What are ways of presenting ideas in logical order, rather than merely in the order in which they came to mind?

Chapter Seven, "Persuasion," stresses the relationship between the writer and his *audience*. How can you hope to reach and influence a skeptical reader? How is awareness of your audience going to affect your strategy, your use of language? Why are some familiar techniques of persuasion ineffective with an educated reader?

Chapter Eight, "Tone and Style," directs attention to the writer's choice of stylistic means. What is the appropriate degree of formality in serious writing? What is the role of the *imaginative and creative* elements in expository prose? What are the uses and limitations of humor, irony, satire? How can you develop a forceful, natural personal style?

Chapter Nine, "The Research Paper," concentrates on the writer's use of *sources.* It helps you select the kind of topic that you can profitably investigate and takes you step by step through the preparation of a typical paper.

Chapter Ten, "Writing About Literature," deals with kinds of critical papers most frequently assigned in a composition class or an introduction to literature class: explication, studying a character, tracing a central symbol, tracing the theme, defining a critical term, comparison and contrast.

The Standards of Written English

The second part of this book, "A Concise Handbook," serves for study, review, and reference. The handbook shifts attention from the larger questions of substance, purpose, and effect to specific problems of expression and mechanics. This part of the book summarizes the standards of written English, ranging from the requirement for continuity in a paragraph to correct spelling and conventional punctuation.

The handbook stresses positive features that make prose clear and effective. In recent years, the teaching of English in school and college has moved away from an overemphasis on mere mechanical correctness. The purpose of good writing is not to avoid "errors" but to communicate effectively with the reader. Several major chapters of the handbook stress the relationship between words and ideas, between outward form and the *substance* of what is said:

Chapter Eleven, "The Paragraph," deals with the paragraph as a meaningful unit, structured to serve a *purpose.*

Chapter Twelve, "Diction," will help you extend your range of words and strengthen your grasp of their exact meanings and implications. The chapter will help you express your ideas directly, forcefully, and economically.

Chapter Thirteen, "Sentence Style," demonstrates how appropriate sentence structure produces emphasis, continuity, appropriate perspective.

Chapter Nineteen, "Practical Prose Forms," discusses the summary, the business letter, and the essay exam, paying attention to both form and substance.

At the same time, writing is not merely a set of functional signals, like a traffic light or the Morse code. Like other forms of human behavior, language is governed in part by *convention*. A young businessman conventionally is well shaved; he wears a suit and tie. A young poet is likely to have longer hair and to wear more informal clothes. No law regulates the appearance of either the businessman or the artist. But when either departs too far from what is expected, his friends and associates stop and stare. They are distracted from his message — his sales talk or his poem — and they become caught up in externals.

This book teaches the conventions of serious writing for a double purpose: When you observe them, you will help your message reach the reader without avoidable distraction. When you depart from them for good reasons of your own, you will be prepared for the possible negative reactions of your reader.

The following chapters most typically combine attention to function and convention:

Chapter Fourteen, "Grammar," stresses the construction of sentences that clearly communicate the intended meaning and at the same time conform to the conventions of written English.

Chapter Fifteen, "Punctuation," stresses punctuation practices that facilitate reading and clarify meaning, and that at the same time conform to what is *customary* in formal writing. It examines in detail the most noticeable departures from convention: the sentence fragment, the comma splice.

Chapter Seventeen, "Glossary of Usage," presents in alphabetical order brief discussions of current status for expressions — *different than, reason is because,* the split infinitive — that have frequently been ruled *inappropriate* to formal writing.

Like other conventions, the conventions of written English are subject to a certain amount of variation. Journalistic writing is more informal than scholarly writing; creative writing is more hospitable to experiment than expository writing. Over the years, educated written English has generally moved closer to the informality of speech. Nevertheless, certain features of language and of style are widely recognized as appropriate to the discussion of serious issues, to the treatment of ideas of some consequence. The advice given in this book on matters of mechanics, grammar, and word choice is designed to help you write the kind of English that is acceptable to many educated readers, regardless of region, profession, or social status.

Making Use of Criticism

The amount of evaluation and criticism that your writing receives will vary with different institutions and instructors. One function of a writing course is to break the ice, to make the student overcome his inhibitions, to help him express himself freely and honestly. Sooner or later, however, a writer reaches the point where he profits from studying the detailed reactions of a critical reader.

Regardless of when, and in what quantities, such criticism comes, you may at first have difficulty in making constructive use of it. Most of us instinctively yearn for recognition and praise. When instead we find our shortcomings analyzed or our conclusions questioned, we feel resentful and discouraged. Few people are less popular than the professional critic—the teacher, reviewer, or examiner who passes judgment on the work of others.

Few experiences, on the other hand, are more instructive for us as writers than the encounter with an experienced critic who stubbornly refuses to accept our own rosy estimate of ourselves. Such an encounter dramatizes for us the basic problems of communication: how to make our ideas clear, acceptable, persuasive—without meekly accepting standards that we do not share. Criticism, whether worded positively or negatively, can teach us to make our writing less open to misunderstanding, less vulnerable to attack. In later life, criticism often takes the form of reactions that are final and irremediable: a letter of application is quietly filed; a report is turned over for revision to a rival; an article is returned with a printed rejection slip attached. In a writing course, criticism is an invitation to profit from advice.

When a paper is returned to you, you may find general comments on its effectiveness and suggestions for improvement. You may find marginal comments on specific points of style. You may find symbols, like G 5b or P 3, referring you to the relevant section of the handbook for a discussion of problems of punctuation, grammar, diction, or organization. A reference chart of these symbols is printed inside the back cover of this book. You may find abbreviations like *frag* or *MM*, whose significance is explained in the guide printed inside the front cover.

Follow your instructor's suggestions concerning revisions and corrections. Treat revision not as a mechanical exercise but as an opportunity to study the strengths and weaknesses in your past performance. Try to show in your subsequent writing that you have learned to deal with problems pointed out to you in earlier papers.

Criticism has served its purpose when in your future writing you begin to anticipate the reader's reactions. Even when writing a first draft, you will tell yourself: "This paragraph is too thin. Better look for a more solid example." "This isn't the right word. How can I say this more exactly?" "This sentence is getting too involved. Let me try again." The effective writer is the one who has learned to be his own critic. He has learned to revise and edit his work *before* it reaches the reader.

The Need for Practice

Composition is not the kind of subject that can be taught and learned once and for all. Proficiency in writing comes from practice. It comes from tackling many different kinds of writing assignments and from exploring the problems they present. A competent writer has written a great deal, and he has learned from the experience. He has learned even from false starts — from a project he gave up as a bad job; from a paper he finished but then decided to keep in his desk. But above all, he has learned from projects that he *did* carry through and that *did* reach the intended reader.

A writer cannot keep going by merely doing finger exercises, practicing this or that limited aspect of composition. He needs the sense of accomplishment that comes from putting together a piece of writing, however short or informal, that was worth attempting and that is worth reading. This book is designed to provide you with opportunities for this kind of accomplishment.

Five Principles of Good Writing

Each writing assignment presents its own problems and calls for somewhat different skills. But some basic principles apply equally to different kinds of writing. Whether your writing is descriptive or autobiographical, whether you are defining a term or developing an argument, remember the following requirements:

Your writing should be your own.   It should reflect your own first-hand observation, your honest attempts to work out your own answers to questions and problems. Your first task is not to follow a prescribed formula or to please the reader but to write with conviction.

Your writing should be concrete.   Keep in mind the reader who asks: "What is there for me to *see*? What does it *feel* like to be there? What does this mean *in practice*?" Back up generalizations with examples; anchor abstract terms to concrete reference.

Your writing should have focus.   Learn to do justice to one point at a time. Though you are fully entitled to your opinions on many different subjects, limit your writing to the kind of idea you can fully examine, explain, and support. Concentrate on a limited area, but cover it well.

Your writing should be coherent.   When you move from one point to another, your reader should be able to move with you. He should see the logical connection between one paragraph and the next. He should see the direction in which you are headed or perceive the trend of your argument.

Your writing should be responsible.   Learn to forego sweeping claims and drastic charges. Learn to respect evidence that goes counter to your assumptions, objections that might weaken your case. Respect the reader's right to think for himself. Present your sources and your reasoning in such a way that he can examine and verify.

First Themes

1. Discuss and illustrate fully one important way in which the kind of English spoken in your family, or among your friends, differs from that taught in the schools.

2. Discuss a work by a modern writer with whom you are familiar. Explain what makes him "modern," addressing yourself to someone not familiar with his writings. Make use of specific references to his work.

3. Among books that a whole generation of students have chosen for "unrequired reading" are Salinger's *Catcher in the Rye* and Heller's *Catch-22*. Have you recently read a book that could be called a current campus favorite? Write a book review explaining to someone over thirty what the book has to offer to young people.

4. Television has been called "a cruel caricature, aimed well below the lowest common denominator of American life." How true is this charge? Limit yourself to one area of American life that you know well, and examine the way it is reflected on commercial television.

5. Many people love traditional campus architecture—with spires and arches harking back to medieval cathedrals, or columns and gables reminiscent of classical temples. Others prefer a modern style, reflecting the values of our own time. Are you a "traditionalist" or a "modernist"? Defend your point of view.

6. Many students complain that lessons and exams are too rigidly structured, with the student's own contribution seeming minimal. Looking back over your own schooling, do you feel that too often you were expected to repeat approved opinions and established facts? Or did you have a chance to participate, to develop your own interests and point of view?

7. Is racial prejudice on the decline? Are the barriers of prejudice gradually breaking down? Or is discrimination merely taking new forms, with most American Negroes as segregated or discriminated against as before? Cite specific instances from your own experience.

8. Someone recently said that the average young American has seen "some pretty offensive wars fought in far places, without even the patina of glory. The idea of war as a cause or a crusade is quite comic to him." What and how does the average young American of your own age know about war?

9. To judge from your own observation, what is the role of "intellectuals" in American society? What are they like, and what is their influence? Use specific illustrations.

10. Write an account of the vocation or profession that you plan to follow or that interests you most. Explain and defend your choice to a reader suspicious of public-relations prose.

A College Rhetoric

There is excitement in the very act of composition. Some of you know this at first hand—a deep satisfaction when the thing begins to take shape. Actually, I wonder if life holds a deeper satisfaction.
Catherine Drinker Bowen

CHAPTER ONE

The Whole Theme

1. Exploring the Subject

2. The Need for Focus
   - Limiting the Subject
   - Choosing a Key Question
   - Defining Your Purpose

3. Four Kinds of Themes
   - The Process Theme
   - Thesis and Support
   - Classification
   - Comparison and Contrast

4. Beginnings and Endings
   - Titles
   - Introductions
   - Conclusions

5. Continuity and Transition
   - Key Sentences
   - Transitions
   - Synonyms and Recurrent Terms
   - Logical Continuity

6. Using Outlines
   - Working Outlines
   - Final Outlines

Sample Themes
Theme Topics 1

1. Exploring the Subject

The finished theme is the result of a process. Ideally, the process of composition moves through five overlapping stages:

(1) The writer *explores his subject,* gathering and examining possibly relevant material.

(2) The writer *limits his subject* to what he can treat in the necessary detail.

(3) The writer *works out a pattern of organization* that fits his material.

(4) The writer *writes his first draft,* presenting his material to advantage.

(5) The writer *revises* his first draft for continuity, clarity, and effectiveness.

If the finished paper is going to be substantial, the writer must be sure not to neglect the first step. No one can write a substantial paper from an empty mind. The most common complaint about student writing is "This paper doesn't *say* anything." The writer who wants to say something must first "work up" his subject. He must take time to get acquainted with his subject, to think about it, to gather relevant material.

Assume that you have been asked to discuss a quotation that deplores an alleged modern trend toward the "welfare state." Your first question should not be "Do I agree or disagree with this quotation?" Your first question should be: "What do I know that *might* prove relevant to a discussion of this topic? What could I draw on that might help me give substance to a paper on this topic?" Here are some of the avenues you might explore:

"Where has the term *welfare state* come up in my own experience?" Perhaps it entered the discussion when elderly relatives were concerned about the passage of Medicare legislation. Perhaps it also came up when a neighbor complained about a welfare recipient's driving a sports car and spending her days on the beach. These two situations have several things in common: Government is taking active measures to assure the welfare of a citizen. Often, what is done seems too little to the recipient; too much to the taxpayer, who feels he is paying the bill. With these tentative generalizations in mind, you might look for other government programs that have in one way or another touched the lives of your family, friends, acquaintances. You might thus be led to consider what you know from experience about social security, unemployment insurance, slum clearance, or retraining programs.

"What role does the concept of the welfare state play in current discussion and controversy?" Is it currently in the news? Does it appear in campaign oratory? Is it related to campaigns currently conducted by the PTA, the League of Women Voters, a local taxpayers' organization? Everyone has read newspaper reports about investigations into alleged welfare chiseling. You may have heard political candidates complain that the "welfare state" conditions citizens to rely on government "handouts." According to the same candidates, many government programs are ill conceived or mismanaged, and lead to the growth of a huge government bureaucracy. You may have heard other candidates defend government programs by appealing to your compassion for the unfortunate, your belief in equal opportunity, your belief in the worth and dignity of every individual. You may in fact come to feel that for many "welfare state" programs the pros and cons are surprisingly similar, and that people take sides in fairly predictable fashion.

"What reading have I done that might prove related in some way to the current trend toward the welfare state?" Some of the most memorable, widely read, and influential books castigated the *conditions* that called for government intervention through various types of "welfare state" legislation. The reader of Charles Dickens's *Hard Times* remembers the workers putting in long hours of hard work for a pittance, the pennyless victims of technological unemployment, the children growing prematurely old in the factories, the unsuspecting traveler falling down an abandoned mineshaft. The reader of Upton Sinclair's *The Jungle* remembers workers working in filth and mortal danger on the job, and falling prey to profiteers after hours. The reader of John Steinbeck's *The Grapes of Wrath* remembers the sufferings of those uprooted by economic conditions beyond their control. Books such as these vividly show the original need for many "welfare state" features that we have come to take for granted: minimum wage laws, laws restricting child labor, unemployment insurance, factory safety laws. They also throw light on matters currently disputed: consumer protection, the responsibility of industry for keeping its environment habitable.

As your preliminary exploration proceeds, you are accumulating material to work on. By now, you will have come to see how large and sprawling a topic the alleged trend toward the welfare state really is. You will see the need for limiting your subject. Your sense of the full *range* of your topic will guide you in making an intelligent choice. For instance, you may decide to concentrate on how the trend toward the welfare state affects *one* group of people or type of person: the businessman, the worker; the young or the aged; the privileged, the unfortunate, the handicapped. Or you might want to concentrate on one major cause, or one major effect.

By now you will also have come to see the need for sharpening your key terms. Is "welfare state" merely a faintly derogatory catch-all term for all kinds of government intervention in the lives of citizens? Or are there specific assumptions or goals that make a modern welfare state go beyond more basic obligations of government? If "individualism" is pitted against "welfare statism," how specifically can the kind of "initiative" and "self-reliance" we expect of the individual be spelled out?

By now you will also have accumulated the kind of evidence on which you could base a cautious, limited opinion of your own. You are coming closer to the point where you could venture an assertion, select evidence to support it, and arrange the evidence in some kind of intelligible order. In short, you are reaching the point where you could start writing.

Obviously, the kind and extent of your preliminary exploration will vary greatly for different kinds of assignments. Usually, however, you will be able to draw on one or more of the following sources of material:

- Current *observation* — close first-hand study of scenes, people, objects, events.
- Past *experience* — the vast but often untapped memory bank of everything you have experienced and read.
- Informed *opinion* — the sometimes contradictory views of others who have studied the same subject.
- Scholarly *research* — the systematic sifting of evidence from relevant records, documents, and other printed sources.
- *Critical reading* — the close study of one or more literary works: poems, novels, plays.

These five major sources of material will each in its turn be given detailed attention in the following chapters of this book: Chapter 2, "Description"; Chapter 3, "Personal Experience"; Chapter 4, "Opinion"; Chapter 9, "Research"; and Chapter 10, "Writing About Literature."

Exercises

A. Prepare a tentative *inventory of material* for a paper on one of the following topics: camping, cliques, the handicapped, grades, school discipline, city government. In a phrase or two, jot down possible examples, incidents, arguments, references to your reading, and the like.

B. Find an exceptionally substantial recent magazine article in the area of education, politics, or social problems. Prepare a short report on the *sources* that the author has drawn on to give substance to the article. What kind of material has he brought together? From the finished article, can you tell how he has gone about "working up" his subject?

2. The Need for Focus

Every writer must learn to heed familiar advice: *Write more about less.* The novice almost always tries to cover too large an area. He moves too quickly from point to point. The frustrated reader feels like saying, "Slow down. Stay with one point and develop it in detail. Instead of rushing on, do justice to the claims you have already made."

There are three things you can do to bring your subject into focus:

• Narrow down the *area* to be covered.

• Close in on one limited *question* to be answered.

• Make your paper serve a limited *purpose*.

Limiting the Subject

The shorter the paper, the greater the need for restricting the area to be covered. No one could write a paper on a vast subject like "Education in America." A writer interested in American education may restrict this field according to *kind:* academic, physical, religious. He may restrict it according to *area:* a state, a town, the nation's capital, Indian reservations in Arizona. He may limit himself to a particular *level:* kindergarten, grade school, high school, college. He may limit his discussion to a certain *type of student:* gifted, retarded, emotionally disturbed. A manageable topic might look like this:

Space-age science at Washington High
"Released time" and the Winchester Public Schools: No time for God
Talking typewriters for the retarded
Home economics for boys
Stagnant schools and the migrant child
How to succeed in a military academy

Each large subject can be split up into several medium-sized subjects. Each of these in turn will yield many limited subjects narrow enough to serve as topics for short papers:

General Area:	City life
Intermediate:	The inner city
	Suburbia
	Urban sprawl
Topics:	One major cause of urban blight
	Redeveloped vs. grown neighborhoods
	An alternative to teen-age gangs
	A new trend in city architecture
	Keeping up with the Joneses
	The suburb and the sense of community
	Who pays for the schools?
	Why I don't like supermarkets
	The passing of the neighborhood store
	Kids with nothing to do
	My church is a country club
	Good fences make good neighbors

Choosing a Key Question

Often, the most effective device for bringing a subject into focus is to formulate a key question that the paper as a whole is designed to answer. Merely writing *about* a subject often results in a catalog of miscellaneous impressions. The freshman who writes "about" his first week on campus may ramble from one thing to another: the mass of humanity swirling around him at registration, the confusing layout of the campus, a chance meeting with a hometown acquaintance, the difficulty of adjusting to dormitory food, the pleasure of finding a compatible roommate (or the disappointment of finding an incompatible one). To give direction to his paper, he should ask a question that helps him to sort out his impressions: "What kind of advice would I give to an incoming freshman? What makes a person a good roommate? What can be done to help students find adequate housing?" He can then select those of his impressions that help him answer his question. He can reject those that do not. His paper will no longer be aimless and incoherent; it will be focused on a query to be satisfied, an issue to be settled, a problem to be solved.

The more *specific* the key question you choose, the more likely your paper is to have a clear focus. "How do crime comics shape their readers' attitudes?" is a very *general* question. Crime comics could affect the reader's attitude toward many things: police work, violence, minority groups, criminals, courts — to mention only the most obvious. Try to point your question at a more limited issue:

Is it true that crime comics equate physical ugliness with moral depravity, thus encouraging the reader to judge by appearances?

Is it true that heroes tend to look white, Anglo-Saxon, and Protestant, while villains are made to look Latin, for instance, or Oriental?

Is it true that in the crime comics people are either all good or all bad?

Do crime comics reveal the political sympathies of their authors?

A paper attempting to answer any one of these questions would have to discuss in detail several examples from familiar comic strips. In a short paper, the author could hardly take on more without seeming to skim the surface.

Remember that a *pointed* question is more likely to produce a focused paper than a question that is open or merely exploratory. Avoid questions like "What are some of the causes of adolescent crime?" or "What are some of the things every freshman should know?" The "What-are-some" kind of question almost always leads to a paper in which many different things are *mentioned* but too few of them studied in detail. Substitute a "What-is-the-most" or "What-is-the-best" kind of question: "What is the most important thing a freshman should know?" "What is the most serious obstacle to communication between a teenager and his parents?" "What are three key features shared by successful television comedians?" The question with the word *some* in it often leads to tedious inventory taking and is hardly likely to create suspense. The question with the word *most* or *best* or *key* in it implies a promise to concentrate on what is most significant.

Defining Your Purpose

Often a confusing subject comes into focus when the writer limits the purpose he is trying to achieve. To get a subject under control, you will often have to ask yourself: "What am I trying to do for my reader?" Lack of focus often results when you try to do too many things at once. It is one thing to *explain* to your reader how a machine functions. It is another thing to *persuade* him that the machine will serve his needs. It is one thing to *define* a term like "modern liberalism." It is another to *convert* the reader to the cause so defined. The main purpose of a writer may be:

- *to inform:* to pass on to the reader facts gathered by first-hand observation or compiled from other sources;
- *to explain:* to show the workings of a process or trace the causes of an event;

- *to define:* to give definite meaning to a confusing or difficult term;
- *to argue:* to show the logic behind a conclusion or decision;
- *to persuade:* to influence the reader's opinions, decisions, actions.

These purposes are not mutually exclusive. Explanation, definition, and argument, when well done, have a persuasive effect on the reader. Nevertheless, failure to settle for one major purpose can easily make a writer's efforts seem scattered and ineffectual. When you feel defeated in your effort to lick a formless subject into shape, ask yourself: "What exactly am I trying to do?"

Exercises

A. Choose *two* of the following general areas. For each, write down *five topics limited enough* to be covered in a short paper.

Recreation
Religion
Industry
Minority groups
Transportation

B. Assume you are preparing five pointed questions for an *interview* with one of the following: a college president, a police chief, a Negro minister, a conscientious objector, a diplomat from a country currently in the news. Formulate questions *significant* enough to be worth following up but *limited* enough to steer the interview away from vague generalities. The class as a whole may want to choose the two or three sets of questions most likely to produce significant, detailed responses.

C. Write two paragraphs covering roughly the same area but serving a *different purpose.* Choose one: (1) In one version *describe* a product factually; in the other, *persuade* a skeptical customer to buy it. (2) In one version *report* an incident objectively; in the other, use it to *entertain* the reader. (3) In one version *explain* a current political slogan or idea; in the other version *make fun* of it.

3. Four Kinds of Themes

To organize a theme is to give suitable shape to the material at hand. That shape has to be discovered. When you impose a ready-made pattern on your material, your writing becomes mechanical.

The right pattern of organization for a given theme is the one that will do justice to your topic. Let the material help you make up your mind. Let the task you have set yourself suggest the best strategy for tackling it.

Four kinds of themes often assigned toward the beginning of a composition course illustrate well what is involved in giving shape and direction to a paper as a whole. Each kind of theme confronts you with a *limited task.* You can thus give full attention to problems that with more demanding writing assignments become merely a part of a larger undertaking. Each type of theme described here can teach you something that will prove of wide general application in many different kinds of writing.

The Process Theme

The process theme teaches us to present essential steps in the right order. Describing the process of paper making, we trace the necessary steps that turn wood chips first into pulp, then into a paper web, and finally into sheets of paper. Describing the process of radio transmitting, we follow the newscaster's voice through microphone and transmitter to the receiving set and the listener's ear. What we learn from the process theme has many applications. We apply it when we

- explain a *scientific* process:
    how energy of motion converts into electricity
    how sediments build up on the ocean floor
    how a translation machine scans a sentence
- give *directions:*
    how to plant a lawn
    how to make wine from your own grapes
    how to make pottery
- trace a *historical* chain of events:
    how nomads became villagers
    how the railroad transformed rural America

The following instructions will help you write better process themes:

(1) *Learn to pay patient attention to detail.* No one can make a machine work, or produce an enameled vase, who does not have a loving concern for the *little* things that add up to the whole. No one can write a good process theme who is too impatient to take in details like those in the following paragraph:

A black and white garden spider dropped down from one of the higher branches of the tree. He picked a flimsy, forked twig, covered with large drops of water from the rain, and swung in on it like a toy glider coming in for a landing. As he caught hold of it, it sagged under his weight, and several large water drops slid off to the ground below. The spider sat on the twig until it ceased vibrating. Then he carefully moved to the end of one of the forks. He first walked rather fast, but halfway down the twig fork he slipped and turned upside down. He tried to right himself but failed, so he moved along the twig upside down, fighting both the vibrations of the twig and the large water drops. When the spider reached the end of the twig fork, he carefully fastened a silver thread to the end of the fork. Then he slowly righted himself on the twig. He proceeded to crouch in a peculiar position, somewhat like a sprinter set in his starting blocks. With a mighty leap, he jumped toward another twig fork, but he missed it. He swung down below the twig and hung by his silver thread until the vibrations and his swinging stopped. He climbed up the thread and repeated the maneuver, and again he failed. The third time he jumped, he caught the other twig and proceeded to fasten his silver thread to it. Running back between the two forks the spider began to build his web.

(2) *Concentrate on what is essential.* At a given stage of the process, ask yourself: "What is needed to make the work proceed? What, if left out, would prevent my reader from duplicating the process and producing the desired result?" Note the grimly businesslike fashion in which the author of the following passage makes us see "how it works":

The sergeant turned to the captain, saluted and placed himself immediately behind that officer, who in turn moved apart one pace. These movements left the condemned man and the sergeant standing on the two ends of the same plank, which spanned three of the crossties of the bridge. The end upon which the civilian stood almost, but not quite, reached a fourth. This plank had been held in place by the weight of the captain; it was now held by that of the sergeant. At a signal from the former the latter would step aside, the plank would tilt and the condemned man go down between two ties. — Ambrose Bierce, "An Occurrence at Owl Creek Bridge"

(3) *Relate the new and technical to what is familiar.* How is the process you describe similar to something the reader already knows? In the following short process theme, a student makes use of extended **analogy** to make us understand the process of vision:

The eye operates like a simple box camera. Such a camera has four essential parts: a shutter, a lens, a chamber or box, and a sensitized plate or film. The shutter's job is to allow light to pass through the lens. The lens is a circular piece of glass with curved faces to concentrate the light upon the plate or film. After being concentrated by the lens, a beam of light must pass through the chamber to reach the sensitized plate. The sensitized plate or film then receives an impression of the projected image.

The four corresponding parts of the eye are the iris, the lens, the vitreous body, and the retina. The iris is a muscular diaphragm which can close or dilate to regulate the passage of light to the lens. The lens is composed of a semi-solid, crystalline substance. Like the lens of the camera, the lens of the eye serves to concentrate and focus light. The vitreous body is a large area between the lens and the retina. It is void of any material save a transparent liquid. The retina, through its rods and cones, receives an impression of the projected image.

In the camera, a beam of light passing through the shutter strikes the lens. It is then focused and projected through the chamber to the rear wall of the camera. There, a sensitized plate or film registers an impression of the image carried by the beam of light. In the eye, a beam of light passing through the iris hits the lens. The lens focuses the beam and projects it through the vitreous body to the rear wall of the eye. There, the retina receives an impression of the image carried on this beam of light. From the retina, a stimulus is then flashed to the brain through the optic nerve.

(4) *Explain the necessary technical terms.* Without technical terms, the typical process theme soon becomes cumbersome. Once the term is clearly explained, *piton* is more efficient than "the kind of metal spike used as a support in mountain climbing." But the writer must *limit* his use of technical terms to those his audience can take in. The reader will soon get lost if every sentence in an article about paper making contains terms like *digester, cyclones, knotter, centri-cleaner,* and *jordan.*

Ask yourself: "Which are key terms I need—because they are the names of the most important parts or operations, or because what they stand for will have to be mentioned *repeatedly* in the paper?" Then ask: "Which of these terms do I have to explain?" When in doubt, explain: "Braise—that is, cook the piece of meat by browning it in fat and then letting it simmer with a little liquid in a closed pot." "Differential—the part of the automobile transmission that allows the inner wheel to turn a curve with fewer revolutions than the outer."

(5) *Break up the whole sequence into major divisions, or emphasize the most significant steps.* A monotonous "and-then" sequence becomes confusing, because it gives equal emphasis to many parts, events, or operations. Suppose your paper follows the assembly line in an automobile factory: the basic parts of the body are welded together; the doors are hung; the body shells are dipped into a chemical solution; they are spray-painted; they are dried in ovens; electrical wiring is laid; door locks and other mechanisms are installed; glass is installed; interior lining is installed; and so on. To protect the reader against fatigue, break up the body's progress into three major stages:

I. Building the body shell

II. Painting the body

III. Outfitting the painted shell

Thesis and Support

Supporting a thesis requires us to relate a mass of material to a single major point. It thus teaches us to *limit* ourselves to one major point, and to drive it home. The writer of a travel article would not simply claim that people in Eastern Europe are fascinated with things American. He would go on to give example after example. A developer would not just casually mention to the planning commission that a new suburb needs a shopping center. He would support his claim with a mass of statistics. We call the central idea that the rest of the presentation supports the **thesis**. The thesis is the assertion, generalization, or claim that is backed up by examples, evidence, statistics.

Writing that first states a thesis and then supports it has almost unlimited uses. We use it, for instance, when we

- defend a *generalization* in an essay exam;
- call for *action* in a letter to the editor;
- make good a *promoter's claim* in an advertising brochure;
- establish someone's aptitude for a job, in a letter of *recommendation;*
- defend a political candidate against a rival's *charge.*

In the following excerpt, from Gordon Parks' *A Choice of Weapons,* the first sentence serves as a thesis; and each of the three paragraphs of the excerpt takes up one incident that bears out the point made by the thesis:

thesis	*When I was eleven, I became possessed of an exaggerated fear of death.* It started one quiet summer afternoon with an explosion in the alley behind our house. I jumped from under a shade tree and tailed Poppa toward the scene. Black smoke billowed skyward, a large hole gaped in the wall of our barn. . . .
first incident	
second incident	Then once, with two friends, I had swum along the bottom of the muddy Marmaton River, trying to locate the body of a Negro man. We had been promised fifty cents apiece by the same white policeman who had shot him while he was in the water trying to escape arrest. . . .
third incident	One night at the Empress Theater, I sat alone in the peanut gallery watching a motion picture, *The Phantom of the Opera.* When the curious heroine, against Lon Chaney's warning, snatched away his mask, and the skull of death filled the screen, I screamed out loud. . . .

The following instructions will help you write papers that successfully support a thesis:

(1) *Make sure your thesis is a clear statement of a limited point.*
Whenever possible, state your thesis in a *single* sentence:

Topic:　　　　　Urban Redevelopment

Thesis:　　　　"Redeveloped" neighborhoods lack the varied life of the "grown" neighborhoods they replace.

Topic:　　　　　Life in Suburbia

Thesis:　　　　Living in the suburbs does not prevent people from developing a sense of community.

The thesis should be a true statement, a true assertion. It cannot be a question, though an excellent way of *arriving at* a thesis is to sum up in one sentence the answer to a question like "What is missing in the typical redeveloped neighborhood?" The thesis should not merely map out the general territory but focus on a limited issue:

Too Vague:　　　　A modern suburb is a good place to live.

Focused More
Clearly:　　　　Modern suburbs have kept alive the American tradition of being a good neighbor.

Too Vague:　　　　Today's children are spoiled.

Focused More
Clearly:　　　　Grade school teachers lack the means of disciplining their students.

(2) *Make your thesis pull together your previous observations or impressions.* Writing about the heroine of an Ibsen play, you may wish to say that she was bored and frustrated, cruel and selfish, hungry for excitement but at the same time afraid of scandal. Formulating a thesis, you try to make these various points add up to a coherent overall view: "This woman was dissatisfied and resentful because she was unable to adjust her desires to the limitations of her environment." Your paper could then give several examples of her acting frustrated and cruel when the setting she lived in thwarted her desires. Or perhaps you formulate a thesis like this: "She expected too much of people and as a result was invariably disappointed." Your paper could then give several examples of her approaching people with high hopes and then acting bored, frustrated, or cruel when her expectations fail to come true.

(3) *Use your thesis to help you keep out what is immaterial.* A thesis sentence helps you check for **relevance**. It helps you to eliminate or play down things that are not directly related to the issue under discussion. A thesis claiming that football players are as intelligent as other students focuses the discussion on the question of

intelligence. It will help you realize that your description of the song girls you observed at football games may be irrelevant.

(4) *Arrange your supporting material in an intelligible order.* Try to sort out your examples under three or four major headings, as in the following sample outlines:

THESIS: My high school teachers insisted on strictly formal language.

SUPPORT: I. Colloquial language was forbidden in *student themes.*

II. *Books* with outspoken and slangy dialogue were put on the "don't-read" list.

III. *Classroom discussion* had to be carried on in strictly formal phrases.

THESIS: A part-time job supplements a student's education.

SUPPORT: I. Part-time work can provide a valuable *practical education* (training for do-it-yourself projects; knowledge useful to future housewife, car owner).

II. It can provide field work related to the student's *major field of study* (hospital work for future nurses, tutoring for future teachers, playing in a commercial band for music student).

III. It can provide valuable *psychological training* (association with people from different backgrounds, taking orders from superiors).

The thesis-and-support paper provides invaluable training for the writer learning how to give unity and direction to a piece of writing. Several of the problems raised by the thesis-and-support paper will be explored more fully in later chapters of this book: how to formulate responsible opinions as the result of first-hand observation and inquiry (Chapter 4, "Opinion"); how to arrive at logical conclusions that meet the requirements of straight thinking (Chapter 6, "Logic"); how to make the material we offer in support of a thesis persuasive for a critical reader (Chapter 7, "Persuasion").

Classification

Papers devoted to classification teach us how to sort out material into plausible categories. Classification is the most widely applicable method for breaking up a sprawling, formless subject into manageable parts. When we classify things, we group them together on the basis of what they have in common. No two people are exactly alike. Yet we constantly sort them out according to features they share: extrovert and introvert; single, married, and divorced; native-born, naturalized citizen, resident alien, visitor; joiners and loners; upper class, upper middle class, lower middle class, lower class.

Classification is the most common way of determining the *internal* organization of a piece of writing. As you collect material for a theme, your most basic task is to start grouping things together that belong together. Here is a typical preliminary collection of material for a paper about a person:

SUBJECT: Last semester's psychology teacher
  (1) had a loud, clear voice
  (2) told some interesting stories about students helped by psychology
  (3) came to class late several times
  (4) explained difficult words
  (5) wasn't sarcastic toward students
  (6) wore colorful neckties
  (7) walked with a limp
  (8) had been an exchange teacher in France
  (9) outlined subject clearly
  (10) spaced assignments well
  (11) talked over test I did poorly on
  (12) served in the Army Signal Corps

What goes with what? Here are four possible categories:

I. *Teaching methods:* (2) relevant anecdotes, (4) explanation of terms, (9) clear outline, (10) spacing of assignments, and perhaps (1) effective speech habits

II. *Attitude toward students:* (5) absence of sarcasm, (11) assistance after class

III. *Personal traits:* (6) sporty clothes, (7) limp, (3) lack of punctuality

IV. *Background:* (8) teaching experience abroad, (12) service in Signal Corps

A student concerned about his success in school would probably conclude that categories I, II, and IV are most significant. A second look at III might suggest an effective strategy for the paper as a whole: an introduction describing an unpromising first impression, belied by the teacher's effectiveness. The outline of the finished paper might look like this:

I. Unpromising external characteristics

II. Effectiveness as a teacher
    A. Interesting background

B. Effective presentation of subject

C. Positive attitude toward students

III. Lesson learned
("Don't judge a teacher by his ties.")

Here are some other subjects with relevant material sorted out into major categories:

SUBJECT: Types of comic strips

I. Righteous crime fighters (Dick Tracy, Robin Malone)

II. Comic stereotypes (Dennis the Menace, Blondie, Bugs Bunny)

III. Social satire (L'il Abner)

IV. Amusing human foibles (Peanuts, Pogo)

SUBJECT: Types of high school teachers

I. The *authoritarian* personality (strict discipline, one-way teaching, heavy assignments, severe grading)

II. The *journeyman* teacher (reliance on the textbook, moderate assignments, "don't-rock-the-boat" attitude)

III. The students' *friend* (chummy attitude, many bull sessions, unusual projects, fraternizing outside of school)

Remember the following advice when setting up and presenting such major categories:

(1) *Let the subject of your paper help you determine appropriate categories.* Writing about campus social life, you might divide students into Greeks, Coop dwellers, and Independents. Writing about "cultural" subjects for vocational students, you might divide them into nursing majors, engineering majors, police majors, and so on.

(2) *Avoid a confusing mixture of criteria.* It does not make sense to divide students into graduates of local high schools, disadvantaged students, and Catholics. It *does* make sense to sort them out according to geographical origin (local, rest of the state, out of state, foreign), *or* according to belief (Catholics, Protestants, Jews, agnostics), *or* according to social and economic background.

(3) *Try not to vary thoroughness of treatment drastically from one category to the next.* Some papers seem unbalanced because the writer has tried to analyze the subject exhaustively instead of

fully developing perhaps three major categories. A paper on teen-age marriage might proceed like this:

THESIS: Often teen-age marriages result from motives other than mature affection.

   I. One possible motive is the desire for independence from parental control. (Several case histories are discussed.)

   II. Another motive may be the sense of satisfaction derived from marrying a popular boy or a popular girl. (No details or examples are given.)

   III. A person may marry "on the rebound," marrying one person to spite another. (A sketchy and inconclusive case history is provided.)

   IV. A couple may mistake physical attraction for love. (Several cases are discussed; similar cases in fiction and drama are cited.)

   V. A boy about to be drafted may marry a girl for fear of losing her. (A case in point is discussed at length.)

The paper is likely to be unconvincing, because the author is stretching himself too thin. In a long paper, he might successfully tackle I, IV, and V. In a short paper, he might do well to limit himself to either I or IV.

(4) *If the major divisions of the paper vary in importance, make your presentation follow a consistent pattern.*   Many effective papers move from the less important to the more important. This order produces a **climactic effect** and leaves the most important point firmly embedded in the reader's memory. The paper on teen-age marriage, for instance, might start with motives related to external circumstances (I, V) and end with the problem that is probably the most important and the hardest to discuss (IV).

Comparison and Contrast

Comparison and contrast requires us to establish meaningful connections between things normally considered separately. The immediate need for comparison and contrast arises when we are faced with a choice. We often engage in systematic comparison and contrast to justify a *preference.* To justify our preference for a lack-luster incumbent over a more dynamic challenger, we may compare their records on a number of crucial points. To justify our endorsement of a policy of "confrontation," we may contrast the results produced by an aggressive and a more conciliatory approach in a number of situations.

More basically, comparison and contrast helps us *notice* things we previously took for granted. We learn to identify a style of architecture by noting the features it shares with other styles and those features that set it apart. We are more vividly aware of the American way of doing things after we spend a year in Mexico or in France. We become aware of some of the distinctive features of the American high school after we spend some time in college.

The most common failing of the comparison-and-contrast paper is that the author has left the actual brainwork for his readers. He has collected the necessary material but has failed to *work out* the parallels or differences. Often such a paper breaks apart in the middle: a discussion of the Volkswagen followed by a separate discussion of the Ford; a discussion of the villain in a Shakespeare play, followed by a discussion of the villain in a play by Ibsen. To make possible fruitful comparison and contrast, the author must *line up* his material so that one thing throws light upon the other.

Here are the two basic ways of organizing the comparison-and-contrast paper:

(1) *The author discusses two things together—feature by feature, point by point.* A **point-by-point comparison** takes up one feature of, say, the Volkswagen, and then immediately asks: "Now what does this look like for the Ford?" A typical outline would look like this:

I. Economy
   A. Initial cost (data for both cars)
   B. Cost of operation (data for both cars)
   C. Resale value (data for both cars)

II. Comfort and convenience
   A. Space for passengers and luggage (data for both cars)
   B. Maneuverability (data for both cars)

III. Performance
   A. Acceleration and speed (data for both cars)
   B. Durability (data for both cars)

Here is the same scheme applied to a discussion of two Dutch painters. The author is trying to show that the two, though superficially very different, share important traits.

THESIS: There are basic resemblances between Rembrandt and Van Gogh.

I. Both were interested in people, in what is called "character" or "expression" (this point applied first to Rembrandt and then to Van Gogh).

II. Both were deeply religious—but not in a remote or abstract way (applied first to Rembrandt and then to Van Gogh).

III. Even formally, in their brushwork and use of color, the two men are akin (applied first to Rembrandt and then to Van Gogh).

(2) *The author discusses two things separately but takes up the same points in the same order.* Such a **parallel-order comparison** makes it possible to give a coherent picture of each of the two things being compared, while at the same time helping the reader see the connections between the two. In the following portrait of two types of baseball fans, notice that the same three points are taken up both times in the identical order: I. absorption in the game; II. attitude toward fellow fans; III. interest in the players.

thesis	The true baseball fan is found in the bleachers, not in the grandstand.
point 1	The man in the bleachers *forgets himself in the game.* When he gets excited . . .
point 2	He is apt to *turn to a total stranger,* tap him on the shoulder, and say, "Ain't that boy Aaron the berries!" . . .
point 3	Though his seat is farthest from the diamond and he cannot see the batters' faces, he *recognizes each one* of them as they come up. . . .
transition	The man in the grandstand looks at the game differently. . . .
point 1	He never quite *gives himself up to the game.* He never cuts loose with a wild yell. . . .
point 2	If he is sitting among people who are strangers to him, he *treats them like strangers.* . . .
point 3	He has to refer to his scorecard to get the *names of the players.* . . .

Here is the same scheme applied to a comparison and contrast of the villain in a Shakespeare and an Ibsen play:

thesis	Shakespeare's Iago represents spectacular and triumphant evil, whereas the villain in Ibsen's *The Pillars of the Community* represents the unheroic evil brought about by ordinary men.
point 1	Iago is a *deliberate* villain, freely admitting his evil intentions to his audience. . . .
point 2	Iago is forever plotting *ingenious schemes,* producing dramatic results. . . .
point 3	Iago goes about his villainies with tremendous *gusto,* finding ever new objects for his cynical sense of humor. . . .
transition	Ibsen's villain is much less spectacular, and is in fact revealed as the villain only after a close second look. . . .
point 1	Ibsen's villain is constantly *rationalizing* his guilt. . . .
point 2	The evil he does is represented by *acts committed half-heartedly and furtively.* . . .
point 3	Ibsen's villain is a *brooding, unhappy man,* ineffectually revolving his problems in his own mind. . . .

Exercises

Process

A. Identify the ten or twelve *essential steps* in a complicated process that is well known to you from first-hand observation or experience. Try to group the various steps into several major stages. Use the following outline form to report your findings.

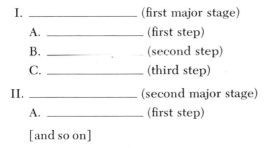

I. _____ (first major stage)

  A. _____ (first step)

  B. _____   . ___ (second step)

  C. _____ (third step)

II. _____ (second major stage)

  A. _____ (first step)

  [and so on]

B. Assume you are giving your reader instructions for a complicated task. Write a paragraph describing *in full detail* one essential step. Try to include everything that the reader would have to know and do to produce the right results.

C. In one sentence each, explain the six most essential *technical terms* that you would need in tracing one of the following processes: generating electricity, pollination, the life cycle of a butterfly, transmission of a visual image by television, the making of sugar, preparing a French (Spanish, Italian) dish.

Thesis and Support

D. Of the thesis sentences presented in the following brief passages, select the three that come closest to your own views. For each one, jot down briefly what *supporting material* you could supply from your own experience and reading to back up the point made.

    1. In today's high schools, *there is too much competition for grades.* The student constantly worries about tests and has little chance to think and explore on his own.

    2. *Students profit as much (or more) from a summer of work, travel, or reading as from additional coursework in summer sessions.* Though such experiences are less systematic than academic learning, they are educational in the sense that they broaden the student's perspective.

    3. *The public schools do not fully practice the constitutional principle of separation of church and state.* Students, whether of Christian,

Jewish, or agnostic parents, participate in Christmas plays and Easter pageants, and sing religious songs.

4. *Teen-age fads and fashions have increasing influence on the adult world.* Teen-age styles set the pace for much advertising and strongly influence adult fashions and even hair styles.

5. *The population of the typical big city is declining in income and social status.* The unskilled and the less educated remain, while the middle class moves out to the suburbs to find living space and better schools for the children.

6. *Fear of violence restricts the activities of many Americans.* People stay away from public parks; older people are afraid to venture out into the streets.

E. Consult recent issues of several of the following general-interest magazines: *The Atlantic, Harper's, The New Republic, National Review, Commentary, Commonweal.* Choose *three thesis sentences* that illustrate exceptionally well the kind of thesis that makes a definite assertion on a limited point.

F. State *three possible theses* that your experience or background equips you especially well to support. For each thesis, outline the paper you would write in support of it. Your instructor may ask you to write a thesis-and-support paper based on the most promising of your outlines.

Classification

G. The following "interest inventory" was adapted from a student paper. How would you *classify* the items in order to present them in a plausible sequence? Prepare a brief outline showing how you have sorted them out.

1. contact sports
2. coffee dates
3. religious retreats
4. taking a girl to the movies
5. work for worldwide disarmament
6. long hikes
7. beach barbecues
8. vacation trips
9. fellowship meetings
10. swimming
11. social work
12. student government

H. A student paper listed the following points as guidelines for parents. How would you sort these points out into *major categories?* Prepare an outline reflecting what you would consider the most plausible classification.

1. Parents should avoid swearing or vulgarity.
2. Parents should not contradict each other in the presence of their children.
3. Parents should provide encouragement when children do something constructive.
4. Punishment should be impartial when there are several children.
5. Parents should not shower their children with gifts.
6. One parent should not overrule the other in matters of discipline.
7. Parents should show affection, whether by a pat on the back or a good word.
8. Parents should respect children as individuals, letting them develop their own likes and dislikes.
9. Parents should not be overprotective.
10. Children should be allowed to learn from their own mistakes.
11. Parents should refrain from quarreling in the presence of their children.
12. Parents should teach good manners by example.
13. Parents should allow their children to choose their own friends.
14. Parents should not give vent to their frustrations or irritations by punishing their children.
15. Parents should not take notice of a child only when it does something wrong.

I. Sort out the suggestions in the following list into major categories. Arrange both your major categories and their subdivisions in the *most plausible or the most logical order.*

STUDY HINTS

1. Make study time as regular as possible.
2. Work out an understanding with friends and roommates concerning unnecessary interruptions.
3. Avoid dim or glaring light.
4. Get an understanding of the purposes and organization of a course from course outlines, introductory materials in a textbook, or chats with the instructor.
5. If you can, work at an uncluttered desk.
6. Ask yourself practice questions about what you study.

7. Make a point of not protracting lunch hours and coffee breaks indefinitely.

8. If you can, find a congenial corner in a library or study hall.

9. Start studying the first week of each term.

10. Take two or three *short* breaks during each two- or three-hour period of study.

11. In studying a textbook, try to relate what you read to the instructor's lectures or to class discussion.

12. If a subject does not seem immediately practical or interesting, treat it as a challenge to your resourcefulness, agility, and perseverance.

13. Break up the material to be studied into convenient chunks.

14. Reserve the cramming session before final examinations for review and for attention to special difficulties.

15. Summarize, review, and think about one major section before going on to another.

J. What is your favorite reading matter? Have you ever sorted it out into recurrent types? Choose one of the following: science fiction, detective novels, Western novels, historical novels, nineteenth-century British fiction, current American short stories, biographies, autobiographies, books on travel or exploration. Sort the books you have read in this major category out into a few major types. For each, write a short paragraph indicating the major features that examples of the type have in common.

Comparison and Contrast

K. Of the following topics, choose the one that seems most promising for fruitful comparison and contrast. Write *two* rough outlines — one for a point-by-point comparison, the other for a parallel-order comparison. Choose one: your high school campus and your present college campus, two successful television comedians with different styles, old-style and "adult" Western movies, a student hang-out and an expensive restaurant.

L. Write a rough outline for a comparison and contrast of *two major characters* from imaginative literature. Choose the central figures of two Shakespeare plays, two nineteenth-century British novels, or two modern American novels. Make it *either* a point-by-point or a parallel-order comparison, and be prepared to defend your choice.

M. Write a rough outline for a comparison and contrast of *two sets of attitudes*, of two distinct positions, on some major aspect of education: discipline in high school, sex education, supervision of the private lives of college students. Use either a point-by-point or a parallel-order comparison and be prepared to defend your choice.

4. Beginnings and Endings

Many writers worry too much about how to begin and how to conclude. Often, the best advice to such a writer is to begin in the middle and to stop when he is through. In many a student paper, the introduction takes too long to get to the point, and the conclusion is merely an expendable summary of points already made — sometimes in exactly the same words. Nevertheless, the experienced writer increasingly thinks about his audience as his paper begins to take shape. How can he attract and hold his readers' attention? How can he make clear to them what he is trying to do? How can he leave them with a strong final impression?

Titles

The ideal title attracts the reader without promising more than the author is going to deliver. It is specific enough to stake out a limited area, honest enough to prevent later disappointment, and striking enough to compete with other claims on the reader's time. A good title often has a dramatic or humorous touch:

AT LAST LINCOLN FOUND A GENERAL
THE CRIME OF PUNISHMENT
SECOND THINGS FIRST
ON BECOMING HUMAN

Bad titles tend to be vague, colorless, sprawling, or deceptive. Here are some weak titles followed by a choice of possible improvements:

Before:	BUSINESS SUCCESS
After:	SELLING HOME ENCYCLOPEDIAS
	WHERE THE CUSTOMER IS KING
Before:	QUALITIES OF A FUTURE HUSBAND
After:	WHAT MAKES ELIGIBLE MEN ELIGIBLE
	BREADWINNER OR PRINCE CHARMING?

Before: JUVENILE DELINQUENCY

After: MY STAY AT JUVENILE HALL

THE BOY FROM A GOOD FAMILY

Before: NEUTRALITY OF POLITICAL SCIENCE TEACHERS

After: IMPARTIALITY IN THE CLASSROOM

TEACHERS, TOO, HAVE OPINIONS

Introductions

The ideal introduction attracts the reader but at the same time does important groundwork for the paper. An effective introduction *creates interest;* it hooks the reader into the essay or story. It *sketches out the territory* to be covered, often by narrowing down a more general subject. It *sets the tone* for the rest of the essay. Above all, it *heads straight for the central idea* to be developed in the rest of the paper.

You will seldom write a paper requiring more than *one short introductory paragraph.* Here are some typical examples, each serving one or more of the purposes for which an effective introduction may be designed:

(1) The writer may attract the reader's attention by relating his subject to a *topical event or a current controversy:*

RUSSIAN, ANYONE?

On August 12 . . . the Soviet government announced the construction of Russia's first . . . Though Russian scientific journals had published detailed accounts of . . . , the lack of qualified translators had kept American scientists unaware of the Russians' rapid progress in this field. . . .

(2) The writer may make the reader take a *new look at a familiar situation:*

THE LIFE OF STRESS

A lot of sympathy is being wasted on executives for leading lives so full of stress and strain that it impairs their health. Actually, their subordinates suffer more from high blood pressure and artery disease. These surprising findings . . . *— Time*

(3) The introduction may limit the subject by *proceeding from a general situation to a specific instance:*

THE WASTELANDS REVISITED

School people have to put up with a lot, not only from the kids, who must be bad enough, but also from the grown-ups, who probably are worse. Pummeled, pressured, and advised from every side, still bearing the wounds inflicted by super-patriots, super-religionists, super-taxpayers, and super-superintendents, the educators now have to deal with yet another attack from Arthur E. Bestor, Jr. — William Lee Miller, *The Reporter*

(4) An *initial quotation* may serve as the keynote for the rest of the paper:

WHO IS HAMLET?

"It is a commonplace that the character of Hamlet holds up the mirror to his critics."[1] Shakespeare's Hamlet has been aptly described as the sphinx of the Western world, with each critic giving his own subjective answer to the riddle it proposes. . . .

(5) *Striking facts or statistics* may dramatize the issue to be discussed:

MONOLINGUALISM IS OBSOLETE

Last year, only one out of ten American high school graduates had studied a foreign language. In spite of the publicity recently given to the teaching of foreign languages in primary and secondary schools . . .

(6) A *striking contrast* may heighten the point to be made:

AMERICAN CHILDREN ARE SPOILED

Not too many decades ago, young children were early taught the difference between what they were, and were not, allowed to do. Today, many American parents treat their children as if they could do no wrong. The most obvious manifestation of this change . . .

(7) An *initial definition* may clarify a key term:

WHAT IS AUTOMATION?

Economists do not agree among themselves on what "automation" means. Some writers use the term for any type of large-scale mechanization of industrial or administrative processes. Others, more plausibly, use it in referring to the mechanization of planning, supervision, and control.

(8) Biographical or personal comment may help establish the *writer's qualifications* for dealing with his subject:

VICTORY AND AFTER

When I first came to Germany in November 1945, all the major cities seemed to be curiously alike. . . .

(9) A *provocative statement* may challenge a familiar belief or ideal:

FREEDOM IS IMPOSSIBLE

Freedom in society is impossible. When the desires of two people do not agree, both cannot be satisfied. Who is going to be free to realize his desire—the man who wants to walk down the street shouting and singing, or his neighbor who seeks peace and quiet? The man who wants to build a new highway, or the one who wants to retain the unspoiled natural beauty of the land? . . .

(10) A *controversial question*, provocatively worded, may stir up an apathetic reader:

DIVIDED LOYALTIES

Should a man put loyalty to his country above loyalty to a friend? Does loyalty to the government come before loyalty to one's family? How we answer such a question depends on . . .

(11) By *anticipating damaging objections*, the writer may disarm would-be critics:

THE HIGH COST OF MISFORTUNE

Nowadays anyone who advocates public health insurance is called a socialist. Thanks to years of skillful and well-financed publicity . . .

(12) An *amusing anecdote* may at the same time convey an important idea:

MEDICAL JOURNALISM— WITH AND WITHOUT UPBEAT

As a veteran writer of medical and psychological articles for the mass-circulation "slicks," I have a fellow feeling for the violinist who rebelled after having been with an orchestra for thirty years. One day, so the story goes, he sat with his hands folded during rehearsal, and when the conductor rapped on the podium with his baton and demanded furiously, "Why aren't you playing?" replied, with a melancholy sigh, "Because I don't like music." Sometimes I feel like sitting at my typewriter with my hands folded. I don't like popularization. It has gone too far. The little learning—with illustrations— which the magazines have been pouring into a thirsty public has become a dangerous thing. . . .—Edith M. Stern, *Saturday Review*

Some common ways of introducing a theme are usually *ineffective:*

(1) A *repetition*, often verbatim, *of the assignment.*

(2) A *colorless summarizing statement:* "There are many qualities that the average college graduate looks for in a job. Most of them probably consider the following most important. . . ."

(3) An *unsupported claim to interest:* "Migratory birds are a fascinating subject. Ever since I was a little child I have been interested in the migration of birds. Studying them has proved a wonderful hobby. . . ."

(4) An *unsubstantiated claim that the paper is going to deal with a burning issue:* "There has been much controversy over the question of whether public schools should give their students released time for religious instruction. This question has been debated many times. . . ."

(5) *Complaints:* "I find it hard to discuss prejudice in a paper of 500 words. Prejudice is a vast subject. . . ."

(6) *Apologies:* "I am really not very well qualified to write about the qualifications that good children's books should have. . . ."

(7) *Evasions:* "Everyone feels differently about the merits of required courses. I think everyone has a right to his own opinion. . . ."

(8) A *dictionary definition* that is not really followed up, applied, or argued with in the rest of the paper.

Conclusions

An effective conclusion ties together different parts of a paper and reinforces its central message. Avoid conclusions that are merely a lame restatement of points you have made abundantly clear. Instead, make your reader feel that your conclusion was *needed* to make your paper a satisfying whole. Try making your conclusion fulfill an expectation created earlier in your paper. For instance, make it give a direct answer to a question asked in your title or introduction, tie it in with a key incident treated early in your paper, or allude again to a central unifying symbol.

Here are some examples of effective conclusions:

(1) A *memorable restatement* of the central idea:

. . . Underneath our shiny fronts of stone, our fascination with gadgets and our new toys that can blow the earth into a million stars, we are still outside the doorway through which the great answers wait. Not all the cameras in Christendom nor all the tricky lights will move us one step closer to a better understanding of ourselves, but only, as it always was, the truly written word, the profoundly felt gesture, the naked and direct contemplation of man which is the enduring glamour of the stage. — Arthur Miller, "The American Theater," *Holiday*

(2) A *final anecdote* that reinforces the central idea without explicit restatement:

. . . Only once did I ever hear of an official football speech which met with my entire approval. It was made by a Harvard captain. His team had lost to Yale but by a smaller score than was expected. It had been a fast and interesting game. At the dinner when the team broke training the captain said, "We lost to Yale but I think we had a satisfactory season. We have had fun out of football and it seems to me that ought to be the very best reason for playing the game."

A shocked silence followed his remarks. He was never invited to come to Cambridge to assist in the coaching of any future Harvard eleven. His heresy was profound. He had practically intimated that being defeated was less than tragic. — Heywood Broun, "A Study in Sportsmanship," *Harper's*

(3) An apposite *final quotation:*

. . . Should there be codes of ethics for honesty in government? Must public men declare themselves in writing to be honest men just as some professors have been required to swear solemnly that they do not really intend to overthrow the Government of the United States? Personally, I have no faith in such oaths. A gentleman who much influenced my early life once told me:

"Son, by God, when I invite a man to dinner I do not propose to count the silver — before or after he leaves the table!" — William S. White, "The American Genius for Hypocrisy," *Harper's*

(4) A sober estimate of the *significance of the conclusions* reached:

. . . Criticism by outsiders will not miraculously transform the quality of network programs. But as long as criticism finds its way into print, and as long as network presidents take their critics seriously enough to cajole or denounce them, the cause of informative and satisfying television is not lost.

(5) A *forecast or warning* based on facts developed in the paper:

. . . In education we have not yet acquired that kind of will. But we need to acquire it, and we have no time to lose. We must acquire it in this decade. For if, in the crucial years which are coming, our people remain as unprepared as they are for their responsibilities and their mission, they may not be equal to the challenge, and if they do not succeed, they may never have a second chance to try. — Walter Lippmann, "The Shortage in Education," *Atlantic*

(6) An essential *condition for future progress:*

. . . When public relations people become as a group more forthright, less designing, more strict in their standards, and more respectful of the public, then — and only then — will the discerning public accept them as real professionals. — Vance Packard, "Public Relations: Good or Bad," *Atlantic*

(7) A suggestion for *remedial action:*

. . . If the leading citizens in a community would make it a point to visit their state prison, talk with the warden, then return to their communities with a better understanding of actual down-to-earth prison problems, they would have taken one of the most important and most effective steps toward a solution of our crime problem. — Erle Stanley Gardner, "Parole and the Prisons — An Opportunity Wasted," *Atlantic*

(8) A *return from the specific to the general,* relating the findings of the paper to a general trend:

. . . Inge's family plays constitute a kind of aesthetic isolationism upon which the world of outside — the world of moral choice, decision, and social pressures — never impinges. Although he has endowed the commonplace with some depth, it is not enough to engage serious attention. William Inge is yet another example of Broadway's reluctance or inability to deal intelligently with the American world at large. — Robert Brustein, "The Men-Taming Women of William Inge," *Harper's*

Here are some examples of *ineffective* conclusions:

(1) The *platitude:* "This problem deserves the serious attention of every right-thinking American."

(2) The *silver lining:* "When things look their grimmest, a turn for the better is usually not far away."

(3) The *panacea:* "The restoration of proper discipline in the nation's schools will make juvenile delinquency a thing of the past."

(4) The *conclusion raising problems* that weaken or distract from the point of the paper: "Of course, a small car has obvious disadvantages for a family with numerous children or for the traveler in need of luggage space."

Exercises

A. Study the following *book titles* and rank the three best titles in order of their effectiveness. Explain what makes them effective.

1. *George Washington, Man and Monument*
2. *Freedom in the Modern World*
3. *The City in History*
4. *The New Radicalism in America*
5. *The Free World Colossus*
6. *Number: The Language of Science*
7. *Lost Worlds of Africa*
8. *The Feminine Mystique*
9. *The Naked Ape*
10. *The Second Sex*

B. Look through recent issues of general-circulation *magazines* to find five articles whose titles you consider exceptionally effective. Defend your choices.

C. What would you do to improve the title of a theme you have recently written? Write down the original title and *three* alternative titles that seem equally or more effective. Make sure the new titles do justice to the content of the actual theme.

D. Describe the approach chosen in each of the following introductions. Comment on the effectiveness of both *introduction and title*. Do they make the reader want to go on reading? Do they seem to lead clearly and directly into a specific subject? What kind of paper would you expect in each case?

1.   HYDROPONICS IN THE HOME

Hydroponics is a subject about which many people have little or no knowledge, yet there is nothing really new or mysterious about it. It is merely a system by which plants are grown in water solutions containing the essential minerals for plant growth. The terms *water culture* and *water gardening* refer to this same system. . . .

2.   THE LATEST STYLE

If you picked this paper up expecting a dissertation on frills, frocks, and new brassieres to dream in, you had best put it down again. I am concerned here with a new style in automotive power plants, the free-piston turbine engine. You may ride behind one sooner than you think. . . .

3.   THE NEW ILLITERACY

We hear much about the reawakening interest in the humanities, the new appreciation of the generalness in the liberal arts, the growing dissatisfaction with overspecialization. Maybe so. But these signs are minute, I suggest, [compared with] those coming from the other direction. I offer the proposition that the trends that have been working against the humanities are likely to increase, not decrease, in the decade ahead. . . . —William H. Whyte, Jr., *Saturday Review*

4.   MARY HAD A LITTLE DELINQUENT

In today's world, the worst kind of juvenile delinquent is not the one who has become a public blotch on the good name of society, or who has been blasted to fame in a newspaper headline. More frightening is a silent, sneaking kind of young rebel. Normal enough in looks, this person creeps through our culture until suddenly—POW—his disrespect for authority is revealed. The delinquent of this second variety with whom I am most intimately acquainted is—*me*! I am very good at being bad.

5.   THOREAU AND HUMAN NATURE

Our histories of American literature are deficient in a number of categories. They seldom or never, for example, recognize the greatness of American biographical writing. . . . They do not know what to do with the powerful library of travel literature written by Americans. . . . But I think the greatest deficiency in these manuals is their failure to recognize the existence of that type of writer the French call the moralist. — Howard Mumford Jones, *Atlantic*

6.   COLLEGE — FROM THE OUTSIDE LOOKING IN

Why waste four years going to college? In four years an ambitious high school graduate can become happily established with a company and have a sizable lead on the road to fame and fortune over his former schoolmates. This is how I felt when I left high school. Three years of pursuing fame and fortune altered my thinking radically. . .

7.   THE EDUCATED ANTI-INTELLECTUALS

It is a curious fact that the American people spend more per capita on the schooling of their children than any other people on this globe and yet they persist in proclaiming their anti-intellectualism. Consider the epithets "brain trusters" and "eggheads." Look at the general disdain for the very word "intellectual". . . .

8.   BRUTE STRENGTH IS NOT ENOUGH

Football has often been called a game for men who are all muscle and have no brains. This charge may have been justified in the infant years of the game, when it consisted entirely of running plays and when the players used brute strength to crash through the opposing line. To-day, a team may use as many as fifty different plays, involving complicated deception and a wide variety of passes. . . .

9.   THE ROLE OF GOVERNMENT

The decision between a strong government which governs the people or a weak government is one of importance and one that needs careful thought and consideration. Throughout history, the proper role of government has been a subject of discussion. . . .

10.   THE BENT AND BLUNTED FREE LANCE

In the chivalry of the thirteenth century, an important figure was the free lance, an independent knight who sold his fighting skill to the highest bidder and, so legend says, tilted his bold weapon in defense of the helpless against all sorts of dragons and outrages. So far in the twentieth century an important adjunct to communication has been the free-lance writer who has made a living, and a considerable social impact, with his pen. . . . — Hartzell Spence, *Saturday Review*

E. Examine the introduction or "lead" in three current articles from different general-interest magazines. Write a well-developed paragraph about each one. Describe the approach followed and evaluate its effectiveness.

F. Formulate a central idea for a short theme on a topic of your choice. Then write *three different possible introductions,* each time using a different approach.

G. Describe the function and estimate the probable effectiveness of the following conclusions:

1. (A paper describing the game of badminton)

. . . Badminton can be very exciting. If you are ever looking for a good time I suggest that you try this game. I know from experience that it can really be a lot of fun.

2. (A paper discussing a veteran's visit to his former high school)

. . . As I walked, alone, down the familiar and yet strangely different hall, I began to realize a truth that nostalgic people like myself find hard to learn: Distance gives glamor to the past.

3. (A paper defending women against the charge that they are poor drivers)

. . . that the woman driver, inexperienced and timid as she may be, is less of a highway menace than the arrogant, inconsiderate male. Of course, this is only one woman's opinion, and yours may be different from mine.

4. (A paper trying to demonstrate the futility of censoring comic books)

. . . the parents can do most to counteract the comic-book habit. If they read to their children from good books, if they teach their children to treat good books as treasured possessions, if they make it a habit to talk about good books in the home, the positive attraction of good literature may prove more effective than censorship possibly can.

5. (A paper discussing several examples of "tolerance")

. . . We thus conclude that by "tolerance" we mean allowing beliefs and actions of which we do not wholly approve. Since many of us approve wholeheartedly of only very few things, life without tolerance would be truly intolerable.

6. (A paper examining the proposition that "that government governs best that governs least")

. . . Government must effectively govern to be a true government, but it must govern with restraint and not to excess. The government that governs least is not necessarily the best one. I would rather say that the government that governs ablest, in the interest of most of its citizens, is the best government.

7. (A paper on race prejudice)
. . . What can the individual do to combat racial prejudice? This question is very hard to answer, because nobody can predict the future.

8. (A paper on the democratic process)
. . . The benefits society derives from the democratic process are often unspectacular, and slow in coming. Its weaknesses and disadvantages are often glaringly evident. By its very nature, democracy, in order to survive, must give its enemies the right to be heard and to pursue their goals. As Chesterton has said, "The world will never be safe for democracy — it is a dangerous trade."

H. *Rewrite the conclusion* to one of your recent themes. Write two new versions, each reinforcing in a different way the same central idea as the original.

5.   Continuity and Transition

A paper has continuity when it takes the reader along. An effective writer knows how to make his readers follow from point to point. Good writing has a pied-piper effect; it is accompanied in the reader's mind by a running commentary somewhat like the following: "This I have to hear"; "I can't wait to see how this will turn out"; "Now I can see where you are headed"; "I hope you can make this stick"; "That's what I *thought* you were leading up to"; "Yes, I see"; "That certainly does follow"; "How right you are!" When continuity is lacking, the running commentary is of a quite different sort. It consists mostly of exasperated questions: Where are we going? How does this fit in? What are you leading up to? What is the point?

Every writer must learn how to make his readers see the connections that hold his paper together. In writing, but especially also in revising the paper, he can take the necessary steps to help the reader follow.

Key Sentences

Emphatic key sentences serve as guideposts to the reader. Thus, a **topic sentence** becomes a guide to the intention of a paragraph (see 0 1a). A **thesis sentence** gives direction to the paper as a whole.

From paragraph to paragraph, and even within a paragraph, the most basic method of moving a paper along is to make a key statement that calls for an explanation, to make an assertion that calls for proof.

Notice how a typical passage from Toynbee's *A Study of History* raises questions in the reader's mind that make him move on to the next sentence:

We have said that primitive societies are as old as the human race, but *we should more properly have said that they are older.* Social and institutional life of a kind is found among some of the higher mammals other than man, and it is clear that *mankind could not have become human except in a social environment.* This mutation of sub-man into man . . .

(How can this be? Let me see how this is going to be explained.)

(How did this work? Let me follow this in detail.)

To improve continuity in a theme, state such key ideas clearly and directly — often in a short separate sentence. They will then begin to stand out as the *framework* that your examples, explanations, and other supporting material fill in. Study the following excerpted version of an article that is exceptionally deliberate and clear-cut in its organizational scheme. Can you see how the key sentences the author formulates in response to his four major questions help the reader follow him step by step?

What are the students like? They come from all sorts of backgrounds. . . .
Only one thing they are certain to have in common: they are roughly in the same age group. . . .
Why do they come to college? They come because it is assumed that they will come, because almost everyone they know does. . . .
A second and related reason why students come is to make good contacts. . . .
Many come simply to learn to make a living. . . .
To have fun is still another motive. . . .
There are students who actually come because they want to learn. . . .
What happens to students in college? It is the students' first meeting, most likely, with a national and perhaps international group of men and women of their own age. . . .
Furthermore, college is the students' first encounter with live intellectuals. . . .
Students are surprised, too, at their first meeting with really violent political opinion of all possible varieties. . . .
It is in college, too, that the sharp bitter sting of failure is first experienced to any appreciable extent. . . .
What does the student learn? On the simplest level he has acquired a considerable amount of information. . . .
He will also have learned to question. . . . — James K. Feibleman, "What Happens in College," *Saturday Review*

Transitions

Apt transitional phrases help the reader move smoothly from one point to the next. In a well-written paper, the reader can see how and why the writer moves from point to point. But the connection is seldom as obvious as the writer thinks. Transitional phrases are directional signals that help the reader move along without stumbling.[2]

Here are common transitional phrases:

addition	too, also, furthermore, similarly, moreover
illustration	for example, for instance
paraphrase or summary	that is, in other words, in short, to conclude, to sum up
logical conclusion	so, therefore, thus, accordingly, consequently, as a result, hence
contrast or objection	but, however, nevertheless, on the other hand, conversely, on the contrary
concession	granted that . . . , no doubt, to be sure, it is true that . . .
reiteration	indeed, in fact

The following advice should help you make effective use of transitional phrases:

(1) *Avoid transitions that merely add without showing why.* Shun expressions like "Another interesting point is . . ." or "We might also take a look at . . ." These make it sound as though the writer asked himself: "What else?" They make the reader feel that what follows is at best optional and at worst mere padding.

(2) *Use enumeration sparingly, for emphasis.* Lining major points up in a numerical sequence makes for a formal, systematic presentation. In the following discussion of language, the key points gain force from marching across the page in a 1-2-3 order:

There are *five simple facts* about language in general which we must grasp before we can understand a specific language or pass judgment on a particular usage. . . .

In the first place, language is basically speech. . . .

In the second place, language is personal. . . .

The third fact about language is that it changes. . . .

The fourth great fact about language . . . is that its users are, in one way or another, isolated. . . .

The fifth great fact about language is that it is a historical growth of a specific kind. . . .—Donald J. Lloyd, "Snobs, Slobs, and the English Language," *The American Scholar*

[2] For transitions within the paragraph see 0 lb.

Though effective when used for special emphasis, such enumeration easily becomes too rigid and unimaginative. When used in a perfunctory manner, it makes for heavy, plodding reading. The next example, though also presenting several major points in order, uses less obtrusive transitional expressions:

thesis	An arrangement of shapes is satisfying, or otherwise, to the human eye, because of certain elementary natural laws. *The most*
first point	*essential of these* is the law of balance. . . .
second point	A picture *also* demands harmony. . . .
summarizing definition	*In speaking* of the harmony, or unity, of a picture, *we mean* that . . .
further development of point 2	The colors, *too,* must be related harmoniously. . . .
summary of points 1, 2 third point	*Thus* we have balance and harmony as necessities in a picture. We must *also* have variety and subtlety. . . .
definition summarizing points 1-3	The design of a picture, which includes *these qualities of* balance, harmony, and variety, is its basis and essential skeleton. . . .—K. W. Maurer, "On the Appreciation of Paintings," *Queen's Quarterly*

(3) *Fill in the logical connections that help the reader follow an argument.* Take special care to take your reader along when an argument moves systematically through a number of essential steps:

introduces main point	It is plain that . . .
begins to enumerate reasons	Here are some reasons for . . .
elaborates on one of several points	The second of these . . .
summarizes what precedes	In short, . . .
raises a possible objection	Yet . . .
concedes a point	It is true that . . .
returns to original trend of thought	Nevertheless, . . .
draws balanced conclusion	At the very least, . . .

Often a complete sentence, and in longer papers a complete paragraph, may be needed to establish the transition from one major point to another. Overuse of transitional expressions like *however, therefore,* and *all things considered* can make a paper awkward and mechanical. But when used sparingly, and when varied to avoid monotony, they help to keep both writer and reader from leaving the tracks.

Synonyms and Recurrent Terms

In much well-focused discussion, key terms and their synonyms echo from one paragraph to the next. In a paper on academic freedom, terms and phrases like "freedom," "liberty," "independent thought," "free inquiry," "responsible choice," "absence of interference," and "self-government" show that the writer is never straying far from the central issue. Learn to look for the network of synonyms and near-synonyms that helps keep together much well-written prose.

> Throughout his public career, Taft was lampooned as an *anachronism*, a man *out of touch with modern needs* and aspirations. . . . Reading over his speeches and debates, one detects an *antiquarian* flavor. . . . the lawyerly precision and the candor are decidedly *old-fashioned*. . . .

The echo effect of such synonyms reassures the reader that he is not expected to take unexplained sudden jumps. In the following excerpt, notice how the repetition of key terms like *work, toil,* or *labor* helps lead the reader through a passage consisting of several substantial paragraphs:[3]

> What elements of the national character are attributable to this long-time agrarian environment? First and foremost is *the habit of work.* For the colonial farmer ceaseless striving constituted the price of survival. . . .
> The *tradition of toil* so begun found new sustenance as settlers opened up the boundless stretches of the interior. "In the free States," wrote Harriet Martineau in 1837, "*labour* is more really and heartily honoured. . . ."
> One source of Northern antagonism to the system of human bondage was the fear that it was jeopardizing this basic tenet of the American creed. "Wherever *labor* is mainly performed by slaves," Daniel Webster told the United States Senate, "it is regarded as . . ."
> Probably no legacy from our farmer forebears has entered more deeply into the national psychology. If an American has no *purposeful work* on hand . . .
> This *worship of work* has made it difficult for Americans to learn how to play. As Poor Richard saw it, "Leisure is . . ."
> The first mitigations of the daily grind took the form of hunting, fishing, barn-raisings and logrollings — *activities that* had no social stigma because they *contributed to the basic needs of living.* . . .
> The importance attached to *useful work* had the further effect of helping to make "this new man" indifferent to aesthetic considerations. . . . —Arthur M. Schlesinger, *Paths to the Present*

Logical Continuity

Effective writing moves forward in logical patterns that the reader can recognize and follow. Key sentences, transitional phrases,

---

[3] For the use of recurrent terms within the single paragraph see 0 lc.

and repeated terms can point up continuity of thought where it exists, but they cannot make up for the lack of it. If transitions prove hard to establish, the logical patterns that keep the paper moving forward from point to point may need strengthening. Familiar logical patterns that the reader is prepared to follow are from a *problem* to its *solution;* from a decision to one or more possible *alternatives;* from one major cause to several *contributing* ones; or from a hypothesis to several major *objections.*

Can you see the logical pattern that helps move forward the following student paper?

PROBLEM	In any family, there is a network of antagonistic desires. A young girl might want to practice her violin, while her brother insists that the noise interferes with his studying. . . .
SOLUTION first alternative	These situations must be solved or managed. If one parent dictates without consideration of the others, the family will be run in an authoritarian manner. Women used to bend to the wishes of an authoritarian husband. . . .
second alternative	If no authority figure guides and directs these daily decisions, the individuals in the family must create some method of living together. . . .
LARGER PARALLEL	Society presents the same picture on a much larger scale. The disagreements found in the family unit are multiplied in society. . . .

Similar logical relationships account for the purposeful forward movement of much professional writing. Study the following excerpt from a magazine article. Notice how the opening sentences of each paragraph suggest well-planned, systematic forward movement. Notice the frequent use of a *this* or *these* pointing back to a preceding paragraph. Notice the use of a *the one . . . the other* pattern tying two paragraphs together:

thesis	The diversity of higher education in the United States is unprecedented. . . .
first problem is taken up; one alternative is considered	Consider the *question of size.* The small campus offers . . .
second alternative is considered	Others feel hemmed in by these very qualities. They welcome the *comparative anonymity and impersonality* of the big university. . . .
second problem is taken up; first alternative is considered	Another familiar question is whether the student should go to a *college next door, in the next city, or a thousand miles away.* By living at home . . .

second alternative
is considered

Balanced against this, there are considerable advantages to a youngster in *seeing and living in an unfamiliar region* of the country. . . .

alternatives are
weighed

But this question too must be decided in terms of the individual. . . .

third problem is
taken up; first
alternative is
considered

Co-education poses still another problem. Those who favor it argue . . .

second alternative
is considered

Others believe that *young men and women* will work better if . . .

alternatives are
weighed

There is no pat answer. It might be healthy for one youngster . . .

fourth problem is
taken up

The so-called *"prestige" colleges and universities* present a special problem. . . . —John W. Gardner, "How to Choose a College, if Any," *Harper's*

NOTE: Chapter 6 of this book discusses in detail some of the logical patterns that determine the structure of a paper as a whole.

Exercises

A. In each of the following pairs of sentences, a transitional word or phrase has been left out. Fill in a transition that will help the reader move smoothly from the first sentence to the second.

1. There are many special schools which should be considered by the young person who is not going on to college. The boy who wishes to be an X-ray technician and the girl who wishes to be a practical nurse, _____, will find many schools at which they may receive training.

2. Apprenticeship systems are still operating in every industry and offer wide opportunities for the ambitious youngster. He must be warned, _____, that in some of the older crafts entry is jealously guarded.

3. The home environment is the largest single factor determining the grade school youngster's "scholastic aptitude." _____, how well he learns in school depends on what he has learned at home.

4. Rennie was lazy, self-indulgent, spoiled. _____, he did remarkably well in his favorite subjects.

5. The basic promise that American society has always held out to its citizens is equality of opportunity. The typical substandard big-city school, _____, is profoundly un-American.

6. Negro athletes are not as pampered as some white sports fans seem to think. _____ the outstanding Negro athlete enjoys many privileges, but when a black and a white man are equally well qualified, coaches are likely to give preference to the latter.

7. The European system of education very early separates youngsters permanently on the basis of ability. The American system, _____ _____, is designed to make possible numerous second chances.

8. In many Latin-American countries, more young men study to be lawyers than are needed in their country. _____, in many underdeveloped countries more young men study to be engineers than a pre-industrial society could support.

9. A highly specialized skill limits a person's job opportunities. It _____ makes the specialist a potential victim of technological unemployment.

10. Our leaders are fond of the phrase "the free world." In actual fact, _____, societies that foster political freedom are the exception rather than the rule.

B. Point out the *logical connections* that give continuity to the following excerpted student paper about the work of an American painter.

> . . . The "window series" captivated me for it implied glimpses into the privacy of humanity; each soul was shielded, barely, by a fragile lace curtain, or a shade, or perhaps a shadow . . . Exquisite and delicate, the details of the curtain, for instance, were so tangible that I was tempted to push it aside; but then, I'd have been intruding.
>
> In contrast, the civil rights drawings almost scream for involvement—they beg to be studied, and to study them means to lose one's complacency. . . .
>
> Perhaps his interest in the civil rights struggle helped the artist to identify with Lincoln. Certainly he created a striking interpretation in his Lincoln portrait. . . .
>
> If it could be said that Lincoln symbolizes the simplicity of the Midwest, then the artist's prairie landscapes glorify it. There is a sense of infinity in the vast expanse of heavens over rain-soaked fields and rolling prairies. . . .

C. Study the following key sentences from a magazine article about the Presidency. As fully as you can, trace the network of *key terms* and synonyms that helps keep the article together; the *logical connections* from paragraph to paragraph; and the *transitional words and phrases* that help make these connections clear to the reader.

    In [the] received formulation, the growth of Presidential power is historically associated with the assertion of federal as against state sovereignty, and of executive over legislative initiative: a collective triumph of liberalism over conservatism, welfare-state concern over laissez-faire indifference, . . . internationalism over isolationism. . . .

    In the last few years this kind of interpretation, seemingly so self-evident to men of good will, has been jarred by events. . . .

    . . . In these disturbed, confused circumstances there are signs of an attempt to rethink the received view of the Presidency.

    The effort is easier talked about than made. In the first place, there is much historical truth in the conventionally respectful view of the office. . . .

    Other factors would appear to reinforce the familiar estimates. The almost permanent crisis situation of the past quarter-century shows little sign of easing. In foreign affairs, both tradition and necessity seem to locate authority in the hands of the executive. . . .

    Similarly, the trend toward centralized governmental authority has been conspicuous and seems an unavoidable movement, observable in many other countries. . . .

    Again, historically the legislative branch has not been dazzlingly impressive. . . .

    Embedded within the historical record, and stretching back as far as the creation of the office, are recurrent schemes to reform and even to abolish the Presidency. Their very profusion, and the lack of effect they have had, weaken any present-day proposals. . . .

    Nor do the experiences of other countries offer encouragement to Americans to change their own executive system. . . .

    We seem to be left where we started: namely either with the cheerful belief that the Presidency comes as near perfection as can be achieved in an imperfect world, or with the pragmatic belief that it is unwise to tinker with long-established mechanisms. . . .

    But such testimony leaves much unsaid. The historical record is in actuality less clear and less unanimous. . . .

    One of the worst effects has been on Congress. The federal legislature, while certainly not lacking in aggressive impulses, has over the decades been mainly thrust on the defensive. . . .

    Moderate Presidents have themselves had to pay a price for the performances of aggrandizing predecessors. . . .

    "Strong" Presidents, in other words, store up trouble for themselves and for their successors. . . .

    Perhaps something is to be learned after all from the misgivings of 19th-century American liberals, and from the plethora of plans for

executive reorganization. . . . —Marcus Cunliffe, "A Defective Institution?" *Commentary*

D. In a page of expository prose selected by your instructor, point out all
key sentences, transitional phrases, and words or devices making for continuity.

6. Using Outlines

The written outline is a device for working out and strengthening the organization of a piece of writing. It is true that many experienced writers do most of their outlining in their heads. They
mentally fit possible ideas into tentative patterns while shaving, taking a shower, or walking the dog. But a written outline helps a writer
visualize the structure of his paper, and to confront and solve problems of organization.

Working Outlines

*Construct a working outline by jotting down major points in a
tentative order.* To be useful as a help in *writing* a paper, an outline
should be informal and flexible. Such a working outline resembles an
architect's preliminary sketches rather than the finished blueprint.
When jotting down a working outline, the writer is in effect saying to
himself: "Let's see what it would look like on paper." Here is a first
tentative outline for a short paper on anti-intellectualism in the high
schools:

        emphasis in high school on
            athletics
            social activities

        little recognition for intellectual achievement
            honor roll
            debating society
            drama society ("intellectual"?)

        attitude now changing?
            stress on college entrance

One of the most essential skills you can learn as a writer is to use
such an informal outline as a *tool* in working out a plausibly organized
paper. As you look at your tentative points, you ask: Would this order
make sense to the reader? Perhaps you will reverse the order of two
major points to make the scheme as a whole follow a rough *chronologi-*

cal or historical order. Or you will shift the easiest and most familiar point to the beginning to make the scheme proceed from the *simple to the difficult.*

Suppose a writer wants to discuss an important common element in books that have enjoyed a tremendous vogue with adolescents. He might first jot down titles as they come to mind:

Catcher in the Rye
Goethe's *Young Werther*
Catch-22
The Prophet
The Stranger
Lord of the Flies

To arrange these titles in a plausible order, he might decide to start with the *classic* example: Goethe's *Werther*, the book that "invented adolescence." He would then discuss outstanding *recent* examples, taking them up roughly in the order in which they became popular. Finally, he would discuss in detail a *personal* example – a book that meant a great deal to him as an adolescent. His working outline might look like this:

classic example: Goethe's *Werther*

recent examples
   Catcher in the Rye
   The Stranger
   Lord of the Flies
   Catch-22

my own favorite
   poems of Dylan Thomas

Final Outlines

The final outline serves both as a final check on organization and as a guide to the reader. Your instructor may require you to submit a final outline with any paper presenting a substantial argument or organizing a substantial body of material. The final outline of a library or research paper is usually a carefully developed chart, without which the investigator may lose his way (see Chapter 9).

The outline you submit with your paper will have to follow conventional outline form. Two major forms are common:

(1) The **topic outline** is most useful for quick reference. It presents, in logical order, the topics and subtopics (and often the subsubtopics) that a paper covers. Like other outlines, it is often pre-

ceded by a thesis sentence summarizing the central idea of the paper. Here is a representative example:

SORORITIES AND THE SINGLE GIRL

THESIS: The social activities of a sorority are designed to help girls conclude desirable middle-class marriages.

I. Keeping girls away from undesirable men

   A. Dating arrangements with fraternities

   B. Busy social calendar discouraging independent dating

II. Husband-hunting opportunities

III. Emphasis on formal courtship rather than casual dating

   A. "Pinnings" as formal ceremonies

   B. The role of pinnings and engagements in sorority "news"

(2) In a **sentence outline**, the writer sums up, in one complete sentence each, what he has to say on each topic and subtopic. The sentence outline thus forces him to think through his material thoroughly and systematically. It reveals vagueness, indecision, and lack of continuity more reliably than the topic outline, which merely indicates the ground to be covered. A sentence outline might look like this:

MAIN STREET ISN'T PENNSYLVANIA AVENUE

THESIS: A successful business career alone does not qualify an executive for government work.

I. Prominent businessmen have often occupied high positions in the federal government.

II. Businessmen often have qualifications that government officials tend to lack.

   A. They are in close contact with the wishes and opinions of the general public.

   B. They have thorough training in organizational problems.

     1. They are trained in administrative efficiency.

     2. They are cost-conscious.

III. But business executives often lack preparation for other aspects of government work.

   A. They tend to lack the tact and experience necessary for dealing with people from foreign cultures.

     1. They may alienate foreign diplomats.

     2. They tend to ignore public opinion abroad.

   B. They tend to lack the legal training required in interpreting and administering laws.

C. They have had little experience with the delays inherent in democratic processes.

IV. The personal qualifications of the individual executive are more important than his business background.

The divisions of an outline do not always correspond exactly to the paragraph divisions in the paper—though in a well-organized paper the two often coincide. Several minor subdivisions may be treated in the same paragraph; one subdivision, developed by detailed examples, may spread through several paragraphs; short transitional paragraphs may intervene between subdivisions.

To eliminate common weaknesses, check your finished outlines against the following list of suggestions:

(1) *Be consistent* in the use of symbols, indention, and spacing.

(2) *Avoid using "Introduction," "Conclusion,"* etc., as substitutes for individual headings.

(3) *Avoid single subdivisions.* If there is a subdivision A, there should be a subdivision B. If there is a section numbered 1, there should be a section numbered 2. If a section covers only one major point or one major step, leave it undivided.

(4) *Avoid a long sequence of parallel elements,* such as I—X, A—F, or 1—8. Unless the subject matter justifies mere undifferentiated enumeration, try to split the sequence into two or three major groups.

(5) *Use parallel grammatical structure* for headings of the same rank in order to emphasize their logical relation. For instance, if A 1 reads "To revive the student's interest," A 2 and A 3 should also be worded as infinitives: "To promote the student's participation"; "To develop the student's independent judgment."

(6) *Make sure the thesis is a complete statement*—not a question, not a phrase without a predicate, not a dependent clause.

(7) In a topic outline, *make each topic specific and informative.* In a sentence outline, make each subdivision a complete sentence. *Make each sentence sum up an idea* rather than merely indicate a topic.

Exercises

A. Sort out the following material and arrange it in a topic outline:

EDUCATION WITHOUT REPRESENTATION

THESIS: Students would profit greatly from being given greater influence on curricula and teaching methods than they now have.

1. Training for citizenship through active participation
2. Present lack of student influence
3. Sense of belonging through participation.
4. Attitudes toward elective as compared with required courses
5. Success of experimental programs
6. Attitude of night school and business college students toward freely chosen subjects
7. Training for adult responsibilities in business and family through participation
8. Improved motivation through active participation

B. Sort out the following material and arrange it in a sentence outline:

THE VALUE OF GROUP DISCUSSION

THESIS: Training in the techniques of group discussion is an indispensable part of the student's general education.

1. Discussion teaches us to look for evidence that will withstand criticism.
2. Discussion teaches us to control emotional reactions.
3. The primary goal of a discussion is to solve immediate problems.
4. Successful discussion requires ability to focus on the subject at hand.
5. In modern American society, more and more decisions are reached as the result of group discussion.
6. Successful discussion requires willingness to consider the viewpoints of others.
7. Discussion teaches us to estimate the reliability of evidence submitted by others.
8. Comparison of different views enables us to distinguish valid from invalid arguments.
9. The give-and-take of discussion is a humane alternative to one-sided propaganda and the use of force.
10. Discussion teaches us to get along with others.
11. Discussion teaches us to respect people whose knowledge or ability is superior to ours.
12. A successful discussion has educational value.
13. Discussion teaches us to be patient with people whom we assume to be wrong.
14. Discussion teaches us to evaluate evidence.

15. Successful discussion requires careful investigation of the relevant facts.

16. Discussion teaches us how to think.

17. Disagreement forces us to reexamine our views.

C. Select a current magazine article whose organization you find exceptionally clear or effective. Prepare both a topic and a sentence outline. Your instructor may wish to suggest a maximum number of words for each outline.

Review Exercise: Sample Themes

Study the following *student themes*. How successful has the author been in gathering relevant material? Is the subject adequately restricted? How effective are title, introduction, and conclusion? What features make for continuity? Rate these papers from most to least successful, and be prepared to defend your choices.

1.   CERAMICS — MY HOBBY

Have you ever picked up a piece of free-form earthenware and thought how very satisfying and enjoyable it must have been for the person who worked it up from mere earth and water? By "free form," I mean the potter's own creative idea modeled in clay. Such free-form modeling is rather an involved process — many times, it is true, heart-breaking, but nevertheless an enjoyable and thoroughly gratifying experience.

It is possible to dig one's own clay from the earth. By moistening it with water and adding certain chemicals, one can make the clay mass more elastic, more workable, and stronger. Then follows the mixing of a glaze which, according to a specialized formula, will have an affinity to the original clay body. This in itself can become a long and tedious procedure . So, unless one has a pioneering spirit, it is better to find a standard clay body and glazes which have already been processed according to the manufacturer's own formula.

Cutting, shaping and molding the clay mass into the desired form with one's own hands is one of the biggest thrills imaginable. It is surprising what can be done with moist clay! A creative spirit can really go "wild" and still come up with something both beautiful and practical — say a flower vase or planter in the exaggerated form of some sea shell.

When the piece is thoroughly dry, it is known as "greenware" and is very fragile, but it becomes hardened through firing in a kiln. The firing is done slowly. The heat goes up to about 2000°F. It is measured by a cone-shaped pin set in a clay base and made to melt at the desired temperature. This is known as the pyrometric cone. The entire firing period takes about eight hours. Then the kiln is cooled slowly. It should not be opened or disturbed during the cooling time, which may take twelve hours or more. The greenware is now referred to as "bisque."

Bisque may be painted in a variety of colors, called underglaze, and then dipped in a transparent glaze. It may be sprayed or brushed with or dipped in any of the colored glazes. A second firing to bring out the glaze effect is now necessary. Usually, this firing is slow too, with the temperature not as intense as before—about 1800°F. However, the pyrometric cone must be watched more closely than in the bisque firing, especially with certain glaze formulas.

Glazes are extremely difficult to control, and many unexpected effects are obtained—probably caused by moisture in the air, uneven firing elements, firing time, dirt particles, or some chemical reaction. Many unique and unusual effects can be obtained through experimentation with underglazes, overglazes, colored clay bodies, sifted sands, crushed colored glass and even salt! I remember my first experiment. I used sifted sand which I found in my backyard. I dusted the sand over the glaze coating and, after firing, found there were bright red and black raised granules throughout the glaze.

One can look at this hobby from a practical point of view. Gifts alone, especially at Christmas time, make it worth while. But it is the ideas and experiments that make it a truly fascinating and worthwhile hobby.

2.   MY FRIEND, MY ENEMY

Mimi is practically my best friend. On the outside, she is a loud-talking, big-mouthed, obnoxious girl. At a party, her only aim seems to be fun, with no feelings about anyone else. During the course of a conversation, she tells all she knows about her friends and their personal lives, never leaving out a detail or personal remark. Though Mimi is my best friend, her utter disregard for other people's feelings also makes her my worst enemy.

After seeing Mimi once, you won't forget her. She has a wild mop of short blond hair, which is combed once a day. Her big blue eyes are continually covered by a pair of heavy, coke-bottle lens glasses. She weighs well over her quota, a fact she explains by saying "there's more of me to love" and "I was thin once, but I wasn't as jolly." Her clothes are in the casual range of tennis shoes, big sweaters, and skirts.

What's ticking inside her head? Most noticeable is a bad, bad temper. She has the idea that no man is good enough to be his brother's keeper. This is her basic philosophy: If she decides to swear or dress sloppily, it's her business and nobody else's. Her temper makes her rage at people who make noise while she sleeps and at such things as a dirty bathroom basin. Usually her rage is a short atomic blast, but it never has a fallout of grudges. After waking, Mimi speaks to no one for at least two hours. She simply glares at any bystander.

A greater sense of humor never was found in one human being. In high school she called herself "Sherman" because she was as big as a tank. Everyone loved and hated her at the same time. Some people claimed that she sold

beer and wine from her hall locker and made stencils of the teachers' signa-
tures. When she was sent to the dean, she presented her ideas on how to
improve the school honor code.

The parties Mimi goes to are never boring. She cuts everyone to pieces,
including—and especially—me. At one time, she told everyone that I mixed
my make-up in a huge vat and spread it on with a spatula. She is always talking to my friends and warning them about my numerous shortcomings.

Mimi lives across the hall in our boarding house. There she can sit for
hours with a piece of clay or even a cigarette box and create small things for
her enjoyment. Her jolly laugh is heard around the house when small things
amuse her.

Few people understand what provokes Mimi, and they resent her carefree attitude. When I see her sitting like a fat little baby on the floor reading
the college daily or a letter from home, enjoying every word like a piece of
candy, I would like to hug her. However, as she slowly reveals my life to all
present, I would like to kill her.

To many people, Mimi is just another coed. But to me she is a villain,
the Medusa, Eleanor Roosevelt, Jerry Lewis, and Jack the Ripper, with a
heart as big as a statue, all rolled into one fat, fun-loving, childlike package.

3.   THOU SHALT NOT LIE

Although most people believe it is wrong to lie, it is doubtful that anyone can go through his entire life without ever telling a lie. But are all lies
equally wrong? Or are some lies actually justified? To answer this we must
examine the four basic types of lies. Each type is told for a different reason.

The first, and probably the most common type of lie, is the lie of exaggeration. This is the type of lie we tell to make an incident sound more interesting. Or we may lie about our achievements to make ourselves seem more
intelligent or clever. We justify this type of lie by convincing ourselves it cannot harm anyone. But there is one disadvantage to this type of lie. If we are
found out, we are left feeling like a fool and wondering why we bothered to
lie about something so unimportant.

The second type of lie is the one told to avoid hurting someone. This
type of lie is often considered necessary. When someone asks, "Do you like
my new dress?" we prefer to answer yes because we know that is what she
wants to hear. But even this type of lie is not always wise. For example, if a
patient asks his doctor if he has terminal cancer, he wants and expects an
honest answer in most cases.

The third type of lie is the exact opposite of the second. It is the deliberately malicious lie told for the express purpose of hurting someone. Few
mature adults tell this kind of lie, but it is fairly common among children.
They may shout "I hate you" at another child one day but be back playing
with him the next day.

The last type of lie is the one we tell to cover up something we should
or should not have done in the first place. Rather than admit we made a mistake, we lie about it. This is the type of lie that gets us into the most trouble.

No one has a good enough memory to tell this type of lie. One lie leads to another. Then before we know it, we have forgotten what we said to whom, and we are afraid to open our mouth for fear we will put our foot in it. Then we realize what is meant by the phrase, "Oh, what a tangled web we weave when first we practice to deceive."

4.   NO MORE FAVORS, PLEASE

Many times in a conversation I have heard it said that "a boss's son has it made." I doubt whether a person who makes this statement has ever worked for his father. At any rate, during the four years that I worked for my father's water softener firm, I was not treated nearly as well as were the other employees.

With them my father was generous and tolerant. They received $2.50 an hour or $100.00 for their standard forty-hour week. And if Jerry or Fred helped to sell a new water softener to one of our customers, he was awarded a $20.00 commission. Whenever Jerry asked for a little time off to go fishing, my father promptly granted his request. And once Fred got two days off to take a trip to Chicago, and Dad didn't even dock his pay. If Jack and Kenny botched an installation job, my father would reprove them in a kindly tone and explain how they could have avoided the mistake. Once Kenny failed to tighten a packing nut on a valve, and the water leaked all over the customer's floor. Father sent over a man to clean up the mess and just told Kenny to be more careful next time. On another occasion Jack and Kenny dropped a softener down a customer's stairs, ruining the softener and damaging several steps. When they reported the incident to him with worried and anxious looks, Father calmed their fears and told them his insurance would cover the loss. If one of his men became involved in a dispute with a customer over a repair bill, it was his employee, and not the customer, who was always right.

But where I was concerned, my father was a close-fisted and harsh employer. My weekly paycheck was an unvarying fifty dollars, whether I worked forty hours or fifty-five, and the occasional salary raises the other employees enjoyed were never extended to me. I rarely received a commission on the sales I made; my father would either say that he couldn't afford to pay me any extra just then, or else that I wasn't really entitled to the money. If I wanted to take part in some school activity or go on a beach party with some friends, my father would not only refuse to give me time off, but he would often find extra jobs that would force me to work overtime. My mistakes called forth only anger from my father, never understanding. If anything went wrong with one of the company trucks while I was driving, he always assumed I had been driving like my "hot rod friends." If a customer complained about my service or her bill, my father bawled me out for giving him and his business a bad name. Once when I forgot to reduce the water pressure in the backwash machine and caused about twenty dollars worth of mineral to be washed down the drain, he spent half an afternoon sarcastically analyzing my mistake and showing me, in minute detail, how my carelessness had "cut into the profits for the year." Insurance never covered *my* accidents; their cost was deducted from my salary, "to teach me to be more careful."

I don't know whether my father was so harsh with me because he didn't want to appear to be favoring me; but I do know that his constant criticism convinced me that the role of boss's son is a role I don't want to play for a lifetime.

Theme Topics 1

Process

1. Assume that your reader is a high school graduate with little detailed knowledge of science or engineering. Describe the *process* underlying one of the following: the operation of a television set, jet engine, or computer; the life cycle of a butterfly or frog; the manufacture of paper, sugar, or other product that goes through numerous stages in the production process.

2. Write *instructions* that will help your readers perform a difficult task well. Choose one requiring a skill that you have acquired but that is not generally shared. Preferably the task to be performed should require loving care: the preparation of an unusual and difficult dish; the grafting of a bush or tree; the grooming of a horse.

3. Write a *job description* that would help a newcomer do a fairly complicated kind of work. Make it a step-by-step account that would take the novice through a typical hour (morning, evening) on the job.

4. For a foreign student with a good command of English but little experience with *American sports*, prepare a step-by-step account of a typical quarter in football or a typical inning in baseball. Make sure your reader will have a clear and graphic picture of how the game proceeds. Make sure to cover features that you have long taken for granted but that are essential to the outsider's understanding of the game.

Thesis and Support

5. Write a paper in which you support as fully as you can *one limited assertion* in one of the following areas: learning how to drive, learning a foreign language, P.E. in American schools, women teachers and high school boys, student journalism, the school band or orchestra.

6. Of the following statements, select the one you most wholeheartedly *endorse or reject*. Make your affirmation or denial of it the thesis of your paper, and support it as fully as you can.

  a. High school administrators are too authoritarian in their exercise of discipline.

  b. Students seldom receive meaningful vocational guidance.

  c. Girls today receive little encouragement to become truly feminine.

  d. Popular songs repeat the same sentiments over and over.

  e. American society is intolerant of unconventional dress or appearance.

  f. The typical American male takes sports too seriously.

Classification

7. Write a paper in which you divide *a group of people* into three or four major categories. For instance, you might classify children as leaders, followers, and loners; or teachers as authoritarian, chummy, and withdrawn. Make sure to establish categories that reflect your own experience and that you can fill in with graphic detail.

8. Have you found that one of the following labels covers an exceptionally diverse assortment of *different things*? Classify them, setting up several major categories and describing them as fully as you can. Choose one of the following: jobs, hobbies, comics, popular songs, television game shows, poems. Do not rely on conventional categories; set up divisions that reflect your own experience.

9. Have you ever watched closely the people present at a demonstration, riot, protest march, "confrontation with authority," or similar occasion? Can you *classify* them, setting up three or four major categories? For instance is it possible to distinguish between "demonstrators" and mere "spectators"?

Comparison and Contrast

10. Compare and contrast two fairly complicated pieces of *equipment or machinery* designed for basically the same job. For instance, compare and contrast an ordinary car motor with a diesel or jet engine. Or compare and contrast two related forms of *music or dance*: the polka and the waltz, dixieland and progressive jazz, gospel and blues.

11. Compare and contrast one of the following: current men's fashions and women's fashions, girls' talk and boys' talk, men's and women's ways of dealing with children. Limit your subject so as to make possible a unified, well-focused paper.

12. Compare and contrast *two styles of talk* used by the same person on different occasions: shop talk and sports talk, customer talk and "insider's" talk, talking with friends and talking with strangers, or the like. Base your paper on your *own* use of language or that of people to whom you listen frequently.

The first time I became aware of the power of writing was when I sent a postcard to a German friend who was in America at the time. The side of the card on which I was to write was white and crinkly, somewhat like snow, and it was that surface which made me evoke snow and Christmas. Instead of writing some commonplace sentiment, I wrote about the quality of the paper. That was what got me started.

Jean Genet

CHAPTER TWO

Observation and Description

1. The Uses of Description

2. The Need for Detail
    General and Specific
    Sensory Detail
    Relevant Detail

3. Finding the Right Word
    Specific Words
    Concrete Words
    Figurative Language

4. Organizing the Descriptive Theme
    The Key Idea
    The "Detail-First" Paper
    Consistent Progression
    The "Then-and-Now" Paper

5. The Lessons of Descriptive Writing

Sample Theme
Theme Topics 2

1. The Uses of Description

A good writer is first of all an alert observer. He has an eye for scenes, people, and events. He *notices* things. He takes in things that the eyes of routine spectators pass over. Where the ordinary tourist in the Southwest sees only a vaguely Spanish-looking building, he sees the whitewashed plaster walls; the roofs of curved red tile; the small slit-like windows of a tower; the palm trees in the courtyard, clipped like French poodles. Where the casual spectator sees only a brash person, an alert observer sees the sidelong glance or the forced smile that hints at the real person behind the brash façade.

Effective description is the record of alert first-hand observation. The descriptive writer puts into words what he has seen, heard, and felt. There are three main uses of effective description:

(1) *Imaginative description* enables the reader to share in an experience by making him visualize objects, people, scenes. It satisfies the need for reading that appeals to the reader's senses and emotions as well as to his intellect. It satisfies the reader's curiosity about places others have seen, people they have encountered. Imaginative description may be the main purpose of a personal letter, an account of travel, a descriptive essay devoted to a memorable person or place.

The following example of imaginative description aims at making the reader share in the sights and sounds of the natural world:

> I climbed up the gully slowly, for the icy air hurt in my lungs, and all the while over my head a hawk made his sound. . . . Almost I could make out the notching of his outer primaries as he wheeled in slow spread-winged arcs above me, peering and crying. The red-tails are always leisurely, even at their killing. Sometimes — once or twice in a season — we surprise one of those slaty hawks called Cooper's in the thick pine woods on the mountain, and always they flash from sight almost before we know what they are, and there is only the harsh staccato of their cac-cac-cac! receding in the far distance. But the red-tails, seeking their meat from God, move with so slow and indolent a grace that it would not be hard to imagine it were a studied thing. With unbeating wings they sidle down the wind, and the scream wells slowly from their throats. — Alan Devoe, *Down to Earth*

(2) *Incidental description in a narrative* creates an authentic setting. It makes events seem real by providing graphic, vivid impressions of characters and scenes. Fiction, biography, and historical writing all profit from competent use of incidental description. Here are two passages that help give the reader of Ralph Ellison's *Invisible Man* the feeling of "I was there":

We stopped before an expensive-looking building in a strange part of the city. I could see the word *Chthonian* on the storm awning stretched above the walk as I got out with the others and went swiftly toward a lobby lighted by dim bulbs set behind frosted glass, going past the uniformed doorman with an uncanny sense of familiarity; feeling now, as we entered a soundproof elevator and shot away at a mile a minute, that I had been through it all before. Then we were stopping with a gentle bounce and I was uncertain whether we had gone up or down.

I looked past their heads into a small crowded room of men and women sitting in folding chairs, to the front where a slender woman in a rusty black robe played passionate boogie-woogie on an upright piano along with a young man wearing a skull cap who struck righteous riffs from an electric guitar which was connected to an amplifier that hung from the ceiling above a gleaming white and gold pulpit.

(3) Effective *descriptive details* make for graphic illustration in prose of opinion and argument. They help a writer make his discussion of issues and ideas concrete rather than abstract. They help him explain and convince by linking ideas to what the reader himself could have observed. The following passage is from an article about the role of the novelist in contemporary America. The author's aim is to sketch for the novelist a role that avoids a lying optimism on the one hand and an oversensitivity to banality and ugliness on the other. But the author *starts* with an impression of a trip through Illinois, recording the kind of ordinary existence that the novelist can choose either merely to chronicle or to "humanize":

Here and there, in some of the mining counties and in the depopulated towns along the Mississippi there were signs of depression and poverty, but these had the flavor of the far away and long ago, for the rest of the state was dizzily affluent. "Pig Heaven," some people said to me. "Never nothing like it." The shops were filled with goods and buyers. In the fields were the newest harvesting machines; in the houses washers, dryers, freezers, and refrigerators, air conditioners, vacuum cleaners, Mixmasters, Waringblenders, television and stereophonic high-fi sets, electrical can openers, novels condensed by the *Reader's Digest* and slick magazines. In the yards, glossy cars in giddy colors, like ships from outer space. — Saul Bellow, "The Sealed Treasure," *Times Literary Supplement*

For someone who is serious about writing, practice in description is not just an elegant pastime. Accurate observation is a prerequisite of straight thinking. We do not expect clear thinking from a writer whose observation of the world is blurred. Logic is not a useful tool unless it is brought to bear on a rich fund of data, and unless the person using it is willing to adjust his logical categories in the light of new observation. Description can teach us how to keep our writing and thinking honest by keeping it close to what we have observed.

2. The Need for Detail

Much ordinary language is perfunctory or merely polite. When we ask a friend about the pueblos of the Mesa Verde, he may say that they are "interesting." When we want to hear about the dancing of a Russian ballerina, he may say that it was "enjoyable." Such answers do not really inform, let alone make us *share* in the excitement of the trip or of a virtuoso performance. The real question is What *makes* the pueblos interesting? What *made* the ballet enjoyable? Every student in a writing course should declare a moratorium on the use of words like "interesting," "enjoyable," "impressive," "magnificent," "beautiful," "exciting," and "rewarding." Instead, he should practice showing his readers *what made* a building impressive, *what makes* the desert beautiful, *what makes* a famous painting magnificent.

General and Specific

A descriptive writer needs a firm grasp of specific detail. Words like *interesting* or *beautiful* are general labels that sum up the overall impression of the observer. Such words can tell the reader *about* the overall impression, but they cannot make him share in it. To make the reader share in his reactions, the writer has to reconstruct what brought them about. He has to make his readers see what he saw, hear what he heard, touch what he touched. He has to fill in sufficient detail to make the reader visualize a scene or a person. An effective writer has to be patient enough to take in the little things that make up the larger picture.

As you describe a person or a scene, imagine a reader at your elbow who keeps saying: What was actually there? What did it look like? What was it made of? As you respond to his nudging, you will start to observe the first rule of descriptive writing: *Give your reader things to see.* Writing is not description unless it becomes specific enough to provide details like the following:

The elementary school was a *big brick cube* set in a *square of black surfacing chalked and painted with the diagrams and runes of children's games.*   (John Updike)

As we continued down one of the canyons, we spotted several of the *low redstone structures,* with their *neat rectangular openings, perched like swallows' nests* high above us in the canyon wall. One was easy to reach, and I climbed up to explore it. The roof had long since fallen in, but the walls still stood. In the *mud daubing between the stone blocks* was a *thumbprint* that could have been made last week, the *whorls sharp and clear* enough to satisfy any detective who might be on that Indian's trail. (Paul Brooks)

In October, Halloween masks appeared, *hung on wire clotheslines. Hanging limp, these faces of Chinamen and pirates and witches were distorted, and thickly clustered and rustling against each other,* they seemed more frightening masking empty air than they did mounted on the heads of my friends.   (John Updike)

Effective description requires greater attention to detail than is necessary in casual everyday observation. The casual tourist can look at Indian pottery with mere passive enjoyment. The writer who wants to describe it needs to pay careful attention to shapes, ornaments, and shades of color. In fact, a writer who tries to focus on important details about a person or a piece of machinery often finds that for the first time he is really looking with open eyes.

Sensory Detail

Choose details that appeal to the reader's senses. Not all details are equally useful in making description come to life. The exact measurements of a cabinet will help a carpenter build one like it, but they will not help a reader imagine what it looks like. Sensory details make writing concrete and tangible because they appeal to the reader's sense of sight, hearing, taste, smell, and touch.

Would you agree that in each of the following pairs the concrete version helps us share in *how it felt to be there?*

Bare: The person walking down the path behind the house cannot help noticing the many spiders and other insects that are always present.

Concrete: Spiders, large black ones with red markings, stretch their webs across the path to catch the flies humming and buzzing in the afternoon sun.

Bare: At noon we got ready for lunch.

Concrete: At noon, when the threshing machine fell silent, we straightened up, glanced at the burning sun, pulled out our pocket watches, wiped the moisture from under the sweatbands of our caps, relaxed, and sought the cool shade for lunch.

Bare: Stacking hay is one of the dirtiest and most uncomfortable jobs I know.

Concrete: The hay is burned crisp and with every jab of the fork black dust flies out; it sticks on the wet arms and face, this sharp chaff, and under the collar it grits against raw sunburn.

Bare: I always passed the neighborhood saloon with an instinctive feeling of dislike.

Concrete: Through the doorway of the saloon, in the dim light, I could see people sitting around a small round table. As I stood there in the hot, humid evening, the rancid smell of smoke, liquor, and garbage turned my stomach.

Relevant Detail

Make your descriptive detail add up. A writer must learn to *guide* his selection of detail. Great chunks of miscellaneous detail tire and bewilder the reader. Details become significant when they become part of a larger picture. Effective detail is more than detail for detail's sake; it is relevant to a larger purpose.

Here are the kinds of questions that can guide you in your selection of detail:

(1) *What is distinctive about what I want to describe?* What is it about a collie that makes him stand out among more nondescript dogs? What makes a eucalyptus tree look *different* from all other trees? Describing a Gothic cathedral, we are likely to stress the features that make it different from a Roman Basilica or a Greek temple: the pointed arches, the filigreed spires, everything that breaks up solid blocks of masonry and makes for airiness, height, and upward thrust. Writing about modern skyscrapers, we are likely to stress what makes for their boxy, flat-topped quality; the absence of the cornices, Aztec towers, and the like, that cap similar buildings from earlier decades.

(2) *What is the overall effect I am trying to reproduce?* Details become relevant when they help to build up one **dominant impression**. Perhaps the prevailing impression you took home from a football game is one of color and excitement. In a paper aimed at this effect, the uniforms of the band, the reactions of the crowd, the shouts of the hot dog vendors, and the gyrations of the cheerleaders all become relevant. But perhaps you were struck mainly by the stresses and strains of a sport in which there is no substitute for victory. You will then shift attention to the tension in the locker room, the exhortations of the coach, the drawn face of a player as he limps off the field.

In the following passage, descriptive detail is unified by a dominant impression sustained through the italicized phrases until the passage reaches its climactic ending:

In that instant, in too short a time, one would have thought, even for the bullet to get there, *a mysterious, terrible change had come over the elephant.* He neither stirred nor fell, but every line of his body had altered. He looked suddenly *stricken, shrunken, immensely old,* as though the frightful impact of the bullet had *paralysed* him without knocking him down. At last, after what seemed a long time—it might have been five seconds, I dare say—he *sagged flabbily to his knees*. His mouth *slobbered*. An enormous *senility* seemed to have settled upon him. One could have imagined him *thousands of years old*. I fired again into the same spot. At the second shot he did not collapse but climbed *with desperate slowness* to his feet and stood *weakly* upright, with *legs sagging* and *head drooping*. I fired a third time. That was the shot that did for him. You could see the agony of it jolt his whole body and knock *the last remnant of strength* from his legs. But in falling he seemed for a moment to rise, for as his hind legs *collapsed* beneath him he seemed to tower upwards *like a huge rock toppling*, his trunk reaching skywards like a tree. He trumpeted, for the first and only time. And then down he came, his belly towards me, with a crash that seemed to shake the ground even where I lay.—George Orwell, *Shooting an Elephant and Other Essays*

(3) *What is the point I am trying to make?* A thoughtful observer does not merely take in data the way a tape recorder registers sounds. He draws conclusions about what he sees and hears. In the following passage about a trip to Utah, descriptive detail supports a major point:

Farther along we came to a cool moist cave beneath a great ledge of overhanging rock, like the opening of a giant clamshell. At the inmost recess, where the sloping roof came down to the dirt floor, lay a spring-fed pool, with maidenhair fern growing in the crevices above it, as it might have grown in a mist-filled mountain gorge. The contrast between the cave's microclimate and the arid heat outside underscored the obvious fact, which we sometimes forget in the East, that *water is life.* — Paul Brooks, "Canyonlands," *Atlantic*

In the most loosely organized descriptive writing, a paragraph will often be devoted to a unified effect, but *the whole* may simply be in the form of impressions jotted down—the notes of a traveler, for instance. What holds such notes together is the writer's and reader's common interest in what is freshly observed. We tire of advertising and travelogues in which every mountain is "majestic Mount So-and-So," every big city a "bustling metropolis," every subtropical island an "enchanted isle." We read phrases like "springtime riot of flowers" and "sweet fragrance of cherry blossoms" half a dozen times every spring. When a writer clears away the haze of familiar phrases and takes a first-hand look, he revives our natural curiosity about the world in which we live.

In your own descriptive papers, remember what your basic claim is on the reader's attention. What you are saying in so many words is: "Here—look at this! See what I have found!" To make that look worthwhile for the reader, you have to honor a basic principle of *all* good writing: *Trust your own eyes and ears.* Revive your natural curiosity about the sights and sounds around you, and let it become contagious for your reader.

Exercises

A. Write three sentences, each a *one-sentence portrait of a different person.* Pack each sentence with specific, concrete detail. Try to make your readers see the person by the time they have finished reading each sentence. You might use the following student-written sentences as models:

> A sad little old man with a scraggly beard and a shabby coat was walking along the curb, selling rooter buttons.

> A sour middle-aged woman with frowsy hair and wearing a faded chenille bathrobe leaned out of a tenement window, wondering what was making the neighbor's dog bark.

B. Write down half a dozen phrases that bring to mind the most characteristic *sights, sounds, and smells* of one of the following: registration day, a football game, a political rally, a rodeo, a circus, Sunday morning in church.

C. Write three sentences, each a capsule description that captures the *characteristic atmosphere of a place*—a hotel, dormitory, city hall, police headquarters, draft board office, or the like. Here is a possible model:

> The Military Park is a soup-stained hostelry, its one-time elegance worn at the cuffs, the carpets trod thin by Rotarian feet.

D. Write a paragraph describing a scene that you consider exceptionally beautiful or ugly, magnificent or shoddy. Concentrate on *what makes it so.* Rely on specific, concrete detail. Do *not* use the key term or any of its synonyms anywhere in the paragraph.

E. Choose three of the following. For each, write a one-sentence description stressing the *distinctive features* that would help the reader tell

> a Siamese cat from other cats;
> a trout from other fish;
> a robin from other birds;
> a mule from a horse;
> a clarinet from an oboe;
> a banjo from a guitar.

3. Finding the Right Word

We cannot share what we have observed unless we can put it into words. Effective descriptive language is like a clean window, giving us a clear look at the outside world. Language that is impoverished or too routine is like a fogged-up window through which only blurry outlines are visible.

Specific Words

An effective writer knows things by their names. He uses words
that are accurate, specific, informative. Instead of using *thing, gadget,*
or *contraption,* he uses *lid, lever, valve, tube,* or *coil.* A dictionary
may describe a revolving door as "a door consisting of four vanes
hung on a central vertical axle and so arranged in a wall that a person
using it turns it around by pushing on one of the vanes." This definition relies for accurate description of two essential parts on the
words *vane* and *axle,* which not only identify the parts but give the
reader definite ideas concerning their shape and function.

The author of the following passage not only was a loving observer of flowers and plants; he also knew their names and the names
of their parts:

In my front yard grew the strawberry, blackberry, and life-everlasting, johnswort and
goldenrod, shrub oaks and sand cherry, blueberry and groundnut. Near the end of
May, the sand cherry *(Cerasus pumila)* adorned the sides of the path with its delicate
flowers arranged in umbels cylindrically about its short stems, which last, in the fall,
weighed down with good-sized and handsome cherries, fell over in wreaths like rays
on every side. I tasted them out of compliment to Nature, though they were scarcely
palatable. The sumach *(Rhus glabra)* grew luxuriantly about the house, pushing up
through the embankment which I had made, and growing five or six feet the first
season. Its broad pinnate tropical leaf was pleasant though strange to look on. The large
buds, suddenly pushing out late in the spring from dry sticks which had seemed to be
dead, developed themselves as by magic into graceful green and tender boughs. — Henry
David Thoreau, *Walden*

Specific words may become too technical for the general reader.
(How many of Thoreau's readers would know that *pinnate* means
"structured like a feather"?) Rather than fall back on a blurry general
term, however, try one of the following: Briefly *explain* a technical
term that the reader is not likely to know. Or *prefer* the less technical
term when two words both adequately describe the same thing:
lady slipper rather than *Cypripedium* as the name of a plant; *tree-
dwelling monkey* rather than *arboreal brachiator* to identify a kind
of animal.

Concrete Words

An effective writer uses words that appeal to our senses. Concrete words do not merely convey information but conjure up a
picture. They call to mind sounds, textures, odors, and flavors. *Speak*
is merely a convenient all-purpose term. To make us visualize an
actual speaker, an effective writer uses a word like *chat, mumble,
coo, whisper, shout, rant, quip, orate, jeer, scold, brag, proclaim,*

argue, bluster, assert, drone, stammer, or *blurt.* A word like *mumble* makes us imagine a person actually mumbling; the word has visual and auditory associations. In a more general word like *speak,* all the variables of gesture, tone, and intention that make an individual speaker stand out from the rest have been smoothed over.

Would you agree that the writers of the two following passages know how to choose words that make us *see?*

There are hotter places than a hayfield, but I doubt if there is another place where as many things remind you of the heat. In the next field, the corn is yellow, the blades are *rolled tight* for lack of water. A buzzard *hangs* becalmed above the field; his shadow *creeps* along the hillside. Brown grasshoppers *clatter* out of the dead grass as you walk. Sometimes they fly against your face and hang *clawing* at an eyebrow. Swarms of gnats *swirl* along the ground. Yellow nit-flies sing above the lathering horses and *swing down* to sting them under the jaw and to make them *tangle* the lines and shy. — Student paper

Nick laid the bottle full of *jumping* grasshoppers against a pine trunk. Rapidly he mixed some buckwheat flour with water and stirred it smooth, one cup of flour, one cup of water. He put a handful of coffee in the pot and *dipped* a lump of grease out of a can and *slid* it *sputtering* across the hot skillet. On the smoking skillet he poured smoothly the buckwheat batter. It spread like lava, the grease *spitting* sharply. Around the edges the buckwheat cake began to *firm,* then *brown,* then *crisp.* The surface was *bubbling* slowly to porousness. Nick pushed under the browned under surface with a fresh pine chip. He shook the skillet sideways and the cake was loose on the surface. I won't try and *flop* it, he thought. He slid the chip of clean wood all the way under the cake, and flopped it over onto its face. It sputtered in the pan. — Ernest Hemingway, "Big Two-Hearted River"

Note how the author of the following passage uses words that suggest the way different people talk:

The word is everything in Harlem. The *long word* or the *book word* beautifully *uttered* by the man driving his cab or talking in his shop; the *rambling* or the *inciting* word of the street meeting; the *Biblical* or *inflaming* word of the *unctuous ranting* preacher. These people have the gift of tongues which is scarcer among American whites; indeed conversation is commoner there than in white New York. On Sunday mornings in Harlem the word rules. *Roars* as of murder come from upper rooms over the cleaner's or the grocer's: it is a preacher in a one-room chapel *screaming* the name of Jesus, in paroxysms about Emmanuel. — V. S. Pritchett, "Striverstown," *The New Statesman*

Colorful or unusual words do not by themselves make for effective description. They have to fit. A student who writes that he "ambled" into the cafeteria is not really trying to describe how he walked (more likely he *slouched, marched, plodded,* or *drifted* into the cafeteria). He is probably just having fun with the word *amble.* To make sure he chooses the *right* word, the writer has to keep his eye on the object.

Figurative Language

An effective writer uses figurative language to stretch the resources of language. When we do not have a specific and concrete word for something, we try to tell the reader what it is *like*. We compare the shape of a blimp to that of a huge cigar, the shape of an imported car to that of a beetle. Figurative language makes use of such similarities, exploiting them in shorthand comparisons. A **simile** is a compressed but still explicit comparison, introduced by *as* or *like* ("The great fantastic arch of the Delaware River bridge loomed ahead of me *like a preposterous giant's toy*"). A **metaphor** is an implied comparison, using one thing as the equivalent of another ("The candidate *surfed* to the speaker's table on a nice *wave* of applause"). A common kind of metaphor involves **personification**, giving human qualities to objects or ideas ("The sound of the passing cars was *a steady whisper out of the throat of the night*").[1]

Everyday language is full of *ready-made* figurative expressions. We are constantly warned not to turn back the clock, put the cart before the horse, or change horses in midstream. We are told to keep our powder dry or to put our shoulder to the wheel. With many of these, what was once a vivid picture has become trite through constant repetition. What was once a fresh metaphor has become a **cliché**. We recognize such trite figures of speech by their coming to mind *all in one piece* — ready to be pasted together, with others of the kind, in a piece of writing that required no fresh thought or first-hand observation.

Descriptive writing has its share of clichés: "apple-pie order," "fresh as a daisy," "brown as a berry," "the cloak of darkness," "a carpet of green," "heaven's candles," "a blanket of snow." In effective description, figurative language is fresh; it makes us pay attention. It is apt; it makes vivid and concrete something that would otherwise be hard to put into words.

Would you agree that in the following passages figurative language helps us see, hear, and feel?

When they are on the alert, a flock of sparrows, or pigeons, or cedar-birds, or snow-buntings, or blackbirds, will all take flight as if there was but one bird, instead of a hundred. The same impulse seizes every individual bird at the same instant, *as if they were sprung by electricity.* . . . . A brood of young partridges in the woods will start up *like an explosion, every brown particle and fragment hurled into the air at the same instant.* (John Burroughs)

[1] For a more general discussion of figurative language and its pitfalls, see D7b.

Cornelia's voice *staggered and bumped like a cart in a bad road.* (Katherine Anne Porter)

Many men can chord a guitar, but perhaps this man was a picker. There you have some-thing—the deep chords beating, beating, while the melody runs on the strings *like little footsteps.*   (John Steinbeck)

He lay down in his shirt and breeches on the bed and blew out the candle. Heat *stood in the room like an enemy.*   (Graham Greene)

Figurative language requires of the writer a quick eye for un-suspected similarities. At the same time, it requires him to be wary of differences that might prove distracting. Figurative language defeats its purpose when it is too artificial or far-fetched. If you say that the setting sun was a huge candied apple descending into a sea of honey, you may put the reader in the mood for a candy bar rather than for a descriptive essay on an evening at the sea. If you say that the setting sun made the sea look like a wrinkled face full of blood, the reader is likely to forget the sunset but remember the gory picture of the blood-filled wrinkles. Figurative language is most effective when it does its work without calling attention to itself.

Exercises

A. A British writer discussing the "vocabulary of the future" predicted that "man will be less in touch with the natural world" and that "as more and more land comes under cultivation, the ability to distinguish between the forms of wild life is bound to diminish and eventually die. . . . The general term *bird* will swallow the swallow, the finch, the green linnet. *Vegetation* will have to serve for most of the varieties of green life—plant and weed alike." What *names of animals and plants* do you know that the city dweller may no longer be sure of? Choose one of the following categories and explain, in one sentence each, *six* names that you consider worth preserving: birds, game, fish, trees, flowers, weeds.

B. In one sentence each, explain six *technical terms* that you would have to use in describing the characteristic features of one of the following: this year's women's fashions; one of the traditional styles of architecture (classic, Romanesque, Gothic, baroque); one of the major schools, traditional or modern, of painting.

C. How accurate is your knowledge of the following descriptive words? Look up those that you are not sure of: (colors) *azure, beryl, crimson, emerald,* *livid, maroon, ocher, sepia, tawny, vermilion;* (tastes and smells) *acrid, dank, fetid, musty, pungent, rancid, redolent, tangy, tart;* (sounds) *crackle, grate, gurgle, rasp, rustle, snarl, sough, thrum, whir;* (movements) *hover, jounce, lope, lunge, lurch, plod, plummet, quiver, saunter, slosh, totter, trudge, yaw;* (moods) *dour, ferocious, frenetic, languid, lethargic, lugubrious, morose, somber, sultry, torpid, wistful.*

D. Discuss the *figurative language* used in each of the following sentences. Is it fresh, appropriate, effective?

1. When the bee landed on a blossom, it would move its legs back and forth like a man wiping his feet before entering a house.

2. The reporters fell upon the candidate like so many cats on a bowl of chopped liver.

3. In the flat, rich field of oats, the men worked like drones drowsily loading themselves with golden nectar-sheaves for their queen, the thresher.

4. The trees were covered with layers of ice, and when the wind blew them, they made a creaking noise like the sound of someone's tiptoeing on loose floor boards.

5. In the laughing, chattering crowd, I was a stick tossed about on a fast moving river — at times I could float along with the current, and at other times I would hit a dam and have to push and shove until I reached open space once more.

6. The ivy twined to the very top of the structure, and in the wind it rustled like dry leaves in the fall.

7. Century-old trees stood like sentinels at the entrance to the park.

E. Study the way the following paragraph carries through the same figurative analogy. Then write a similar descriptive paragraph making use of such a *sustained metaphor*.

Squatting in the middle of the field, the threshing machine was a weird-looking mass of rumbling wheels, spouts, and conveyers. A metal rack with a conveyer extended from one end of the machine. Bundles of oats thrown onto this belt crept to the *mouth* of the machine and suddenly disappeared within the huge *belly* of the thresher. Inside, meshing steel separated the grain from the stalks and hulls and sent them into separate compartments. Scooping up the grain, a second conveyer belt *spewed* it from the spout in a golden stream that filled the wagon waiting below, while the straw and hulls were blown through a large funnel extending twelve to fifteen feet beyond the rear of the machine. The funnel was periodically cranked up as the straw stack was built to a conical peak. So our harvest machine *ate* its way through the morning; and at noon, when the air was suddenly still, all that remained of the field were two straw piles and a bin full of grain.

F. Study the *use of language* in the following passages. How does each author use words to make the reader see, hear, and feel? Discuss each author's use of specific words, concrete words, and figurative language. How apt, expressive, or effective is his use of words? What makes the passage unusual, striking, distinctive?

1. In a shoe box stuffed in an old nylon stocking
   Sleeps the baby mouse I found in the meadow,
   Where he trembled and shook beneath a stick
   Till I caught him up by the tail and brought him in,
   Cradled in my hand,
   A little quaker, the whole body of him trembling,
   His absurd whiskers sticking out like a cartoon mouse,
   His feet like small leaves,
   Little lizard-feet,
   Whitish and spread wide when he tried to struggle away,
   Wriggling like a miniscule puppy.

   Now he's eaten his three kinds of cheese and drunk from his bottle-
       cap watering trough—
   So much he just lies in one corner,
   His tail curled under him, his belly big
   As his head, his bat-like ears
   Twitching, tilting toward the least sound.—Theodore Roethke, from
       "The Meadow Mouse"

2. The house was left; the house was deserted. It was left like a shell on a sandhill to fill with dry salt grains now that life had left it. The long night seemed to have set in; the trifling airs, nibbling, the clammy breaths, fumbling, seemed to have triumphed. The sauce-pan had rusted and the mat decayed. Toads had nosed their way in. Idly, aimlessly, the swaying shawl swung to and fro. A thistle thrust itself between the tiles in the larder. The swallows nested in the drawing-room; the floor was strewn with straw; the plaster fell in shovelfuls; rafters were laid bare; rats carried off this and that to gnaw behind the wainscots. Tortoise-shell butterflies burst from the chrysalis and pattered their life out on the window-pane. Poppies sowed themselves among the dahlias; the lawn waved with long grass; giant artichokes towered among roses; a fringed carnation flowered among the cabbages; while the gentle tapping of a weed at the window had become, on winters' nights, a drumming from sturdy trees and thorned briars which made the whole room green in summer.—Virginia Woolf, *To the Lighthouse*

3. To get there you follow Highway 58, going northeast out of the city, and it is a good highway and new. Or was new, that day we went up it. You look up the highway and it is straight for miles, coming at you, with the black line down the center coming at and at you, black and slick and tarry-shining against the white of the slab, and the heat dazzles up from the white slab so that only the black line is clear, coming at you with the whine of the tires, and if you don't quit staring at that line and don't take a few deep breaths and slap yourself hard on the back of the neck you'll hypnotize yourself and you'll come to just at the moment when the right front wheel hooks over into the black dirt shoulder off the slab, and you'll try to jerk her back on but you can't because the slab is high like a curb, and maybe you'll try to reach to turn off the ignition just as she starts the dive. . . .

But if you wake up in time and don't hook your wheel off the slab, you'll go whipping on into the dazzle and now and then a car will come at you steady out of the dazzle and will pass you with a snatching sound as though God-Almighty had ripped a tin roof loose with his bare hands. Way off ahead of you, at the horizon where the cotton fields are blurred into the light, the slab will glitter and gleam like water, as though the road were flooded. You'll go whipping toward it, but it will always be ahead of you, that bright, flooded place, like a mirage. — Robert Penn Warren, *All the King's Men*

4. I had expected the Taj to be exquisite, but small and jewel-like. Actually, it is imposing and exciting in its very size. The sunlight burns white on its sleek gigantic surfaces, which imperceptibly become a rich antique yellow in the shadows. It seemed like a vast, fabulous ivory carving, set in a wonderful garden of clipped grass, roses, bougain-villea, trumpet flowers, and blossoming trees. The still pools in which it is mirrored are filled with darting fish, and from those pools dark men fill big animal skins for watering the grass and the fuchsias.

Conquerors and thieves have stolen the diamonds and other jewels with which the actual tombs were once crusted, and the looted golden doors have been replaced with carved wood; but nowhere else on earth remains such a vastness of pierced and fretted marble. And all over those gigantic sweeping surfaces, both inside and out, are inlaid patterns — lotus blossoms, poppies, lilies, and long quotations from the Koran in graceful Arabic script. Jade, lapis lazuli, agate, carnelian, onyx, and porphyry are laid into the marble with the most beautiful taste and skill to make up those flowing patterns. — Leslie C. Stevens, "The Grand Trunk Road to Agra," *Atlantic*

5. The stream wound its burrow into the jungle. Already they had forgotten how the mouth appeared in sunlight. Their ears were filled with the quick frenetic rustling of insects and animals, the thin screech-ing rage of mosquitoes and the raucous babbling of monkeys and para-keets. They sweated terribly; although they had marched only a few

hundred yards, the languid air gave them no nourishment, and black stains of moisture spread on their uniforms wherever the pack straps made contact. In the early morning, the jungle was exuding its fog drip; about their legs the waist-high mists skittered apart for the passage of their bodies, and closed again sluggishly, leisurely, like a slug revolving in its cell. For the men at the point of the column every step demanded an inordinate effort of will. They shivered with revulsion, halted often to catch their breath. The jungle dripped wetly about them everywhere; the groves of bamboo trees grew down to the river edge, their lacy delicate foliage lost in the welter of vines and trees. The brush mounted on the tree trunks, grew over their heads; the black river silt embedded itself in the roots of the bushes and between the pebbles under their feet. The water trickled over the stream bank tinkling pleasantly, but it was lost in the harsh uprooted cries of the jungle birds, the thrumming of the insects. — Norman Mailer, *The Naked and the Dead*

6. A few lithesome young people, clad in informal, patchy-looking ballet outfits, bounded about on the stage in time to the remote jangle of a piano. The slithering footsteps made a sound infinitely faint in the center of that silent scarlet circle of chairs. We put our elbows on a wall whose concrete was exhaling a delicate damp scent, and watched. The last time we leaned on this wall and watched, there had been skaters down below, gliding, weaving, tottering, tumbling. A priest, we remembered, had brought some children, and was himself ravishing on skates, black against the white ice, his arms folded behind him, skimming on one foot, then the other . . . Behind this elegant crow, his childish flock, a muffled bunch of sparrows and chickadees, fluttered along as best they could, extending stumpy wings for balance, chirruping with delight. — John Updike, "Cancelled," *The New Yorker*

4. Organizing the Descriptive Theme

Compared with argument or narration, description often is only *loosely* organized. Some of the best descriptive writing is found in journals, diaries, travel notes — which record the changing observations of the author from day to day. Yet even in the kind of description that offers us great variety, individual sketches and some longer passages will have the unified impact of successfully organized writing.

Here are sample patterns for short sketches and longer descriptive themes of your own:

The Key Idea

This pattern applies the familiar "thesis-and-support" scheme to descriptive writing. The thesis sentence sums up the dominant impression or overall effect that the paper is trying to convey. Such a thesis sentence, stated at the end of a short introduction (or, in a short sketch, as the very first sentence) gives clear direction to the description that follows. The writer can simply ask himself: Do the details I am using *reinforce* the overall effect?

Here is the beginning of a descriptive sketch in which the initial thesis sentence sums up a *prevailing mood:*

Tropical fish create an atmosphere of peace and relaxation. It is soothing to observe some of the fish *hanging motionless* in the water, as if suspended by a fine thread, while the angler fish *glide silently* across the tank. . . .

The "Detail-First" Paper

The "detail-first" sketch or paper turns the usual thesis-and-support pattern upside down. It first provides the related details, making them *build up* to the intended effect or key point. The key sentence, or thesis sentence, then appears at the end—after it has been earned, so to speak.

Writing with "detail first" has the great advantage of being modeled on the actual process of observation. Authentic observation *starts* with detail and then gradually funnels it into general impressions or conclusions. Writing that imitates this process is an education for the writer who is used to starting with second-hand ideas and then hunting about for details that might fit. Practice in putting detail first helps a writer get the most basic requirement for effective description into his bones.

Can you see the funnel effect in the following "detail-first" passages?

When he was done shaking hands with me, the Judge smoothed back his thick, black mane, cut off square at the collar, like a senator's, put one hand in his pocket, played with the half-dozen emblems and charms on his watch chain with the other, teetered from his heels to his toes two or three times, lifted his head, smiled at me like I was the biggest pleasure he'd had in years, and drew a great, deep breath, like he was about to start an oration. I'd seen him go through all that when all he finally said was, "How-do-you-do?" to some lady he wasn't sure he hadn't met before. *The Judge had a lot of public manner.*—Walter Van Tilburg Clark, *The Ox-Bow Incident*

Throughout the press conference, the public address system kept going off and on, with raucous squeaks of feedback anguish. A few minutes before the candidate's arrival, a hotel crew had arrived with ladders and stapling guns to fasten some bunting to the molding. Now a worker returned to retrieve a forgotten ladder. As he left, a swash of bunting collapsed like a broken wing. One of the closed-circuit TV receivers went berserk, rolling the candidate's image endlessly up and off the screen. *It was, in brief, an utterly amateur staging.*

Consistent Progression

This pattern is designed to counteract two weaknesses of descriptive writing. Description easily becomes too *static*. It then gives us a mere picture postcard view, without movement. Secondly, description easily becomes too *scattered.* Too many different things call for our attention, leaving us in the end without any sense that we have made headway or covered ground. To overcome these defects, the writer can try to build into his description a sense of *purposeful forward movement.* He can make us follow him as he moves in a consistent direction in space or in time.

For instance, a writer may give a descriptive essay a sense of forward movement by making the plan of his paper follow the course of a river through a valley; a hike from the valley floor up through the green foothills into the dry sierras; or a walk from the outskirts of a town to a central landmark. He may trace the course of a typical afternoon for a souvenir peddler at a stadium; or the course of history as he makes us look at a house built by an early settler, one next door built in the 1880s, and one going up across the street.

The following paper describes the scene at a Lake Michigan beach as a drowning victim is given artificial respiration. Note how the paper moves through three plausible stages:

focus on the victim	The woman looked as though she was lifeless. Appearing as though she were some form of statuary caked with wet sand, her body lay in a motionless prone position. . . .
focus on the rescuer	A young man was desperately trying to restore her normal breathing pattern. His whole sun-tanned body moved rhythmically up and down in the cycle of artificial respiration. . . .
focus on bystanders	The drowning seemed no more than an attractive diversion for many of the people on the beach. A graying middle-aged man was instructing his wife to stay and watch the food while he was taking the children "to have us a look." . . .

The "Then-and-Now" Paper

This pattern is one way of using comparison and contrast for the purposes of descriptive writing. *Change* is one of the most effective ways of making us take notice: the highway where we used to play in the fields; the cluttered commercial buildings where orchards used to be; the concrete office building that replaced a wooden Victorian mansion; the glass-and-steel palace that superseded the turreted old City Hall.

The following passage records the kind of experience that provides promising material for a "then-and-now" paper:

I went down from this ancient grave place eighty or ninety rods to the site of the Van Velsor homestead, where my mother was born (1795), and where every spot had been familiar to me as a child and youth (1825-'40). Then stood there a long, rambling, dark-gray, shingle-sided house, with sheds, pens, a great barn, and much open road-space. Now of all those not a vestige left; all had been pull'd down, erased, and the plough and harrow pass'd over foundations, road-spaces and everything, for many summers; fenced in at present, and grain and clover growing like any other fine fields. Only a big hole from the cellar, with some little heaps of broken stone, green with grass and weeds, identified the place. Even the copious old brook and spring seem'd to have mostly dwindled away. The whole scene, with what it arous'd, memories of my young days there half a century ago, the vast kitchen and ample fireplace and the sitting-room adjoining, the plain furniture, the meals, the house full of merry people, my grandmother Amy's sweet old face in its Quaker cap, my grandfather "the Major," jovial, red, stout, with sonorous voice and characteristic physiognomy, with the actual sights themselves, made the most pronounc'd half-day's experience of my whole jaunt. —Walt Whitman, *Specimen Days*

Exercises

A. Write a descriptive paragraph in which the first sentence sums up and the rest of the paragraph develops a *prevailing mood.*

B. Write three *"detail-first"* sentences in which several descriptive details are funneled into a general impression. You may use the following student-written sentences as models:

> Red, white, and blue banners; crowds of people cheering, booing; men with tired eyes, smiling and shaking hand after hand: *this is a political rally.*

> The shape and texture of a paper bag; the delight of a scarlet ribbon; the bareness of an almost empty room: *these show the painter's fascination with simplicity.*

> The portrait captured Lincoln's lanky ungainliness; the ill-at-ease, though resigned, submission to the crackling stiff formal shirt; the unruly hair, resisting brush or comb—*the complete lack of pomposity in Lincoln's nature.*

C. Study the way the student author has *organized descriptive detail* in the following short portrait of a person. Is there a sense of consistent progression? How is it achieved? Your instructor may ask you to write a similar portrait of a person you frequently observed as part of a scene familiar to you as a child.

THE FLOWER VENDOR

Shortly before six o'clock on a sunny tropical morning, a flower vendor would walk alone along one of the narrow, winding streets of

Old Havana. On his head, he gracefully balanced a round wicker basket, heavily loaded with dozens of long-stemmed roses — dark red, light pink, pale yellow, and brilliant orange; sweet-smelling spikenards; white lilies; and multi-colored carnations.

He was a tall man, thickly muscled through the arms and chest. He had the short, dark, curly hair and full lips of the African, with a sharp pointed nose and light cinnamon color skin. His forehead was narrow and slightly wrinkled, his dark eyebrows set apart. His eyes were perpetually atwinkle, and his lips seemed ever ready to part in a smile. His face was freshly shaved, his small black mustache trimmed neatly to expose a thin line of cinnamon flesh above a thick upper lip.

He wore a faded blue denim shirt from which the buttons had long since departed, a white T-shirt, sharply pressed white duck trousers, and white shoes that could have used a touch-up of polish.

At this early hour, the vendor's footsteps on the uneven, shiny cobblestones were the only sound to interrupt the morning silence. He would pause at the middle of the block to wait for his usual customers. He would let his eyes scan the empty street, taking in the smooth narrow sidewalks, the old stone houses with heavy wooden doors, their ground floor windows protected by intricately designed lattices, their upper floors graced by balconies with wrought-iron railings.

At about six o'clock the bells of a nearby church would begin to peal, calling the faithful to Mass and signaling to the vendor to start his business day. His cry of "Flowers . . . . flowers!" filled the air, causing sleepy-eyed customers to appear at the balconies and windows. Greeting them with a cheerful "Good morning," he would put down the big basket tilted against his legs, the better to display his merchandise. Occasionally, an animated chit-chat developed between the flower vendor and one of his clients about baseball or politics, the two most popular and inexhaustible topics of conversation in pre-Castro Cuba.

As the weight of the basket lightened with each sale, the flower vendor's spirits seemed to become brighter. He would wander off through other streets, until his basket was empty or the day was over. Wherever he went, he added a touch of color and charm to the streets of Old Havana. I'd like to think he still does.

D. Write an *outline* for a "then-and-now" paper in which you make use of the kind of point-by-point comparison described in Chapter 1.

5. The Lessons of Descriptive Writing

When we first develop an enthusiasm for writing, our goal often is to "express ourselves" — to express what we honestly feel. We are often disillusioned to find how hard it is to reach out and share these feelings with a reader. To share our feelings, we have to anchor them to something the reader can recognize. One way of doing this is to concentrate on our impressions of the outside world in which both we and our readers live. Here lies our first best chance to get the reader to say: "Yes, that is the way it is." It is in this way that descriptive writing teaches us something essential about what it means to *communicate.*

Specifically, here are the ways practice in descriptive writing will help you communicate with your readers:

(1) Description makes you *notice and appreciate detail.* Mere unsupported expressions of feelings and ideas are usually too thin and merely verbal to establish any meaningful contact with the reader. In the following paragraph, the author talks about her mother's work as a seamstress at a Ford plant. Note how weak the word *fatiguing* would be without the telling detail that follows it:

> My mother works a tight eight-hour day, with half-an-hour for lunch; the routine is so demanding that she has nothing left for herself. As fatiguing as the job is (her index finger is swollen to more than twice its natural size from tugging on the "decking" and her eyes are similarly injured from staring eight hours a day at a moving needle) . . . yet she does all her own housework when she leaves the shop, including floor scrubbing, window washing, and other heavy duties.—Patricia Cayo Sexton, "Speaking for the Working Class Wife," *Harper's*

(2) Description helps you *develop your ability to sort out and select.* Mere unsorted experience is too miscellaneous to hold the attention of the reader. Practice in descriptive writing will develop your feeling for what is characteristic, revealing. To convey the memorable quality of an unusually successful camping trip, you will sift out many minor incidents to concentrate on what made the trip exhilarating: the sunlight filtering through branches and leaves onto the forest floor; the echo of laughter in a cathedral-like nave of big trees; the glow on the cheeks of campers huddled around a fire.

(3) Description provides basic practice in how to *put what you have observed into words.* A competent writer has the knack of finding the right word for something that we easily recognize but find hard to communicate. Notice how in the following passage a skillful writer uses expressive and figurative language to distinguish different kinds of laughter:

> There are four different kinds of laughter in the theater. One is the gag laugh: the *short, sharp bark* of reaction to a funny line. The second is the *nervous titter*, with an edge of hysteria, that greets a grotesquerie or a sick and special joke. A third is the *warm and rippling laughter* of an audience happily involved in the play's characters. And the fourth is commonly known as the belly laugh: *loud, released, and visceral.*— Marya Mannes, "Just Looking," *The Reporter*

Of the writing you do, and of the material you read, comparatively little will have description as its main goal. However, the lessons to be learned from descriptive writing apply to many other kinds of writing. Accurate observation, discriminating selection of detail, and graphic, expressive language are essential characteristics of any competent writer's work. They should become second nature to you even if little of your writing is devoted primarily to description.

Review Exercise: Sample Theme

How effective is the following student theme? Examine its use of descriptive detail and expressive language. Examine the organization and explain its relationship to the overall idea. Do you sympathize with the writer's feelings and attitudes? Why, or why not?

CUSTOM BALING — PLEASANT AGONY

For four years it has been my joy and sorrow to earn my livelihood during the summer as a custom baler operator. Every spring I scan the pages of the calendar in restless anticipation of the haying season. It is at this time of mid-summer harvest that I couple up my tractor and baler into a mechanical team of which I am the undisputed master and begin earning a few dollars in this supposedly profitable vocation.

Perhaps before I go any further, I should explain, mostly for the urban population, just what the term "custom baling" means and what it involves. "Custom baling" is the name given to the type of seasonal enterprise in which a farmer or some other individual with a tractor and baler at his disposal makes himself available for hire by neighboring farmers who wish to have their hay baled. The operator is paid on a piece-work basis, that is, he receives a predetermined amount of money for each bale of hay he makes.

This entire operation may seem exceedingly simple to the casual observer, but a closer look will unveil custom baling as the complex undertaking that it really is. For the money which the farmer pays for the service, the baler operator is under obligation to complete the job in reasonable time regardless of the odds. His machinery is expected to be in such dependable condition that no trouble should come from that source. The operator is supposed to be so familiar with his machinery, the topography of the field and its effect on his machines, as well as the type of hay he is baling, that he can spot trouble before it actually occurs. In short, all the farmer does in the baling operation is to reimburse the operator at the predetermined rate. The rest is up to the man on the baler.

It is he who fights to remove the rocks which were swallowed along with the hay from the innards of his machine. It is he who must take care to avoid mud holes and soft ground. If he gets stuck he must not only engineer his way out, but later he must apologize for the unsightly ruts he made in his employer's property. It is he who sits cramped under his machine in the hot sun with the chaff falling in his eyes, ears, and neck, trying to free the hopelessly ensnarled moving parts from their tangled wraps of hay. It is he who, covered with grease and dirt, must restore his machine to working condition. Often at the same time he is put into a cold sweat as he sees the sun lowering toward the west over acres of hay which he cannot possibly finish in the few short hours before sunset. In such cases custom baling is agony.

It may seem strange then that there could possibly be any room for pleasure in such a disagreeable task. Still, for every agony there is at least one pleasure. How can one adequately describe to listeners who have never had such an experience the satisfaction felt by the operator when he rises early and when going outdoors he is greeted by the sparkling freshness of the morning? When he mounts to the seat of his tractor he is about to know an experience shared only by those who love fine machinery and earn a living with it. It is the satisfaction of hearing his tractor burst into action with an authoritative roar the instant he pushes the starter button. To listen to the smooth, flawless operation of machinery which he himself has tuned to perfection is to the ears of the operator as the harmonious music of an accomplished symphony orchestra is to the lover of fine music. How, too, can one describe the sweetness which rises from the new-mown hay in the adjacent field as the operator directs his machinery into the first windrow of a new field?

It is such things as these that make custom baling something to which one becomes attached. Even an ordinary sunset acquires a special significance. As the operator heads for home with his tractor and baler, he sits relaxed at the wheel, the cares of the day left behind. Only memories of the pleasant things seem to survive in the serenity of this unique state of mind. He rides along happily tired. To him sunset is the crown of glory to an honest day's labor, the signal to forget the cares of the day and look forward to a refreshing night's rest. From his perch on the tractor he may even watch the fading glow of red in the west and quietly say to himself, "Amen."

Theme Topics 2

1. Write a paper in the form of *journal entries* or *traveler's notes*. Make the length of your notes vary from short thumbnail sketches to full paragraphs. Choose one of the following as the subject of your notes: a downtown street, an amusement park, a construction site, a factory. Rely on fresh, authentic observation to hold the reader's interest.

2. Write a short paper (200–300 words) in which you develop a *dominant impression* derived from your observation of the crowd at a bus terminal, a country fair, a church picnic, the scene of an accident, or a political rally. State the dominant impression in your first sentence.

3. Write a *"detail-first"* sketch of a person, a room, or a building. Select details that build up to a general effect or key point, and state the intended effect or point in your last sentence.

4. Write a paper in which you give unity to descriptive detail by clear *progression in space or in time* (or a combination of both).

5. Compare and contrast two buildings representing *different styles of architecture*: a skyscraper fifty years old and one recently completed, a church in the city and one in the suburbs, the oldest and the most modern building on campus. Concentrate on *distinctive* detail.

6. Write a *"then-and-now"* paper about a scene or a place you know well: a downtown area before and after redevelopment; a factory before and after automation; a farm, a section of town, or a waterfront that has either been upgraded or gone downhill.

7. Describe the characteristic *visual effects* of an art form on which you are more of an expert than the general public. For instance, can you make your reader visualize a modern ballet or a particular type of modern painting? Concentrate on characteristic shapes, forms, colors, movements.

8. Describe a place or a scene that turned out *different from what you had been led to expect*: a national monument, an often-visited city, a famous site, a scenic wonder. Concentrate on re-creating your own authentic, first-hand impression.

9. Describe the characteristic *sound effects* of two composers, or two kinds of music, in such a way as to help the uninitiated listener tell them apart. For instance, can you help your reader distinguish between Bach and Mozart? Dixieland and rock-and-roll? Two different kinds of current popular music?

10. We are sometimes told that even the modern outdoorsman is cut off from much of nature by modern conveniences and by his own blunted habits of observation. Describe a *natural scene* or an outdoor setting in such a way as to demonstrate to your reader how close an attentive observer can get to nature.

CHAPTER THREE

Personal Experience

1. The Strengths of Autobiography

2. Words and Experience
        The Authentic Note
        Overdramatization

3. Organizing the Autobiographical Theme
        The "I-Was-There" Paper
        The Incident with a Point
        The Study in Contrasts
        The Unifying Theme
        The Process of Growing Up

4. The Uses of Autobiography

Sample Theme
Theme Topics 3

1.   The Strengths of Autobiography

We write what we know. And only the most impersonal part of what we know is what we learn from textbooks. What we know in the most real sense of the word is what we have lived. In the words of John Keats, our truest knowledge is knowledge "proved upon our pulses."

Writing that relies on this kind of knowledge is **autobiography**. In autobiographical writing, the author gives an accounting of his own life. He takes stock of his background and personality. He writes about where he comes from, what he is, and where he is headed. He looks at his failures and his successes. He tries to come to terms with his doubts and aspirations.

Autobiographical writing is a crucial part of a writer's apprenticeship. It is not surprising that many successful professional authors keep diaries, which force them to take stock of their experience from day to day. It is not surprising that some of the most powerful books are autobiographies, or autobiographies thinly disguised as fiction. Training in autobiographical writing prepares a writer to draw on personal experience for several important purposes:

(1) *First-hand experience makes writing real.* Much writing is unreal because it remains too impersonal. The following sentiments do not *sound* like anybody; they could be lifted from any one of a dozen dutiful articles on the values of education:

A willing mind is all the more easily trained. The student who comes to college with little or no intention of training his mind does not long remain among his new-found friends. With his failure to meet the intellectual challenge, he is asked to leave and is quickly replaced by the earnest, more conscientious newcomer.

This passage sounds like a recorded announcement from the dean's office. Contrast the following autobiographical passage, which gives us a sense of real people moving onto a real campus:

Its high, iron-runged, Gothic gate, which swung open on this day to receive the stream of cars laden with luggage, tennis rackets, phonographs, lamps, and musical instruments, was for most of us outlanders, still in our neat cloche hats and careful little traveling suits, a threshold to possibility. — Mary McCarthy, "The Vassar Girl"

(2) *Personal experience provides evidence with which to back up the writer's claims or assertions.* The most convincing answer to the question "How do you know?" is "I know *from experience.*" Notice how the account of an actual incident gives substance to the following paragraph:

A lively street always has both its users and watchers. Last year I was in the Lower East Side of Manhattan, waiting for a bus on a street full of errand-goers, children playing, and loiterers on the stoops. In a minute or so a woman opened a third floor tenement window, vigorously yoo-hooed at me, and shouted down that "The bus doesn't run here on Saturdays!" Then she directed me around the corner. This woman was one of thousands of New Yorkers who casually take care of the streets. They notice strangers. They observe everything going on. If they need to take action, whether to direct a stranger or to call the police, they do so. — Jane Jacobs, "Violence in the City Streets," *Harper's*

(3) *An account of first-hand experience has a chance of getting the reader involved.* A sociologist's analysis of hidden prejudice will leave us better informed. But it will not stir our sympathies or enlist our support as effectively as a single authentic incident from a writer's own experience:

I and two Negro acquaintances, all of us well past thirty, and looking it, were in the bar of Chicago's O'Hare Airport several months ago, and the bartender refused to serve us, because, he said, we looked too young. It took a vast amount of patience not to strangle him, and great insistence and some luck to get the manager, who defended his bartender on the ground that he was "new" and had not yet, presumably, learned how to distinguish between a Negro boy of twenty and a Negro "boy" of thirty-seven. — James Baldwin, *The Fire Next Time*

In a composition text, obviously, the emphasis will be on what autobiography does for the writer as writer. But autobiography also does something important for the writer as a person. It makes him stop and think. It makes him question what normally is most nearly self-evident to him: his beliefs, preferences, and dislikes. Autobiographical writing is enlightening because it confronts us with our personal history. It makes us think through our feelings and commitments.

2. Words and Experience

Writing about oneself is difficult because it makes public what is personal. It puts into words what is normally only thought and felt. In technical and scientific writing, a major goal is **objective** reporting that rules out unreliable personal elements. Science needs procedures and measurements that stay the same regardless of the thoughts, preferences, and emotions of the observer. Autobiography takes stock of the subjective, personal elements that the scientist and technician typically bypass in their work. Since these elements *are* subjective, they vary greatly from one piece of autobiographical writing to another. The reader must be prepared to be tolerant of material that does not fit conventional categories, of writing that does not follow familiar patterns. Nevertheless, how receptive the reader is will be greatly influenced by how well the writer has solved a number of basic, predictable problems.

The Authentic Note

Make your reader feel that your major aim is to give an honest accounting of your experience. The reader will soon become restless and dissatisfied if he feels that your major aim is to make a good impression. He will be disappointed if he feels that on the most important matters you are holding him at arm's length. Here are some ways you can assure your reader of your candor, your good faith:

(1) *Be frank enough to mention what is unflattering as well as what is creditable.* Note the refreshing candor of the following passage:

> My school days were not all golden. In my senior high-school year, I became deeply unsettled, by life and literature, and came to reject the whole scheme of things, including the silly data the school had poured into me and the monster they had tried to make me—competitive, aggressive, snobbish. My family was bewildered, as was everyone else including myself, but had no way of helping as my grades dropped from all A's to failures. I've never been the same since. Though I've developed a genuine passion for learning, it has been on my own terms, and what I have learned and done has been guided almost exclusively by my own stubborn will. Naturally enough, this caused serious problems for me in school from time to time. If assignments appealed to me, I did them—if they didn't, I didn't. . . . Moreover, I never received a cent of tuition aid, being too proud, uninformed about how to do it, and uncertain about the future to apply for scholarships or even loans.—Patricia Cayo Sexton, "Speaking for the Working Class Wife," *Harper's*

(2) *Do not shy away from admitting unresolved problems and contradictory attitudes.* As Oscar Wilde said, the truth is seldom pure and never simple. Cardboard heroes have simple (and always noble) motives. Real people have mixed feelings and divided loyalties. In a famous essay, George Orwell describes his experience as a police officer in British Burma. On the one hand, he describes the sights — the prisons, the flogged convicts — that reinforced his sympathy with the hatred of the Burmese for their British oppressors. On the other hand, he describes the constant baiting he as a European suffered at the hands of the Burmese:

> All I knew was that I was stuck between my hatred of the empire I served and my rage against the evil-spirited little beasts who tried to make my job impossible. With one part of my mind I thought of the British Raj as an unbreakable tyranny, as something clamped down, in *saecula saeculorum*, upon the will of prostrate peoples; with another part I thought that the greatest joy in the world would be to drive a bayonet into a Buddhist priest's guts.—George Orwell, *Shooting an Elephant and Other Essays*

(3) *Resist the temptation to tell your reader things that he would be pleased to hear.* Suppose you are writing a paper on why you plan to choose teaching as a profession. A reader who is seriously interested in you as a person will be disappointed if you merely say, "I want to teach because I love children." This sounds too much like a routine answer, like "the thing to say." If you mean it, you should provide an explanation or an illustration that will make your statement seem less secondhand. Perhaps you like the clever way young children make fools of adults, their skill in dodging embarrassing questions, their resourcefulness in making up answers that serve their own purpose. If you do not mean it, however, you should try to purge your paper of insincerity. You may discover that one reason you like teaching is that it gives you a chance to influence the lives of other people. Or perhaps you are somewhat of an actor and like to perform in front of a group. Your paper should bring some of these things out into the open. If it does, you and your reader will learn something about you as a person, about teaching, and about the motives and ideals of people in general.

Eagerness to adopt attitudes apparently expected of you will fill your writing with **cant** phrases. In talking about teaching and teachers, you may find yourself constantly using words like *wonderful* and *enthusiastic,* simply because you have been taught to consider a highly articulate enthusiasm the mark of a good teacher. You may find yourself constantly describing your experiences as "challenging," "thrilling," and "rewarding," because you have been made to feel that admiration and prestige do not go to people with experiences that are boring, frustrating, or routine. If a person meets "wonderful" people and has a "wonderful" time everywhere he goes, the word *wonderful* becomes automatic and meaningless. Therefore, when you are writing about experiences that are genuinely wonderful and thrilling, you should find words without such overtones of insincerity.

NOTE: Cant is not always allied with optimism. A student may have come to use phrases expressing world-weary disillusionment. Instead of constantly telling his readers that "people are wonderful," he may insist that life is a farce and that all is vanity. He may delight in pointing out the greed and stupidity of his fellow men. His attitude will smack of cant if it is the result of imitation.

Overdramatization

When your subject calls for emotion, develop it unobtrusively, without fanfare. Even a writer who is trying to give an honest accounting of himself may have trouble finding the right tone. He may use self-conscious, apologetic phrases like "After all, I was only a child," "This may not sound very exciting to a person who wasn't there," or "I know this sounds silly, but . . ." Trying to avoid an apologetic attitude, he may go to the opposite extreme. Inexperienced writers often exaggerate for effect. They posture and pose to impress their audience. They overdramatize their experiences, making them sound impressively tragic, hectically exciting, or hilariously funny.

Would you agree that the following passages are overdramatized?

When a surfer looks at the sea, he feels the power of the waves and a surge of independence overcomes him. The surfer sees the sea as a challenge to his surfboard, and he accepts this challenge with all his skill, for he knows he must win or else he may lose his game of life.

I realized as I put my doll back in her place in the trunk that a million yesterdays had been relived and rolled back into a couple of hours spent in the attic with my best childhood friend, Raggedy Annie.

Overdramatization is encouraged by much reading matter intended for popular consumption. It is found, for instance, in popular journalism ("Into the vortex of the crisis flew the President of the United States, his forehead deeply furrowed, his mood somber"). It is equally common in advertising ("Out of the pages of history comes the stupendous story of the love that shook an empire!"). The skeptical reader has had so many things advertised to him as exciting, stunning, or thrilling that mere promises of excitement leave him cold.

Obviously, some subjects call for emotion genuinely powerful or even violent. The following autobiographical passage describes the anguish of a stammering child in a school where his speech defect meets with incomprehension and ridicule:

The word was my agony. The word that for others was so effortless and so neutral, so unburdened, so simple, so exact, I had first to meditate in advance, to see if I could make it, like a plumber fitting together odd lengths and shapes of pipe. I was always preparing words I could speak, storing them away, choosing between them. And often, when the word did come from my mouth in its great and terrible birth, quailing and bleeding as if forced through a thornbush, I would not be able to look the others in the face, and would walk out in silence, the infinitely echoing silence behind my back, to say it all cleanly back to myself as I walked in the streets.—Alfred Kazin, A Walker in the City

But note that even in this passage the major aim of the writer is not to impress us or to plead for our sympathy, but to make us *understand*. The violent birth metaphor powerfully conveys the desperate anxiety of the child. The plumbing metaphor makes us share in the awkward and often futile circumspection of the handicapped.

Generally, the modern reader is wary of direct appeals for sympathy. He is quick to accuse the writer of **sentimentality** — of emotion in excess of what is called for by the occasion, indulged in for its own sake. As a result, a statement in a low key is often more effective than one with strong emphasis.

You may find the following advice useful when trying to do justice to the emotional dimension of experience:

(1) *Do not merely talk about attitudes and feelings but act them out.* More effective than putting exact labels on shades of feeling is to show the reader a situation in which he can sense them. What people say and do can suggest what they think and feel. Notice how effectively the following dialogue suggests the tensions just below the surface, with the Negro boy sensing and trying to protect himself against his employer's hostility to the boy's moving "North" from where he grew up:

> When I broke the news of my leaving two days before I left — I was afraid to tell it sooner for fear that I would create hostility on the part of the whites with whom I worked — the boss leaned back in his swivel chair and gave me the longest and most considerate look he had ever given me.
>
> "Chicago?" he repeated softly.
>
> "Yes, sir."
>
> "Boy, you won't like it up there," he said.
>
> "Well, I have to go where my family is, sir," I said.
>
> The other white office workers paused in their tasks and listened. I grew self-conscious, tense.
>
> "It's cold up there," he said.
>
> "Yes, sir. They say it is," I said, keeping my voice in a neutral tone.
>
> He became conscious that I was watching him and he looked away, laughing uneasily to cover his concern and dislike.
>
> "Now, boy," he said banteringly, "don't you go up there and fall into that lake."
>
> "Oh, no, sir," I said, smiling as though there existed the possibility of my falling accidentally into Lake Michigan.
>
> He was serious again, staring at me. I looked at the floor.
>
> "You think you'll do any better up there?" he asked.
>
> "I don't know, sir."
>
> "You seem to've been getting along all right down here," he said. — Richard Wright, *Black Boy*

(2) *Experiment with conveying emotions by projecting them into objects and scenes.* Emotions can become tangible for the reader if the narrator's environment reflects them like a mirror. Can you see how in the following passage from a student paper the setting mirrors the writer's feeling of loneliness?

As I walk down the hard sidewalk, the sunlight is behind me, and I stare blindly into my dark shadow. A group of people pass me talking happily among themselves. It seems as if they are in a moving box, and I can only see the walls. I smile, but there are no windows to see me through. A gusty cold wind blows and has crept into my mind. A dark concrete building looms ominously above me. No lights, no colors, just gray unfinished concrete. My mind is cold; I feel the hollowness, the hurt, but cannot rid myself of these bitter feelings.

(3) *Use figurative language to communicate feelings and states of mind.* Can you see how in the following examples figurative language effectively communicates attitudes, feelings, motives?

She would look for dark spots in his character and drill away at them as relentlessly as a dentist at a cavity.   (Mary McCarthy)

"I couldn't beat the system. . . ." He was speaking more rapidly and confidently . . . he was cutting the cloth to fit his faults, as everyone did at some time or other.   (John P. Marquand)

An innavigable sea washes with silent waves between us and the things we aim at and converse with.   (Ralph Waldo Emerson)

Exercises

A. Write a paragraph in which you make the *setting* in which you find yourself mirror what you feel. Make the whole paragraph project one dominant attitude or emotion. Choose an emotion *not* overexploited in popular entertainment: apprehension rather than fear, affection rather than passionate love.

B. Write *two different reports* on a game, dance, meeting, or party that you have recently attended. Make the reports reflect the feelings and reactions of two different people—one jovial and one sour, or one excitable and the other bored.

C. Select *one* of the following general terms: *cruelty, curiosity, dignity, extravagance, forgiveness, kindness, naïveté, patience, poise, rudeness, shyness, spite, touchiness.* Write a well-developed paragraph describing in detail an incident from your personal experience or observation that illustrates the quality you have selected.

D. Study the following brief passages from autobiographical student papers. From which of the authors would you expect an honest stock-taking of their attitudes or emotions? Why or why not?

1. My uncle was no ordinary hypochondriac. He owned a drugstore, inherited from his father, and had been practically brought up in it. He talked to doctors and nurses every day. When some infectious disease was making the rounds, he would worry for hours over whether he had the symptoms. When he was positive that he did, his mind was in a way relieved and he went to bed. The next morning he woke up in perfect shape.

2. I must have been nine or ten when my family moved into a small farming town in the northwest corner of Wisconsin. Before, when we lived on a farm several miles out, I had been unable to attend the activities held in the Town Hall, the school, and the churches. I was happy to move, for now I could go to the out-of-date movies on Wednesday and Sunday nights. I could go roller skating. I could attend the Halloween and Valentine's Day parties, the church socials, and the Sunday school picnics. Most important, I had friends to share these experiences. Every year, Old Ray Brewer would draw his rifle on us when we went trick-or-treating. Every year we pushed over his woodpile and his outhouse. How we laughed and cried the night Teddy fell into the hole when he tripped over the wire old Ray had strung around the building. On bright summer days, we swam till our hands became wrinkled and rough, and we lay in the sun till we were cozy and warm. In the winter, we went to the pond and skated on the ice till our toes twinkled with cold; then we sat by the bonfire and toasted our toes and the marshmallows and sipped hot chocolate. When we went to the station to watch the train, we pretended that we boarded it and took the long journey to Chicago.

3. Let me cite my experience as a lover of folk music, aspiring to become a professional in that field. Because my parents had never heard any genuine folk music and had never even thought about its origins, they immediately associated it with the "Oakie" (or to them "low-class") element in society. In their over-hasty judgment, they could not know that real folk music is superior and more "respectable," musicologically, than the schmaltz they listen to.

4. Then I heard people screaming that there was a man trapped under the front tire of the other car. I found Jack, who was completely stunned by the whole event. He told me that he put on the brakes at the intersection and that the brakes had failed. He just couldn't stop the car. Within minutes the police and ambulance arrived, and the car was tediously lifted off the trapped, quiet man. I observed a girl sitting in the ambulance, and I realized that she also had been riding the other car.

5. At first, finding a job was very difficult. There was no work for a boy nine years old anywhere. After five days of cutting school, I saw a sign

in the window of a little grocery that said "Delivery Boy Wanted." When I walked through the door, I thought my heart would never stop pounding. When I told the man inside that I wanted to apply for the job, his first reaction was to look over the counter and laugh. But then he asked me a few questions and seemed to become interested. His next reaction was to go over to the sign in the window and take it down. I was so excited I wanted to scream. What would my mother say? How happy she would be! With great effort I controlled my emotions. The sweat was pouring down my back and face. Then the man said, "I hired a boy yesterday. He should be in any minute now. I guess he forgot to take the sign out of the window."

6. Any job I have ever had has been taken under duress. I am a moody, indolent, dreamy individual, and once, in a fit of pique, I quit school and wandered off to seek my soul. My parents took a dim view of the search and, becoming hungry, I found myself taking employment with the Union Oil Company, a well-fed crew. Here I found I could be moody, indolent, and dream-prone on company time.

E. The following are brief excerpts from autobiographical passages by well-known modern writers. What makes each passage graphic, effective, memorable? Show in detail how each writer *uses language* to re-create a setting or a scene, and to convey his feelings or attitudes.

1. I was born in a large Welsh town at the beginning of the Great War—an ugly, lovely town (or so it was and is to me), crawling, sprawling by a long and splendid curving shore where truant boys and sand-field boys and old men from nowhere, beachcombed, idled and paddled, watched the dock-bound ships or the ships steaming away to wonder and India, magic and China, countries bright with oranges and loud with lions; threw stones into the sea for the barking outcast dogs; made castles and forts and harbours and race tracks in the sand; and on Saturday summer afternoons listened to the brass band, watched the Punch and Judy, or hung about on the fringes of the crowd to hear the fierce religious speakers who shouted at the sea, as though it were wicked and wrong to roll in and out like that, white-horsed and full of fishes.— Dylan Thomas, *Quite Early One Morning*

2. Now, the First War, with its massed artillery, was the noisiest of all time; the sound hit you harder and harder as the months passed; some things you got used to—sniping and machine-gun fire if you were not entangled in the open and a sitting duck, hand bombs and rifle grenades if you had sandbags and room to dodge—but as time went on the vast cannonading, drumming hell into your ears, no matter whether it was their guns or yours, began to wear you down, making you feel that flesh and blood had no place in this factory of destruction. So in that war it was not the recruit but the veteran who began to feel he was being ham-

mered into the ground. Every time I went back into the line, especially after being out of it long enough for my ears to open to civilization again, I felt more and more apprehension. In that listening post I was the gallant Tommy of the home-front legends; but as time wore on I was more and more a chap who wondered what the hell he was doing there and how he could get out of it — a mouse in a giant mincing machine. — J. B. Priestley, *Margin Released*

3. I had forgotten, in the rage of my growing up, how proud my father had been of me when I was little. Apparently, I had a voice and my father had liked to show me off before the members of the church. I had forgotten what he had looked like when he was pleased but now I remembered that he had always been grinning with pleasure when my solos ended. I even remembered certain expressions on his face when he teased my mother — had he loved her? I would never know. And when had it all begun to change? For now it seemed that he had not always been cruel. I remembered being taken for a haircut and scraping my knee on the footrest of the barber's chair and I remembered my father's face as he soothed my crying and applied the stinging iodine. Then I remembered our fights, fights which had been of the worst possible kind because my technique had been silence.

I remembered the one time in all our life together when we had really spoken to each other.

It was on a Sunday and it must have been shortly before I left home. We were walking, just the two of us, in our usual silence, to or from church. I was in high school and had been doing a lot of writing and I was, at about this time, the editor of the high school magazine. But I had also been a Young Minister and had been preaching from the pulpit. Lately, I had been taking fewer engagements and preached as rarely as possible. It was said in the church, quite truthfully, that I was "cooling off."

My father asked me abruptly, "You'd rather write than preach, wouldn't you?"

I was astonished at his question — because it was a real question. I answered, "Yes."

That was all we said. It was awful to remember that that was all we had *ever* said. — James Baldwin, *Notes of a Native Son*

4. Throughout my life I have longed to feel that oneness with large bodies of human beings that is experienced by the members of enthusiastic crowds. The longing has often been strong enough to lead me into self-deception. I have imagined myself in turn a Liberal, a Socialist, or a Pacifist, but I have never been any of these things, in any profound sense. Always the skeptical intellect, when I have most wished it silent, has whispered doubts to me, has cut me off from the facile enthusiasms of others, and has transported me into a desolate solitude. During the War, while I worked with Quakers, non-resisters,

and Socialists, while I was willing to accept the unpopularity and the inconvenience belonging to unpopular opinions, I would tell the Quakers that I thought many wars in history had been justified, and the Socialists that I dreaded the tyranny of the State. They would look askance at me and while continuing to accept my help would feel that I was not one of them. — Bertrand Russell, *Autobiography, 1914-1944*

F. Investigate current television dramas or Hollywood movies. To what extent do they bear out the familiar charge that their treatment of love is cliché-ridden and sentimental? More generally, what ideas about people — their standards and their motives — do they convey to their audience?

G. Study the letters written by people with personal or emotional problems in a question-and-answer column in a newspaper or magazine. Can you generalize about these letters — their candor, their tone? How useful, mature, or responsible is the advice these people receive?

H. From your current reading, gather five phrases or sentences that seem especially effective in using *figurative language* to express attitudes, emotions, or states of mind.

3.   Organizing the Autobiographical Theme

Ordinary experience is miscellaneous, one thing after another. Writing that merely chronicles this flow of experience remains formless; it does not seem to lead anywhere. Good autobiographical writing is more than the unedited record of the past, compiled by the camera eye of nostalgic memory. To give an autobiographical paper shape and point, you will have to

- *restrict your subject.* Obviously, no one can tell the story of his life in 500 words. Only when the scope of a paper is narrow enough to allow the reader a close look at specific persons, incidents, and problems does the ordinary person's experience become interesting. When writing about a trip, do not give your reader a mere neutral itinerary that might have been followed by a hundred people other than yourself. Focus on something that happened to *you* somewhere along the way.

- *sift out the insignificant.* Themes about "My Spring Vacation" or "A Labor Day Outing" seldom have the unity suggested by the neat temporal limitation of their titles. The events of a week or of a single day can be as miscellaneous as those of a month or of a year. A paper discussing a change in Christmas customs that you have experienced over the years can be more unified than the paper that assembles the unrelated trivia of a single holiday weekend.

- *work your material into a unifying pattern.* Make your reader feel that you are getting at something. Help your reader see that your paper as a whole is designed to pinpoint a problem, or work out a contrast, or justify a point of view. Make him see that you have organized your paper to make it serve a unifying purpose.

Here are sample patterns for a unified autobiographical theme:

The "I-Was-There" Paper

Much forceful autobiographical writing has a documentary quality; its purpose is "to tell it the way it was." The eyewitness at some serious turn of events—a demonstration, a strike, a riot—often finds reports of it partial or superficial, colored by preconceived notions. He then determines to "set the record straight." At its best, the resulting paper has a grim loyalty to what happened, *in the order* in which it happened. It observes rigorous **chronological order** so that the reader may clearly see action and reaction, cause and effect. The author may

- start in a low key and let events gradually build up to a **climax;**
- keep the outcome in doubt and thus create **suspense.**

The Incident with a Point

Autobiographical writing easily becomes rambling reminiscence, moving from one thing to another in a loose "and-then . . . and-then" sequence. You can counteract this tendency by concentrating on a *single meaningful incident.* This may be an episode in which an erroneous impression is first created and then corrected, an incident that revealed a character trait you had long suspected, an event that destroyed a cherished illusion. The point made is most convincing when it *emerges* plausibly and vividly from the incident. It effectively ties the paper together if stated as the lesson learned, in the final sentence of the paper; or if summed up in the "punch line" of a dialogue. The basic pattern of such a paper is "This-is-what-happened-and-this-is-what-it-means."

The more naturally the point emerges from the event, the less likely the reader is to object to it as the tacked-on "moral of the tale." Modern readers are wary of too obviously edifying conclusions.

Notice how clearly, and yet how unobtrusively, the student's main point emerges from the following autobiographical sketch:

ENJOY

My father is a ten-gallon-hat man, big and tall. At home, when he opened a bag of potato chips, he never ate any himself; he gave them to me: this was satisfaction, knowing I was happy. My brothers and I could never enjoy ourselves enough for him. "Enjoy life while you can. Have fun," he would say. "Don't study so hard."

Sometimes I carried my books home, wearing them between my shirt and my chest, and then hid with them and some crackers in the attic next to the grayed windows with light filtering through and down upon me. The attic smelled of stale dry air. There I could lie and read.

Then my father would roar up the stairs. "Why don't you go play baseball? Enjoy yourself!"

I stood up without answering.

"Your mother said you were playing baseball, but I said I'd find you reading!"

I studied his watch.

"I worked hard, studied long hours, and got little sleep all my life. Saturday is not a day to study. Hah?"

I couldn't say anything.

"What's the matter, cat got your tongue? Don't you feel good? You want to lay down?"

"I want to go outside and enjoy myself," I finally said. Instead of taking it up or carrying it any further, he would let it drop.

My father had worked hard all his life. He never had any time to enjoy life until he was older. For these reasons he always wanted me to enjoy life.

The Study in Contrasts

Much autobiographical writing attempts to come to terms with conflicting influences in the author's life. Young people, especially, are often pulled in contradictory directions by friends, parents, teachers, and their own inclinations. A well-focused paper may work out a contrast between two such conflicting forces:

- a businesslike, efficient father and a sensitive, artistic mother;
- the foreign customs of immigrant parents and the Americanizing influence of school;
- two teachers that strongly influenced the writer but represented strongly opposed views of life or models for conduct;
- a strongly religious family but friends with a different outlook.

The Unifying Theme

At a given stage in our lives, a major new interest may develop; a problem may loom large. Such an interest or problem can provide the unifying theme, the common thread, for experiences dissimilar on the surface. It can thus become the focus for a paper that traces the common element in *several related incidents*. Thus, the author may find a unifying theme in his encounters with a type of person. A student from a well-to-do family, for instance, might write about his encounters with people who first made him understand what it means to grow up, like Moss Hart, with "the dark brown taste of being poor forever in my mouth and the grim smell of actual want always at the end of my nose" (*Act I*).

In the following excerpt from a magazine article, can you see how the italicized passages strike the recurrent note that helps the author unify autobiographical detail?

I was *a strong patriot*, a peppy, idealistic fellow living in a walkup near Union Square. I *had hitchhiked all over America*, dragging my suitcase to forty-three states. I'd seen the Snake and the Rio Grande and San Diego and Aberdeen, Wash. In fact I'd turned down a trip to Europe in order to go out and see more. And so in the evening I often went to the Square to hear the accents of the soapbox speakers, *scanning the Kentucky and wheat-belt faces*. It seemed the whole country was represented there, old men of every occupation, scallop-boat men and soybean farmers. The Communists spoke under an equestrian statue—"under the horse's ass," as they said. Early birds saved the platform for them and they scheduled themselves: first a small, dedicated Jewish bookkeeper who spoke seriously from notes; after him, a rangy Dos Passos Communist *with Idaho still in his voice* and the vocal cords of a Wobbly organizer; . . . last, an emotive, fair-minded Russian, a family man with an earthy, demonstrative face who rode up from Delancey Street on his bicycle with a white terrier running alongside. . . .

The other speakers hadn't the training or the podium but they did their best—a prototype black nationalist, a hollering atheist, a thin Catholic proselytizer and retired businessman who lived on West 72nd Street. He tore his voice shouting at all of them. They brought up the Inquisition so many times that at last he started defending it. There were also a couple of opera singers, a vaudeville comedian, and a pacifist who knelt on the pavement after every pugnacious remark that he made. . . .

I loved Steinbeck and Dos Passos and, though my blood beat at the stories of injustice I was told, it was mainly the faces I came to see, *the map of the continent*, from the tunafish cannery where I'd worked one July to the Platte River that I'd hitchhiked along.—Edward Hoagland, "The Draft Card Gesture," *Commentary*

The Process of Growing Up

As autobiographical writing becomes more ambitious, it goes beyond limited topics and begins to confront its larger underlying subject. That subject is a process of growth, of development. The writer looks back at what he once was and ponders what he has become. In the more serious kind of autobiographical paper, he maps *one important stage in the process* of gradual change that has shaped his personality. The author may retrace the road from expectation to reality, from the creed he was taught to his present convictions, from the values of the society in which he grew up to his own personal sense of values. A classic theme of great autobiography is the individual's attempt to make traditional formulas fit his own experience, and to work out his own salvation.

Even a short paper can be modeled on the basic process of growing up that much true autobiography explores. It can trace a *change* from

- promising appearance to the discovery of sober reality—for instance, in a paper about a person;
- a taught dislike to genuine preference—for instance, in a paper about friends frowned upon by one's parents;
- hostility to tolerance—for instance, in a paper about political associations.

Exercises

A. Write an "I-was-there" paragraph about an incident that has been, or is likely to be, misrepresented or misinterpreted. For instance, write about the crucial stage of a quarrel, a classroom incident, or an accident.

B. Write a one-paragraph theme describing an incident that revealed something significant about the character of a friend or relative. Sum up the point of the episode in a key sentence placed at the end of the paragraph.

C. Young people today are said to be nonideological in politics and uninterested in dogma in religion. How specifically can you state your own personal convictions? Write down three sentences, each stating a conviction or belief you held, say, three years ago. Then, in the same form, write down the version of each as you would accept it today. (Is it different? about the same? more strongly held? drastically modified?)

D. Describe the organization of each of the following short autobiographical papers. How has each author given *unity* to his material? Does he succeed in going from something of personal interest to him to something of *general significance* to the reader? Your instructor may ask you to use one of these sketches, or the earlier one entitled "Enjoy," as a model for a short paper of your own.

1.   SATURDAY AFTERNOON

He cut. The scalpel made a teeth-gritting noise as it hit the cartilaginous callus. His hands were steady, the skin tight over blue veins and white tendons—wide, strong hands, the kind that could comfort a crying child and pat a big black dog's velvet head.

He swore as he sliced a fraction of an inch too deeply. Smells floated up from the table. Formaldehyde—sickly sweet, like pickled worms and frogs—but a cadaver has its own peculiar smell. Almost musty—like a house that's been locked for a long time.

Sweating now, he peeled back the uppermost layer to expose the acetabulum, into which the head of the femur fits. "Sacrum, coccyx, ptaylin, mylohoids . . . it's all here."

"Liss—let's go fly kites—run in the sun at the park." How good he is: the kite-flyer, cutter-of-cadavers; lover of hunting, the outdoors, nature, people. How gently he touches.

His hands stiffened as he pulled the hepatic artery up to reveal its bluish hepatic sphincter. He sliced the thick wall—all peripheral resistance gone, the reddish fluid oozed out. He examined carefully, noticing every fissure.

"You'll make a wonderful nurse," he mumbled. He would make a wonderful doctor. . . .

Without looking up, he held out his hand, placing in my thin, tiny one some vital organ. It was cold and very slimy. I gulped, the swallow sticking slightly below the larynx-joins-the-trachea area. It was terribly hot in the minute anatomy dissecting room.

"Next weekend," I murmured, "do you think we could go to the beach?"

2.   A CHANGE OF PLACES

I lived in a neighborhood that respectable white people like to think does not exist. Ninety percent of its people were poor Negroes. The rest, like me, were poor whites. I was a minority. All my friends were black, as were my enemies. I lived by their standards, and, consequently, I felt the pains of being different. Whenever we played games, my name was not Dick, but "Milky," or "Sugar," or that old standby "Whitey." If a new club was formed in the neighborhood, I was always left out because I couldn't be trusted with any secrets. If I made a new friend and he asked me to come play at his house, I had to prepare myself for that same chilling, motherly line, "You can't have any friends in, Georgie, because your father is sleeping, and you'd better come in anyway because it's time to eat." Whenever I got into a fight with another kid, I knew that there would be no help from any of my friends, because I was white and they were black, and the bonds of color were much stronger than the ties of friendship. I had to stand alone.

My soul was not that of a young child, in those days. As a matter of survival, I had encased myself in a callus of bitter acceptance. Smiles became a strange, bewildering phenomenon to the muscles of my face. The usual childhood tears were never able to find an escape route through my eyes. Crying is not allowed when one is a minority, for one doesn't show his feelings, or else his weaknesses may be exposed. And so I existed, very cold and all alone.

But my father, unlike the other fathers in that neighborhood, was able to increase his income enough to take us out and into a new environment. Left behind were those cluttered streets and crowded apartment buildings, and those cold black faces. I soon found myself in a new world, a world of front lawns, and pastel-colored toilet bowls, and two-car garages. As for the people, they were not black, as I had expected them to be, but white like me. For a while then, I was happy. But then a Negro family moved into our neighborhood, and they had a boy my age. He was a raisin in a sugar bowl, and he knew it. He was cold and lonely as I had been, and I remembered that awful feeling that I had left behind.

4. The Uses of Autobiography

Few people become important enough to have the world clamor for the publication of their memoirs. More people at some time keep a diary, which both gives them pleasure and teaches them something about themselves. Most people limit what little autobiographical writing they do to personal letters to family and friends. Even if you intend to do no more, practice in autobiographical writing can teach you several things essential for success in *other* kinds of writing:

(1) Autobiographical writing can teach you to *mobilize your own resources*. It can help you discover your personal experience as the most immediate, the most legitimate, and often the most interesting source of material. You may never become an authority on troop movements during the Civil War or on the behavior of subatomic particles. But nobody can question your right to act as an authority on what you have personally observed, undergone, and felt.

(2) Autobiographical writing can give you the habit of approaching possible subjects from a personal perspective. It will encourage you *to speak for yourself*. Suppose you start a paper by saying "History proves that the pursuit of luxury causes the downfall of nations." Who is History? But suppose you start the paper by saying "A history textbook I recently read led me to believe that the pursuit of luxury causes the downfall of nations." This version sounds less impressive, but that a college student should be reading a history textbook seems natural and convincing.

Many familiar phrases pretend to authority more sweeping and definitive than the writer can reasonably claim. Often "It is a known fact" means "All my friends think so"; "Experience shows" means "Father tells me"; "Science has proved" means "My high school biology teacher claimed." If you present yourself as a spokesman of History, Common Knowledge, Experience, or Science, you will render your credentials automatically suspect. Talk to your reader as one fallible human being to another.

(3) Autobiography can help you develop the most important single quality of effective writing: *good writing carries conviction.* Whatever good writing is, it is not the repetition of thin generalities about the American way of life. Your writing must be something that you yourself are willing to stand up for, something to which in some way you are personally committed.

For a time, a reader may be carried away by the writer who can argue glibly either side of an issue. But the writer who makes a lasting impression is the one whose writing expresses his personal commitment. Good writing means recording one's own observations, pinning down one's own reactions, interpreting one's own experience, formulating one's own judgments, and making one's own mistakes. To profit from instruction in writing, you have to consider it as more than perfunctory practice. Papers dealing with personal experience can help you take your writing seriously by making you focus on some of the matters important to you in your own life.

Review Exercise: Sample Theme

How effective is the following student theme? Does it seem self-conscious or self-confident, authentic or overdramatized? What strategy does the writer employ in organizing the material? How effective is the selection of detail?

WHAT AM I?

When people ask where I was born, they often seem disappointed when I reply, "California." Because of my Oriental features and name, they seem to have anticipated something exotic like Japan, Siam, or at least Hawaii!! My parents were born and raised in Japan. They came to America when they were in their teens, but they have retained the language, music, and some of the customs of Japan in our home. They have reared my brother and sisters in the ways of the old country in preparation for becoming good citizens in America. Bridging the gap between home and school is sometimes as hard as trying to build a bridge across the Atlantic.

One difficulty is the transition from our home language to the school language. My father prefers to speak Japanese. Therefore, my mother refused to teach us how to speak English, because she did not want us to learn both languages poorly or to mix both in broken English. After her first week in school, my little sister came home from school and announced that she had learned a new song at school. In proud innocence she sang: "Teacher,

teacher, ring the bell; teacher, teacher, go to hell." She was forbidden to speak English from then on unless she knew the *exact* meaning of her new words. She received an "A" in deportment during her first semester of school. The second semester's card, however, was accompanied by a note from her teacher ("Hideko chatters constantly") and a "C" in deportment. Evidently, she had learned to understand English.

The problems of adjustment are not usually as humorous, however. It is not just one generation's ideas against another's, but the moral standards of Japan conflicting with those of America. Dating did not exist in the Japan my parents left thirty years ago. The only respectable procedure was for a "bishakunin," a go-between, to arrange the engagement of the young couple. After that, the two principals involved were introduced and often allowed to go around together. It is strange to hear my parents saying that the time seems to have come when girls and boys will marry whomever they please, that these foolish young people should leave an important thing like the selection of one's mate in the hands of an impartial and wise elder. It is a far cry from the world of steadies, pinnings, and engagements that are so much a part of college life.

The moment I leave home, a conflict arises because the Japanese and Caucasian Americans seem to form into separate groups. In grammar school, I did not face this problem, since there were too few of us to be considered a minority group. We were considered to be individuals who had nothing special in common with each other. In high school, however, the Japanese seemed to stay together as a group. The majority of the students seemed to make generalizations about each group as a whole and to expect everyone who was Japanese to be like the others. "Oh, yes," someone would say, "I know her. She's Japanese." The sense of disinterest, of finality, and of cool classification seemed unjust to me. I rebelled against losing my own sense of identity; I didn't want to be a generalization, by any means!

I resolved to find out where I belonged by developing my interests and by following them through into whichever society they would bring me. In other words, I stopped thinking and got busy. In the four years of high school, I found that those who allow themselves to be taken over by racial bondage do not develop themselves. Their areas of interests seemed to lie only where other Japanese were active. For example, the majority of Japanese girls joined either one of two clubs — both of which had a majority of members of Japanese descent. My interests led me to join clubs of service, sports, and art as well as the other two. Others often expressed a desire to join a new club, but only if several Japanese joined together. Such conformity, to me, was like swimming in a stagnant pool.

I was happy being active in school affairs until my senior year. All went well until I began to attend parties where I began to feel like the "lone wolf" because I was the only Japanese and was always a "stagette." The latter was irrelevant because my parents would not allow me to date anyway, but the element of being irrevocably "different" entered my mind. In college, I joined a Japanese social club where I felt that I would "belong." But this kind of belonging came about through no effort of my own, but simply by virtue of being Japanese — an accident of birth. The depth of what the members had in common was apparent to the eye in a single glance.

At this time, I asked myself: "What happens to the person who is brought up in two different cultures or societies? Should he choose between the two in his adult life? What factors would influence his decision?" I think that I was frustrated for months. However, I reached the following conclusions: First, one should strive to develop the finer aspects of both cultures and their ideals; secondly, one should wear a race as he wears clothes — as just one expression of his personality. It should neither dominate nor undermine the presence of the person. It is like an attractive pin, however, that draws attention to the person.

A person with a negative attitude toward his race wraps it around himself like a huge coat. He keeps from developing the natural potentialities within because of the skin that covers them. Not to venture outside is like saying, "I wanted a different coat, but, through no fault of my own, I ended up with this one. I suppose I must arrange my other clothes to go with this coat because I can't exchange it." Eventually, that person will have a wardrobe of clothes (abilities and friends) which have one thing in common — their relationship to a coat (race) for which he had no freedom of selection.

What am I? What does it matter? To me, as with everyone else, it is *who* I am that matters.

Theme Topics 3

1. Write an *"I-was-there"* paper to set the record straight on an event to which you were an eyewitness, or in which you were a major participant. Try not to talk *about* the event but to show how it really happened.

2. Write a paper focused on a *single incident* that taught you something about a matter that up to then you had only *heard about*: juvenile delinquency, drug use, race prejudice, poverty, crime in the streets, the role of the police, the authoritarian personality, intolerance, snobbery, or the like. Make the point of the incident emerge clearly toward the end of the paper.

3. Work out a *comparison and contrast* between two people who strongly influenced you: parents, relatives, teachers, friends, idols. Limit yourself to a few crucial features that you can illustrate in authentic detail.

4. Have you ever found yourself torn by conflicting advice, contradictory standards, divided loyalties? Discuss one such *contrast or conflict* in detail.

5. Trace *one major theme* in your upbringing or past history through several related incidents. For instance, write about a strong interest you developed, a recurrent obstacle, a type of person you gradually came to know and understand.

6. Write a paper focused on an important *change* in your outlook—a change in attitude toward someone important in your life or toward a public figure; a changed attitude toward a group, institution, tradition, kind of work, or endeavor; a basic change in your ambitions, expectations, ideals, or beliefs.

7. A favorite modern term is *complexity*. We constantly hear statements like "our generation must learn to deal with the complexities of the modern world" or "Sigmund Freud began to unveil the true complexity of man." Have you had something that at one time seemed simple to you turn out to be complicated? Rely on authentic detail from your own experience.

8. Writing about the Vassar girl, Mary McCarthy said, "The Vassar freshman still comes through Taylor Gate as I did, with the hope of being made over. . . . The daughter of a conservative lawyer, doctor, banker, or businessman, she will have chosen Vassar in all probability with the idea of transcending her background." Are you, or those of your friends that you know best, trying to "transcend" your background? In what sense, or in what way? Limit yourself to one major area: ideas, manners, habits, associations.

9. It has become a cliche to talk about the "generation gap," with young people expected to reject the "complacent" views of their elders. In what area, or in what way, did the generation gap become most real to you, or to close friends?

10. Today's college students may hear a campus chaplain call his a "discussing church," or they may hear a student editor from a Catholic university explain how far his school has gotten away from a "stereotyped" Catholic mentality. Have you had any close first-hand experience with changing religious attitudes or standards?

An enormous amount of other learning must take place before one can write worthwhile essays of ideas; that is in the nature of the whole abstraction process.
James Moffet

CHAPTER FOUR

Opinion

1. Opinions Worth Writing Down

2. Anchoring Opinion to Fact
   Fact and Inference
   A Respect for Facts

3. Developing Opinions of Your Own
   Identifying an Issue
   Forming an Opinion
   Changing Your Mind
   Revising for Clarity

4. The Opinions of Others
   Cross-Examining Your Witnesses
   Questioning Conventional Views
   Staying Clear of Verbal Traps

5. Organizing the Essay of Opinion
   Defending a Thesis
   The "Yes, But" Paper
   The Change of Mind

Sample Theme
Theme Topics 4

1. Opinions Worth Writing Down

Most writing in one way or another expresses the author's opinions. It shows how he interprets and reacts to what he has observed, experienced, and read. We call an article we read an "essay of opinion" if in studying the material presented we are at the same time vividly aware of the *person* who is selecting data, who is appraising a situation, who is making judgments. We do not ask a person's opinion on how far it is from Philadelphia to Baltimore. For such questions, we rely for answers on records or measuring instruments that tell the same story to different observers. We do ask for people's opinions on subjects like student riots, the generation gap, the draft, capital punishment, hair styles, or violence on the screen. We know that on these subjects people hold different views.

Among the statements offered to us as opinions, we recognize familiar types. Some speculate about causes ("The recent campus riot was the result of a nationwide conspiracy"). Some generalize, pointing to the common element in diverse situations ("The generation gap is merely our modern version of the gulf that has always separated older people from adolescents"). Some offer judgments of value ("The draft is inequitable"). Some offer a program for future action ("Capital punishment should be abolished"). In practice, however, these categories overlap. The person who ascribes riots to a conspiracy is not merely explaining the riots; he is at the same time condemning them. (He is also implying that they should be treated as a sinister threat, to be dealt with by drastic means.) The person linking the current generation gap to a more general pattern is by implication judging it to be normal and acceptable. He is suggesting that no special remedial action is necessary or possible.

The basic question that confronts you as a writer is: "What opinions are worth writing down?" Later chapters of this book will examine in some detail the problems of logic you will encounter in trying to arrive at sound opinions, the problems of definition you will encounter in trying to state them clearly. The more serious your topic, the more ambitious the scope of your argument, the more important your close attention to these problems will become. But even a short opinion paper, on a limited subject close to your experience, must meet some fundamental requirements if you want to make a claim on your reader's time.

Here are the most basic requirements your writing will have to meet if you want your reader to take your opinions seriously:

.   (1) The opinion you offer should be an *informed* opinion. It should be clearly related to facts you have studied, events you have observed. Whatever your interpretations and judgments may be, you should offer enough of the data on which they are based so that the reader can form his *own* opinion. A good reader does not simply stop reading because he disagrees with the author. He can disagree and still feel that he is learning something, that he is given something to ponder.

(2) The opinion you offer should be your *considered* opinion. It should show that you have wrestled with your subject and, if necessary, changed your mind. It should show that you have learned to consider objections and to make the necessary adjustments in your own position, painful as that process may be. Your reader will not be willing to learn from you if you do not sound like the kind of person willing to learn something new himself.

(3) The opinion you offer should be *your own*. Obviously, many people who speak of the need for "law and order" are merely repeating the views of others, using to a large extent the very words we have heard others use. Anonymously, and in the mass, such shared opinions carry considerable weight. But when your paper merely repeats ready-made views in pre-assembled phrases, the reader's reaction is going to be: "I have heard all this before." To make him pay attention, you will have to answer questions like "Why do *you* share this view? How does it fit *your* experience? How have you *adjusted* it to fit your experience?"

When written as a routine exercise, the essay of opinion is merely an occasion to vent our prejudices or to play oracle. When we take our assignment seriously, however, it is likely to remind us that writing is a creative process. *The art of writing well is the art of making up one's mind.* For a serious writer, the invitation to state his opinion is a challenge to seek out information, sharpen his observation, and clarify confusion. His finished paper is the result of exploration and discovery.

2.   Anchoring Opinion to Fact

The first step toward an effective presentation of opinions is to become aware of them as opinions. The mind is not a mechanical recording device. What it takes in, it tries to explain, to interpret. It relates what is new to established preferences, likes and dislikes. It tries to shape from what it has observed a guide to future action. When we deal with opinions, we focus attention on what the human observer has done to make sense of experience.

Fact and Inference

Learn to distinguish between readily observable facts and the conclusions you draw from them. Ideally, a fact is something we can verify by direct observation or measurement. We can see a car in a ditch; we can measure skid marks; we can take an injured man's pulse. The more factual a policeman's report is, the more it stresses exact time, location, dimensions; the exact extent of damage done to the car; the observable outward condition of the victim. When we conclude that there has been an accident, we take a large step away from fact to **inference**. We infer something we have not actually observed. To help support our inference, we would probably look for the testimony of eyewitnesses who actually saw a car spin around, or the like.

The closer they stay to the facts, the better the chance that two competent observers will bring back the same data. We would be surprised if two policemen disagreed violently on the length of the skid marks. But we are not surprised when we hear two different *interpretations* of the same facts. Even though our inference about an accident stayed fairly close to the facts, an insurance adjuster might investigate the 1-in-a-100 chance that the "accident" was *staged* to defraud his company. The farther our inferences move beyond direct observation, the more chances there are for them to differ from those of others.

If we were to take a sampling of opinion from motorists who stopped at the scene of the accident, we would encounter many inferences that come close to merely being *one person's view:*

• the type of car involved in the accident is unsafe;

• people in the age group of the victim tend to be careless drivers;

• speed limits in this state are too high;

• the driver was probably drunk.

Notice that much of what we are offered as "fact" is far removed from what can be directly verified. It turns out to be something the speaker has *inferred*, something that is a matter of *interpretation*. Suppose someone says: "It's against the law to kill people. Isn't that a fact?" This assertion turns out to be not a fact at all but a very *general* statement that badly needs narrowing down: It is against the law to kill people *except* in self-defense, or in the pursuit of a policeman's duties, or as part of a military operation in times of war. What constitutes "self-defense" is a matter of interpretation — just as what is "insanity" is a matter of interpretation when a person accused of murder pleads not guilty on those grounds. It is matters of interpretation such as these that keep judges, lawyers, and juries occupied.

For the writer, the distinction between fact and interpretation, between fact and inference, is fundamental. As long as he considers something a simple "fact," he does not feel the need to support, to defend it. He simply presents it, assuming that right-minded people will agree with him. Once he realizes that he is really presenting an inference, he feels the need to support it — and to reconsider it if necessary.

A Respect for Facts

A reader will respect an opinion if the writer shows a respect for facts. The opinions you present to your reader will be inferences, resting on a more or less factual foundation. Your most basic task is to reassure your reader that the superstructure of inference that you are erecting is indeed founded in observations and experiences that he himself could share, duplicate, or verify.

To make the reader respect your opinion, observe the following advice:

(1) *Keep your inferences close to the facts you present.*   Do not try to erect a large superstructure of theory on a meager supply of data. The more freely you editorialize, the more difficult you make your basic task: to give solid substance to one major point at a time. In each of the following pairs, both passages offer an interpretation of available facts. But the first version goes too far too fast; the second version has a better chance of carrying the reader along:

Debatable:	The voters of the fifth district expressed their resentment of Republican policies by sending a Democratic congressman to Washington.
More Factual:	Though voter registration in the fifth district is 58 per cent Republican, a majority of the voters voted for a Democratic congressman. The results show a sizable crossover to the Democratic side by normally Republican votes.
Debatable:	Without provocation, the police attacked the demonstrators, brutally beating boys and girls alike.
More Factual:	After a plate glass window was broken, the police moved in to disperse the demonstrators. In the ensuing melee, a dozen students were injured. Three boys and two girls were treated at the Student Health Service for cuts and bruises.

Most of us need little encouragement to venture an opinion. We have to learn to ask "What do I know about it?" before we ask "What do I think of it?"

(2) *Avoid unnecessary comment on side issues.*   Concentrate on the opinion that the paper as a whole is designed to support. Do not scatter throughout your paper statements of likes and dislikes that you do not have time and space to back up. If you are taking a stand against censorship of textbooks by school boards or state boards of education, you *weaken* your paper by unsubstantiated references to "managed news," or to the undue influence of industry on university research. Many readers are annoyed by *obiter dicta* — opinions offered merely in passing.

(3) *Be content to leave moot points unresolved.*   Often, an issue is too large, the facts too contradictory, for us to form a sound opinion. We may have hunches or preferences, but we do not expect the reader to accept these on our mere say-so. Opinionated people can be recognized by the firm stand they take on such highly debatable subjects. They have high admiration for their own judgment but little patience with contradictory data. Here are some subjects on which a writer with a respect for facts hesitates to make emphatic pronouncements:

- What are the results of *permissiveness* in child rearing? Does it make children on the whole more natural, well-adjusted people? Or does it spoil children, making it impossible for them to accept or respect authority?

- What is the long-range effect of constant exposure to *violence through the mass media*? Does it provide a healthy vicarious outlet, or is it an incitement to imitation?

What you need to keep in mind about the relationship of opinion and fact can be summed up in one sentence: *Consider every statement of opinion as a promise to the reader.* Much factual information is complete in its own terms: "It is now six o'clock." The response, if any, is simply "Correct." But a statement of opinion is a different matter: "It is too late for college freshmen to start learning a foreign language." The predictable response is: "What makes you think so?" The mere statement is an implied promise to supply the data, the facts, the arguments that would make the reader think so too.

Exercises

A. A prominent speaker at a recent convention of professional journalists said that "to the true newsman, partisanship is the original sin":

It is this striving for objectivity that places the journalist apart from society today; it is this struggle for objectivity that keeps him awake at night as he wrestles with the facts; . . . a journalist deals in facts, and they continually come back to haunt him—because facts are often contradictory.

Examine the *news reports* in several recent issues of a major newspaper. Can you cite specific examples of respect for "contradictory" facts? Can you cite facts that a partisan spokesman might have refused to recognize?

B. Columnists are typically men with strong opinions. Examine the following passages, adapted from newspaper and magazine *columns and editorials*. For each, cite concrete facts or incidents that you could use to relate the opinions expressed to the world of fact. For which passages is this hard to do? For which easy? How would you describe the author of each passage? Can you *predict* his opinion on one or two other issues?

1. One wonders what progress the black people of the South have made in the hundred years since their emancipation. On paper they have made a lot. Belatedly they have the right to vote. Theoretically they have the right to sit beside white children in equal schools. They can patronize the same restaurants, use the same restrooms, buses, hotels, and railroad trains. The days of Jim Crow are over.

But do they have the equal right to make a living? Are they permitted to enter the skilled labor unions? Are the cards stacked against them when it comes to the land laws? Above all, are they forced off the land which they have plowed and hoed and cultivated through the generations? The laws are written so they favor the big landowner, not the tenant farmer who is made homeless by the laws written by a Congress where the key committee chairmanships, the power establishment, stem from rural areas of the United States.

2. Several communities in my state, and I presume in others, are busily enacting local ordinances which make it illegal for me to leave my key in my own car. Presumably, the mere sight of my battered Plymouth with its key protruding nakedly from its modest dashboard is enough to trigger the beast in the passing teen-ager so that he will leap incontinently into the front seat and ravish away my hapless sedan. Said youth is thus tempted into a sordid life of crime, with guess who in the role of Satanic tempter.

Sorry. I can't buy this. I can't even rent it temporarily. It's not my duty to lock up my own property just so some passerby with latent larceny in his heart may the more easily subdue his own worst instincts. Once we legitimate burghers meekly fall for this whopping non sequitur reasoning, we will be sitting ducks from then on for every ivory-tower nut who wants us to chain the front wheels together every time we put the car in a parking lot . . .

Unless we step firmly upon this burgeoning toadstool of a trend, we will end up with laws compelling us to bar all the doors and shutter the windows before we leave the house to walk the dog. I resent legal harassment which implies so smugly that it's somehow my fault that some sneering scofflaw roars off with my jalopy and thus proposes to fine me for making his lawbreaking easier.

3. What we call organized crime is the result of a busybody, Puritan approach to private sin. The Mafia, the Syndicate, the Mob, the Cosa Nostra, or whatever you call it, originated out of that monstrous bit of folly called Prohibition. This is the classic example of laws breeding crime.

While most of the able-bodied men in this country were caught up in the conduct of World War I, the busybodies organized themselves into a group to show their strong disapproval of boozers and boozing. They got their law. As a result, boozing simply increased, and the cops who were assigned to enforce this loony law were corrupted wholesale all over the country. Deceit and dishonor became the commonplaces of existence. Thus did morality end up by strangling itself.

4. The voices of America are a little shrill these days. Listening in a journey across the land, one is almost overwhelmed by the torrent of self-analysis and self-criticism. The voices of the radio, the debates by the universities, and the campaign speeches from the stump are all trying to fix something or improve something. . . .

Maybe life will not bear all this self-analysis and self-improvement, but even so there is something aspiring and even majestic in all these noisy debates. For whatever else can be said about America today, it is grappling with the great issues of human life. It is asking momentous questions: What is the purpose of all this wealth? Is poverty inevitable or intolerable? What kind of America do we want, anyway? And what are its relations to be with the rest of the world?

There are, of course, many ways of looking at all this contention. In the middle of the battle, it often seems senseless and even hopeless, but from the wider perspective of the nation as a whole, the agitation has its purposes and results. It will not be easy to "tear up" or "burn down" this country. It is too big and too adaptable. It is not very good at dealing with theories in advance, but it deals in its own way and time with facts.

It may not have the right answers but it is asking the right questions, and it is changing faster than most people think.

5. The right to disagree, to speak out freely, and to demonstrate peacefully against injustice, must be protected both on and off the campus. But any student or college administrator who cannot understand the difference between peaceful demonstration and destructive attack, between freedom of speech and the harassment of opposing speakers,

or between asking for changes in the law and breaking laws, is not intelligent enough to deserve a place within the halls of academe. The majority of students who do understand these distinctions — who are willing to listen to both sides without booing and jeering and who accept the need for law because they comprehend the dangers of anarchy — have failed to make their position clear. Until the majority speaks out and lends its support to administrators who make the necessary distinctions and act upon them, a few extremists will continue to give the impression that they — and only they — represent the views of those within the colleges and universities. And public confidence in higher education will continue to decline.

C. Study the proportion of *fact and inference* in a series of editorials in a major newspaper. Are the facts to which editorial opinion is anchored kept clearly in view? Would you call the editors opinionated or open-minded? Use specific evidence to support your conclusions.

3. Developing Opinions of Your Own

When asked for their opinions on college life or freedom of the press, students sometimes have a dim feeling that they are for it. Otherwise their minds are somewhat of a blank. When writing a paper on one of these topics, they will put down a number of sentences to the effect that college life or freedom of the press is a very important subject. They will point out that it is a very important part of the democratic way of life, and that everybody should be aware of this fact. Inevitably, the reader of the resulting paper is going to ask himself: "*Why* am I reading this? What is there here that I have not heard a hundred times before?"

In your own writing, you should obviously aim at a quite different response from your reader. Your main goal should be not so much to make him agree with you as to *make him pay attention.* You want him to say: "Is that so? I see what you mean. Can you make this stick? Perhaps you are right. This certainly seems to support your point of view." If you can start this kind of running commentary in the reader's mind, you have satisfied the most elementary requirement for a successful essay of opinion: You have something to say. You have succeeded in developing substantial, significant opinions that the reader will respect as your own.

Identifying an Issue

Identify an issue open enough to allow for differences of opinion and limited enough to be explored in a short paper. Your first task in writing an essay of opinion is to raise a question that is open and significant enough for the reader to want to know your answer. Even when you are writing on an assigned topic, it will be part of your job to identify, within the general area suggested by the topic, an issue that will arouse and focus the reader's attention.

What, for instance, are issues on your own campus? You might find some of the following by reading the student newspaper or listening to a campus debate: Is student government a waste of time? Should students be required to live in dormitories? Is there room for military training on a college campus? Should students have a voice in decisions about courses to be offered? Is old-fashioned "school spirit" obsolete? Do present admission standards discriminate against minority groups? Is intercollegiate athletics irrelevant to the purposes of a college education? Do college professors stifle dissent?

Here is an outline for an essay of opinion answering a question that is unspectacular but nevertheless an *open* issue of concern to many college students:

THESIS: Athletics deserves a place in American higher education.

SUPPORT: I. Even in the so-called "spectator sports," athletes set a standard of *physical fitness* that serves as a model to others.

II. Though too much lip service has been paid to "character building" through sports, athletics *does* build—and set a standard for—qualities like *determination and perseverance.*

III. Colleges help train athletes that greatly enhance the *prestige of our country* in international competition.

Note that this outline reveals several of the qualities that make an essay of opinion worth writing:

• *The thesis has been, or is likely to be, contested.* Teachers and students who equate "academic" with "intellectual" have strongly attacked collegiate athletics as a sideshow distracting from the true purposes of higher education.

• *Something is at stake.* A threatened de-emphasis on athletics jeopardizes jobs, scholarships, career opportunities for the future, as well as alumni loyalty to their alma mater.

• *The issue can be argued in relatively objective terms.* The paper can be based on something more solid than "I happen to like it" or "I happen to think this is true." The writer can appeal to the reader's own observation of possible alternatives and results.

• *Much of the evidence is in the public domain.* We do not need expert testimony to convince a reader that victory in the Olympic games confers prestige. We can cite newspaper articles to show that, while U.S. diplomats abroad have at times been spat upon, athletes have often been warmly welcomed. We can quote what distinguished foreigners have said about their admiration for Jesse Owens or other American athletic stars.

Forming an Opinion

Let your opinion take shape in the process of gathering and organizing your material. Ideally, an opinion is the result of a process of investigation. Rather than find facts to fit a preconceived opinion, we develop an opinion to fit the facts we have found. Thus, most of what makes a paper substantial takes place *before* we actually start writing. Ideally, when asked for his opinion on a key issue, the writer would say: "I don't know, and what I do know I'm not sure of, but I am willing to *find out.*"

How would you go about developing the kind of opinion that you could present and support in a short paper? To show the process in operation, let us assume that you have selected from a list of ten theme topics the following: "The football player, once a campus hero, is today regarded by some of his fellow students as a student without the necessary intellectual qualifications but kept in school to please the alumni. Do you think football players are less intelligent than other students?" You start by asking yourself: "What do I know about football players?" You remember the quarterback of your high school team who never opened his mouth in your English class. But you also remember a close friend who played football in both high school and college and who seemed no less "intelligent" than other college students you know. You try to recall what he said about courses he took and grades he made. You remember reading a magazine article about a Negro athlete who quit as member of a college football team and went to a different campus to devote himself full time to his studies, in order to prepare himself for a successful professional career. You go back to the article itself and find it developing the point that Negro students of high IQ but economically disadvantaged find it possible to attend college through athletic scholarships.

If you have taken or are now taking a psychology course, it may occur to you that psychologists do not really seem to agree on what skills, verbal and nonverbal, they should include under the general heading of "intelligence." In your own paper about football players, you decide to retreat to the somewhat safer ground of "academic performance, as measured at least in part by grades, and as predictable at least in part on the basis of IQ." So far, the material you can gather from your experience and reading seems to point to the conclusion that at least some players do well academically — and that others *could* do well if they were not devoting most of their time and energy to the team. At this point, you may be able to talk with one of the assistant coaches about members of the present team. What courses do they take and why? What problems do they have meeting academic standards? Is there any information on the average IQ of football players?

As you look over the material you are accumulating during the course of this exploration, a tentative scheme of organization begins to suggest itself. In a first major section of your paper, you might present those of your data and personal experiences that would tend to bear out the familiar stereotype of the "slow" college athlete. In the next major section, however, you would present material that would counteract the stereotype: material that shows that many football players have considerable academic potential. In the third major section, finally, you detail the reasons why that potential is not always realized: the amount of study time a player loses through practice and traveling to games; the way physical exhaustion and nervous tension interfere with study.

You now try to sum up the opinion that has crystallized in your mind as the result of your investigation: "One major reason that football players as a group seem less intelligent than other students is that they are football players. To judge from what I have observed and read, many of them would do better academically if they would quit the team." You state this opinion early in your paper and then make sure that the material in the three major sections of your paper explains, develops, and supports this view. The resulting paper will do something that many people find hard to do: to present a considered opinion in a straightforward manner. It will *not* provide a conclusive or definitive answer to the question raised in the topic. But it will be considerably stronger than a paper written on the principle of "This is what I happen to think."

Changing Your Mind

Be prepared to change your mind in the light of new evidence. In practice, we seldom approach a subject with a completely open mind. Often we bring to it opinions distilled from hearsay or previous experience. Even when we are determined to treat the subject as an open question, we will early in our investigation of it form first guesses and tentative hypotheses. The test of open-mindedness is our willingness to *modify* first impressions as it becomes necessary.

Here are some examples of the kind of change of mind that is necessary for the development of opinions worth paying attention to:

Previous Opinion: People on welfare are loafers who prefer the easy money of welfare to honest hard work.

Results of Inquiry: Of the about eight million on relief, more than two million, mostly women, are 65 or over; more than 700,000 are totally blind or disabled; almost four million are children whose parents cannot support them; about one million are their mothers; about 100,000 are their physically or mentally incapacitated fathers. Less than 100,000 are "able-bodied men."

Adjusted Opinion: The great majority of those on relief are either too young, too old, too sick, or too disabled to be self-supporting.

Previous Opinion: In a capitalistic society like ours, economic power is in the hands of a few individuals of great wealth.

Results of Inquiry: Few large corporations are now run by their owners; those like Du Pont, where, for many generations, a talented family has had a decisive influence on the enterprise it owns, are becoming a rarity. Typically the power lies with the professional managers. These make elaborate obeisance to the stockholders. But they select the Board of Directors, which the stockholders then dutifully elect, and in equally solemn ritual the Board then selects the management that selected it. In some cases, for example the Standard Oil Company of New Jersey, once dominated by the first Rockefeller, the Board consists exclusively of managers selected by the managers who were selected by the Board. . . .

Some of the worst cases of corporate misfortune in recent times have been those in which the owners of the capital have managed to use their power to keep the professionals out. In the thirties and early forties the elder Henry Ford used his power as the sole owner of the Ford Motor Company to remain in command. It is now freely acknowledged that the company suffered severely as a result. Following his death the management was professionalized and much improved. The great merchandising house of Montgomery Ward under Sewell Avery provided a parallel example. —John Kenneth Galbraith, *The Liberal Hour*

Adjusted Opinion: Much of the effective economic power in our society is exercised not by stockholders but by a professional class of salaried managers serving as executives of large corporations.

When you find yourself changing your mind, you can tell that you are learning something about your subject. Far from destroying our confidence in the writer's judgment, evidence of open-mindedness reassures us that his mind is in good working order.

Revising for Clarity

Make your finished paper spell out clearly the results of your thinking. Since an honest opinion results from a ferment of ideas, the first draft of your paper may still mirror the contradictions and indecision of your investigation — rather than present strongly the conclusions you have reached. As you revise the first draft, ask yourself: What have I learned? What am I trying to say? Can I point to a sentence that clearly spells out the central idea of the paper?

To make sure that your opinions clearly emerge from your paper, observe the following suggestions:

(1) *State both your thesis and the key idea of each paragraph in preferably short and emphatic sentences.* Are both the central and the supporting ideas clearly and succinctly stated, or must the reader infer them for himself? If they are stated, does position and wording mark them clearly as important points? (See also S 3a.)

(2) *Make sure that each point receives adequate support.* Have you shown your reader that the ideas he is supposed to accept are important to you as a writer? Have you concentrated on each of the main points in succession, trying to do them justice? Are examples and illustrations relevant to the point at issue?

(3) *Make sure to devote special care to points that the reader might find difficult or unfamiliar.* What points confused you when you first started to think about your subject? Have you made sure they will be less confusing for your reader?

The mere fact that you have presented an opinion clearly does not assure it general acceptance. As your instructor or your classmates read your finished paper, they will not necessarily like it or agree with it. However, their very disagreement will in a sense be a measure of your success. It will be first-hand proof that you have succeeded in saying something. It is hard to disagree with hazy generalities about the teaching of sportsmanship or the values of a college education. If your paper provokes detailed comment, it probably has meaning and point.

Exercises

A. Identify as specifically as you can *three major issues* that are currently the subject of debate on your own campus. Sum up each issue in a one-sentence question. Then write a paragraph explaining fully what you take to be at stake. Your instructor may ask you to write a paper presenting *your* position on one of these issues.

B. Each of the following passages presents and develops briefly an opinion that could become the thesis of a theme or article. On which of these would you feel best qualified to *form an opinion of your own*? In a rough collection of notes, sketch out the material you could supply from your own observation, experience, or reading to support, modify, or refute the point made.

1. Under our system a student's progress up to the point of entering college has been largely automatic, as he went along from one grade to another. But at about the college level the intellectual demands on the student's capacity suggest that not all may be capable of profiting by further study. *College calls for a different kind of intellectual effort, and a more difficult one.* — Laird Bell, "Admit and Flunk," *Atlantic*

2. The casual horrors and the real disasters are thrown at newspaper readers without discrimination. *In the contemporary arrangements for spreading the news, an important element, evaluation, is always weak and often wanting entirely.* There is no point anywhere along the line where someone puts his foot down for certain and says This is important and That doesn't amount to a row of beans, deserves no one's attention, and should travel the wires no farther. The junk is dressed up to look as meaningful as the real news. — Philip M. Wagner, "What Makes a Really Good Newspaper," *Harper's*

3. The cool adolescent finishing high school or starting college has a skeptical view of virtually every institutional sector of his society. He knows that government is corrupt, the military dehumanizing, the corporations rapacious, the churches organized hypocrisy, and the schools dishonest. But *the one area that seems to be exempt from his cynicism is romantic love and marriage.* When I talk to teen-agers about marriage, that cool skepticism turns to sentimental dreams right out of *Ladies' Home Journal* or the hard-hitting pages of *Reader's Digest*. They all mouth the same vapid platitudes about finding happiness through sharing and personal fulfillment through giving (each is to give 51 percent). — Mervyn Cadwallader, "Marriage as a Wretched Institution," *Atlantic*

4. *In recent decades, planners have rarely given much thought to creating a psychologically satisfying focal point or heart for their city, town, or neighborhood.* . . . Americans in earlier centuries built their communities around a focal point. Witness Boston, with its Common and its Public Garden. Most New England towns and cities still have a clearly perceived heart, and many of the smaller, older-fashioned Midwestern towns such as Woodstock, Illinois, still do, too (and so do a few larger cities, such as Indianapolis). But in the majority of American

cities, the heart of downtown typically is the street intersection where the largest bank faces the largest department store. Downtown Dallas, Oklahoma City, Los Angeles, Sioux City, Des Moines, Milwaukee, Birmingham, and Winston-Salem seem a blur of almost indistinguishable commercial buildings. — Vance Packard, "America the Beautiful — and Its Desecraters," *Atlantic*

5. The crude ideas advanced by many of the successful mass movement leaders of our time incline one to assume that a certain coarseness and immaturity of mind is an asset to leadership. However, it was not the intellectual crudity of an Aimee McPherson or a Hitler which won and held their following but the boundless self-confidence which prompted these leaders to give full rein to their preposterous ideas. A genuinely wise leader who dared to follow out the course of his wisdom would have an equal chance of success. The quality of ideas seems to play a minor role in mass movement leadership. *What counts is the arrogant gesture, the complete disregard of the opinion of others, the single-handed defiance of the world.* — Eric Hoffer, *The True Believer*

C. How much is your thinking affected by what you read? In one paragraph, summarize material from an article or book that *made you change your mind* on an important point. For instance, summarize a set of facts, a report on conditions, an account of an incident, a portrait of a type of person.

4.   The Opinions of Others

We do not form our opinions in a vacuum. Even when trying to make up our own minds, we constantly have to come to terms with the opinions of others presented to us *ready-made*. On many subjects, we merely adopt, or adapt, the opinion of parents, teachers, or friends, frequently without the possibility of checking it against first-hand experience. We thus repeat ideas about law and order before we have ever been inside a police station or court of law. We absorb opinions about communism without ever having argued with a real communist.

Ideally, contact with the ideas of others should have an enlightening effect. By listening attentively to others, we can become aware of gaps in our information and flaws in our reasoning. Seeing our own half-formed ideas challenged, we are forced to make them take more definite shape. In the clash of opposing views, we become more knowledgeable, our position less vulnerable.

In practice, however, we too often find ourselves merely echoing opinions that we have not examined. If a writer wants to know his own mind, he has to become critical of opinions that are the result of mere hearsay or mere tradition.

Cross-Examining Your Witnesses

Learn to sift the testimony of authorities. An alert reader does not believe everything he is told, but neither is he cynical about everything he sees in print. The following pointers will help you to profit from *authoritative* opinion:

(1) *Distrust mere unsupported general impressions.* Many a general judgment or expression of preference is meaningless until you find out on what it was based. Suppose a friend tells you that John Doe is a smart fellow. Your friend may have derived this opinion from a careful study of John's high school record and of various intelligence tests John has taken, as well as from interviews with several of his former teachers. But more likely your friend has concluded that John is smart after watching him make up a good excuse for not having his English theme ready on time the day before.

(2) *Discount the testimony of interested parties.* If a coach talks about the character-building virtues of football, you will ascribe his enthusiasm to his loyalty to his work rather than to a careful study of the actual moral growth of his players. When writing about alcoholism in your home town, you will be as skeptical of material put out by the whisky companies as of pamphlets distributed by the Women's Temperance Society. You will turn for data to investigators who are neither prohibitionists nor heavy drinkers nor employees of a brewery.

(3) *Guard against excessive reliance on any single source.* When you are trying to form an opinion about the adequacy of teachers' salaries, pay attention to the arguments of teachers, administrators, government officials, and taxpayers alike. Even when you can draw on the impartial outside expert, compare the views of another expert equally competent. This way you will become alert to contradictions that might result from professional rivalries or doctrinaire attachment to theory. You can then identify the areas on which there is solid agreement.

Questioning Conventional Views

Question opinions that seem to be everybody's and nobody's at the same time. In examining our opinions we often come up against ideas with obscure credentials. We seem to have derived them from the climate of opinion in which we grew up, without examining them for their validity or even for their exact significance. The more uncertain their origin, the more thoroughly we need to investigate them before we make them definitely our own.

To forestall the objections of a critical reader, examine your writing especially for the following:

Approved Opinions   Often we find ourselves repeating opinions that merely seem the approved thing to say for a person of good will. Perhaps you find yourself saying in one of your papers that "other people's ideas should be respected, even though different from those of the majority." To discover whether you really mean it—and to discover *what* you really mean—apply this statement to a number of specific instances. Perhaps your next-door neighbor has the opinion that every first of the month ten virgins should be sacrificed to the rain gods. You probably didn't mean to include opinions that were *that* different. Then the question becomes: "How different can these opinions be and still be respected? And what does 'respect' mean in practice? If we dismiss a teacher for his opinions on loyalty oaths or on marriage, can we at the same time respect those opinions? What is such respect good for?" As you start examining these problems, you find that your original statement covers up many questions that you have not really thought about.

Stereotypes   Stereotypes provide us with a prepackaged set of attitudes toward a whole group of people or things. They thus keep us from a fair appraisal of the individual. Familiar stereotypes are the bungling woman driver, the monocled Prussian Junker, the ivory-tower intellectual, the money-grubbing businessman, the corrupt politician. A familiar stereotype in American political journalism is the windbag member of Congress — "illiterate hacks whose fancy vests are spotted with gravy, and whose speeches, hypocritical, unctuous, and slovenly, are spotted also with the gravy of political patronage" (Mary McCarthy).

The limiting effect that stereotypes have on the mind is most forcefully revealed to the person at the receiving end: the American who hears his European visitor hold forth on the superficial smiles of Americans and their incapacity for true friendship and deep affection; the woman who hears a junior executive hold forth on the emotional instability of women employees.

A writer with a vigorous, independent mind is wary of stereotypes, ready to test them against more searching observation:

It was the habit of proponents for the repeal of the Eighteenth Amendment during the 1920's to dub Prohibitionists "Puritans," and cartoonists made the nation familiar with an image of the Puritan: a gaunt, lank-haired killjoy, wearing a black steeple hat and compounding for sins he was inclined to by damning those to which he had no mind. Yet any acquaintance with the Puritans of the seventeenth century will reveal at once, not only that they did not wear such hats, but also that they attired themselves in all the hues of the rainbow, and furthermore that in their daily life they imbibed what seem to us prodigious quantities of alcoholic beverages, with never the slightest inkling that they were doing anything sinful. True, they opposed drinking to excess, and ministers preached lengthy sermons condemning intoxication, but at such pious ceremonies as the ordination of new ministers the bill for rum, wine, and beer consumed by the congregation was often staggering. — Perry Miller and Thomas Johnson, *The Puritans*

Prejudice   Prejudices are hostile preconceptions, usually widely shared, and sometimes handed on from generation to generation. Prejudice makes a stereotype the basis for systematic exclusion or discrimination. Prejudice enables people to feel superior to others who may be, and often are, their moral and intellectual superiors. If he is not to lose the critical reader's respect, a writer must take great care to make sure that negative judgments on representatives of a faith, race, or nationality do not seem to proceed from prejudice.

Staying Clear of Verbal Traps

Keep ready-made phrases from channeling your thinking. On most subjects we write about, we encounter convenient verbal formulas, phrases that strikingly seem to sum up a key idea. But such phrases often commit us to more than we are ready for, more than our own exploration of the matter warrants. They often carry with them a set of built-in attitudes — and keep us from developing our own.

Check your writing for ready-made formulas that might make your reader suspect your mind is not your own:

Pregummed Labels   Be wary of repeating formulas that are becoming catchwords — suggesting a definite point of view that may or may not be the same as yours. Would you agree that each of the following labels carries with it its own set of ready-made attitudes? Can you spell these out?

> law and order
> crime in the streets
> centralized federal bureaucracy
> white power structure
> military-industrial complex
> law-abiding citizen
> alien ideologies
> hard-core pornography
> guilt by association
> police brutality

Slogans   We repeat slogans because of their rousing, focusing power: "Black Power," "Freedom Now." Decades later, American schools still show the impact of the slogans of progressive education: "Learn by doing," "Teach the whole child," "Teach children, not subjects." Though such slogans can help break down fossilized systems of ideas, they in turn set our thinking in a new mold. They are a great comfort to one-track minds. Many familiar slogans are devices for *warding off* disturbing new suggestions: "You can't change human nature," "The mind is not a muscle," "Peace with honor."

Not surprisingly, slogans flourish in countries where Big Brother does the thinking for all: "Four legs good, two legs bad." But even elsewhere, the true believer eagerly repeats ideas simple enough to fit on a placard. By unthinking adoption of other people's slogans in your own writing, you will make the reader suspect that you too have surrendered the right of private judgment.

Proverbs   "Look before you leap" and "He who hesitates is lost" cancel each other out. Knowing that horses can be led to water but not made to drink avails us little in trying to improve the training of retarded children. Avoid the kind of saying that makes you sound wise without requiring you to think about the issue at stake.

Exercises

A. Assume that you are investigating *one* of the following subjects: (1) urban renewal, (2) rehabilitation of juvenile delinquents, (3) *de facto* segregation in public schools, (4) enforcement of narcotics laws in your state. Spell out as fully as you can the cautions you would observe in trying to obtain reliable and instructive material on your subject. What qualifications would you set up for *authorities* you would be willing to trust?

B. The following passages have been adapted from published comments on President Wilson. What accounts for such *contradictory judgments* on public figures whose record is presumably well known? What do these judgments reveal about the people who made them? Your instructor may ask you to compile and examine a similar collection of contradictory opinions on a more nearly contemporary public figure.

1. Woodrow Wilson will be held in everlasting remembrance as a statesman who, when others thought of revenge and material gain, strove to bring nearer the day which should see the emancipation of conscience from power and the substitution of freedom for force in the government of the world.

2. Mr. Wilson in dealing with every great question thought first of himself. He may have thought of the country next, but there was a long interval.

3. Woodrow Wilson was in many respects the most remarkable figure in American politics since Jefferson. A scholar and an intellectual,

unaccustomed to the hurly-burly of public life, he was nevertheless astute, hard-headed, and resourceful. A visionary and an idealist, he was at the same time the most thoroughly realistic and adroit political leader since Lincoln.

4. First it was "neutrality in thought and deed," then "too proud to fight" when the *Lusitania* sinking and the danger to the Morgan loans and the stories of the British and French propagandists set all the financial centers in the East bawling for war, but the suction of the drumbeat and the guns was too strong; the best people took their fashions from Paris and their broad "a's" from London. . . . Five months after his re-election on the slogan "He kept us out of war," Wilson pushed the Armed Ship Bill through Congress and declared that a state of war existed between the United States and the Central Powers.

5. Wilson at length chose war, but not without the gravest of misgivings engendered both by his somewhat reluctant recognition of the essentially non-ideological nature of the world struggle and by his basic antipathy to war itself. To a less scrupulous, less self-demanding statesman such misgivings would have brought balance and humility, but to the perfectionist Wilson they brought only confusion and a tortured sense of guilt, which convinced him that the war must be a holy crusade to "make the world safe for democracy."

C. What do the authors of the following passages do to attack or modify *stereotypes*? How familiar, how strong, or how current are the stereotypes attacked?

1. "This-here is a internal combustion engine," Joe said. Lee said quietly, "So young to be so erudite." The boy swung around toward him, scowling. "What did you say?" he demanded, and he asked Adam, "What did the Chink say?"
    Lee spread his hands and smiled blandly. "Say velly smaht fella," he observed quietly. "Mebbe go college. Velly wise." — John Steinbeck, *East of Eden*

2. What is imputed to Americans is an abject dependence on material possessions, an image of happiness as packaged by the manufacturer, content in a can. This view of American life is strongly urged by advertising agencies. We know the "others," of course, because we meet them every week in full force in *The New Yorker* or the *Saturday Evening Post*, those brightly colored families of dedicated consumers, waiting in unison on the porch for the dealer to deliver the new car, gobbling the new cereal ("Gee, Mom, is it good for you too?"), lining up to bank their paychecks, or fearfully anticipating the industrial accident and the insurance-check that will "compensate" for it. We meet them also,

more troll-like underground, in the subway placards, in the fero-
ciously complacent One-A-Day family, and we hear their courtiers
sing to them on the radio of Ivory or Supersuds. The thing, however,
that repels us in these advertisements is their naïve falsity to life. Who
are these advertising men kidding, besides the European tourist? Between the tired, sad, gentle faces of the subway riders and the grinning
Holy Families of the Ad-Mass, there exists no possibility of even a
wishful identification. . . . It is true that America produces and con-
sumes more cars, soap, and bathtubs than any other nation, but we live
among these objects rather than by them. Americans build skyscrapers;
Le Corbusier worships them. Ehrenburg, our Soviet critic, fell in love
with the Check-O-Mat in American railway stations, writing home
paragraphs of song to this gadget — while deploring American materialism. When an American heiress wants to buy a man, she at once crosses
the Atlantic. The only really materialistic people I have ever met have
been Europeans. — Mary McCarthy, "America the Beautiful," *Commentary*

3. The white South said that it knew "niggers," and I was what the
white South called a "nigger." Well, the white South had never known
me — never known what I thought, what I felt. The white South said that
I had a "place" in life. Well, I had never felt my "place"; or, rather, my
deepest instincts had always made me reject the "place" to which the
white South had assigned me. It had never occurred to me that I was in
any way an inferior being. And no word that I had ever heard fall from
the lips of southern white men had ever made me really doubt the worth
of my own humanity. — Richard Wright, *Black Boy*

D. *Prejudice* is easy to denounce but hard to fight. Read the following account
of fruit workers, written by a farmer's daughter. Is there any way of affecting
the writer's prejudices? Write a letter in which you try.

Caring for fruit trees and harvesting the crops at times requires the
help of many men. I have worked alongside drunkards, prostitutes, and
men literally from skid row. These people are generally the epitome of
laziness, foul language, and deceit. I have frequently found fruit boxes
with leaves or dirt filled in to provide a cushion for the few peaches on
top. I have seen workers gather discarded fruit from the ground, or even
cheat among themselves by claiming another's stock. The area in which
the fruit workers live is typically rundown, dirty and depressing. These
people don't care; it is the way they were brought up, and for most of
them, this is the way they will live until they die. I knew families on
welfare who worked harvesting crops during the summer and spent the
time drinking during the summer. The more kids they produce, the
more money flows in for cars, color T.V., and drinks. What an easy life!

E. Prepare a report in which you examine the *verbal formulas* of one: (1)
current campus debate; (2) state politics; (3) chamber of commerce promotion;

(4) an aggressive labor union. Look for promising material in published speeches or debates, editorials, pamphlets, leaflets, and the like.

5. Organizing the Essay of Opinion

The inexperienced writer often starts writing on a subject before he has thought the matter through. His work then reflects the digressions, confusions, and uncertainties of a man thinking on his feet. As a result, it is hard for the reader to follow, and makes little lasting impact. The experienced writer presents material that he has *brought under control*. Whatever his backtrackings while taking notes and writing his first draft (or drafts), his final version presents a finished product. Writing an essay of opinion then breaks up into two major (though overlapping) stages: working out the matter to his own satisfaction, and then presenting the results effectively to the reader.

Here are strategies of organization that will help you present your opinions effectively to your reader:

Defending a Thesis

To make your point as clear and emphatic as possible, state your thesis early and devote the rest of the paper to defending it. The essay of opinion presents the most frequent and most typical opportunities for the "thesis-and-support" paper described in Chapter One (see pp. 25–30). Such a paper from the beginning clearly focuses the writer's and the reader's attention on the point at issue. The writer from the beginning has his work cut out for him; the reader is protected against a rambling "some-thoughts-I-want-to-share-with-you" approach.

In writing this kind of paper, you would typically present your opinion as the central idea at the end of a short introduction. You would then support it by devoting the rest of the paper to one or more of the following:

- several detailed *examples* (or sometimes *one* key example examined at length);
- one or more *case histories;*
- *precedents* offering convincing parallels to the current situation;
- the probable *consequences* or benefits;
- the testimony of *experts.*

Here are some opinions, staying close to the student's own experience, that might provide the unifying thesis to be defended in a "thesis-and-support" paper:

Living in a fraternity and pursuing a highly competitive field of study are rapidly becoming mutually exclusive.

For the children of recent immigrants from rural Mexico, the transition to the Anglo school causes difficulties that most teachers neither understand nor know how to handle.

A job gives a married woman something to talk about and someone to talk to; it gives her life a focused interest and an organized purpose.

Here is a possible scheme for a paper supporting such a thesis:

THESIS: The prestige of sororities is rapidly declining on today's campuses.

I. Declining number of rushees

II. Declining amount of space given to sororities in campus newspapers

III. Adverse comments by student leaders

The "Yes, But" Paper

To establish common ground, present a generally accepted opinion and then proceed to make the necessary modifications. The "yes, but" paper shows a decent respect for the opinions of mankind. It reassures the reader that he is not going to be frontally assaulted. At the same time, it involves both writer and reader in the kind of process by which opinions are actually formed.

Here is a possible outline for a magazine article using the "yes, but" pattern:

I. COMMON VIEW: Much of the American press is owned by conservative Republicans, biased against the liberal or progressive elements in American politics. (References to several famous presslords are offered in support.)

II. COMPLICATIONS: Reporter and editors often seem to be people of liberal sympathies. For example,

A. Republican Presidential candidates have at times bitterly complained about hostile treatment by reporters.

B. Southern conservatives often attack the "left-wing" press.

C. Initial press coverage of revolutionary movements (for instance, Castro) has often been sympathetic.

III. ADJUSTED VIEW: Like other American institutions, the American press functions as the result of compromise between conflicting interests and opposing views.

The "yes, but" approach is ideal for correcting stereotypes, for enlarging the reader's horizons. By agreeing with the probable views of his readers at the start, the writer keeps them from erecting their defenses. Putting them in an assenting mood, he has a better-than-average chance of making them receptive to the different or the new.

The Change of Mind

Make your statement of opinion dramatic rather than static by tracing an important change in your views. Ideas come to life when the author is seen as someone engaged in the *search* for truth, not merely one of its self-appointed guardians. A writer with unpopular views may secure a sympathetic hearing by the honesty with which he exposes his earlier mistaken assumptions, by the candor with which he retraces his steps.

Here is a possible outline for a paper tracing an important change of mind:

I. EARLIER VIEW: Coming from a conservative business family, I used to be convinced that big government more and more determines the course of the individual's life.

II. CONTRARY EVIDENCE:

    A. Acquaintance with local politics has convinced me of the power of big private organizations — unions, chambers of commerce, the AMA — to bring about or to block change.

    B. Working with members of minority groups has made me familiar with some of the set social patterns and attitudes hard for any government to change.

    C. Service in the army and study at a big university have shown me the force of mere custom and tradition.

III. NEW VIEW: Government is often helpless in trying to change the patterns that determine our lives.

Obviously, the sample patterns described here will not fit all subjects. They are for you to experiment with: to try out, to adapt. Sooner or later, you will encounter problems that will interfere with the kind of smooth sailing that these sample outlines seem to promise. The most important of these will be treated in the next three chapters of this book:

- How can we keep a discussion of ideas from ending in a dispute over *words*? (Chapter Five, "Definition")

- How can we be sure that the conclusions we draw from the evidence are *logical*? (Chapter Six, "Logic")

- What can we do to *persuade* a recalcitrant reader? (Chapter Seven, "Persuasion")

Review Exercises: Excerpts and Sample Theme

A. The following passages about American education are from magazines that many readers turn to as sources of *informed opinion*. Would *you* consider the opinions of the authors worth listening to? Why or why not? How does each author develop, support, or defend his views? How close does he keep them to first-hand observation? Is there any evidence of stereotypes or prejudice? Which of these observations could you support or challenge by comparable observations of your own?

1. At Indiana University, where I am at the moment, the freshman and even sophomore courses in language and literature represent, in both content and level of teaching, what is taught in Britain two or even three years before the end of secondary education. And yet this is not altogether true. For the American freshman and sophomore has often a kind of curiosity, a provocative, uninformed but insistent "show me" attitude, an insistence on pitting his own limited experience against his teacher's knowledge, that makes the American college classroom at these levels very different indeed from the classroom of either the British grammar school or the British university.

"Why did Ulysses spend all that time in getting home to his wife after he left Troy?" a freshman asked one of my colleagues here the other day, during a lesson on the Odyssey. "If he'd really wanted to get home quickly, he would have managed it. I think he was kidding himself when he said he was so anxious to get back." This is naive, but it is not stupid, and it is not the kind of thing an English schoolboy would ask. The bright English schoolboy would mug up the standard works on the Homeric world and turn out a sophisticated essay on "Homer and the Heroic Age" based on a conflation of half a dozen books he had read in the school library; but it would never occur to him to ask whether Ulysses was kidding himself when he expressed his anxiety to return home quickly. The English schoolboy tends to relate knowledge to other knowledge, in order to form an elegant pattern (the bright essay being always the standard of achievement in the humanities); the American freshman wants to relate everything he reads or is told to his own experience. The latter as a rule has no sense of history or of form or of the *otherness* of different times and places; the former often lacks a sense of personal implication in what he studies.

To British — and indeed European — eyes, American education seems to waste some of the best learning years, at least for the brighter pupils, and to postpone until an unnecessarily late stage the essential core of education. But there is another side to the picture. The better American students are less blasé and work harder than their British opposite numbers, and by the end of their four undergraduate years have often achieved a kind of sophistication in terms of their subject which is at the opposite pole from the attitude revealed by the freshman's question about Ulysses. That kind of sophistication, which is particularly noticeable among the brighter students of literature, is consciously won by hard effort; it is (and I am talking of the best students) often the prelude to the use of specialized techniques in graduate work. The English student, building on his school training, will develop his accustomed skills with a kind of leisurely elegance and often, by the time he gets his degree, is not fundamentally any better educated than when he left school. He is likely to be less ambitious, more skeptical, less fundamentally serious than the American.

In such fields as literature, philosophy, and history, at least, the bright British student will most appreciate the lecturer who plays with ideas cleverly and suggestively, but the bright American student resents that: he wants the truth, or the right methods, and no nonsense. "Do you believe in that view of literature you were developing in your lecture this morning?" a Cornell student once asked me. I said that I did not, but I thought it was interesting to play with the idea a little and see where it led us. He replied, almost angrily, that if I did not believe the theory to be true I should not waste my own and the class's time discussing it at such length; it was sheer verbal gymnastics, and the students were there to *learn*, not to be played with. "Is C. S. Lewis's book on sixteenth-century literature a book to be read?" a graduate student asked me the other day at Indiana. I replied that it was a fresh and sometimes brilliant reading of the texts of the period, and though I quarreled sharply with some of the views expressed in it, I thought it a most stimulating book, well worth reading. "But will it give me a proper view of the period?" she persisted. "I don't know," I replied. "I'm not sure what the 'proper' view of the period is. Read it and make up your own mind about it." This answer was not regarded as satisfactory. — David Daiches, "Education in Democratic Society," *Commentary*

2. Notre Dame has its social and intellectual activists, but compared to the major secular universities its undergraduate culture still appears to lack ironic detachment, wit, and irreverence. One can hear rock' n' roll in the dormitories, and occasionally a folk guitar, but no Mozart or Beethoven. The place seems isolated from the world, as well as from the city of South Bend (which most students visit only to drink). Most, though not all, of its students come from the Midwest and from middle-class homes and schools where they have been drilled in obedience to authority. Those who read newspapers (many watch television) tend to buy the Chicago press. The *New York Times* is available a day or two late, and *Time* and *Newsweek* are sold in the cafeteria, but hardly anyone seems familiar with the weekly journals of opinion, right or left. The military, on the other hand — with its large ROTC units — is conspicuous, as is the clergy. Both tend to reinforce native Midwestern Catholic Americanism, and to weaken any incipient liberalism or rebellion.

Undergraduates are demanding more responsibility — the right to have cars and entertain women (the rules against drinking in the dormitories seem to be largely ignored). But the tone of protest and questioning is far more subdued than at Chicago, Stanford, or Yale. No one seems to have read (or even heard of) Paul Goodman, the author of *Growing Up Absurd*, a major hero on other campuses. While the college bookstore has sold nearly a thousand copies of the Tolkien trilogy, there are no signs at Notre Dame saying "Frodo Is Alive." A student editor acknowledged that he cannot find either under-graduate humorists or serious writers who are outspoken on contemporary issues. Even arguments in support of the status quo — involvement in Vietnam, for example — are anemic. "They look on Vietnam like a football game," said a young teacher. "It's them against us." How would the administration re-spond to any serious political demonstration on the campus? ("We're not sure we would allow it," said the vice-president in charge of student affairs.) Un-less the undergraduate mood changes, the question is academic.

This is not to say that either the faculty or the students are fettered. Echo-ing many other professors, one teacher, who is considered a reformer, said, "There are no checks on you. No one is handing you a syllabus or telling you how to teach." The university and its president have gone out of their way to protect academic freedom. A few years ago, after Michigan State parted com-pany with Professor Samuel Shapiro, a historian who defended the legitimacy of Fidel Castro's government, Notre Dame hired Shapiro. The first Jew in the Notre Dame history department, he was assigned to teach Peace Corps trainees in a summer program. When Washington questioned Shapiro's suitability for the program, the university replied that if the government didn't want Shapiro, Notre Dame didn't want the Peace Corps. Similarly, when James Silver, author of *Mississippi, The Closed Society*, resigned (under harassment) from the Ole Miss history department, Notre Dame took him on. Plainly, Notre Dame — with its independence from legislatures, and even from formal control by higher Church authorities — can be at least as free in its appointments and in its treatment of faculty as many state or private in-stitutions.

Men with a strong religious commitment or a keen interest in problems of value find the South Bend academic community more congenial than the secular institutions where they previously taught. "Notre Dame's concern about values," said its president, "is probably an asset for the kind of people I'm trying to get. If a man feels that this quality is not relevant to an institu-tion, then I'm not sure he ought to come." The president's own prestige in American life — what one teacher called "his clout on the outside" — apparently gives him almost total freedom from Church interference.

Yet, Notre Dame's freedom is freedom with a frame around it — a frame its president would call commitments. The Catholic university, he said, "touches the moral as well as the intellectual dimension of all the questions it asks itself and its students; it must emphasize the rightful centrality of philosophy and theology among its intellectual concerns. . . . The Catholic university must be a witness to the wholeness of truth, from all sources, both human and divine . . . [it] must reflect profoundly, and with full commit-ment, its belief in the existence of God and in God's total revelation to man."

On the university's shelves of ideas and commitments, students can now find two or three brands of Catholicism, but little support for atheism or agnosticism. An undergraduate on a secular campus swims in a maelstrom of relativistic questions — in scientism, and in various forms of liberalism. In contrast, the Notre Dame student's choices are anchored firmly to something called value or philosophy. In the campus bookstore, the ratio of psychology to theology is roughly comparable to the proportions in which the average supermarket stocks caviar and soap powder. Windows have been opened in psychology and other social sciences, religious doubt, and many aspects of personal responsibility. "If a boy wants to sin," said an administrator, "he can sin." An increasing number of teachers are, in a sense, secularists more concerned with their own disciplines than with philosophical values. Nevertheless, many still believe that everything must be taught with an eye to values. ("You can't read Shakespeare without confronting religious questions," said a member of the English department.) An important goal for them is "building bridges between the world and the wisdom of the Church." — Peter Schrag, "Notre Dame: Our First Great Catholic University?" *Harper's*

3. The idea of the "talent search" for engineering and scientific skills, scholarship awards for high scholastic averages, special programs for the "gifted," advanced placement for special students, are all ways of meeting certain of the country's educational and social needs, but they do so not in order to build a new and more enriching social order, but to staff the manpower needs of the present conservative establishment to which science, technology, and education have now been harnessed. This is to put the cart before the horse.

The recent changes in educational practice have therefore consisted largely in new mechanical and structural arrangements for the high schools and colleges — the use of television to handle more students by the lecture method, the development of standard curricula, the consolidation of smaller schools into bigger, the proliferation of scholastic tests at every point in the system, the shift of college curricular material into selected classes in the high school, the construction of buildings and classrooms — while the central mode of education through academic credit hours, examinations, tests, grades, and competition for admission to the next stage of the educational hierarchy has become more and more dominant.

Going to high school is conceived as a way of getting into college. Going to college is a way of either getting into a graduate school or into a satisfactory place in the business system. In the process, the purpose of education as a means of recreating the culture and renewing its social ideals has been lost in the shuffle.

The intellectual freedom of the student is accordingly inhibited, not so much by specific legislation, but by the requirement that he submit to one kind of success symbol, one kind of academic achievement, and one set of subject matter taught and learned in one particular way — lectures, textbooks, examinations, grades. The control by the college and the society over the student is gained through administering grades and awarding credits. Thus the student cannot find in his education a means of achieving his spiritual, moral, and intellectual maturity, since that is not a concern of the educator. If the student does not play the system and win the requisite grades, no matter how sterile and irrelevant the courses, or how talented he may be, he is blocked from the professions and the higher vocations. He therefore submits to the system and lives a double life, while his real education goes on out-side the curriculum. — Harold Taylor, "Portrait of a New Generation," *Saturday Review*

B. How successful is the author of the following student paper in presenting an opinion that his readers are likely to take seriously? What type of person is the author? Does he strike you as opinionated or prejudiced? How success-fully does he relate personal opinion to common experience? How has he organized his material? How would you expect teachers and administrators to react to this statement of opinion?

THE FALLACY OF EXAMINATIONS

I have only a vague hope that what I am going to say about examinations will shake the foundations of education. Perhaps our present system is after all the only safe method of determining the grades that a student should receive. But certainly I am not the only student who has had his ability tested in ways that made him want to cry out, "Unfair!"

You ask, "Why are you against examinations?" And my answer is, "I am not against examinations." In fact I'm not even against the basic reasons that exams are given. But I am strongly against what has developed into the "in-stant recall" examinations, or maybe even a better term would be the "mara-thon" examinations. Let me give you two examples which will illustrate this type of test. But first let me set the scene. Class periods here are fifty minutes long. Many of the classes have from fifty to eighty students in them, which means that by the time the instructor can count and pass out the exam and then pass out the "easy-grade" I.B.M. answer cards approximately five to ten minutes of the class period has been used. The instructor then spends another few minutes to make corrections on a few of the questions in the exam. This means that the student has forty minutes to take a test that will not only determine a portion of his final grade but will supposedly show what knowl-edge he has gained from the class.

My first example involves my Business Law 130B class. The last mid-term counted twenty-five per cent of our final grade, and this is the type of test it was. There were thirty "fill-in" questions. There were twenty "match-ing" questions, and there were 140 "multiple-choice" questions. In short we had 190 questions to read and answer in forty minutes. This is an average time of twenty-one seconds per question.

Second example: Last Friday, I took my second midterm in my Account-ing 117A class. This exam constituted five pages of accounting problems with an average of three problems per page. Each of these problems is roughly equivalent to the homework problems that are given to us in account-ing classes. The point herein is that the author of the text book estimates that the average accounting student at this level will take from three quarters to one hour to do each homework problem. We are expected to do fifteen of these problems in one class period in order that the instructor may determine our grade and determine what we are learning in his class. No wonder so many instructors feel that they are failures as they grade this type of test.

Let me give you another brief example of what I feel is an unfair way to judge the performance and capability of anyone. I have heard the comment that we write English papers in class because for some reason students tend to do better when they do outside papers. This comment is usually said from the side of the mouth with a knowing smirk on the face of the speaker. But I feel that it stands to reason that it must be better. Again we have that knowing smirk and the question, "Why must it be better?" My answer, and I can only speak from my own experience, is that a student will spend two or three hours, and many times more, in writing his out-of-class papers, he will rewrite the out-of-class papers at least twice (especially if it is typed) and the student will be able to use a wider choice of words because in out-of-class papers he has the opportunity to use his dictionary. Add to this the opportunity to predetermine what line of thought and reasoning will go into the paper, and it will bound to be better than the student's forty-minute in-class papers.

At the beginning of this paper I said that I was not against examinations. I also said that I was not against the basic reasons behind examinations. But let us look at the reasons for examinations. First in the mind of students is that examinations are given in order to give the student a grade. Second, the examinations are given to determine the education that a student is receiving due to his own abilities and the abilities and capabilities of the school he is attending. Better yet, they determine the knowledge the student obtains because of the guidance of the instructors at the school.

Now we have the question stripped to the bare bone. That question is, "Is the student obtaining an education that will enable him to seek out the facts and to apply them to any given situation *and* are examinations to test this education given in such a manner as to determine which students can apply the subject matter to a hypothetical life-situation?" I think not. I feel that examinations such as the business law example serve only to test how many business law terms and facts a student can memorize but do not test his ability and knowledge to apply these facts and, even more important, to apply the principles of business law to a life-situation. I feel that the accounting test example shows that a student who is slower but much more thorough will receive a lower grade. I think the English example can only speak for itself.

Theme Topics 4

1. A girl said of the rulebook given to her as she entered a women's college: "It said what a young lady may not *wear*. That's so superficial, it makes me sick." Does a college have any business regulating the dress, appearance, or manners of its students?

2. Some colleges publish "recommended housing" lists including only

landlords willing to sign an anti-discrimination pledge. Is this an example of unwarranted official meddling in private transactions?

3. A sociology professor has said, "Our schools, both high schools and colleges, teach sentimental rubbish in their marriage and family courses. . . . If taught honestly, these courses would alert the teen-ager and young adult to the realities of matrimonial life in the United States and try to advise them on how to survive marriage if they insist on that hazardous venture." To judge from your experience, how honest or how relevant are such courses?

4. Is intercollegiate athletic competition an anachronism in today's society? Does it perpetuate an image of American higher education as remote from the real problems and challenges of contemporary America?

5. Is it true that American teachers do not encourage, or even tolerate, dissent in their classes? Is it the better part of wisdom for the student to tell his teachers what they want to hear?

6. In recent years, students rebelling against adult authority have enjoyed a tremendous amount of publicity. To judge from your experience, how representative are student rebels of the feelings of students generally? Is it true that they represent only a "tiny minority"?

7. Captain Cook said, "I . . . had ambition not only to go farther than any man had ever been before, but as far as it was possible for a man to go." Is it true that the student's "peer culture" today discourages ambition?

8. How much truth is there in the stereotype? Select one that you at one time shared or still in part share: the welfare chiseler, the militaristic ex-marine, the bookworm, the back-slapping Rotarian, or the like.

9. If well-intentioned words could cure prejudice, this country would by now be free of it. To judge from your experience and reading, what makes prejudice hard to combat?

10. Have you changed your mind on a significant issue since you started college? Write a paper about the change.

Certain kinds of "intelligence" are not to be encouraged too wholeheartedly. A man who handles abstract ideas fluently, and the more fluently because he never feels them as anything more than abstract ideas, can do only a limited amount of good and may, in many circumstances, do harm.
John Wain

CHAPTER FIVE

Definition

1. The Need for Definition
   Vague Words
   Relative Words
   Ambiguous Words
   Specialized Terms

2. The Search for Concrete Reference

3. Formulating and Supporting Definitions
   Dictionary Definitions
   Formal Definitions
   Aids to Definition
   Stipulated Definitions

4. Writing an Extended Definition
   The History of a Term
   Providing the Key
   Finding the Common Denominator
   Drawing the Line

5. The Uses of Definition

Sample Theme
Theme Topics 5

1. The Need for Definition

Until we examine the way language works, we usually assume that words have definite, permanent meanings. Once we have found the words to express what is on our minds, we expect them to carry our message. We feel that what we are trying to say should be obvious to all people of good will. However, when dealing with issues of some consequence, we soon learn that different people use the same words in widely different ways. As a writer found when he set out to explain what the term *excellence* means in education:

. . . "excellence" is a curiously powerful word — a word about which people feel strongly and deeply. But it is a word that means different things to different people. It is a little like those ink blots that psychologists use to interpret personality. As the individual contemplates the word "excellence" he reads into it his own aspirations, his own conception of high standards, his hopes for a better world. . . .

It isn't just that people have different opinions about excellence. They see it from different vantage points. The elementary school teacher preoccupied with instilling respect for standards in seven-year-olds will think about it in one way. The literary critic concerned with understanding and interpreting the highest reaches of creative expression will think of it in a wholly different way. The statesman, the composer, the intellectual historian — each will raise his own questions and pose the issues which are important for him. — John W. Gardner, *Excellence*

Once a writer realizes that such differences exist, he will feel obligated to make clear what his *own* vantage point is, what ideas and aspirations *he* reads into a term. The first step is to become aware of the types of words that are most likely to need such narrowing down; that is, words in need of definition.

Vague Words

Many familiar words cover too much ground to be useful in detailed discussion. The word *weather* is convenient when we are trying to indicate whether it is pleasant or unpleasant to be outdoors. But the meteorologist needs more precise terms to make distinctions between wind, temperature, humidity, cloudiness, precipitation, and other factors that together determine atmospheric conditions. The tour director, the airplane pilot, the sailor, and the surfer all want something more informative than a vague prediction of bad weather.

Similarly, a reader interested in educational reform expects something more meaningful than a commitment to "well-rounded" education and a "modern" curriculum. The familiar call for a "well-rounded" education is so vague that it can be used to justify inclusion in the curriculum of anything from finger painting and baby care to

Chinese philosophy and Inca music. If we use the term at all, we will have to specify what *we* would include to give balance to education.

Here are some statements with vague terms that call for definition:

Vague: New educational programs will be developed in close *consulta-tion* with representatives of the student body.
(Who will select the "representatives"? How and when will they be "consulted"? Will they have a chance to propose programs of their own? Will they be allowed to vote on anything? How much will their vote count?)

Vague: A military academy does more than the typical public school to build a boy's *character.*
(*What* character traits does the writer have in mind? When and how are they demonstrated by graduates of military academies?)

Relative Words

Many words cover a range of meaning. Their exact meaning depends on circumstances: *Hot* may mean 95 degrees or 9,500 degrees; a "large" sum of money may suggest $500 to you and $500,000 to your next-door neighbor. To make such words less relative, we often have to indicate a precise point on the scale. Exactly how rich is "rich"? How intelligent does a boy have to be before we classify him as "gifted"? Our estimate of how many Americans are "poor" depends on where exactly we draw the "poverty line."

Many less obviously relative words do not become fully meaningful until we specify *degree.* When someone promises us "freedom," asks us to assume "responsibility," or admonishes us to act "unselfishly," the key question often is "How much?" How *far* can a teacher go in exercising his promised "freedom to discuss controversial issues"? How *much* responsibility is society asked to assume for the disabled and unemployed? How *completely* are we expected to subordinate self-interest?

Ambiguous Words

Many terms that we tend to take for granted have several different, and at times contradictory, meanings. We all early learn to manage words that do double duty: *sense* means both "sense perception" and "intelligence." Your dictionary lists both "potency" and "chastity" as synonyms of *virtue.* Ambiguity becomes a problem when a double meaning remains unresolved; when an unexpected disagreement over a key term tangles the thread of discussion.

Have you ever been tripped up by the ambiguity of one of the following terms?

Honor   One of the meanings of *honor* is implied in the expression "to honor a person"; this meaning centers on recognition, esteem, prestige, reputation. The other is implied in an expression like "an honorable person"; this meaning centers on the person's own standard of conduct. We might call the first external honor and the second internal honor. The first is used in "honor roll," a list of students honored by a school. The second is used in "honor system" or "school code of honor," which appeals to the students to behave honorably. The difference in meaning becomes clear when a student is found to have acquired his school honors dishonorably, through cheating on examinations.

Justice   To some people, the term *justice* implies that the strong, the intelligent, the competent should be rewarded: "Let the best man win." It then seems "only just" that a shrewd, hard-working businessman should earn considerably more than less aggressive, less able members of our society. But other people invoke the term *justice* when they call for greater *equality* of rewards. It then seems "just" that the weak and disadvantaged should be allowed to share in the good things of life. Because of the fundamental ambiguity of the term, mere insistence that "justice be done" will not resolve the differences between the conflicting points of view.

One sign of the ambiguity of a term is our groping for labels that would help eliminate *unintended* meanings: "Western democracy," "people's democracy," "representative democracy," "direct democracy," "participatory democracy." By confronting the ambiguities of key terms directly, and by clearly ruling out unintended meanings, we can keep from saying one thing while our audience hears another.

Specialized Terms

Much serious writing relies for precision on the specialized use of terms that have a more general meaning in everyday use. In popular journalism, for instance, the term *tragedy* usually means "disaster," any event involving fatal loss or great suffering. A drama critic is likely to use the term in its more technical sense of "a serious play having a disastrous or unhappy ending." He will probably restrict the term further by setting up more specialized criteria. He may specify a certain type of plot and define tragedy as "a play about a great man who brings about his own downfall by choices inherent in his character." He may apply the term only to a play with definite philosophical implications — for instance, a play that raises questions about a moral order or divine plan behind all existence. The layman reading scholarly studies and technical reports has to watch out for the exact implications of terms used in a limited technical sense.

Every competent reader has learned to infer the intended meaning of a word from where and how it is used. The word *law* usually stands for written law, enforced by policemen. But it means "unwritten standard of behavior" when an author uses the phrase "the moral law" in a discussion of conscience and individual responsibility. The word *honor* used in a speech about the Civil War is likely to mean the prestige or glory of a nation. The same word used in a sentimental novel is likely to mean the innocence of the heroine.

As a result, you can often do without definition when the meaning of an otherwise confusing term is clear from the **context** in which you use it. There is no need to define *conservative* in the following sentence: "The present owner, being an extremely conservative man, still follows the daily routine first instituted by his father." But suppose you are saying, "Powerful conservative forces are at work in American society." Here *conservative* needs to be carefully defined. It may mean "dedicated to the preservation of law and order," "irrationally attached to outmoded conventions," or perhaps "cautious in spending public funds."

Exercises

A. What is the meaning of the words italicized in the following sentences? Compare your answers with those of your classmates. Do you find it easy or difficult to pin down the meaning of these words?

1. When I meet a person, I try to be interested and express an interest through a warm handshake and a *sincere* smile.

2. Her family are nice people, but they have absolutely no *class*.

3. She was good-looking, but I soon found she was very *shallow*.

B. Can you and your classmates arrive at a consensus on the following questions? Your instructor may ask you to write a paragraph to present your answer to one of these.

1. What is the difference between love and infatuation?

2. When does a demonstration become a riot?

3. When does a conservative become a reactionary?

4. Are extremism and radicalism the same thing?

5. When does self-interest become selfishness?

C. What minimum requirements does a person have to meet for you to call him Christian? Jewish? A liberal? Compare your stipulated requirements with those of your classmates. How much divergence is there? How much agreement?

D. From a Shakespeare play, select five quotations that all use the word *honor.* Does the word mean the same each time? If not, how many different meanings can you identify?

2.   The Search for Concrete Reference

The general principle for successful definition applies to all successful writing: *Anchor the general to concrete reference.* Give substance to abstract terms by relating them to people, places, and events. Notice how the writer in the following example uses the first paragraph of an essay to anchor the general term *work* to her account of a character who throughout the essay serves as an example of what hard, lifelong work means:

> Whenever I think of the word "work" I first think of my Aunt Clara. Next I think of the hymn we used to sing so often in our North Dakota village church: *Work, for the night is coming,/Work in the noonday sun./Work, for the night is coming,/When man's work is done.* The logic of those verses has always eluded me, but their meaning has always been mysteriously clear, perhaps because I knew my Aunt Clara and so many others almost like her. Because I knew my Aunt Clara I am astounded at the number of people who seem to think of work as an abstraction — like Truth or Beauty. — Lois Phillips Hudson, " 'Work, for the Night Is Coming,' " *The Reporter*

When a term covers much ground, and is used in many diverse situations, anchoring it to concrete reference may require careful thought. For instance, many students who accept *freedom* as a basic democratic concept find it difficult to give a coherent account of what it means in practice. Asked for a definition, they may say that it means "freedom to do as you please" or "freedom to follow the dictates of your own conscience."

Such a definition appeals partly because it is still almost as vague and inspirational as the original term. A consistent attempt to live up to it would require us to abolish all zoning laws, traffic regulations, criminal statutes, health controls, and numerous other arrangements that make life and the pursuit of happiness possible. All known societies, free or unfree, have imposed *some* external restraints on their members, if only to keep Jesse James and Typhoid Mary from doing the rest of society in.

What does it take to make a word like *freedom* meaningful? Here is an abstraction that has been invoked impartially by Whig and Tory, Democrat and Republican, Communist and Fascist alike. Hitler's storm troopers carried the word *freedom* in golden letters on their banners. Anyone using this much-abused word must be prepared to answer the question: "What specifically do you mean?" Here are some questions that might help you give concrete substance to your use of the word:

(1) What *specific freedoms, sometimes denied,* would you include? These might include, for instance,

- *freedom of movement.* The slave, the serf, the deportee, as well as the actual prisoner or inmate of a labor camp, are denied the fundamental freedom to move on, to "grab a train and ride," to start over again at the other end of the rainbow.

- *free choice of employment.* The government that sends intellectuals to work on farms, the employers that blacklist political undesirables, the union that reserves apprenticeships for nephews of members, the college department that does not hire woman teachers — all these restrict a person's opportunities to find satisfying, productive, profitable work of his own choice.

- *freedom of artistic creation.* How free a society is depends in part on how much regulation of literature and the arts there is on political, religious, or moral grounds. How much banning, blacklisting, or censorship is there of heresy, blasphemy, pornography, "degenerate art," alien ideologies, counter-revolutionary writers, decadent bourgeois influences, or any other deviations from approved norms?

(2) What *basic limitations* on freedom would you accept as necessary? Businessmen strenuously argue in favor of "free enterprise," while academic liberals often favor government regulation of logging firms, strip miners, drug manufacturers, pesticide sprayers, and a host of other businesses whose business, for better or for worse, affects the public weal. College professors demand "academic freedom" to pursue the truth wherever it will lead; their critics ask the professor to deliver services that the taxpayer is willing to pay for. American Protestants have historically favored "freedom of worship" yet have often balked at allowing free advocacy of unreligious or atheistic views.

(3) What procedures for *implementing* the necessary restrictions on freedom would you approve? To the person accused of subversive

activities, it makes a difference whether he is arrested and freed on bail after a night in prison, or whether he disappears in the dark of night and is never seen alive again. Many societies have found it necessary to rely on compulsory military service. But to the person refusing to serve, it makes a difference whether he is allowed to do noncombatant duty as a conscientious objector, or is put in jail for years for violating the draft laws, or is executed as a coward.

A meaningful definition of freedom would have to pull together the results of an investigation similar to the one here sketched out. What would be a common denominator for some of the answers suggested above? First, we might want to stress the idea of *personal choice*. A free society would try to provide the largest possible scope for our choice of job, mate, friends, place to live, hobbies, religion, intellectual pursuits, and means of artistic expression. Second, we might want to stress the idea of *consent*. A free society would impose the necessary restrictions of freedom not only with the consent of the majority but also with respect for dissenting views and minority interests. Third, we might want to stress the idea of procedural safeguards. A free society would implement restrictions on freedom with regard for *due process*, with ample opportunity for appeal and review, and through a system of checks and balances that keeps the exercise of authority from being swift and deadly.

If we thus succeed in putting together, in a few sentences or in a paragraph, a definition of *freedom*, we should realize what such a definition *does not* accomplish. It is not binding on everybody, since much political controversy hinges on *disagreements* over what kinds of freedom are desirable and how they might be achieved. What such a definition does accomplish is something less ambitious but basic to successful communication. Basically, a successful definition helps the reader understand what the writer had in mind. It enables the reader to take in not only the author's words but what the words stand for as well.

Exercises

A. A writer with an eye for the concrete defined sewage as "whatever goes down the drain in home, factory, or office." In one sentence each, write a similar capsule definition for three of the following: credit, prestige, glamor, charm, influence.

B. The president of a large urban college recently asked himself what we mean by "urban." Here is part of his answer. How, and how successfully, does it give concrete substance to an abstract sociological term?

The urban society means crowded neighborhoods, poor housing, sometimes shacks on the fringes of the city inhabited by the fringes of humanity, more often fine old houses, tottering with age, wrinkled and cross-veined with partition. . . . Urban means poverty, hunger, disease, rats; it means unemployment, placement below skills, welfare and dependence perpetuated now to the third generation. . . . Urban means the decay of the central city, the moving out of business, the proliferation of "For Rent" signs, the boarding up of windows, the transformation of pride to embarrassment. . . . What once was city is now largely deteriorating buildings, empty stores, buildings about to empty themselves, and open spaces where buildings once stood.

Using the above passage as a model, write a paragraph in which you give concrete substance to one of the following terms: *downtown, suburbia, rural, slum, metropolitan.*

C. Study the way the following paragraph gives concrete substance to a familiar term. What is that term? What effect does the author achieve by *not* stating the term at the very beginning? Using this paragraph as a model, write a passage in which you *first* present the concrete experiences that make a familiar term truly meaningful, and *then* present the delayed abstraction.

It was an old black man in Atlanta who looked into my eyes and directed me into my first segregated bus. I have spent a long time thinking about that man. I never saw him again. I cannot describe the look which passed between us, as I asked him for directions, but it made me think, at once, of Shakespeare's "the oldest have borne most." It made me think of the blues: *Now, when a woman gets the blues, Lord, she hangs her head and cries. But when a man gets the blues, Lord, he grabs a train and rides.* It was borne in on me, suddenly, just why these men had so often been grabbing freight trains as the evening sun went down. And it was, perhaps, because I was getting on a segregated bus, and wondering how Negroes had borne this and other indignities for so long, that this man so struck me. He seemed to know what I was feeling. His eyes seemed to say that what I was feeling he had been feeling, at much higher pressure, all his life. But my eyes would never see the hell his eyes had seen. And this hell was, simply, that he had never in his life owned anything, not his wife, not his house, not his child, which could not, at any instant, be taken from him by the power of white people. This is what paternalism means.—James Baldwin, *Nobody Knows My Name*

3. Formulating and Supporting Definitions

Like other meaningful statements, a meaningful definition is the result of inquiry. It sums up what the writer has *found out* about a term. It states how he proposes to limit the territory the term covers, how he has resolved its ambiguities. How does a writer pull together the results of his investigation? How does he present them to the reader?

Dictionary Definitions

Take into account but do not simply repeat a dictionary definition.[1] Dictionary definitions are most useful when they give the layman a reliable, exact account of a technical term. They bring to bear both the expert's knowledge of the subject matter and the lexicographer's knowledge of the history and use of words. They make us check our incomplete personal impressions against an impersonal stock-taking of essentials. Once we penetrate the polysyllabic terminology, a definition like the following sums up for us conveniently what makes a horse a horse:

A graminivorous quadruped of the genus *Equidae,* distinguished from other species of the genus by excessive elongation of the metacarpus and the metatarsus and by a mane and tail of coarse hair.

Dictionary definitions are much less helpful when we grapple with a vague term hard to relate to concrete experience, or when much depends on the personal commitments of the user. Sometimes, a dictionary definition of such a term can serve as a point of departure, alerting us to a key problem that needs attention. If *free enterprise,* for instance, is defined as "a minimum of government regulation of business," we may start thinking about whether, why, how, and when regulation is necessary.

But more often, repeating the dictionary definition merely gives the student writer a false sense of accomplishment. Suppose you are asked to write a paper on some problem of maladjustment. You start by saying,

The *New American Standard Dictionary* defines *adjustment* as "the process of fitting individual or collective patterns of activity to other such patterns made with some awareness or purposefulness."

Your reader is likely to ask: "How is this definition related to your own knowledge and interpretation of adjustment? What does it mean? Why do you accept this definition rather than some of the other possible ones? Can you think of any concrete cases that this definition seems to fit? Can you think of any cases that it does not fit?"

[1] See D 1 for a discussion of college dictionaries.

These questions are not designed to discourage you from making use of your dictionary. However, *to make effective use of a dictionary definition, you have to relate it to your own investigation of the subject.* You have to show why you accept the definition, or how it needs to be modified.

Formal Definitions

A *formal definition first places a term in a larger class and then sums up distinctive features.* One general lesson you can learn from dictionary definitions is to sort out the parts of a definition into two types of information. First, you can list things that classify the term to be defined as a member of a group, or **class**. Second, you can list characteristics that distinguish the term to be defined from other members of the same group. Thus, a formal definition of *horse* first places horses in the general category of four-legged mammals that have solid hoofs and feed on grass or grain. It then points out characteristics that distinguish horses from other animals in the same general category. Here are some examples of formal definition:

Term to be Defined	Class	Differentiation
An autobiography	is the story of a person's life,	written by himself.
Oligarchy	is a form of government	in which power lies in the hands of a few.
A martyr	is someone who suffers persecution	for refusing to renounce his faith.

This simple formula proves useful for several reasons: It focuses on essentials and yet can be packed with relevant *information:*

A faun	is a Roman wood god	who is half man and half goat.

It trains us to take in the important *nuances:*

To double-cross	is to betray someone	whom we have deliberately impressed with our trustworthiness or loyalty.

It forestalls predictable *confusion.* Careful choice of the class may by itself clarify a confused argument. For instance, a debate concerning free enterprise is likely to profit from general agreement that free enterprise is not "a form of government" but "an economic system" or "an economic theory." Careful choice of the differentiating qualities can exclude things or ideas that a term might mistakenly be thought to include. For instance, revolutionary communism is excluded by a definition of evolutionary socialism as "a political movement that aims at bringing about government ownership of the means of production, *using peaceful or constitutional means.*"

Several precautions have to be observed if a formal definition is to be informative. Check your definitions for the following shortcomings:

(1) *The class in which a term is placed may be too inclusive.* Classifying a cello as "a musical instrument" is less informative than classifying it as "a string instrument of the violin family." Classifying an epic as "a type of literature" is less informative than classifying it as "a long narrative poem."

(2) *The definition may place the term in a group without supplying adequate differentiation.* Defining *Puritanism* as "the religion of the Puritans" makes it clear that we are dealing with a religion but does not tell us what kind. Defining *tragedy* as "a play concerned with a tragic situation" clarifies the meaning somewhat but leaves the key term undefined. Definitions that repeat the key term in a slightly different guise are called **circular definitions**. Their circularity is often less obvious than in the preceding examples. Take, for instance, the familiar definition of *liberty* as "the right to do whatever does not interfere with the liberty of others." "Liberty of others" is vague unless *liberty* has already been defined in some other way.

(3) *The distinctive features stated may not be adequate to rule out things that are similar or closely related.* This is the weakness of a definition of *patriot* as "a person who promotes the best interests of his country." This definition does not exclude the person who serves his country for the sake of gain or personal glory. Adding the words *zealously* and *unselfishly* to the definition would make it more discriminating.

(4) *A definition may be too restrictive.* A definition referring to a *senator* as "an elected representative of a state" would exclude the minority of senators who are not elected but appointed. Defining *patriot* as "a person who wholeheartedly supports his country's policies" would exclude persons who have served their country well but who criticize or oppose unwise policies.

(5) *Instead of enumerating the characteristics of the term to be defined, a definition may offer another term covering approximately the same area of meaning.* **Synonyms** are useful when they provide a familiar equivalent for an unfamiliar or difficult term, such as "double meaning" for *ambiguity.* But a writer makes little headway if he explains that by *just* he means "right in action or judgment" and by *equitable* "fair or equal." Substituting one set of familiar general

terms for another does not help a writer pin down the exact meaning he intends to give to flexible and elusive words.

(6) *What looks like a definition may actually be only a tangential observation.* Many statements that use an *is* or *means* are not intended to define but to comment on some aspect of a term whose definition is already known. Such a comment is George Bernard Shaw's remark that "martyrdom is the only way in which a man can become famous without ability." To feel the edge of this irreverent observation, the reader has to know beforehand what *martyrdom* means.

Aids to Definition

Use supporting material that will give your definition depth and force. A formal definition is typically designed to sum up rather than to explain or convince. To drive home a definition you have presented, use supporting material that will answer questions like the following: What does this mean in practice? How would this actually work? How did this term acquire this meaning? How is this term different from terms that are closely related?

(1) *Definitions often need the support of examples.* We would probably merely nod our heads dutifully at a definition of "news" as what is out of the ordinary. But a graphic example makes us realize what this definition implies:

The fact that 6,000,000 students read books yesterday is not news because that is what students are supposed to do. The fact that a thousand staged a demonstration, a hundred booed and shouted down a speaker who had been invited to the campus, or a dozen threw rocks at the police, is news because that is not what we expect of students.

Notice how the author of the following passage, after first making a distinction between different kinds of freedom, gives us a series of graphic examples of what freedom means in everyday life:

A man's free condition is of two parts: the instinctive free-ness he experiences as an animal dweller on a planet, and the practical liberties he enjoys as a privileged member of human society. The latter is, of the two, more generally understood, more widely admired, more violently challenged and discussed. It is the practical and apparent side of freedom. The United States, almost alone today, offers the liberties and the privileges and the tools of freedom. In this land the citizens are still invited *to write plays and books, to paint their pictures, to meet for discussion, to dissent as well as to agree, to mount soapboxes in the public square, to enjoy education in all subjects without censorship, to hold court and judge one another, to compose music, to talk politics with their neighbors without wondering whether the secret police are listening, to exchange ideas as well as goods, to kid the government when it needs kidding, and to read real news of real events instead of phony news manufactured by a paid agent of the state.* — E. B. White, *One Man's Meat*

(2) *Many definitions are incomplete without instructions show-ing how to produce the result being described.* Children's definitions stay close to this level of "How does it work?" and "What does it do?" ("A genius is a fellow who gets into trouble. Then some moron comes along and gets blamed.") Scientists, engineers, businessmen, and politicians all expect from a definition an account of essential causes, functions, and effects. A physicist looks for an **operational definition**, showing how a given phenomenon can be experimentally reproduced. He may decline to comment on what "matter" is, but will talk freely about how it behaves.

(3) *The history of a term can help to explain its present mean-ing.* For instance, a cultural historian may be discussing the influence of Puritanism on life in nineteenth-century America. In defining *Puritanism*, he might start from the efforts of seventeenth-century Puritans to go beyond their fellow Protestants in restoring Chris-tianity to what they considered its original purity. Seen from this per-spective, the Puritan's strictness of standards and austerity of be-havior will fit into a meaningful context. Many of the terms used in previous illustrations—*freedom* and *free enterprise, tragedy* and *epic*—cannot be fully defined without reference to their historical background. Here is the way one writer puts the term *freedom* in historical perspective:

> The eighteenth century was the matrix from which most contemporary ideas of freedom have come. As Carl Becker pointed out, "the eighteenth century was the mo-ment in history when men experienced the first flush and freshness of the idea that man is master of his own fate." The American and French Revolutions testify to the extent and passion of this conviction. Men were to be freed from coercive institutions— from tyrannical government and dogmatic creeds—by their own efforts. Had not Rous-seau declared that man is naturally good but is corrupted by institutions, and is born free but is everywhere in chains? Men were to be freed from superstition, and Voltaire's iconoclastic wit did a great deal to accomplish this purpose. Men were to be freed from autocratic government: the contents of the American Bill of Rights reveal that government was regarded as the chief danger to individual liberty.—Liston Pope, "Does Faith Impair Freedom?" *Saturday Review*

(4) *Often, effective definition is impossible without comparison and contrast with closely related terms.* One major section of an essay on liberal education may explain in what ways it resembles general education; another section may explain how it differs from vocational education. Often the major problem in defining a term is to set it over against a term with which it is popularly confused. Notice how emphatically the author of the following passage contrasts "old-style" liberalism with "new-style" radicalism:

If liberals are defined roughly as those who accept the basic characteristics of the existing political and economic systems and who believe that the government should be an active instrument for improving the lot of our citizenry and perhaps of mankind as a whole; and if radicals are defined as those who seek fundamental changes in the political, social, and economic systems—some adhering to democratic norms and some not—then it is obvious that the relationship between liberals and radicals will usually be strained and often nonexistent. . . . these radicals, whatever may be their personal motives and however real and profound their grievances, do not offer liberal democrats an acceptable alternative, nor are they acceptable allies. They detest compromise, conciliation, and accommodation, the necessary elements of a democratic, tolerant, and humane policy; they accept violence as an appropriate means. . . . Many of them have explicitly rejected liberal democracy as a sham and a fraud.—William P. Gerberding, "Liberals and Radicals," *The Reporter*

Often a large part of a definition is taken up by an explanation that A is *not* B, that it is *not* C, and that, though it overlaps with D to some extent, it is not D either.

Stipulated Definitions

Keep a stipulated meaning clearly in view to prevent inconsistency and confusion. Terms like *liberalism, materialism,* and *idealism* have a long and confusing history, and a number of different or opposed current meanings. *Liberalism* used to mean a political doctrine favoring free enterprise, but is now usually taken to mean the opposite. To cut through the thicket of conflicting meanings and associations, a writer using the term may have to stipulate clearly the meaning of *liberalism* "as used here." He can then proceed to show that his use of the term is apt, convenient, or historically justified. The more this use varies from its more current popular uses, the more careful the writer has to be to reinforce it by reminders.

It is such stipulated definitions that we look for when a writer uses terms like *true love, true integrity,* or *true democracy.* "True" love is simply the kind of love the writer believes in or aspires to, and the term does not become meaningful until the writer shows what love must have to win his approval.

Exercises

A. If necessary, rewrite the following definitions to make them more exact or more informative. Explain what made the original version inexact or uninformative.

1. A barometer is an instrument used in predicting the weather.

2. Classical music is the type of music played in concert halls.

3. A sorority is a private association which provides separate dormitory facilities with a distinctive Greek letter name for selected female college students.

4. Tyranny is rule by a tyrant.

5. Jazz is a form of strongly rhythmic music played by Negro musicians.

6. Islam is the religion of the Moslems.

7. A strike means that workers leave their jobs in order to get higher pay.

8. An alien is a person born in another country.

9. Pacifism makes people refuse military service in times of war.

10. A plebiscite is a method of giving the public a voice in political decisions.

B. State as briefly and as accurately as possible the difference between (1) murder and manslaughter, (2) blasphemy and sacrilege, (3) a trade and a profession, (4) tactics and strategy, (5) a college and a university, (6) a democracy and a republic, (7) intuition and instinct, (8) a revolt and a revolution, (9) legend and myth, (10) poetry and verse.

C. Examine and evaluate the following student-written definitions of *sportsmanship*. Is there a common denominator? Which of the definitions would be most useful to you in working out your own definition of the term?

1. Sportsmanship means playing a game according to the rules and obeying the instructions of the referee. If a player does not obey rules, he is penalized.

2. Sportsmanship is applauded by crowds at boxing events when the boxer allows his opponent to stagger to his feet before being smashed to the canvas again.

3. Sportsmanship is the quality of wanting to let another fellow have a chance. It is parallel to the ideal embodied in the Ten Commandments. Religion teaches a way of life that will always have the sportsman as a part of it.

4. Sportsmanship is the ability to get along with one's fellow man and at the same time oppose him. It enables a player to congratulate an opponent who has just handed him a crushing defeat.

5. The American athlete is known for his high sense of sportsmanship. Sportsmanship is hard to explain, but most people recognize it when they see it. It means being friendly, fair, just, and sincere.

6. Sportsmanship is a luxury. The gentleman hunter who hunts for amusement can afford to observe a sportsmanlike code in shooting animals. The hunter who has to find food for a starving family cannot afford to be particular about his methods.

7. Sportsmanship is the quality of being sportsmanlike. A sportsman, in other words, is the person who adopts a standard of sportsmanlike behavior and lives up to it.

8. Sportsmanship is the willingness to live up to the established traditions of a sport. Through the years, a certain kind of conduct has come to be expected of the players. A player is unsportsmanlike when he violates the traditions of the sport.

9. The most important ingredient in sportsmanship is courtesy. Consideration and restraint make the difference between a courteous player and a ruffian.

10. Sportsmanship means playing not in order to win but for the love of the sport. The sportsman who plays primarily for profit or for personal glory is not a sportsman in the true sense of the word.

D. How accurately can you distinguish between the two key terms in each of the following passages? Define each term so as to set it off clearly from the other.

1. The young people today are much closer in their views on civil rights to the abolitionists of a century ago than they are to yesterday's liberals. The oppression of the Negro is to them a *sin* rather than a *wrong*.

2. "Yes," a student said to me, "I want to be *intelligent*, but I don't want to be a detached, emotionless *intellectual*."

3. Many people today hold strong religious *beliefs* while rejecting *dogma*.

4. The author described her father as "a tough, taciturn, *uneducated* man but also a deeply *learned* and handsome one."

4. Writing an Extended Definition

Devoting a whole paper to the definition of an important term gives you a chance to become fully aware of words as words. It gives you a chance to ponder the relationship between words and experience, and between words and ideas. Here are some possible patterns for a theme devoted to definition:

The History of a Term

Explain a word's range and characteristic ambiguities by tracing its development. Often the best way to clarify a confusing term is to trace major stages in its history. College dictionaries provide at least some historical information; the *Oxford English Dictionary* traces the history of words in great detail, with many authentic quotations (see D 2). But your paper will be the more substantial if you can draw on your own first-hand reading—of a Shakespeare play, of an eighteenth-century novel, of Romantic poetry.

Here is a possible outline for a paper tracing the history of a term with an unusual range:

I. The word *virtue* derives from the same root as *virile* and originally meant "manliness," or "manly strength."

II. More specifically, the term came to stand for manly performance in battle, or warlike prowess.

III. In a more generalized sense, *virtue* came to mean "competence" or "power," as in the phrase *by virtue of.*

IV. Between the general sense of "competence" and the more limited sense of "valor" lies the meaning still most widely in use: "desirable moral quality."

V. By focusing on the moral quality considered most desirable in a woman, we arrive at the familiar nineteenth-century meaning of "feminine chastity" or "purity."

Providing the Key

Give clear focus to your discussion of a term by making your definition the thesis that the rest of the paper will support. By modeling an extended definition on the familiar thesis-and-support paper, you can provide a clear and direct answer to the question that may be uppermost in the reader's mind: "What is the clue? What is the secret?" For instance, you may have concluded that the key element in a narrow-minded person's makeup is his quickness to *judge*— to make judgments that put others in the wrong and himself in the right, to pronounce hasty judgments that at the same time tend to be harsh and extreme. You state this key element as your definition of narrow-mindedness early in the paper. You then devote the rest of your paper to examples showing how well your definition fits actual cases of narrow-mindedness.

Here is a rough scheme for a similar paper on romantic love:

Romantic love is a love *strong enough to overcome formidable obstacles.* It makes a lover persevere in an apparently hopeless passion. It makes lovers go against the opposition of parents, church, and state. . . .

The most striking representative of the persevering lover is the knight of the *medieval romance*. . . .

More recent examples of all but hopeless and yet persevering passion can be found in such *nineteenth-century novels* as Flaubert's *Sentimental Education.* . . . In *modern literature*, . . .

Finding the Common Denominator

Make your reader participate in the search for an elusive meaning. When again and again we find two contending parties each shouting "Unfair!" it may seem presumptuous for us to announce a definition of *fairness* or *fair play* as though it were obvious and binding on everyone. We might get a more respectful hearing if we assumed the stance of the impartial observer, approaching the subject with an open mind. We could take the reader through a series of test cases, each raising an issue of fair play. We could in the process call attention to what they seem to have in common, and then, at the end, sum up the definition thus discovered.

Here is a rough scheme for the kind of paper that would ask the reader to join in the search for the common denominator:

First Test Case:	An honor code states that it is not "fair" to cheat.
Second Test Case:	According to a newspaper story, a mother considered it "fair" to steal food for her starving children.
Third Test Case:	A tennis player considers it "fair" to let his opponent find his footing after stumbling.
Fourth Test Case:	Students consider it "unfair" to penalize a sick student for failure to take a test.
Common Denominator:	Fair play makes us impose limits on competition — and sometimes *suspend* normal limits — in order to assure greater equality of opportunity; it shows our desire to "give everybody a chance."

Drawing the Line

Give force and point to your definition of a term by setting it off from a more familiar term to which it is closely related. Systematic comparison and contrast with a familiar synonym or near synonym is often the most effective way to give concrete substance to a term that is at best blurry in the reader's mind. In the statement excerpted below, the spokesman of a militant student group uses the familiar term *protest* as a foil for the term summing up his own more aggressive position:

definition of first term	To protest is to speak out against. To let it be known that you do not like a certain action of another. To protest is an act of intellectual commitment. It is to say, "Sir, I protest" when you are slapped in the face. . . .

first example　　　　　To protest is to play a game. You go to a demonstration, listen to speeches, wave signs, and go home to see if you got on television. There are many toys in the game of protest.

second example　　　　There is the picket line. Originally a picket line was formed by striking workers to keep strike-breakers out. If anyone tried to cross that picket line, the strikers tried to kill him. Today you get a permit from the police to protest. . . . We have allowed the form that our protest takes to be defined for us by those whom we protest against. Thus our protest is drained of its power because we do not have the power to make our protest effective. We are no longer outraged at what is being done to us. If we were, we would resist.

definition of
second term　　　　　To resist is to say, NO! without qualification or explanation. To resist is not only to say I won't go. It is to say, I'll make sure nobody else goes, either.

first example　　　　　To resist is to not go to jail when sentenced, but only when caught and surrounded and there is no other choice but death.

(second example)　　. . . . .

summary　　　　　　To protest is to dislike the inhumanity of another. To resist is to stop inhumanity and affirm your own inhumanity.

As you grapple with a difficult term, you may have to adapt or combine these relatively simple patterns. Writing about *free enterprise,* for instance, you may want to mark it off from both capitalism, as a near synonym, and socialism, as a possible opposite. Before you do, however, you may want to show how often the term serves someone's interest, being the kind of word whose meaning varies as different users suit it to their own ulterior purpose. You may also have to distinguish carefully between free enterprise as a myth, handed on in inspirational speeches, and as a working reality. The more serious your attempt at definition, the more likely your pattern of organization is to reflect some of the inherent complications or contradictions of the term.

When you ask someone to read an extended definition, you have to do two somewhat contradictory things. To make your problem worth the reader's attention, your position has to be "This is not as simple as you think." But to assure the reader that his attention will be rewarded, you attitude also has to be "But I am getting this under control." As in much serious writing, your double task will be to call attention to a problem and help the reader resolve it at the same time.

Exercises

A. Write a paragraph about an important or widely used term that has changed in meaning or application since you first became aware of it. Give examples of its different uses.

B. Write a paragraph in which you first sum up and then explain and illustrate the key element in one of the following: *fanaticism, integrity, pluralism, surrealism.*

C. Much modern philosophical analysis is concerned with the meanings of words in common use. After pondering the following paragraph, how would you sum up the most basic similarities and relationships that give meaning to the term *games?* Can you find a common denominator that would satisfy this skeptical a reader?

> Consider the proceedings that we call "games." I mean board-games, card-games, ball-games, Olympic games, and so on. What is common to them all? Don't say: "There *must* be something common, or they would not be called 'games'" — but *look and see* whether there is anything common to all. For if you look at them you will not see something that is common to *all*, but similarities, relationships, and a whole series of them at that. To repeat: don't think, but look! Look for example at board-games, with their multifarious relationships. Now pass to card-games; here you find many correspondences with the first group, but many common features drop out, and others appear. When we pass next to ball-games, much that is common is retained, but much is lost. Are they all "amusing"? Compare chess with noughts and crosses. Or is there always winning and losing, or competition between players? Think of patience. In ball-games there is winning and losing; but when a child throws his ball at the wall and catches it again, this feature has disappeared. Look at the parts played by skill and luck; and at the difference between skill in chess and skill in tennis. Think now of games like ring-a-ring-a-roses; here is the element of amusement, but how many other characteristic features have disappeared! — Ludwig Wittgenstein, *Philosophical Investigations.*

D. The following passages define terms of special interest to students of language and literature. Examine and compare the methods of definition employed. Comment on the clarity or adequacy of each passage.

> 1. Sophistication is the quality that results from wide experience and mature observation. The sophisticated person both feels and thinks, but he does so with an attitude which is generally accepted as sound by the world. Sentimentality is, in a way, the opposite of sophistication, for it is an unreasonable appeal for emotion. The sophisticate accepts emotion as a natural part of life and controls it; the sentimentalist is carried away by emotion and over-emphasizes what that emotion deals with. — Robert O. Bowen, *Practical Prose Studies*

> 2. An inference, as we shall use the term, is *a statement about the unknown made on the basis of the known.* We may *infer* from the hand-

someness of a woman's clothes her wealth or social position; we may *infer* from the character of the ruins the origin of the fire that destroyed the building; we may *infer* from a man's calloused hands the nature of his occupation; we may *infer* from a senator's vote on an armaments bill his attitude toward Russia; we may *infer* from the structure of the land the path of a prehistoric glacier; we may *infer* from a halo on an unexposed photographic plate that it has been in the vicinity of radioactive materials; we may *infer* from the noise an engine makes the condition of its connecting rods. Inferences may be carelessly or carefully made. They may be made on the basis of a great background of previous experience with the subject matter, or no experience at all. For example, the inferences a good mechanic can make about the internal condition of a motor by listening to it are often startlingly accurate, while the inferences made by an amateur (if he tries to make any) may be entirely wrong. But the common characteristic of inferences is that they are statements about matters which are not directly known, made on the basis of what has been observed. — S. I. Hayakawa, *Language in Thought and Action*

3. I am not sure that I can draw an exact line between wit and humor. Perhaps the distinction is so subtle that only those persons can decide who have long white beards. But even an ignorant man, so long as he is clear of Bedlam, may have an opinion.

I am quite positive that of the two, humor is the more comfortable and more livable quality. Humorous persons, if their gift is genuine and not a mere shine upon the surface, are always agreeable companions and they sit through the evening best. They have pleasant mouths turned up at the corners. To these corners the great Master of marionettes has fixed the strings and he holds them in his nimblest fingers to twitch them at the slightest jest. But the mouth of a merely witty man is hard and sour until the moment of its discharge. Nor is the flash from a witty man always comforting, whereas a humorous man radiates a general pleasure and is like another candle in the room.

I admire wit, but I have no real liking for it. It has been too often employed against me, whereas humor is always an ally. It never points an impertinent finger into my defects. Humorous persons do not sit like explosives on a fuse. They are safe and easy comrades. But a wit's tongue is as sharp as a donkey driver's stick. I may gallop the faster for its prodding, yet the touch behind is too persuasive for any comfort. — Charles S. Brooks, *Chimney-Pot Papers*

4. Snobbery is not the same thing as pride of class. Pride of class may not please us but we must at least grant that it reflects a social function. A man who exhibited class pride — in the day when it was possible to do so — may have been puffed up about what he *was*, but this ultimately depended on what he *did*. Thus, aristocratic pride was based ultimately on the ability to fight and administer. No pride is without fault, but

pride of class may be thought of as today we think of pride of profession, toward which we are likely to be lenient.

Snobbery is pride in status without pride in function. And it is an uneasy pride of status. It always asks, "Do I belong—do I really belong? And does he belong? And if I am observed talking to him, will it make me seem to belong or not to belong?" It is the peculiar vice not of aristocratic societies, which have their own appropriate vices, but of bourgeois democratic societies. For us the legendary strongholds of snobbery are the Hollywood studios, where two thousand dollars a week dare not talk to three hundred dollars a week for fear he be taken for nothing more than fifteen hundred dollars a week. The dominant emotions of snobbery are uneasiness, self-consciousness, self-defensiveness, the sense that one is not quite real but can in some way acquire reality.—Lionel Trilling, *The Liberal Imagination*

5.   The Uses of Definition

When we first start thinking about language, we usually feel that the meaning we ascribe to a word is its "real" meaning, that this real meaning is obvious, and that to tamper with it is both frivolous and futile. As we gather experience, we sometimes go to the opposite extreme. We conclude that words are "just words," that anyone can define any word in his own way, and that attempts to give a term a generally binding meaning are necessarily misdirected.

Neither view prepares us to meet the problems we encounter when trying to make ourselves understood. In practice, we have to know what ideas the reader is likely to connect with a given term and what ideas we ourselves want him to attach to it. Definition is our means of giving substance to terms that are in danger of remaining mere words. It is our means of making words carry the message that we intended.

The study and practice of definition helps a writer develop habits indispensable to the effective use of language. Your own experience with the process of definition should help you strengthen your writing in several basic ways:

(1) *Learn to "fill in" terms that are subject to interpretation.* When you label something "propaganda" or "rationalization," anticipate the inevitable question: "What *kind* of propaganda is this? And what is *wrong* with it?" Become aware of how effectively many published writers fill in even terms that allow considerably less leeway for interpretation (or misinterpretation):

... He studied Latin and Greek and became increasingly **ascetic,** *denying himself a bed, and eating frugally.* Abandoning formal theology, he decided to go among the poor as an **evangelist.** Living among Belgian miners, *he read to them from the Bible, taught and cared for their children, visited their sick.* —Robert Coles, book review in *New Republic*

(2) *Develop what one writer has called "the passion for the clear and necessary distinction."* Refuse to muddle an issue by settling for the *almost* appropriate word. Study, for instance, the way a judge must know how to draw the line between terms that shade over into each other:

Disobedience is a long step beyond dissent. In this country, at least in theory, no one denies the right of any person to differ with the government, or his right to express that difference in speech, in the press, by petition, or in an assembly. But civil disobedience, by definition, involves a deliberate and punishable breach of a legal duty. However much they differ in other respects, both passive and violent resisters intentionally violate the law. —Charles E. Wyzanski, "On Civil Disobedience," *Atlantic*

(3) *Use well-defined key terms to give focus to a program or argument.* A new idea, a political program, a set of attitudes often remains inarticulate and ineffectual until it crystallizes around one or more key terms. Here is how Paul Goodman defines a term that for many young people has become a rallying cry and a program for action:

What the American young do know, being themselves pushed around, itemized and processed, is that they *have a right to a say in what affects them.* They believe in democracy, which they have to call "participatory democracy," to distinguish it from double-talk democracy. . . . they want the *opportunity to be responsible, to initiate and decide,* instead of being mere personnel.

(4) *Define your standards of judgment.* Definition is indispensable when you try to move beyond "I happen to like this"; when you try to set up criteria of judgment that the reader can understand and respect. By merely calling a concert "enjoyable" you convey little to readers who do not know what kinds of things you enjoy. By merely calling a proposal "impractical" you do not convince readers who cannot judge how narrow or how imaginative your standards of practicality are. Observe that much writing about art and literature is devoted to setting up categories that serve as a guide to interpretation and evaluation. Much writing about comedy, for instance, tries to find a more intellectual basis for laughter than the pratfalls of the "pie-in-your-eye" school of comedians.

I believe the best rule-of-thumb-guide to comedy was suggested some years back, in a little book by Harold K. Munroe, entitled *The Argument of Laughter*. Mr. Munroe suggests that laughter is occasioned by the *juxtaposition of disparate worlds* and he offers a good deal of evidence to support such a thesis. Consider the cartoon, the simplest example of this juxtaposition of disparate worlds. Perhaps it's one with two men quietly drinking on an African verandah, with a gorilla, in the background, carrying away a struggling woman. The husband, in total indifference, is remarking, "personally, I don't know what he sees in her." Or maybe it's a row of British soldiers, each wearing dark glasses, marching up what has to be Bunker's Hill, with one of the defenders asking the commander of the Revolutionary Army: "When did you say to shoot?" Or it is two little children in a gloomy Charles Addams forest, looking over a hedge, at a dinky little cottage, which abides by food regulations having printed on its side—"contains oil of peppermint, sugar, glucose, etc."—G. S. McCaughey, "Shakespeare Today," *Humanities Association Bulletin*

The more serious your writing becomes, the more likely you are to be making judgments of value that need support by careful definition. Words like *good, wholesome, inspiring, ridiculous, challenging, practical,* and *absurd* mean little unless we know about the standards of the person who uses them. To give meaning to words like *truth, beauty,* and *goodness,* we have to explain what makes a statement truthful, a picture beautiful, and an action good.

The space a writer devotes to definition varies greatly for different subjects and different kinds of writing. At one extreme, an author, in one brief sentence, illuminates his interpretation of an important term. An example is the educator who defined *education* as "a lifelong discipline of the individual by himself." Another example is the philosopher who defined *individualism* as the conviction that "everyone should paddle his own canoe, especially on the high seas." At the other extreme, an author defines a term like *liberalism* by tracing its history, examining its associations, distinguishing it carefully from similar or related terms, and giving detailed illustrations of its use. Between the two extremes is the writer who, while infrequently using a formal definition, makes a constant effort to keep his key terms stable and meaningful.

Review Exercises

A. What are the problems of definition suggested by the following passages? How would you deal with the terms that cause difficulty?

1. Southern Democrats are not really true Democrats at heart. For years they have opposed programs advocated by Democrats representing the northern and western sections of the country.

2. The trouble with my high school teachers was that they used absolutely no psychology. They tried to argue recalcitrant students into changing their ways, instead of cracking down.

3. I believe people should have the right to speak as they wish, and criticize the government if they have a legitimate reason. But as for letting the communists or groups like them speak out against the government, I say no. As soon as they advocate the beliefs of communism, they are no longer Americans, and are not entitled to the rights of Americans. Any American should have the right of freedom of speech, but a communist is no longer an American and is therefore not entitled to that right.

4. The college administration has definitely taken its stand on the side of reaction and against the forces of progress. It has been an outstanding characteristic of progressive American society that it has made available a college education to ever increasing numbers of students. Nevertheless, the administration has decided to reduce the number of freshmen to be enrolled next year by raising admission standards.

5. At its last meeting the local school board decided that an "enriched" and accelerated program would be set up for children who show exceptional aptitude for academic work. The community should reject this program as undemocratic.

6. One kind of inflation is caused by the law of supply and demand. Prices go higher in a time of shortage because demand exceeds supply. The other kind of inflation is caused when people are paid higher wages without producing more. To distinguish between these two kinds of inflation is to distinguish between a natural law and a man-made condition.

7. Theft means taking things that belong to others. The businessman who inflates prices for the sake of excessive profits takes what belongs to me as surely as the thief who picks my pockets.

8. I was surprised to see that a prominent teachers' organization opposed a bill requiring the removal of obscene publications from school libraries. The organization claimed that the bill could be used against books of educational and cultural value. Since when have obscene books contributed to the culture of a nation? There is more than one way of sabotaging a nation, and placing undesirable literature in school libraries is one of them.

9. Many people do not recognize that all our freedoms are based on individual property rights. Freedom of speech is based on the individual's private property right to his voice and the use of his voice in his own

defense. Freedom of the press is based on the newspaper owner's private property right to control his own newspaper. Freedom to keep and bear arms is based on the individual's private property right to defend his property from outside encroachments when all other methods fail. And freedom of religion is dependent on the private right of a church to conduct whatever ceremonies or acts it pleases on its own property.

10. Insanity means a serious derangement of the mental faculties. Anyone who is deranged enough to commit murder must be considered at least temporarily insane.

B. Study the following extended definition of *courage*. Describe in detail the technique employed by the author. Point out features that add to or detract from the effectiveness of this student-written paper.

COURAGE

The word *courage* has the power greatly to stimulate the imagination. All one has to do is to see the word in print or hear it spoken to be prepared for an account of stirring deeds of bravery and selfless sacrifice. Because of this immediate appeal to the emotions, we often pay little attention to causes that effect courage in a person or in animals. I believe that human courage and animal courage are completely different, both in nature and origin.

First I would like to consider courage in man and offer some ideas about what human courage is and why it manifests itself in man. Imagine that you are witnessing a hunter stalking a wounded lion in dense brush. It undoubtedly takes great courage to hunt lions, and even more so under the conditions I have described. Let it be presupposed that the hunter is fully aware of the possible consequences of hunting lions and, further, that the hunter is one of that vast group of people who show a marked antipathy toward being eaten by a lion. Why is he there at all, especially if he realizes that lion-hunting is not conducive to longevity? If the hunter is responsible for the lion's being wounded in the first place, it is possible that he is acting to conform to a hunter's code that forbids leaving a wounded animal to suffer. However, in addition to the influence of the hunter's code there is a strong chance that other pressures are holding the hunter on the trail of the lion.

If the hunter were to lose his nerve and break off the hunt, he would have to face up to the fact that he had lost his nerve. Even with the anesthetic of rationalization this would be a painful blow to his ego. In addition to self-esteem, there are the love of excitement and the desire for the acclamation that is accorded someone who has killed such a formidable beast as a lion. Add to these the awareness that his friends would censure him should he show fear in the face of danger and you can see that the hunter is more or less pushed along by these combined pressures.

Let us turn to the lion who lies a few yards deeper in the brush licking his wounds and waiting for the hunter to get just a little closer. Since the instant the lion was slammed to earth by the impact of the hunter's bullet, he has been bathed in agony, and this agony has fanned his instinctive spark of hatred for man into a blazing inferno. Why does the lion wait for the hunter when he could run and avoid the possibility of another wound or perhaps death? It is clear that the lion does not have the same reasons for being there that the man has. The reason for the lion's ambush is his instinctive hatred for man and his instinctive fear that if he doesn't kill the man, the man will kill him. Whatever "courage" the lion has is strictly the result of instinct.

While the word *courage* might be used to describe the actions of both hunter and lion, the motives behind their actions are quite different. The basic difference between animal courage and human courage is that animal courage is purely of instinctive origin, while courage in man is a result of many factors that lie mostly outside of himself. These factors consist of the attitudes of his friends, the ideals he pursues and the codes he conforms to, and his particular desires or appetites. All these combine to produce the attribute we call courage.

Theme Topics 5

1. Trace the major stages in the history of one of the following words: *gentleman, chivalry, wit, humor, romance*. If you can, draw both on a historical dictionary and your own reading of earlier literature.

2. Explain your idea of a lady, a snob, a cynic, or an opportunist. Present a formal definition as your thesis early in the paper. Support it with authentic examples from your own experience and reading.

3. Write an extended definition of one of the following terms: *tact, respectability, bigotry, prejudice, sarcasm, sentimentality, militarism*. Try to identify a key element and sum it up early in your paper. Support it with authentic examples from your own experience and reading.

4. Write an extended definition of one of the following: *fair play, tolerance, liberalism, social justice*. Start by examining actual uses of the term and try to find a common denominator.

5. Can you draw a clear line between the terms in one of the following pairs? Help your reader to distinguish reliably between the "amateur" and the "professional" athlete, between "highbrow" and "lowbrow" art, or between "classical" and "pop" music.

6. Write a paper helping your reader distinguish between two terms that are hard to keep apart. For instance, when does self-interest become selfishness? When does patriotism become chauvinism? When does liberty become license? When does autocratic rule become tyranny?

7. Write a paper presenting your definition of a term that in your opinion is often used too loosely or superficially. For instance, how would you define true individualism, true charity, a truly religious person?

8. Writing about the University of California at Berkeley, the former editor of a campus newspaper referred to its "diffuse and splintered student radicalism." Does student radicalism seem "diffuse and splintered" where *you* have a chance to observe it? Or can you find a common denominator for student radicalism on your own campus? Draw on sources such as student publications (official and otherwise), speeches, discussions, personal interviews.

9. Writing about Henry Luce, the founder of *Time* magazine, a recent critic said that "through the agency of his magazine, he . . . contributed more to the Gross National Product than to American culture." Study several recent issues of *Time*. What idea of "American culture" is implied or illustrated by *Time*'s treatment of cultural topics?

10. Choose a term often heard today when young people define their goals or ideals. For instance, choose a term like *commitment* or *relevance*. Explain the term in as concrete terms as possible for a reader over thirty.

That is what I call living by ideas: when one side of a question has long had your earnest support, when all your feelings are engaged, when you hear all round you no language but one, when your party talks this language like a steam-engine and can imagine no other,—still to be able to think, still to be irresistibly carried, if so it be, by the current of thought to the opposite side of the question, and, like Balaam, to be unable to speak anything but what the Lord has put in your mouth.
Matthew Arnold

CHAPTER SIX

Logic

1. Writing and Thinking

2. Generalizing Soundly and Effectively
   Kinds of Induction
   Hasty Generalization
   Generalization and Example
   Levels of Generalization

3. The Uses and Abuses of Deduction
   From Induction to Deduction
   Valid Deductions
   Faulty Premises
   Hidden Premises
   Equivocation
   Misleading Statistics
   Circular Arguments

4. Guarding Against Pseudo-Logic
   Oversimplification
   Post Hoc Fallacy
   False Dilemma
   Arguments from Analogy
   Foregone Conclusions
   Rationalization
   Thinking Straight

5. Constructing an Argument
   The Inductive Approach
   The Method of Dialectic
   The Argumentative Drive

Sample Themes
Theme Topics 6

1. Writing and Thinking

One of the most basic questions we ask of a writer is "How does this follow? How did you get from *A* to *B*?" Sometimes we do not see the connection at all, and may at best come to regard the writer as a gadfly, better at raising questions than at answering them. Sometimes we can see where we are asked to go, but the leaps we are asked to take are too big, or the turns too obviously in the wrong direction. Sometimes, finally, we encounter the writer who makes us say: "Yes, I see why this is so. I cannot help accepting your conclusion. I can see that *A* and *B* are both true, and that *C* logically follows, as you say."

Such a writer carries us along as he takes an argument through the necessary steps to a valid conclusion. He makes us feel that we are guided from point to point by logic rather than by mere precedent, prejudice, or whim.

For any serious kind of writing, much of the running commentary in the reader's mind deals in one way or another with questions of logic:

Most women who work would rather stay home raising a family.
("How do you know? Has anyone recently polled these women? Are you generalizing from two or three examples?")

Women are kept out of professional and executive jobs by male prejudice.
("Is that the *only* reason?")

Men who do not wish to fight should not be drafted.
("*Why*? What premises would I have to accept so that this conclusion would follow?")

The right of private citizens to own guns is guaranteed by the Second Amendment to the U.S. Constitution.
("What exactly does it say? Does everyone agree with your interpretation?")

In turn, a strong motive in much serious writing is the need to *challenge* someone else's logic, to correct the faults in his thinking:

The language of the Second Amendment is crystal clear: "A well regulated militia being necessary to the security of a free State, the right of the people to keep and bear arms shall not be infringed." This language has nothing, but nothing, to do with guns for sport, or guns for target practice, or mail order guns, or guns for private collections. It protects the right to bear arms for members of individual State *militias* only. . . .

It is easy to see why so much of the talk of business investments in the ghettos is a sham: The return on investing in improvements—say in decaying downtown property—cannot compete with the capital gains to be realized in land speculation or with the profits in "growth" industries. Relying on the private sector to cure our social problems has not worked in the past and is not likely to work in the future. . . .

How much attention you pay to logic in your own writing is a measure of your respect for your reader. Though the educated reader is not immune to short-cut logic and panic thinking, he will basically expect you to respect his judgment. He will be suspicious of the kind of argument that in a series of crudely simplified steps blames the problems of a nation on the Yankees or the Jews, poverty on the rapaciousness of a clique, war on foreign devils.

At the same time, sound logic is not something we cultivate merely to escape the censure of the critical reader. Straight thinking helps us deal with our own confusions and perplexities. It helps us order our impressions, test our tentative conclusions, clarify our convictions. The ability to marshal ideas in a theme cannot be separated from the ability to think through a problem in orderly and systematic fashion.

2. Generalizing Soundly and Effectively

Occasionally someone will call a statement a "mere generalization." To discredit the statement, the charge that it is a generalization is scarcely enough. "Paint fumes are toxic" is a generalization. It merits consideration nevertheless. No one can go about his daily affairs without relying on generalizations of all kinds. What concerns you as a writer is that some generalizations are more reliable than others. If you want a generalization to survive in the rough-and-tumble of critical discussion, you have to show that it is both genuine and sound. It has to be a general conclusion actually derived from the information available, and carefully formulated to do justice to the evidence.

To generalize means to extract the common element from a number of different situations. A group of educators studying high school curricula may find that the senior class in the first high school they visit is, among other activities, reading *Macbeth.* In the next school, a senior honors section is scheduled to read *Macbeth* later in the year. In the third or fourth school visited, the senior class is studying *Hamlet.* If this pattern persists, the educators' final report will generalize that high school seniors in the area visited usually study a Shakespeare play, often *Macbeth.*

This process of drawing general conclusions from individual observations is known as **induction,** or inductive reasoning. Without inductive reasoning, each observation would remain a mere isolated fact. Induction pulls different observations together; it makes data add up.

Kinds of Induction

Reasoning that aims at finding a common element has many applications. Here are three of the most common:

(1) Induction makes us find the *common pattern linking individual instances*. It makes us conclude that the "hot pursuit" of juvenile offenders by police cars is a grave danger to life and property. The same kind of induction is at work when we correlate data: We read that 18 per cent of our skilled workers are women, 15 per cent of our executives, 12 per cent of our technicians, 7 per cent of our doctors, 3 percent of our lawyers. We conclude that women have only a small share of highly skilled and responsible work.

We constantly find the results of this kind of induction in serious writing:

The very best of the American young are rejecting, as Keynes did forty years ago, the "money-making morbidity." In 1964, the *Wall Street Journal* reported that 14 per cent of Harvard's senior class entered business, as contrasted with 39 per cent in 1960. In 1966 the Harris Poll surveyed college seniors for *Newsweek* and found that this trend was deepening. Only 12 per cent of the sample were looking forward to business careers — and twice as many wanted to be teachers. Harris further reported that the acceptance of business as an institution in American society declined as education increased. — Michael Harrington, "Taking the Great Society Seriously," *Harper's*

(2) Induction makes us classify superficially different things as *members of the same category*. A whale may look and act like a huge fish, but the zoologist can list many *shared features* that make us classify it with other mammals. The more such points of contact there are, the more convincing the classification. The followers of Darwin in the nineteenth century used this kind of induction to show that man and the apes belonged to the same zoological order. The astronomers of the sixteenth century used it to challenge the medieval view of the heavenly bodies as perfect, and different in kind from our imperfect earth:

Galileo, beginning with the moon, proved its similarity in every particular to the earth; its convex figure, its natural darkness when not illuminated, its density, its distinction into solid and liquid, the variations of its phases, the mutual illuminations of the earth and moon, their mutual eclipses, the inequalities of the lunar surface, etc. After many instances of this kind, with regard to all the planets, men plainly saw that these bodies became proper objects of experience; and that the similarity of their nature enabled us to extend the same arguments and phenomena from one to the other. — David Hume, *Dialogues Concerning Natural Religion*

(3) Induction makes us construct a *hypothesis to account for a set of phenomena*. When we try to explain a puzzling state of affairs, we often model our reasoning on the following example:

The house across the street has shown no signs of life in some days;
Some rolled-up, rain-soaked newspapers lie on the front steps;
The grass needs cutting badly;
Salesmen who ring the doorbell get no answer; . . .
    Therefore:
    The people across the street are away on a trip. — Monroe C. Beardsley, *Thinking Straight*

Each of the original observations here is interpreted as an instance of a generalization of the type "Some houses show no life because the owner is away"; "Some lawns remain uncut because the owner is away"; and so on. Since a number of generalizations of this kind intersect, we assume that their common element provides the clue to the present instance. How reliable a hypothesis is depends on our caution and skill in correlating relevant observations, and on our determination not to ignore clues that point in unexpected directions.

In much ordinary thinking, the "inductive leap" merely takes us from familiar observations to the obvious conclusion. But the power and the risks of inductive reasoning derive from its ability to take us *beyond* ordinary experience. Cautiously employed, induction takes us far beyond what meets the eye. Allowed to go astray, induction makes us believe firmly in things that aren't so.

Hasty Generalization

The basic logical weakness of much student writing is the excessive scope of many of its generalizations. Our minds tend to be far ahead of the evidence actually collected. We talk to Professor Smith and find that he is a Democrat. We talk to Professor Brown and find that he is a Democrat. We talk to Professor Miller and find that he is a Democrat. By now, we may have reached a sweeping general conclusion: "All professors are Democrats." It costs us an effort to revise our conclusion to read: "Some (three, to be exact) of the college professors I know are Democrats." As more and more information accumulates, we can replace the *some* with *many* or even with *a great many*. Only on the basis of comprehensive statistical information can we claim that the "majority of them" or "most of them" are Democrats. Only rarely are we entitled to a generalization containing words like *all, nobody, everything,* or *nothing.*

Hasty generalizations like the following will undermine the

reader's confidence in a writer's ability to draw conclusions justified by his evidence:

Every week we read newspaper reports of some college hiring a professor who holds Marxist views. We are turning our colleges into centers of indoctrination in the Marxist view of economics and history.

Every young Negro I have talked to has rejected the materialistic ideals of middle-class America. Negroes today no longer aspire to becoming black counterparts of the organization men of white suburbia.

Writers like Carl Sandburg and e. e. cummings rejected traditional meter and rhyme. The modern poet rejects traditional poetic form.

A writer must learn to respect the resistance that things and people offer to easy generalization. No one wants to be a "typical" freshman, a typical Republican, a typical Jew. Whenever we use a phrase like "a typical Catholic," we have to remember that St. Francis is not Torquemada. When we use a phrase like "Renaissance man," we have to remember that Henry VIII is not Shakespeare. Make it a habit to *look for sweeping generalizations in need of scaling down:*

Sweeping: Armenians are an exceptionally gifted people.

Cautious: A number of Armenians have done exceptional work in music and art.

Sweeping: Americans are the most generous people on earth.

Cautious: Over the years, Americans have given impressive support to private charity and to such government programs as foreign aid.

Even when generalizing on a fairly large scale, an effective writer can gain the confidence of his readers by *careful wording.* Notice how the author of the following passage presents his generalizations as tentative first impressions, how he explains terms that might prove misleading or offensive:

American women are particularly conspicuous to the European observer. *They strike him first* as being *generally* better groomed and better dressed than their European sisters, *even if* they rarely show individual and critical taste. *Then they strike him* as being more sure of themselves than are the women of any other nation, even those of Northern Europe. *There seems to be* little hesitation and shyness, even in a very young American girl. American women, to the European, *may even seem* "tough," *not in the sense that* they are vulgar in any way, *but in the sense that* they are both resilient and forthright. These are qualities which the European is accustomed to find only among men. —Gunnar D. Kumlien, "America: Image and Reality," *Commonweal*

Generalization and Example

Support your generalizations with representative examples. The way to make generalizations meaningful is to anchor them firmly to the first-hand experience from which they are derived. Make it a habit to provide at least some concrete detail with every general statement you make. Even one example or illustration is better than none: "My father is a mechanical wizard; only last night, for instance, he repaired the wiring in our electric toaster." "History 21 is a difficult course; two of my friends failed it last year." But obviously one occurrence does not set a trend; one example does not prove a point. Ideally, you should back up a generalization with enough examples and illustrations to make your reader feel that you have presented a fair sampling of the evidence. Notice how the author of the following passage provides a solid array of examples to substantiate his original generalization:

> *Americans* are a sententious people and *are taught at an early age to moralize.* They learn it in Sunday school. They learn it from Poor Richard — at least they did so in my time. In Chicago during the twenties we were filled up with Poor Richard: "Little strokes fell great oaks." "Plough deep while sluggards sleep." These formulas seemed true and sound. Longfellow, whom we had to memorize by the yard, was also strongly affirmative: "Life is real! Life is earnest! And the grave is not its goal." And finally there was "The Chambered Nautilus": "Build thee more stately mansions, O my soul." — Saul Bellow, "The Writer as Moralist," *Atlantic*

In your presentation of examples, try to avoid two common weaknesses:

(1) *Avoid the example that is striking but atypical.* It is tempting to document the American need for "constant expensive amusement" by citing slot machines installed in its toilet booths by a gambling casino in Nevada. But obviously many readers will feel: "You are not talking about *me*." There must be a better example than a reference to a place that caters to the *unusual*, that promises Americans what they do *not* typically get at home.

(2) *Avoid the sample that is too narrow or too weighted to be representative.* You cannot reach a general conclusion about the attitude of college professors toward their students by observing a Latin professor about to retire, a part-time Greek instructor, and a graduate student who plans to teach Hebrew. At the least, you will have to branch out into other specialties: science, engineering, English. Ideally, you would sample teachers of many different opinions and backgrounds: young men and old men, teachers at large universities and small colleges, conservatives and radicals. A small sample, care-

fully chosen to cover different possibilities, can be more representative than a large sample favoring one type of person.

Levels of Generalization

Many student papers move on such a high level of abstraction that the writer has trouble getting down to earth. He says, "My father is a wonderful man" when he means "He let me use our new car over the weekend." He says, "Farm income is deteriorating" when he means "My uncle has been complaining about the price of hogs."

Once you adopt the habit of translating the general into the specific, it is likely to bring about a general downgrading of your generalizations. When there is an obvious gap between the general and the specific, a concrete example may not support the generalization but rather deflate it. Notice how the original generalization in the following example becomes more obviously untenable the closer the writer comes to first-hand observation:

Very General:	The younger generation has no morals.
Less General:	Students are careless in their conduct.
Less General:	College students present a casual appearance.
Less General:	Freshman girls dress casually.
Specific:	Betty wore shorts to class.

The various levels of generalization form a pyramid. There are countless concrete, factual observations at the bottom ("My feet are blistered"). There are a limited number of sweeping general pronouncements at the top ("Man is born to suffer"). At the bottom of the pyramid, Betty, like millions of her kind, goes about her daily business. Seen from a more elevated point of view, she loses her individual identity and fits into the general category of "girl." Soon she joins her brothers and boy friends to appear under the more inclusive heading of "mankind" or "humanity." As the categories become fewer and more comprehensive, she is included under "organism." At the very top of the pyramid, there is still a trace of her in an all-embracing term like "life" or "creation."

Some writers are most at home on the ground level, talking about individual human beings. Others are most at home in the clouds, generalizing about life and existence. The most instructive kind of writing occupies the space between, presenting generalizations large enough to be of general interest and yet limited enough to be firmly tied to individual instances.

Exercises

A. What kind of evidence would you need to support the following generalizations? Point out generalizations that are difficult or impossible to support. Suggest how you would scale down generalizations that are too sweeping.

1. Women are poorer drivers than men.

2. For the current generation of students, the importance of athletics is rapidly becoming null.

3. Teen-agers smoke to prove that they are grown up and mature.

4. The quality of motion pictures put out by Hollywood producers has improved over the last five years.

5. The crime rate among Americans of Oriental descent is lower than among the rest of the population.

6. Businessmen tend to support the Republican party.

7. Grade schools used to be more effective in teaching reading.

8. College teachers are more impersonal than high school teachers.

9. Young people today consider World War II as merely another meaningless war, to be blamed not on Hitler and Hirohito but on the older generation.

10. Americans form new friendships more easily than Europeans.

11. The American Negro is worse off than he was ten years ago.

12. European girls make better housewives than American girls.

13. Television breeds in children an inclination toward violence.

14. Capital punishment does not·have a deterrent effect on crime.

15. Students rebelling against adult authority are a small vocal minority.

B. Examine the use of generalizations in the following passages. On what level of generalization does the author move? Which of his generalizations would you *challenge*, and on what grounds? Which of his generalizations could you *buttress* with evidence of your own?

1. It seems our mad quest for material objects is a national characteristic. We constantly desire more than we know rationally we need. But instead of curbing our desires, as mature persons seemingly should, we let our desires command us. We allow ourselves to fall into the most outrageous financial arrangements in order to finance all the material goods we feel are essential for the "good life." Of course these goods

usually supply no real satisfaction and, paradoxically, their attainment seems usually to be followed by an even greater desire for more possessions — a kind of fever.

We seem as a result to be an unsatisfied, uneasy people, living in a society which has a crazy, frenetic quality. A drive down a freeway at night is all one needs to confirm this. The sight of thousands of human beings hurtling through the night, each sealed in a steel capsule, cannot but instill in the observer the feeling of aimless urgency which seems to characterize our society. It is as if there is a basic need to stay in constant motion, to be always *active* (a favorite word in advertising). It is as if we know instinctively that if the cars were ever to stop, or the televisions to be silenced, or the insane longing after material goods to abate, our society would deflate like a punctured tire, so unsubstantial are the institutions upon which it rests.

2. We can do something about that all too prevalent attitude that intellectual honesty requires emphasis upon our national mistakes and downgrading our attributes. There are those who feel that promoting instinctive patriotism is intellectually dishonest. They contend that if Democracy is good, it should survive the injection of doubt. This may be true for those who possess mature judgment. Certainly any American has the right to question our system and the obligation to seek its improvement. But to think that a student, for example, has such judgment at the start of the learning process is to ignore psychological reality. A young mind must first be taught to believe in something before it can intelligently doubt. To stifle unquestioned pride in our heritage and love of our flag is to deprive this, the greatest of all nations, of men and women who will understand and urgently rededicate themselves to the ideals of Democracy.

3. Most activists — and with them many of the apathetic and excluded — are alienated because they feel that our society and its institutions prevent people from determining their own destinies; that society robs people of their individuality and leaves them depersonalized and alone. As students they see a bureaucratic educational system whose teachers are remote and uninterested in them; whose administrators never listen seriously to their views on issues (housing, academic problems, regulations, student activities) which vitally affect them; and in whose classrooms they are expected not to participate but merely to listen. As potential employees they see vast corporations and unions which cynically manipulate and depersonalize people rather than liberate them and provide interesting and challenging work. Such a society, many activists believe, cannot possibly fulfill the hopes and talents of the individual.

3.   The Uses and Abuses of Deduction

Plato, in his Dialogues, frequently shows Socrates engaged in the following kind of argument with his disciples (who are often no match for their master). "Don't you think, Adeimantus, that such and such is true?" "Yes, Socrates." "And would you not further agree that such and such is also true?" "Of course, Socrates." "And does it not therefore follow that such and such a conclusion is fully justified?" "Yes, Socrates — if you say so."

The strength of this kind of argument is that it establishes a climate of assent. Once a reader has found himself agreeing with two or three initial points, he is predisposed to keep on saying "yes" as the writer spells out their full implications. Both as a writer and reader, you will have to be alert enough to say "no" when an argument moves from sound assumptions to dubious conclusions. Not every triumphant "therefore" is justified.

From Induction to Deduction

Deduction helps us put to work what we already know. The generalizations and hypotheses produced by inductive reasoning tell us how to react and what to expect. In the absence of reliable induction, life becomes a matter of constant experiment. Without established guidelines on what mushrooms are edible, our cooking will have to proceed by trial and error — possibly with fatal results. Without general ideas about what animals make good transportation, we have to test the suitability of each individual horse and donkey. Once induction has furnished us with generalizations about mushrooms and animals, we simply establish what category each specimen belongs in. Our reasoning proceeds somewhat as follows:

> All the horses that I have observed were suitable for riding.
> This animal seems to be a horse.
> Therefore, this animal should be suitable for riding.

In contrast to the generalizing, inductive kind of reasoning, the process of applying general knowledge to specific instances is called deductive reasoning, or **deduction**. Induction and deduction are two sides of the same coin. Once you have established inductively that students who cut classes do poorly on examinations, you can apply this knowledge to your own case and predict that you will do poorly on tests unless you attend class. Accurate deduction makes generalizations pay off; it helps you to convert your general knowledge into solutions to specific problems.

When fully and explicitly stated, a deductive argument, moving from two initial assumptions to a conclusion, is called a **syllogism**. The statements representing what we already know or assume are called **premises**. *Syllogistic reasoning deduces conclusions that are implied in, or follow from, accepted premises.* The common term ("horse") that accounts for the partial overlapping of the two premises and thus makes a conclusion possible is called the **middle term**. Here are some formal syllogisms, with the middle terms italicized:

First Premise: All *members of the Pegasus Club* are English majors.
Second Premise: Claire Benton is a *member of the Pegasus Club.*
Conclusion: Claire Benton is an English major.

First Premise: No *round-headed Irishmen* are eligible to join the Phi Beta Gamma
                    Fraternity.
Second Premise: I am a *round-headed Irishman.*
Conclusion: I am not eligible to join the Phi Beta Gamma Fraternity.

First Premise: Only *seniors* can be elected to the student court.
Second Premise: Gerald is not a *senior.*
Conclusion: Gerald cannot be elected to the student court.

Valid Deductions

In applying a generalization to specific instances, pay special attention to its scope. There is an implied difference in scope between "*All* pacifists read Gandhi" and "*Only* pacifists read Gandhi." Only the second version clearly *limits* the ranks of Gandhi's readers: If someone reads Gandhi, he *must* be a pacifist. The first version does not make such an exclusive claim. It does not rule out the possibility that many people who are not pacifists *also* read Gandhi. "All pro-Peking communists read the thoughts of Chairman Mao" does not mean that every reader of Chairman Mao's thoughts is a communist, let alone pro-Peking.

We call a deduction **valid** if it draws only those conclusions that are actually implied in the premises. To draw valid conclusions, we must remember that a generalization may apply to some members of a group but not all, to all members of a group and no one else, or to all members of a group and possibly members of other groups. *Assuming the premises to be true*, the following arguments would result in the following justified conclusions:

First Premise: Some redheads are passionate.
Second Premise: Horace is a redhead.
Conclusion: Horace *may or may not be* passionate.
                    (The greater the percentage of passionate people among redheads,
                    the stronger the likelihood that Horace is passionate.)

First Premise:	All redheads are passionate.
Second Premise:	Horace is a redhead.
Conclusion:	Horace is passionate.
	(A quality ascribed to *all* members of a group applies to each individual member.)

First Premise:	All redheads are passionate.
Second Premise:	Horace is passionate.
Conclusion:	Horace *may or may not be* a redhead.
	(Horace shares *one* quality with all members of the group "redheads," but that does not make him a member of the group.)

First Premise:	Only redheads are passionate.
Second Premise:	Horace is passionate.
Conclusion:	Horace is a redhead.
	(Horace has a quality possessed *only* by redheads; it therefore identifies him as a member of the group.)

First Premise:	No redheads are passionate.
Second Premise:	Horace is a redhead.
Conclusion:	Horace is not passionate.
	(A quality *ruled out* for all members of a group is necessarily ruled out for each individual member.)

First Premise:	No redheads are passionate.
Second Premise:	Horace is not a redhead.
Conclusion:	Horace *may or may not be* passionate.
	(When both premises are negative, neither an affirmative nor a negative conclusion can be drawn.)

Logicians sort out arguments such as these into two types. The first is the true syllogism, in which a definite conclusion *necessarily* follows from the premises. If the premises are true, and the logical operations valid, the conclusion is necessarily true. The second type leads to a merely *probable* conclusion; it allows a degree of more or less reliable prediction. In your writing, you will seldom present generalizations that start with "all" or "no" and thus can function as the first premise in a true syllogism. More typically, you will present the conclusions you can reasonably draw from generalizations neither all-inclusive nor all-exclusive.

Faulty Premises

Examine the premises on which you base your arguments. Any argument based on previous knowledge can be no more accurate than that previous knowledge itself. If it starts from unreliable assumptions, the argument itself may be technically valid and yet the results untrue. In other words, even when the logical machinery is operating correctly, it cannot produce true results from misleading information.

When you present an argument like the following, your reader may challenge one of your premises rather than your conclusion:

> Students learn best in a relaxed, permissive atmosphere.
> The present system of exams induces tensions and anxieties.
> Therefore, exams work against true learning.
> (But is it *true* that a relaxed atmosphere is best for learning? Do not at least some people perform better under pressure?)

When your readers find one of your arguments unconvincing, the flaw may be not in the way you have conducted the argument but in what you have taken for granted. Critical readers will not accept without question such premises as "Football promotes unselfishness," "High taxes cause inflation," or "The voters can be trusted to detect insincerity." Before you make such statements the basis of a deductive argument, you should carefully examine, qualify, and support them.

Hidden Premises

Be prepared to bring hidden assumptions into the open. The assumptions on which an argument rests are not always stated. Such unstated premises become a handicap when the writer himself does not realize what his assumptions are, and when the hidden assumptions would not stand up to scrutiny once they are brought into the open.

An argument based on hidden premises frustrates the reader. He may feel that something is wrong, even though he cannot put his finger on what it is. To find his bearings, he might outline the argument something like this:

Premise:	Jones is a fascist.
Conclusion:	Don't listen to him.
(Hidden Premise:	Fascists are not worth listening to.)

Premise:	That camera was made in Japan.
Conclusion:	I won't buy it.
(Hidden Premise:	Cameras made in Japan are not good buys.)

Premise:	Professor Metcalf is from a middle-class background.
Conclusion:	He cannot be expected to sympathize with the poor.
(Hidden Premise:	People always take over the attitudes of their parents.)

The less likely the reader is to agree with you, the more necessary will it be for you to bring your hidden premises into the open. On many controversial topics, discussion is futile until the participants succeed in identifying some of their basic assumptions.

Equivocation

Keep your key terms from shifting in meaning during the course of an argument. An intentional shift in the meaning of key terms in order to deceive or mislead is known as **equivocation**. A political speaker may be equivocating when using a versatile word like *radical*. As he argues for censorship of radical views expressed in an economics textbook, the word *radical* may at first seem to mean "a person who wants to destroy our political and economic system." But as the argument moves closer to specifics, we may find that the word *radical* really points to "a person who advocates a revision of collective bargaining laws." In an argument over improved provisions for social security, *weak and helpless* may at first seem to point to "sick and disabled." But it may later turn out to include "able-bodied but temporarily out of work." By careful definition of key terms at the beginning, you can assure your reader that you do not intend to equivocate later.

Misleading Statistics

When you base logical arguments on statistical figures, make sure you understand the information they provide. Of the various generalizations whose bearing you may misinterpret, the most deceptive ones are those given to you in the form of statistical data. Statistical figures have something solid about them and are a powerful tool of persuasion. However, unless you interpret them cautiously, they may lead you to make claims they do not justify.

Suppose a set of statistics indicates that the average income of the twenty families living in Blueberry Park is $10,000 — a figure that is said to represent an increase of 100 per cent during the last two decades. If you read them hastily, these figures might conjure up a picture of twenty well-to-do families. The figures themselves, however, do not exclude the possibility that nineteen of the twenty families earn $2,000 a year and live in shacks, while the twentieth family earns $162,000 and lives in a mansion on the hill. In that case, it would be no contradiction to say that the average income is $10,000 but that the average family makes only $2,000. *Average*, in other words, does not always mean "typical." The reported increase offers similar problems of interpretation. It may be an increase in dollar earnings, which could be largely nullified by a corresponding increase in the cost of living. It could be an increase in actual purchasing power as determined by the cost of basic commodities.

Skeptical readers will not be impressed by what you deduce from statistics unless you show that you understand the assumptions and procedures of the statistician. When you wish to quote the data provided by an intelligence test, try to find out what kinds of intelligence the test measures and what measurements it applies. If the results of the test are described in terms of norms, medians, and percentiles, make sure that you understand the technical terms before you start quoting any of the figures.

Circular Arguments

Many would-be arguments merely reiterate initial assumptions. Some arguments, though they have the appearance of moving from premises toward a conclusion, in fact merely tread water. Consider the following example:

> True ability will always assert itself.
> A man of true ability sees to it that his talents are recognized.
> Therefore, true ability will not want for recognition.

The supposed conclusion, except for differences in wording, is identical with the initial premise. We gather at the very beginning that the speaker is not going to label as "true ability" the abilities of a man who cannot gain recognition for his talents. What accounts for this position we are not told. The supposed argument makes no contribution toward showing that such a way of labeling ability is helpful or reasonable. It moves in a circle; it leaves us exactly where we started.

Exercises

A. Examine the arguments presented or implied in the following. Spell out hidden assumptions. How sound are the *premises* on which the argument rests? How valid is the *logic* by which it proceeds?

1. There are certain four-letter or Anglo-Saxon words which we could not accept in a campus magazine. Our standards, as a university, are naturally high. This is our main restriction: No four-letter words.

2. A white man is better than Africans because he is a member of a superior race.

3. All members of the imperial bodyguard had to be at least six feet

tall. Kim's grandfather was a member of the guard. He must have been very tall.

4. All members of the imperial bodyguard had to be at least six feet tall. Kim's grandfather was rejected when he tried to join the guard. He must have been too short.

5. A law is passed by the majority of the people before it becomes a law; therefore, everyone should obey the laws.

6. Public colleges are financed through taxes. They therefore should provide the kind of education that taxpayers want them to provide.

7. After two world wars, every American realizes what General Sherman meant when he said, "War is hell." I firmly believe that nobody in America desires a war. Therefore, the oil companies that are promoting a price war by selling gasoline at cut-rate prices are going against the desires of the American people.

8. For many years, the destiny of our nation has been guided by men whose views of the world were shaped in the thirties and forties. It is high time for a change to new blood and fresh ideas.

9. When I went to see Professor Smith, he had a copy of the *Daily Worker* on his desk. He must be a communist.

10. The X Company produces a battery additive. The additive has enjoyed a steady sale for many years. Therefore, the battery additive must be effective.

B. Study the use of logic in the following passages. Where necessary, spell out the assumptions on which the argument rests. Which premises would you accept as sound; which would you challenge? Where would you challenge the logic by which an argument proceeds, and on what grounds?

1. Colleges should not set up facilities to accommodate political rallies or debates. For colleges are not intended to be institutions for the advancement of aspiring statesmen, but to prepare our young citizens for their place in society. I am not against voicing our opinions; in fact, I feel that we are extremely fortunate to be able to express our views openly. Nevertheless, there is no place for the luxury of such provisions on campus. The money needed to build a hall or a meeting place could be put to better use in the addition of new classrooms or laboratories. Furthermore, the majority of students on campus are not eligible to vote and would therefore be spending their time needlessly. A student should be studying while he is fresh—later or when he takes a break he may read about political events in the paper. When he graduates, his employer will look at his grade-point average, not at his views on a bygone political issue.

2. Compulsory military service interferes with my God-given right to live peacefully. I cannot live peacefully knowing that I am causing harm to another person. With Thoreau, I feel it is better to break the law than to be an agent of injustice to another. I do not believe in killing, yet the present draft laws would force me to kill. Thus, the government is partially destroying my right to be an individual. I agree that a state could not exist if all laws were disregarded. But if some laws are broken because the citizens think these laws to be wrong, these laws should be amended. Laws cannot be upheld if they are against the beliefs of the majority of the citizens.

3. Detention is implemented as a disciplinary measure to curtail offenses committed by chronic offenders. The chronic offender has little or no respect for the school and what the school attempts to do for him. Therefore, the discipline imposed by detention has little or no effect upon the chronic offender. Furthermore, the most effective punishment is direct punishment meted out nearest to the time an offense has been committed. Detention is delayed indirect punishment served at least a day or more after an offense has been committed. Therefore, detention is not effective.

4. You may recall the old adage to the effect: "There is no good war and no bad peace." But that is not always true. Jesus once declared a local war on the moneychangers who were desecrating the Temple in Jerusalem. He resorted to force! He uspet the tables of the money-changers. And he drove them out with a whip!

"But," you may protest, "wasn't that a violation of Christ's own advice to turn the other cheek?" No, it did not conflict with his "dove" policy concerning personal insults. Jesus Himself submitted to all sorts of indignities.

"Then did they spit in his face, and buffeted him; and others smote him with the palms of their hands." (Matthew 26:67)

Yet Jesus answered not a word nor did he make any attempt to strike back. For when Christ urged us to "turn the other cheek," he was referring to personal affronts. By contrast, threats to those basic freedoms which it has taken mankind thousands of years to acquire were not to be permitted without a fight!

C. State as fully as you can the hidden premises or unstated assumptions in a political speech, an editorial, or a letter to the editors of a newspaper or magazine.

4. Guarding Against Pseudo-Logic

Ambrose Bierce, in *The Devil's Dictionary*, defined logic as "the art of thinking and reasoning in strict accordance with the limitations and incapacities of the human misunderstanding." Traditionally, much study of logic has focused on common **fallacies**, errors recurring in the reasoning of people of widely different backgrounds and convictions. Many of these errors result when we allow preference to interfere with the requirements for straight thinking. We prefer the simple to the difficult; and we prefer what confirms our views to what contradicts them.

Oversimplification

Beware of ascribing complicated situations to a single cause. When we look for a solution to an urgent problem, we are naturally impatient with detailed explanations, with elaborate arguments pro and con. We readily turn to someone who can give us a simple and forceful answer. Often, the simple answer is not the right one. The simple answer cannot do justice to situations brought about by a variety of different causes. Perhaps there have been wars that were caused mainly by the monomania of one single person. But among the many other causes of war identified by historians are fear of the power of others, desire for national glory, land hunger, economic rivalry, injured pride, hatred of foreigners, desire to spread the true faith, imperialism, militarism, and the scorn of "womanish peace."

Whenever we discuss causes and effects, we must learn to ask: "Is that the *only* reason?" When we look at the sorry state of public transportation, and at the huge sums spent for expressways and interstate highways, we may well identify as one reason the economic interest of car makers and oil companies. They have a large stake in the matter, and they can and do influence public opinion and legislation. But we *oversimplify* if we ignore other factors. For instance, many people prefer to use their own cars, no matter what pleas are made by experts about the need for efficient public transport to alleviate congestion.

How would you react to a magazine article that begins as follows?

> Some time ago my wife and I spent a year traveling through Eastern Europe, the Middle East, and the Far East. . . . Wherever we found any large element of individual freedom, some beauty in the ordinary life of the ordinary man, some measure of real progress in the material comforts at his disposal, and a live hope of further progress in the future — there we also found that the private market was the main device being used to organize economic activity. — Milton Friedman, "Myths That Keep People Hungry," *Harper's*

A skeptical reader is likely to say: "How beautiful if it were true!" But a little voice in the back of his mind will keep saying: "Too *simple*. We cannot simply rely on the 'private market' to produce freedom, beauty, progress, and hope." The skeptical reader may then look for an expert prepared to recognize some of the "other factors." He would be reassured to find a writer who first of all recognizes that the poverty of backward nations "is the product of a plurality of causes":

> . . . Few poor countries are without a minority of exceedingly rich. And it is difficult to understand why an Andean or Middle Eastern peasant should seek to enhance his income by irrigation, improved seed, or acceptable livestock when he knows that anything in excess of subsistence will be appropriated by the landlord, tax collector, money-lender, or merchant. *Yet* the world has much poverty without evident exploiters. In India and Pakistan there are millions of small landowning peasants who are very poor but whose poverty cannot be related to the enrichment of any landlord, moneylender, tax collector, or other visible oppressor.
> . . . Low income allows of no saving. Without saving there is nothing to invest. Without investment there can be no economic advance, and so poverty is self-perpetuating. *Yet* in several countries of the Middle East, as also in South America—Venezuela is particularly a case in point—oil provides a rich source of revenue and capital is not scarce. But the vast majority of the people remain exceedingly poor.—John Kenneth Galbraith, "The Poverty of Nations," *Atlantic*

Such an ability to go from "on the one hand" to "on the other hand" does not prevent a writer from deciding which causes are most important or what remedial action is most urgently needed. A writer should be able to make up his mind and to present his conclusions vigorously and effectively. He should, however, make up his mind by weighing the possibilities, not by going straight for the one that is closest to the surface or dearest to his heart.

Post Hoc Fallacy

A second event following closely after another is not necessarily a result of the first. The kind of short-cut thinking that makes us look for a single, simple cause often makes us seize on some striking event immediately preceding the effect that we are trying to explain. The result is called the *post hoc* fallacy, from Latin *post hoc ergo propter hoc*—"*after* this, therefore *because* of this." We eat potato salad at a picnic and return home violently ill—cause and effect? Not necessarily—though very likely if others who ate the salad also fell ill, whereas several picnickers who did without are feeling fine.

A partygoer smokes marijuana and has a bad accident driving home—cause and effect? A girl is assaulted and later goes insane—cause and effect? The regents select a permissive university president, and some months later rioting erupts on the campus—cause and effect? A "yes" answer to such questions is hard to support unless the same cause can be shown to produce similar results in similar situations. In the absence of other evidence, the only logical course often is to suspend judgment. That Chinese foreign policy changes *after* a speech by the American Secretary of State does not mean that the speech *caused* the change in policy. That a young man proposes to a girl *after* he learns of her wealth does not mean that he proposed *because* he learned of her wealth.

False Dilemma

Resist oversimplified "either-or" choices. When we are asked to choose between black and white, we may find ourselves preferring different shades of gray. A true dilemma leaves us only two ways out, both undesirable. A false dilemma presents us with two ways out, while the author is trying to block our view of the third. A salesman might seem to offer a worried parent a choice between buying a home encyclopedia and allowing his children to grow up ignorant. A third alternative is to trust in the educational efforts of the schools.

To resist the "either-or" fallacy, we have to remember that often there are *more* than the proverbial "two sides" to an issue. Looking back at the Spanish Civil War, most observers agree that it was more than a simple question of "Democracy versus Fascism." The struggle was in various ways complicated by the role of the Catholic church, of the Spanish monarchist tradition, of many different shades of democratic thought, and of the Communist International. After the end of World War II, the simple slogan of "Democracy versus Fascism" soon proved deceptive to observers of events in the Soviet-dominated countries of Eastern Europe. There are many similar alternatives: "Conservatism versus Liberalism," "Socialism versus Free Enterprise," "Censorship versus Freedom of Thought," "Traditional versus Modern Education."

The appeal of a thoughtful writer often lies in his ability to re-examine such oversimplified contrasts in order to make us see the underlying, more complex relationships. Here, for instance, is Walter Lippmann discussing the familiar distinction between "straight news" and "editorial comment." It is naive to assume that a journalist *either* reports the facts *or* "editorializes":

It is all very well to say that a reporter collects the news and that the news consists of facts. The truth is that, in our world, the facts are infinitely many and that no reporter could collect them all, no newspaper could print them all, and nobody could read them all. We have to select *some* facts rather than others, and in doing that we are using not only our legs, but our selective judgment of what is interesting or important, or both. . . .

Because we are newspapermen in the American liberal tradition, the way we interpret the news is not by fitting the facts to a dogma. It is by proposing theories or hypotheses, which are then tested by trial and error. We put forward the most plausible interpretation we can think of, the most plausible picture into which the raw news fits, and then we wait to see whether the later news fits into the interpretation. — "The Job of the Washington Correspondent," *Atlantic*

Simplified alternatives appeal to us because they make us feel that we have a firm grip on our subject. Being able to divide many confusing items into two or three main categories makes us feel that we have a clear overall view of what is going on. For instance, suppose you are discussing the motives of business executives who come to Washington to work for the government. You set up three possible categories: They enter the government for the sake of money, for the sake of prestige, or for the sake of wielding influence in favor of their former businesses and associates. You then write a paper demonstrating that most of the businessmen coming to Washington stand to lose rather than to gain both money and reputation. After thus eliminating these first two possibilities, you then conclude that the third one must be true. Actually your paper proves no such thing. There may be a fourth and a fifth possibility you have not mentioned. One such possibility is that they feel qualified to serve their country.

Arguments from Analogy

Guard against carrying an analogy too far. Just as there is a difference between *after* and *because,* there is a difference between *similar* and *alike.* Two objects, or two situations, may share several important features and yet be different in crucial respects. A man who in his youth saw a land boom end in a spectacular crash may watch the real estate prices shoot up in his neighborhood, noting many factors at work that remind him of the earlier boom. Noting the similarities, he may confidently wait for a crash—that may never come. In spite of the many similarities, there may also be crucial *differences* between the two situations.

Analogies are most valuable when used for explanation and illustration. When we try to explain something that is complicated or abstract, we compare it to something the reader already knows. For instance, we might compare the human brain to a telephone switchboard or to an electronic calculator. The switchboard analogy, for instance, could explain how the brain sorts out the many incoming impressions and establishes relevant connections. But in order not to mislead the reader, we should also point out some of the things that make a brain different from a machine. For instance, a brain is not produced in a factory, its components are not half so well known, it is largely self-directing, and it suffers from quirks and ailments more mysterious than a short circuit.

To use an analogy to advantage in your own writing, make sure you realize *where it breaks down.* Show your reader in what respects analogous situations are similar and in what respects they are dissimilar. Suppose you are trying to show a relationship between business experience and government employment. You say:

Our nation is in a way a big business. To prevent businesses from failing, one has to have qualified business executives. So why not give high offices in the federal government to business executives qualified to deal with business problems?

This argument, if really developed in detail, would depend too exclusively on alleged similarities between business and government. The analogy you have in mind could become instructive if you followed up *both* similarities and differences. On the one hand, you could point out such assets of the business executive as training in organizing and coordinating many different activities, in selecting and directing personnel, in handling legal and financial problems, or in maintaining good public relations. On the other hand, you could point out that unlike most businesses government is owned and run by and for the customers. There is one vote per head rather than per share. And whatever the main purpose of government may be, it is not financial profit or giving employment to its employees.

Foregone Conclusions

Logic becomes unproductive when it is used to defend views already strongly held and not about to be reexamined. People with strong convictions naturally look for arguments to support their own point of view. Instead of using logic as a means of arriving at the truth, they assume that they know the truth and put logic to work to support it. They eagerly seize on evidence and arguments that bolster their own predetermined position.

The way foregone conclusions inhibit productive thinking is most strikingly demonstrated by the competitive debate. We would be surprised, and the purpose of the debate would be defeated, if one of the contestants were to stop suddenly in mid-rebuttal and say: "I've changed my mind. What you just said has convinced me. I am now *for* the admission of Mainland China to the United Nations."

In the debate, of course, two opposing views are represented; and the audience, at least, is free to change its mind. Often when we are invited to defend foregone conclusions, the road is more clearly marked for one-way travel only. Such a one-way street is the kind of contest offering a $400 fall wardrobe or a $1,000 scholarship for the best essay on "The Influence of Manufacturers' Brand Names on Better Retailing." There will obviously be no scholarship for the essayist who finds that the influence of brand names is for the worse. When the topic is "What the Flag Means to Me," there is not likely

to be a prize for the writer who finds that the flag as a symbol of patriotism has been much abused.

Apart from the spirit of debate, and the cash awards for saying the
right thing, what makes us support foregone conclusions? We all tend
to fit the evidence to the desired conclusion when our professional
or personal loyalties are engaged. The public relations director of a
university may be fully aware of current questions about the relevance
of much academic research to the problems of our society and to the
questions asked by students. In his official capacity, however, he may
spend much of his time disseminating news of new research programs
in order to reinforce the conventional image of the university as the
center of a vigorous, forward-looking intellectual life. When our
readers are mainly concerned with the problem itself, and not with
our personal interests and loyalties, we must learn to say to ourselves:
"Now that I have said the pious thing, or the dutiful thing, what are
the actual facts of the case, and what conclusions do they justify?"

Rationalization

*Logic makes for self-deception when we use it to support the
most flattering or least damaging hypothesis.* Rationalization enables
us to construct explanations more satisfying or less threatening than
the grim truth. When the issues under discussion are of great concern
to us, rationalizations are hard to avoid. A mother whose child did
poorly on an intelligence test is more likely to claim that the test is
unreliable than a mother whose child did well. Such claims may be
based on careful investigation, and the person who makes them may
be ready to adjust his findings in the light of new evidence. Often,
however, they are based on a desire for reassurance or self-justification.
If so, they may keep us from looking for adequate solutions to important problems. A habit of praising and glorifying her child may keep
a mother from taking the corrective steps necessary to prevent the
child from becoming a failure. A habit of rationalizing his scholastic
inadequacies may keep a student from finding out what is wrong and
what he can do about it.

Thinking Straight

Develop habits that make for straight thinking. Awareness of
common logical errors is indispensable insurance against elementary
blunders. When carried to excess, however, it may immobilize thought
altogether. When a student first becomes aware of the imperfections
of many familiar arguments, he may conclude that any idea he might
adopt is bound to involve a logical flaw. Like a man finding himself on

thin ice, he may refuse to move another step. He may decide that the safest course is not to commit himself, to suspend judgment on all issues that present a choice among several alternatives.

Such complete skepticism is of course impossible in everyday life. A businessman has to make decisions, even though his estimate of market conditions cannot be absolutely foolproof. If his guesses are intelligent guesses, he will, with luck, be more often right than wrong. A voter cannot be sure about the qualifications and intentions of a candidate. He will nevertheless vote for the most attractive or the least objectionable one. In making up our minds, as in all other aspects of life, we can never eliminate error and chance. What we can do is to cultivate mental habits that make for truth and accuracy in the long run, and on the average.

Some of the habits that make for straight thinking may be summed up as follows:

(1) *Be prepared to change your mind.* Pursue possibly important questions, and examine possibly relevant evidence, even when they go counter to your original assumptions or your present tentative conclusions. When investigating any subject of importance, you are bound to discover things you did not know, problems you were not aware of.

(2) *Take your time in formulating conclusions.* A thoughtful person has explored a range of examples and evidence before formulating a carefully limited generalization. He develops his argument step by step, paying attention to the soundness of his assumptions and the validity of his inferences.

(3) *Distrust the simple answer.* Gross oversimplification is the stock in trade of the demagogue. Few problems in education or politics are limited and clear-cut enough to permit simple solutions. Few social or cultural ills can be cured by a single drastic remedy.

(4) *Examine your views for consistency.* Although a rational person may be slow to arrive at conclusions, he takes them seriously once he has adopted them. He does not make a generalization and a few minutes later contradict himself. If his salary is paid out of city taxes, he does not charge that city taxes are too high when he pays his taxes and complain that city taxes are too low when he picks up his paycheck. If you change your mind while writing, you will have to revise what you have already written to make sure there is no inconsistency. Do not claim on page 1 that the chief cause of highway accidents is lax law enforcement only to assert on page 3 that the chief cause of highway accidents is careless driving. Make clear from the beginning that there are several important causes and, if possible, show how they are related.

Exercises

A. Identify the *logical shortcomings* of the following arguments:

1. The establishment of a universal language is a difficult problem. Man has solved many other difficult problems, such as that of flight or of harnessing atomic energy. Therefore, man will succeed in establishing a universal language.

2. John is opposed to infant baptism. He must be an atheist.

3. George is above the national average in intelligence He is below the national average in reading ability. Therefore, the school's system of teaching reading must be defective.

4. Statistics are unreliable as a means of determining public opinion. After careful tabulation of the answers on more than 1,200 questionnaires, I have concluded that 70 per cent of those questioned felt that statistical opinion polls misrepresent public opinion.

5. In periods of rapid expansion, the American economy gorges on time payments and capital investment. It needs to chew this cud sufficiently before it resumes eating. Therefore, recessions are a natural and organic part of the business cycle.

6. College students are interested in learning all they can while in college. Unlike high school, college is not required by law; therefore, a person who goes to college is going because he desires to further his education.

7. Where there is smoke there is fire. If a public official comes under attack for stealing public funds, it is a good sign that some kind of wrongdoing has been committed. Officials accused of dishonesty should be removed from their jobs before they can do any further harm.

8. The most important thing I have been taught is a strong sense of what is right. You determine what is right, and then you do it. For instance, as a dedicated patriot, I support my country, right or wrong, in whatever tasks it may face.

9. Today, columnist Y criticized the Democratic leadership in Congress. Columnist Y must be a Republican.

10. Last semester I disagreed with my history teacher's opinion of Thomas Jefferson. I received a failing grade in the course. The teacher failed me because I contradicted him.

B. Point out the *strengths and weaknesses* of the logic employed in the following excerpts from newspaper columns, magazine articles, letters to the editor, congressional newsletters, and similar sources. Pay special attention to arguments concerning cause and effect, arguments from analogy, and problems of consistency.

1. The person fighting some racial or economic abuse is usually told, "The problem is very complex." But what contributes most to the complexity of social issues is apathy. A simple example is that of a fire in a building in a city. If one does not take sufficient steps to put the fire out in the first building, it will spread to others, until whole city blocks are ablaze. At that point, putting out a fire becomes indeed a complex undertaking. Our lack of initiative in dealing with social problems contributes greatly to their complexity.

2. With her A.B. in hand, tomorrow's college graduate should be encouraged to enter a profession and to stick with it even if this involves postponing motherhood and eventually delegating some of its responsibilities. The delusion that every woman must be a chambermaid, cook, and nurse—in addition to any other work she may do—is archaic. It makes no more sense than insisting that a research chemist take time out to wash the test tubes and scrub the lab floor. Women, like men, should give their highest skills to a society which badly needs them.—Marion K. Sanders, "A Proposition for Women," *Harper's*

3. Eighteen-year-olds should be allowed to vote. Take for example a young couple that married when they were about seventeen or eighteen. They should have some say about the political future of the country their children will grow up in. These young people have the right to want their children to live in a democratic country. They want each child to have the same freedoms and privileges that they themselves enjoy.

4. A biological axiom explains that progress is made only through differences. The breeders of race horses succeed only because some animals are born different from the ordinary. The same is true of roses or potatoes or grapefruit—or thinkers! If we all tend to think, or to appear to think, the same way, under compulsion or from any other motive, the laws determining intellectual evolution cease to operate. —Claude M. Fuess, "The Perils of Conformity," *Saturday Review*

5. Haven't we advanced farther and faster than any other nation in the past one hundred and eighty years? Isn't our standard of living the highest in the world? The answer is *yes*, even though every four years violent claims are made to the contrary, and disaster is foretold by one of our temporarily unseated politicians. Since we are governed under a two-party system and since we enjoy the highest standard of living under this system, it certainly follows that attempts to form a third major party in the United States should be discouraged.

6. A democracy, unlike a Communist government, is only as strong as the combined *individual* strength of its people. Strength, like muscle, can be built only through exercise. Moral strength comes from the

exercise of our religious and parental training through prayer and practice. Physical strength comes not from watching a steamshovel move dirt but from shoveling it ourselves. Strength of any kind is improved by exercise. Can anyone name one major proposal which has come before Congress this year that is not a transfer of responsibility from ourselves to federal government? Can anyone deny that today there are more individuals and local governments following the easy course to the federal treasury than ever before? I can't help feeling that we are growing soft and weak from lack of exercise.

C. Which *common fallacy* or familiar problem of logic do you encounter most frequently in the debates and controversies of today? Examine its role, presenting detailed examples from editorials, speeches, discussions, press conferences, magazine articles, or similar sources. Remember that we are much quicker to see logical shortcomings in the arguments of others than in our own; do not engage in mere fault-finding.

5. Constructing an Argument

In much of the writing we do, we present the *results* of our thinking. We present a thesis, a definition, or a program for action, and then support it with examples, reasons, precedents. But when we seriously try to change the reader's mind, we may instead lead him to the intended conclusion through the *actual steps in the argument.* If we are to be successful in this attempt, the reader must feel that we have matters firmly under control. He must have a clear sense of where he is headed. He must see how one step leads logically to the next.

These patterns of organization follow the order of a logical argument:

The Inductive Approach

Use the inductive approach to overcome the resistance of a skeptical or hostile reader. An inductive paper or article presents examples, case histories, or evidence and then draws a general conclusion. Inductive order is especially effective when a writer has to overcome prejudice or distrust. It deprives the reader of a chance to say early: "I don't believe it!" Instead, he finds himself paying attention to the evidence, and perhaps step by little step changing his mind.[1]

---

[1] For the application of an inductive approach to other kinds of writing, see the "detail-first" paper in Chapter 2 (Observation and Description) and "Finding the Common Denominator" in Chapter 5 (Definition).

An inductive approach may be especially advisable for a subject on which the reader has already endured much lecturing or exhortation. The writer may then spend most of his time "letting the evidence speak for itself":

> Whites outnumber Negroes in the population about ten to one, but in the colleges they outnumber them thirty to one. . . .
> In 1963, one of 42 white Americans was in college, but only one of 110 Negroes. . . .
> According to a study published some years ago, the average expenditure per student in the nation's colleges was $1,334; in Negro colleges it was $888. . . .
> In 1960, Negro colleges were getting 2.7 per cent of the money given by states for higher education, and a pitiful .66 per cent of federal money given to higher education. . . .

As the writer proceeds, he begins to funnel these figures, and comparable ones for more recent years, into the generalizations that they clearly point to. Instead of sounding like yet another repetition of what all well-meaning people say, his charge of inequality of educational opportunity will sound at the end of his paper like a conclusion *well earned.*

A similar procedure may work best when much previous discussion has taken place on a subject; when interpretation has been piled upon interpretation. Who wants to listen to yet another theory explaining the enigma of Hamlet? The best way to proceed may be to wipe the slate clean, to pretend that we know nothing about the subject, and simply to take the reader along on a reading of the play — always watching out for evidence about Hamlet's character. As we proceed, we piece the evidence together into an interpretation of our own after all. But for having *emerged* gradually from the text, it will seem that much less a mere theory.

The inductive approach makes the reader share in discovery. It can hold the reader's attention by going

• from *surface differences* to *underlying similarities:*
   At first glance, the sources of evil are different in Shakespeare's *Romeo and Juliet* and in *Macbeth.* In the story of the "star-crossed lovers," chance, misunderstanding, and accident play a large role. In Macbeth, "vaulting ambition" provides the driving force. Is there nevertheless a common pattern?

• from *apparent contradictions* to *underlying relationships:*
   Among the billboards put up by a right-wing organization, some may proclaim "freedom," others strongly endorse "law and order." Can *freedom* and *order* be defined in such a way as to become necessary parts of a consistent conservative view of society?

The Method of Dialectic

Use the dialectic method to play opposites off against each other. The dialectic process makes us move from narrow or one-sided views to a larger perspective through the clash of opposites. It starts with a strong statement of one extreme, the **thesis**. This statement in turn provokes a counterstatement, or **antithesis**. An attempt to reconcile or balance the two statements produces the resolution, or **synthesis**. For instance, we may use the dialectic method when we set a paper in motion by first presenting but then attacking a familiar point of view:

I. FIRST STEP: A familiar idea is confirmed:
It is true that many required courses do not help to prepare the student for his professional career (detailed illustrations).

II. SECOND STEP: An objection is stated:
But a responsible citizen must be able to recognize competence and quackery in fields other than his own (detailed illustrations).

III. THIRD STEP: A balanced conclusion is drawn:
Therefore, a student needs at least some required courses that give him a basic understanding of some important disciplines outside his own field.

The dialectic scheme is applicable to more general or more demanding subjects:

I. THESIS: It is true that modern industrial society makes for unprecedented interdependence among its citizens.

II. ANTITHESIS: But such interdependence is an essential condition of mass production and mass consumption.

III. SYNTHESIS: Interdependence is the price modern society pays for a high standard of living.

Can you see the dialectic process at work in the following excerpt, adapted from a discussion of "U.S. imperialism"?

Thesis   The United States has the physical potential—both human and material—for implementing even greater international commitments than those we have hitherto assumed. Our population includes more than 16 million young men between the ages of eighteen and thirty, and we have the industrial potential to equip whatever armed forces we raise with more firepower than any other nation of the world. Our gross national product exceeds $700 billion, an amount that is quite sufficient to supply a military machine with all of its needs. . . .

Antithesis   What is missing, of course, is the will. Americans value their private comforts and pleasures, and are unwilling to make the sacrifices that are necessary for the success of imperial ventures.

Synthesis
> Young men are not volunteering to fight for manifestly destined causes these days. Our citizens look upon their personal incomes as sacred vessels, not to be tapped by the tax-collector for ambitious expenditures on armaments. . . .
>   Thus to say that our power is "limited" is really to admit that the citizens of America are unwilling to devote more than a minor fraction of their population or their prosperity to the enterprise of empire.

The *result* of the dialectic method typically is to produce balanced views. But its great advantage is that it reaches these views as the result of a dramatic confrontation. What often defeats the spokesman of a moderate position is that his views sound sensible, dutiful, and dull. We would expect only politely disguised yawns if we were to announce that the great early political leaders of the United States were only human. But we might create some interest if we first sketched the moral paragons of schoolbook and patriotic speech: honest George Washington, thrifty Ben Franklin. We could then counter by taking the reader through the debunker's gallery of American statesmen: a disciplinarian Washington, a slave-holding Jefferson, a Franklin peopling the world with illegitimate children. We could then work toward a balanced view of men with quite human failings and yet setting *political* precedents of tremendous importance for modern times.

The Argumentative Drive

Work from premises to a desired conclusion. Much forceful writing carries us along because it suggests an air of determination, a sense of purpose. We sense that the groundwork is being done for conclusions to be reached in due time. Each paragraph is a link in a chain; each point being established is necessary as a step in an ongoing argument.

Sustained logical reasoning makes unusual demands both on writer and reader. It is necessarily rare in popular or informal exposition and most common in scholarly controversy. Here is a rough outline of a **deductive argument**, which draws conclusions from premises previously established or applies generalizations to specific instances:

I. A college should develop in its students a sense for spiritual values (elaboration and support).

II. Architecture gives tangible expression to such values as dignity and permanence (elaboration and support).

III. The buildings facing the traditional Inner Quad of the college exhibit several of these qualities (elaboration and support).

IV. Of the modern classroom buildings on this campus, few suggest a sense of tradition, a sense of style, a feeling of dignity (elaboration and support).

V. Therefore, the buildings surrounding the Inner Quad should not be torn down to
make room for additional "cell block" structures.

Induction, deduction, and the dialectic process are not the *only* logical patterns that can give shape to a paper as a whole. Here are some other ways of modeling the organization of a paper on a sustained logical argument:

- *eliminating alternatives.* The less desirable alternatives are examined first and found wanting. The writer thus prepares the way for the presentation of his own choice (in the process guarding against the kind of oversimplification that produces false dilemmas).

- *tracing a chain of causes and effects.* The writer may try to disentangle major contributing causes, presenting them in historical order or settling questions of relative importance or priority.

The more clearly the organization of a paper reflects a logical scheme, the less likely the reader is to ask: "Why should I go on to the next paragraph? Why should I turn the page?" A logically organized paper keeps the reader going as the result of his own sense that the argument is still *incomplete.*

Exercises

A. A writer trying to resist *premature* generalization can apply the inductive approach not only to a paper or a paragraph but even to an individual sentence. Write three sentences in which a limited generalization emerges from detail presented earlier in the sentence. Here is a possible model:

Dogs bark at the door to be let in; rabbits thump to call each other; the cooing of doves and the growl of a wolf defending his kill *are unequivocal signs of feelings and intentions to be reckoned with by other creatures.* (Susanne Langer)

B. Write an *inductively organized* paragraph on a subject of your choice. Make a special effort to avoid hasty generalization and unrepresentative sampling.

C. Write a paragraph on the *dialectic* model: going from "on the one hand" to "on the other hand" and on to a balanced conclusion.

D. Write an outline for a paper modeled on the dialectic method. Have you recently become strongly aware of two different or opposed views on a familiar problem or current issue? Use your outline to line up the *pros and cons* and to lead up to your own conclusion. Among possible topics are

> Antisemitism in Shakespeare's *Merchant of Venice*
> The commitment to nonviolence in political demonstrations
> Legal control of the ownership and sales of guns
> Stepped-up freeway construction in urban or scenic areas

Your instructor may ask you to write a paper following your outline.

E. Write an outline for a paper in which you derive a *specific, limited proposal* for the reform of high school or college education from basic assumptions about the nature or purposes of education. Try to make each major point in your outline a necessary step in your argument. Your instructor may ask you to write a paper following your outline.

Review Exercise: Sample Themes

Study the *uses to which logic is put* in the following examples of student writing. What kind of reasoning predominates in each example? Examine the nature and scope of generalizations; premises, stated or implied; the logical steps in an argument. To what extent do logical patterns help shape the organization of each paper?

1.   STAYING FREE

When he is alone, no man is compelled to consider the welfare of others in making his decisions. On the proverbial desert island, a man would be free to take any license he wished. If smoking were satisfying to him, he would smoke. If drinking were pleasing to him, he would drink. If taking drugs were gratifying to him, he would take drugs. If killing himself were to seem the best course, he would kill himself. His range of choice would be limited only by the limits of his *physical* resources. Within the range of what is physically possible, the man would have complete freedom to do whatever he wishes. Where is the man who is not envious of such freedom?

There is, perhaps, one consideration that mitigates this envy. For if one begins to smoke, he may soon feel the need to smoke more. If one begins to drink, he may not be able to stop. If one begins to take drugs, he may come under an absolute compulsion to take more. And if one kills himself, he is forever dead. It is much as in a game of chess, when one player has fallen into an opponent's trap. Then, though at the beginning he had complete freedom, he has no choice in his play, and in the end he is checkmated. The mitigating consideration, then, is that freedom, to be truly freedom, must be self-perpetuating.

If one is not to diminish by his actions the amount of freedom he has, how can he act? Any decision would limit the number of available alternatives and thus would eventuate ultimately in a loss of freedom.

Fortunately, it is possible to look at this situation in a more positive light. Freedom may be understood as a choice among creative possibilities. The concern is only that the choices be creative, that they do not rob us of paths or pursuits we know to be good. Freedom is not an end in itself; it must be a tool for producing good. The ideal is not so much to be *free to* do whatever we please. Rather, it is to be *free for* doing what we know, or think, we should.

2.   NO VACANCY

Last weekend, I went to a picnic with the girls from the women's co-op where I live. We were joined by the members of a newly formed men's co-op. We engaged in an impromptu football game and happily charred hot dogs and marshmallows. We finished the afternoon singing around a dying fire. The high point of the afternoon, for me, came when I did a vaudeville routine with one of the boys. The boy, by the way, is a Negro. This fact was of no great interest to me until I chose to look into the attitude which college students in general have toward minority groups.

I made a personal survey of forty students at the college I attend and found that ninety per cent of them would theoretically live in a house with a member of a minority group. Three-fourths of those I questioned said they would share a room with a member of a minority group. Ninety-eight per cent said they would attend a party where members of minority groups were present. The same percentage said they had close friends who are members of minority groups. However, when I studied the results of a survey of one thousand students, which was compiled by a Student Housing Survey Committee last spring, I found the results were less favorable. According to the report of the committee, approximately one-third of the student body would refuse to share a room with a colored student and fourteen per cent would refuse to share a room with an Oriental.

The ladies, it seems, take top honors for prejudice. On the question "Would you share a room with a Negro girl?" more than forty per cent of the girls indicated they would refuse. Twenty per cent of the males said they would refuse to share a room with a Negro boy. The reason for the higher percentage of women students who would refuse may be that their parents usually take a more active part in choosing their housing accommodations than those of the men students. Even more of the householders who rent rooms to students said they would discriminate. Forty-eight per cent of them said they would refuse to rent rooms to members of racial minority groups.

According to the advisor of the College Religious Council, an attempt was made to have only non-segregated houses put on the approved housing list. This attempt failed because the housing office personnel stated that many students would be unable to live at school if only non-segregated houses were on the approved list. These students' parents would not permit their children to live with those of minority races.

In reading the "Letters to the Editors" column of the college daily, I found two students who felt that investigating housing conditions for minority groups was creating "much ado about nothing." However, after reading letters by Negro students describing their attempts to find housing, I feel that there has been too little ado. One Negro student describes how he and his wife looked at over a hundred apartments without finding one available to them. Their final solution to the problem was to live respectively in the YMCA and the YWCA. Another student states that he put a deposit down on an apartment and later received his check back in the mail with a note which he describes as saying, "It would be better for all concerned if you found someplace to live with your own kind."

I have learned of many other cases where students of minority groups have experienced much the same sort of rebuff. However, in social matters, most of the students I talked to seemed willing to accept minority group members as equals or at least near equals. Most of those I interviewed also seemed to feel that there is little need to worry about a racial problem at their college.

Before investigating this problem for myself, I too had the comfortable feeling that discrimination against races was something which was reserved for the Southland of the United States. Granted, the racial minority problem at colleges in other parts of the country is not as serious as it is in the South. However, it is foolish to believe that no problem exists. There is not much sense in acting like the little boy who breaks the cookie jar, then closes his eyes and pretends it never happened. As long as one-third of the students of a fairly representative college freely admit that they are racially prejudiced we can hardly boast of a truly democratic respect for all individuals, regardless of race, creed, or color.

What is the answer? It would be fine if we could make racial prejudice stop existing just by saying that it is not right. Obviously, this can not be done. For the present at least, we must face the fact that some students will discriminate. It is impossible to force them not to discriminate.

There is a practical solution, however, to one phase of this problem. Why not establish more cooperative houses for those students who are not prejudiced? This would give members of minority groups better housing than they now have. It would also help to improve racial understanding. I have found that when I learn to know a person as a person I tend to forget that he is a member of a racial group. This is, I think, a start in the right direction.

Theme Topics 6

1. Present and support a general conclusion you have reached about a *group of people* or a type of person. For example, present a generalization concerning first-generation Americans, campus leaders, science teachers, rural politicians, city policemen. Beware of hasty generalizations and unrepresentative sampling.

2. Present and support a generalization about the *quality of life* in present-day America as you know it. For instance, has the concept of the "good neighbor" been lost in both city and suburb? Is it true that the large city park is no longer safe? How dependent have we become upon the automobile? Is highway design as aesthetically barren as some critics claim?

3. We are often told that a whole generation of boys took as a model the Horatio Alger hero, who made his way to fame and fortune through self-reliance, honesty, and hard work. Do young people today find any such *culture hero* in what they read or watch? Can you identify a recurrent type that might serve as a model or ideal for large numbers of young people? Use the *inductive approach* in presenting your findings.

4. After visiting the United States in the 1880s, Matthew Arnold gave his countrymen in England the following account of the American press:

> On the whole, and taking the total impression and effect made by them, I should say that if one were searching for the best means to efface and kill in a whole nation the discipline of respect, the feeling for what is elevated, one could not do better than take the American newspapers. The absence of truth and soberness in them, the poverty in serious interest, the personality and sensation-mongering, are beyond belief.

How true would such an indictment be of American newspapers today? Test one major part of the indictment against your own study of one week's supply of a "typical" American paper. Use the *inductive approach* in presenting your findings.

5. Americans are often said to think of themselves as open, generous, compassionate, motivated by sympathy for the underdog. Would you say that Americans widely share this image of themselves? Use the following for evidence: current newspaper and magazine editorials, columns, letters to the editor, and material from similar sources.

6. Study the following greatly condensed account of the "black image" as projected by film and television in years past. Then prepare to write a paper on the *current* situation:

For over forty years, almost all images of black were in one direction—negative. The blacks were always depicted as irresponsible, uninhibited, and generally mentally inferior. In World War II, the government suggested to the movie industry that it try to reflect black people in a more positive manner. Thus, in war films, you saw a few Negro servicemen. Generally, the image was patronizing. Then there was a wave of mulatto films, showing black Americans light enough to pass. More recently, there has been a "supernigger" character emerging in films and on television. He has no particular background. He is usually a loner and always has lots of qualifications. If he is a spy, he cannot just be an ordinary spy; he has to be a Rhodes scholar. He is unmarried, so the producer doesn't have to deal with love scenes. Also, he has absolute integrity. He is so one-dimensional that it is impossible to think of him as a real being.

Can you identify *one major current trend* in the treatment of Negroes by movies and television? Use detailed examples from recent movies or television programs. (You may want to limit your discussion to *one* of these media.)

7. Have you ever examined in some detail the arguments *on the opposite side* of some cause that you yourself support? For instance, have you ever seriously considered the arguments for tuition-supported over free public education, violence over nonviolence, separation over integration, necessary wars over peace, natural inequality over equality, materialism over idealism? Write a paper in which you present and analyze as fully and as sympathetically as you can the arguments "on the other side."

8. Argue as fully as you can your position on one of the following issues. Try to make your reader see as fully as you can the assumptions on which your argument rests and the steps by which it proceeds.

a. Should a newspaper represent the opinions of its journalists, its publishers, its advertisers, or its public?

b. Should a college make it a policy to bar undesirable or controversial speakers?

c. Should college professors be allowed to bring their own political views into the classroom?

d. Is there ever any justification for censorship of the arts?

9. Write a paper in which you examine the pros and cons in order to lead the reader to a balanced conclusion. Choose a topic for which you can identify *two strong opposing views*. For instance, should the primary goal of higher education be the creation of an intellectual élite equipped to understand and deal with the complex issues of our time? Or should higher education aim at providing the best possible education for everyone?

10. John F. Kennedy said, "Let every nation know, whether it wishes us well or ill, that we shall pay any price, bear any burden, meet any hardship, support any friend, oppose any foe to assure the survival and the success of liberty." On the other hand, it is often argued that the United States cannot play policeman to all the world, that it should become involved only when its own national security is clearly at stake. Argue your own position on this issue.

I have wondered whether we might legitimately try to introduce . . . some new test for exclusion of the inessential. Suppose, for example, that a man were permitted only to say something that he could grow eloquent about.
Kenneth Burke

CHAPTER SEVEN

Persuasion

1. Knowing Your Reader

2. Avoiding Distortion
        Rhetorical Exaggeration
        Slanting
        Appeals to Emotion
        Ad Hominem
        Appeals to Authorities

3. The Language of Persuasion
        Denotation and Connotation
        Interpreting Emotive Language
        Statement and Implication

4. The Strategies of Persuasion
        Appealing to a Common Cause
        Dramatizing the Issue
        Persuading by Degrees
        Demolishing the Opposition

5. Persuading the Critical Reader

Student Themes
Theme Topics 7

1. Knowing Your Reader

We write to be read. Sooner or later we ask ourselves: "Is any-body listening? If so, what is he thinking? Does any of what I am say-ing make an impression on him? *Why* is he so uninterested, or so sarcastic? What can I do to make him sympathize with my point of view?" The more we depend on the reader's approval, the more ur-gent these questions become. In writing devoted to persuasion, pro-ducing the desired effect on the reader has become the writer's central purpose.

The art of persuasion is the art of making ideas, suggestions, and advice palatable. Persuasion aims at producing results. Its effective-ness can often be judged, at least indirectly, by tangible consequences: products sold, bond issues passed, officials forced to resign or to mend their ways. But the results of persuasion are at least as important when they are harder to measure: attitudes hardened or changed, resent-ments reinforced or allayed, expectations created or doubts raised.

A writer who wants to persuade must know his reader. He must know what information he has to fill in, what prejudices he has to over-come, what arguments he has to refute. He knows that a policeman's view of people living in slums is likely to differ from that of a social worker. He knows that businessmen are often against higher school taxes but teachers in favor of them. An effective persuasive writer takes into account the reader's background, interests, and preferences. He knows how to put himself in the reader's place. An effective writer can persuade his readers for the same reason that a mother or wife can manage the ones she loves: She knows their weaknesses; she under-stands their needs and desires.

Effective persuasive writing offers the author the satisfaction of a strong positive response. But at the same time it raises problems not faced by the author writing mainly for the "record." The writer aim-ing at persuasion has to ask himself questions like the following:

(1) *How far should I go in humoring the reader?* Is it best to be conciliatory, "reasonable"? Or is it not sometimes more effective to confront the reader directly, to challenge his prejudices?

(2) *Where is the dividing line between making the strongest pos-sible case and engaging in distortion?* When does an advertiser stop showing his product in the best possible light and begin to deceive his customers? When is a political charge merely exaggerated, and when does it turn into a falsehood?

(3) *Where does persuasion become manipulation?* What can keep an advertiser from exploiting deep-seated needs or frustrations

unsuspected by the customer? What can keep a writer from exploiting the fears and stereotypes of his audience?

From the point of view of effective writing, one general observation applies regardless of the answers you work out to questions such as these. A critical, informed person will want to feel that you are appealing to his own honest judgment. He will resent writing that has too obvious a design on the reader. You can antagonize critical readers simply by trying too hard to persuade. They do not like to be wheedled, bullied, or threatened. An appeal to fear had better be well grounded. Flattery had better be subtle. Skillfully used, persuasive techniques can help your writing get all the attention and consideration it deserves. Used indiscriminately, they can make the reader dismiss your writing as brash and unscrupulous.

2.   Avoiding Distortion

Most writers feel that their ideas, no matter how meritorious, will not prosper unless they are dressed up to advantage. As a reader, it is part of your job to separate reliable information from the simplifications, exaggerations, and embellishments that an author uses to make you adopt his point of view. As a writer, it is part of your job to keep the same persuasive devices from discrediting you with readers who object to being misled.

Rhetorical Exaggeration

Tone down sweeping charges and exaggerated claims. We all at times exaggerate for rhetorical effect. There is always the temptation to state a weak position forcefully in the hope that its weakness will not be apparent. There is a temptation to word disagreement strongly in the hope that it will prove contagious. Editorials, speeches, and advertisements are full of **superlatives**, absolute claims to superiority or singularity: "the biggest," "the best," "available now for the first time," "threatening us with utter extinction," "fatal to our most cherished institutions," "unparalleled in recorded history."

It is easy enough to discount rhetorical exaggeration when it obviously serves someone's ulterior purpose:

> The American Aspirin Company is gratified to announce the climax of its relentless search for the absolute truth about pain relief.

The advertiser himself is the first to disregard such language when off duty: The real estate salesman who uses terms like "tremendous values," "unique opportunities," and "once-in-a-lifetime savings" in advertising a housing development will ignore them when he himself buys a house. Instead, he will try to find out what grade of materials was used, whether the sewer assessments have been paid, and whether the neighborhood is going to be industrial, residential, or commercial. He will compile all the information which a customer needs to make an intelligent decision, but which an advertiser seldom provides.

We are much less likely to be aware of exaggerated claims when we make them ourselves. When writing in the heat of passion, we often feel at a loss for statements drastic enough to do justice to our feelings. The test of such writing is how it stands up when reread in the cold light of another day. What was meant to be forceful may merely sound shrill; what was meant to be indignant may sound crudely unfair. Whenever you write in an angry or enthusiastic mood, *put the result aside for a sober second reading.* Blow off steam in your first draft. Then, in revising it, trim down all statements that seem extravagant when reread.

Exaggerated:	The mayor's program for urban reconstruction is diametrically opposed to the best interests of the business community.
Balanced:	The mayor's program for urban reconstruction does not pay sufficient attention to the interests of downtown businessmen.
Exaggerated:	The bald truth is that railroads are being starved to death through government regulation.
Balanced:	The railroads lack adequate funds for modernization and expansion because of the government's failure to approve higher rates.

Slanting

Keep slanting from discrediting your writing with a fair-minded reader. Though parallel in effect to exaggeration, **slanting** is more subtle in method. A writer can slant his material by consistently selecting from several equally true statements the ones most favorable to his cause. A lawyer defending his client may describe him as a veteran, a homeowner, and a father of three children. A lawyer representing the plaintiff may describe the same man as an ex-convict, a man twice divorced, and a heavy drinker. Both descriptions may be quite truthful, but each creates an entirely different picture.

Slanting takes a variety of forms:

(1) A *slanted selection of evidence* may make the reader draw conclusions not justified by the facts known to the writer. Such slanting is hard to detect and hard to resist. Its insincerity or inaccuracy

lies not in what the writer says but in what he *omits*. Thus, an article about a college campus may describe expensive modern classroom buildings and ignore the temporary wooden structures around the corner. The article may be quite factual in what it does describe; it just happens to create a wrong impression.

(2) *Verbal slanting* is illustrated in the familiar example of the pessimist, who calls a bottle half empty, and the optimist, who calls it half full. Verbal slanting helps steer the reader's reactions in much effective writing:

Enterprising shopping centers are setting up day nurseries. So are bowling alleys. This gives the nation's ten million *female bowlers* a considerable edge over the seven million *working mothers.* — Marion K. Sanders, "A Proposition for Women," *Harper's*

Is it merely a coincidence that the bowling mothers are called "female bowlers" but the female workers "working mothers"?

(3) Strategic *juxtaposition* can make something big look small and vice versa. A writer can belittle protests against the draft by pointing out that during the Civil War draft riots in New York City between 400 and 500 rioters were killed, and that the rioters killed ninety-eight federal registrars in the North. This strategy is sometimes called "putting the problem in perspective."

(4) Flattering or invidious *analogies and figures of speech* can steer the reader's feelings in the desired direction. A writer may say that education should be like the lighting of a fire rather than the filling of an empty pot. Nobody is going to opt for the banal pot. Leo Tolstoy, in a letter to a draftee written in 1899, said,

No matter how dangerous the situation may be of a man who finds himself in the power of robbers who demand that he take part in plundering, murder, and rape, a moral person cannot take part. Is not military service the same thing? Is one not required to agree to the deaths of all those one is commanded to kill?

The association of soldiering with plunder and rape produces a revulsion that is hard to resist.

Like exaggeration, slanting ceases to persuade when it becomes consistent, determined, obvious. What makes people cynical about wartime propaganda is the predictable slant it gives to everything it touches. Bombs dropped by the one side destroy bridges, factories, convoys, and troop concentrations; bombs dropped by the other side hit churches, hospitals, refugee camps, and densely populated residential areas.

In writing for a critical reader, you will have to protect yourself against charges of one-sidedness. In attacking the dangers of one-man rule, do not limit your examples to notorious tyrants and demagogues. If your reader thinks of the less evil examples first, you have put him in the position of attorney for the defense. Try to keep your reader from saying "Yes, but . . ."

Appeals to Emotion

Do not use emotional appeals as a substitute for valid arguments. A writer who wants to move men to action will often appeal to their passions rather than to reason. Passionate appeals can move men toward decision in times of crisis; they can strengthen morale in times of danger. Like Thomas Paine in "The American Crisis," a writer may appeal to love of freedom and fear of oppression, to the desire for glory and fear of infamy, to love of country and hatred of it enemies:

The summer soldier and the sunshine patriot will, in this crisis, shrink from the service of his country; but he that stands it NOW, deserves the love and thanks of man and woman. Tyranny, like hell, is not easily conquered; yet we have this consolation with us, that the harder the conflict, the more glorious the triumph. What we obtain too cheap, we esteem too lightly: 'tis dearness only that gives everything its value. Heaven knows how to put a proper price upon its good; and it would be strange indeed, if so celestial an article as FREEDOM should not be highly rated.

The great power such appeals can exercise invites abuse. Every day we hear appeals to our love of freedom that are designed to promote someone's private motive or ulterior goal. Learn to recognize emotional appeals that are more likely to turn the reader against you than to make him join your cause:

(1) *Beware of substituting flattery for argument.* Advertisers often work with statements like "Women know values," "Discriminating buyers prefer Lusterol," "Men of distinction drink Sunlight soda water." Such statements are not well-deserved recognition of discriminating customers but an attempt to ensnare undiscriminating ones. Political candidates assure the public that they have "faith in the intelligence of the American people." Such assurances flatter the voter, but they do not help him decide whether the candidate's program is sound.

(2) *Be skeptical of appeals to fear, and hesitate to employ them to sway the reader toward your way of thinking.* Some people represent every minor departure from their own views as a national disaster. Too often and too rashly they predict runaway inflation, large-scale depression, or totalitarian tyranny.

(3) *Do not cheapen such ideals as love of country by invoking them in support of every minor project or conviction.* Many (says

e. e. cummings in "Humanity i love you") "unflinchingly applaud all /
songs containing the words country, home, and mother." But many
also object to the use of such words to put a halo effect on the passing
causes of the day. A pamphlet that praises the use of phonics in the
teaching of reading as "soundly American," and attacks the "whole
word" method as "education for socialism," will make many readers
flinch.

These warnings are not meant to imply that all your writing
should be unemotional. To discuss without emotion the martyrdom
of the Jews in Hitler's Europe, or the fate of the people of Hiroshima,
one would have to be, in Thomas Hardy's words, as "cold as a fish
and as selfish as a pig." But too often, recourse to emotional appeals
is an easy way out or, worse, an attempt to block discussion. As one
authority on logic observed,

It would be a mistake to condemn, or even to mistrust, all discourse that appeals to
our emotions. A statement can arouse emotions and still be true. Some facts are de-
lightful and some are damnable. But to get at the truth about anything you have to do
something more than feel strongly about it. And that is why it is necessary to recognize
these emotional appeals. For if they do not paralyze clear thinking, they make it very
difficult. As the immortal John J. McGraw (who was occasionally known to take offense
at umpires' rulings during the thirty years he managed the Giants) once remarked,
"When a man sees red, it's not likely he sees much of anything else." — Monroe C.
Beardsley, *Thinking Straight*

Ad Hominem

Do not evade the issue by dealing in personalities. The argument
ad hominem, directed "at the person," diverts attention from the
merit of ideas to the merits of their advocates. Instead of refuting an
economist's analysis of economic trends, his critics may let it be
known that his wife is suing him for divorce or that his brother recently failed in business. Such tactics boomerang with a responsible
audience. An author, a judge, or a political candidate is entitled to
respect for his privacy. His looks, loves, friends, and hobbies are
normally his own business. Regardless of his private problems, his
ideas and decisions in his special area of competence may still be
sound.

An opponent who drags in extraneous personal matters may
render not the victim's judgment questionable but his own. When
a candidate calls a Supreme Court Justice a "child-marrying mountain
climber," his gibes, instead of invalidating the decisions of the judge,
may merely stamp the speaker as a booby. In your own writing, remember that *ad hominem remarks do not have the force of argument.* At best they provide a facetious aside:

Francis Bacon, *a man who rose to eminence by betraying his friends,* asserted, no doubt as one of the ripe lessons of experience, that "knowledge is power." But this is not true of *all* knowledge. . . . (Bertrand Russell)

Sometimes, of course, a man's background or conduct *is* the issue. In that case, make sure your reader can see the *relevance* of any personal remarks.

Appeals to Authorities

Cite authorities to profit from their wisdom, not to borrow from their prestige. Too often, a writer will invoke science, the Bible, or the Founding Fathers, not in order to learn from them but in order to silence a skeptical reader. Magazine advertisements often use scientific-sounding terms and pictures of white-clad people working in laboratories. Few of these advertisements give a scientific evaluation of the product being advertised. Candidates and lobbyists link their proposals with symbols of patriotism: the Pilgrims, George Washington, Thomas Jefferson, Abraham Lincoln.

It is of course possible that a speaker who quotes Thomas Jefferson has studied Jefferson's life and works and is convinced that Jefferson's ideas are relevant to twentieth-century problems. But some orators who refer to Jefferson in their speeches have never read him. A critical reader is not easily impressed by references to famous or learned authorities. He knows that Lincoln's name, for instance, has been invoked in support of different and mutually contradictory programs.

In trying to bolster your own ideas, use references to people widely respected or admired not as evidence that your ideas are true but as evidence that they are worthy of consideration. In a paper attacking censorship, you may well wish to point out that the President of the United States said on such and such an occasion that censorship is bad in principle. This shows that the President agrees with you, but it does not show that he is right. You will still have to present arguments against censorship, whether they be the President's or your own.

The basic difficulty with many of the persuasive devices here examined is that they try to push the reader beyond what the evidence warrants. Sometimes there is *no* connection between the device employed and the merits of the case, as when a baseball player endorses a breakfast cereal he has never eaten. More typically, a writer aiming at the most forceful way of presenting his case comes close to the kind of distortion that alienates the fair-minded reader.

Exercises

A. Examine and evaluate the methods of persuasion employed in the following passages. What, in detail, does each writer count on to influence the reader's reaction? Which passages strike you as relevant to the issue and likely to carry weight with a critical and fair-minded reader? Which passages are *least* likely to influence an intelligent audience?

1. By a 5-to-4 decision in mid-April the United States Supreme Court nudged our economy back towards the era of handwritten ledgers and the hand loom. This, in an age of computers and high-speed cost cutting machines!

The learned Justices decided that labor unions have a right to strike over automation. Some building contractors in Pennsylvania tried to cut the cost of modestly priced homes by installing 3600 prefabricated doors. The carpenters struck because they wanted to construct these doors by hand on the site. The Court's decision in this and a companion case upheld the strikers because of the "employer's efforts to abolish their jobs."

If United States industry must protect specific jobs at whatever cost, instead of trying to serve the American public by adopting improved methods of production which lower costs and prices, the vaunted dynamism of the United States, obviously, would be destroyed.

2. The New Leftists are busily undermining their own best defense: the American traditions of free speech and tolerance. Increasingly they are taking the position: "I'm right. You are wrong. Therefore I cannot permit you to be heard." So, in the name of morality, they are stoning and howling down anyone who might disagree with them — setting a precedent, in short, for mob violence. They don't seem to realize that their doctrine is identical with that of the Spanish Inquisition, and with Hitler's justification for gas chambers.

3. The author of the article claims that we live in an "age of sexual ambiguity." American men, he claims, are abandoning their traditional dominant, masculine role in order to become more feminine. I feel that one look at American sports, for instance, would show the opposite. Perhaps the author should take a good look at his own masculinity before he begins to downgrade the entire male population of today.

4. Heywood Broun once said, "A case of sorts could be made for censorship if you imagine the job being administered by the wisest man in the world." The extent to which American censors fall short of this standard can be partially indicated by a look at the cross-examination of Police Captain J. Ignatius Sheehan in the case of "The Game of Love," as reported in *Chicago* for February, 1956. At that time it was

Sheehan's function, assisted by five widows of police officers, to decide what the citizens of Chicago should see or hear on the picture screen. Here are some excerpts from the cross-examination:

Q. Have you taken any courses subsequent to your high school?
A. No, sir.
Q. How many literature courses did you have during high school?
A. I don't remember.
Q. How many books on an average do you read a year? . . . A dozen, two dozen?
A. No.
Q. It is less than that?
A. Yes.
Q. How many plays do you attend each year?
A. Very few.
Q. Would you say one or two?
A. No.
Q. . . . Do you attend the art exhibits in Chicago?
A. No.
Q. Do you read the book review sections of . . . any newspapers?
A. No, sir.
Q. Are the members of the board required to have any special qualifications?
A. No, sir.
Q. Are any of them writers or recognized in other forms of art?
A. I wouldn't know.
Q. . . . Do any of them have any special literary qualifications?
A. I wouldn't know. . . .
Q. . . . In the course of events is the producer of the film ever called in to explain ambiguities in the film?
A. No, sir.
Q. Is the distributor ever called in?
A. No, sir.
Q. Are other people's views invited, such as drama critics or movie reviewers or writers or artists . . . ? Or are they ever asked to comment on the film before the censor board makes its decision?
A. No, sir. — Arthur Mayer, "How Much Can the Movies Say?" *Saturday Review*

5. For many decades, American retailers have given savings stamps which their customers can redeem for merchandise. Savings stamps have become a tradition as truly American as fireworks on the Fourth of July and turkey on Thanksgiving. Though there are thoughtless people who attack savings stamps, the wise customer realizes the advantages savings stamps offer and the place they occupy in the American economy. When you trade with merchants who show their appreciation by giving savings stamps, a veritable bonanza of America's finest merchandise awaits you—absolutely free. Mom can get just about anything she wants for home decorating and equipping. Dad can get those do-it-yourself tools or sports needs. The youngsters can save for toys, sports equipment, bikes, and many other "musts" for happy children.

B. Study the following two passages by an author who is expert at steering the reactions of his readers. *What* does the author want his readers to think and feel? *How*, in detail, does he achieve his aim? Your instructor may ask you to rewrite one of these passages so that it will describe the same basic situation but produce the opposite, or at least a sharply different, effect.

1. Before being killed and canned, the turtles swim in dense kraals, bumping each other in the murky water, armor clashing, dully lurching against the high pens. Later, trussed on a plank dock, they lie unblinking in the sun, their flippers pierced and tied. The tough leather of their skins does not disguise their present helplessness and pain. They wear thick, sun-hardened accumulations of blood at their wounds. Barbados turtles, as large as children, they belong to a species which has been eliminated locally by ardent harvesting of the waters near Key West, but the commercial tradition still brings them here to be slaughtered. Crucified like thieves, they breathe in little sighs, they gulp, they wait.

At a further stage, in the room where the actual slaughtering occurs, the butchers stride through gore in heavy boots. The visitor must proceed on a catwalk; a misstep will plunge him into a slow river of entrails and blood.

2. Before the ambulance arrived, the police were there. They came strolling into the classroom with their legs apart, as if they remembered ancestors who rode the plains. Their mouths were heavy in thought. They had noses like salamis, red and mottled with fat. They were angry at the weather, at the crowd, and especially at the prostrate man at our feet. . . . They stared at him in the classic pose—one cop with a hand resting lightly on the butt of his gun and the other on his butt, the younger cop with lips so pouted that his breath made a snuffling sound in his nose. They both had head colds. Their Ford was pulled up on the snow-covered lawn outside, with raw muddled marks of tread in the soft dirt. When the snow melted, there would be wounded streaks in the grass. The cab driver closed his eyes under the finicking, distasteful examination. At last one spoke: "See your driver's license."

The cab driver made a clumsy gesture towards his pocket. The cop bent and went into the pocket. He flipped open the wallet, glanced briefly at the photographs and cash, glanced at me, and then began lip-reading the license. —Herbert Gold, *The Age of Happy Problems*

C. Newspaper headlines are often more clearly slanted than the actual news reports, in which there may be some real attempt to balance conflicting points of view. It is one thing to headline a story about teenagers protesting a new curfew "Kids Against the Law"; it is quite another to headline it "The Law Against Kids." Study some *provocative recent headlines*. To judge from the articles, how fair or how slanted are they? Write several alternative headlines for one or more of the articles.

3. The Language of Persuasion

Suppose that in writing a theme you have made the point that majority rule or fraternity hazing is a tradition. You can now continue, "I approve of this tradition" or "I disapprove of this tradition." You will then have to show *why* you approve or disapprove of it. On the other hand, you may want your reader to share your approval or disapproval without your examining the issue on its merits. You may then act as though the very fact that majority rule is a tradition decides whether or not the reader should approve of it. You will say, "Majority rule is a *time-honored tradition*" if you favor it. You will say, "Majority rule is *just a tradition*" if you are opposed to it. This procedure may save you the trouble of starting a long argument — unless an alert reader asks, "How exactly does time honor?" or "Why did you use the word *just* in this sentence?"

Part of the secret of persuasive writing is skillful use of language — often in ways of which the reader is unaware. While seeming to convey information, language can at the same time convey the writer's preferences and dislikes. Persuasive writing relies heavily on **emotive language**, on words charged with attitudes and emotions. Whatever the actual data presented, or the causes and effects analyzed, the writer is likely to keep up a steady drumfire of words designed to shape the reader's reactions. Look at typical phrases from an article on the urban crisis:

> *antisocial* allocation of transportation funds
> irresponsible *self-seeking* of large corporations
> pressure from *lobbyists*
> metropolitan *chaos*
> *vested interests*
> *segregated, bureaucratic* high-rise projects
> *speculators robbing* the public

The more your own persuasive writing relies on such strongly charged language, the more you have to become concerned with the probable reactions of your reader.

(1) Emotive language can fire up the enthusiasm of readers in-

clined to agree with you, but it will also *make your opposition more hostile.* A passage like the following will please people who deplore "leftist" tendencies, but among the people attacked it is likely to increase the very "animosity" the writer deplores:

Because of their *dogmatism, violence, disrespect for the rights of others,* intellectual *rigidity,* belief in *class hostility* and *social insurrection,* and *animosity* toward the American political system, the *"anti-Americans"* of the Left have severed all connections with the *accommodating, cooperative* nature of American liberalism.   (letter to the editor)

(2) Even if the reader does not feel attacked, he may feel pushed. In reading a passage like the following, an independent reader may well say: "You are leaving me no choice!"

Even if the *corporate obstacles to the common good* were overcome, there is still another *status quo* which must be dealt with—the *Balkanized political map* of the United States, which has more to do with the *accidents of our history* and the desire of the white middle class to *shirk its responsibilities* than with the *needs of the nation.* (Michael Harrington)

Who could come out *for* a "Balkanized" United States, and *against* the "common good"? Who would want to say a good word for a "corporate obstacle"? Or even a "status quo"?

Emotive language, in other words, produces emotional reactions—but not always those intended by the writer. To handle it effectively, and to keep it under control, he has to be aware of its possibilities and limitations.

Denotation and Connotation[1]

A difference in connotation is typically a difference in the attitude of the observer rather than in the nature of the thing observed. The very words used to name an object or an idea may be colored by the writer's or the speaker's attitudes. Pairs like *cur* and *man's best friend, politician* and *statesman, war hero* and *militarist* can be applied to the same individual. In discussing the meaning of the words concerned, we can separate "what is out there" from that part of the meaning which expresses the attitudes, preferences, or emotions of the person who uses them.

The objective meaning of a word is often called its **denotation**. The attitude or emotion it suggests is often called its **connotation**. While the denotation of both *cur* and *man's best friend* may simply be "dog," *cur* has unfavorable or derogatory connotations, *man's best*

[1] See also D 1b.

friend has flattering or complimentary connotations. Words with strong connotations bring into play a wide range of associations, commitments, affections, fears, and resentments. *Dagger* simply denotes a short weapon for stabbing, but it connotes treachery. *Sword* denotes a somewhat longer weapon; it connotes valor, chivalrous adventure.

The power of words to suggest attitudes is most obvious in fields like politics, where attitudes differ widely. From the broad range of possible terms, the political propagandist will select those with either favorable or unfavorable connotations. When a public official is accused of dishonesty, his opponents say that he has been "exposed," while his friends say that he has been "smeared." When the same official is cleared for lack of sufficient evidence, his opponents say that he has been "whitewashed," while his friends say that he has been "vindicated." To indicate that its foreign policy is changing, the administration calls it "dynamic" and "alert," whereas its political opponents call it "aimless" and "confused."

Such verbal slanting is hard to resist. Most of us associate the word *statesman* with public-spirited wisdom and the word *politician* with crafty, self-seeking manipulation. *Bureaucrat* makes us think of red tape; *public servant* makes us think of somebody looking out after our own best interests. In a discussion of a road-building program, the phrase *government funds* makes us think that we are getting something for nothing, while the phrase *taxpayers' money* makes us feel that the money is coming out of our own pockets.

Some words are so strongly charged as to evoke an almost automatic response. If a writer refers to the killing of John Doe as the "murder" of John Doe, the word *murder* will cause an almost automatic reaction of horror, disgust, and violent disapproval. If he speaks of the "execution" of John Doe, the killing will sound respectable and official. If he refers to it as "administration of justice," most readers will feel reassured. To "liquidate" one's political opposition makes killing sound businesslike and scientific; "exterminate" or "eradicate" makes it sound as though one were getting rid of vermin. Goebbels, minister for propaganda under Hitler, made the killing of political prisoners sound reassuring by announcing that certain elements had been "rendered harmless."

Interpreting Emotive Language

To maintain a clear view of people and events, we need to separate the objective meaning of words from the attitudes and emotions they imply. For instance, the words *constitution* and *constitutional* have a strong emotional coloring. They suggest pride, approval, assurance that things are regulated for the best. A careful reader will not let this feeling of approval carry over into his attitude toward provisions of state constitution that were adopted in a spirit of partisan spite. *Alien, foreigner,* and *un-American* may evoke suspicion and uneasiness. However, they often need to be treated as dispassionately as "originating outside the continental United States" or "coming from another part of the world."

You will find that it is not easy to keep from cheering an idea when it is stated in flattering terms and booing it when it is stated in unflattering ones. One possible precaution is practice in matching corresponding complimentary and derogatory terms in order to neutralize whatever unexamined attitudes they may suggest. For instance, examine the relationship between *courageous* and *reckless, loyal* and *servile, tolerant* and *indiscriminate, devout* and *sanctimonious.* Or pair the "plus words" and the "minus words" for familiar political ideas: *democracy—mob rule; leader—demagogue; conciliation—appeasement; grant-in-aid—handout.* Such pairing of related terms, like the confrontation of contradictory witnesses, will remind you of your responsibility to draw your own conclusions.

Another helpful precaution is to chart the emotive expressions typical of a writer in order to prevent them from subtly subverting your own better judgment. Many journalists and public figures habitually use one set of terms when reporting the activities of their favorite "statesman," another set of terms when reporting those of an opposition "politician." Statesman knows, understands, is aware of, is firmly convinced; Politician guesses, theorizes, speculates, or suspects. Statesman gravely points out, forthrightly declares, bluntly states, eloquently sets forth; Politician excitedly sputters, theatrically proclaims, brazenly alleges, or stridently asserts. Statesman consults with his advisers, reaffirms basic convictions, makes decisions, and finds solutions; Politician listens to his cronies, hunts for issues, jumps to conclusions, and gets bright ideas. Statesman presents a sound program, guards basic rights, and works for the good of the nation; Politician indulges in Utopian dreams, caters to special interests, and plays politics. Statesman shows his skill in facing the realities of political life; Politician demonstrates his political deviousness and lack of candor. When exposed to such consistent verbal slanting, even an alert reader will have to remind himself that the difference between Statesman and Politician may be all in the words of the reporter.

Once we make allowance for it, emotive language ceases to mislead and becomes instructive instead. *When skillfully interpreted, emotive language provides valuable clues to preferences and commitments that a writer does not openly admit.* A man who represents himself as an impartial observer will often reveal his sympathies by the words he uses to identify issues and personalities. An editorial writer who speaks of "labor strongmen," "labor politicians," and "union bosses" is not likely to be a champion of organized labor. The parent who refers to "warming a youngster's tail" is less likely to be a foe of corporal punishment than the parent who refers to "beatings administered to children."

Changes in vocabulary are often a symptom of changes in attitude. Changing moral standards are reflected in gradual shifts from *vicious* to *antisocial* to *maladjusted;* from *perversion* to *abnormality* to *deviation;* from *modest* to *shy* to *inhibited.* Paying attention to the values implied in such words is one way of reading between the lines.

The Weaknesses of Strong Language

Avoid the routine use of strong language. In your writing, emotive language will be as much of a problem as in your reading. When you use it too freely and routinely, it may well produce a clash of emotions rather than a meeting of minds. Learn to tone down the emotional implications of the words you employ. You can often keep a discussion focused on the issues at stake by substituting neutral terms for words that are complimentary or derogatory. For instance, you can learn to keep irrelevant associations out of references to other people by studying alternatives like the following:

Complimentary	Derogatory	Neutral
public servant	bureaucrat	government employee
financier	speculator	investor
law officer	cop	policeman
legislative consultant	lobbyist	spokesman of group interests
stage personality	ham	actor
manufacturer's representative	huckster	salesman
labor leader	union boss	union official
captain of industry	tycoon	successful businessman
investigator	spy	detective
captive	jailbird	prisoner
soldier of fortune	hired killer	mercenary

Even a writer who is trying to present an objective argument or a scientific report sometimes has trouble with emotionally weighted words. A psychologist describing typical or frequent behavior may inadvertently use terms which, contrary to his intention, suggest approval or dislike. *Healthy* would imply strong approval; *normal* would be taken to imply approval by many readers; *mediocre* sounds negative and implies that to be average is not good enough. However, the systematic procedure and the careful attention to detail of a scientist's report can do much to cool off emotions that a word would ordinarily arouse. Similarly, a dignified and objective context can do much to neutralize the derogatory implications of *politician, socialism, lobbyist,* or *vagrant.*

The limitations of emotive language are most obvious with words that express strong feelings of disapproval and contempt. In moments of emotional stress, we are tempted to employ **invective,** more popularly known as name calling or abuse. When we are angry at motorists who dump eggshells, beer cans, and waste paper along scenic highways, we derive strong satisfaction from an article attacking "rampant slobbism," "careless boobs," and the "spreading desecration of the American landscape." Even such an article, however, is likely to owe its more lasting effects not to invective but to more substantial means of persuasion. Compare the following two passages by the same writer:

Acquisition of new parkland has not kept pace with population growth, and in many cities the planners have been *stealing* land from existing parks for projects with higher priority, such as super-highways and parking lots. The newer the metropolitan area, the more likely it is to be short of a *decent minimum* of greenery. I suppose Los Angeles has a park somewhere, but I have never seen it.

Much of Denver's beauty comes from trees that were planted and parks that were established more than forty years ago. I would say, on the basis of having very recently viewed some of the jam-packed, look-alike houses now springing up on the north side of Denver, that *not much is being done to make the city beautiful forty years hence.* — Vance Packard, "America the Beautiful — and Its Desecraters," *Atlantic*

In the first passage, the term *steal* will strike as unfair many people who are aware of the conflicting pressures and interests that planning commissions must reconcile. The second passage, by contrast, does without abusive language; instead, it effectively appeals to a sense of obligation that many readers will share: We enjoy the fruits of the investments by earlier generations, and we should make similar investments to benefit our children and grandchildren.

No one wants your writing to be bland, noncommittal, colorless — and dull. But as you use language that *does* have color and verve, keep the following problems in mind:

(1) *Some words have different associations for different readers.* To some readers, the word *progressive* suggests awareness of the demands of the modern world. To other readers, it suggests newfangled schemes. The term *socialism* may suggest strong disapproval to an American businessman, but merely suggest an eminently respectable

political alternative to a teacher from Britain. Words with such **variable connotations** can easily short-circuit discussion.

(2) *When overused, strong language loses its sting.* Terms like *reactionary, radical, fascist,* and *communist* have so often served as ignorant abuse that they have lost their power to influence a thoughtful reader. A fuller glossary of used-up vilifiers might include *leftist, fellow traveler, do-gooder, militarist, aggressor, appeasement, egghead, beatnik,* and *Uncle Tom.* Add your own favorites to this list.

(3) *Abusive language often backfires.* The emotional relief and the sense of triumph that we derive from it are likely to be short-lived. We have to ask not only "What does this do for me?" but also "What does this do to my reader?" Often the answer is "It will bring out the worst in him." A well-aimed insult may on occasion succeed in shaming or reforming the reader. But more often, the reader who feels insulted will turn a deaf ear to all further attempts at persuasion. We do not make police officers more humane by telling them that their calling tends to attract bullies, sadists, and people with paranoid inclinations.

(4) *Verbal violence breeds physical violence.* It is an exceedingly grave matter to call a civil rights leader "a notorious liar" or a President of the United States "a murderer." Such words tear at the fabric that precariously holds together a pluralistic society. Thomas Hobbes, in the *Leviathan,* set out to show men how they could emerge from the jungle and live in peace. He set down the avoidance of hateful and contemptuous language as one of the conditions for the emergence of civilized society:

And because all signs of hatred or contempt provoke to fight . . . we may in the eighth place, for a law of nature, set down this precept, that no man by deed, *word,* countenance, or gesture, declare hatred or contempt of another. The breach of which law is called *contumely.*

(5) *Where everything is emphasized, nothing is emphasized.* When someone always shouts at the top of his voice, nothing stands out. When a responsible writer *does* use strong language, it gains force from its contrast with more dispassionate, more coolly argued passages. It carries authority because it comes from someone who weighs and ponders before he accuses and denounces. The following statements owe their power in part to their coming from writers who do *not* make grave charges lightly:

The glorification of one race and the consequent debasement of another — or others — always has been and always will be a recipe for murder. (James Baldwin)

In the earlier part of the century scores of thousands of children, aged sometimes as young as six, were literally worked to death in the mines or cotton mills, and even at the fashionable public schools boys were flogged till they ran with blood for a mistake in their Latin verses.   (George Orwell)

The science, the art, the jurisprudence, the chief political and social theories, of the modern world have grown out of those of Greece and Rome—not by favour of, but in the teeth of, the fundamental teachings of early Christianity, to which science, art, and any serious occupation with the things of this world, were alike despicable. (T. H. Huxley)

Even when you feel strongly about a subject, your readers will want to feel that you respect their judgment enough to give them a chance to make up their own minds. They will welcome emotive language that helps transform a dry treatise into a lively and emphatic piece of writing. They will respect emotive language that is the sincere expression of strong convictions. But they will resent emotive language if you consistently use it to prejudge issues and to prevent rational appraisal.

Statement and Implication

Be prepared to assume responsibility for what you hint as well as for what you state outright. Much persuasive language exploits the difference between statement and implication. Suppose a senator calls an enterprise undertaken by the Secretary-General of the United Nations "a failure by any standards that Americans can use." This statement implies that those who consider the enterprise a success are not good solid Americans. Mentioning two things together can suggest a causal relationship: "He is Irish and drinks a great deal" (because he is Irish?). The mere fact that something is mentioned at all can suggest that it is newsworthy. "Salvex is now 100 per cent pure" suggests that purity is important. "Salvex now contains *three* active ingredients" suggests that impurity is important.

Implications can cause bad feelings because the author is usually ready to accept responsibility for what he states but not for what he suggests. The investigator who admonishes a witness to tell the truth seldom admits that he is trying to make the witness look like a liar. The congressman who says "Most college professors are loyal, competent Americans" is seldom prepared to substantiate charges against that minority of college professors who, by implication, are disloyal and incompetent. Suggestion thus becomes **innuendo**, a means of insinuating things that the writer or the speaker is unable and unwilling to defend.

Here are some uses of implication that many readers find evasive or annoying:

Vague Charges   Implied charges are often left deliberately vague, so that the victim has little chance to refute them. "Scientist So-and-So associated with communists" might conceivably damage So-and-So's career and reputation. It may, however, mean many different things: He may have met a communist or two at a cocktail party. He may have had long arguments with communist fellow scientists. He may have associated with communists in planning legal activities, such as fund raising, strikes, or propaganda campaigns. He may have associated with them in planning illegal activities, such as revolution or espionage.

Loaded Allusions   An editorial writer may have been blaming the opposition party for being too friendly toward a foreign power. His last sentence reads, "If we listen to these people, we may be engulfed by disaster, without so much as a Trojan horse for a souvenir." What exactly is implied in the **allusion** to the "Trojan horse"?

Rhetorical Questions   The **rhetorical question** has a built-in answer: It *seems* to leave the decision up to the reader, but it is worded in such a way that only one answer is possible. "Would you deprive your wife of a convenience that is essential to her health and peace of mind?" "Would you recommend a teacher who doesn't care whether his students succeed or fail?" It is hard to answer "yes" to such questions.

An occasional rhetorical question can serve to dramatize an important point. However, when rhetorical questions are used to cover up a scarcity of good arguments, they easily become annoying. Do not try to settle difficult issues by simply inquiring: "If the government can send an eighteen-year-old boy to war, can it deprive him of the right to vote?" or "Can a law that goes against the desires of millions of citizens be called just and fair?" An impatient reader is likely to reply: "Well, can it? If not, why not?"

Exercises

A. Spell out as fully as you can the *attitudes implied or suggested* by the words italicized in the following passages.

1. The President *trimmed* $8 billion from the budget, and the *howls* went up from the afflicted.

2. *Going after* students as formerly politicians went after labor and farmers, the candidate was being *pawed* by the *adoring*.

3. The *ritualistic* "anti-cop" attitude of many liberals is *sophomoric* and *escapist*.

4. Because he doubted the wisdom of *backdoor entry* into World War II, he was *tarred* as a Nazi.

5. Last December, college presidents *wrung* an assurance from the White House that draft boards would not be used to "repress unpopular views."

6. To preserve the inculcation of reverence in your public schools may not be possible under the *regime* of the present Chief Justice.

7. The New Left ranges from slightly *disguised* representatives of the Old Left to political *fauna* so bizarre as to defy classification.

8. The *intelligentsia's* affinity for left-wing politics results from the fact that American conservatism is an intellectual wilderness, populated by *Babbitts* and *ex-plebeians* who have acquired *split-level homes*.

B. Examine the differences in attitude suggested by the *changes in the wording* of the following passages.

1. Jones was a portly man with a healthy glow in his cheeks.
   Jones was a stout man with a ruddy complexion.
   Jones was a pudgy man with a complexion like a boiled lobster.

2. Last night, vandals defaced a patriotic monument by smearing yellow paint over a statue of the Father of Our Country.
   Some youngsters out for a lark last night painted a yellow mustache on a weather-beaten statue of George Washington.

3. Simon withdrew from college because he had difficulty keeping up with the pressure of college work.
   Simon flunked out of school because he was unable to do the assignments.
   After one semester on probation, Simon dropped out of college.

4. An economy-minded legislature has called a halt to additional spending.
   A penny-pinching legislature has refused to appropriate adequate funds.
   The legislature has cut the budget submitted by the governor by approximately 3 per cent.

5. John studies little and often quarrels with his classmates.

John needs to improve his study habits and his relations with other children.

John, in addition to being lazy, is a constant troublemaker.

6. Former prisoners were continually spied upon even after their return to civilian life.

Ex-convicts were kept under surveillance after their release from penal institutions.

Criminals were carefully watched as a potential menace to society.

7. Her father was unemployed and received relief payments from the County Welfare Department.

Instead of working, her father lived on government handouts.

Her father was out of work and had to accept help from the county.

8. The school board fired Mr. Smith for insubordination.

The school board dismissed Mr. Smith for refusing to answer questions about his home life.

The school board deprived Mr. Smith of his job for resisting their attempts to pry into his private affairs.

9. The governor compromised standards of official integrity by condoning John Smith's misconduct.

The governor refused to turn his back on a trusted subordinate involved in legal difficulties.

C. The following passage is addressed by Don Juan to the Devil in Act III of George Bernard Shaw's *Man and Superman*. Explore as fully as you can the common core and the contrasting connotations of each pair of words. Which words have *unfavorable* connotations for Shaw (or Don Juan) but *favorable* connotations for you, and vice versa? How do you explain the difference? To judge from the description here provided, who are the Devil's friends?

Pooh! Why should I be civil to them or to you? In this Palace of Lies a truth or two will not hurt you. Your friends are all the dullest dogs I know. They are not beautiful: they are only decorated. They are not clean: they are only shaved and starched. They are not dignified: they are only fashionably dressed. They are not educated: they are only college passmen. They are not religious: they are only pew-renters. They are not moral: they are only conventional. They are not virtuous: they are only cowardly. They are not even vicious: they are only "frail." They are not artistic: they are only lascivious. They are not prosperous: they are only rich. They are not loyal, they are only servile; not dutiful, only sheepish; not public spirited, only patriotic; not courageous, only quarrelsome; not determined, only obstinate; not masterful, only domineering; not self-controlled, only obtuse; not self-respecting, only vain; not kind, only sentimental; not social, only gregarious; not considerate, only polite; not intelligent, only opinionated; not progressive, only factious; not imaginative, only superstitious; not just, only vindictive; not generous, only propitiatory; not disciplined, only cowed; and not truthful at all: liars every one of them, to the very backbone of their souls.

D. Examine and evaluate the techniques of persuasion used in the following selections. Pay special attention to the use of *emotive language.*

1. The editorial policy of the campus daily seems to be directed by a mid-Victorian Sunday school teacher with an inferiority complex. As a result, this chicken-hearted, lily-livered, weak-minded, professor-parroting, know-nothing, do-nothing, say-nothing fish wrapper refuses to take a stand on anything (assuming that it is capable of such). Any news with the magic word "instructor" in it gets top coverage, while other news, no matter how important, is put on the back page under the obituaries. Why this lack of backbone? Is it because the editors do not realize that the world has changed since 1870, and that tomatoes aren't really poisonous? Open up your eyes, student journalists of the Daily! It's hard to see unless you do.

2. Deficit financing never accords with the public weal. Government spending in excess of tax revenues and the resulting inflation both indicate either ignorance or neglect of duty on the part of the legislators and executives responsible. Clearly, inflation is always reprehensible, for it surreptitiously robs every bank depositor and every owner of bonds, notes, or mortgages of part of his property. Indeed, it is an especially pernicious type of theft, for it even filches away the pensions going to the disabled or decrepit and the life insurance accumulated through the years by thoughtful and considerate men for the protection of their loved ones. Therefore, to prescribe inflation as a remedy for recession indicates that the person doing so is either an economic illiterate or a knave.

3. Students are politically disenfranchised. Many of them can vote in national elections, but they have no vote in the decisions that affect their academic lives. The students are, it is true, allowed to have a toy government of their own. It is a government run for the most part by Uncle Toms and concerned principally with trivia. The faculty and administrators decide what courses will be offered; the students get to choose their own Homecoming Queen.

4. The publication of patently pornographic books and magazines for distribution on newsstands seems to us a clear abuse of the privilege of a free press, and those who profit from these sultry ventures know perfectly well, in spite of self-righteous denials, that this profitable filth will fall under some eyes too young to be exposed to such matters. Our feeling about four-letter words and pornography has always boiled down to a simple equation: We would no more allow this sort of material to fall into the hands of small fry than we would hand them a glass of

straight gin. They simply aren't ready for such strong doses of adult stimulant. Yet scarcely a night goes by that network TV does not step over this commonsense line in a medium that goes straight to the heart of every home.

5. Best deodorant beauty bar is a truly unique bath and beauty product. Before you take your first Best bath, we would like to tell you just a few things about Best . . . a few of the reasons why it's so wonderfully different. Open the luxurious foil wrapper and notice first of all the delicate pastel color . . . smell that fragrance of fine perfumes. Then, step into your Best bath and see how billows of rich lather appear almost like magic. And Best is so wonderfully mild . . . so gentle to your complexion . . . leaves your skin clearer, fresher, cleaner. After your first Best bath, you'll discover the new sensation of "feeling really clean." You see . . . Best leaves your skin free of the unseen sticky film that all ordinary soaps leave. Perhaps most wonderful of all . . . you'll find that Best's amazing new deodorant action helps keep you fresh and protected all day. That's because Best's wonderful new deodorant ingredient destroys odor-causing bacteria all over your body.

E. Select a piece of writing which shows that the writer's emotions are aroused. For example, choose a *newspaper editorial*, a *letter to the editor* of a newspaper or magazine, a strongly favorable or unfavorable *book review*. Discuss and evaluate the methods of persuasion used, paying special attention to the use of emotive language. Your instructor may ask you to provide a copy of the selection you discuss.

F. Study samples of *advertising* for a nationally known product or company. Select a full-page ad and examine the methods of persuasion used, paying special attention to the use of emotive language. Your instructor may ask you to provide a copy of the ad.

G. Discuss and evaluate the techniques of persuasion illustrated in all or portions of a famous document from *American history*. Choose a document like the Declaration of Independence, Thomas Paine's *The Crisis*, one of James Madison's contributions to *The Federalist,* or a selection from the speeches and writings of Daniel Webster, John C. Calhoun, or William Lloyd Garrison.

4. The Strategies of Persuasion

In working out his general strategy, the effective persuasive writer moves between two extremes. At one extreme, the writer with a message or with a grievance spontaneously gives vent to his feelings, flailing away at his opposition, real and imagined. At the other extreme, the retained propagandist, all in a day's work, plots the campaign designed to work the desired effect on his carefully analyzed public. Between the two extremes, a writer writing from conviction works out the strategy that will help his message reach his readers.

Appealing to a Common Cause

Find the common interests or the shared convictions that will bring the reader over to your side. If you were a teacher arguing for smaller class sizes before a school board, would you stress the benefits in more leisure time for teachers released from paper-reading chores? Or would you stress the benefits to the taxpayers' children, such as more individual attention? Probably, teachers and school board would find a common interest in improved education for the children.

When the reader is expected to change his mind on an important issue, the writer is not likely to succeed unless he can appeal to a strong common motive or commitment. In 1849, Thoreau published his essay on the right of civil disobedience to a government that was a party to slavery and that was engaged in what he considered an unjust foreign war. He appealed to the "right of revolution" asserted by his countrymen in the War of Independence — "the right to refuse allegiance to, and to resist, the government, when its tyranny or its inefficiency are great and unendurable."

In our time, the civil rights movement owes its force to its appeal to widely held principles, to basic American beliefs. As one social critic has said, in recent years the American Negro "demanded that this society live up to its own pieties. Words about equality and justice which had been as ceremonial as a Fourth of July speech suddenly became the programs and slogans of a militant mass movement." Richard Wright in his autobiography, James Baldwin in his essays, and Ralph Ellison in his fiction powerfully appeal to ideals we all recognize: the belief in human dignity, the right of a human being to be respected as an individual.

Dramatizing the Issue

Translate abstract issues into personal or human terms. Grave issues have *general* significance; they may seem far from the reader's personal frame of reference. The statistics of misfortune and injustice, however grim, are also *impersonal*. Accident statistics can make us shudder, but they do not jolt us as witnessing a single actual accident does. To the persuasive writer, one striking case, dramatizing the issue, is worth a thousand anonymous ones, reflected in statistical percentages.

The fate of a single individual can fire our imagination the way large figures cannot. When statistics about violence in our cities fall on deaf ears, a single horrible event, involving someone widely loved or admired, can arouse and focus public concern. In nineteenth-century France, much anti-semitism was of the country club and officers' mess variety—practiced covertly by eminently respectable people. To expose and discredit their complacency became possible through the Dreyfus affair, the case of a Jewish officer convicted of treason but cleared after years of bitter controversy. In Germany after World War II, it took the story of Anne Frank to make many Germans fully realize for the first time the enormity of the Nazi crimes.

An effective persuasive writer will often build his case entirely or in part on a single striking instance. The foe of capital punishment may devote all or most of his argument to the detailed examination of a *cause célèbre*, a man executed after years of legal battle and bitter debate.

Persuading by Degrees

Take the reader from where he is to where you want him to be. Contrary to the stereotype of the ranting demagogue, a striking characteristic of a truly persuasive speaker is his patience. He sizes up the mood of the moment, estimates what his audience is ready for, holds his most important points in abeyance until the time is ripe. "I come to bury Caesar, not to praise him"—there will be plenty of time to praise him in a little while.

"Meet them where they are, but don't stay there" is an elementary principle of effective teaching. In trying to introduce a student to the principle of gravity, an instructor might start from a trivial everyday manifestation of gravity, such as a pencil dropping to the floor or an apple dropping from a tree. In order to explain the workings of a steam engine, he might start from such a familiar observation as that of steam lifting the lid of a pot or blowing the whistle of a kettle.

Like an effective teacher, a persuasive writer will often move

- from the simple to the difficult;
- from the familiar to the new;
- from the safe to the controversial;
- from the plausible to the paradoxical.

Can you see how the following paper on "tolerance" gradually leads the reader from the trivial and familiar to the significant and controversial?

I. The most basic quality of a tolerant person is *patience*. A teacher must be tolerant when the person being taught to play tennis or run a mimeographing machine gets the same simple operation wrong for the fourth time.

II. A tolerant person demonstrates his tolerance by his *willingness to live and let live*. He has learned to put up with noisy neighbors, dogs running over his lawn, a radio blaring next to him on the beach.

III. But the true test of a tolerant person is his *willingness to listen and to learn* — the willingness of a strongly religious student to listen to an astronomer's lecture denying supernatural existence, the willingness of a no-nonsense science major to look at the evidence for extrasensory perception.

Demolishing the Opposition

Attack opposed views likely to carry much weight with your reader. Writers like Thomas Paine or Jonathan Swift do to the opposition what the wrecking crew does to a venerable old building. Often, more positive arguments would be unavailing, because basic misconceptions on the part of the reader might not have been touched. Though the writer might make a strong case *for* his point of view, the stubborn reader would say, "That is all very well, but . . . "

When a persuasive writer aggressively moves in on his opposition, his writing becomes **polemical**. A polemical writer often exposes the weaknesses in his opponent's premises, and the flaws in his argument, with great gusto. He will look for vulnerable spots like the following:

• *extreme praise* or *rash promises* that can be ridiculed by being juxtaposed with imperfect reality. This is the strategy we expect the writer to adopt when he starts a paper as follows:

THE CAUSES OF THE PULLMAN STRIKE

The last paragraph of a small pamphlet entitled *The Story of Pullman*, which was prepared by the Pullman Company for distribution at its exhibit at the World's Fair in 1893, reads:

> Imagine a perfectly equipped town of twelve thousand inhabitants, built from one central thought to a beautiful and harmonious whole . . . a town, in a word, where all that is ugly and discordant and demoralizing is eliminated, and all that inspires to self-respect, to thrift, and to cleanliness of person and of thought is generously provided. Imagine all this . . . and you will then have some idea of the splendid work, in its physical aspects at least, which Mr. Pullman has wrought.

• *premises* or *arguments* adopted to bolster a particular point of view but yielding absurd results when applied elsewhere. Eighteenth-century thinkers argued for the existence of a divine Creator by comparing the universe to a machine built by a master mechanic or a house built by a master craftsman. However, as David Hume pointed out, machines and houses are usually built by more than one person, so that the analogy would support a polytheistic hypothesis even more strongly than the existence of a single deity.

Sometimes, a whole paper or article may be devoted to attacking obstacles to reform, or views blocking the acceptance of a new idea. More often an attack on the opposition is only one part of a larger strategy. In the following excerpted theme, positive arguments in favor of dissent, and its defense against the most important objections, combine to give shape to the paper as a whole:

THE IMPORTANCE OF DISSENT

appeal to a common cause
    The right to dissent, to disagree and differ in opinion, is one of the most precious rights of an American citizen. . . .

appeal to historical precedent
    It was the exercise of dissent that first led the American colonists to assert their independence in the Revolutionary War. . . .

first objection refuted
    It is sometimes made to seem as if the right of dissent is claimed mainly by self-important people who must always make known their own views. But the true purpose of dissent is not to indulge those who want to speak their minds, but to help "prevent error and discover truth." . . .

second objection refuted
    Many find dissent distasteful because it is disorderly and disruptive; because it is often shrill or unmannerly. But it is universally painful to have to rethink established premises. . . .

third objection refuted
    Probably the most significant objection to dissent is that it is unpatriotic in a time of crisis. Dissent is said to weaken our nation in external conflicts because it gives opponents the impression that the American people are divided. But, in the words of one U.S. Senator, our country has "rarely been far from a crisis of sufficient magnitude" for someone to call for the suspension of dissent. . . .

appeal to authority
    The importance of dissent was well summed up by John Stuart Mill: "If all mankind minus one were of one opinion, and only one person were of a contrary opinion, mankind would be no more justified in silencing that one person than he . . . would be justified in silencing mankind."

Exercises

A. Study important editorials in a major newspaper over a period of weeks. What are the standards, interests, or ideals most consistently appealed to? Write a composite portrait of the person whose attitudes and standards would make him the *ideal reader* of the paper.

B. Write a brief account of an *individual case* that strongly influenced your views on an important issue.

C. Write a brief outline of a speech, a lecture, or an article that you found especially effective in *leading the audience up* to the major point(s) aimed at by the author.

D. How effectively does the author of the following passage, adapted from a longer student paper, deal with the *objections* to his own point of view?

CAPITAL PUNISHMENT

To my mind, none of the usual arguments advanced in its favor are sufficient to justify capital punishment.

(1) It cannot be shown that capital punishment is an effective deterrent to crime. Statistics on the ratio of murders committed in a country or state before and after the abolition of capital punishment seem to vary from slightly fewer to slightly more murders committed.

(2) It is often argued that it is not worth the taxpayer's money to pay for the room and board of a murderer who can never again benefit society. I can see no reason why a man in prison cannot benefit society, or at least why he cannot pay for his own costs. If I in such a situation had the choice between solitude and engaging in a work project, I would be happy to put in eight hours a day. Of course the question would arise whether the man allowed to work is receiving the full punishment of rotting in confinement.

(3) We are told that no one would suggest abolition of the death penalty after seeing a close relative or friend of a murder victim, or having been the parent of a murdered daughter. These same arguments have been used to justify lynch mobs. Are we to base our laws on the irrational behavior of those struck with grief? If you can imagine yourself when you are moved by extreme anger, would you want the law based on the type of logic you formulated then?

(4) We are often told that the deed must be avenged and that the murderer must pay his debt to society. This raises the moral question: What is a human life worth after someone has committed the act of taking another? Does this act mean that this human being can only be the object of revenge rather than be helped? Most of the advocates of revenge are followers of the Christian religion. That very religion denounces revenge. There are no exceptions listed under "Thou shalt not kill."

(5) We are told that it is immoral to execute a man who is insane, but that a sane man must accept responsibility for what he did. It seems more moral that a man, sane or insane, good or bad, who takes the life of another should be allowed to live so that he might rehabilitate and reconcile himself before God and society.

5. Persuading the Critical Reader

Some of the most familiar techniques of persuasion antagonize critical readers. Often, when we are being carried away in presenting our case, we must stop and tell ourselves: "With readers who think, this will do more harm than good."

Check your finished papers for the elements that help persuade thinking readers:

(1) *Readiness to make qualified judgments.* An effective writer builds confidence by recognizing pros and cons, by arriving at judgments that if necessary cross party lines to give credit where credit is due:

. . . His essay on "Conservative Thought" in *Essays in Sociology and Social Psychology*—while truculent and somewhat Marxist in motivation—is one of the most brilliant studies of conservatism ever written.—book review in *National Review*

The abuse meted out to Presidents has a healthily scurrilous element. Some commentators see it as a guarantee that Americans will never accept a real dictator: their natural irreverence protects them against such psychological radiation. *But the scurrility has a hysterical tinge.* John F. Kennedy may not have deserved all the praise that was heaped upon him: he *certainly did* not *deserve the corrosive denunciations that were circulating before his death.*—Marcus Cunliffe, "A Defective Institution?" *Commentary*

(2) *Willingness to make concessions, to meet the reader halfway.* Many intelligent readers are heartily tired of the lily-white, true-blue champion of truth and justice who always finds himself 100 per cent in the right on every issue. A writer addressing a critical reader may at times have to go out of his way to avoid an imputation of self-righteousness.

The sins of omission and commission of the over-thirty generation (if it makes any sense to speak in such general terms) *are many and serious;* so it has always been and so it will always be. But unless one is willing to compare reality only with utopia, then the nation into which these young people are entering as adults cannot be simply or reasonably characterized as a "sick society." It is, among many other things, a nation that enjoys and has always enjoyed more political, cultural, and religious freedom than any—or almost any—other society, past or present; it is a nation with an economy of almost unbelievable productivity; and it is a nation that has, since having leadership thrust upon it, generally played an honorable role in international affairs.

I know all the arguments against such positive and optimistic statements, and I know how many qualifications and disclaimers need to be added. Especially it must be said that the unemployed and the Negroes do not share appropriately in wealth and status and that American foreign policy has its darker side. That there is plenty of room for improvement is all too obvious.—William Gerberding, "Liberals and Radicals," *The Reporter*

(3) *Full discussion of whatever is startling, controversial, or difficult.* A writer throwing out a multitude of unexpected or original ideas can stir up discussion, suggest possibilities, impress his readers.

He seldom produces lasting conviction. To be effective, persuasion needs to concentrate on driving home one major point at a time.

(4) *Willingness to identify doubtful conclusions and open questions.* A writer addressing critical readers weakens his position by pretending to omniscience. He should not feel obligated to have a ready answer on every aspect of a complicated problem. If conflicting evidence prevents clear-cut conclusions, he should say so.

(5) *Serious consideration of objections.* To many readers, a writer's handling of adverse evidence is a touchstone of his sincerity and competence. He should show that he has thought of important objections and has found a satisfactory way of dealing with them. By taking this precaution, he makes it harder for the reader to resist his arguments and for the critic to find fault with them.

Review Exercises (including student themes)

A. How persuasive is the following *letter to the editor?* Does it persuade *you?* Point out in detail the features that you consider most effective and those you consider least effective. How much depends on the audience?

A Life with Guns

When I was seven, happiness was a toy six-shooter, with which I banged around the neighborhood and felt as powerful as Tom Mix.

When I was eleven, Christmas brought a Daisy Air Rifle with which I promptly killed a few sparrows, and almost shot out a playmate's eye while playing cops and robbers. When I was fourteen I graduated to a .22 rifle, which was deadly on song birds, but which consistently missed the bounding local jack rabbits. At fifteen I began collecting old unfireable guns and miscellaneous cartridges. I day dreamed of what could be killed with this or that bullet, and felt vicariously potent.

I don't think I was an uncharacteristic product of the American culture — a culture which has made folk heroes of not only Daniel Boone and Kit Carson, but also Billy the Kid and Bonnie and Clyde.

Modern anthropologists have become aware that our pre-human primate ancestors were not tree dwelling vegetarians like present day apes, but ground dwelling, weapon-using carnivores. Our heritage then is aggression, and it is hard to change our ingrained instincts in a few thousand years of semi-civilization. In America, having no history of battles won with sword or bow, the gun has been our aggressive tool. With it we killed off the buffalo and the Indians, conquered a continent and fought some wars. And guns are still our "thing." Boys still grow up as I did, never hearing of Thoreau, but steeped in Wyatt Earp.

I still feel this romantic attachment for the things. I occasionally still day dream of defending my home from some dastardly criminal with my trusty Colt. But this is unrealistic — it is a dream. The day of the Frontier is past, and guns no longer represent security. Rather they are the symbol of the murderer, the robber, the rioter, the suicide.

In this decade we have seen ostensibly "hunting" rifles used to kill a President, Martin Luther King, and thousands of lesser folk. It is said that guns would not kill if there were not people to shoot them. It could also be said that people would rarely kill if they lacked the weapons to do so. There is no prospect of our being able to recognize and adequately deal with the potential killers among us in the near future. A more practical solution for the present is to remove the primary method of homicide — the gun.

But there is a more pressing threat than even the sniper or assassin. The Negro after two centuries of exploitation is openly rebellious, and, given the weapons, their youth could ignite the most bloody revolution this country has seen since the civil war. On the other side there are the white racists arming in fear, and the militant right wingers storing up arsenals against the omni-present Communists that pervade their paranoid world.

The measures so far suggested or adopted to control guns are ludicrously inadequate. Registration will accomplish little or nothing. In spite of my life-long infatuation with the things, reason tells me that guns must be eradicated from our cities.

What I would propose is that there be State or even national laws that guns be illegal anywhere that there is no legitimate use for them. Except in the hands of law enforcement personnel, guns would be kept locked up at target ranges and at depositories in hunting areas. They could be checked out only for those acceptable uses. The ramification of this proposal is that the mere possession of an unauthorized gun in a city would be cause for arrest.

To the anticipated argument that this would breach the Second Amendment, it should be pointed out that the right to bear arms refers to a "well regulated militia." None of our gun-carrying civilian organizations, white or black, can be seriously considered such.

B. Study the following *student papers* on subjects on which readers are likely to have strong opinions. What does each writer do to persuade readers inclined to disagree with him? How successful is he? Describe as fully as you can the writer's strategy and his use of persuasive language.

1.   THE EVILS OF COMIC BOOKS

"Garishly presented in clashing colors and cheaply printed in forty-eight paperbound pages of pulp" lies an imaginary children's world which has yet to be surpassed in terms of enjoyment, quality, and price. This world is not the wasteland of violence and the corrupter of young minds against which many people have self-righteously protested. Rather, it is a world in which a young boy or girl may spend hours of contented learning and preparation. In short, the comic book is the most misinterpreted and slandered of childhood's unsung heroes.

For years now, the "experts" have preached with hellfire-and-brimstone enthusiasm against all the violence and sordid excitement contained in the comic books. There have even been attempts by irate mothers and other concerned people to have state and even federal legislatures pass laws of censorship concerning comic books and their publishers. All of this activity has arisen from the belief that comics provoke the young mind to thoughts of violence and crime by somehow giving the underworld a romantic appeal, which destroys the developing conscience nurtured by the child's parents. This claim, however, is all an unsubstantiated alarmist's myth.

I feel that I speak with some degree of authority on this subject, having been a dedicated and impassioned young follower of Superman, Batman, Green Lantern, and the rest. Likewise, my father and my uncle before me, and all my friends have also walked through the valley of moral and spiritual death of the comic book. I am sure that you, the reader, have also read at least two or three of these subversive publications in your younger days. And, somehow, all of us, I, my father, my uncle, and perhaps you yourself, have weathered the destruction, the incurable damage perpetrated upon our once young and impressionable little brains. Indeed, thousands upon thousands and by far the vast majority of young comic book readers, like ourselves, have matured into the adult world without any latent effects whatsoever.

I consider myself to have been a somewhat typical fan of the funny books, and, in retrospect, they were actually an important benefactor of my development. The comics were an intermediate step between first-grade "Run, Spot, run, run, run!" and the later, more sophisticated enjoyment of *Black Beauty*. It is because of the comics that my interest in reading developed, for, at the age at which one masters its techniques, the plots must be simple, the action funny or exciting (and in the comics they certainly are) in order to retain the wandering attention of young readers. Comics helped to carry me through this struggling period of reading development until I had matured enough to find pleasure in more solid material.

Certainly the quality of the moral implications in these magazines is acceptable. A comic, as a rule, concerns the exploits of some champion of justice who, through a combination of brains *and* brawn, gets his or her man or monster. Evil, however, is always the loser.

But perhaps the most immediate factor concerning the young is the vast amount of pleasure they find in lying on the floor on a drizzly day and donning Superman's uniform to apprehend Evil and to make things right for Metropolis. This is what is important: letting a child have the food his hungry imagination desires, food of which comic books are a source.

Besides, what logic is there in forbidding children the privilege of reading comic books? No one gives a moment's thought to the newspapers that children also read.

2.   CAPITAL PUNISHMENT: RELIC OF THE PAST

Capital punishment is a barbaric, pointless anachronism from the primitive period of man's history. In medieval times, the death sentence was the usual form of punishment for nearly all felonies. In the seventeen and early eighteen hundreds, English law listed one hundred and sixty offenses as punishable by death. One thirteen-year-old British boy in 1801 was even hanged for stealing a spoon. Today, however, capital punishment has fallen into near-international disuse. Thirty-four nations, including Great Britain and the U.S.S.R., have completely abolished the death penalty.

Capital punishment also seems to be on its way out in this country. Thirteen states, including New York, have completely abolished the death sentence, five of this thirteen during the last four years. A chart which appeared in a recent Friends Committee on Legislation Newsletter indicated that since the number of executions in the U.S. peaked at two hundred in 1936, it has slowly dwindled to only fifteen in 1964, seven in 1965, and only one execution in all of the United States in 1966.

I believe that capital punishment should be abolished in the United States because it is not a deterrent to crime, because it is applied to some groups in society more than others, and because capital punishment can put an innocent man wrongfully to death.

Let me begin with my first contention that capital punishment is not a deterrent to crime. The only way to prove that it is or is not a deterrent to crime is to compare the crime rates of states which have capital punishment with states which have abolished it. Dr. Thorsten Sellin, a criminologist at the University of Pennsylvania, in a pamphlet entitled "The Death Penalty," stated, "It is impossible to distinguish the abolition states from the others. . . . The trends of homicide rates of comparable states are similar. . . . The death penalty, as we use it, exercises no influence on the rates of capital crimes. It has failed as a deterrent." Anyone who would execute a man to keep others from committing the same must prove such deterrence. The homicide rates are not significantly different from abolition states. Capital punishment has not successfully deterred crime.

Secondly, capital punishment is applied to some groups in society more than to others. Minority racial groups are hit hardest by this imbalance of justice. Between 1930 and 1959, 3666 prisoners were put to death. 1972 were Negroes; 42 were from other minority racial groups. That makes 2,013 of the total, almost two-thirds, from minority racial groups. Then, too, wealthy people seldom receive the death penalty because they can afford better counsel. All of the people executed in the United States in 1964 were represented by court-appointed attorneys. A former governor of California stated, "As for the poor of all races, it is clear we execute them in disproportionate numbers, because they lack the resources to retain the most skillful counsel or to press their cases to the ultimate." If there is enough money behind you, you can usually avoid the chair.

Finally, the death penalty can wrongfully execute an innocent man. There are documented cases of this happening. Dr. Hugo Adam Bedau, author of the book *The Death Penalty in America,* states, "I have abstracted 74 cases occurring in the United States since 1893, in which a wrongful conviction of criminal homicide has been alleged and in most cases, proved beyond doubt; 8 probably erroneous executions and an additional 23 erroneous death sentences have been discovered." From Dr. Bedau's statement then, it is possible for an innocent man to be executed. I believe that killing a man for any crime he has committed is morally wrong, but while there is any chance that he is innocent, it is clearly murder.

In conclusion, I oppose the death penalty because it is not a deterrent to crime, because it is applied to some groups in society more than others, and because it can execute an innocent man. A governor working for the abolition of the death penalty in his own state summed up my feelings in this statement: "I oppose capital punishment because it is more vengeful than punitive; because it is more an act of hate than of justice. We kill the murderer because we fear him, not because he is beyond rehabilitation or control. We kill him not for his crime but in the blind hope that others may not commit his crime." We must put an end to this barbaric, primitive form of punishment.

Theme Topics 7

1. Write a letter to the editor in which you criticize an institution, a custom, or a practice of which you disapprove. Try to make your letter as persuasive as you can for the "typical" newspaper reader, or for a large representative cross section of the newspaper audience.

2. Study editorials, letters to the editor, lead articles, and the like, in one of the following publications in order to determine the attitudes and standards of its "ideal reader": *National Review, The Wall Street Journal, The New Republic, The Nation*. Then write a letter to the editor in which you try to change this hypothetical reader's mind on a current issue on which he is likely to have strong convictions.

3. Write a full-page ad designed to advance a project or cause that you believe in. Write two versions: one addressed to the readers of the *Reader's Digest* or *TV Guide;* the other, to the readers of *Harper's, The Atlantic,* or *The Saturday Review*. Or address one version to the readers of *True* or a similar men's magazine, the other version to the readers of a magazine like *McCall's* or *Vogue*.

4. Argue the case *for or against* one of the following in a paper addressed to an audience strongly committed to the opposite point of view: capital punishment; abolition of the draft; use of state lotteries to help finance public education; pacifism; legalized abortion.

5. Write a brief article for a student newspaper or magazine in which you argue a cause *unpopular* with many students. For instance, say something *good* about the "value system" of their parents or about a "paternalistic" administration. Find a topic on which you can write with conviction.

6. In recent years, students have increasingly registered their loss of faith in the "academic definitions of what is worth knowing or doing," their objection to the lack of "personal relevance" in the curriculum. Write a plea for more "relevance" that will sound concrete, feasible, and persuasive to readers over thirty.

7. People with conventional values are likely to deplore the "alienation" of the modern artist; they may accuse him of preoccupation with the for-

bidden, the morbid, the negative, or of a desire to shock or subvert. Write a paper in which you defend the modern artist against criticism from a middle-class audience. *Or* write a paper in which you convince a supporter of modern art of the seriousness or validity of such charges. Limit yourself to one major branch of art or one major artistic movement; focus on a specific charge.

8. Modern clergymen are often accused of being too aggressive in their social criticism. Assume that you are asked to write a brief *lay sermon* addressed to an audience with strong religious convictions. Choose a topic of strong current concern to your audience, such as taxation of church property, or prayer in the public schools. Choose a topic on which you will have to argue with your audience, but try to make your presentation as persuasive as possible.

9. Have you ever felt that one of the following groups is at times *misrepresented* by people who are part of the academic community? Have you ever felt moved to come to the defense of businessmen, military officers, Southern politicians, state legislators, the "mass audience," advertisers, or a similar category that is often the subject of recrimination? Come to its defense in a paper addressed to students and teachers that might attend a typical discussion session on campus.

10. The German novelist Günter Grass was asked why he failed to join the Social Democratic Party even though campaigning for its candidates. One reason, he said, was to save the party constant debate over whether to expel him for independent ideas at odds with the official position of the party. Should a true individualist refuse to become identified with any one party?

there are two
kinds of human
beings in the world
so my observation
has told me
namely and to wit
as follows
firstly
those who
even though they
were to reveal
the secret of the universe
to you would fail
to impress you
with any sense
of the importance
of the news
and secondly
those who could
communicate to you
that they had
just purchased
ten cents worth
of paper napkins
and make you
thrill and vibrate
with the intelligence
                    Don Marquis

CHAPTER EIGHT

Tone and Style

1.   Style and Substance

Style gives writing individuality. We read imaginative writers from Dickens and Mark Twain to Hemingway and Faulkner at least in part because of their characteristic manner. We turn to a favorite columnist in part because we have come to like his way of approaching a subject. Expository writing, though showing less variety of style than imaginative literature, must have its own kind of individuality. It cannot simply be gray, averaged-out committee prose. The reader wants to feel that what he reads was put together by a human being, not a ditto machine. In the best expository writing, we feel in contact with a person; we hear the echoes of a human voice.

Effective style does not merely convey the intended meaning in a businesslike fashion. It conveys the intended meaning aptly, freshly, or vigorously. It effectively calls attention to what is being said. It makes what is being said readable, striking, or memorable. Each of the following passages, for instance, has more bite than would a more routine statement of the same idea:

Official war propaganda, with its disgusting hypocrisy and self-righteousness, tends to make thinking people sympathize with the enemy.   (George Orwell)

The price the immigrants paid to get into America was that they had to become Americans.   (LeRoi Jones)

In my own house I was never left in the care of baby-sitters or left behind while my parents vacationed. But then my parents never traveled, never went anywhere. Neglect would have been too expensive a luxury.   (Patricia Cayo Sexton)

The writing assignments most likely to confront you directly with problems of style are those on the borderline between expository prose and imaginative literature. Similarly, you will have your best opportunity to *identify* distinct elements of style when studying kinds of writing in which the imaginative and creative ingredients in expository prose are strongest. Among such kinds of writing are the following:

(1) The **informal essay** (sometimes called the "familiar essay") provides pleasant, casual discussion of subjects of general interest. Its aim is to entertain as well as instruct. It often deals with a topic that the author takes seriously but not too seriously: amusing human foibles, matters of taste. Pedantry, for instance, can be infuriating, but in the following excerpt the author chooses to treat it lightly. Joseph Addison, who helped found the tradition of the informal essay, here

reports on his conversation with "Tom Folio" concerning Tom's reading of Virgil's *Aeneid:*

I found . . . that Tom did not believe a future state of rewards and punishments, because Aeneas, at his leaving the empire of the dead, passed through the gate of ivory, and not through that of horn. Knowing that Tom had not sense enough to give up an opinion which he had once received, that I might avoid wrangling, I told him "that Virgil possibly had his oversights as well as another author." "Ah! Mr. Bickerstaff," says he, "you would have another opinion of him, if you would read him in Daniel Heinsius's edition. I have perused him myself several times in that edition," continued he; "and after the strictest and most malicious examination, could find but two faults in him; one of them is in the *Aeneid,* where there are two commas instead of a parenthesis; and another in the third *Georgic,* where you may find a semicolon turned upside down." "Perhaps," said I, "these were not Virgil's faults, but those of the transcriber."

(2) The **humorous essay** provides the relief that we experience when we can temporarily suspend our concerns and anxieties. A humorist like S. J. Perelman provides comic relief by doggedly pushing aside the requirements imposed by common sense and propriety and substituting a mad logic of his own. Most of us can read the instructions concerning an electric blanket with equanimity, but we can trust Mr. Perelman to lie

in the dark with eyes protruding, . . . expecting at any moment to be converted into roast Long Island duckling. The possibility is evidently far from academic, to judge from the question a little later on: "Can the Comforter overheat or give an electric shock?" The manufacturers shrug aside the contingency in a breezy 450-word essay, easily comprehensible to wizards like Steinmetz but unhappily just out of my reach. One passage, nevertheless, is all too succinct:

> Even if the full 115 volts went through the Comforter, the body would have to be moist . . . a worn spot on the web wire inside the Comforter would have to touch the body . . . and another part of the body, as a hand or leg, would have to come in contact with a piece of metal, in order to get the sensation of an electric shock.

Given half a chance, I know I could fulfill these conditions, difficult though they seem. — "To Sleep, Perchance to Steam"

(3) **Satire** shows the object of its attack to be not only deplorable but also ridiculous. Many moralists have deplored the obsequiousness of those who aspire to high honors, but few have depicted them as memorably as Jonathan Swift, the master of English satire. Here, from *Gulliver's Travels,* is his account of the "trial of dexterity" required of those aspiring to special tokens of the Emperor's favor:

The Emperor holds a stick in his hands, both ends parallel to the horizon, while the candidates advancing, one by one, sometimes leap over the stick, sometimes creep under it backward and forward several times, according as the stick is advanced or depressed. Sometimes the Emperor holds one end of the stick, and his first minister the other; sometimes the minister has it entirely to himself. Whoever performs his part with most agility and holds out the longest in leaping and creeping is rewarded with the blue-colored silk; the red is given to the next, and the green to the third.

Study and practice of kinds of writing like those illustrated here will make you aware of different stylistic effects, and it will help you extend your control over a writer's stylistic resources.

NOTE: See Chapters Twelve and Thirteen for such elements of style as direct and expressive diction, apt and varied sentence style.

2. Setting the Right Tone

In expository writing, the element of style that we are likely to notice first is tone. **Tone** reflects the writer's *attitude* toward his subject and his reader. Speaking to a friend in need of help, we can give much the same advice in a nagging, teasing, or quietly encouraging tone. Similarly, a writer can vary his tone to express patience or exasperation, amusement or resentment. In supporting a community project, he can adopt the coaxing tone we use with children; the curt, impatient tone of someone pointing out the obvious; the pleading tone of someone deeply involved.

A writer learns to *control* his tone in order to make it fit his subject, and in order to achieve the desired effect. Whether the writer intends it or not, his tone does shape the reactions of his readers. A book reviewer, for instance, will produce quite different results depending on whether he adopts a tone of crude sensationalism ("the shock-by-shock confessions of a sorority girl") or a tone of judicious evaluation ("a sensitively told story of college life"). The first version will whet the reader's appetite for scandal; the second will put him in a more thoughtful mood. In your own writing, a serious tone may succeed in making the reader pay serious attention; a casual tone may put him in a more leisurely frame of mind.

Formal Writing

Serious writing is formal without being stuffy or unnatural. The most obvious differences in tone are due to the level of formality or informality on which the writer moves. At one extreme is the dignified, impersonal, carefully polished style most appropriate to the **formal** discussion of serious issues. At the other extreme is the chatty, personal, improvised style most appropriate to **informal** letters among friends. Your own writing in college will generally stay closer to the former extreme than to the latter. In technical reports, in themes of opinion and argument, and in scholarly discussion, a relatively formal style is the most appropriate choice. In autobiographical writing, in accounts of travel, and in essays devoted to personal impressions, an informal style is often appropriate, with the degree of informality depending on the intentions of the writer.

A formal style owes its distinctive quality to a number of features. Its vocabulary tends to be more extensive, more discriminating, and more technical than that of everyday English. Unlike their equivalents in parentheses, the words in the following list are likely to appear only in relatively formal writing: *arduous* (difficult), *felicitous* (appropriate), *incongruous* (queer), *indigenous* (homegrown), *lucid* (clear), *precarious* (risky), *serene* (peaceful), *spurious* (false); *frivolity* (silliness), *jeopardy* (danger), *leisure* (free time), *unison* (harmony), *virtuosity* (skill); *abound* (have plenty of), *beguile* (seduce, cheat), *compel* (force), *rejoice* (be glad). Closely related to the scope of vocabulary is the range of **allusion** and comparison. A writer cultivating a formal style is likely to draw freely on references to history, literature, the fine arts. He may expect his readers to know what a "Utopia" is, what "Napoleonic airs" are, or how an "interregnum" comes about.

A formal style does not use "big words" to impress the reader. It uses the less common word or the learned allusion where it makes possible distinctions or associations passed over in casual talk. The best formal writing uses much of the *common stock* of the language as well as resources not usually drawn on in everyday speech.[1]

The sentences and paragraphs of formal writing are usually more elaborate, or at least more carefully planned, than ordinary conversation. The following two sentences illustrate several features that help make formal writing different from improvised speech:

Many critics through the years have pointed out that almost all anti-war novels and motion pictures are, in fact, pro-war. Blood and mud and terror and rape and an all-pervading anxiety are precisely what is attractive about war — in the safety of fiction — to those who, in our overprotected lives, are suffering from tedium vitae and human self-alienation.   (Kenneth Rexroth)

Note the careful balance of opposites ("anti-war . . . pro-war"); the lining up of a long series of related terms ("blood and mud and terror and rape and an all-pervading anxiety"); the qualifications worked into an already complicated sentence without breaking its rhythm or muddying its meaning (" — in the safety of fiction — "; "in our overprotected lives").

[1] See D 9b for a warning on jargon.

The organization of a formal essay is likely to be systematic. Formal writing is usually easier to outline than informal writing. The subdivisions are often clearly labeled; transitions are likely to be explicit, often signaled by relatively heavy connectives like *however, nevertheless,* and *moreover.*

Formal English, finally, is *edited* English. It shows the standardizing influence of editing designed to make it generally acceptable to educated readers. In matters of usage, it is likely to observe the traditional distinctions between *who* and *whom, like* and *as, if he was* and *if he were.* (See the handbook chapter on grammatical usage, and the glossary of usage, for a discussion of many of these.) Often, formal writing does without the subjective *I* and the direct *you.*

Much of the earnestness and impersonality of a rigorously formal style used to be edited *into* a text in response to the criticism of editors, reviewers, and teachers. In recent decades, editors and teachers — some reluctantly, some gladly — have steadily moved toward greater permissiveness. Generally, today, even a formal style stays closer to idiomatic, natural speech, and allows a stronger personal element, than used to be possible.

Informal Writing

Informal writing can be casual or entertaining without being brash. The kind of informal style that you will have use for in college-level writing is not the shirt-sleeve informality of much advertising and popular journalism. Though easygoing and relaxed, an informal paper can have the thoughtful, well-mannered quality of polite conversation. Informal writing of this kind may make occasional use of the folksy, **colloquial** phrase. It occasionally uses **slang**, usually in tongue-in-cheek fashion.[2] Its range of reference and allusion is likely to be that of patio, garage, and playing field rather than that of library or study. Its sentence structure and its punctuation sometimes suggest the pauses, ramblings, and afterthoughts of speech. Its unity may derive less from step-by-step development than from the continuity of an underlying mood. It tends to be subjective; it makes room for personal impressions, reminiscences, and whims. It often tells the reader as much about the author as about his subject.

The following three selections move *from a relatively formal to a relatively informal style:*

(1)   Of escapes from the pressure of an increasingly mechanized life to occasional outbursts of excitement or triviality there is much to be said. At least it may be said for

[2] See D 3 for a fuller discussion of informal diction.

them that they are natural, perhaps needful, refuges from a world whose tightly woven days would otherwise be unbearable. It is perhaps a sad commentary on the angular and constricted lives we lead that we should have to seek such lurid or futile ways to peace. But it is not to be wondered at that, living in such a world of routine, we should plunge ever so often into the loud nonsense of inane parties, wallow in the absurd pathos and comedy of the screen, or fall enraptured victims to successive crazes of bootless puzzles and dull games. We may be forgiven our excursions to musical comedies without wit or music, and conversational evenings without humanity or ideas. The contemporary citizen is vexed beyond his own realization by the humdrum unthrilling pressure of his days; he craves naturally now and then an opportunity to be trivial, irresponsible, and absurd. — Irwin Edman, *Adam, the Baby and the Man from Mars*

This selection, while concerned with trivial amusements, is scholarly and formal in style. Its vocabulary departs enough from the level of everyday language to be reserved and dignified: *needful, enraptured, excursion, vexed.* Its metaphors are fresh and expressive rather than familiar or amusing: "tightly woven days," "angular and constricted lives." Sentence structure departs from the ordinary by inversion ("Of escapes . . . there is much to be said") and by frequent use of parallelism ("plunge . . . of inane parties, wallow . . . of the screen, or fall . . . of bootless puzzles and dull games"; "excursions . . . without wit or music, . . . evenings without humanity or ideas"). Throughout, the impersonal passive reinforces the tone of dignified detachment ("it may be said," "it is not to be wondered at," "may be forgiven").

(2)   It happens to be a fact that all classic works without exception deal directly or indirectly with problems of conduct. That is their great virtue for school use. Not that they teach a plain goody-goody morality, but that they show and discuss and solve dilemmas that a shipping clerk or an athlete can be made to understand. For this understanding, the discussion of any classic *must be superficial.* If you dive below the surface with your pupil you drown him. Certain teachers are always terrified of superficiality; they seem to think other teachers will scoff or that the dead author will scold. Let them remind themselves that their colleagues' profundity would strike the great author as either surface scratching or pedantry; and let them remember that for every reader there is a time when a given book is being read for the first time. — Jacques Barzun, *Teacher in America*

This selection illustrates a less reserved, more urbane formal style with informal touches. It uses the conversational phrase ("it happens to be a fact that . . ."), the occasional colloquialism ("goody-goody morality"), the informal *you.* Its metaphors have a homely, familiar quality ("if you dive . . . you drown him"; "surface scratching"). Its sentences, on the whole, are shorter, more abrupt, and more emphatic than those in the preceding selection ("That is their great virtue for school use"). The author, however, does not *limit* himself to the familiar, the simple. His vocabulary ranges beyond the conversational: *terrified of superficiality, scoff, colleagues' profundity, pedantry.* His sentences are deliberate and effective; they repeatedly become insistent ("show and discuss and solve"; "let them remind themselves . . ."; "let them remember . . .").

(3)   If television is ever to amount to anything of cultural importance, it should rid itself of the idea that it's the motion picture industry, the book business or the stage. It's a big, new art form of its own. It was radio's lack of standards that led to that dizzy lunacy known as the giveaway program. Radio programs gave away washing machines, Cadillacs, $1,000 bills, houses — everything, in fact, except women. I could never quite understand that lone omission. If Bert Parks had thrown a beautiful 18-year-old babe into the jackpot of *Stop the Music,* even I would have stayed home and listened for the telephone. But he wouldn't. Some faint moral scruple — or conceivably fear of the Federal Communications Commission — stayed the broadcaster from this final depravity. The Roman emperors who gave the populace bread and circuses — which is what radio was imitating with its giveaway programs — also threw in sexual orgies, and it always seemed to me inconsistent of the broadcasters not to follow through with the thing. I brought this to the attention of several vice presidents, but they failed to see any humor in the suggestion. They also failed to see anything wrong with the giveaway program, which shows where a lack of moral standards leads. — John Crosby, "Seven Deadly Sins of the Air," *Life*

This selection illustrates the kind of distinct informality that would be inappropriate in a more objective, less personal context. There is no doubt about the literacy and skill of the writer, suggested by such phrases as "faint moral scruple" or "stayed . . . from this final depravity." However, his style is in keeping with his brash, no-holds-barred attack on his subject. The tone of the passage is set by the colloquial phrases ("amount to anything," "follow through with the thing"), the slang expressions ("babe," "jackpot," "threw in"), the informal contractions ("it's," "wouldn't"). Overstatement runs wild ("dizzy lunacy," "sexual orgies"). Sentence structure ranges from the short half-sentence ("But he wouldn't.") to the overloaded last sentence, with its parenthetical *which*-clause reaching half-heartedly for an antecedent. Serious students of the mass media might object to the writer's flippancy; but readers not otherwise interested in the subject might be attracted by the writer's treatment of it.

Formality is a matter of degree. Finding the appropriate tone is not a simple matter of right or wrong, correct or incorrect. Just as it is possible to be overdressed at a party, so it is possible to be too stiffly formal in a piece of writing. But it is also possible to be so casual as to suggest "I don't care." Usually, we can place a statement on a *scale of informality:*

Very Formal: In our society, performance is a primary determinant of status.

Less Formal: What an individual can deliver more than anything else determines how far he can go in our society.

Very Informal: You have to come through if you want to make it in this society.

In your own writing, you will have to avoid two extremes. The first is the stiff formality of a pseudo-scholarly jargon, in which an outing is a "recreational activity" and a college an "institution of higher learning." The other extreme is the breezy informality of a too casual conversational style, misapplied to subjects that deserve serious attention. In a serious paper about the dilemmas of college education, it is inappropriate to refer to teachers as "Prof" and "Doc," to fellow students as "kids," to campus policemen as "the fuzz." Between the two extremes, your problem will be to *make the degree of formality fit the seriousness of the occasion.*

Exercises

A. How *formal or informal* is the style of each of the following passages? Take into account such factors as diction, range of allusion, sentence structure, and degree of objectivity. How appropriate is the style of each passage to its subject matter?

1. My first affection for the University of Michigan was due, simply, to their accepting me. They had already turned me down twice because my academic record (I had flunked algebra three times in my Brooklyn high school) was so low as to be practically invisible, but the dean reversed himself after two letters in which I wrote that since working for two years — in a warehouse at $15 a week — I had turned into a much more serious fellow. He said he would give me a try, but I had better make some grades. I could not conceive of a dean at Columbia or Harvard doing that. — Arthur Miller, "University of Michigan," *Holiday*

2. Above Albuquerque begins the lyric grace of the river in its richest passage of the pastoral life. Where life is fed by water, the landscape here recalls the opulence and grandeur and occasional vistas of order in the image of classical country painted by Nicolas Poussin, who left so many celebrations of grove and meadow, shady leaf and column of light, reflecting stream and stepped mountain and composed bodies.

There is more than a reminder here, there is a real likeness. It is a likeness of grace and plenty in the midst of dramatic nature; nourishment in the desert; bounty summoned by the most ancient of agricultural rites out of the most inscrutable of antiquities; cool for the heated, slaking for the parched, food for the hungry, rest for the weary, ease for the eye blinded in the unimpeded sun. — Paul Horgan, "Pages from a Rio Grande Notebook," *The New York Times Book Review*

3. Then there is another hazard — the hazard of owning a camera that is just too complicated for the beginning photographer. It's really advisable to have a simple camera. That leaves him free to have fun. Whether he's an artist working with a camera or an amateur working with a camera, the instrument must become a part of him. He must be just as free as you are with a fork when you're eating mashed potatoes. You don't sit down and figure out how you should hold the fork; you do that unconsciously.

Worrying about technique is inhibiting. There was a time, during a very weak period in painting, when Sargent had such an influence, when long, suave brush strokes were considered important. It amounted to a closed system, and that's always pernicious. Today in modern painting they put it on with a trowel, they put it on with their feet, they drip it out of a can, they do anything with it. It's unimportant. It's what the fellow *feels* about the thing, what he has to give, what he sees, what he experiences, that counts. — Edward J. Steichen, "The Living Joy of Pictures," *Holiday*

4. There are more people than ever before, at least in the sense of mutations in our national botany, and this is probably due to mobility — cross-fertilization. Take as an example a gangster who was in the slot-machine racket, decided to go straight and became a laundromat king, sent his daughter to Bennington, where she married a poet-in-residence or a professor of modern linguistic philosophy. There are three characters already sketched out in that sentence and all of them brand-new: the father, the daughter, and the son-in-law. Imagine what one of the old writers might have made of the wedding and the reception afterward at the 21 Club. The laundromat king or his equivalent is easy to meet in America; there are hundreds of him. . . . People speak of the lack of tradition or of manners as having a bad effect on the American novel, but the self-made man is a far richer figure, from the novelist's point of view, than the man of inherited wealth, who is likely to be a mannered shadow. — Mary McCarthy, "Characters in Fiction," *Partisan Review*

5. Einstein knocked out space and time, as Rutherford knocked out matter. The general viewpoint of relativity toward space is very simple. Einstein explains that there is no such place as *here*. "But," you answer, "I'm here; here is where I am right now." But you're moving, you're

spinning around as the earth spins; and you and the earth are both spinning around the sun, and the sun is rushing through space toward a distant galaxy, and the galaxy itself is beating it away at 26,000 miles a second. Now, where is that spot that is here! How did you mark it? You remember the story of the two idiots who were out fishing, and one said, "We should have marked that place where we got all the fish," and the other said, "I did; I marked it on the boat." Well that's it. That's *here.* — Stephen Leacock, *Last Leaves*

B. What is the *range of formality* that you encounter on the editorial page (and in related matter) of a major newspaper? Are there editorials or columns written in a very formal style? Are there others more informal? Provide examples.

3. Humor, Irony, and Satire

Among the elements that contribute to the informality of a writer's tone, humor needs special attention. *Humor puts the reader at ease and helps break down his reserve.* A writer who lacks a sense of humor often lacks a sense of balance. A piece of writing seems to lack proportion when it treats solemn and trivial matters with the same deadly seriousness. There is something reassuring about the detachment that enables a writer to see whatever might be ridiculous about his subject or about himself. Some of the most readable writing combines a basic seriousness with touches of dry wit:

There is another possibility to be taken account of, which is that of manufacturing food chemically. There seems no good reason why we should continue to grow our food laboriously in soil and allow ourselves to be dependent on the vagaries of sun and rain. Why not make beefsteaks in factories? And flour in workshops? I dare say that food made in this way would not taste very nice, but in time people would get used to it and a little "real" food would still be produced for wedding feats and the banquets of Heads of States. Some very rich men would occasionally issue invitations saying in one corner, "Decorations will be worn" and in the other corner, "Real peas." — Bertrand Russell, "The Next Eighty Years," *Saturday Review*

Your study of the way other writers use humor should pay off in two ways. It should make you experiment with the leavening effect that touches of humor have upon otherwise serious writing. But it should also help you in writing papers where the use of humor is not just incidental: humorous essays whose main purpose is to entertain; satirical essays using humor as a weapon.

Verbal Humor

The writer who wants to be serious without being dull makes at least some use of verbal humor. Verbal humor can be quite unintentional ("There are several million alcoholics in the world. This is a staggering number"). When it is intentional, the writer makes use of unexpected twists in his choice of words ("Bear it like a man, even if you feel it like an ass" — G. B. Shaw). He lines up contrasting ideas in parallel form for antithetical heightening.

The idols of every campus generation have always been *against* everything and *for* nothing.   (Peter F. Drucker)

Mannerism consists in the allowing of a form of speech that has now & again *served* us well to *master* us.   (H. W. Fowler)

The playful use of long or learned words is a onesided game *boring the reader* more than it *pleases the writer*.   (H. W. Fowler)

Democracy substitutes *selection by the incompetent many* for *appointment by the corrupt few*.   (G. B. Shaw)

Here are some other familiar devices of verbal humor:

(1) A **paradox** is an apparent contradiction; it goes "counter to what people think." A paradox at first seems absurd but then turns out to *contain a valid point*. "When peace breaks out" is a paradoxical phrase. We usually speak of war, rather than peace, as "breaking out," but on second thought we may agree that in a period of constant international tension the arrival of genuine peace would be as momentous as the outbreak of open war. Similarly, a bachelor may startle us by mentioning the possibility of "committing matrimony." The term *commit* is usually applied to crimes rather than to something as respectable as marriage. To the speaker, the thought of marriage is as abhorrent as the thought of crime is to others. The apparent contradiction of a well-turned paradox annoys the literal-minded but delights more nimble-witted readers:

To be natural is such a very difficult pose to keep up.   (Oscar Wilde)

(2) The **pun** exploits ambiguity, or similarity between two words, to make the same word suggest *two different but equally possible meanings*. A writer is punning when he accuses a college president of having an "edifice complex"; when he speaks of a contemporary as having left "footprints on the sands of *Time*." Most puns are irreverent enough to give a flippant tone to a passage as a whole.

(3) A related play on words is the **garbled cliché**. It revives a trite phrase by *turning it upside down* or twisting it in some other unexpected way. A publisher, referring to unsold books returned to him by booksellers, might complain that his stock is "gone today and

here tomorrow." A writer might list a number of important questions but go on to say that "space and ignorance" do not permit his answering them.

Irony and Sarcasm

A writer using irony has to make his ironical intention clear to the reader. **Irony** exploits the comic juxtaposition of things that don't go together. Verbal irony uses statements that mean the opposite of what they seem to say. A student is likely to be ironical when he says, "I just love to write my English themes!" or "How I enjoy dormitory food!" Several things help to make such irony obvious: the pained look on the student's face, the knowledge that students often have a prejudice (however unfounded or unfortunate) against English themes and dormitory food.

Unable to rely on looks and gestures, a writer must rely on context and wording to suggest his ironical intention. What the reader knows about the *New York Times* is enough to make the following statement clearly ironical:

We had an Engineer Officer who wrote confidential letters to the Office of Naval Intelligence requesting emergency security checks on officers who read the *New York Times.*

The clues to irony are more clearly built into the text itself when a writer says, "Bill's political ideas happened to correspond exactly to those of the employer he worked for at a given time." The wholeheartedness of Bill's agreement with his employers, combined with the opportune changes in his convictions, is obviously *not* a coincidence; the word *happened* is therefore being used ironically.

Special uses of irony are as follows:

(1) Irony can be indulgent, as when Mary McCarthy describes the spirit of Vassar College as "the passion for public service coupled with a yearning for the limelight." But irony can also become *bitter, cutting, insulting.* Irony turned sour becomes **sarcasm:**

At the University every great treatise is postponed until its author attains impartial judgment and perfect knowledge. If a horse could wait as long for its shoes and would pay for them in advance, our blacksmiths would all be college dons. (G. B. Shaw)

(2) **Understatement** achieves an ironical effect by *belittling something that is of serious importance to the speaker,* as when a man with double pneumonia says, "I don't feel quite as sprightly as

I might wish." In the following passage, a familiar point gains fresh impact through vast understatement:

Among the enterprises currently attracting the energies of man, one of considerable moment is his effort to launch himself across space. A second, less grand, less costly, *but perhaps not less important,* is the effort to improve the position of *those who will stay behind.* —John Kenneth Galbraith, "The Poverty of Nations," *Atlantic*

(3) Similar in effect to verbal irony is **irony of situation**. Not only the writer's statements or opinions but also the *details and events* he describes may go counter to expectation. For instance, he can ridicule what is pompous by placing the pretentious next to the trivial. He can point out the shabby rear of a building with an imposing façade, or he can emphasize the gaudy medals on the chest of a small-time dictator. An easy prey of this kind of irony is the person whose theory points one way and whose practice another: the traffic-safety expert who has an accident or the marriage counselor whose wife sues for divorce.

Satire

Satire employs ridicule as a means of persuasion. When you make systematic use of humor, irony, or sarcasm to attack something you disapprove of, you are employing **satire**. Satire criticizes short-comings by holding them up to ridicule and scorn. For instance, you may use satirical exaggeration. In a paper entitled "The Quick and the Dead," you might say of the gentleman hunter, "Death awaits anything foolish enough to place itself in front of his gun, be it a cow, mule, fellow hunter, or even, in rare instances, a deer." By exaggerating the occasional failure of the inexperienced hunter to aim at a legitimate target, you would emphasize and ridicule his lack of competence.

The following passage is satirical in intention:

Harvard (across the river in Cambridge) and Boston are two ends of one mustache. Harvard is now so large and international it has altogether avoided the whimsical stagnation of Boston. But the two places need each other, as we knowingly say of a mismatched couple. Without the faculty, the visitors, the events that Harvard brings to the life here, Boston would be intolerable to anyone except genealogists, antique dealers, and those who find repletion in a closed local society. Unfortunately, Harvard, like Boston, has "tradition" and in America this always carries with it the risk of a special staleness of attitude, and of pride, incredibly and comically swollen like the traits of hypocrisy, selfishness, or lust in the old dramas. At Harvard some of the vices of "society" exist, of Boston society that is—arrogance and the blinding dazzle of being, *being at Harvard.* —Elizabeth Hardwick, "Boston: The Lost Ideal," *Harper's*

The author's target is stagnation, a "closed society," "tradition," staleness, snobbery. Her aim is to make her target look comical, "whimsical." Her method is to use details and analogies that are comical and belittling at the same time: "two ends of one mustache," "mismatched couple," "genealogists, antique dealers." She makes use of satirical exaggeration ("incredibly . . . swollen"); she mimics the people she attacks *("being at Harvard")*.

In writing a satirical paper, you will have to keep satire from becoming a mere indiscriminate flailing out. *A satirical paper is most effective when it clearly implies the positive standards by which its target is judged.* For instance, a paper on hunting, no matter how merciless in its attack upon hunters, can have a constructive purpose. The reader can be made to realize that the author is, indirectly, setting up two basic requirements: minimum competence in the handling of firearms and a respect for human life strong enough to keep the hunter from firing at just anything that moves.

By clarifying your standards, you will be able to avoid the most common defect in student-written satire: lack of focus. A satirical description of a hike, for instance, can concentrate on incidents that illustrate inconsiderate or thoughtless behavior. It can dwell on the hiker who is suddenly consumed by an unquenchable thirst, and on his companion who consistently finds the scenery inferior to that in the Black Forest or that in the Kize-Kazuyo Mountains. Other incidents, though amusing, could obscure the target of the satire. The alarm clock that goes off late and the sudden rainstorm might help to create a hysterical slapstick atmosphere, but they might also keep the reader from getting the point: A cooperative enterprise will be a success only if everyone learns to subordinate some of his personal whims and complaints to the common good. In preparing a satirical paper, ask yourself: Does my paper have a definite point? Or am I merely taking potshots at miscellaneous abuses? A satirist who fails to ask such questions easily becomes a kind of court jester, whose barbs nobody takes seriously.

Parody

In a good parody, a writer uses his gifts of mimicry in order to satirize the work of another writer. A **parody** is a comic imitation, exaggerating traits that are vulnerable to ridicule. But a good parody results only from loving attention to the original, and often becomes a kind of backhanded tribute to the individuality and force of the writer being parodied. Writing parodies is in fact one of the best ways a writer can develop his own feeling, and respect, for style.

Would you say that the following passage is a recognizable

parody of Holden Caulfield's style in J. D. Salinger's *Catcher in the Rye?*

OLD GILES

I've had this thing about math ever since I was a kid. I mean I wasn't good at it, but there was just something about it. I probably could have been good at it if I had had any kind of a decent teacher; the teachers I had were about as stimulating as track shoes to a polio victim. I mean these guys are standing in front of the room going on about x's and y's and I'm still thinking about the alphabet. I wanted to be good. I mean I always did my homework and that stuff, but I knew I wasn't getting out of math what those Euclid- and Newton-type guys had put into it.

Then in junior college I had this guy for a math teacher who had more math in his left ear lobe than all my other teachers put together. Old Giles wasn't much over twenty-five, but he could really deliver a math lecture. I mean each lecture was well-prepared and to the point. I figured he must have spent about eight million years workin' up each one. I was beginning to see what this math thing was all about. My poor algebra background was really making things hard, but old Giles made those triangles jump off the blackboard and into that grey stuff that holds your ears apart. He sure made up the goddamnedest tests. I don't think I ever did completely finish one. I mean he had to fight me at the end of the hour to get it back. Giles had this thing about tests—he figured that the only way to find out who's the best swimmer is to throw everyone into the water and see who drowns last.

Limitations of Humor

Whether you use humor in a few incidental touches, or whether you make it part of your basic strategy, it creates special problems of appropriateness and consistency. Humorous anecdotes are inappropriate in a funeral sermon, just as whistling is inappropriate in church. How far a writer goes in making his writing humorous or satirical is a matter of taste—both his own and that of his readers. Some uses of humor, however, are certain to strike a false note:

(1) *The strained facetiousness by which a writer seems to apologize for taking up a serious subject.* Some writers seem unable to refer to themselves, to their readers, or to their country without a would-be humorous variation: "Yours truly," "the gentle reader," "these Yew-nited States." They overwork the facetious circumlocution, which substitutes an impressive roundabout phrase for a simple everyday word: a toothbrush becomes a "denture scrubber"; women become "the female gender"; a dog's tail becomes a "caudal appendage."

(2) *A tone of contemptuous, sarcastic familiarity.* Some papers address the reader in the tone of a parent addressing a misbehaving and not very bright child. Beware, for instance, of condescending or bullying questions put directly to the reader: "I believe in honest government. How about you?"

(3) *The kind of flippancy that results from ·discussing serious or solemn subjects in racy, colloquial language.* Suppose that in answering an examination question, you write: "Poor Othello finally blows his top when he sees Cassio fondling Desdemona's hanky." If the person so unceremoniously discussed is, like Othello, a figure of considerable dignity, your reader is likely to feel that you are not taking the material – and the examination – seriously.

Exercises

A. What is the *characteristic tone* of each of the following passages? Is it indulgent, impatient, angry, nostalgic, bitter? Is it humorous, ironical, sarcastic? What is its effect on the reader?

1. The present state of things on the planet earth would be rather a puzzle to an observer from another planet. If he landed in the United States, the most conspicuous animals in sight would be automobiles, and if he examined these vigorous hard-shelled creatures, he would find that each contains one or more soft, feeble organisms that appear notably helpless when removed from their shells. He would decide, after talking with these defenseless creatures, that they have no independent existence. Few of them have anything to do with the production or transportation of food. They need clothing and shelter, but do not produce them for themselves. They are dependent on their distant fellows in thousands of complex ways. When isolated, they usually die – just like worker ants that wander helplessly and hopelessly if separated from their colony. – Jonathan Norton Leonard, *Flight into Space*

2. There are rumors that when dying of the thirst you can save soul *and* body by extracting water from the barrel cactus, but this is a dubious proposition and I don't know anyone who has made the experiment. It might be possible in the low desert of Arizona where the barrel cactus will often grow as high as a man and big around as a beer keg. In Utah a similar species of cactus grows no more than a foot up and bristles with needles curved like fishhooks. To even get close to this devilish plant you need leather gloves and a machete, or at least a big hunting knife. Slice off the top and you find inside not a little tun of precious water but only the green pulpy core of the living plant. To get a few drops of liquid from that you would have to hack the cactus into manageable chunks and wring what water you could from each piece. Meanwhile you are sweating badly from the labor and the exasperation, dehydrating rapidly, doomed anyway. You'd actually be better off to

stay at home with the TV and a case of beer. If this happy thought arrives too late, relax and enjoy your demise as best you can; it's the only one you are likely to know. See those big, black, scrawny wings far above, waiting? Console yourself with the thought that within only a few hours, if all goes well, your human flesh will be working its way through the gizzard of a buzzard, your essence transformed into the fierce greedy eyes and unimaginable consciousness of the vulture — you too will soar on motionless wings far above the ruck and the rack of human existence, part of the Oneness of the One. — Edward Abbey, "The West's Land of Surprises," *Harper's*

3. People who should know tell us that during the Paleolithic Age man's store of knowledge doubled every 100,000 years, give or take a month or two. Even then it didn't amount to much. Man learned to build fires, say, and then in another 100,000 years he learned to put fires out. That sort of thing.

 Today, however, our knowledge is doubling every five years, or several hundred times as fast as it did even in Grandpa's day. There is, we are told, at least 300 per cent more knowledge right now than there was in 1930, although you certainly can't tell by looking at people. In case you think you may be looking at the wrong people, you will be comforted to know that Dr. George Gallup recently demonstrated that while knowledge is exploding all over the place it is hitting remarkably few targets. Dr. Gallup found that only 11 per cent of the population is behaving knowledgeably. A whopping 76 per cent of the population is still carrying on in pretty much the same damn fool way their ancestors did. Thirteen per cent is undecided. — Patrick Butler, "Phoenix Nest," *Saturday Review*

4. As more and more people have painful reason to know, the press has a nasty kind of power, the same kind of power a bully has; that of hurting somebody smaller and weaker than himself. An individual's only defense against the press is the law of libel, but considerable harm and much pain can be caused without going so far as to commit an actionable libel. Journalists themselves generally have a horror of being interviewed, "written up," or even noticed by the press; they know too well from their own experience how inept and cruel a distortion the result is likely to be — even in photographs — which, in the lying phrase, "cannot lie." — T. S. Matthews, "What Makes News," *Atlantic*

5. We should behave towards our country as women behave towards the men they love. A loving wife will do anything for her husband except stop criticising and trying to improve him. That is the right attitude for a citizen. We should cast the same affectionate but sharp glance at our country. We should love it, but also insist upon telling it all its faults. The dangerous man is not the critic, but the noisy empty

"patriot" who encourages us to indulge in orgies of self-congratulation. —
J. B. Priestley, *Rain upon Godshill*

B. Study the satirical techniques used in the following passages. For each
passage, describe the possible reactions of different kinds of readers.

1. As advertising men by the tens of thousands bring their wiles to
bear to stimulate sales of products, we are seeing a massive straining
for greater impact. Some months ago a distiller sent a photographic
team to the edges of the Sahara Desert in order to obtain a photograph
of a martini-filled glass in a setting which would suggest dryness. The
photographers faced a crisis when, in searching the fruit markets of
Cairo for a sliver of yellow lemon peel to go with the drink, they discovered that lemons sold in Egypt are green. This problem was solved
when they arranged for a yellow lemon to be flown over from Italy. —
Vance Packard, "The Growing Power of Admen," *Atlantic*

2. A young man walked into my office a few weeks ago and announced
that he was ready to sell out. What he wanted, I discovered eventually,
was a job. He had been out of college for about a year, making the
scene, as he put it, around New York. Recently his parents had stopped
sending him money; so now, strictly for want of bread, he had to go
to work.
     Publishing, he confided, struck him as less distasteful than any
other occupation he could think of. Consequently he was prepared to
sacrifice his integrity to the sordid demands of book or magazine publishing—he didn't care which—but since he valued it highly he trusted
that *Harper's* would pay him handsomely for it. In our further conversation it turned out that he had nothing else to sell, such as a marketable
skill. Like many students who have a hard time deciding what to do
with their lives, he had majored in English literature. He knew virtually
nothing, it seemed, about the contemporary world, aside from rumors
he had picked up from other students and his teachers, most of them
almost equally innocent. He was convinced, however, that work in
almost any business firm was certain to be both dull and debasing, and
that corporations were by definition corrupt institutions. Only after
much anguished wrestling with his conscience had he decided that it
was better to let himself be co-opted and corrupted than to starve. —
John Fischer, "The Perils of Publishing," *Harper's*

3. One of the difficulties of crowding so much honor and tribute into
the calendar is that there is a good deal of overlapping, some of it a
little trying to respectful people who want to do the right thing. Is it
possible, for example, to give due recognition to Jewish Book Month
when right smack in the middle of it you have to celebrate National
Long Underwear Week and Holiday Eggnog Time? Not to mention the
fact that November also happens to be National Contact Lens Month.
Or consider the predicament of the man who starts out on a Monday to

observe National Weight-Watchers Week, sponsored by the "Lite Diet" bread people, only to find that Thursday marks the beginning of Kraut and Frankfurter Week, a festive rite presided over by the National Kraut Packers Association.—Robert Bendiner, "Fifteen Weeks Hath September," *The Reporter*

4. "What do we call the three organizations, Archer, that are to blame for the way the world is?"

"The establishment, the power elite and the white power structure."

"And what kind of democracy do these organizations militate against?"

"Participatory democracy. Through highly structured institutional patterns reinforced by an uncommitted technological bureaucracy and a depersonalized hierarchical management system, they deny all men a voice in making the decisions that control their lives."

"Well spoken, Archer, you have a gift for the abstruse latinate polysyllabic. . . . What must a man be, Warelson?"

"A man must be involved, engaged and committed."

"And if he is not?"

"He is a fink. He has copped out. He has opted for middle-class affluence."

"Now Shuster, name ten isms that have been thoroughly discredited and tell me why."

"Communism, anti-communism, reformism, liberalism, socialism, Uncle Tomism, militarism, nationalism, industrialism and puritanism. All have been thoroughly discredited by the residue of psychic trauma they have left at the very core of American life."

"Not the very core of American life, Shuster. The very heart and core of American life. The use of understatement in New Leftspeak is tantamount to cooptation. Phelps, would you please overstate in one word the story of America's history?"

"Genocide, sir."

"Excellent. What odious organism has proved in our time to be the principal beneficiary of our long and disgraceful history of genocide?"

"The military-industrial complex, sir."

"And by what four-syllable word must the power of the military-industrial complex be overthrown?"

"By confrontation."—Russell Baker, *New York Times*

C. Study and evaluate the following samples from *student-written satire*. Describe as fully as you can the weapons chosen by each author. How effectively does he use them?

1. We often hear from foreigners that Americans are provincial, that we think everything in America is the best in the world, that we know little of the world outside of our boundaries, that we are a shallow

people without value, without culture and without purpose. How provincial of them to believe this!

In "Kibbutz; Venture in Utopia" by Melford E. Spiro, the author quotes an Israeli girl who, after visiting the United States, remarked that "they have no values. Of course, in Israel we have austerity, but we have values; we are absorbing immigrants, building a new society. Hence, you feel that your life has meaning. But what meaning does it have in America?"

How clever she is! How astute she must be to determine all of this on a brief visit. It reminds one of the columnist or politician who goes to Vietnam for a week's "look for himself" and comes back an expert on that complex problem. Of course, it is very bad form for Americans to answer their critics. We are considered immature and overly sensitive if we object to their generalities and over-simplifications. . . .

2. Herbie, our modern advertising man, is awaking refreshed from a good night's sleep. Last night he may have had a splitting headache, muscular pain, neuralgia, nervous tension, sluggish liver, abdominal distress, and tired blood. But no matter. This morning he obviously got FAST FAST FAST relief.

He takes his shower and rolls on something that takes away the fear of offending. He is now not just half safe, but for the first time in his life he really feels clean. Brushing his teeth, he finds he has twenty-two per cent fewer cavities, because he uses his toothpaste along with a scientifically approved program of oral hygiene and regular professional care. Shaving, he gets fourteen more shaves with his new blade than with a boop-boop. Afterwards, he uses an after-shave lotion that makes him irresistible to women—and okay for the office too!

Our modern advertising Herbie has, of course, a breakfast of champions, rich in iron and protein and high in big, body-building energy. And it's all topped off with a cup of coffee that's so mmm mmmm good! Getting into his automobile—which he chose by a 114-mile grueling test on a deserted mountain road—he could, if he wished, put himself in the driver's seat, but prefers, instead, to ride in comfort and leave the driving to us! Finally, though he finds that some things he likes separate him from the boys—they don't from the girls. Indeed, after work, he steps almost at once into a wonderful world of softness, and a wonderful world of freshness, that is not only friendly to his taste, but also apparently contains no harsh irritants for his girl friend! In any case, he and she wander around brooks and waterfalls and horses' necks and scarecrows, and he gets a smile every time, just asking himself what do guys look at second?

3. Sociologists and people-watchers interested in the patterns of conformity should invade the college dormitory, for a peek inside the coed's room exposes her dominant instinct—to be in with the college crowd.

The room is full of standard items essential for imparting that improved collegiate atmosphere. Beneath a light dusting of cigarette ashes, crumpled candy wrappers, ethnic folk records, and unanswered masculine letters scattered indifferently about, one notes a Princeton bedspread, Harvard bookcovers, Michigan State pencils, M.I.T. ashtrays, and a Washington University bear (teddy and stuffed). Mementoes of all major campus events and snapshots of the standard Boy Back Home and of men in every branch of the service and on every Big Ten campus are tacked obtrusively on the bulletin board to advertise the coed's maddening social whirl. ("Isn't it terrible?" she sighs.) Of course she would never betray the Image by leaving certain give-away items lying around — high school pennants (who ever heard of high school?), Lawrence Welk albums, *American Girl* magazines, and pictures of the REAL Boy Back Home bending tenderly over his smoking hot-rod. If her private cache of "out-of-it" treasures were discovered, the Image would be shattered, and the poor American Coed might have to face her true identity — a fate worse than being caught reading her ancient history text instead of the latest copy of *Mademoiselle, Vogue,* or *Bazaar.*

D. Report on the *use of satire* in one of the following: Lil' Abner, Pogo, Peanuts, *Mad.*

E. Report on the *use of humor* in the writings of one of the following: Max Shulman, Dick Gregory *(From the Back of the Bus)*, a humorist currently popular with college students. Identify recurrent features of his type of humor; provide brief examples.

4. Developing a Style of Your Own

What your writing sounds like and feels like is determined in part by how formal or informal you make it, and by how serious or humorous you allow yourself to be. Beyond these qualities are more personal features that help give good writing an individual touch. As you try to develop your personal style, you encounter a familiar dilemma. To be readable, your writing must have personality. The reader must be kept from saying to himself: "But I have just read twenty papers *exactly* like this one." But the more personal your style becomes, the more it brings the reader's *own* personal preferences into play. The more distinctive your style, the greater the risk that it may not be to the reader's taste.

Anonymous, look-alike writing is safe, but it is also dull and often ineffectual. A strongly individual style is interesting, provoking, and risky. As you develop your own style, you should study some of the reactions a writer risks by giving his writing a distinctive personal quality.

Distinctive Styles

Develop your feeling for the stylistic effects that give writing individuality. The following passages illustrate some of the strengths and weaknesses of expository writing with a distinct style:

> In CBS's *Gandhi*, the scrawny, jug-eared little man in the white loincloth looked as Author John Gunther once saw him: an inscrutable "combination of Jesus Christ, Tammany Hall, and your father." Fuzzy images from old films showed the gentle ascetic all but engulfed by the worshiping, hysterical throngs on the mass pilgrimage to the sea to carry out a plan of passive resistance during the British salt monopoly. There was the shrewd lawyer-diplomat putting his hand over an inquisitive British reporter's mouth or quipping on arrival in London in 1931: "You people have your plus fours. These are my minus fours." In the best sequences, faded with age, there was "your father" — with metal-rimmed spectacles, a big, near-toothless grin, the dollar watch dangling from the dhoti — who tenderly encircled a little girl with a garland of flowers that she had brought for him. — *Time*

This passage illustrates a sophisticated and very successful kind of journalism whose trademark is its slick, bright-eyed quality. The tone is irreverent and ironical ("jug-eared little man"; "big, near-toothless grin"). The account owes its graphic quality to a selection of striking external detail ("the white loincloth," "the dollar watch dangling from the dhoti"). It owes its dynamic quality to its habitual exaggeration of the dramatic ("worshiping, hysterical throngs"; "all but engulfed"), heightened by contrast ("gentle ascetic"). The "little girl" keeps the exotic scene from escaping beyond the scope of ordinary human interest. There is a smattering of brief, striking quotations — too short to give an insight into the speaker's character, too simple to require careful interpretation, but either startling ("Jesus Christ, Tammany Hall, and your father") or witty ("minus fours"). Even a demanding reader may find this passage clever and entertaining. But he may also find it too cleverly superficial to do justice to the CBS program, let alone Gandhi.

> In pre-movie days, the business of peddling lies about life was spotty and unorganized. It was carried on by the cheaper magazines, dime novels, the hinterland preachers and whooping politicians. These combined to unload a rash of infantile parables on the land. A goodly part of the population was infected, but there remained large healthy areas in the Republic's thought. There remained, in fact, an intellectual class of sorts — a tribe of citizens who never read dime novels, cheap magazines or submitted themselves to political and religious howlers.
> It was this tribe that the movies scalped. Cultured people who would have blushed

with shame to be found with a dime novel in their hands took to flocking shamelessly
to watch the picturization of such tripe on the screen.

For forty years the movies have drummed away on the American character. They
have fed it naïveté and buncombe in doses never before administered to any people.
They have slapped into the American mind more human misinformation in one evening
than the Dark Ages could muster in a decade. — Ben Hecht, *A Child of the Century*

This passage illustrates a deliberately "tough" style, marked by
a boisterous disregard for standards of refinement, politeness, or tact.
Its tone is that of a heavy-handed facetiousness ("tribe of citizens,"
". . . that the movies scalped"). It produces the effect of **caricature** by
a combination of habitual extreme overstatement and heavy invective
("business of peddling lies," "rash of infantile parables," "flocking
shamelessly," "buncombe in doses never before administered to
any people"). Its vocabulary is a mixture of slang ("unload . . . on the
land," "tripe," "slapped into the American mind"), archaic tags
("a goodly part"), outlandish phrases ("hinterland preachers"),
and facetious neologisms ("picturization"). Many readers find this
kind of writing invigorating and entertaining, in a beer-garden sort of
way. Others, more finicky, react to it the way they would to a too loud
and insistent gregarious stranger.

The radio has made sentimentality the twentieth century Plymouth Rock. As a
discipline, I have forced myself to sit a whole morning listening to the soap operas,
along with twenty million moms who were busy sweeping dust under carpets while planning to drawn their progeny in honey or bash in their heads. This filthy and indecent
abomination, this trash with which, until lately, only moron servant girls could dull
their credulous minds in the tawdry privacy of their cubicles, is now the national saga.
Team after team of feeble-minded Annies and Davids crawl from the loudspeaker into
the front rooms of America. The characters are impossible, their adventures would
make a saint spew, their morals are lower than those of ghouls, their habits are un-
cleanly, their humor is the substance that starts whole races grinding bayonets, they
have no manners, no sense, no goals, no worthy ambitions, no hope, no faith, no information, no values related to reality, and no estimate of truth. They merely sob and
snicker — as they cheat each other. — Philip Whlie, *Generation of Vipers*

This passage, though it resembles the preceding selection in its
reliance on overstatement and invective, has a more exasperated,
more serious tone. It has some of the profuse, passionate eloquence
of the moralist denouncing and belaboring his fellows. It owes its
insistent, emphatic quality to the skillful use of repetition and parallel
grammatical structure. Starting with a concise statement of the key
idea, the paragraph warms up until it launches into the sustained
parallelism of the last but one sentence. It keeps piling up resounding
abstractions that, though they overlap somewhat in meaning, reinforce each other's emotional impact ("goals," "ambitions," "hope,"

"faith," "values"). Reading a book written in this style is like frequenting a Turkish bath: not everyone likes the steam and the heat.

A Natural Style

Develop a style that does not call attention to itself, that does not distract attention from the subject at hand. English prose styles of earlier centuries were often ornate, laid out in elaborate decorative patterns. Modern expository prose generally employs a much less obtrusive style. As George Orwell has said, good modern prose "is like a window pane." It does not come between the subject and the reader. Your best protection against an artificial style is to keep your eye on your material. Choose not the unusual or the startling word, but the *right* word. Choose words and phrases because they set the right tone, reflect the right shade of emotion, convey the precise shade of meaning.

Remembering the following advice should help you make your writing more readable without making the reader feel that you are straining for effect:

(1) *Write from an independent, personal perspective.* Show your willingness to take a new look. Good writing is fresh and different, not from a desire to bait the bourgeois, or from a conditioned reflex for dissent, but because the writer's attitude is "This is the way it looks from here." Much of the vigor of Thoreau's prose stems from his refusal to repeat the dutiful conventional view:

Nations are possessed with an insane ambition to perpetuate the memory of themselves by the amount of hammered stone they leave. What if equal pains were taken to smooth and polish their manners? One piece of good sense would be more memorable than a monument as high as the moon. . . . Most of the stone a nation hammers goes toward its tomb only. It buries itself alive. As for the Pyramids, there is nothing to wonder at in them so much as the fact that so many men could be found degraded enough to spend their lives constructing a tomb for some ambitious booby, whom it would have been wiser and manlier to have drowned in the Nile, and then given his body to the dogs. — Henry David Thoreau, *Walden*

(2) *Translate the abstract into the concrete.* Good writing is graphic. The author has the knack for translating attitude into gesture, ideas into acts. He uses the concrete example, the vivid figure of speech, that makes us imagine, visualize, remember:

Habit is habit and not to be *flung out of the window* by any man but *coaxed downstairs a step at a time.* (Mark Twain)

The principal effect of our material well-being has been to set *the children's teeth on edge.* (James Baldwin)

Pre-eminently among American college women, the Vassar girl is thought of as *carrying a banner*. The inscription on it varies with the era or with the ideas of the beholder and in the final sense does not matter — *the flushed cheek* and *tensed arm are what count*. (Mary McCarthy)

When books pass in review *like the procession of animals in a shooting gallery,...* *the critic has only one second in which to load and aim and shoot and may well be* *pardoned if he mistakes rabbits for tigers, eagles for barndoor fowls, or misses al-* *together and wastes his shot upon some peaceful cow grazing in a further field.* (Virginia Woolf)

The young, of course, are always questioning values, *knocking the status quo about,* *considering shibboleths to see if they are pronounceable.*   (Edward Albee)

(3) *Develop a love and respect for words as words.* Language is more than a neutral code. Each word has its own shape, sound, history, associations. *Squander* is not just another word for *waste*. *Toil* is not just another word for *work*. A good writer has a feeling for nuance, for words that are closely related and yet different. He is aware of the echoes and cross references from one word to the other:

The way to be *safe* is never to be *secure*.   (Benjamin Franklin)

The new head of the Central Intelligence Agency, who looks more like a man of the *cloth* than of the *cloak*, does not make friends easily.

For the gifted young woman today, such a life ... is not a *destiny* but a *fate*.   (Mary McCarthy)

Some writers have a knack for finding the inevitable, illuminating way of putting ideas into words. Most people, however, have to train their powers of expression through careful listening and reading. They read a magazine article and stop to repeat an apt quotation or a striking phrase. They start reading a short story and are caught up by its arresting first sentence.

Attentive reading of other writers' work will help you develop your sense of what makes expression appropriate and effective. What it is that makes the style of an essay adequate is often hard to put into words. Many writers rely on a sense of fitness rather than on rules or instructions. They feel that a piece of writing fails to "come off," and they keep tinkering with it until it does. A word sounds strained, a metaphor doesn't fit, a conclusion is too obvious. The writer tightens a relationship here, cuts out a phrase there, not because of theories he has about stylistic effects but because as a result his work reads better, seems more finished.

Exercises

A. Study the following sentences, written by writers with a strongly individual style. What, in detail, gives each passage its characteristic quality? For each, write a passage of your own, imitating as closely as possible its distinctive features.

1. The bank, as will happen in Vermont, was right across the street, and we found there the ball-point instruments usual in local temples of deposit, insultingly chained to their tuberous sockets. (John Updike, in *The New Yorker*)

2. Hungry Joe ate voraciously, gnawed incessantly at the tips of his fingers, stammered, choked, itched, sweated, salivated, and sprang from spot to spot fanatically with an intricate black camera with which he was always trying to take pictures of naked girls. (Joseph Heller, in *Catch-22*)

3. If it all blew up, if it all came to so little, if our efforts, our loves, our crimes added up to no more than a sudden extinction in a minute, in a moment, if we had not even time before the bomb (as civilians did once) to throw one quick look at some face, some trinket, some child for which one had love, well, one could not complain. That was our fate. That was what we deserved. (Norman Mailer, in *The Presidential Papers*)

B. The following two passages are by authors widely read for their unmistakable individual style. In detail, what makes each passage different from ordinary expository prose? How do you think different kinds of readers would react to each author's style?

1. If a man, being ill of a pus appendix, resorts to a shaved and fumigated longshoreman to have it disposed of, and submits willingly to a treatment involving balancing him on McBurney's spot and playing on his vertebrae as on a concertina, then I am willing, for one, to believe that he is badly wanted in heaven. And if that same man, having achieved lawfully a lovely babe, hires a blacksmith to cure its diphtheria by pulling its neck, then I do not resist the divine will that there shall be one less radio fan later on. In such matters, I am convinced, the laws of nature are far better guides than the fiats and machinations of medical busybodies. If the latter gentlemen had their way, death, save at the hands of hangmen, policemen and other such legalized assassins, would be abolished altogether, and the present differential in favor of the enlightened would disappear. I can't convince myself that that would work any good to the world. On the contrary, it seems to me that the current coddling of the half-witted should be stopped before it

goes too far—if, indeed, it has not gone too far already. To that end nothing operates more cheaply and effectively than the prosperity of quacks. Every time a bottle of cancer oil goes through the mails *Homo Americanus* is improved to that extent. And every time a chiropractor spits on his hands and proceeds to treat a gastric ulcer by stretching the backbone the same high end is achieved.—H. L. Mencken, *A Mencken Chrestomathy*

2. The first comic books appeared in 1935. Not having anything connected or literary about them, and being as difficult to decipher as the *Book of Kells,* they caught on with the young. The elders of the tribe, who had never noticed that the ordinary newspaper was as frantic as a surrealist art exhibition, could hardly be expected to notice that the comic books were as exotic as eighth-century illuminations. So, having noticed nothing about the *form,* they could discern nothing of the *contents,* either. The mayhem and violence were all they noted. Therefore, with naïve literary logic, they waited for violence to flood the world. Or, alternatively, they attributed existing crime to the comics. The dimmest-witted convict learned to moan, "It wuz comic books done this to me."

Meantime, the violence of an industrial and mechanical environment had to be lived and given meaning and motive in the nerves and viscera of the young. To live and experience anything is to translate its direct impact into many indirect forms of awareness. We provided the young with a shrill and raucous asphalt jungle, beside which any tropical animal jungle was as quiet and tame as a rabbit hutch. We called this normal. We paid people to keep it at the highest pitch of intensity because it paid well. When the entertainment industries tried to provide a reasonable facsimile of the ordinary city vehemence, eyebrows were raised.—Marshall McLuhan, *Understanding Media*

C. Study the following *student-written* passages. Can you identify features that give each passage its characteristic tone and style?

1. Two years of white shirts, alarm clocks, bus schedules, and a Simon Legree for a boss played havoc with my original ideas about business success. I was established with the company—so was the janitor—but my general conclusion was that working as a clerk was a miserable way to make a living.

2. Boxing has never been stamped out because it is the most fundamental form of competition. It generates a mystique that encompasses its obvious hardness and pain, fashioning a ritual catharsis of the hidden violence within each of us. Even a dilettante such as Norman Mailer, that sly old fabulist and self-proclaimed veteran of innumerable cocktail party four-rounders, can catch a hint of the mystique. He perceives what he calls one of the first rewards of the ring, a marijuana-like deep-

ening of concentration. This is most apparent in amateur bouts and sparring sessions, for the professional is generally too concerned with money to allow himself any aesthetic considerations. But there are psychological rewards as well as material. It is, when one gets down to the nitty-gritty, so to speak, extremely rewarding to hit someone in the face with a fist.

3. Bradbury's office is on Wilshire Boulevard in Beverly Hills. I half expected it to be like that of the thousands of highly paid professional men who do business in the Wilshire district. Offices in that area are usually multi-secretaried affairs, vast, plushly carpeted and littered with examples of the costly tastes of some hired decorator. But Bradbury's working domain was only a microscopic cubicle of a room, stuffed spaceless with wildly abstract drawings, huge printed replicas of Prince Valiant comic strips, stacks of unshelved books, a bicycle, some hats and helmets, scattered unhung photos of rare animals and playing children, a bugle, a vintage 1927 radio and a torn, overstuffed sofa. Amidst this seemingly impassible sargasso rested a desk, a wide, shining metal island, whose drawers bulged open with papers and bric-a-brac, but whose top was perfectly clear of clutter, save several pencils and a mammoth IBM typewriter.   (from a student magazine)

4. In one of his writings, Plato indicates a mode of being which exists only as a mode of interaction between two persons. Experiences are communicated directly from one person to another, much as a "flame is kindled by the leaping fire." This mode of being cannot be reduced to the physical or psychical and only exists "between" two persons each of whom recognizes the naked authenticity of the other. It is a flower which can only blossom in a soil from which the weeds of manipulative games have been tenaciously removed. It is a reciprocal "growing together" in which perhaps most of the potentialities of man in his concreteness are actualized. In some ways the usage of drugs represents a flight from the leaping fire of a genuine dialogue and shared experiences. While drugs occasionally generate a moment of shared being, they invariably embed such moments in a diffuse matrix of peripheral entanglements and freaked associations and identifications, so as to totally trivialize the meaningful pursuit of being-in-the-world. (from an underground student newspaper)

Review Exercises

A. What makes each of the following sentences different from humdrum workaday prose? What gives it an individual touch? Your instructor may ask you to select three of these and for each write a sentence of your own imitating it as closely as you can.

1. The forward guywire of our mast began to sing under the wind, a deep and yet penetrating tone like the lowest string of an incredible bullfiddle. (John Steinbeck)

2. The role of the U.S. Commission on Civil Rights is to move the U.S. government forward, inch by agonizing inch, on civil rights. (Elizabeth Brenner Drew)

3. I was gratified to be able to answer promptly, and I did. I said I didn't know. (Mark Twain)

4. He carried under his arm a flat, grey portfolio of black-and-white sketches, which he had sold with more or less success to publishers ever since his uncle (who was an admiral) had disinherited him for Socialism, because of a lecture which he had delivered against that economic theory. (G. K. Chesterton)

5. The day arrived when he warned his companion that he could hold out — or hold in — no longer. (Henry James)

6. Not all of the President's programs receive overwhelming support in Congress. In some cases, the support is barely whelming, and may even be underwhelming.

7. She wasn't given to thinking very far, but she did a lot of intelligent feeling. (Walter Van Tilburg Clark)

8. The human back can become the seat of more aches and pains than are registered in books for the composite anatomy of a regiment. It is a limited area, but it can become the theatre of innumerable muscular conflicts, tangles, wrenches, knots, and other comforts. (Stephen Crane)

9. The guest took a large piece of cake and exception to the hostess's remarks.

10. He sat forward nervously on his chair; and she knew herself to be acting the Ancient Mariner, but her dignity would not allow her to hurry. (Mary McCarthy)

B. Report on the characteristic tone and style of one of the following departments: "Cinema" in *Time;* "Notes and Comment" in *The New Yorker;* "The Editor's Easy Chair" in *Harper's;* "On the Right" in *The National Review;* "Trade Winds" in the *Saturday Review*. Pay attention to word choice, sentence style, figurative language, use of humor, attitude toward the subject and the reader. Provide appropriate brief quotations to support your points.

C. What makes the style of the following student theme different from that of much average expository prose? What distinctive features can you identify? How do you react to them?

A MOST UNUSUAL CHARACTER

"Are you with him?"

"Yes, sir," I said in a high pitched voice.

"Follow me, both of you."

The image of the man speaking stood framed in the shadows of the rear exit door way. His corpulent body appeared to touch the sides of the door way and when he turned to lead the way to his office I noticed that his grey cotton pants were wrinkled and dirty at the knee, only at the back of the leg. The crotch hung practically halfway to the floor, perhaps because the man lacked a waist, and the butt of his slacks was shiny and blackened from his being seated so much.

I remember counting the steps leading to his second floor office, but I forgot the number immediately. I was so nervous and scared! Moreover I noticed the stains on the stair carpet which were probably made when the fat man spilled his coffee while waddling to and from his cagy working quarters.

I can still see him tearing in half a pink sales slip, giving half to me and half to my accomplice. He ordered us to write our name, address, and phone number—and no phoney info! Meanwhile he sat behind his cluttered desk, pushed his thick glasses up his long sweaty nose and lifted the telephone receiver. "Fatty" mumbled something into the phone but I knew who he was calling, the sinister gleam in his beady little black eyes was a dead give away. Besides, what is the usual procedure when one is holding two desperate shop lifters? I just wanted to get out of that horrid cell-like office but I couldn't make a run for it and leave my friend holding the yo-yo. That's what we took, a one dollar yo-yo. All this melodrama for a lousy buck.

When the interrogation began the questions came hot and heavy. "Fat man" was on his feet pacing the creaky floor in his massive wing tip shoes that just happened to be well polished and out of place in contrast with the rest of his grubby half dressed appearance. Why did you do it? Who put you up to it? How long have you been involved with this type of behavior? You know what's going to happen to you don't you? This kind of jazz went on for over ten minutes. All I could say was yes, sir; no, sir; I don't know, sir; I think so, sir; shut up, sir; you make me sick, sir! I was so scared I could die and melt away, and if he had breathed on me I would have.

"You boys know that I'm doing you a big favor, don't you. I'm giving you guys a break. This episode could mold your lives."

The policeman arrived and looked all very formidable and impressive as policemen should look. I enjoyed the trip to the station, but the waiting room there, painted in a sickly finger-marked yellow, depressed me no end.

The adventure lasted a little over three hours. I was involved in the world of crime for that short period of time. I was only nine years old and I have never stolen anything since. I've never wanted to. Even the memory of the fat man with beady eyes and long nose who probably had his tail coiled up in the seat of his pants makes me shudder. I never want the same thing to happen again. That fat old man did give me a break. He did do me a favor. He had the compassion to be so terrible and ugly and crass and just down right humane to blow the whistle and scare the bug of crime from my young dishonest body. Thanks, fat man!

Theme Topics 8

1. Write an informal letter to a friend about your difficulties in adjusting to college life.

2. Write a humorous paper on a subject usually treated with too much glum seriousness.

3. Write an ironical endorsement of a product or a policy that you disapprove of. Make sure your reader is aware of your ironical intention.

4. Write a satirical attack on features of college life that you think could be improved. Try to employ a type of satire that will appeal not only to students but also to teachers and administrators.

5. Write a satirical paper attacking a type of behavior, or some feature of contemporary American society, of which you disapprove. Avoid trivial subjects. Make your paper effective and acceptable for a fair-minded, well-informed audience.

6. Write a parody of a type of speech, lecture, or editorial that annoys or amuses you.

7. Study the manner and technique of an author who has attracted your notice because of his distinctive style. Modeling your style on his, write a composition on a subject of your own choice.

8. Select an object that to you symbolizes a set of attitudes or a way of life — the motorcycle, the guitar, the beard, blue jeans, bare feet, the hunting rifle,

a policeman's boots. Write as a spokesman for the set of attitudes involved, suiting your style to the interests and feelings expressed. (Draw on authentic observation rather than on stereotypes.)

9. Write a paper about the current scene as you would imagine it if written by one of the following in his characteristic style: a blues singer, a gospel singer, a modern jazz musician, a Shakespearean actor, a Baptist preacher, a disc jockey for a Country-and-Western station.

10. Write an article for an underground student newspaper.

Usually we are content to gather knowledge carelessly, taking life as it comes, reading as institutions decree and our tastes decide. Research, however, leads to a different kind of knowledge, for the researcher gathers knowledge systematically. And because research is conducted systematically, it results in knowledge that is not merely personal but also public—at its best, man's knowledge.
Frederick Schepman

CHAPTER NINE

The Research Paper

1. Choosing a Subject

2. Using the Library
    General Reference Works
    Specialized Reference Works
    Sifting Evidence

3. Using Bibliographical Information
    Library Catalogs
    Bibliography Cards
    Annotation

4. The Technique of Note-Taking
    Gathering Material
    Recording Material
    Note Cards

5. Writing and Revising the First Draft
    Organizing the Research Paper
    Outlining the Paper
    Adapting Quoted Material
    Integrating Quoted Material
    Form of Quotations
    Revision

6. Preparing Footnotes and Bibliographies
    Footnotes
    First References
    Subsequent References
    Abbreviations
    Final Bibliography

7. The Standards of Responsible Investigation

Sample Research Paper

1. Choosing a Subject

An effective writer has learned to assemble, interpret, and correlate material from a variety of sources. He has learned to build on the work of previous investigators. He knows how to present his findings in such a way that they will be accepted as the result of detailed and comprehensive exploration, conducted by a competent and responsible observer.

As a student writing a research paper, you need to produce definite results in a limited time. The result of whatever research you do is supposed to be a substantial and coherent paper. Your first task, therefore, is to select a subject that you can profitably treat within the time and with the materials at your disposal. Obviously, you will avoid subjects for which you are completely unprepared. For instance, recent developments in the natural sciences or in medicine make interesting subjects, but most of them call for a knowledge of mathematics, physics, or chemistry that many college freshmen do not have. If you can, try to start from a foothold of previously acquired knowledge. If you grew up in the South, you might be prepared to investigate the influence of a Confederate leader like Jefferson Davis. If your home state is known for its Indian reservations, you might profitably investigate the cultural traditions of an Indian tribe.

A research paper need not be on a highly technical subject. Many subjects of general interest provide fruitful topics for a paper of this kind. A research paper will give you a chance to focus on a familiar idea and to assess its significance. For instance, you might trace the concept of "rugged individualism" in the speeches and writings of Herbert Hoover. Or you might compare Mahatma Gandhi's concept of nonviolence with Western ideas of passive resistance.

Select a subject that will allow you to observe a number of basic requirements for a successful paper:

(1) *The paper should center on one limited aspect of a general subject.* Avoid subjects that would lead you to compile miscellaneous information. Many research papers are unsuccessful because they cover too much ground. They are too broad in scope, too shallow in treatment. Restrict your general subject area until you arrive at something that you can explore in detail. "The early history of American universities" is a general subject area; "the training of Puritan divines at Harvard" is a specific subject.[1]

(2) *The paper should show that the author has made detailed use of several different sources.* Avoid subjects that would tempt

---

[1] See the section on limiting the subject in Chapter One, "The Whole Theme."

you to summarize preassembled information from one main source. Avoid subjects that you find conclusively and satisfactorily treated in a textbook or in an encyclopedia. A research paper is more than a condensation of easily accessible material. Whatever points you make should require careful sifting and comparing of evidence from different, and possibly conflicting, sources.

(3) *The conclusions elaborated in the paper should stay close to the evidence actually presented.* When you write a research paper, the stance you adopt toward your audience is: "Here is the evidence. This is where I found it. You are welcome to verify these sources and to check these facts." Avoid subjects whose discussion would require you to appeal frequently not to objective evidence but to personal preference or partisan allegiance.

Here are some general areas for research:

1. The past history and future prospects of English spelling: reasons for its irregularity; causes that led to standardization; attempts at spelling reform.

2. The history of dictionary making: the principles and practices of lexicographers like Samuel Johnson or Noah Webster; the history of the *Oxford English Dictionary;* problems of lexicography.

3. Bilingualism: problems encountered by French Canadians, Mexican-Americans, or Flemish-speaking Belgians; assimilation versus the preservation of a separate linguistic and cultural tradition; the schooling provided for children who speak a different language at home.

4. Foreign-language teaching in the public schools: arguments for and against the study of Latin; current trends toward increased study of foreign languages; public school offerings in Russian and other languages not often taught.

5. The early history of outstanding universities or colleges: the philosophical, religious, or political motives of their founder; the purposes, vocational or otherwise, for which the institutions were originally intended; the educational principles of their founder or their original faculties.

6. The education or the reading of a prominent early American: books that influenced Washington, Jefferson, Franklin, or Madison; the influence of the classics or of contemporary trends of thought.

7. The public reception of a controversial author: Henrik Ibsen, D. H. Lawrence, James Joyce, Henry Miller, Jean Genet; changing standards of taste and public morals.

8. The history or the extent of the censorship of imaginative literature: standards applied by critics, courts of law, civic groups; legal means and indirect pressures at the disposal of would-be censors.

9. The self-image of the young Negro in white society as reflected in several books by Negro authors: Richard Wright, James Baldwin, Ralph Ellison.

10. Religious trends: the growth of Catholicism; the spread and influence of evangelistic movements; the prospects for closer association of the various Protestant denominations; tendencies within American Judaism; interest in religious subjects among college students.

As you start your investigation, remember that your purpose is to *tell your reader something worthwhile* about your chosen or assigned topic. It is easy for a research paper to sink under the weight of its scholarly paraphernalia, to become a mere exercise in footnoting and the writing of bibliographies. Do not allow your paper to live up the definition of research as "a minimum of thought about a maximum of data." Think of your research paper throughout as a piece of writing—an attempt to communicate something to a reader.

2. Using the Library

In an adequate college library, every imaginable subject is covered by books, articles, and reports that are often the result of painstaking and comprehensive study.

General Reference Works

A writer must learn to use the reference tools available to every investigator regardless of his specific subject.

Encyclopedias. An encyclopedia is a good place to start—but not to finish—your investigation. Typically, the encyclopedia provides a convenient summary of what is generally known, or easily accessible to the layman, on your subject. The purpose of your investigation is to go *beyond* the encyclopedia—to take a closer first-hand look.

The *Encyclopaedia Britannica,* now an American publication, is considered by many the most authoritative of the general encyclopedias. It provides extended articles on general subjects, with exceptionally full bibliographies at the ends of articles. It is brought up to date each year by the *Britannica Book of the Year.* Although you would normally consult the most up-to-date version, you will occasionally find references to scholarly articles in earlier editions.

The *Encyclopedia Americana* is sometimes recommended for science and biography. General subjects are broken up into short articles, arranged alphabetically. The annual supplement is the *Americana Annual.*

Collier's Encyclopedia is another multivolume general encyclopedia, aiming somewhat more directly at a popular audience.

The one-volume *Columbia Encyclopedia* provides a bird's-eye view. It serves well for a quick check of people and places.

Bibliographies.   At the end of many encyclopedia entries you will find a short bibliography, a list of important books and other sources of information. The encyclopedia may suggest only very general books, but these in turn will often contain more detailed bibliographical listings or direct you to book-length bibliographies. Any general survey of a subject is likely to provide information about more detailed studies. College textbooks often provide a short bibliography at the end of each chapter.

Take up first those books that a bibliography labels "standard," "indispensable," or "the best introduction" to your subject. If the bibliographies you have consulted merely *list* books, take up those that are most frequently mentioned. Study their tables of contents, prefaces, introductory or concluding chapters. Find out what each book is trying to do and whether all or parts of it would be useful for your project.

The *Book Review Digest* contains short selections from book reviews written shortly after publication of the book reviewed. These can give you an idea of the intention and importance of books on subjects of general interest.

Periodical Indexes.   When writing on a current problem, you may have to rely primarily on articles in both general and technical magazines. Often a well-written magazine article is the most convenient survey of and guide to information on a subject. Often magazine articles contain detailed discussion of points treated very briefly in available books. Since the card catalog of your library lists magazines but not individual magazine articles, you will have to locate the latter in the **periodical indexes**. These are published in monthly or semimonthly installments and then combined in huge volumes, each listing articles for a period of one or more years.

The *Readers' Guide to Periodical Literature* indexes magazines written for the general reader. If you are. writing on American policy in the Far East, the *Readers' Guide* will direct you to speeches by government officials reprinted in full in *Vital Speeches of the Day* or *U.S. News & World Report*. It will direct you to discussions of American foreign policy in such magazines as *Newsweek* and *New Republic*. The *Social Sciences and Humanities Index* (formerly *International Index*) lists articles in more scholarly magazines. If you are writing on the status of the American Negro, this index will direct you to articles in sociological and psychological journals.

Poole's Index to Periodical Literature lists articles published between 1802 and 1906. It can help you find contemporary reviews of Noah Webster's dictionary or the novels of James Fenimore Cooper.

NOTE: Whatever index or bibliography you use, read its introductory pages and study its list of abbreviations. *Study the list of the periodicals indexed* — it may not include a magazine that you have seen mentioned elsewhere and that you know to be important. Look at sample entries to study the listing of individual articles (usually by subject) and the system of cross references.

Specialized Reference Works

A writer must learn to use the reference tools of his special area of study. Every major area, such as education, history, or art, has its own specialized reference guides: yearbooks, specialized encyclopedias, dictionaries of names and technical terms, general bibliographies.

To find specialized reference works revelant to your research project, turn to Constance M. Winchell's *Guide to Reference Books*, including the supplements bringing it up to date. It lists the standard sources of information for all major fields of study and contains many helpful hints for the inexperienced research worker.

Biography.   One type of library project that is often assigned in writing classes is the biographical paper. In addition to the biographical entries in the major encyclopedias, most libraries have ample material for this kind of project.

Who's Who in America, a biographical dictionary of notable living men and women, provides a brief summary of dates and details on important contemporaries. The *Dictionary of American Biography (DAB)* contains a more detailed account of the lives of important persons. The British counterparts of these two volumes are *Who's Who* and the *Dictionary of National Biography (DNB)*.

The *Biography Index* is a guide to biographical material in books *and* magazines. By consulting both recent and earlier volumes, you can compile a comprehensive bibliography of material on the married life of George Washington or on the evangelistic campaigns of Billy Graham.

Literature.   Courses that stress reading and discussion of imaginative literature may include a library project on a subject from literary history — an author's schooling or early reading, recurrent themes in the books of a well-known novelist, the contemporary reputation of a nineteenth-century American poet.

The fifteen-volume *Cambridge History of English Literature* and the *Cambridge Bibliography of English Literature* provide comprehensive information about English authors and literary movements.

The Spiller-Thorp-Johnson-Canby *Literary History of the United States,* with its supplementary bibliographies, lists as its contributors an impressive and representative roster of contemporary American literary scholars.

Harper's Dictionary of Classical Literature and Antiquities is a comprehensive scholarly guide to Greek and Roman history and civilization. (Robert Graves' *The Greek Myths* and Edith Hamilton's *Mythology,* both available as paperbacks, provide an introduction to famous names and stories.)

Current Events. A number of special reference guides are useful for papers on a political subject or on current events.

Facts on File (published since 1941) is a weekly digest of world news, with an annual index. It gives a summary of news reports and comments with excerpts from important documents and speeches. It can serve as a convenient review of day-to-day happenings in politics, foreign affairs, entertainment, sports, science, and education. The *New York Times Index* (published since 1913) is a guide to news stories published in the *New York Times.* By looking up an event or a controversy in either index, you can ascertain the approximate dates for relevant articles in newspapers and magazines.

The annual index to the *Monthly Catalog of the United States Government Publications* lists reports and documents published by all branches of the federal government.

Sifting Evidence

A writer must learn to evaluate the library resources available to him. He must learn to choose authoritative sources and to evaluate conflicting evidence. An inexperienced writer often shows an uncritical acceptance of other writers' views. He tends to accept statements as factual or true on the say-so of a single source: "Economic rivalry between Germany and Great Britain was the primary cause of World War I" (because a book I have just read developed this theory). An experienced writer will accept such conclusions only after comparing the evidence offered by different authoritative sources. He is likely to consider to consider such points as the following:

(1) Is the author an *authority on his subject* or merely a casual observer? If you can, find out whether a book was written by an econo-

mist whose specialty is Russian agriculture or by a columnist who spent four weeks surveying Russian agriculture from the windows of a train.

(2) Does the author have an *established reputation in his field?* Keep an eye open for comments on the background and the scholarly competence of authors you are reading, or on the reputation of institutions and organizations with which they are connected.

(3) Does the publisher of the book or magazine represent a *tradition of scholarly and serious work?* Does he have a reputation to maintain? Know whether your material comes from a university press or from a popular book club, from a technical journal or from a mass-circulation magazine.

(4) Regardless of the reputation of the author and the publisher, *is the present work a thorough and carefully documented study* or a sketchy, improvised survey of the topic? Is it short on opinion and long on evidence, or vice versa? Does it weigh the findings of other authorities, or ignore them?

(5) Does the author settle important questions by *referring to primary sources* — that is, legal documents, letters, diaries, eyewitness reports, transcripts of speeches and interviews, reports on experiments, statistical surveys? Or does he rely exclusively on *secondary sources* — other authors' accounts and interpretations of primary materials?

(6) Is the author's treatment *balanced or one-sided?* An early phase in the history of the American labor movement is likely to be treated one way in the success story of a famous industrialist, another way in the biography of a pioneering labor leader. An objective historian will weigh both pro-business and pro-labor views. He will draw on a variety of contemporary accounts and documents by both interested and disinterested parties.

(7) Is the work *recent enough to have profited from current scholarship?* If it was originally published ten or twenty years ago, is the current version a revised edition? Consider the possibility that an author's views may have been invalidated by new findings and changing theories in a rapidly expanding field of study.

Exercises

A. Select one of the three major encyclopedias discussed in this section and one other encyclopedia not mentioned here. Compare their treatment of *one* of the following subjects: atonality, cybernetics, Gestalt psychology, impressionism, quantum theory, semantics, stream-of-consciousness technique, surrealism, transcendentalism, transformational grammar.

B. Study the general scheme of the *Book Review Digest* and check it for reviews of books you have read. Describe its treatment of one or two of the books.

C. Study the general scheme and sample entries of *one* of the following reference works: *American Universities and Colleges, Art Index, Business Periodicals Index, Cambridge Modern History, Catholic Encyclopedia, Concise Dictionary of American History, Dictionary of World Literature, Education Index, Grove's Dictionary of Music and Musicians, Oxford Companion to American Literature, Standard Jewish Encyclopedia, Van Nostrand's Scientific Encyclopedia.* Report your findings, commenting on the scope, usefulness, and possible limitations of the work.

D. Select *one* of the following books and study its preface, table of contents, bibliography (if any), and introductory or concluding sections. Study its treatment of one or two limited topics. Then write a brief report on the intention, scope, level of difficulty, and special features of the book: (1) Ruth Benedict, *Patterns of Culture;* (2) James B. Conant, *On Understanding Science;* (3) Myron Lieberman, *The Future of Public Education;* (4) Erwin Panofsky, *Meaning in the Visual Arts;* (5) Otto Jespersen, *Growth and Structure of the English Language;* (6) David Riesman, *The Lonely Crowd;* (7) Marshall McLuhan, *Understanding Media;* (8) René Wellek and Austin Warren, *Theory of Literature.*

E. Study the general scheme of Constance M. Winchell's *Guide to Reference Books* and report on its treatment of a field that is of special interest to you, such as journalism, medicine, business, folklore, or religion.

F. Consult the *Readers' Guide* and find recent articles on *one* of the following: Benjamin Franklin, Alexander Hamilton, Andrew Jackson, Thomas Jefferson, Thomas Paine, George Washington. Compare the intention, tone, and level of difficulty of articles taken from three different periodicals.

G. Consult the *International Index (Social Science and Humanities Index)* to find a scholarly article on *one* of the following: (1) the hypothetical parent language of all Indo-European languages, (2) the historical background of Homer's epics, (3) the Roman occupation of ancient Britain, (4) the earliest extant versions of the Old Testament, (5) the origins of medieval drama, (6) Freud's view of imaginative literature. Examine the author's use and identification of the source materials on which he has drawn.

H. Consulting more than one index, locate at least five reviews or critical discussions of one of the following: an essay by James Baldwin, a play by Peter Weiss or Richard Hochhuth, a novel by Günter Grass, the poems of Theodore Roethke. Report on your success in locating relevant material.

3. Using Bibliographical Information

When you make extensive use of printed sources, you will real-ize the usefulness of systems of description and classification that help you to identify and to locate books. You will have to be able to interpret information about books that describes their origin, author-ship, publication, content, and the like.

Library Catalogs

A writer should learn to make efficient use of the card catalog. Your research projects will ordinarily be geared to the resources of your college library. Its central card catalog is a complete alphabetical index of the materials available to you.

A card for a general-interest book brought out by a commercial publisher will look something like this:

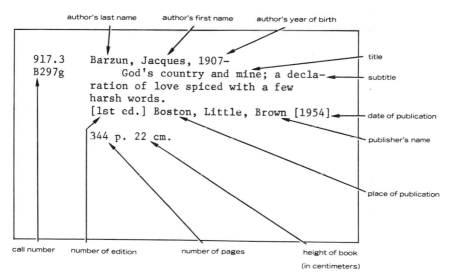

Such cards give you several kinds of information:

(1) After the *full name of the author,* you will find the *date of his birth* and, if applicable, his death.

(2) After the title of the book, you will find *the number or de-scription of the edition.* If the catalog lists both the original edition and another one marked "2nd ed." or "Rev. ed.," you will generally choose the one that is most nearly up to date.

(3) The *name and location of the publisher* can be a clue to the nature of a book. For instance, a book published by a university press

is more likely to be a scholarly and specialized study than a book published by a commercial publisher. The *date of publication* is especially important for books on scientific, technological, or medical subjects, since new scientific discoveries can rapidly invalidate old theories.

(4) The *number of pages*, with the number of introductory pages given as a lower-case Roman numeral, can indicate whether the book is a short pamphlet or a full-scale treatment of the subject. If the book contains *illustrations* or a *bibliography*, the card will carry a notation to that effect.

In most card catalogs, the same book is listed several times: by *author* (under the author's last name), by *title* (under the first word of the title, not counting *The, A,* or *An*), and by *subject*. Often, a card lists the several major *subject headings* under which the book can be found. For instance, a catalog card for a sociological study of a town in the Middle West may carry the following notation concerning various headings under which the study is listed:

1. U.S.—Social conditions. 2. Cities and Towns—U.S. 3. Cost and standard of living—U.S. 4. U.S.—Religion. 5. Social surveys. 6. Community life.

Subject cards can direct you to many books that are relevant to your topic. Look for subject headings under which books on your topic might be listed. Books on progressive education might appear under *Education—Aims and Objectives*, under *Education—Experimental Methods*, or under *Educational Psychology*. Books on the Civil War might appear under *U. S.—History—Civil War*, under *U. S.—History—Military*, under *Slavery in the United States*, or under *Abolitionists*.

Once you decide that you should consult a book, copy its call number. The **call number** is the group of letters and numbers usually found in the upper left-hand corner of the card. It directs you, or the librarian, to the shelf where the book is located. Your library may use either of two numbering systems: the Library of Congress system or the Dewey decimal system. The **Library of Congress system** divides books into categories identified by letters of the alphabet. It then uses additional letters and numerals to subdivide each main category. For instance, the call number of a book on religion would start with a capital *B;* the call number of a book on education starts with a capital *L.* The **Dewey decimal system** uses numerals to identify the main categories. For instance, 400-499 covers books on language; 800-899 covers books on literature. The 800 range is then further subdivided into American literature (810-819), English literature (820-

829), and so on. Additional numerals and letters distinguish among individual authors and among individual works by the same author.

Along with the call number, you may find a notation directing you to a special section of the library. The book you are looking for may be located in a *reference room*, where encyclopedias, dictionaries, and other reference works are kept. It may be located in a *special reading room* where books for a particular field of study are on reserve.

NOTE: Although the card catalog lists magazines and newspapers, most libraries have a separate, compact catalog for periodicals. It lists, in alphabetical order, all periodicals to which the library subscribes. For each periodical it indicates the location of recent issues (often on the shelves of a separate periodical room) as well as of back issues (usually in bound volumes in the book stacks of the library).

Bibliography Cards

Make your own card catalog of all materials that seem promising or worthy of investigation. Include a separate note card for each book, pamphlet, or magazine article you intend to use. Your instructor may suggest a minimum number of sources he wants you to consult.

On each bibliography card, include the library call number or the place in the library where the publication is to be found. (This information is for your own personal use; do *not* reproduce it in your finished paper.) Other entries on your cards will serve as the basis for references to a source in your final manuscript. Check all entries carefully against the title page of the book or the heading of the magazine article in order to correct discrepancies. Be especially careful to get the *exact spelling* of unfamiliar names.

Often, a bibliography card for a book need list no more than the following information:

509   Conant, James Bryant
C743o   *On Understanding Science: An Historical Approach*
        New Haven: Yale University Press, 1947

Usually, the first item you record is the *full name of the author.* Put the last name first to facilitate alphabetizing. If a work has been collected or arranged by a person other than the author (or the authors), you may start with that person's name, followed by "ed." for "editor." Ordinarily, however, the name of an editor or of a translator (followed by "trans.") appears on a separate line below the title. If an article in an encyclopedia is identified only by the author's initials, you may be able to find his full name by checking the initials against a list of contributors.

Start a new line for the *full title of the publication,* including a subtitle, if any. Underline the title of a book, pamphlet, or other work published as a separate entity. (Underlining in a typed manuscript corresponds to italics in print.) Put the title of an article or short poem in quotation marks and underline the title of the magazine, collection, or encyclopedia in which it appears.

Use a separate line for the *facts of publication.* For a book or pamphlet these may include a number of different items:

(1) The *number or description of the edition* (unless a book has not been re-edited since publication).

(2) The *number of volumes* (if a work consists of several, and all are relevant to your investigation).

(3) The *place of publication* (usually the location of the main office of the publishing house, or of the first branch office listed if several are given).

(4) The *name of the publisher.*

(5) The *date of publication* (not always given on the title page, though it can usually be inferred from the copyright date, found on the reverse side of the title page).

(6) The *number of the specific volume used* (if only one of several volumes is relevant to your investigation).

A bibliography card for an article is likely to contain something like the following:

Periodical   Whyte, Lancelot Law
Room   "Can We Grow Geniuses in Science?"
             Harper's, 114 (June 1957), 46–50

For a magazine or newspaper article, the facts of publication ordinarily do *not* include the name of the publisher and the place of publication, though the latter is sometimes needed to identify a small-town journal. The pages of most professional or technical magazines are numbered consecutively through the several issues comprising one volume, usually the issues published during one year. For an article in such a magazine, record the *number of the volume* (in Arabic numerals), the *date of the issue,* and the *page numbers of the article.* For articles in other magazines and in newspapers, record the date of the issue and the page numbers. If the pages in separate sections of a newspaper are not numbered consecutively, identify the section where the article is to be found.

Annotation

You will greatly increase the usefulness of your bibliography cards by annotation. Write down brief reminders concerning characteristic features of your sources. You might note, for instance, that an article on atomic energy is extremely technical; perhaps it requires more knowledge of physics than you command. Another article on the same subject may be a popularized treatment and give none of the specific data you need. Or you may want to note that a book has a glossary of technical terms, or an annotated bibliography, or a convenient summary of historical facts.

```
Humanities    Neville, Mark A.
Room          "Who Killed Poetry?"
              The English Journal, 47 (March 1958), 133-38

      Examines, with examples, conventional methods
of teaching poetry in high schools.  Concludes
that teachers of poetry should stress appreciation
and enjoyment rather than the study of versifica-
tion.
```

NOTE: If your project is to provide the basis for further study on the part of your reader, you can help him by annotating the final bibliography which you furnish with your paper.

Exercises

A. Study the arrangement of cards in the central card catalog of your college library in order to answer the following questions: (1) What are the major subdivisions for subject cards under the heading "Education"? (2) Where would you find a book by an author named John McMillan (under *Mc, Mac, Mi?*), George St. John (under *St., Sa, Jo?*), Antoine de Saint-Exupéry (under *De, Sa, St.?*)? (3) Do subject cards for books on the Civil War precede or follow cards for books on the War of Independence? Is the arrangement alphabetical or chronological?   (4) Are books about George Washington listed before or after books about the State of Washington, or about Washington, D. C.?   (5) Check under *John Keats:* What is the relative order of the author's individual works, his collected works, and books about the author?

B. Transcribe and explain the information that the card catalog of your college library provides concerning *one* of the following books: Leonard Bloomfield, *Language;* H. W. Fowler, *A Dictionary of Modern English Usage;* Otto Jespersen, *Modern English Grammar;* H. L. Mencken, *The American Language;* Stuart Robertson, *The Development of Modern English.*

4.   The Technique of Note-Taking

While you are investigating source materials, your reading will be primarily exploratory. You may read an article in an encyclopedia or a chapter in a textbook. You may glance through introductory material and selected chapters in a number of promising books. Even at this stage you may be jotting down tentative questions and observations. It will be some time, however, before you have a clear idea of the scope and point of your paper. Only then will you be ready to start taking notes in a thorough and systematic manner.

Gathering Material

Select material for its relevance to the tentative generalizations that you formulate as you go along. Ideally, you should become better able to decide what material is relevant to your purpose with every step in your investigation.

Suppose you are writing a research paper on trends toward increased teaching of foreign languages in the public schools. You are consulting a number of books published in the fifties and sixties and devoted to the improvement of American public education. By glancing over the table of contents and consulting the index of each book, you locate a number of discussions bearing on your subject. The following passages seem particularly relevant:

The school board should be ready to offer a third and fourth year of a foreign language, no matter how few students enroll. . . . I have met no teachers of foreign language who felt that anything approaching mastery could be obtained by the study of a foreign language for only two years in high school, nor have the students felt that two years of study had given them any real working knowledge of the language. Four years of study, on the other hand, will yield dividends for those capable of handling foreign languages. This is the recommendation of the foreign language panel of the NEA Conference on the Identification and Education of the Academically Talented held in Washington in February, 1958.

Almost without exception, I found a deplorable state of affairs in regard to foreign languages. . . . —James B. Conant, *The American High School Today*, p. 69.

. . . In the third field of importance today—foreign languages—the situation is even more serious. One consequence is that we have a diplomatic service where only 50 per cent now have command of a foreign language and where—still worse—a mere 30 per cent of the incoming recruits speak any foreign language; clear evidence of the deterioration of foreign-language teaching in the last generation. . . .

Progressive education must be blamed in large part for our neglect of foreign-language teaching. . . . We are the only major country which neglects the early years when a child can learn foreign languages most easily—from 10 onward.—H. G. Rickover, *Education and Freedom*, p. 109 and App., p. 65.

The American attitude toward the study of foreign languages has changed remarkably in the last decade. Twenty years ago, the future for these subjects seemed bleak indeed. Greek was gone, Latin was going, and enrollments in French and German were steadily declining. . . . In the early fifties, the Modern Language Association of America received from the Rockefeller Foundation a substantial grant for the purpose of setting up a Foreign Language Program. . . . It collected and disseminated information of all sorts and tried with some success to persuade the nation that a revival of foreign languages was in the national interest. The movement called FLES—Foreign Languages in the Elementary Schools—was greatly encouraged by this project.

The shudder that the launching of the Russian satellite sent through the world accelerated the swing back to foreign languages, as to other solid subjects. . . . The most dramatic response was the National Defense Education Act of 1958, which provided funds for the improvement and expansion of instruction in science, mathematics, and modern foreign languages.—Albert R. Kitzhaber e.a., *Education for College*, pp. 113–116.[2]

From these and related passages, a number of tentative areas of agreement emerge. The first is the relatively low state of foreign-language teaching in the past. The second is a growing concern in the last one or two decades with the improvement of foreign-language instruction, reflected in the recommendations of educational authorities like Dr. Conant, in the efforts of professional organizations, and in government support. In further reading, you will look for material that will support or clarify these tentative points. At the same time, these passages suggest avenues for further exploration. You will try to find some of the "information of all sorts" disseminated by the Modern Language Association, some of it likely to be found in its official quarterly, *PMLA*. You will try to find out more about the role of the National Education Association (NEA), again perhaps turning first to an official publication like the *NEA Journal*. You will try to locate authoritative accounts of the original National Defense Education Act, both its original intent and its impact on the schools.

[2] Albert R. Kitzhaber, Robert M. Gorrell, and Paul Roberts, *Education for College: Improving the High School Curriculum.* Copyright © 1961 The Ronald Press Company.

Recording Material

While recording information and ideas, you will have to employ a combination of techniques:

(1) *Learn to extricate important points from long passages, to summarize or condense lengthy quotations.* A formal abridgment, sometimes called a **précis**, preserves all essential generalizations and qualifications while curtailing or omitting altogether such material as explanations, examples, and incidental comments. It uses the most economical kind of wording, substituting one-word equivalents for lengthy phrases wherever possible. (See the section on summarizing in Chapter 19, "Practical Prose Forms.")

When you condense material for reproduction in the finished paper, you are likely to be more selective than in preparing a formal précis. You will pick out only those points of a report or of an argument that are directly relevant to your investigation. For instance, you may be investigating Woodrow Wilson's unsuccessful defense of the Treaty of Versailles and the League of Nations in 1919. After reading several pages of a historical study that reviews relevant political facts, you may decide to summarize them for use in an introductory paragraph. Your note might look something like this:

```
American Politics 1918-1920

     Election of Republican Congress in 1918.
Bitter opposition to President's role in peace
conference from such men as ex-President
Roosevelt and Senator Lodge.  Unprecedented
Republican majority in congressional elections
of 1920.  Final rejection of treaty and of
League of Nations by U.S. Senate in March
1920.


Commager, History, pp. 411-13
```

(2) *Learn to translate information and ideas into your own words.* Many of the notes you will take for a research project will record information fairly specifically and fully. A flexible method of recording such material is the **paraphrase**. This method enables you

to select and emphasize points you consider important while at the same time working them smoothly into your text:

Wilson's Campaign in Support of League

    Speech at Pueblo, Colorado, shows that Wilson is very much aware of the activities of men creating what he considers erroneous impressions concerning the League of Nations. Speech is designed to dispel mistaken impressions created in the public's mind.

    The proposed peace treaty is based not on the desire for territorial acquisition but on the principle that people should freely choose their own governments. The League of Nations is needed to mobilize the united moral force of the great nations of the world in support of the principles of non-agression and of self-determination for all nations.

Heffner, Documents, p. 235

---

(3) *Use well-chosen quotations to pinpoint key ideas or to clinch an argument.* Also, preserve characteristic phrases that give an insight into the personality of an author, whether by illustrating his aspirations, his sense of humor, or his style. The following note reproduces verbatim an author's position on a debatable point:

Dangers of Conformity

    "The idea that men are created free and equal is both true and misleading: men are created different; they lose their social freedom and their individual autonomy in seeking to become like each other."

Riesman, Lonely Crowd, p. 349

Use **direct quotation** sparingly or not at all in reproducing information, in outlining an author's argument, and in covering minor or noncontroversial points. Unselective recording of verbatim material in your notes is likely to lead to the kind of paper that consists primarily of lengthy excerpts from the original sources, held together by a thin tissue of phrases like "He further says . . ." and "We should also remember that . . ." Frequent use of undigested direct quotations tempts the reader to skip the quoted material and to look in the accompanying text for your main point.

NOTE: Make sure that your notes differentiate clearly between paraphrase or indirect quotation on the one hand and direct quotation on the other. In other words, *use quotation marks to identify all material quoted verbatim.*

Note Cards

Separate note cards enable you to sort out and reshuffle information. Most composition instructors require that their students take notes for a research project on 3x5 or 4x6 cards. Observing the following suggestions will help you make efficient use of your cards:

(1) Each card should record either *one single item of information or material so closely related that there is no chance of your having to separate it* in order to use it in different parts of your paper. However, generalizations should be accompanied by the specific detail that you will need to illustrate or support them in a paragraph. Include selected examples, statistical figures, definitions of difficult terms.

(2) The *material on each card should be full and clear enough* to make sense to you even after the context in which it originally appeared is no longer fresh in your mind. Excessive use of condensation and of abbreviations may make notes worthless later.

(3) The *material on each card should be representative* of the source from which it was taken. Be careful not to copy, as bare assertion, statements that are modified or qualified by the context in which they originally appeared.

(4) Each card should clearly *identify the source of the material recorded.* Use a shortened form of the author's name and the title of the work. (Some instructors recommend using a code number that you have assigned to the work in your preliminary bibliography.) *Include the exact page reference.*

(5) If you have arrived at tentative subdivisions for your paper, the *heading to which the material on the card relates* should appear at the top of the card. Use headings that will divide your material into sizable but convenient units. Having too many cards per heading

will make your notes unwieldy. Having too few cards per heading will make your notes confusing.

Exercise

Select an article (or chapter from a book) for its possible relevance to a future research project. Prepare a dozen note cards, grouped around two or three related headings and illustrating the various techniques of note-taking.

5. Writing and Revising the First Draft

By taking notes on separate cards, you can sort your notes into tentative categories while you are still studying your sources. When you have done most of the necessary reading, you should review your note cards to consider the main divisions they suggest.

Organizing the Research Paper

Group together cards that contain related material. The major weakness of many research papers is that the connections between the recorded facts are not clearly worked out. Make sure your finished paper will not strike the reader as a collection of loosely connected bits of information. Often a group of cards will record details pointing to a common generalization, evidence backing up the same major point. Often a group of cards will record related causes combining to produce a common result. Two related groups of cards may contain parallel sets of data for detailed comparison.

As your paper begins to assume definite shape in your mind, remember the following advice:

(1) *Work toward a unifying thesis.* Ask yourself: "What is this paper as a whole going to tell the reader?" Suppose you are writing a paper on the present state of gambling in the United States. Your problem will be to keep your paper from becoming a repository of miscellaneous facts about gambling laws, famous gamblers, different games of chance, and tourist life in Las Vegas. To unify your paper, you might concentrate on the legal aspects of gambling. You could then review in some detail the laws of Nevada as exceptions to anti-gambling laws in other states, the legal status of horse and dog races, the question of lotteries and games conducted for charitable purposes.

Everything you say in the paper could support one single major point: "Gambling laws in the United States are as paradoxical and unpredictable as we would expect them to be in a pluralistic society."

(2) *Plan to state your thesis early in your paper.* To give thrust and direction to your paper, do not merely start by indicating the *direction* of your inquiry. Instead, early state the *conclusion* you have reached. No one can quarrel with a program like the following, but no one will get excited about it either:

Volumes have been written about the character of Hamlet. Careful study is required to separate the mere fanciful theories from those that deserve our attention. . . .

Have the courage to *commit* yourself to an assertion that can be argued, challenged — and remembered:

The great majority of Shakespeare's critics agree that the ghost's appearance, urging Hamlet on to revenge, imposes a task on a man unfitted by nature to accomplish such an undertaking.

(3) *Do not take the line of least resistance in working out your overall scheme.* When writing about critical interpretations of Hamlet's character, do not simply give a dreary survey following straight chronological order. Instead, try to identify three or four major schools of thought. Group together critics interested in the *lone* Hamlet, listening to him most intently in his monologues and solitary musings. Group together critics interested in the *social* Hamlet and absorbed by his playacting and verbal fencing. Group together critics interested in the *child* Hamlet, listening, in psychoanalyst's fashion, for hints of his early psychological history.

If you want to assure your reader that you have brought your material under control, your paper as a whole will have a strong and clear logical scheme. (You may want to review the section on organizing a paper in Chapter One, "The Whole Theme.")

Outlining the Paper

After arranging your cards in a tentative sequence, write a preliminary outline that reflects their order. Formulate a tentative thesis sentence summarizing the conclusion that your paper seems to suggest. Your outline and your thesis sentence will enable you to decide which of your note cards contain irrelevant material and should be set aside. They will also help you to decide in which areas your notes need to be supplemented by further reading. A definitive outline preceding the final paper usually shows whether the paper has a unifying purpose, whether the major subdivisions of the paper contribute to that purpose, and whether unrelated odds and ends have been eliminated. (For forms of outlines, see Chapter One, "The Whole Theme.")

Once you have a preliminary outline, you can start writing a first rough draft of your paper. Keep your eyes on your overall plan and decide to be temporarily satisfied with less than perfection in details. Where necessary, modify your plan or reorganize your note cards as you proceed. If you notice unanswered questions or missing evidence, note the inadequacies in the margin and follow them up later.

Adapting Quoted Material

In writing a research paper, you will be working into the text an often considerable amount of quoted material. The following examples illustrate some legitimate, and some illegitimate, ways of incorporating material from a source into the text of a paper:

(1) *Extensive quotation — to be used sparingly:*

such a view. In an article in <u>Fortune</u> that has been fre-

quently reprinted, Adlai Stevenson stated his belief that

American postwar prosperity was due to the cooperation of

business and government:

> It is a curious thing that the two institutional
> forces in the democratic capitalistic society that
> contributed most directly to this emergence of the
> powerful consumer during this quarter-century seemed
> to snarl at each other every step of their common way.
> The bounding prosperity of postwar America has been
> due in large measure to processes in which government
> and business have in effect played complementary and
> cooperative roles. The New Deal legislation of the
> Thirties helped to provide a "built-in" consumer
> demand that business could then work to satisfy, and
> the increase of 70 per cent in the scale of the
> American economy between 1939 and 1944 was achieved
> by the closest cooperation between government and
> industry in America's war effort.[7]

---

[7]Adlai E. Stevenson, "My Faith in Democratic Capitalism," <u>Fortune</u>, October 1955, p. 126.

In this example, a lengthy excerpt from a source is used to buttress an important point. The excerpt is indented and set off from the text as a **block quotation** — *no quotation marks, single-spaced lines*. The sentence introducing the excerpt gives credit to author and publication; the footnote numeral at the end directs the reader to the footnote providing the name of the article and an exact page reference. *The introductory sentence also summarizes the main point or the significance of the quotation.* A reader easily becomes bored and discouraged if he cannot make out why he is given numerous lengthy quotations.

(2) *Plagiarized version — illegitimate, unacknowledged paraphrase:*

has had lasting effects. But it is surprising that the

two forces in our society that contributed most to the

emergence of the powerful consumer seemed to snarl at each

other every step of the way. The prosperity of postwar

America has been due to the fact that government and

business have played complementary and cooperative roles.

The New Deal legislation of the Thirties provided a built-in

consumer demand for business to satisfy. The increase of

70 per cent in the American economy was achieved by the

cooperation between government and industry in America's

war effort.

Much **plagiarism** takes this form: a slightly abridged version of the original source. Even if the source were identified, this way of adapting the material would be unsatisfactory. It preserves far too much of the original author's way of putting things — without using direct quotation. Sentence structure corresponds closely to that of the original. Much of the characteristic phrasing is preserved ("emergence of the powerful consumer," "seemed to snarl," "complementary and cooperative roles"). The only changes are the omission or shortening of incidental phrases. As in much hasty adaptation, qualifications that made the original cautious have been lost ("due to" for "due *in large measure* to"; "provided" for "*helped* to provide").

(3) *Legitimate paraphrase — attributed to the original author:*

Like other observers, Mr. Stevenson points out the

irony in the apparent hostility of the two major institutions

that made the American consumer a powerful force in the

nation's economy. He attributes the rapidly growing pros-

perity of postwar America at least partly to the cooperation

intentional or unintentional, of government and business.

Thus, legislation enacted under the Roosevelt administration

helped to increase consumer purchasing power. Similarly,

the extraordinary growth of the American economy between

1939 and 1944 was the result of government and industry

working together in building up the country's military

strength.[7]

This **paraphrase**, documented by a footnote, preserves the essential meaning of the original. At the same time, by translating the passage into his own words, the adapter shows that he has understood it. He shows how he interprets phrases that are in any way unusual or metaphorical. For instance, he takes the phrase "a curious thing" to express irony. For the graphic "seemed to snarl" he substitutes its literal equivalent, "apparent hostility." Instead of using percentage points, the adapter describes the growth of the economy as "extraordinary." Though general, this term does justice to the intention of the original. Although some of the sentences are roughly parallel to the original in grammatical construction, others — for instance, the first and second ones — are completely reorganized. This kind of close paraphrase is useful when detailed interpretation and evaluation of a source is desirable.

(4) Part paraphrase, part direct quotation—worked closely into the text:

Like economists and sociologists before him, Mr.

Stevenson emphasizes that government and business in this

country have in effect worked together in assuring postwar

prosperity--even though they "seemed to snarl at each other

every step of their common way." As he implies but does

not directly state, business has never openly acknowledged

that "New Deal legislation . . . helped to provide a

'built-in' consumer demand that business could then work

to satisfy." He attributes an "increase of 70 per cent in

the scale of the American economy between 1939 and 1944"

to "the closest cooperation" between government and

industry.[7]

This technique is the most flexible and most generally useful one for adapting source material to the adapter's own use. He condenses, restates, and interprets the material he has selected, at the same time using brief direct quotations for important points and characteristic phrases. Competent use of this technique can effectively break up the deadly "So-and-So says such-and-such" pattern found in many library papers.

(5) Legitimate summary:

Mr. Stevenson feels that postwar prosperity in this

country was to a large extent the result of cooperation

between government and business. Specifically he refers to

the role of New Deal legislation in restoring consumer

demand and to the joint participation of government and

industry in the war effort.[7]

This **summary** gets at the gist of the passage. At the same time it lists briefly arguments or details supporting the main point in the original.

Integrating Quoted Material

Work material from different note cards into a coherent paragraph of your own. Do not simply stitch together the material on your cards more or less in the order in which you took your notes. Instead, draw on material from the cards when you need it to *support a point.* Pull out a striking example; select a key phrase; use several lines verbatim as a key quotation. Use only what helps you carry forward your argument; never feel you have to use material merely because you went to the trouble of recording it on your cards.

Can you see how material from the note cards on "Hamlet as thinker" (on page 320) has been excerpted and rearranged in order to produce the integrated paragraphs based on these cards? On page 321 are the two paragraphs based on these cards.

To keep your text moving smoothly in spite of the bulk of quoted material, remember the following points:

(1) *Link quoted and paraphrased material clearly to its source.* There is considerable difference between "Capitalism is a moribund system" and "According to Marx, capitalism is a moribund system." If you are citing several authors, make sure that references like "he," "this author," or "the writer" point clearly to the person you have in mind. Show clearly where a paraphrase stops and your own comment starts:

Lewis Theobald, an eighteenth-century critic, sees Hamlet as the heroic prince. *Theobald* is engrossed with the neoclassical principle of decorum as he criticizes Hamlet's coarseness and obscenity toward Ophelia. *The modern reader* is not likely to think of this part of Hamlet's behavior in the same terms. . . .

(2) *Tell your reader what the point of a quotation is, and why you quote it.* As you introduce a quotation, steer the reader's attention in the right direction. Make him look for a key point; show the relevance of the quote to the rest of your argument:

Weak: In 1870, William Hazlitt expressed his views on Hamlet's character *in the following manner:* "He seems incapable of deliberate action and is only hurried into extremities on the spur of the occasion. . . ."

Better: Hazlitt, like Coleridge, *saw Hamlet as a man kept from action by excessive thought:* "He seems incapable . . ."

Hamlet as thinker

  Charles Lamb (1811) prefers <u>reading</u> the plays
to seeing them performed; in drama, speech is
only an often artificial medium for letting us
see the inner workings of a character's mind:
"nine parts in ten of what Hamlet does, are
transactions between himself and his moral sense,
they are the effusions of his solitary musings,
which he retires to holes and corners and the
most sequestered parts of the palace to pour
forth; or rather, they are the silent meditations
with which his bosom is bursting, reduced to <u>words</u>
for the sake of the reader."
in Smith, pp. 195-96

Hamlet as thinker

   "Hamlet's character is the prevalence of
the abstracting and generalizing habit over the
practical. He does not want courage, skill, will,
or opportunity; but every incident sets him
thinking; . . . I have a smack of Hamlet myself,
if I may say so."

  According to Coleridge (1818?), Shakespeare
meant to show the need for a healthy balance
between observation and thought, between reality
and the world of imagination. "In Hamlet this
balance is disturbed: his thoughts, and the
images of his fancy, are far more vivid than
his actual perceptions . . . Hence we see
a great, an almost enormous, intellectual
activity, and a proportionate aversion to real
action. . . he vacillates from sensibility,
and procrastinates from thought."

in Smith,

Hamlet as thinker

   "It is <u>we</u> who are Hamlet. . . . Whoever has
become thoughtful and melancholy through his own
mishaps or those of others; whoever has borne
about with him the clouded brow of reflection,
and thought himself 'too much i' th' sun;' . . .
whose powers of action have been eaten up by
thought, he to whom the universe seems infinite
and himself nothing; . . . this is the true
Hamlet." (pp. 287-88)

   "His ruling passion is to think, not to act."

William Hazlitt, <u>Characters of Sh.'s Plays</u> (1817)
in Smith, pp. 287-91

The Romantic critics saw in Hamlet a man paralyzed by thought. They saw in him a reflection of their own temperament: a love for solitude, an extreme sensitivity, a tendency to be kept from effective action by melancholy reflections. "It is we who are Hamlet," said William Hazlitt. The true Hamlet is someone "whose powers of action have been eaten up by thought"--"whoever has become thoughtful and melancholy through his own mishaps or those of others; whoever has borne about with him the clouded brow of reflection, and thought himself 'too much i' th' sun.'"[7] Coleridge, who said "I have a smack of Hamlet myself," saw in Hamlet a lack of balance between thought and reality-- "a great, an almost enormous, intellectual activity, and a proportionate aversion to real action."[8]

As a result, the Romantics tended to disregard the dramatic action of the play to concentrate on the study of Hamlet's thought and motives. To Charles Lamb, the dramatic action of the play was little more than a pretext for letting us study the inner workings of Hamlet's mind:

> Nine parts in ten of what Hamlet does, are transactions
> between himself and his moral sense, they are the
> effusions of his solitary musings, which he retires
> to holes and corners and the most sequestered parts
> of the palace to pour forth; or rather, they are the
> silent meditations with which his bosom is bursting,
> reduced to words for the sake of the reader.[9]

(3) *Quote key words and phrases as part of your own sentence.* Avoid the seesaw motion of a paper in which a sentence of your own is predictably followed by "So-and-so says: . . ." in support. In addition to full-length quotations, use apt quoted words and phrases in wording your own conclusions, comments, interpretations:

The eloquent and sardonic Renaissance prince became for Romantic critics like Charles Lamb "the shy, negligent, retiring Hamlet."

To critics like Hazlitt, Hamlet was the "prince of philosophical speculators" rather than a real prince likely "to have proved most royal."

Form of Quotations

Review carefully the conventions governing the punctuation of quoted material. Pay special attention to the distinction between direct and indirect quotation, to differences in handling long and short passages, and to ways of indicating omissions and insertions. (See chart.)

(1) When a quotation becomes part of one of your own sentences, fit it into the *grammatical pattern* of your sentence, *without* changing the original wording of the material enclosed in quotation marks:

Unsatisfactory: Pope Pius described a just war in this way: "If it has been forced upon one by an evident and extremely grave injustice that in no way can be avoided."

Satisfactory: Pope Pius stated that a war is just "if it has been forced upon one by an evident and extremely grave injustice that in no way can be avoided."

Unsatisfactory: The writer suggests that Whittaker Chambers, "Having experienced at first hand the evils of communism, he now sees himself clad in shining armor, engaged in deadly combat with that evil."

Satisfactory: The writer says of Whittaker Chambers that "having experienced at first hand the evils of communism, he now sees himself clad in shining armor, engaged in deadly combat with that evil."

(2) Quotations must be *logically complete;* they should not require explanations that you do not provide. Suppose you quote Albert Schweitzer as saying, "I therefore stand and work in the world, as one who aims at making men less shallow and morally better by making them think." To keep the quotation from being logically incomplete, you will have to let your reader know what the "therefore" stands for. If you don't want to include the reasons to which it refers, you will have to shorten or paraphrase the quotation in such a way as to omit it.

HOW TO PUNCTUATE QUOTATIONS
A Brief Guide (see also P 8)

Word or phrase directly quoted, becoming part of a larger sentence (quotation marks, but *no* comma or colon):

> A. E. Housman is generally known as "a writer of elegiac pessimism in strikingly simple form." [1]

Indirect quotation or paraphrase (no quotation marks, no comma or colon):

> These dissertations on death and its aftereffects are merely Housman's stoical explanation of actuality. He once observed that the love of truth with most people is the faintest of passions. [14]

A sentence or more, directly quoted (quotation marks, introduced by comma or colon):

> George Santayana, American poet and philosopher, commented on the use of melancholy in many of Housman's poems: "I read *A Shropshire Lad,* always with tears. There is not much else than tears in them, but they are perfect of their kind." [4]

Long prose passage, set off as block quotation (indented, single-spaced — *no* quotation marks):

> During Housman's teaching career at Princeton, his work was very influential on those close to him. According to one of his students,
>
>> Instinctively we felt he knew all about us, that some would die young, some fail in love, some end in jail. His wisdom was a bitter brew, but it did not inspire bitterness or despair, and his poems with a marvelous economy told us the strengthening truth that we were very ordinary fellows whose only portion was the estate of man. Those of us who learned this young owe him much. [6]

Words or phrases from poetry, becoming part of a larger sentence (quotation marks; diagonal line to show start of a new line in original poem):

> The poet and his guide journey "like the cloudy shadows / Across the country blown . . ." (p. 55), and the entire expedition Is a very pleasant one with no hardships or miseries.

Complete lines of verse, set off as block quotation (indented, single-spaced, centered on the page):

> Housman does not deny his use of despondency but rather seems to think it essential to the universality of his work:
>
>> They say my verse is sad: no wonder;
>> Its narrow measure spans
>> Tears of eternity, and sorrow,
>> Not mine but man's. [3]

Revision

Careful revision of the first draft is an essential step, and your timetable should make adequate allowance for it. A first draft usually makes jerky reading. The writer is likely to have concentrated on arranging his material in the most logical or the most convenient order, without always explaining to his readers how he got from one paragraph to the other. He is likely to have concentrated on getting the main body of the paper into shape, providing no more than a routine introduction and allowing the paper to run out without a definite conclusion.

In revising your first draft, you will make changes ranging from the substitution of a semicolon for a comma to the rearrangement of major sections of your paper. However, regardless of the specific improvements needed, your revision should concern itself with several basic requirements for a successful paper:

(1) Check for *adequacy of detail.* See to it that individual points are clearly stated and well illustrated or documented. Make sure that the evidence you present in support of your generalizations is adequate to prevent questions such as "Is this really so?" "Is this merely a superficial impression?" or "Do the experts agree on this point?"

(2) Check for *clarity of explanation.* Many papers suffer from too much quotation, too much paraphrase, too much summary, and not enough explanation and comparison. Examine key terms to see whether they need to be more explicitly defined. Explain terms like *Hellenistic, psychosomatic,* or *lingua franca.*

(3) Check for *adequate paragraph structure.* Avoid sequences of short paragraphs that give bits of information or quotation from different sources. Instead, work material from different note cards into a coherent paragraph that coordinates, compares, contrasts. Choppy paragraphing makes continuous reading difficult, if not impossible.

(4) Check for *clear attribution.* If you are comparing different sources, keep your reader from getting hopelessly confused about who says what. Constant repetition of phrases like "according to Dewey" or "as his biographer observes" can make a paper seem heavy-handed. However, awkward but exact identification is preferable to elegant but misleading continuity of discussion.

(5) Check for *coherence.* Make your reader see the relationship between different parts of your paper. Anticipate and answer the questions of a reader mired in a mass of details: "How did this get in here?" "Why do I have to study this particular set of statistics?" Make sure there is a clear **transition**, implied or explicitly stated, from paragraph

to paragraph. Inserting a *therefore,* a *nevertheless,* or a *for instance* in a few strategic places can help transform a rambling discussion into a tightly knit argument. Check the organization of the paper against your tentative outline and adjust your outline to reflect any changes you made while writing the first draft and while revising it.

(6) Check for *clarity of overall intention.* Make sure that the main points you are trying to bring out are not merely implied but clearly and fully stated. State them preferably at the beginning of the paper following your introduction or, if more appropriate, toward the end of the paper in the form of a summary. Don't take it for granted that your reader will automatically arrive at the same conclusions that you did if you merely present "the facts."

Exercises

A. Select a passage of paragraph length from an article or book relevant to a future research project. Illustrate various legitimate ways of quoting, excerpting, or summarizing it in the text of a research paper.

B. In the following passage from *Eminent Victorians,* Lytton Strachey documents the period of spiritual unrest that Cardinal Manning experienced before his conversion to Catholicism. Study the way Strachey has worked *short, revealing* quotations from Cardinal Manning's diary into a coherent paragraph. Your instructor may ask you to write a similar paragraph, using quotations from the autobiography, diary, or memoirs of one of the great Victorians—Cardinal Newman, Charles Darwin, General Gordon, or another major figure of your choice.

> He decided to mortify himself, to read St. Thomas Aquinas, and to make his "night prayers forty instead of thirty minutes." He determined during Lent "to use no pleasant bread (except on Sundays and feasts) such as cake and sweetmeat"; but he added the proviso "I do not include plain biscuits." Opposite this entry appears the word "*kept.*" And yet his backslidings were many. Looking back over a single week, he was obliged to register "petulance twice" and "complacent visions." He heard his curate being commended for bringing so many souls to God during Lent, and he "could not bear it"; but the remorse was terrible: "I abhorred myself on the spot, and looked upward for help." He made out list upon list of the Almighty's special mercies towards him, and they included his creation, his regeneration, and (No. 5)
>
> the preservation of my life six times to my knowledge—
> (1) In illness at the age of nine
> (2) In the water.

(3) By a runaway horse at Oxford.
(4) By the same.
(5) By falling nearly through the ceiling of a church.
(6) Again by a fall of a horse. And I know not how often in shooting, riding, etc.

At last he became convalescent; but the spiritual experiences of those agitated weeks left an indelible mark upon his mind, and prepared the way for the great change which was to follow.

C. After finishing the first draft of a research paper, write a *one-page abstract* that spells out the thesis and summarizes the argument. (Your instructor may ask you to submit a *preliminary* summary of findings at an earlier stage of your investigation.)

6. Preparing Footnotes and Bibliographies

Documentation enables your readers to identify, trace, and check your sources. Its purpose should not be to impress your readers but to provide exact and comprehensive information in condensed form.

Footnotes

In your own paper, the main purpose of footnotes will be to document your sources. Use footnotes to indicate the origin of facts, opinions, and illustrative material. Use them not only when you quote an author directly, but also when you merely paraphrase or summarize what he said.[3] A footnote is *not* necessary when the author has merely repeated something that is widely known or believed.

No Footnote: George Washington was elected to the Virginia assembly in 1758. (This is "common knowledge," the kind of fact likely to be recorded in public documents and found in many history books.)

Footnote: Samuel Eliot Morison describes Washington as "an eager and bold experimenter" in new agricultural methods.[17] (This is a judgment the historian made on the basis of first-hand investigation. The text already mentions his name; the footnote, not reprinted here, will give the exact source.)

---

[3] Not all footnotes serve exclusively for documentation. **Explanatory footnotes,** of which this note is an illustration, may define technical terms unfamiliar only to some of the readers. They may provide information not necessary to the main trend of the argument. They may contain reservations that would confuse ordinary readers but are needed to satisfy critical ones. Use such material sparingly. Many readers check all footnotes to make sure they miss nothing of importance. Do not make them interrupt their reading for the sake of something trivial or irrelevant.

When a critic mentions that Hamlet kills Polonius at a given point in the play, he merely reminds you of something easily verified. You need not mention the critic, or footnote the source, when referring to the killing of Polonius in writing your own paper. But when a critic shows that a phrase used by Hamlet in Act V echoes one used in Act I, he is calling your attention to something that most readers have missed. If you refer to the parallel in your own paper, a footnote is in order.

Current practice favors consecutive numbering of all footnotes for a paper, article, or chapter of a book. In other words, footnotes are not indicated by asterisks or similar symbols. Nor do the footnote numbers start anew on each individual page. The **footnote number** is placed outside whatever punctuation goes with the item to which it refers. The footnote itself is indented like a paragraph and is introduced by a raised numeral; the numeral is *not* followed by a period or other punctuation. The footnote begins with a capital letter and ends with appropriate terminal punctuation, most commonly a period.

In printed publications, the footnotes for each page appear in small print at the bottom of each page. In typed manuscripts, footnotes are usually single-spaced and placed in one of three possible positions:

(1) Footnotes may be placed *between two unbroken lines immediately below the line of typed material* to which they belong. This system, when permitted by the instructor, helps the inexperienced researcher to make the right footnote go with the right portion of the text.[4]

---

[4]Even when a different system of placing footnotes is required in the final paper, students may find the system of which this footnote is an illustration the most convenient one to follow in the first draft. It prevents errors when footnotes have to be renumbered because of changes in the manuscript.

---

(2) Footnotes may be placed *at the bottom of the page,* separated from the text by an unbroken line or by triple spacing. This system is convenient for the reader, who is used to a similar arrangement in printed material, but it is hard on the amateur typist. It requires him to type his footnotes on a separate sheet of paper so that he can estimate the amount of space needed for each and leave exactly enough space at the bottom of each page for the footnotes that go with it.

(3) Footnotes may appear *on a separate sheet at the end of the paper.* This system is usually required when a manuscript is submitted for publication.

First References

Fully identify a source the first time you refer to it. The most common type of footnote gives full information about a source the first time it is mentioned or drawn on in the text. The following sample footnotes illustrate the standard form for such a first reference, as well as the most important variations. *Pay special attention to the way punctuation marks are used in these sample footnotes.* Use commas, colons, parentheses, and quotation marks exactly as here illustrated unless you are otherwise instructed by the teacher or editor who is to pass judgment on your work.

(1) *Standard reference to a book.* Give the author's full name, putting the first name *first.* After a comma, add the title of the book — *underlined* in typescript (italicized in print). Give the facts of publication in parentheses. (Include place of publication, name of publisher, date of publication.) After a comma, add the page reference ("p." for single page; "pp." for several pages: pp. 163–65).

    [2] Albert H. Marckwardt, *American English* (New York: Oxford Univ. Press, 1958), p. 17.

    [4] Irving H. Anderson and Walter F. Dearborn, *The Psychology of Teaching Reading* (New York: Ronald, 1952), pp. 70–72.

    [7] Henry James, *The Portrait of a Lady* (New York: Random House, 1951), p. 140.

(2) *Newspaper or magazine article.* Enclose the title of the article in quotation marks; underline the title of the newspaper or magazine: "How to Deep-Freeze Bait," *The Fisherman's Monthly.* Give the date of issue, separated from what precedes and follows by commas. If a magazine provides a volume number, give it as an Arabic numeral, enclose the date in parentheses, and give the page reference *without* using "p." or "pp.": 15 (Sept. 1969), 47.

    [3] "U.S. Asked to Aid Youth Exchanges," *New York Times,* 15 June 1968, p. 8, col. 1.

    [6] Jeanne Contini, "The Illiterate Poets of Somalia," *The Reporter,* 14 March 1963, p. 36.

    [9] Constance M. Drake, "An Approach to Blake," *College English,* 29 (April 1968), 545.

NOTE: Linguists often follow an alternative style used in the sciences: The volume number is separated from the page number by a period: *College English,* 29.545 (April 1968).

(3) *Partial footnote.* If the text of your paper has given the author's full name, do not repeat it but start your footnote with the title. If you have given both the full name and the full title, start your footnote with the facts of publication (without parentheses):

[2]*American English* (New York: Oxford Univ. Press, 1958), p. 17.

[2]New York: Oxford Univ. Press, 1958, p. 17.

(4) *Work with subtitle.* Separate the subtitle from the title by a colon unless the original has other punctuation. Underline the subtitle of a book; enclose both the title and the subtitle of an article in the same set of quotation marks.

[11]Marshall McLuhan, *Understanding Media: The Extensions of Man* (New York: McGraw-Hill, 1964), p. 20.

[2]John J. Gross, "The Writer in America: A Search for Community," *Queen's Quarterly,* 63 (Autumn 1956), 387.

(5) *Edited or translated work.* Insert the editor's or translator's name after the title, separating it from the title by a comma. Use the abbreviation "ed." or "trans." The editor's name may come *first* if the author is unknown, if the editor has collected the work of different authors, or if the editor has brought together an author's work from different sources.

[2]H. L. Mencken, *The Vintage Mencken,* ed. Alistair Cooke (New York: Vintage, 1956), p. 49.

[8]André Siegfried, *America at Mid-Century,* trans. Margaret Ledésert (New York: Harcourt, 1955), p. 227.

[5]Kenneth Sisam, ed., *Fourteenth Century Verse and Prose* (Oxford: Clarendon, 1948), p. 14.

(6) *Revised editions.* If a work has been brought up to date since its original publication, indicate the number of the edition you are using. Place it before the facts of publication, separating it from what precedes it by a comma.

[2]Albert C. Baugh, *A History of the English Language,* 2nd ed. (New York: Appleton, 1957), pp. 7–8.

[9]M. B. Forman, ed., *The Letters of John Keats,* 3rd ed. (London: Milford, 1948), pp. 67–68.

(7) *Work published in several volumes.* Specify the number of the volume you are citing. Use a capital Roman numeral, insert it after the facts of publication, and separate it from what precedes and follows it by commas. Remember that after a volume number "p." and "pp." are omitted.

[3] Vernon Louis Parrington, *Main Currents in American Thought: An Interpretation of American Literature from the Beginnings to 1920* (New York: Harcourt, 1930), III, 355.

(8) *Article in a collection.* Identify fully both the article and the anthology of which it has become a part.

[13] Eliseo Vivas, "Kafka's Distorted Mask," in *Kafka: A Collection of Critical Essays,* ed. Ronald Gray (Englewood Cliffs, N.J.: Prentice-Hall, 1962), pp. 137–38.

(9) *Encyclopedia entry.* Page numbers and facts of publication are unnecessary for *short* entries appearing in alphabetical order in well-known encyclopedias or dictionaries. Date or number of the edition used, however, is sometimes included because of the frequent revisions of major encyclopedias.

[2] M. J. Politis, "Greek Music," *Encyclopedia Americana,* 1956.

[4] "Drama," *Encyclopaedia Britannica,* 1958, VII, 596.

(10) *Bible or literary classic.* References to the Bible usually identify only book, chapter, and verse. The name of a book of the Bible is *not* underlined or put in quotation marks. References to a Shakespeare play available in many different editions may specify act, scene, and line; references to an epic poem book, canto, and stanza.

[4] Judges 13:5.   or   [4] Judges xiii.5.

[3] *Hamlet* II.ii.311–22.

Note, however, that you will have to specify the edition used if textual variations are important, as with a new translation of the Bible. No identification is necessary for well-known or proverbial lines: "To be or not to be"; "The quality of mercy is not strained"; "They also serve who only stand and wait."

(11) *Quotations at second hand.* Make it clear that you are not quoting from the original or complete text.

⁵William Archer, letter of October 18, 1883, to his brother Charles; quoted in Henrik Ibsen, *Ghosts,* ed. Kai Jurgensen and Robert Schenkkan (New York: Appleton, 1965), p. 135.

(12) *Pamphlets and unpublished material.* Indicate the nature and source of materials other than books and magazines: mimeographed pamphlet, unpublished doctoral dissertation, and the like. Start with the title if no author or editor is identified. Use quotation marks to enclose unpublished titles.

⁶Walter G. Friedrich, ed., "A Modern Grammar Chrestomathy" (Valparaiso, Indiana, mimeo., 1961), p. 12.

⁷U. Fuller Schmaltz, "The *Weltschmerz* of Charles Addams," Diss., Columbia 1959, p. 7.

⁸*Grape Harvesting* (Sacramento: California Department of Viticulture, 1969), pp. 8–9.

Subsequent References

Keep subsequent references short but clear. There is no need to repeat the full name and title, or the facts of publication. Here are the most common possibilities:

(1) *Shortened reference.* Once you have fully identified a book, use the author's last name to identify it in subsequent footnotes. Separate the name from the page reference by a comma.

¹¹Baugh, p. 9.

When you are using *several works by the same author,* use the author's last name and a shortened form of the title:

¹¹Baugh, *History,* p. 9.

(2) *One footnote for several quotations.* Avoid long strings of footnotes giving different page references to the same work. If several quotations from the same work follow one another in the same paragraph of your paper, incorporate the page references in a single footnote. Use this method only when *no* quotations from another source intervene.

¹³Harrison, pp. 8–9, 12, 17.

(3) *Page references in the text.* If all or most of your references are to a single work, you may put page references in parentheses in the body of your text: (p. 37). Identify the source in your first footnote and explain your procedure.

[1] Jerome S. Bruner, *On Knowing: Essays for the Left Hand* (New York: Atheneum, 1965), p. 3. All page references in the text of this paper are to this source.

(4) *Latin abbreviations.* An alternative system for shortened reference is frequently found in earlier scholarship but no longer in frequent use. Instead of repeating, in a shortened form, the author's name or the title, the writer may use *ibid.*, an abbreviation of Latin *ibidem*, "in the same place." When used by itself, without a page reference, it means "in the last publication cited, on the same page." When used with a page reference, it means "in the last publication cited, on the page indicated." Like other Latin abbreviations used in footnotes, *ibid.* is no longer commonly italicized. It can refer only to *the last source cited.*

[1] G. B. Harrison, *Introducing Shakespeare* (Hammondsworth, Middlesex: Penguin Books, 1939), p. 28.

[2] Ibid., p. 37.

If a reference to a *different* work has intervened, the author's name is followed by *op. cit.*, short for *opere citato*, "in the work already cited." (This abbreviation cannot be used when *several works* by the same author have already been cited.)

[1] G. B. Harrison, *Introducing Shakespeare* (Hammondsworth, Middlesex: Penguin Books, 1947), p. 28.

[2] B. Ifor Evans, *A Short History of English Drama* (Hammondsworth, Middlesex: Penguin, 1948), pp. 51–69.

[3] Harrison, op. cit., p. 37.

Abbreviations

Footnotes in scholarly books and articles employ a number of abbreviations and technical terms in addition to those you will regularly use in your own work. The meaning of many of these will be clear from their context or position; for example, *anon.* for "anonymous," *ch.* and *chs.* for "chapter" and "chapters," *col.* and *cols.* for "column" and "columns," *l.* and *ll.* for "line" and "lines," *n.* and *nn.* for "note" and "notes." Others are not self-explanatory:

©	copyright (© 1961 by John W. Gardner)
c. or ca.	Latin *circa,* "approximately"; used for approximate dates and figures (c. 1952)
cf.	Latin *confer,* "compare"; often used loosely instead of *see* in the sense of "consult for further relevant material" (Cf. Ecclesiastes xii.12)
et al.	Latin *et alii,* "and others"; used in references to books by several authors (G. B. Harrison et al.)
f., ff.	"and the following page," "and the following pages" (See pp. 16 ff.)
loc. cit.	Latin *loco citato,* "in the place cited"; used without page reference (Baugh, loc. cit.)
MS, MSS	manuscript, manuscripts
n.d.	"no date," date of publication unknown
passim	Latin for "throughout," "in various places in the work under discussion" (See pp. 54-56 et passim)
q.v.	Latin *quod vide,* "which you should consult"

Final Bibliography

The final bibliography, based on your bibliography cards, includes all the information required to identify a source when first cited. Its main purpose is to describe in one single alphabetical list all sources you have used. You may include sources that you have found helpful or enlightening but have not had occasion to quote from in your paper. However, do *not* list every book or article whose title you have come across during your investigation.

Entries in the bibliography differ from footnotes both in the arrangement and in the punctuation of the material presented:

(1) The *last name of the author* (or of the first author listed when a book has several authors) is placed first — since the bibliography is an *alphabetical* listing. The full name of the author is separated from what follows by a period.

(2) The *facts of publication* for a book include the place and date of publication and the publisher's name. They are *not* enclosed in parentheses and are separated from what precedes and what follows by periods.

(3) Entries for books do not include page references; entries for parts of books or items in magazines give the *inclusive page numbers* for the whole selection.

In a typed manuscript, single-space each individual item but leave a double space between items. Indent five spaces for the second and for subsequent lines of each item. If you list *several publications by the same author,* substitute a line composed of six consecutive hyphens for his name in second and subsequent entries. If *no name of author or editor is known to you,* list the publication alphabetically by the first letter of the title, not counting "The," "A," or "An."

The following might be the final bibliography for a paper investigating theatrical conventions and stage techniques in the time of Shakespeare. Study the different kinds of entries it includes. (See also the bibliography at the end of the sample research paper.)

BIBLIOGRAPHY

Adams, John Cranford. The Globe Playhouse: Its Design and
    Equipment. Cambridge, Mass.: Harvard Univ. Press, 1942.

Bailey, Margery. "Shakespeare in Action," College English, 15
    (March 1954), 307-15.

Brooke, C. F. Tucker. "The Renaissance." A Literary
    History of England. Ed. Albert C. Baugh. New York:
    Appleton, 1948.

Chambers, E. K. The Elizabethan Stage. 4 vols. Oxford:
    Clarendon, 1923.

Davies, W. Robertson. Shakespeare's Boy Actors. London:
    Dent, 1939.

Frye, Northrop. "The Argument of Comedy." Shakespeare:
    Modern Essays in Criticism. Ed. Leonard F. Dean, 2nd ed.
    New York: Oxford Univ. Press, 1967.

Granville-Barker, Harley, and G. B. Harrison, eds.
    A Companion to Shakespeare Studies. New York:
    Macmillan, 1934.

Greg, W. W., ed. Henslowe's Diary. 2 vols. London:
    A. H. Gullen, 1904-1908.

Harbage, Alfred. Shakespeare's Audience. New York:
    Columbia Univ. Press, 1941.

-----. Theatre for Shakespeare. Toronto: Univ.
    of Toronto Press, 1955.

"A New Shakespearean Festival." The Oakland Herald,
    12 Aug. 1958, p. 7, col. 2.

North, Sir Thomas, trans. Shakespeare's Plutarch: The Lives
    of Julius Caesar, Brutus, Marcus Antonius, and Coriolanus.
    Ed. T. J. B. Spencer. Baltimore: Penguin, 1964.

Rosenberg, Marvin. "Elizabethan Actors: Men or Marionettes?"
    PMLA, 69 (Sept. 1954), 915-27.

Shaw, G. B. Shaw on Shakespeare. Ed. Edwin Wilson. New York:
    Dutton, 1961.

Spargo, J. W. "The Knocking on the Gate in Macbeth, An
    Essay in Interpretation." John Quincy Adams Memorial
    Studies. Ed. J. G. McManaway et al. Washington, D. C.:
    Folger Shakespeare Library, 1948.

Sprague, A. C. Shakespeare and the Actors: The Stage
    Business in His Plays (1660-1905). Cambridge, Mass.:
    Harvard Univ. Press, 1948.

Exercises

A. Interpret the information provided in the following footnotes:

[3] Robert E. Spiller et al., *Literary History of the United States,*
rev. ed. (New York: Macmillan, 1953), p. 1343.

[1] James Brown, "Eight Types of Puns," *PMLA,* 71 (March 1956),
20.

[9] Euripides, *The Trojan Women,* trans. Richmond Lattimore, in
Greek Plays in Modern Translation, ed. Dudley Fitts (New York: Dial,
1947), p. 161.

[2] "America—the Beautiful?" *Life,* 3 June 1957, p. 34.

[8] Kenneth Muir, ed., *Collected Poems of Sir Thomas Wyatt* (Cambridge, Mass.: Harvard Univ. Press, 1950), p. xx.

[7] I Corinthians iii.18–20.

[6] Joannes Caius, *Of English Dogs,* trans. Abraham Fleming (1576),
in *An English Garner,* ed. Edward Arber (London: A. Constable, 1877–
83), III, 225–68.

[12] Cf. *The Complete Works of William Hazlitt,* ed. P. P. Howe
(London: Dent, 1932), XI, 88 ff.

B. Study the style of documentation followed in a scholarly journal in your
major field of interest. Determine to what extent its style coincides with that
outlined in the preceding discussion and in what respects it differs from it.

7. The Standards of Responsible Investigation

In preparing a research paper, the student must guard against a common danger: Preoccupied with procedure and format, he may lose sight of the purposes the procedures serve. He may come to regard the research paper as an elaborate ritual rather than as an introduction to the standards of scholarly investigation. In completing your own research project, you should review in your mind some of the lessons to be learned from the experience.

First, *writing a research paper can help you understand the scholar's respect for fact.* Reliable information on important subjects is not as easy to come by as the average newspaper reader thinks. Establishing a fact as fact rather than hearsay often takes considerable time and effort. As a judge must be able to tell relevant evidence from the immaterial, so the biographer, historian, or sociologist must learn to tell fact from fiction.

The careful investigator soon learns to guard against influences that tend to make information unreliable. The most obvious of these is partisan bias: A Democratic reporter may find it hard to give an objective account of the campaign tour of a Republican candidate. National and ideological bias even more irresistibly colors accounts of alleged historical fact. A careful investigator is on his guard in reading either a French or a German account of the causes of World War I, in reading about the history of Marxism either in a militantly conservative pamphlet or in the official Soviet encyclopedia. Where historical accounts are not obviously polemical, they may be designed to edify rather than record. Thus, the historian finds it difficult to verify accounts such as that of Washington's prayer at Valley Forge, which was not reported by witnesses of the incident and seems out of keeping with Washington's well-documented habits and convictions.

Second, *study of competent scholarship shows that facts become instructive only when carefully interpreted.* Facts do not speak for themselves. To make them meaningful, the investigator must sift out the insignificant. He must correlate his data in such a way that they begin to explain a situation or help settle a debated point. Competent scholarly work combines accuracy and thoroughness with a grasp of meanings, relationships, and purposes.

Interpretation of the facts must be patient, balanced, and systematic. A research paper has even less room for superficial conclusions and hasty judgments than the ordinary expository theme. A historian will call a policy "shortsighted" only after fully exploring the nature of the policy and its relation to views and expectations current at the time. A researcher writing about the disaster that struck the *Titanic* will ascribe it to the negligence of her owners only after a careful study of both their obligations and their failure to fulfill them.

Third, *practice in scholarly investigation trains a writer to make his sources and procedures available for inspection and review.* He learns to identify his sources of information. He enables his readers to consult these sources to see whether the selection of material was judicious and in keeping with the original context. He enables his readers to check whether opinions and judgments attributed to an authority fairly represent the authority's point of view.

Such emphasis on accounting for the sources of his material helps the writer overcome characteristic temptations. The crudest temptation is that of plagiarism: the unacknowledged appropriation of the product of another investigator's labor. Plagiarism is to the scholar what shoplifting is to the businessman. It is true that many facts and ideas are common property and need not be credited to any specific source. Major historical dates and events, key ideas of major scientific or philosophical movements — these are generally accessible in reference books. However, whenever a writer makes use of information recently discovered or compiled, and whenever he adopts someone's characteristic, personal point of view, it is necessary for him to identify his source.

More subtle is another temptation to dishonesty: the reliance on testimony favorable to one's own point of view, the ignoring or playing down of material that would complicate the thread of one's argument. Once the investigator has correlated points *A*, *B*, and *C* to establish a thesis, he is inevitably tempted to play down a point *D* that interferes with his tentative conclusions. Careful consideration of such complications, due attention to authorities who *disagree* with the investigator, reassures his readers that he has not simply solved problems by ignoring adverse evidence. Detailed documentation helps to convince the reader that an author has nothing to hide.

To sum up, training in scholarly research can make a writer at once more skeptical and more responsible. It can train him to read patiently and well, and to discount the biased, the sensational, the superficial. Instead of delivering improvised opinions on all possible subjects, he comes to accept, as a matter of course, an often prolonged period of study between question and answer. He habitually takes into account what has been said on a given subject by qualified observers.

Obviously, writing a research paper will not make a rash person cautious, or an opinionated person open-minded. However, once a writer acquires a scholarly frame of mind, it will help him produce the kind of writing that represents balanced views and rests on solid foundations.

Review Exercise: Sample Research Paper

Study the following sample research paper, adapted from a student-written paper. Pay special attention to the way the author has adapted and worked into the text a variety of quoted material. Compare the different kinds of footnotes used. Contrast the way sources are identified in the footnotes and in the final bibliography. How successful has the author been in meeting the standards outlined in the preceding chapter?

THE FUROR OVER IBSEN

by

John Balfour

English 2, Section 5

March 22, 1969

OUTLINE

<u>Thesis</u>: Ibsen's plays were denounced as immoral and at
the same time celebrated as advancing a new
morality.

Introduction: The divisive effect of Ibsen's plays

    I. Ibsen's plays and his time

        A. The morality of his plays

        B. The moral views of his contemporaries

    II. The attack on Ibsen

        A. Scott's denunciation

        B. Archer's collection of criticism

    III. Shaw's defense of Ibsen's plays

    IV. Ibsen's portrait of his critics

        A. The moralist in his plays

        B. Ibsen's letters

Conclusion: Ibsen as father of the modern drama

THE FUROR OVER IBSEN

What did Henrik Ibsen do?   According to Granville-Barker, he "split the English theater in two."[1]   Indeed, "as everyone knows, the introduction of Ibsen into England was not a peaceful one.   In its wake came one of those great outbursts of critical frenzy and inflamed controversy which at regular intervals enliven literary history."[2]   In England, as in the rest of Europe, the public was split into two factions: those who placed Ibsen on the blacklist as "immoral"; and those who saw in him the champion of a new morality.

Ibsen's plays aroused both indignation and enthusiasm because he fought against maintaining appearances at the expense of happiness, or what he termed hypocrisy.   Una Ellis-Fermor, a translator and lifelong student of Ibsen, said that he "took upon himself the task of exposing the makeshift morality of his contemporaries in private and public life":

---

[1]Harley Granville-Barker,   "When Ibsen Split the English Stage in Two,"   Literary Digest, 28 April 1928, p. 24.

[2]"A Retrospective Eye on Ibsen,"   Theatre Arts Monthly, 12 (March 1928), 199.

-2-

> In <u>The Pillars of the Community</u> he examines
> the lie in public life, the tragic struggle
> of Karsten Bernick to hide his sin and pre-
> serve his reputation at the expense of another
> man's good name. . . . In <u>A Doll's House</u> and
> <u>Ghosts</u> the subject is the lie in domestic life;
> the first shows the destruction of a marriage
> by an unreal and insincere relationship between
> husband and wife, and the second the destruction
> of the lives and souls of the characters by the
> oppressive tyranny of convention.[3]

In <u>Ghosts</u>, a dutiful and unloving wife keeps up an elaborate

façade of respectability for a profligate husband. She

finds herself defeated when her cherished son returns home

suffering incurably from the syphilis he has inherited from

his father. According to Bernard Shaw, the play was "an

uncompromising and outspoken attack on marriage as a useless

sacrifice," the story of a woman who had wasted her life in

manufacturing a "monstrous fabric of lies and false appear-

ances."[4]

Against the tyranny of middle-class standards, Ibsen

pitted his own concept of individual integrity. He felt,

according to Georg Brandes, that "the individuality of the

human being is to be preserved for its own sake, not for

---

[3] Henrik Ibsen, <u>Three Plays</u>, trans. Una Ellis-Fermor
(Hammondsworth, Middlesex: Penguin Books, 1950), pp. 9-11.

[4] <u>The Quintessence of Ibsenism</u>, 3rd ed.   (New York: Hill,
1957), pp. 86, 88.

-3-

the sake of higher powers; and since beyond all else the

individual should remain free and whole, all concessions

made to the world represent to Ibsen the foul fiend, the

evil principle."[5] One of the main ideas fused into Ibsen's

plays, according to an article in the Encyclopaedia

Britannica, is "the supreme importance of individual char-

acter, of personality: in the development and enrichment

of the individual he saw the only hope for a really cul-

tured and enlightened society."[6]

A Doll's House was particularly loaded with the "first

duty to oneself" theme. Nora, in the last act, wakes to the

fact that she is not worthy to be a good mother and wife

because she has been merely a submissive servant and foil

first for her father and then for her husband; she has been

so protected and guided by them that she has no individual

conception of life and its complexities. Nora realized that

she did not know enough about the world and her place in it

to be really "a reasonable human being," and she felt a

duty to become one.[7] Her life all at once seemed so

---

[5]Creative Spirits of the Nineteenth Century, trans.
Rasmus B. Anderson (New York: T.Crowell, 1923), p. 373.

[6]"Ibsen, Henrik Johan," Encyclopaedia Britannica, 1958,
XII, 38.

[7]Henrik Ibsen, Four Great Plays by Ibsen (New York: Dutton,
1959), p. 65.

-4-

artificial and meaningless to her that she felt like a doll

living in a doll's house, Nora left her husband and chil-

dren to try to gain an understanding of real life, and when

she "banged the door of A Doll's House, the echo of that

violence was heard across the continent."[8]

Ibsen wrote these plays at a time when people felt a

general ferment, a "spirit of the age" or "movement of the

century" that had introduced everywhere a tendency toward

change. Spokesmen for the modern age referred to the "new

phase into which humanity is passing" and expressed the

conviction that "society must undergo a transformation or

perish."[9] But the voices resisting the clamor for "inno-

vations" were equally strong. Their watchword was devotion

to duty--toward God, country, one's family and husband.

Self-denial for the sake of greater forces was the commend-

able action. The churches taught it was sinful to assert

one's own wishes and desires. The people, especially the

dominated wife with whom Isben frequently deals, were

exhorted to live for the good of everyone but themselves.

---

[8]"Drama," Encyclopaedia Britannica, 1958, VII, 600.

[9]William Barry in The Nineteenth-Century (1889); quoted
in Michael Goodwin, ed., Nineteenth-Century Opinion: An
Anthology (1877-1901) (Hammondsworth, Middlesex: Penguin,
1951), pp. 124, 122.

-5-

Spokesmen for the emancipation of women were told in the
public press that "men are men and women, women"; that
"sex is a fact--no Act of Parliament can eliminate it";
that "where two ride on a horse, one must needs ride
behind."[10] They were told that in women's hands "rests the
keeping of a pure tone in society, of a high standard in
morality, of a lofty devotion to duty in political life."
If she were to enter openly into political conflict, she
would "debase her sex" and "lower the ideal of womanhood
amongst men."[11]

The old-fashioned moralists were shocked by the
"Ibsenist" view that self-fulfillment is more important
than the sanctity of marriage, one's duty to others, and
even business success. According to Arthur Bingham Walkley,
drama critic for the London Times, "Ibsen became a bogey to
many worthy people who had never read or seen a single one
of his plays." To these people, "Ibsenism was supposed
vaguely to connote 'Woman's Rights,' Free Love, a new and
fearful kind of wildfowl called 'Norwegian Socialism,' and

---

[10]Quoted in Nineteenth-Century Opinion, pp. 103, 109.
[11]Nineteenth-Century Opinion, pp. 103-4.

-6-

generally, every manifestation of discontent with the

existing order of things."[12] Clement Scott, a prominent

drama critic, led such formidable opposition against Ibsen's

dramas, especially A Doll's House and Ghosts, that they were

actually banned for a time from English stages. "Ibsen

fails," Scott says, "because he is, I suppose, an atheist,

and has not realized what the great backbone of religion

means to the English race." Scott continues, "He fails

because his plays are nasty, dirty, impure, clever if you

like, but foul to the last degree; and healthy-minded

English people don't like to stand and sniff over an ash-

pit."[13]

Many of the people causing the uproar against Ibsen

used similar exaggerated and irrational language. William

Archer, the first English translator of Ibsen, collected some

of the attacks appearing in the English press when Ghosts

was first produced. The play was called "disgusting,"

"loathsome," "gross," and "revoltingly suggestive and blas-

phemous." It was compared to "a dirty act done publicly"

---

[12]"Ibsen in England," Living Age, 12 (Sept. 21, 1901),
790.

[13]Quoted in "Inside Views of Ibsen in the Nineties,"
Literary Digest, 12 May 1928, p. 24.

-7-

and was called "a piece to bring the stage into disrepute
and dishonour with every right-thinking man and woman."[14]

Those who defended Ibsen--Shaw, Archer, Walkley--
blamed his unpleasant reception in England on both his
revolutionary themes and his new dramatic technique. We
shall steer away from Ibsen's new dramatic technique and
instead discuss the defense of Ibsenism as a new moral
philosophy. Shaw himself has been called one of the men
"who summon their generation to act by a new and higher
standard." He made Ibsen his hero because Ibsen championed
the view that Shaw made the basis for many of his own plays:

> By "morals" (or "ideals") Shaw means conven-
> tional, current standards. Because these stand-
> ards are universal and inherited from the past,
> they often do not fit particular situations and
> present-day societies. Therefore good men--like
> some of Ibsen's characters--often choose to act
> "immorally," contrary to accepted morality.[15]

To Shaw, Ibsen became the first of the two types of
pioneers classified by Shaw in The Quintessence of Ibsenism.
This type of pioneer asserts "that it is right to do something hitherto regarded as infamous." Ibsen felt that it
was right to think first of building himself and secondly

---

[14] Quoted in Shaw, pp. 91-93.

[15] Reuben A. Brower, "George Bernard Shaw," in Major
British Writers, ed. G. B. Harrison (New York: Harcourt, 1959),
II, 687.

-8-

of building the institutions of society. To Shaw, this

change explained the unkindly reception of Ibsen's new

thoughts in England: "So much easier is it to declare the

right wrong than the wrong right. . . . a guilty society

can more readily be persuaded that any apparently innocent

act is guilty than that any apparently guilty act is inno-

cent."[16] Shaw seems to feel that Ibsen would have had more

success telling people it was wrong to work on Monday than

he would have had saying it was right to work on Sunday.

Men could not accept the idea that the obligation of self-

sacrifice could be removed from them--that it would be all

right for them to consider a duty toward themselves first.

Shaw complained of the difficulty of finding "accurate

terms" for Ibsen's new "realist morality." To Shaw, it was

Ibsen's thesis that "the real slavery of today is slavery to

ideals of goodness." Ibsen had devoted himself to showing

that "the spirit of man is constantly outgrowing the ideals,"

and that "thoughtless conformity" to them is constantly

producing tragic results. Among those "ridden by current

ideals," Ibsens plays were bound to be denounced as immoral.

But, Shaw concluded,

---

[16]Shaw, pp. 23-25.

-9-

> There can be no question as to the effect
> likely to be produced on an individual by
> his conversion from the ordinary acceptance
> of current ideals as safe standards of conduct,
> to the vigilant openmindedness of Ibsen. It
> must at once greatly deepen the sense of moral
> responsibility.[17]

Ibsen himself knew well and satirized in his plays the
moralists who inveighed against "the undermining of family
life" and the "defiance of the most solemn truths." In
Ghosts, Pastor Manders, who represents a timid regard for
convention, warns people against books that he vaguely
associates with "intellectual progress"--and that he has
not read. Rörlund, the schoolmaster in The Pillars of the
Community, sums up the position of the guardians of conventional morality when he says:

> Our business is to keep society pure . . . to keep
> out all these experimental notions that an impatient
> age wants to force on us.[18]

Ironically, Rörlund provides a moral façade for "practical
men of affairs" like the ship owner Bernick. Bernick, who
talks about his "deep-rooted sense of decency," has abandoned the woman he loved in order to marry a wealthy girl

---

[17]Shaw, pp. 147-49, 152, 154.
[18]Ibsen, Three Plays, pp. 27-28.

-10-

and save the family business. He has abandoned to need and
shame a married woman with whom he has had a secret affair.
He has saved his own reputation in the community at the
expense of having a younger friend blackened as a libertine
and a thief. Bernick's defense of his conduct is that he
lives in a community in which "a youthful indiscretion is
never wiped out." The "community itself forces us into
crooked ways."[19] But Ibsen's heroes are people who rebel
against the "tyranny of custom and convention"; who hold
that "the spirit of truth and the spirit of freedom" are
the "true pillars of the community."[20]

Ibsen was not intimidated by the controversy caused by
his plays. In a letter to a friend he wrote in 1881, he
said: "Ghosts will probably cause alarm in some circles.
. . . If it didn't do that, there would have been no need
to write it." In a letter written a year later, he said:
"That my new play would produce a howl from the camp of those
'men of stagnation' was something I was quite prepared for."
Shortly afterward, he summed up his faith in the future
in a letter that said in part:

---

[19] Three Plays, pp. 48, 97-98.
[20] Three Plays, pp. 116, 137.

-11-

> In time, and not before very long at that,
> the good people up home will get into their
> heads some understanding of <u>Ghosts</u>. But all
> those desiccated, decrepit individuals who
> pounced on this work, they will come in for
> devastating criticism in the literary histories
> of the future. People will be able to sniff
> out the nameless snipers and thugs who directed
> their dirty missiles at me from their ambush in
> Professor Goos's mouldy rag and other similar
> places. My book holds the future. Yon crowd
> that roared about it haven't even any proper
> contact with their own genuinely vital age.[21]

It was Ibsen's assertion of man's duty to himself,
against the tradition of conformity to custom and convention, that was the main grounds of significant controversy
over Ibsen's works. In presenting this view in his plays,
as a modern critic says, "Ibsen established realism as the
ruling principle of modern drama." Problems of the day had
been aired on the stage before, "but nobody before Ibsen
had treated them without equivocation or without stressing
secondary matters while ignoring primary ones." Because
he was the first, "Henrik Ibsen . . . has long held the
unofficial title of 'father of the modern drama.'"[22]

---

[21]Quoted in Henrik Ibsen, <u>Ghosts</u>, trans. Kai Jurgensen
and Robert Schenkkan (New York: Avon, 1965), pp. 126, 129-30.

[22]John Gassner, Introduction to <u>Four</u> <u>Great</u> <u>Plays</u>,
pp. vii-viii.

-12-

BIBLIOGRAPHY

Brandes, Georg. <u>Creative Spirits of the Nineteenth Century</u>.
    Trans. Rasmus B. Anderson. New York: T Crowell, 1923.

Brower, Reuben A. "George Bernard Shaw." <u>Major British
    Writers</u>. Ed. G. B. Harrison. 2 vols. New York: Harcourt
    1959.

"Drama." <u>Encyclopaedia Britannica</u>. 1958, VII, 576-616.

Goodwin, Michael, ed. <u>Nineteenth-Century Opinion: An
    Anthology (1877-1901)</u>. Hammondsworth, Middlesex:
    Penguin, 1951.

Granville-Barker, Harley. "When Ibsen Split the English
    Stage in Two." <u>Literary Digest</u>, 28 April 1928, pp. 24-25.

Ibsen, Henrik. <u>Four Great Plays by Ibsen</u>. New York: Dutton,
    1959.

-----. <u>Ghosts</u>. Trans. Kai Jurgensen and Robert Schenkkan.
    New York: Avon, 1965.

-----. <u>Three Plays</u>. Trans. Una Ellis-Fermor. Hammondsworth,
    Middlesex: Penguin, 1950.

"Ibsen, Henrik Johan." <u>Encyclopaedia Britannica</u>, 1958, XII,
    37-41.

"Inside Views of Ibsen in the Nineties." <u>Literary Digest</u>,
    12 May 1928, p.24.

"A Retrospective Eye on Ibsen." <u>Theatre Arts Monthly</u>, 12
    (March 1928), 199-211.

Shaw, Bernard. <u>The Quintessence of Ibsenism</u>, 3rd ed.
    New York: Hill, 1957.

Walkley, A. B. "Ibsen in England." <u>Living Age</u>, 12
    (21 Sept. 1901), 790.

> *Literature has its piety, its conscience; it*
> *cannot long forget, without forfeiting all*
> *dignity, that it serves a burdened and*
> *perplexed creature, a human animal*
> *struggling to persuade the universal Sphinx*
> *to propose a more intelligible riddle.*
> *George Santayana*

CHAPTER TEN

Writing About Literature

1. The Function of Criticism
2. Kinds of Critical Papers
   Explication
   Studying a Character
   The Central Symbol
   Tracing the Theme
   Defining a Critical Term

3. Organizing the Critical Essay
   Focusing on a Major Issue
   Following Logical Order
   Using Comparison and Contrast
   Working Toward Synthesis

4. Some Guidelines for Critical Writing

Sample Theme
Theme Topics 10

1. The Function of Criticism

When you write a critical essay about a piece of imaginative literature, you try to explain to your reader what you make of a poem, a short story, a play. The most basic requirement for a successful paper of this kind is your *careful reading of the work itself*. Whether your reader agrees with you or not, he must feel: "This person has read the text." No matter how you argue, classify, or rationalize, your paper should always come back to the actual poem or story. Quote from it, make detailed reference to characters and events, show in detail how it is put together. Never let your writing get too far away from the territory to which it is supposed to serve as a guide.

Once you convince your reader that you have immersed yourself in your subject, he will be willing to listen to your answer to the basic question he asks about a work of literature: "What does it mean? Why do I react to it the way I do? Or, if my reaction is unsatisfying or confused, how *should* I react?"

What a literary work "means" to the reader is not a simple prose statement like "Modern man is alienated from his environment." The meaning of a poem or a play is not simply something we are told. It is something that we are made to *take in*, something in which we become involved. What a play has to say is acted out; it emerges from the conflict of characters and motives. What a novel has to say develops gradually; it takes shape as the plot unfolds. What a poem has to say it says by presenting images that appeal to our senses; objects and events that engage our emotions. In other words, the meaning of a literary work is not merely what it makes us think but also what it makes us feel. The meaning of a literary work is something we live through, something we experience.

For this reason, our question "*What* does it mean?" often shades over into "*How* does it mean?" And the first preliminary answer to that question always is: "It will have its *own* meaning, *in its own way*." We must be patient and open-minded enough to find out how a poem works, how a short story develops, what elements are played off against one another in a play. We should not bring *to* the work ready-made notions about what it *should* say, how it *should* proceed. The casual reader too often approaches a poem or a story with preconceptions that keep him from doing justice to what is there.

In your own writing about literature, try to make your basic attitude that of an open-minded interest in your subject. Don't let attitudes like the following get in your way:

(1) "*If it is a classic, it must be great.*" Mere perfunctory reverence for the great unread dead is not likely to impress your reader. His understanding of Shakespeare, for instance, is not likely

to be helped by yet more praise of the poet's "profound insight into human nature." The reader will learn more from your honest attempt to grapple with one of the *problems* you encountered when reading a Shakespeare play. You show that a classic is *alive* for you if you take him seriously enough to question him, to challenge his assumptions, to argue with him, if necessary.

(2) *"I know what I like."* Too often this means: "I know what I *already* like, and I am not going to learn anything new." Of course, every reader of literature has his favorites—poems he can listen to again and again, plays he has seen several times. But a writer new to us can make us see and feel in new ways. He brings into play capacities for thought and feeling that we did not know we had.

(3) *"Literature should deal with beautiful subject matter."* Great literature, like all great art, does not conform to superficial definitions of what is beautiful—let alone of what is pretty, or heart-warming, or sweet. A poem does not have to be about flowers in the spring or a sunset at the sea. The opening lines of T. S. Eliot's "The Love Song of J. Alfred Prufrock" are not about anything convention-ally beautiful:

> Let us go then, you and I,
> When the evening is spread out against the sky
> Like a patient etherized upon a table;

But these lines are good because they ring true; they authentically project the feelings of a speaker to whom associations with disease and impaired consciousness come naturally, who takes a grim delight in brooding over the things in his life that have gone or are likely to go wrong.

Literature worth reading is often demanding and sometimes ob-scure. It is the function of the critic to explain and interpret, to guide our understanding and to sharpen our judgment. He helps us pull together our scattered impressions, to note differences and similarities. In your own writing about literature, you can sharpen your critical faculties by cautiously generalizing about what you have read, and relating it to other reading and the world as you know it.

2. Kinds of Critical Papers

Among the tasks that a critic performs in interpreting a work of literature, some are especially suited to provide the substance for a short student paper. (In a longer paper, several of these may combine in a fuller study of a poem, play, or story.)

Explication

Trace the full meaning and implications of the writer's language.
The poet—and to a lesser degree other imaginative writers—says
"much in little." We must be patient enough to listen for the full
implications of a word, a phrase, a figure of speech. At its most businesslike, critical writing simply answers the question "What does it
say?" T. S. Eliot has Prufrock say, "women come and go / Talking of
Michelangelo." A student might bring out the meaning and effect of
this recurring phrase as follows:

This to him is the height of irony and absurdity; that Michelangelo, one of the two
great geniuses of the Italian Renaissance, should be talked of by shallow, gossipy
women.

Here is a shortened version of a student paper devoted to **explication**—to spelling out the full meaning of key words and phrases:

THOUGHT

An essential part of Richard Wilbur's poem "Mind" is the simile "the mind is like
a bat," which is developed throughout the poem. When I think of a bat, I think of a creature who lives in darkness, who is confined by a cave. The blind bat protects himself
from colliding into the cave walls by a delicate sensory system. Perhaps, unknowingly,
he sends out sound waves which bounce back from obstacles in his path and thereby
avoids destruction. Wilbur draws a parallel between the bat's method for self-preserva-
tion and the minds's: "Contriving by a kind of senseless wit / Not to conclude against a
wall of stone." The paradox of "senseless wit" suggests an irrationality. Yet "wit"
refers to intelligence. This may imply the unconscious mind. The unconscious mind
acts in continual adjustment against reality's threatening barriers. Wilbur enhances
the allusion between the mind and the unconscious with these lines: "It has no need
to falter or explore; / Darkly it knows what obstacles are there." This seems to express
the unconscious minds's awareness of its deepest fears or "obstacles." But in the concluding lines the author differentiates the mind from a bat: ". . . That in the very
happiest intellection / A graceful error may correct the cave." If the bat commits "a
graceful error, " he may well die. The mind, however, performing in like manner may
discover that a wall was an illusion. The mind may "correct the cave," or man may
change his perception of his environment. The bat will stay in his cave of darkness.
The mind can grow out of its confines.

Studying a Character

*Write a coherent account (or trace the contradictions) of a char-
acter in fiction or drama.* A paper of this kind tests your ability to
bring together from *different* parts of a story or play the evidence that
helps you understand a fictional person. That evidence is of different
kinds, and it often calls for careful interpretation. In the traditional
novel of the kind Charles Dickens and George Eliot write, the
omniscient author may tell us what his characters *think* as well as

what they say and do. In other stories, especially in later fiction, we may see a character only through the eyes of an outside **reflector**. We may have to *infer* thoughts and motives on the basis of perhaps puzzling or contradictory behavior. In a Shakespeare play, we soon learn to listen not only to what a character says about himself but also to what *other* characters say about him. Thus, an important clue to the character of Macbeth is in a speech by his wife:

> Yet do I fear thy nature;
> It is too full o' th' milk of human kindness
> To catch the nearest way. Thou wouldst be great,
> Art not without ambition, but without
> The illness should attend it.   (I.v.)

The following excerpted paper provides a model for a theme studying a character:

A TYPICAL BOY

It is not surprising that Thomas E. Adams' story "Sled" appears in an anthology under the heading "The Beginnings of Awareness." It would be stretching a point to say that the boy in the story grows up and becomes an adult. He *does* become aware of what it is like to be mean (as all people are at some time) and of what it is like to feel remorse for that meanness. . . .

At the beginning of the story the boy is thoroughly typical and believable. He has had a quarrel with his sister, calling her a liar, and his mother is demanding that he apologize. The boy resists and at last apologizes half-heartedly and rather belligerently so that he can go outside to slide on his new sled. Following his apology this bit of dialogue occurs:

> "Put your hat on," his mother said without looking at him.
> His face, toward the door, screwed and tightened with disgust. "Aw Ma."
> "Put it on."
> "Aw Ma, it's not that cold out."
> "Put it on."
> "Honest Ma, it's not that cold out."
> "Are you going to put your hat on, or are you going to stay and help with the dishes?"
> He sighed. "All right," he said, "I'll put it on." . . .

Several other details in the story serve to develop the picture of a typical boy: for example, his delight in the newness and strength of his sled, his great care in running to start a slide, his amazement when he realizes that the sled is irreparably broken, and his coming very close to crying about what to him is a considerable loss. . . .

But the most convincing episode comes at the end of the story when the boy offers his sister a chance to slide on the broken sled, knowing that she will take a spill. He still harbors a grudge against her and is taking his revenge. When he realizes, however, that his sister has been hurt, and that his action has really been a piece of cruel deception, he is immediately sorry. Probably the boy could not, in his own mind, have put the matter quite so clearly; and his somewhat dim realization comes through in his awkward efforts to make his sister feel better.

"It'll be all right," he said. He felt that he ought to do something but he did not move. "I can get it soldered. Don't worry about it." . . .

When the boy knows from the extinguishing of the grocery-store light that it is seven o'clock and that he must go home, he does not return a totally changed person. He has learned something, to be sure, and he has grown up a little. And he has reacted to the experience as a boy would.

The more fully developed a character is, the less likely he is to fit into a simple category. Simply to condemn him as "selfish," for instance, is not likely to do justice to a character substantial enough to engage our attention. Rather, a writer may be interested in the way selfishness is likely to be qualified by unexpected loyalties or sentimentalities. The truly memorable characters of fiction and drama are often people with traits that are contradictory and yet make sense. Michael Henchard in Thomas Hardy's novel *The Mayor of Casterbridge* is such a paradoxical and very human figure. He is capable of the sobriety and grim application that made him rise from laborer to wealthy merchant and mayor of the town. But he is also capable of the impulsive ill-considered gesture, the desperate gamble, the disastrous sudden spiteful act.

The Central Symbol

Trace the role of a symbol that is central to the work as a whole. Even as part of a line-by-line explication, we have to be aware of **symbols**, objects that have a significance beyond themselves. Prufrock says, "I should have been a pair of ragged claws/Scuttling across the floors of silent seas." We imagine a crab-like creature that symbolizes a life less than human, not beset by the disappointments and uncertainties of human consciousness. When at the end of the poem Prufrock mentions the mermaids that are not likely to sing to him, they symbolize the beauty and romance that have escaped him.

When a writer makes continued use of the same symbol, it becomes a clue to the unity of a work. By tracing the recurrences of the symbol, we learn something about the *structure* of the work of which it is a central part. In T. S. Eliot's "The Waste Land," the dry rock "where the sun beats" and the life-giving water that we yearn for in vain become recurrent symbols for the aridity of modern life. The "dry bones," the "dead tree," the "empty cisterns" we encounter in the poem all echo a dominant idea, reinforce a prevailing mood.

Even when a symbol is not actually repeated, it can assume a central role because it sums up many of the meanings that a work has been developing. Toward the end of Arthur Miller's *Death of a Sales-man*, Willy Loman, defeated and alone, is blundering about in his dark back yard planting seeds. That futile gesture sums up much of what we have learned about Willy in the course of the play: his delight in making plans for the future, his happiness in doing useful things with his hands, and his stubborn refusal to face up to the things that will make his happy plans come to nothing.

Examining a central symbol makes us look at a poem, short story, or play *as a whole*. The meaning of a symbolic object or incident is not simply anything that comes to our minds by a process of free association. Its meaning is what is borne out by the rest of the work. Its meaning is *what fits the context*. The last stanza of Robert Frost's "Stopping by Woods on a Snowy Evening" reads as follows:

> The woods are lovely, dark and deep.
> But I have promises to keep,
> And miles to go before I sleep,
> And miles to go before I sleep.

Are we justified in seeing in the dark loveliness of the woods a symbolic hint of restful, peaceful death? Such a symbolic interpretation is supported by many details earlier in the poem. The woods are dark and filling up with snow—and both darkness and snow are hostile to ordinary purposeful activity, that is, to ordinary life. The traveler has stopped "without a farmhouse near," between "the woods and frozen lake." He is, thus, far from a village or other center of human life and activity. His horse acts as if stopping there "is some mistake," since in ordinary life people are usually "getting somewhere." The traveler has to choose between "promises" that keep him going into the future and the "easy wind" and "downy flake" suggesting cessation of activity, rest, sleep. Though the symbolic meaning of the dark woods is not directly spelled out in the poem, the woods do appear throughout the poem as the opposite of life and of going on into the future.

Tracing the Theme

Trace the underlying theme that gives unity of purpose to a work as a whole. When we state the **theme** of a poem, short story, or play, we try to sum up in a sentence or paragraph a dominant idea that seems to pervade it, that helps to give it shape and direction. A true theme is not simply a "lesson for today" tacked on at the end for the edification of the reader. It is organically related to the whole. It may be nowhere directly stated but may emerge gradually from our reading and rereading as we ponder the whole poem, story, or play.

Sometimes the author of the literary work comes close to summing up his major theme in one or more *thematic passages*. We encounter such a thematic passage when Linda says of her husband in *Death of a Salesman*,

I don't say he's a great man. Willy Loman never made a lot of money. His name was never in the paper. He's not the finest character that ever lived. But he's a human being, and a terrible thing is happening to him. So attention must be paid. He's not to be allowed to fall into his grave like an old dog. Attention, attention must be finally paid to such a person.

This is the kind of passage that brings into focus much of what has already been *acted out* in the play. What is here summed up about Willy's performance or accomplishments has already been painfully demonstrated. The plea here made for "attention" has already been implied negatively in scenes arousing the spectator against the callousness of Willy's boss; against the thoughtlessness of his sons, preoccupied with their own casual pleasure. Looking back over the play as a whole, we realize that it does indeed ask us to "pay attention" to an ordinary individual, a man who is outwardly a "failure" and yet entitled to our respect as a human being.

Sometimes we are alerted to the underlying theme by a *key term* that recurs at crucial points. In *Macbeth*, the phrase "vaulting *ambition*" contains such a term, echoing in the play elsewhere. Is the play as a whole concerned with seduction by, and the price to be paid for, ambition? A paper carefully tracing the role of this key term is bound to strengthen our understanding of the whole play. Other clues to the underlying theme may be furnished by a key metaphor, or a recurrent symbol.

Here, in a somewhat shortened version, is a student paper in which the author presents the theme that emerged from his careful reading of a poem by E. A. Robinson:

"MR. FLOOD'S PARTY"

A man may die long before his heart stops beating or his mind stops thinking. On a lonely road between Tilbury Town and his solitary dwelling over a hill, Eben Flood in "Mr. Flood's Party" has come to the realization that his life is ending. Although it is late at night and all around him is deserted, Mr. Flood has a "party" for himself and his memories.

He is returning from the town with "the jug he had gone so far to fill," which is all he has left to ease his loneliness. The town is to him nothing but a "phantom salutation of the dead," for its present inhabitants are strangers to him, "who have shut the many doors that many friends opened long ago." Ahead of him is the "forsaken upland hermitage," which would be his last "home" on earth. Now somewhere between these two places, Eben Flood knows that his only living friend is himself, and even he has changed greatly over the years.

He knows his days are numbered, for as he talks to himself he says of the harvest moon above, "we may not have many more." In one last attempt to recapture the past he drinks and sings out "for auld lang syne."

The theme of "Mr. Flood's Party" is probably most clearly seen in the fourth stanza where, "with trembling care, knowing that most things break," Eben sets the jug so that "on firm earth it stood, as the uncertain lives of men assuredly did not. . . ." To point out how fragile man is and how uncertain is his life (and death) is the poem's central purpose.

"Mr. Flood's Party" is a vivid and emotional portrayal of a lonely senior citizen like millions that exist, abandoned by their own generation because of death, and by succeeding generations because of life. They seem to be alive but have really died long ago, and this is something that can happen to all of us.

When we sum up the theme of a work, we are necessarily making a very general statement. And such statements easily become *too* general. We must not be content with abstractions too sweeping to do justice to the way a particular poem or play shapes experience. It is true, for instance, that Sophocles' *Oedipus Rex*, Shakespeare's *Romeo and Juliet,* and Hardy's *Mayor of Casterbridge* all "show the power of fate." But such a statement tells us little, because we are aware of many different ways of looking at "fate." There is treacherous "fickle Fortune," who raises a man up only to throw him down when he least suspects it, jeering at him as she turns her wheel. There is the kind of cruel, inescapable fate visited on a mortal and his progeny by an angry Apollo or Bacchus. There is Divine Providence, intervening in mysterious ways in the affairs of man. There is the fateful kind of necessity envisioned by deterministic nineteenth-century science, where necessary effects inexorably follow from their causes. There is also mere random chance—the luck of the game.

If we want to say something meaningful about the role of "fate" in a play by Sophocles or Shakespeare, we will have to be specific about the forces (perhaps conflicting) that shape an individual's destiny in the play.

Defining a Critical Term

Sharpen the reader's understanding of an important critical term by applying it to a key example. Critical terms both help and hinder our reading of literature. On the one hand, they help us find our way. They guide our expectations, alert us to characteristic problems, help us put into words important differences and similarities. We would find it hard to talk about drama if we did not have terms like *tragedy, comedy, tragicomedy, farce, theater of the absurd, protagonist, subplot, dénouement.* On the other hand, critical terms can force our thinking into rigid molds. They can channel and distort our responses. We may become prejudiced against a powerful Ibsen play because it does not fit our definition of "tragedy." We may brush off the brilliant chatter of a play by Ionesco because it *does* seem to fit our definition of "mere" farce.

When you try to apply a term like *tragedy* or *farce* to a single major play, you should aim at sharpening your sense of the term; you should put your grasp of it to the test. The following excerpts outline a freshman theme that inductively works out its answer to the question asked in its title:

DEATH OF A SALESMAN – A TRAGEDY?

raising the
question

Ever since Willy Loman trudged into his living room and set down his heavy sample satchel in the first stage production of *Death of a Salesman*, critics have been arguing whether or not Arthur Miller's creation is a tragedy. Some maintain the play is a tragedy of the common man, with Willy Loman as the tragic hero. Others hold that the play does not comply with the dictates of true tragedy and that Willy Loman is incapable of being tragic let alone any other type of hero at all. . . .

DEFINITION
first criterion

There exists a great deal of unity among great tragedies as to the effect they work on their audiences. The Greeks used the words *pity, fear, catharsis* to classify this effect. Tragedy imbues its audience with pity for the tragic hero. This pity is not patronizing but implies equality, a sharing of grief. The word *fear* is not restricted to fright or terror but includes anxious concern, awe, reverence, and apprehension. . . .

second
criterion

Though the point has been overly emphasized through the years, it is necessary that the tragic hero possess some *tragic flaw* which shapes his actions and helps bring about his eventual downfall. We assume that the hero has free will; and we look in his character for a flaw that begins the chain of events leading to ruin. . . .

third
criterion

In the agony, humiliation, and suffering of his defeat, the hero invariably reaches a point of *increased self-awareness*. He comes to a recognition of himself and is able to look back and see the steps leading to his disaster. . . .

APPLICATION
first criterion

Miller certainly achieves the effects of *pity and fear* on his audience. . . .

second
criterion

Certainly, Willy Loman possesses a *tragic flaw*, if not several. But this flaw is not a personal characteristic coming from his own nature, but rather it is a burden given to him by society. Willy believed in the American Dream because he was brought up to do so. . . .

third
criterion

Willy, finally, never enters into the period of *self-realization* characteristic of true tragedy. If the play were tragic, Willy would realize in the last act that "he had all the wrong dreams." But this conception remained beyond him. He died considering himself a greater man, worth more dead than he was alive. . . .

summing up
the answer

By the definition and evidence presented, it is evident that *Death of a Salesman* is not a tragedy. The beauty and stunning effect of tragedy cannot be maintained without the tragic hero's bitter recognition of his true self.

Exercises

A. In one paragraph, explain in as much detail as you can the *implications and associations* that contribute to the full meaning of *one* of the following passages from Shakespeare's sonnets and plays:

> 1.   O, how shall summer's honey breath hold out
>   Against the wreckful siege of battering days,
>   When rocks impregnable are not so stout,
>   Nor gates of steel so strong, but Time decays?
>   (Sonnet 65)

> 2.   That time of year thou mayest in me behold
>   When yellow leaves, or none, or few, do hang
>   Upon those boughs which shake against the cold,
>   Bare ruined choirs, where late the sweet birds sang.
>   (Sonnet 73)

> 3.   Love's not Time's fool, though rosy lips and cheeks
>   Within his bending sickle's compass come;
>   Love alters not with his brief hours and weeks,
>   But bears it out even to the edge of doom.
>   (Sonnet 116)

> 4.   O, she doth teach the torches to burn bright!
>   It seems she hangs upon the cheek of night
>   Like a rich jewel in an Ethiop's ear —
>   Beauty too rich for use, for earth too dear!
>   (*Romeo and Juliet* I.v)

B. Write a paragraph describing the *central character* of a Shakespeare play as seen through the eyes of a minor figure. For instance, have Polonius describe Hamlet; have Desdemona's father describe Othello; have Enobarbus describe Antony.

C. Write a paragraph examining the role of the bird used as the *central symbol* in one of the following poems: Shelley's "The Skylark"; Keats's "Ode to a Nightingale"; Whitman's "Out of the Cradle Endlessly Rocking."

D. Select a *thematic passage* from a play you have read or seen performed. Defend your choice by showing how the passage sums up (or anticipates) major developments in the play.

E. The following passage from an introduction to the reading of poetry defines three important *critical terms*. Find one or more illustrations for each of these terms in a poem by William Blake, John Keats, or a modern poet of your choice. (Or your instructor may provide a copy of a poem.)

Image, metaphor, and symbol shade into each other and are sometimes difficult to distinguish. In general, however, an image means only what it is; a metaphor means something else than what it is; and a symbol means what it is and something more too. If I say that a shaggy brown dog was rubbing its back against a white picket fence, I am talking about nothing but a dog and am therefore presenting an image; if I say, "Some dirty dog stole my wallet at the party," I am not talking about a dog at all, and am therefore using a metaphor; but if I say, "You can't teach an old dog new tricks," I am talking not only about dogs but about living creatures of any species, and am therefore speaking symbolically. — Laurence Perrine, *Sound and Sense*

3. Organizing the Critical Essay

When a short paper is clearly focused on one major aspect of a single work, it is likely to have the unity and coherence we demand of effective writing. But as your papers become more ambitious or more comprehensive, you will have to apply familiar principles of organization to the writing of your critical essays.

Focusing on a Major Issue

Give your essay unity by focusing on one major critical problem or issue. The richer a poem or a story, the more tempted we are to call attention to this and that. As a result, writing about literature easily becomes *impressionistic:* the writer points to something beautiful here, something interesting there, without really working toward an interpretation that adds up and that is systematically supported. To keep a critical essay from rambling, use a familiar method. Ask, "What question am I trying to answer in this paper? What is the issue that I am going to focus on? What is the problem that I am trying to solve?"

In the critical essay, as in other kinds of writing, effectiveness is achieved at the price of restriction, limitation — narrowing down a large sprawling subject to what the writer can treat in depth. A play like Shakespeare's *Merchant of Venice* raises many questions: How seriously are we to take the fairy-tale world of Belmont, where the penniless young hero gains the rich beautiful lady by choosing the right casket — passing up the ones made of gold and silver for the one made of lead? And is the contrasting world of Venice, where the usurer Shylock insists on his "pound of flesh," more real — or is Shylock also a kind of fairy-tale monster? Is Shylock an anti-Semitic stereotype, or does the author make us recognize and respect his humanity? Does the heroine of the play really have a right to lecture

Shylock about mercy, which "droppeth like the gentle dew from heaven"?

As we ponder these and similar questions, we ask: What would be an issue limited enough to be examined in a critical paper? Whatever the final reaction of the *audience* may be to Shylock, we can turn to the play for concrete evidence on a limited problem: What attitude toward Shylock is shown by the characters in the play? Do they *share* a common attitude of contempt? Or are they divided, with the more sensitive among them taking, at least in some way, his side?

This more limited question makes possible systematic investigation. The resulting paper could document in some detail the negative attitude toward Shylock shared by

- the major characters:

> If thou wilt lend this money, lend it not
> As to thy friends . . .
> But lend it rather to thine enemy.   (I.iii)

- their minor associates:

> Never did I know
> A creature that did bear the shape of man
> So keen and greedy to confound a man.   (III.ii)

- civic authority:

> How shalt thou hope for mercy, rend'ring none?   (IV.i)

- Shylock's servant:

> . . . my master who (God bless the mark!) is a kind of devil.   (II.ii)

- Shylock's own daughter:

> But though I am a daughter to his blood,
> I am not to his manners.   (II.iii)

On the basis of these and similar quotations, the paper could plausibly claim that in the play Shylock is universally condemned, but that the anti-Jewish stereotype involved is primarily religious and moralistic in content, rather than "racist" in the modern sense.

Following Logical Order

Make your essay follow a logical rather than a merely chronological order. The weakest kind of critical essay is merely a thinly disguised summary of plot. The writer simply follows the action of a novel from chapter to chapter, or the plot of a play from act to act and from scene to scene. At its weakest, such a paper follows an "and-then, and-then" pattern. It tells us what happened, but not why it happened or what it means. When the reader has read the work in question, he already *knows* what happened.

To keep from boring your reader, you should restrict your use of chronological order to situations where it serves a definite purpose. When you do present material in chronological order, make your reader see that this is the most effective procedure for getting a view of the whole or for settling a major point. When you trace the spiritual growth of a major character, you may have to follow the major *stages* as presented in the work itself. When you examine Hamlet's alleged "indecisive" temperament, you may wish to examine, *in order*, each major occasion where he seems to procrastinate.

But often the best way to show that you have a grasp of the whole poem, play, or story is to *abandon* chronological order as a major principle of organization in your paper. Instead, you bring to bear, on a given point, evidence from *different parts* of the same work. A point about Willy Loman's refusal to "face reality" will be the more convincing if you can give a striking example from a very early scene, one from later in the play, and one from Willy's very last appearance on the stage. Your point about a character trait revealed in the climactic incident of a short story will be the more convincing if you can show how it was already hinted at in a minor incident at the beginning.

As with other kinds of writing, try to arrange your material for a critical paper under several *logical* headings. Suppose you are writing about a play dealing with the alienation of a young Romantic hero. In a given scene, the playwright may bring in or further develop *several* major elements in the character of his hero: his feeling of guilt; his alienation from society; his ambiguous attitude toward nature; his failure to find consolation in organized religion. In the actual scene, these themes are in the process of becoming richer and more fully differentiated through being acted out, explored, echoed. Baldly put next to each other in a paragraph, they merely make the reader move far too fast from one large abstraction to the next.

In a *logical* scheme of organization, each major theme would be fully discussed in a separate paragraph (or several), with supporting evidence brought in from *different* scenes in the play. This way the reader can take in one major point at a time and do it justice. For instance, he can learn enough about the character's sense of guilt to understand how it affected his personality. Rather than moving from scene to scene, the reader would move from point to point.

These points would appear in a logical sequence designed to take the reader along: from cause to effect, or from the more obvious character traits to less obvious complications or nuances.
Here is a rough outline for the resulting paper:

THESIS: Haunted by feelings of inadequacy and guilt, the central character of the play fails to find spiritual fulfillment in God, man, or nature.

   I. His sense of guilt (bringing together the various hints about the character's past to show what light they shed on his guilt feelings)

  II. His rejection of religion (interpreting the various encounters of the character with advocates of religious orthodoxy)

 III. His alienation from society (tracing a common pattern in the character's relationships with other people)

 IV. His disillusionment with nature (tracing the character's progression from a quest for kindred and benign influences in nature to a view of nature as beautiful but impersonal, indifferent, inhuman)

Using Comparison and Contrast

Use systematic comparison and contrast to alert the reader to significant features. Modern critics of literature, it is true, insist that we read a work first and last on its own terms. They ask us to respond to what a short story actually offers—rather than to what we know about its author, other stories he wrote, or stories written by other authors during the same period. Nevertheless, here as elsewhere, comparison and contrast helps sharpen our powers of observation. Striking similarities between two works can alert us to things that are basic or at least important in both. Striking differences between two works *make* us aware of what *makes* each distinctive.

When we read Shakespeare's *Romeo and Juliet,* we may be too intent on the glorious passages given to the young lovers to pay much attention to the bawdy wit of Mercutio, who tells Romeo that being "sociable" is better than "groaning for love." But going on to another play, we may again find the commentator who in witty or bitter asides provides a counterpoint to the more serious main action. Comparing Mercutio to the fool in *King Lear,* or to Falstaff in *Henry IV, Part One,* may teach us something important about the nature of Shakespearean irony.

To make such a comparison add up, have it follow a clear overall pattern. (See the discussion of comparison and contrast in Chapter One, "The Whole Theme.") Here is a possible scheme for a *point-by-point* comparison of two major Shakespearean characters:

Brutus and Macbeth may *appear, on superficial examination, to be very different:* one is an idealistic ancient Roman senator, the other a selfish and ambitious medieval Scottish nobleman; one publicly assassinates a decadent and vain dictator in order to restore the republican form of government; the other stealthily murders a good and generous king in order to usurp the throne.

On closer examination, however, Brutus and Macbeth do turn out to *have something important in common.* . . .

Both Brutus and Macbeth seem to feel that the act of murder they are contemplating is *unnatural* and therefore horrible. . . .

These "horrible imaginings" suffered by Brutus and Macbeth in contemplating murder upset the natural balance of their faculties and cause *inner strife and disorder.* . . .

The strife and disorder in the small world of the two speakers parallels and mirrors the strife and disorder that will result *in the large world of society and nature* from the destruction of established authority.

Here, in excerpted form, is a model paper devoted to a *parallel-order* comparison of the speakers in two well-known poems:

TO MOVE OR NOT TO MOVE

Thesis	Tennyson's "Ulysses" and T. S. Eliot's "The Love Song of J. Alfred Prufrock" are both monologues uttered by the speakers at crucial moments in their lives: Ulysses, the mythical aging Greek king of Ithaca, has decided to embark on his final voyage; and J. Alfred Prufrock, a balding middle-aged bachelor in what passes in twentieth-century America for high society, is trying to decide on visiting a lady to propose to her or to proposition her. . . . Although the monologues are spoken in superficially similar situations, they differ fundamentally in the attitude of the speaker towards adventure represented by the voyage in one and by the visit in the other.

I. Ulysses
  A. Audience
 	
  B. Eager desire
     for voyage
 	
  C. Heroic
     attitude
	Ulysses' monologue dealing with the voyage he has decided to make is addressed partly to himself and partly to his followers. He states that, although he has roamed the known world, he "cannot rest from travel" and be content to live out his days as a king, husband, and father performing safe but routine duties; and that he is "yearning in desire" to make a final voyage into the unknown "beyond the sunset, and the baths / Of all the western stars." He states, further, that he is aware of the dangers posed "by the dark, broad seas" whose "deep moans round with many voices," but that he is willing to face these dangers for the sake of what he may discover and learn regardless of the outcome. . . . Ulysses' attitude towards the adventure of the voyage is courageous expectancy reflecting a heroic view of life. He remarks that by embarking on this dangerous voyage to an uncertain destination he and his followers can still do some "work of noble note" appropriate to their famous past, and he implies that he lived fully—"enjoyed greatly" and "suffered greatly"—on previous voyages and that he is going on his last voyage to return to this kind of life. . . .

II. Prufrock
  A. Audience

      Prufrock's monologue dealing with his attempts to decide on the visit is addressed only to himself; his scattered remarks about his fear of being unmasked and made to look ridiculous suggest that he would not willingly reveal himself to another living creature. He acknowledges that he is dissatisfied and unfulfilled by the "evenings, mornings, afternoons" spent in the safe but meaningless routine of high society; that he is lonely—like the "men in shirtsleeves" whom he has seen "leaning out of windows" in the slums—and yearns desperately for companionship. Yet he

  B. Reluctance
     to visit

confesses that he is afraid of making the visit and putting the "overwhelming question" to the lady, since he is uncertain whether she will accept him or reject him. . . . Prufrock's attitude towards the adventure of the visit is fearful expectancy reflecting a non-

  C. Unheroic
     attitude

heroic view of life. . . . By the end of his "love song," he has decided to forgo the "dangerous" visit to an unpredictable lady and to live out his days, figuratively, on the beach—correctly attired, careful of his diet, hair parted behind to conceal "a bald spot in the middle"—watching the mermaids who "ride seaward on the waves" and hearing them sing, yet knowing that they will not sing to him.

Summary

      Ulysses heroically anticipates and welcomes adventure; Prufrock wistfully desires it but fearfully rejects it. The mermaids who will not sing to the beached Prufrock are the same creatures who have sung to Ulysses on his previous voyages and will sing to him on his last voyage. Their song may bring the voyager joy or suffering, fulfillment or failure, new life or sudden death—but while they sing to him he is drinking "life to the lees"; and when they stop singing to him he has died a hero.

Working Toward Synthesis

Experiment with patterns of organization that allow you to work conflicting elements into a more comprehensive perspective. If our interpretation of a work is not to seem simpleminded, we must be prepared to find, *in the same work,* different versions of the same idea, several ways of looking at the same thing. The kind of organization that is especially well suited to a discussion of such a work moves, in dialectic fashion, from thesis through the antithesis to a hoped-for synthesis. (On the method of dialectic, see the section on "Constructing an Argument" in Chapter Six, "Logic.")

    In writing about "honor" in Shakespeare's *Henry IV, Part One,* we might present as the thesis the glorified concept of honor held by Hotspur, the impetuous young idealist, who would "pluck bright honor from the pale-faced moon" and who is called by one of his comrades-in-arms "the king of honor." We might then present as the antithesis fat, jovial, and cowardly Sir John Falstaff, who eloquently asserts the counter-principle:

Honor pricks me on. Yea, but how if honor prick me off when I come on? How then? Can honor set to a leg? No. Or an arm? No. Or take away the grief of a wound? No. Honor hath no skill in surgery, then? No. What is honor? A word. What is in that word honor? What is that honor? Air. A trim reckoning! Who hath it? He that died o' Wednesday. Doth he feel it? No. Doth he hear it? No. 'Tis insensible, then? Yea, to the dead. But will it not live with the living? No. Why? Detraction will not suffer it. Therefore I'll none of it. (V. i)

We might look for a balance between the two extremes in Prince Hal, the future king, who does not seek out "honor" but who, when called, puts revelry aside and acquits himself honorably.

The same pattern, going from "on the one hand" to "on the other hand," could be applied to the complexities lurking in Shakespeare's characterization of Shylock:

thesis   In *The Merchant of Venice,* the more serious part of the plot centers on Shylock, the Jew. Here we are dealing with the problems of a very real character who is in dead earnest seeking his "pound of flesh." *The picture Shakespeare draws of Shylock is in many ways a very ugly one* and includes the stereotyped conventions of a greedy Jew in his gabardine. And only a man of a villainous nature would lament the loss of his money more than the loss of his daughter. . . .

antithesis   But Shakespeare was trying to do more than paint a stereotyped picture. *There are several passages that show us Shylock as a human being who has suffered injustices.* Who could fail to be moved by the speech he makes: "If you prick us, do we not bleed? If you tickle us, do we not laugh?" . . .

synthesis   For the purposes of Shakespeare's plot, Shylock serves as an all-black villain, who is universally condemned and finally defeated by his enemies. *But Shylock becomes a fuller character than his role in the plot requires.* When he turns on his tormentors, he speaks with an eloquence that makes us temporarily forget the qualities that make him the object of detestation and the butt of the joke.

In the longer critical essay, we are likely to see *several* major organizing principles at work to produce a more complicated overall scheme. A critic may first trace a number of major developments chronologically through a play. He may then line up major characters for comparison and contrast, and finally balance off against each other two opposed interpretations of the play as a whole. Here, as with longer papers on other subjects, the requirement for success is not that the pattern of organization be simple but that it be *clear to the reader.*

Exercises

A. From a poem, short story, or play, select half a dozen short quotations that all bear on the *same limited issue,* or problem of interpretation. In one sentence, state the general conclusion that these quotations support.

B. Write an outline for an extended *comparison and contrast* of two characters from a play or plays you have read.

C. Describe as fully as you can the strategy adopted by the author in each of the short critical essays excerpted below. In each case, how *appropriate* does the scheme of organization seem to the topic?

1.   CHEKHOV BREAKS TRADITION

Anton Chekhov in "On the Road" throws aside the tradition of short story writers which dictates that a character should be static throughout the course of the story. He makes Mademoiselle Marya Ilovaisky a continously developing character who inspires a response at the end of the story which is entirely different from the one she provokes at the beginning.

The first glimpse of Mlle. Ilovaisky reveals a respected lady who seems to do nothing to deserve this respect. In fact she seems to flaunt it in the faces of her inferiors. She has the disposition of a spoiled, demanding child who has no consideration for anyone or anything other than herself. Her first words upon entering the "travelers' room" are spoken in anger. . . . Though she orders her coachman to be quiet because she notices the man and child asleep in the room, she carelessly and thoughtlessly plunks her keys onto the table, causing the sleepers to awaken with a start. . . .

Then Chekhov, as if showing compassion for his creations, begins her metamorphosis by softening her heart toward the child. Her helplessness in dealing with the crying child is rather pitiable. . . .

Her change is, however, interrupted by a relapse in which she speaks contemptuously of her father, her brother, and all men, and arrogantly of their dependence upon her.

Once this spell has passed, she continues on her road of development: she laughs and begins to confide in Liharev and to receive his confidence. For the first time in her life, she is assailed by the sheer beauty of fervent belief as personified in the face of an unhappy man. . . . She weeps without shame when Liharev weeps in sorrow, but she also smiles when he smiles. She is able to understand and to feel compassion for a part of humanity because she understands that Liharev is little more than a child at heart. She cares deeply that he and his child are traveling toward more suffering; she is now aware that a previously stifled part of her has awakened.

2.   THE COLONEL'S "TRUTH"

But all through the Seven Days' Fight,
     And deep in the Wilderness grim,
And in the field-hospital tent,
     And Petersburg crater, and dim
Lean brooding in Libby, there came —
     Ah heaven! — what *truth* to him.

War dispels many illusions and in this way reveals truths which
might otherwise remain obscured. In Melville's poem "The College
Colonel" the reader experiences the truth discovered by one Civil War
colonel. Melville's method is, in part, to make clear what the colonel's
truth is not. Melville cannot, however, say exactly what that truth is.
Only the experiences the colonel has been through can reveal the truth
he discovers, and it is these which are treated most fully in the poem.

Melville implies that the truth discovered by the colonel is not
something he could have learned in college. The title indicates that the
colonel has been to college — perhaps the United States Military
Academy. But in the war the colonel has lived "a thousand years" in
two. . . .

Melville also makes it clear that the truth discovered by the colonel
has nothing to do with patriotism or the glory of war. The third stanza
describes his mixed feelings about the homecoming celebration for his
regiment. People cheer, wave hats and flags, and throw "wreaths
from gay balconies." But to the colonel "there comes alloy," for the
patriotic glorification of war is an inappropriate way to greet men "who
crawl, spent, to shore." . . .

In the next to the last stanza Melville takes special pains to assure
us that the colonel's truth is not simply the recognition of his own
mortality. War does teach the reality of death and pain, but

It is not that a leg is lost,
     It is not that an arm is maimed,
It is not that the fever has racked —
     Self he has long disclaimed.

What then *is* the colonel's truth? Particularly in the second and
last stanzas Melville gives us a sense of the colonel's experiences leading to the discovery of that truth. The extended simile of the second
stanza compares the soldier's experience in war to that of a castaway
sailor: the surf roars like an artillery barrage, some sailors are dragged
back by the surf's ebb just as the dead and wounded fall behind in an
infantry charge, and the undrowned must "again and again breast the
surge" just as the infantrymen must regroup and attack again. When
it is over, there is no celebration or even elation, only exhaustion.
Battered by an elemental force (for the sailors the sea, for the soldiers
war itself), the men are "spent" — not only tired but used up. Even es-

cape leaves them essentially different. This perhaps explains the colonel's coldness and aloofness. Illusions gone, the colonel finds life alloyed. He sees that base metal is fused with precious. . . .

Although Melville makes no statement of what the colonel's truth *is*, by the time he has finished he has indicated what that truth is not. He has also conveyed a sense of the pain and loss that have led the colonel to his truth: war, more horrible than the war college teaches or the stay-at-homes realize, is life.

4. Some Guidelines for Critical Writing

A literary work may seem to be of a familiar type, and it may seem to be similar in important ways to other works we have read. Yet we approach it with the assumption that at the same time it is a law unto itself, that it has to be understood on its own terms. When we write about it, we confront a *new* challenge. It follows that we cannot apply a ready-made formula. Nevertheless, some basic requirements for a successful critical paper remain the same. Here are typical comments likely to recur again and again in a teacher's reactions to student writing about literature:

Good command of the material covered in the course, but not enough specific reference to *actual passages* you have read, and not enough of your own *interpretation* or *reaction*.

Quote (or paraphrase) some actual phrases or passages from the text to make this more authentic.

Not enough *explication* of the actual text — before you judge and react, make sure your reader actually understands what the author is saying in this passage.

You *bring* more *to* this passage from the outside (by way of a second-hand knowledge) than you *draw out* of the actual text.

This is a key term — *develop* it by detailed reference to actual passages or incidents. Where is the term used and by whom? in what context?

Sentimentality, like *cynicism* or *pessimism*, is often used too loosely and superficially as a sweeping derogatory term. Show in detail how or in what sense this work is "sentimental" — earn the right to use this label by working out a definition that will do justice to its significance and *nuances* as it applies to this work.

To forestall these and similar comments, keep the following advice in mind when writing a critical paper:

(1) *Make generous use of the author's own words.* Literary language is rich in personality, force, nuance; and much of this richness is lost in a lame paraphrase. Make ample use of striking, revealing, memorable quotations. In the following excerpt from a paper on

Byron's *Don Juan*, note how much of Byron's actual language the student writer manages to work into her own text:

In the idyllic setting of a Grecian isle, far removed from the taint of civilization, Juan and Haidée find Byron's ideal: unrepressed, unaffected natural feeling. Their love is spontaneous, springing from mutual empathy, needing no words:

> And [Haidée] found, by sympathy,
> The answer eloquent, where the soul shines
> And darts in one quick glance a long reply;
> And thus in every look she saw exprest
> A world of words, and things at which she guess'd.

Their love is one of a kind, and the depth of their feeling excludes all else, is self-contained: "They were all in all to each other," ". . . as if there were no life beneath the sky/ Save theirs." Their passion is innocent, "such kisses as belong to early days," their communion open and natural, linked by a more solemn bond than that of marriage:

> on the lone shore were plighted
> Their hearts; the stars, their nuptial torches, shed
> Beauty upon the beautiful they lighted:
> Ocean their witness, and the cave their bed,
> By their own feelings hallow'd and united,
> Their priest was solitude, and they were wed.

(2) *Explain and defend your likes and dislikes.* When you use a term like "rationalization" or "sentimentality," buttress it with a relevant quotation or a capsule definition. Do not simply use it as a label to paste on something you dislike. When you use a term like "escapism," remember that sometimes escape is from the trivial to the important, as when Thoreau went to Walden Pond to separate what was essential in his life from superfluity and distraction.

(3) *Do not quote from an imaginative creation as if it were a documentary report or a sociological study.* A Gradgrind or a Bounderby in Charles Dickens's *Hard Times* is not "*the* nineteenth-century businessman." He is rather a figure Dickens *created*—to embody his dislike for a certain kind of business philosophy. Dickens shows us in the novel what he *chooses* to see, and the distance between his fantastically narrow-minded "practical men" and the actual species may be considerable. A Puritan minister in a short story by Nathaniel Hawthorne is not "*the* American Puritan." He may rather embody some essential element that Hawthorne *felt* in Puritanism, and that intrigued or obsessed him. What we find in poetry, drama, and fiction is not a photographic reflection of historical reality. Before you cite a novel or a play as evidence of actual historical conditions, remember that an author may idealize or satirize, glorify or belittle.

(4) *Make an effort to get into the spirit of a work, to respond to its characteristic method.* To do justice to a work, you have to pay attention not merely to what is said but also to how it is said. When an author's method is new and different, a critical discussion is likely to be misleading unless it somehow comes to terms with what *makes* the method different. Here is how Mary McCarthy tries to explain her reaction to books written, like *The Catcher in the Rye,* in an assumed first-person style:

> These books are impersonations, ventriloquial acts; the author, *like some prank-ster on the telephone,* is speaking in an assumed voice — high or deep, hollow or falsetto, but in any case not his own. He is imitating the voice of Augie or of Holden Caulfield and the book is written in Augie's or Holden's "style." . . . The reader senses the author, cramped inside the character *like some contortionist in a box,* and suspects (often rightly) some trick.

(5) *Repeat critical opinions only if you have questioned them or made them truly your own.* Do not simply substitute a critic's ready-made opinions for your own honest interpretation and reaction. If you cite a critic approvingly, show why you think he is right.

Review Exercises: Student Writing

A. Study the following poem by Emily Dickinson. Which of the student-written reactions seem to you most successful or instructive? Which seem to contribute most to a valid interpretation of the poem, and which seem misleading? Which respond successfully to manner, method, or style as well as "content"?

> Because I could not stop for Death,
> He kindly stopped for me;
> The carriage held but just ourselves
> And Immortality.
>
> We slowly drove, he knew no haste,
> And I had put away
> My labor, and my leisure too,
> For his civility.
>
> We passed the school, where children strove
> At recess, in the ring;
> We passed the fields of gazing grain,
> We passed the setting sun.

Or rather, he passed us;
The dews grew quivering and chill,
For only gossamer my gown,
My tippet only tulle.

We paused before a house that seemed
A swelling of the ground;
The roof was scarcely visible,
The cornice in the ground.

Since then 'tis centuries, and yet
Feels shorter than the day
I first surmised the horses' heads
Were toward eternity.

1. Emily Dickinson writes about death in a calm and uninhibited way, as though it were just one of the occurrences of everyday life. Her presentation of death is simple, not magnified as is quite often the case. First, death calls whether or not one is ready. There is no hurry, though; there is time to view life's passing incidents. Miss Dickinson talks about passing a school where children are playing, about passing fields of gazing grain, and about the setting sun. All of these things are part of one's everyday life, things one remembers most vividly. In the fifth stanza, she talks about a house, conveying to us that the home is probably the most significant part of one's life. Although death arrives, these things will be present in one's mind for an eternity.

2. When I read the poem I get the idea that someone is near death. The person has led a good life and has probably retired. He is waiting for death to catch up with him. Before death arrives, the person takes an imaginary ride in a carriage and takes in the highlights of his life. He passes a school where children play, and this reminds him of his own youth. He also passes a field of grain, which reminds him of his days as a farmer or of the time when he was working to earn a living. Finally, death catches up with him, as the setting sun indicates. The person is buried, the mound being the symbol of a cemetery. The pause near the mound is probably the funeral service held for him.

3. The poet regards Death as a person always present in the background of life. Death knows "no haste," because once he has made his claim upon a person the only goal is immortality. There is no hurry, the carriage of Death always leads to that one goal. The carriage passes children playing happily. Even though Death is in the background, life, carefree and gay, will continue for them. Other things that are not disturbed by the thought of Death are "fields of gazing grain," for they remain peaceful and serene. The setting sun symbolizes the "twilight" or ending of life. The house that seemed a swelling of the ground is the

last sight which reminds the rider in the carriage of life on earth. He takes a last look at these objects but still moves slowly, though deliberately, toward eternity.

4. The poem gives an impression of calmness and serenity. After the writer has been "kindly" picked up by death for immortality, their progress is slow and orderly, as if there were no rush or limit on time. As soon as she enters the chariot, her labor and her leisure—all worldly ambitions, pleasures, and pursuits—are ended, and she is devoted entirely to death "for his civility." The journey past the various scenes could represent her life in retrospect; the children could represent her youth, the fields of grain could mean maturity or the middle years of her life. The pause at the "swelling in the ground" symbolizes to me the fact that they pause by her grave long enough to leave her material body on earth in the customary manner. Only her spirit accompanies the driver of the chariot on through the centuries of immortality into eternity.

5. I don't particularly like this poem by Emily Dickinson. It feels like sand running through my toes. I'm sure I can't see why she mentions playing children, gazing grain, and a setting sun. Perhaps these are the things she loves best. The lightness of the poem reminds me of a woman riding home and casually remarking about the things she sees that impress her. The last stanza leads me to believe that she knew what it would feel like after death. She thinks she'll know when she is approaching death, because she'll experience some sequence of emotions, or see some particular sequence of objects. I feel as if I were running after the carriage with Emily Dickinson in it and hollering to her to tell me what she means. But she keeps going slowly on toward something mysterious, saying casual things that I don't quite understand. I'm not going to guess what she means. Maybe she doesn't mean anything. Maybe the poem is as light as it feels.

B. The following essay is reprinted from *Orbit*, a magazine of student writing published at Illinois State University. Examine and evaluate it as an example of writing about literature.

IN DEFENSE OF *THE AMERICAN DREAM*

Karen Traficante

Robert Brustein, in his attempt to discredit Edward Albee's play *The American Dream*, claims there is an "absence of any compelling theme, commitment, or sense of life."[1] Are these accusations true? And if so, do they immediately classify the play as a "fumble"?[2] Harold Clurman's review

[1] Robert Brustein, "Fragments from a Cultural Explosion," *New Republic* (March 27, 1961), p. 29.
[2] Tom F. Driver, *Christian Century* (March 1, 1961), p. 725.

advises that Albee "stick closer to the facts of life so his plays may remain humanly and socially relevant."[3] How far does Albee stray?

In order for this play to have a "compelling theme, commitment, or sense of life," a struggle or conflict is needed. But no struggle is found. There is no "man v. society" here. The conventional Mommy and Daddy are relatively content with their lives. It does not matter to them that they are living conformities. There are no carrots in their family tree of apples. Mommy and Daddy are typical Jonathan apples. And they don't care. They carry their dull lives to an extreme. Everything about them points to their lack or originality. Their apartment shows no personality. The hideous gilded furniture and frames with no pictures point to their lack of individualism. Socially accepted Mrs. Barker is actually a "dreadful woman";[4] however, realizing that she is a professional woman and that one is expected to like such elite people, Mommy goes on and explains, "but she *is* chairman of our woman's club, so naturally I'm terribly fond of her." Naturally! No attempts are made to struggle against society and its conformities here either. And thus, with no struggle, no theme. But the play doesn't need a "theme." It is a parable and a parody. It makes it readers question, struggle, and laugh at the absurdity of their human freedoms. It *gives* its readers a theme to live by: that is, man v. society, mechanization, conformity. The play is not a "fumble"; it is a successful defensive play.

Albee's characters and their lives are exaggerated examples of human mass existence and experience. But he does not deviate that far from the truth. "The sense of a radical dehumanization of life which has accompanied events of the past several decades has given rise to the theory of 'mass society.'"[5] And this present mass society has lessened the possibility for "persons of achieving a sense of individual self in our mechanized society."[6] There exists a majority of conventional Mommies and Daddies, and their dull lives are common to many. The uninventive apartment of the play is similar to some modern flats of our society: the rugs blend with the walls which in turn fuse with the upholstery which is highlighted by the paintings on the walls. Why do people tend to buy expensive pictures merely because the wood frame matches their fruitwood cocktail table and the artist's pigments match the color scheme of the room? Paintings are not a part of the furniture. They are unique expressions; they are art.

Mommy and Daddy are overjoyed with the arrival of the new "bumble." He is a "Clean-cut, midwest farm boy type, almost insultingly good-looking in a typically American way . . ."[7] And don't most parents look for these traits in their own offspring? They not only conform, but expect their child to fit the mold as well. Mommy and Daddy's first bumble would not concede, and so he was chopped up and thrown away. Mommy and Daddy wanted

[3] Harold Clurman, *Nation* (February 11, 1961), p. 125.

[4] Edward Albee, *The American Dream*, in *Drama—An Introductory Anthology*, ed. Otto Reinert (Boston: Little, Brown, 1964), p. 838.

[5] Daniel Bell, "The Theory of Mass Society: A Critique," in *The Age of Anxiety*, ed. Clarence A. Glasrud (Boston, 1960), p. 177.

[6] Bell, p. 177.

[7] Albee, p. 858.

only another Jonathan apple. Realistically, modern Mommies and Daddies do not chop up their undesired youth. They may, however, smother their children's individualism or simply break ties with them. Brabantio abandoned his lovely daughter Desdemona in Shakespeare's *Othello*. Why? Because she deviated from his hopes and from society's ideals as well. And so it is true of our modern Mommies and Daddies: unmarried pregnant daughters are banned from their homes; interracial and inter-religious marriages cause conflict or rejection; "flower children" are cursed, punished, and repudiated by their parents. So Albee is not straying far from the truth when his Mommy and Daddy throw away their stubborn bumble.

A predominant condition which exists in our world is an inability to communicate. Mommy and Daddy, though married, are essentially strangers. Their daily conversations are vacuums filled with clichés, small talk, and trivialities. Daddy avoids really talking to Mommy. He simply responds with "Have they!" or "Yes . . . yes . . .",[8] barely recognizing what she is saying. Their marriage exists only in custom. There is no love bond established because they lack the communication necessary to understand one another and thus to love.

Mrs. Barker and Mommy also make some fruitless attempts at social intercourse. With their automatic replies, however, they miss the true substance of what seem to be urbanities: "My, what an unattractive apartment you have!" "Yes, but you don't know what a trouble it is." [9]

With his characters obviously unable to communicate, Albee is illustrating how people are becoming more mechanically respondent and enigmatic in their conversations. The profound importance of communication is exemplified in "Drift and Mastery," by Walter Lippmann: "We live in great cities without knowing our neighbors . . . and our associations are stretched over large territories, cemented by very little personal contact. . . . But this impersonal quality is intolerable. . . ." [10] Albee and Lippmann agree upon this idea and coldly expose it to their readers.

Without a "compelling theme, commitment, or sense of life," Albee successfully brings his readers' attentions to the paralysis of conformity, the failure of communication, and a vision of a future world. The vision is exaggerated to the point of humor and horror. But by its existence, it points out the urgency for alterations, struggle, and reform.

[8] Albee, p. 838.
[9] Albee, p. 845.
[10] Walter Lippmann, "Drift and Mastery," in *The Age of Anxiety*, ed. Clarence A. Glasrud (Boston, 1960), p. 51.

Theme Topics 10

1. Select a short poem by William Blake, Emily Dickinson, or Wallace Stevens. Write as complete an explication as possible.

2. Write a character study of a secondary but important character in a major play you have read: Creon in *Antigone;* Lady Macbeth in *Macbeth;* Claudius in *Hamlet;* Desdemona in *Othello.*

3. Discuss the role of a central symbol in a poem by Robinson Jeffers, D. H. Lawrence, or another modern poet of your choice. Or discuss the role of a central symbol in a short story by John Steinbeck, D. H. Lawrence, or another writer.

4. Trace the role of a key term or concept in a Shakespeare play; for instance, "love" in *Romeo and Juliet,* "honor" in *Henry IV, Part One,* "nature" in *King Lear.*

5. Compare and contrast two short poems dealing with a similar topic or the same subject matter: the same animal, city, mythological figure, legendary hero or event.

6. Compare and contrast Jack London's treatment of the theme of man against nature in "To Build a Fire" with Stephen Crane's treatment of the same theme in "The Open Boat."

7. Compare and contrast John Steinbeck's treatment of the theme of pursuit in "Flight" with Ernest Hemingway's treatment of the same theme in "The Killers." Or, compare and contrast the treatment of man's relationship to nature in a short story by Hemingway and one by William Faulkner.

8. Compare and contrast a Greek tragic heroine, such as Antigone, Electra, or Medea, with the heroine of a modern drama, such as Ibsen's Nora or Hedda Gabler.

9. Examine the treatment of the theme of a young man's alienation from society in *one* of the following: James Joyce, *A Portrait of the Artist as a Young Man;* Albert Camus, *The Stranger;* Ralph Ellison, *Invisible Man.*

10. Discuss fully a poem in which you find strongly contradictory or opposed elements. Select a poem by John Donne, John Crowe Ransom, or another poet of your choice.

A Concise Handbook

CHAPTER ELEVEN

The Paragraph

O 1   Structural Devices
        O 1a   Topic Sentences
        O 1b   Transitional Phrases
        O 1c   Recurrent Terms

O 2   Organizing the Paragraph
        O 2a   Space and Time
        O 2b   Explanation and Illustration
        O 2c   Logical Patterns
        O 2d   Emphatic Order

O 3   Paragraph Revision
        O 3a   Lack of Focus
        O 3b   Filling in Detail

The well-developed paragraph is both the basic unit of, and a model for, the substantial, well-ordered theme. Paragraphs are to the finished paper what concrete blocks are to a wall.

In some kinds of writing, it is true, paragraph division is merely *arbitrary*. In a newspaper article, a paragraph break may occur after every long sentence, and after every group of two or three short ones. In much informal writing, the author starts a new paragraph as nonchalantly as he would pause in conversation. In other kinds of writing, paragraph division is *conventional*. In dialogue, a paragraph break conventionally signals a change from one speaker to another.

Even in an expository essay, some paragraphs are mainly helps to *continuity*: programmatic paragraphs announcing the author's intention, transitional paragraphs helping the reader move from one major section to the next, summarizing paragraphs recapitulating important points. Some are mainly helps to *effectiveness*: introductory paragraphs catching the reader's attention, one-sentence paragraphs setting a statement off for emphasis.

The meat of an essay, however, is likely to be contained in a different kind of unit: the expository paragraph that *does justice to one major point*. It presents and develops an important idea or an important step in an argument. It does not just baldly state an idea but supports or defends it as well. By developing such paragraphs fully and systematically, you can make your papers seem like a sequence of solid, well-placed steps.

O 1   Structural Devices

In serious expository prose, the paragraph is a logical, rather than a typographical, unit.

In studying paragraphs written by professional writers, and in strengthening paragraphs in your own papers, you should look for clues to their logical coherence. You should look for devices that reveal structure and guide the reader.

O 1a   Topic Sentences

By formulating topic sentences for key paragraphs, a writer can greatly improve the clarity and continuity of his discussion. A **topic sentence** states the central idea of a paragraph. Some paragraphs revolve around a central idea without an explicit statement of it. Others range over a number of closely related ideas. In many a typical paragraph, however, a topic sentence serves as the key to the rest of the paragraph.

Typical topic sentences might look like this:

Many animals are capable of emitting meaningful sounds.

Most of us are less tolerant than we think.

The African students I know are suspicious of the motives behind "foreign aid."

"Impulse buying" plays as much of a role in the buying of a car as in other purchases.

Many campus buildings show the influence of imitation Gothic.

Well-chosen topic sentences help you structure your writing in several important ways:

(1) A good topic sentence *pulls together* a mass of closely related material. Notice how much detail has been brought together in the following paragraph. Notice how effectively the topic sentence sums up the generalization to which all the details point.

Latin American culture has been and is a dynamic element in the development of our own. It has, for example, furnished more than 2000 place names to the United States postal directory. Its languages have influenced American English, as such simple examples as "rodeo" and "vamoose" indicate. Its customs are part of our "Westerns" on television. Its housing, its music, its dances, its scenery, its ruins and its romance have been imitated and admired in the United States. One third of the continental area of this republic was for a long period, as modern history goes, under the governance of Spanish viceroys or of Mexico. The largest single Christian church in the United States is identical with the dominant church in Latin America. — Howard Mumford Jones, "Goals for Americans," *Saturday Evening Post*

(2) A good topic sentence *gives clear direction* to a paragraph. It provides a clear test of what fits in and what is irrelevant. Can you see how the topic sentence in each of the following examples steers the paragraph in a different direction?

The dormitory reminds me of a third-class hotel. Each room has the same set of unimaginative furnishings: the same pale red chest of drawers, the same light brown desks. . . .

The dormitory reminds me of a big office building. People who half know each other pass in the hall with impersonal friendliness. . . .

The dormitory reminds me of a prison. The study room is enclosed by windows with lines on them, giving the student a penned-in feeling. . . .

(3) In the theme or article as a whole, a good topic sentence *moves the presentation or the argument ahead* one essential step. Then the rest of the paragraph fills in, illustrates, and supports the point made. Then the next topic sentence again takes a step forward.

Part of an article on the influence of television on political campaigns might proceed like this:

Television continues to change the look of political conventions. Speeches are fewer and shorter. Sweaty orators, bellowing and waving their arms for an hour or more, have yielded almost completely to TelePrompter readers, younger and brisker fellows, some of them very slick and many of them no fun. Both parties have shortened sign-waving, chanting demonstrations. . . .

While many of the changes may be for the best, there is something synthetic about this new kind of convention. There is a lack of spontaneity, a sense of stuffy self-consciousness. There is something unreal about seeing a well-known newscaster starting across the floor to interview a delegate and getting stopped for an autograph. . . .

Nevertheless, television coverage of conventions manages to get across to us a great deal about the way our political system works. We are still a nation of disparate parts. The conventions are the occasions that bring various coalitions together every four years to pull and haul at one another; to test old power centers and form new ones; to compromise and, yes, to raise a little hell together in a carnival atmosphere. . . .

NOTE: The topic sentence is most effective in helping you structure your writing when you place it early in the paragraph. But sometimes a writer will make the paragraph *lead up* to its topic sentence (see O 3b). Sometimes, in fact, the topic sentence appears at the end of an introductory or transitional paragraph rather than in the paragraph that actually develops it.

O 1b   Transitional Phrases

Transitional phrases help the reader see a paragraph as a well-ordered whole. A well-written paragraph does not need elaborate directional signals. When used unobtrusively, however, **transitional phrases** help the reader proceed smoothly from sentence to sentence.[1] Notice their use in the following paragraphs:

Many animals are capable of emitting meaningful sounds. Hens, for instance, warn their chicks of impending danger. Similarly, dogs growl at strangers to express distrust or hostility. Most of man's pets, in fact, have a "vocabulary" of differentiated sounds to express hunger, pain, or satisfaction.

Most of us are less tolerant than we think. It is true that we tend to be tolerant of things sufficiently remote, such as Buddhism or impressionist painting. But we lose our tempers quickly when confronted with minor irritations. My friends, at any rate, will rage at drivers who block their way, at acquaintances who are late for appointments, or at manufacturers of mechanisms that break down.

All the frontier industrial countries except Russia received massive waves of emigrants from Europe. They therefore had a more rapid population growth than their

[1] For a listing of common transitional phrases see Chapter One, "The Whole Theme," p. 49.

industrializing predecessors had experienced. As frontier countries with great room for expansion, *however,* they were also characterized by considerable internal migration and continuing new opportunities. *As a result* their birth rates remained comparatively high. In the decade from 1950 to 1960, with continued immigration, these countries grew in population at an average rate of 2.13 per cent a year, compared with 1.76 per cent for the rest of the world. — Kingsley Davis, "Population," *Scientific American*

Notice how unobtrusive and yet how effective the transitions are in the following excerpt:

. . . What must be *even more surprising* is the thinness of coverage right here at home in the center of our national news, Washington. Washington has a very large press corps. The roster of the National Press Club is substantial, *and* the State Department auditorium is easily filled by a glamour press conference. *The trouble* is that most of the Washington press corps runs as a herd, concentrating on the "big" story of the day to the neglect of much else. The news services have large staffs, *and* a few papers priding themselves on their national news maintain bureaus ranging from a half-dozen full-time correspondents to three times that number. *But* most of the so-called bureaus in Washington are one-man affairs. Except for an hour of gossip at the Press Club or at one of the other informal meeting places, and for what a lonesome man picks up from his home Congressional delegation, and the steady stream of inspired handouts, the average Washington reporter never gets beneath the surface of the day's one obvious story. — Philip M. Wagner, "What Makes a Really Good Newspaper," *Harper's*

O 1c   Recurrent Terms

A unified paragraph is often marked by the repetition or paraphrase of important words and phrases. Such **recurrent** terms reflect continuity of thought and subject matter. Similar in effect is the recurrence of "pointers" like *he, it, they, this, these,* and *those.* Notice in the following excerpt how the idea of change recurs in each successive sentence:

It is an ominous fact that in the long chain of evolution the latest link, man, has suddenly acquired alchemic powers to *alter* whatever he touches. No other species before has been able to *change* more than a tiny fraction of his habitat. Now there is but a tiny fraction that he has *left unchanged.* A bulldozer *undoes* in an hour the work of a million years. — Paul Brooks, "Canyonlands," *Atlantic*

Notice how the following paragraph on the relation of the "ends" and "means" in politics keeps playing off these two terms, and their synonyms or related terms, against each other:

The *technical* man isolates one particular field or activity, in order to concentrate upon the *procedure* within it. In order for his work to proceed, he must assume the worth of the *end* to which his work is addressed; in order to get on to his own question, *"How?,"* he must assume that the *end* he is serving has an assured place in a hierarchy of *values* that he does not himself examine. As a cobbler cannot continually be asking himself whether shoes as such are a *good*, so an economist cannot continually ask himself whether "productivity" or "satisfaction" or — now apparently — "economic growth" is a *good*; he must take that for granted and get on with his job. Where the *end* is simple and noncontroversial, such a *technical approach* raises no problems. But in social policy the *ends* to be served admit of no such description: it is of the essence of politics that their meanings shift, that *values* conflict, and that men differ about them. The *ends* of politics, moreover, are not neatly separable from the *"means"* the *technical man* thinks he deals with exclusively; usually he bootlegs in some assumptions about *ends* in his work on the *means*. One might argue that political leadership, which must interpret the situation and fit together these several and conflicting *ends,* is preeminently the activity that cannot properly be reduced to sheer *technique.* — William Lee Miller, "Some Academic Questions About a New Yale Man," *The Reporter*

NOTE: In the sample paragraphs reprinted in the rest of this chapter, words and phrases that make for unity or continuity are italicized.

Exercises

A. Examine the structure of each of the following paragraphs. Is there a topic sentence? Is all the material in the paragraph relevant to the idea stated in the topic sentence? Does the author use transitional phrases? Does he make use of recurrent terms or their synonyms?

1. All the evidence indicates that the population upsurge in the underdeveloped countries is not helping them to advance economically. On the contrary, it may well be interfering with their economic growth. A surplus of labor on the farms holds back the mechanization of agriculture. A rapid rise in the number of people to be maintained uses up income that might otherwise be utilized for long-term investment in education, equipment and other capital needs. To put it in concrete terms, it is difficult to give a child the basic education he needs to become an engineer when he is one of eight children of an illiterate farmer who must support the family with the produce of two acres of ground. — Kingsley Davis, "Population," *Scientific American*

2. Primarily, the brain is an organ of survival. It was built by nature to search for food, shelter, and the like, to gain advantage — before addressing itself to the pursuit of truth. Hence most human brains are unable to distinguish between truth and advantage, and accept as truth that which is only advantage. We use our brain mainly for finding ways to reach what we want. Simultaneously, we produce the thoughts and arguments which justify our feelings and dealings. I suspect that if I were in the business of selling shelters, my brain would tend to dwell rather steadily on the probability of nuclear war. If I were in politics, I might

find my brain devoting itself less to the next generation than to the next election. — Albert Szent-Gyorgyi, "The Persistence of the Caveman," *Saturday Review*

3. The prestige of science was colossal. The man in the street and the woman in the kitchen, confronted on every hand with new machines and devices which they owed to the laboratory, were ready to believe that science could accomplish almost anything; and they were being deluged with scientific information and theory. The newspapers were giving columns of space to inform (or misinform) them of the latest discoveries: a new dictum from Albert Einstein was now front-page stuff even though practically nobody could understand it. Outlines of knowledge poured from the presses to tell people about the planetesimal hypothesis and the constitution of the atom, to describe for them in unwarranted detail the daily life of the cave-man, and to acquaint them with electrons, endocrines, hormones, vitamins, reflexes, and psychoses. — Frederick Lewis Allen, *Only Yesterday*

4. Detective stories tend to glorify crime. Murderers, gangsters, and crooks of all kinds are described as tough, cunning, and courageous individuals who know how to take care of themselves and who know how to get what they want. In James M. Cain's *The Postman Always Rings Twice*, for instance, the villain is a much more impressive character than his victim. He is casual, brave, smart, and successful with women. It is true that he finally gets caught. But he is punished for a crime that he did not commit, so that his conviction is hardly a triumph of justice. Besides, looking back over the exciting life of the criminal, the reader might conclude that it was worth the risk.

B. Study paragraph division and sequence of material in half a dozen news reports selected from a local newspaper. What is the relation between paragraphing and overall organization? What effect does the paper's system of paragraphing have on its presentation of news? Report your findings.

C. From a current magazine article, select a *model paragraph* that has a clear topic sentence and makes effective use of transitional phrases or other structural devices. Be prepared to defend your choice.

D. From a recent theme, select a substantial paragraph that *could be improved* by use of a clear topic sentence and other structural devices. Hand in both the "Before" and the "After" version.

E. Study in detail the role of topic sentences and other structural devices in the paragraphs from *one sample page* of a current magazine article. Are there any transitional, programmatic, or summarizing paragraphs? Select an article that is exceptionally well structured. (Your instructor may select a page for the class to work on.)

O 2   Organizing the Paragraph

Make your paragraphs follow a clear pattern of organization.

The first requirement for a successful paragraph is that it should be packed with relevant details. But their relevance will show only if they are arranged in a pattern clear enough for the reader to follow.

O 2a   Space and Time

In description, narrative, or technical writing, a well-organized paragraph often follows the most plausible order in space or time. Typically, such a paragraph corresponds to one major unit in the material treated: It takes up one limited aspect of a scene, one episode in a larger chain of events, one step in a process. The reader has to know where he is at the beginning, and where and how he is expected to move from there.

Study the way the two following paragraphs move in space or time:

(1) *Spatial order:*

The jockey *came to the doorway of the dining room, then after a moment stepped to one side* and stood motionless, with *his back to the wall. The room* was crowded, as this was the third day of the season and all the hotels in the town were full. *In the dining room* bouquets of August roses scattered their petals on the white table linen and from the *adjoining bar* came a warm, drunken wash of voices. The jockey *waited with his back to the wall* and *scrutinized the room* with pinched, crêpy eyes. He *examined the room until at last* his eyes reached a table in *a corner diagonally across from him,* at which three men were sitting. *As he watched,* the jockey raised his chin and tilted his head back to one side, his dwarfed body grew rigid, and his hands stiffened so that the fingers curled inward like gray claws. Tense *against the wall of the dining room, he watched* and waited in this way. — Carson McCullers, "The Jockey"

(2) *Chronological order:*

The *greeting ceremony* when one bird of the pair, after having been away at the feeding grounds, rejoins its mate *is also beautiful. Some little time before* the human watcher notes the other's approach, the waiting bird rises on its branch, arches and spreads its wings, lifts its aigrettes into a fan and its head-plumes into a crown, bristles up the feathers of its neck, and emits again and again a hoarse cry. The other approaches, settles in the branches near by, puts itself into a similar position, and advances toward its mate; and *after a short excited space* they settle down close together. *This type of greeting* is repeated *every day until* the young leave the nest; for after the eggs are laid both sexes brood, and there is a nest-relief four times in every twenty-four hours. *Each time* the same attitudes, the same cries, the same excitement; only now at the end of it all, one steps off the nest, the other on. One might suppose that this closed the performance. But no: the bird that has been relieved is still apparently animated by stores of unexpended emotion; it searches about for a twig, breaks it off or picks it up, and returns with it in beak to present to the other. *During the presentation the greeting ceremony is again gone through; after each relief the whole business of presentation and greeting may be repeated two, or four, or up even to ten or eleven times before the free bird flies away.* — Julian Huxley, *Essays of a Biologist*

O 2b   Explanation and Illustration

In many expository paragraphs, developing a key idea is a matter of explanation and illustration. A topic sentence is often intentionally terse and emphatic. It may be developed by material that amplifies it, spells out its implications, clarifies a key term (**definition**). It may be developed by two or three representative examples or by one example that is exceptionally detailed (**illustration**).

Notice how the following sample paragraphs vary the basic pattern of *statement — explanation — illustration:*

key idea	The deep sea has its *stars,* and perhaps here and there an eerie and transient equivalent of *moonlight,* for the mysterious
detailed restatement	*phenomenon of luminescence* is displayed by perhaps half of all the fishes that live in dimly lit or darkened waters, and by many of the
first example	lower forms as well. Many fishes carry *luminous torches* that can be turned on or off at will, presumably helping them find or pursue their
second example	prey. Others have *rows of lights* over their bodies, in patterns that vary from species to species and may be a sort of recognition mark or badge by which the bearer can be known as friend or enemy. The
third example	deep-sea squid ejects a spurt of fluid that becomes a *luminous cloud,* the counterpart of the 'ink' of his shallow-water relative. — Rachel Carson, *The Sea Around Us*

key question	Where do the terms of businesese come from? Most, *of course,* are hand-me-downs from former generations of businessmen, *but*
key idea	many are the fruit of cross-fertilization with other jargons. A businessman who castigates government bureaucrats, *for example,*
first set of examples	is at the same time apt to be activating, expediting, implementing, effectuating, optimizing, minimizing, and maximizing — and at all levels and echelons within the framework of broad policy areas.
second set of examples	*Similarly,* though he is amused by the long-hairs and the social scientists, he is beginning to speak knowingly of projective techniques, social dynamics, depth interviewing, *and* sometime soon, if he keeps up at this rate, he will probably appropriate that hall-
restatement of key idea	mark of the sound sociological paper, "insightful." Businesese, *in fact,* has very nearly become the great common meeting ground of the jargons. — William H. Whyte, "The Language of Business," *Fortune*

introductory anecdote	When Paul Garrett arrived in Detroit twenty-five years ago to begin General Motors' public relations program, the first question

fired at him was: "How do you make a billion dollars look small?"
Garrett said damned if he knew, and furthermore damned if he
thought that was his job. Public relations, he argued, was not an
"act," but a continuing effort on the part of management to win the

key idea   confidence of the people with whom it came into contact. *Hence
you will find General Motors engaged in a host of activities in which*

first example   *altruism and self-interest come together in a creamy blend.* Plant
City and Field Relations, *for example,* stimulates local GM participation in the community affairs of the sixty-eight cities where it has

second example   factories, thereby helping both the community and itself. Educational Relations works with the schools, providing them with such
useful education material as films on safe driving, and providing
itself with a flow of applicants for jobs. The Speakers Bureau is

third example   glad to send a company-sponsored lecturer to your club or association to edify it with an inspirational talk—or to educate it with a
"sound" economic one. Institutional Advertising tells the story of

fourth example   GM's role in supporting some twenty thousand suppliers, and leaves
you with the pleasant impression that what's good for General
Motors is good for small business, too. The billion dollars may not

restatement of   look any smaller as a *result of these efforts. But* it looks much, much
key idea, alluding   nicer.—Robert L. Heilbroner, "Public Relations—The Invisible
to initial anecdote   Sell," *Harper's*

key idea   Not the least remarkable thing about Huck's feeling for
people is that his tenderness goes along with the *assumption that
his fellow men are likely to be dangerous and wicked.* He travels

first example   incognito, never telling the truth about himself and never twice
telling the same lie, for he *trusts no one* and the lie comforts him

second example   even when it is not necessary. He *instinctively knows* that the best
way to keep a party of men away from Jim on the raft is to beg them

further support   to come aboard to help his family stricken with smallpox. And if he
for key idea   had not already had the *knowledge of human weakness and stupidity and cowardice,* he would soon have acquired it, for all his
encounters forcibly teach it to him—the insensate feud of the
Graingerfords and Shepherdsons, the invasion of the raft by the
Duke and the King, the murder of Boggs, the lynching party,

restatement   and the speech of Colonel Sherburn. Yet his *profound and bitter
of key idea   knowledge of human depravity* never prevents him from being a
friend to man.—Lionel Trilling, *The Liberal Imagination*

key idea   Perhaps the most wearing thing about television is that most
of the time it talks in a language so bare, so elementary, and so
lacking in overtones that it can only be called baby talk. *Certainly

narrowed to   the commercials are baby talk,* complete with coo and wheedle;
limited area   and some of them even press the toddlers into service to do the

specific examples   selling for them. *I am thinking of* the little girls who wash their
dolls' clothes in Ivory and of the one little girl who, holding up a roll
of paper, says "Hudson tissues tear so stwaight!"—Marya Mannes,
"Channels," *The Reporter*

NOTE: Observe in these paragraphs the satisfying and self-evident **relevance** of explanations and examples to the central idea. Not only is the illustrative material ample, but its appropriateness is immediately clear.

O 2c   Logical Patterns

Many expository paragraphs, instead of presenting one key idea, weigh several closely related points or work out a conclusion in a series of closely related steps. Such a paragraph may follow a number of different logical patterns:

(1) *Comparison and contrast:*

key idea (linked to preceding step in discussion)	Just as Alger's view of money as something to be made and kept no longer generally operates, [neither] does his view of how it should be given away. There is a great deal of "charity" in Alger, but *it is always man-to-man, even palm-to-palm.* It is a gesture in
first subtopic (situation in Alger's books)	the tradition of the New Testament, a retail transaction between two individuals, spiritual in essence, monetary in form. The adjective that comes first to mind when we think of it is "Christian."
second subtopic (contrasting situation today)	*The adjective that comes first to mind when we think of charity today is "organized."* Via drives, community chests, red feathers, we can give more away more quickly. At the same time the primitive-Christian heart of the process, man-to-man giving, is weakened. Warmheartedness is communized. — Clifton Fadiman, "Party of One," *Holiday*

(2) *Examination of causes and effects:*

key idea	Europeans with time-honored experience in the technique of painlessly extracting cash from foreigners' pockets have correctly gauged that Americans like to travel abroad provided they
cause (with specific examples)	don't really have to leave home. *They've seen* the U.S. armed forces and U.S. oil companies spend millions to give their personnel the illusion of living in a European or African suburbia filled with shopping centers, post exchanges, movie houses, ice-cream parlors, juke boxes, and American-style parking lots. *Smart pro-*
effect (with specific examples)	*moters now give* the American abroad exactly what he wants. Hotel rooms are furnished to please him, meal hours drastically advanced to suit the American habit of eating dinner at 6 p.m., arrangements made to satisfy the Americans' affection for crowds, action, and noise. — Joseph Wechsberg, "The American Abroad," *Atlantic*

(3) *Drawing logical conclusions from evidence* (**inductive order**):

detailed report of experiment	Psychologists studying race prejudice have many times made an interesting experiment. They seat a few people in a row, show a picture to the first in line, and ask him to whisper a description of it in a few words to a second who will whisper the information to the third, and so on. The picture is of a policeman and a badly dressed, uncouth Negro. The policeman is holding a knife in his hand; the Negro is unarmed. Almost never is the description transmitted to more than two or three individuals in succession, before the knife has passed from the hand of the policeman and is now being held in a threatening manner, by the Negro! *In other*
interpretation of experiment	*words,* the picture is transformed until it fits the preexisting concept in the mind, which is that an open knife is far more likely to be held by a Negro than a policeman. *This sort of unconscious*
general application of findings	*alteration* of what is perceived, to make it accord with what is already believed, is universal and is one of the most important of all the facts with which communication has to deal. — Bruce Bliven, *Preview for Tomorrow*

(4) *Drawing logical conclusions from accepted premises* (deductive order):

first observation	In the history books of the future this age of ours may come to be known as the Age of Statistics. In the biological and physical as well as the sociological sciences, statistics have become, as they
second observation	never were before, the most important tool of investigation. *But* as every philosophical scientist knows, the conclusions drawn by a
third observation (specific application of point 2)	science depend to a considerable extent upon the tools used. *And* it is in the nature of statistics not only that they deal with quantity but that they emphasize the significance of averages and medians. What usually exists or usually happens establishes The Law, and
fourth (contrasting) observation	The Law is soon thought of as identical with The Truth. In all the arts, *nevertheless,* it is the exceptional and the unpredictable which really count. It is the excellent, not the average, which is
logical conclusion	really important. And there is, *therefore,* one aspect of the cultural condition of a civilization to which statistical study is curiously inappropriate. — Joseph Wood Krutch, *Is the Common Man Too Common?*

(5) *Choosing among alternatives:*

	History shows that wars between cities, states, and geographic regions cease once the originally independent units have amalgamated under the leadership of a single government with the power of making and enforcing laws that are binding upon in-
first alternative examined and rejected	dividuals. *One might reason on this basis that* if all of the industrialized and semi-industrialized regions of the world were to federate under a common government, the probability of another war would be greatly decreased. It seems likely that this conclusion would be valid if the resultant federation were as complete as was the federation formed by the original thirteen colonies in America.

second alternative presented and supported

On the other hand, it is extremely unlikely that such a highly centralized federation could come into existence at the present time; nationalistic feelings of individual men and groups of men, and conflicts of economic interests, are too strong to permit rapid transition. *Also,* those nations which have high per capita reserves of resources and high per capita production would be most reluctant to delegate their sovereignties to higher authority and to abandon the economic barriers that now exist. — Harrison Brown, *The Challenge of Man's Future*

O 2d   Emphatic Order

Order of presentation in a paragraph is determined in part by the intended effect upon the reader. As in the theme as a whole, the most emphatic positions in the paragraph are at the beginning and at the end. A short, strongly worded topic sentence at the very beginning can throw out a challenge to the reader. A key detail or key point withheld until the end can create suspense; it can make the paragraph as a whole *build up* to a climactic ending.

(1) *Emphatic initial assertion:*

There is little doubt that the draft limits my freedom. Although I have a student deferment, I must carry a full load to maintain it. Since I am not obsessed with the desire to graduate within four years, and because I must work part time during the school term, I would like to take my time and do well in a few courses each semester. In this way I might really learn something. Unfortunately, because of the draft I cannot do this, and so I feel as if I am being rushed through an academic processing plant where education in the form of units is quickly tacked onto me. At the end of four years I will emerge as a finished product with a degree certifying that my processing has been complete. That is not what I want, and yet I am forced to submit to it by a selective service system which leaves military service as my only alternative.

(2) *Climactic order:*

The morning sun was streaming through the crevices of the canvas when the man awoke. A warm glow pervaded the whole atmosphere of the marquee, and a single big blue fly buzzed musically round and round it. Besides the buzz of the fly there was not a sound. He looked about — at the benches — at the table supported by trestles — at his basket of tools — at the stove where the furmity had been boiled — at the empty basins — at some shed grains of wheat — at the corks which dotted the grassy floor. Among the odds and ends he discerned a little shining object, and picked it up. *It was his wife's ring.* — Thomas Hardy, *The Mayor of Casterbridge*

Exercises

A. From your recent writing, select the paragraph that comes closest to following the pattern of *statement — explanation — illustration.* Revise or expand it as needed to make it a clearly and solidly developed example of the type.

B. Select a key sentence from your current writing or reading. Use it as a topic sentence in three different paragraphs. Follow a *different pattern of organization* each time, using different supporting material as far as possible. Concentrate on making each pattern emerge clearly from the paragraph.

C. Describe in detail the pattern of organization in each of the following paragraphs. How clearly does it emerge from the paragraph as a whole? How would you rate these paragraphs as examples of student writing?

1. Newspapers give a distorted view of life. They have a tendency to exaggerate the morbid: the killings, the sex crimes, the fires, and the accidents. Newspapers are prone to overemphasize the unusual, such as a mother giving birth to quintuplets, the development of a Christmas tree that grows its own decorative cones, the minting of two pennies which were only half engraved, gang fights, teen-age drinking, or university riots.

2. Although I never attended a class there, the abandoned main building that crowned the top of the hill was a favorite monument of mine. It was weathered by salt air, wind, and fog; its surface was scarred by dozens of holes where engineers and inspectors had bored into the plaster for samples; many of the windows were broken or missing, and they stared out at the rest of the campus like the huge, vacant eye-sockets of a skull. In spite of these mutilations, the old building radiated an atmosphere of dignity and benevolence. Its massive stone steps extended outward from the barricaded door like the arms of the Lincoln monument, inviting students to gather there.

3. When I attended my first class meeting in World History, I was disappointed to learn that during the year we were not to study and discuss the reasons why an event occurred; we were apparently expected to spend most of our time memorizing dates and names. At least, I thought, when a test came up I would have to think back to remember what happened in 1492, for instance. But when the students sat down for the final examination, the question was not "What important event occurred in 1492, and how did it affect world history?" No! It was as follows: "In 1492, Columbus sailed to the New World—true or false?" or "What year did Columbus sail to the New World? (a) 1942; (b) 1812; (c) 1912; (d) 1492." What kind of thought is provoked by tests such as these?

4. My own pet feature of the magazine are the advertisements. Well I know that their sole purpose is to induce the reader, including me, to spend as many dollars as possible for the product pictured. Knowing this in no way detracts from my enjoyment of the color and pictorial

values of what I see. Fully aware as I am of the appeals being made to my baser instincts (snobbishness and greed, to name just two) by the artful devices of the advertising fraternity, I still enjoy looking at the pictures. The allure of an ordinary metal cooking utensil pictured in a setting more fit for a precious gem can spur me, a representative reader, on to the kitchen with grim determination to substitute for my own quite adequate pots just *such* pots, with or without daisies. Utilized more sensibly, the power of such an imaginative appeal can bring about many small changes in the average home simply by giving a new slant on an old topic.

5. One obvious result of modern technology has been the increasing dependence of one workman upon another. We have "geared the machines and locked all together into interdependence." In Detroit's factories, thousands of workers are specialized; each performs a specific task. On the assembly line, an automobile is mass produced in a matter of hours. One worker installs wires, a second fastens lining in the interior, a third installs the windshield. Further down the line, groups of specialized personnel have assembled the dashboard and the seats. The finished body is lowered onto a chassis that has come down a similar line, operating on the same principle of each man doing a particular job. In a short time, the test driver drives the finished car through the factory gates. This is division of labor. This is specialization.

D. The more sophisticated a professional writer, the more likely he is to combine or adapt familiar patterns of organization in his own way. Can you still recognize the patterns of organization at work in the following paragraphs? Which is the most conventional in organization? Which the least?

1. Nobody has succeeded in explaining the connection between the private sources and the public functions of art. But art does have its public functions, though we often lose sight of them. In primitive agricultural societies, and even in Western Europe until the Renaissance, the functions were more clearly defined. It was the duty of the artist to celebrate the community in its present oneness, in its divine past, and in its glorious future. Thus he invented dances and rituals for the group, he retold the stories of its gods and heroes, he fashioned their images, and he persuaded the "people"—his own tribe that is, the only genuine persons—that they were reenacting the lives of the gods, who would some day return and reinstitute the golden age. Thus the artist played a recognized part in the daily life of the people.—Malcolm Cowley, "Artists, Conscience, and Censors," *Saturday Review*

2. Abstractions are really disguised metaphors (most thoroughly disguised when they derive from the classical languages), and metaphors can only keep their sensuous content when poetry insists on reminding us of it. Take a scientific term like *parthenogenesis*, put it in a poem,

and the poem will not be able to resist digging out the "virgin" image (with the help of the Parthenon and the New Testament) and showing, with reference to the Old Testament, precisely what *genesis* means. Not that etymology is necessarily much help in giving us an anchor for an abstraction; it just happens to be the only source available, with some words, for a concrete image, the sense of a real thing out there in the world of the senses. The vague term "lady" at least takes on an image when we refer it back to the Anglo-Saxon *hlaefdige*, which has something to do with making a loaf. Somebody's there supervising the bread-making, perhaps. Or, even if she's actually baking it herself, her hands are clean. Superiority, neatness, calm, authority—those will do for a beginning.—Anthony Burgess, "The Future of Anglo-American," *Harper's*

3. In many simple societies, the "institutionalized ways" of controlling marriage run to diverse schemes and devices. Often they include special living quarters designed to make it easy for marriageable girls to attract a husband: the Bontok people of the Philippines keep their girls in a special house, called the *olag*, where lovers call, sex play is free, and marriage is supposed to result. The Ekoi of Nigeria, who like their women fat, send them away to be specially fattened for marriage. Other peoples, such as the Yao of central Africa and the aborigines of the Canary Islands, send their daughters away to "convents" where old women teach them the special skills and mysteries that a young wife needs to know.—John Finley Scott, "Sororities and the Husband Game," *Trans-action*

4. Reading is a habit. Once you've got the habit you never lose it. But you must somehow be exposed to reading early enough in life to have it become a part of your daily routine, like washing your face or breathing. Many an unfortunate grade-school child in our highly seasoned, electronic, picture-conscious age has never been exposed to the reading habit and cannot, therefore, read without effort. Some modern children seldom if ever read for fun. Like muscles that are almost never used, their concentration and interest give way quickly. They long for the automatic, pictorial sensation of TV (which can be highly instructive and entertaining at times) rather than the tedium of moving the eyes from left to right, from left to right, from left to right on line after line after line of unillustrated print. There's a certain sadness in realizing that a whopping segment of the exploding new teen-age generation never *really* reads anything, unless forced to do so.—Richard L. Tobin, "Reading Is a Habit," *Saturday Review*

5. When films first broke on the world, let's say with the full-length, full-scale achievement of D. W. Griffith, *The Birth of a Nation*, one of its most persuasive and hitherto unexperienced powers lay in the absolute reality of the moving image. The camera is a scientific instrument,

not a paintbrush: its special virtues are accuracy and actuality. Thus, when Griffith organized a pan-shot which began with a mother and child huddled in terror on a mountain and then moved slowly to a raging battle on the plain beneath, we were left breathless by a juxtaposition in scale—from the individual to the group, from the passive to the active—that was, quite literally, taking place before our eyes. Our belief in the medium had begun with actual railroad trains roaring down actual tracks right at us, with actual ocean waves breaking somewhere near our feet. Griffith moved from simple documentation to high imagination, from fact to fiction, from present to past; and he took us with him because he used his camera as a faithful recorder of something that was really and truly going on: he did not abandon his camera's ability to state visual facts.—Walter Kerr, "What Good Is Television?" *Horizon*

E. Study paragraph division and paragraph development in an essay by a nineteenth-century writer like Thomas Babington Macaulay, Robert Louis Stevenson, or John Henry Newman. Report distinctive features. How does their use of the paragraph differ from modern practice?

O 3   Paragraph Revision

In revising a paper, check your paragraphs for lack of focus and lack of supporting detail.

In revising the first draft of a paper, you will do well to look for common sources of weak paragraph development. Generally, both a sequence of one- or two-sentence paragraphs and a page without any paragraph breaks at all are signals of inadequate paragraphing.

O 3a   Lack of Focus

Focus weak paragraphs more clearly on a central point. Weak writing often is half-finished writing. A paragraph may be weak because the writer has not gone beyond the first jotting down of possibly useful detail. He has not done the kind of sorting and focusing that changes a first inventory of material into structured prose.

Do the following to give clear focus to your paragraphs:

(1) *Give unity to a rambling paragraph by formulating a topic sentence that holds its details together.* Look for a logical connection you previously missed or ignored.

Poor: San Francisco is a city of beautiful parks and public buildings. Golden Gate Park, with its spacious lawns and graceful ponds, enjoys international fame. The city's Bohemian section has become the national headquarters for jazz-age poetry and philosophy. Every tourist must visit Fisherman's Wharf and Coit Tower. The city is famed for its cultural events and conventions.

Revised: *Tourists and convention managers are irresistibly attracted to San Francisco.* Miles of varied waterfront, spacious parks, and impressive public buildings contribute to the city's unique appearance and cosmopolitan atmosphere. Fisherman's Wharf, with its seafood smells and colorful shops, attracts sightseeing crowds. Coit Tower affords a spectacular view of bay and city. Golden Gate Park, with its spacious lawns and graceful ponds, enjoys international fame.

(2) *Give focus to a blurred paragraph by eliminating material that does not bear on the central point.* A paragraph in a paper describing a magazine might contain a comment on a striking cover, information about the price, and a brief summary of an interesting article. However, once the eye-catching qualities of the magazine are mentioned, describing and illustrating them adequately will take at least one full paragraph. Observations and comments not **relevant** to eye appeal will have to make room for more unified material.

(3) *Split up paragraphs that are merely a series of undeveloped observations.* The following paragraph consists of sentences that should each become the topic sentence of a separate paragraph. Each sentence could then be fully developed by supporting detail.

Poor: The poems I liked best were those by A. E. Housman. *His poems were easy to comprehend without being overly simple.* With most other poems I need the assistance of an expert who can "translate" them for me. *The thoughts and attitudes expressed in Housman's poems represent the wisdom of an experienced, educated man. His poems are short and to the point,* a great help to enjoyment. *They are written in such a manner that the reader does not feel the author is preaching to him.*

O 3b   Filling in Detail

Strengthen skimpy paragraphs by supplying relevant detail. The weakest kind of paragraph merely repeats, in slightly different words, an idea that is already sufficiently clear:

Poor: My roommate is very considerate. I have always found him helpful and eager to be of service. He has really taught me something about the role of kindness in everyday living.

But even a paragraph that does develop its topic sentence may remain too thin. Notice how the following passage gains in authenticity through the filling in of detail from the author's experience:

Thin: I like politicians. I have spent a lot of time in their company. Mostly, I have reported their doings, but on occasion I have assisted them. On the whole, they have proved better company than any other professional group I have had a chance to know well.

Authentic: I like politicians. *Ever since I started work as a city-hall reporter in New Mexico some thirty years ago,* I have spent a lot of time in their company—*in smoke-filled rooms, jails, campaign trains, shabby courthouse offices, Senate cloakrooms, and the White House itself.* Mostly I've been reporting their doings, but on occasion I have served them *as speech writer, district leader, campaign choreboy, and civil servant.* On the whole, they have proved better company than any other professional group I've had a chance to know well—*including writers, soldiers, businessmen, doctors, and academics.*—John Fischer, "Please Don't Bite the Politicians," *Harper's*

To keep your paragraphs from remaining too skimpy, try the following by way of both remedy and precaution:

(1) *Practice building up detail in a multiple-example paragraph.* Rarely will your reader exclaim: "Too many good examples!" Try to build up your examples until the reader is likely to say: "Enough! You have made your point, and you have made it well." Here is a paragraph that makes exceptionally ample use of relevant examples:

A person's touch makes what the other senses take in more real to the memory. A *wood carving* appeals to the touch with deep grooves and parts that are rough as well as parts that are smooth. The fingers can interpret the richness of *brocade* and the rough warmth of wool. An ancient *book* becomes even older when one feels the fragile pages. A *puppy* tugging wildly at a leash feels like energy. *Winter* is felt in the hastily prepared snowball and the pine boughs that are brittle in the sharp air. A child must feel a *hot stove* before it becomes a thing to avoid touching, and words become meaningful when he loses the skin from his tongue to the *cold metal pipe* he was warned about. The energy of the *sun* becomes more apparent when one focuses a magnifying glass on his fingers. A *baby chick* is something altogether new when one holds the cotton-like ball of feathers and feels its nervous heartbeat. An *oil painting* is only paint and canvas until one touches the swirls made by the artist's brush. A *rose* is only a flower until one holds it in his hands and pulls the petals from the intricate pattern. A human *voice* becomes more than sounds when one speaks with his fingers to his throat to feel the vibrations. The surface of a *rock* is only light and shadow until one feels its ridges and ripples. Touching helps one to see and hear more clearly.

(2) *Give priority to supporting detail by practicing the examples-first paragraph.* When you reverse the usual order from topic sentence to supporting detail, you force yourself to provide the relevant examples that in the end will add up to a well-earned generalization:

The shops of the border town are filled with many souvenirs, "pinatas," pottery, bullhorns, and "serapes," all made from cheap material and decorated in a gaudy manner which the tourist thinks is true Mexican folk art. Tourists are everywhere, haggling with the shopkeepers, eager to get something for nothing, carrying huge packages and boxes filled with the treasures bought at the many shops. Car horns blare at the people who are too entranced with the sights to watch where they are going. Raucous tunes pour from the nightclubs, open in broad daylight. Few children are seen in the town, but some boys swim in the Rio Grande and dive to retrieve the coins that tourists throw as they cross the bridge above. People come for a cheap thrill, a quick divorce, cheap liquor. *A border town is the tourist's Mexico, a gaudy caricature of the real country.*

Exercises

A. For each of the following paragraphs, formulate a topic sentence that would sum up the *central idea* implied in them. Compare your own topic sentences with those of your classmates.

1. I am sure that the Romans, whose lives were lived under stately porticoes and amid the pomp of great temples, found in that background an ever present dignity which must have followed them even into the poverty and confusions of the crowded, many-storied *insulae*. The wide forums and the glittering *thermae* did not arise merely from the vanity of emperors and the corruption of the people. These were the songs in which the Roman soul made itself known above the cries of the circus and the clash of civil swords. The Gothic cathedrals were, in part at least, prayers of thanksgiving for a joy discovered in the revival of cities, and the *piazze* into which Venice poured her compressed splendor are jubilant with that new enfranchisement. These are not each an ornament added to a city but summations of a city's spirit to which houses and streets, walls, canals, and the domes of public buildings are the harmonious counterparts. Florence, Padua, Cordoba; the Paris of Richelieu, the Philadelphia of Franklin: each of these might have been the work of a single architect so consistent is the ordinance and expression of their streets and structures. — Joseph Hudnut, *Architecture and the Spirit of Man*

2. During my month of vigil and research, I heard an able physiologist who has a radio program say, quite simply, "We do not use up all the food we take in." He wasn't allowed to get away with that piece of clarity, however. "Ah," cut in his announcer, for the benefit of those no longer able to understand simplicity, "the utilization factor!" I turned from this station to a droning psychologist, just in time to hear him say, "The female is sometimes the sexual aggressor." Here a familiar noun of mental illness and military invasion was clumsily at work beating in the skull of love with a verbal bung-starter. The sweetheart now often wears the fustian of the sick man and the Caesar. In the evening, I tuned in on one of the space-patrol programs that gleefully exude the great big blockyisms. "Your astrogation bank will tell you!" cried the captain of

a space ship to another interplanetary pilot, meaning his navigational instruments. In a fairy tale, an astrogation bank would be a "star panel," but the quality of fairy tale is nowhere to be found in these dime novels of the constellations. — James Thurber, "The Psychosemanticist Will See You Now, Mr. Thurber," *The New Yorker*

3. More books have been written about Napoleon than about any other human being. The fact is deeply and alarmingly significant. What must be the day-dreams of people for whom the world's most agile social climber and ablest bandit is the hero they most desire to hear about? Duces and Fuehrers will cease to plague the world only when the majority of its inhabitants regard such adventurers with the same disgust as they now bestow on swindlers and pimps. So long as men worship the Caesars and Napoleons, Caesars and Napoleons will duly rise and make them miserable. The proper attitude toward the "hero" is not Carlyle's, but Bacon's. "He doth like the ape," wrote Bacon of the ambitious tyrant, "he doth like the ape that, the higher he clymbes, the more he shewes his ars." The hero's qualities are brilliant; but so is the mandril's rump. When all concur in the great Lord Chancellor's judgment of Fuehrers, there will be no more Fuehrers to judge. Meanwhile we must content ourselves by putting merely legal and administrative obstacles in the way of the ambitious. They are a great deal better than nothing; but they can never be completely effective. — Aldous Huxley, *Ends and Means*

B. Write a one-paragraph theme describing a face, a dress, the façade of a building, an abstract painting, or a tree. Pack the paragraph with specific detail that all supports the *same dominant impression* or central point.

C. Formulate a limited generalization about youth, education, or campus life. Support it in a *multiple-example* paragraph that presents at least half a dozen clearly relevant examples.

D. Write an *examples-first* paragraph about a place; an actor or a public figure; a type of play, concert, or program. Make all your details help lead the reader up to the final point.

Diction

A good writer knows the power of words. He marvels at the resources of language and exploits them in his work. *He is aware of words as words.* The layman typically notices words only when something goes wrong:

Leprosy invaded Europe in the Middle Ages and was very *popular* among the poor.

From this *vintage* point we could signal to any cars that happened to drive into camp.

Contralto is a *low* form of music that only ladies sing.

In Platonic love, sexual relations are *illuminated.*

Though amused by verbal accidents such as these, the experienced writer studies words with a more positive interest. He knows that in order to study and write in any major field he has to learn its language: the terms for objects and ideas often discussed, for the standards applied, and for the procedures followed. He knows that a student of literature has to become familiar with terms like *monograph, didactic, elegiac,* and *allegory.* He knows that a student of cultural history cannot be content with merely a blurred notion of *metaphysics, asceticism, dogmatism,* or *anthropology.*

In order to use words with confidence, a good writer does more than look for a single basic meaning; he becomes aware of the *different uses* to which a word is put, and the *different effects* it may have on a reader. In its more technical use, *phenomenon* stands for *any* observable fact. But in more popular use, the word often stands for a *rare* or *outstanding* object of observation. *Critical* sometimes means "faultfinding"; but "critical thinking" is sharp and systematic, whether concerned with good points or bad. The effective writer knows how to use words in such a way that they carry the *intended* meaning and produce the *desired* effect.

The effective writer knows that words can work for him, but also *against* him. He knows when the words he uses do their job, but not well—like a knife used in eating peas. He is always looking for words that will help him say what he wants to say more clearly, more directly. He looks for words that are fresh and vigorous rather than stale and tired. Whether merely in odd moments or in systematic studies, he will concern himself frequently with vocabulary and diction; that is, with word resources and word choice.

D 1   College Dictionaries

To make the best possible use of your dictionary, familiarize yourself fully with how it provides information.

Authoritative college dictionaries provide information not only on the full range of meaning of a word but also on its history, implications, and possible limitations. The following dictionaries are widely recommended:

Webster's New World Dictionary (NWD) makes a special effort to explain the meanings of words simply and clearly, using "the simplest language consistent with accuracy and fullness." Historical information *precedes* current meanings, so that the reader is given a sense of how a word developed. Lists of idioms provide an excellent guide to how a word is used in characteristic phrases. Throughout, informal and slang uses of words are so labeled.

The *Standard College Dictionary* (SCD) was first published in 1963. Usually, the most *frequent* (rather than the oldest) meaning of a word appears first. Coverage of informal English and slang is excellent and up to date, with authoritative notes on debatable points of usage. Like the NWD, the *Standard College Dictionary* has valuable introductory materials on the history of English and on modern approaches to the study of language.

Webster's New Collegiate Dictionary, in its current seventh edition, is published by the G. & C. Merriam Company, whose collection of several million citation slips has been referred to as "the national archives of the language." The *Collegiate* is based on *Webster's Third New International Dictionary*, the most authoritative and comprehensive unabridged dictionary of current American English. Historical information precedes meanings, presented in the order of their development. The Merriam-Webster dictionaries have abandoned the practice of labeling words informal as too arbitrary or subjective. They make only sparing use of the label "slang." Unlike the NWD and the SCD, the *Collegiate* lists names of people and places in separate indexes at the end of the book.

The American College Dictionary (ACD) was comparable in coverage and quality to its major competitors and was distinguished for its intelligible definitions. In 1968, the same publisher brought out the college edition of the *Random House Dictionary*, a new work intermediate in coverage between *Webster's Third* and the desk dictionaries. Its college edition, like the SCD, aims especially at students who use the dictionary as a guide to the preferences of conservative teachers. Thus, both informal English and slang are marked; usage

Vocabulary Entry	**beau·ty** (byoo/tē), *n., pl.* **-ties** for 2–6. **1.** a quality that is present in a thing or person giving intense aesthetic pleasure or deep satisfaction to the senses or the mind. **2.** an attractive, well-formed girl or woman. **3.** a beautiful thing, as a work of art, building, etc. **4.** Often, **beauties.** that which is beautiful in nature or in some natural or artificial environment. **5.** a particular advantage: *One of the beauties of this medicine is the absence of aftereffects.* **6.** a person or thing that excels or is remarkable of its kind: *His black eye was a beauty.* [ME *be(a)ute* < OF *beaute*; r. ME *bealte* < OF, var. of *beltet* < VL **bellitāt-* (s. of **bellitās*) = L *bell(us)* fine + *-itāt- -ITY*] —**Syn. 1.** loveliness, pulchritude, comeliness, fairness, attractiveness. **2.** belle. —**Ant. 1.** ugliness.
Pronunciation	
Syllabication Dots	
Synonym Lists	

be·gin (bi gin/), *v.,* **be·gan, be·gun, be·gin·ning.** —*v.i.* **1.** to proceed to perform the first or earliest part of some action; commence or start. **2.** to come into existence; originate: *The custom began during the Civil War.* —*v.t.* **3.** to proceed to perform the first or earliest part of (some action): *Begin the job tomorrow.* **4.** to originate; be the originator of: *Civic leaders began the reform movement.* [ME *beginn(en)*, OE *beginnan* = *be-* BE- + *-ginnan* to begin, perh. orig. to open, akin to YAWN] —**be·gin/ner,** *n.*
—**Syn. 3.** BEGIN, COMMENCE, INITIATE, START (when followed by noun or gerund) refer to setting into motion or progress something that continues for some time. BEGIN is the common term: *to begin knitting a sweater.* COMMENCE is a more formal word, often suggesting a more prolonged or elaborate beginning: *to commence proceedings in court.* INITIATE implies an active and often ingenious first act in a new field: *to initiate a new procedure.* START means to make a first move or to set out on a course of action: *to start paving a street.* **4.** inaugurate, initiate. **—Ant. 1.** end.

bent¹ (bent), *adj.* **1.** curved or crooked: *a bent bow; a bent stick.* **2.** determined, set, or resolved (usually fol. by *on*): *to be bent on buying a new car.*

be·la·bor (bi lā/bər), *v.t.* **1.** to discuss, work at, or worry about for an unreasonable amount of time: *He kept belaboring the point long after we had agreed.* **2.** to scorn or ridicule persistently. **3.** *Archaic.* to beat vigorously. Also, *Brit.,* **be·la/bour.**

belles-let·tres (*Fr.* bel le/tr³), *n.pl.* literature regarded as a fine art, esp. as having a purely aesthetic function. [< F: lit., fine letters] —**bel·let·rist** (bel le/trist), *n.* —**bel·let·ris·tic** (bel/li tris/tik), *adj.* —**Syn.** See **literature.**

bene-, an element occurring in loan words from Latin where it meant "well": *benediction.* [comb. form of *bene* (adv.) well]
be·neath (bi nēth/, -nēth/), *adv.* ① below; in or to a lower place, position, state, or the like. ② underneath: *heaven above and the earth beneath.* —*prep.* ③ below; under: *beneath the same roof.* ④ further down than; underneath: lower in place than: *the first drawer beneath the top one.* ⑤ inferior in position, rank, power, etc.: *A captain is beneath a major.* ⑥ unworthy of; below the level or dignity of: *beneath contempt*

bet·ter¹ (bet/ər), *adj., compar. of* **good** *with* **best** *as* superl. **1.** of superior quality or excellence: *a better coat.* **2.** morally superior; more virtuous: *He's no better than a thief!* **3.** of superior value, use, fitness, desirability, acceptableness, etc.: *a better time for action.* **4.** larger; greater: *the better part of a lifetime.* **5.** improved in health; healthier: *Is your mother better?* —*adv., compar. of* **well** *with* **best** *as* superl. **6.** in a more excellent way or manner: *to behave better.* **7.** to a greater degree; more completely or thoroughly: *I probably know him better than anyone else.* **8.** more: *I walked better than a mile to town.* **9. better off,** a. in better circumstances. b. more fortunate; happier. **10. go (someone) one better,** to exceed another's effort; be superior to. **11. had better,** would be wiser or more reasonable to; ought to: *We had better stay indoors today.* **12. think better of,** to reconsider and decide more favorably or wisely: *She was tempted to make a sarcastic retort, but thought better of it.* —*v.t.* **13.** to make better; improve; increase the good qualities of. **14.** to improve upon; surpass; exceed: *We have bettered last year's production record.* **15. better oneself,** to improve one's social standing, financial position, or education. —*n.* **16.** that which has greater excellence: *the better of two choices.* **17.** Usually, **betters.** those superior to one in wisdom, social position, etc. **18. for the better,** in a way that is an improvement: *His health changed for the better.* **19. get the better of,** a. to get an advantage over. b. to prevail against. [ME *bettre,* OE *betera*; c. OHG *bezziro* (G *besser*), Goth *batiza* = *bat-* (akin to BOOT²) + *-iza* comp. suffix] —**Syn. 13.** amend; advance, promote. See **improve.**

Labels left column: Part of Speech and Inflected Forms; Etymology; Synonym Study; Antonym; Usage Note; Variant Spelling; Hyphenated Entry; Word Element; Consecutive Definition Numbers; Example Contexts; Idiomatic Phrases; Explanation of Dictionary Entries (From *Random House Dictionary*) notes "recognize the existence of long-established strictures." As in the SCD, the most frequently encountered meanings of a word come first.

In the wording of definitions, the major college dictionaries range from the everyday language of the NWD to the more technical and scholarly style of the NCD. Compare the first two meanings of *peach* in the following entries:

> **1.** a small tree with lance-shaped leaves, pink flowers, and round, juicy, orange-yellow fruit, with a fuzzy skin and a single, rough pit.   **2.** its fruit.

From *Webster's New World Dictionary*

> **1.** The drupaceous, edible fruit of a tree (*Prunus persica*) of the rose family, widely cultivated in many varieties.   **2.** The tree itself.

From *Standard College Dictionary*

> **1 a :** a low spreading freely branching Chinese tree (*Prunus persica*) of the rose family that is cosmopolitan in cultivation in temperate areas and has lanceolate leaves, sessile usu. pink flowers borne on the naked twigs in early spring, and a fruit which is a single-seeded drupe with a hard endocarp, a pulpy white or yellow mesocarp, and a thin downy epicarp   **b :** the edible fruit of the peach   **2 :** a variable color averaging a moderate yellowish pink

From *Webster's Seventh New Collegiate Dictionary*[1]

D 1a   Synonyms and Antonyms

A good dictionary discriminates between the exact meanings of closely related terms. Often, it indicates meaning by a **synonym,** a word that has nearly the same meaning as the word you are looking up. Thus, your dictionary may give "sad" or "mournful" as a synonym for *elegiac,* or "instructive" as a synonym for *didactic.* Often, your dictionary will explain a word by giving an **antonym,** a word of approximately opposite meaning. *Desultory,* for instance, is the opposite of "methodical"; *hackneyed* is the opposite of "fresh" or "original."

Synonyms are seldom simply interchangeable. Their areas of meaning overlap, but at the same time there are subtle differences. *Burn, char, scorch, sear,* and *singe* all refer to the results of exposure to extreme heat, but whether a piece of meat is charred or merely seared makes a difference to the person who has it for dinner.

[1] By permission. Copyright, 1963 by G. & C. Merriam Co., Publishers of the Merriam-Webster Dictionaries.

Here is how a dictionary discriminates between the synonyms of *pay:*

syn PAY, COMPENSATE, REMUNERATE, SATISFY, REIMBURSE, IN-
DEMNIFY, REPAY, RECOMPENSE, REQUITE mean to give money or its
equivalent in return for something. PAY implies the discharge of
an obligation incurred; COMPENSATE implies a making up for
services rendered or help given; REMUNERATE more clearly suggests
paying for services rendered and may extend to payment that is
generous or not contracted for; SATISFY implies paying a person
what is demanded or required by law; REIMBURSE implies a return of
money that has been expended for another's benefit; INDEMNIFY
implies making good a loss suffered through accident, disaster, war-
fare; REPAY stresses paying back an equivalent in kind or amount;
RECOMPENSE suggests due return in amends, friendly repayment,
or reward

From *Webster's Seventh New Collegiate Dictionary*[2]

D 1b   Denotation and Connotation

*A good dictionary pays attention to the associations of words
and to the attitudes they imply.* Many words **denote** — that is, point
out or refer to — very nearly the same objects or qualities. At the same
time, they **connote** — that is, suggest or imply — different attitudes
toward the objects or qualities they point out. *Cheap* and *inexpensive*
both mean relatively low in price or cost. However, we may call an
article "cheap" to suggest that we consider it shoddy or inferior; we
may call it "inexpensive" to suggest that we consider it a good bargain,
valuable in spite of its low price. *Unwise* and *foolish* both indicate a
lack of wisdom. However, calling a proposal "unwise" suggests a
certain amount of consideration or respect for the person who made it;
"foolish" suggests ridicule and contempt. Similarly, we may call a
boy of low intelligence a "slow learner" or a "dunce," a new history
of the United States "ambitious" or "pretentious."

Here is how a dictionary discriminates between the connotations of synonyms of *plan:*

SYN.—**plan** refers to any detailed method, formulated beforehand, for doing or making something (vacation *plans*); **design**
stresses the final outcome of a plan and implies the use of skill
or craft, sometimes in an unfavorable sense, in executing or
arranging this (it was his *design* to separate us); **project** implies the use of enterprise or imagination in formulating an ambitious or extensive plan (they've begun work on the housing
project); **scheme,** a less definite term than the preceding, often
connotes either an impractical, visionary plan or an underhand
intrigue (a *scheme* to embezzle the funds).

From *Webster's New World Dictionary*

(On the use of connotative words in persuasion, see Chapter
Seven, pp. 234–236.)

D 1c   Context

Often a dictionary supplies phrases suggesting the kind of context where a given meaning is appropriate. The **context** of a word may be another word ("square meal"), a whole sentence or paragraph ("Square your precepts with your practice"), a whole article or book (a treatment of squares in a book on plane geometry), or a situation (a policeman directing a pedestrian to a square).

Here is an entry showing a word used in different contexts:

> **apt** (apt), *adj.* **1.** inclined; disposed; given; prone: *too apt to slander others.* **2.** likely: *Am I apt to find him at home?* **3.** unusually intelligent; quick to learn: *an apt pupil.* **4.** suited to the purpose or occasion: *an apt metaphor.*

From *The Random House Dictionary*

In an unfamiliar context, familiar words may have a new or different meaning. For instance, an author praising modesty and thrift may describe them as "homely virtues." Looking up the word, you will find that its original meaning, as you might expect, is "associated with the home." Favorable associations of domestic life account for such meanings as "simple," "unpretentious," "intimate"; unfavorable associations account for such meanings as "crude," "unpolished," "ugly." An eighteenth-century writer may talk about the "wit" of a person who does not seem at all "witty" in the sense of cleverly humorous or ironic. *Wit* in this context means general intellectual and imaginative capacity, as in phrases like "half-wit" and "at one's wit's end."

NOTE: Even when the denotation of a word remains fairly stable, its connotations may vary in different contexts. *Academic* basically means "associated with higher learning." "Academic standards," then, may mean standards of responsible and competent scholarship. An "academic argument," on the other hand, may mean an argument that is unrealistic or impractical because, like higher learning, it is removed from the hustle and bustle of economic and political reality.

D 1d   Grammatical Labels

A good dictionary gives reliable information about the functions a word can serve in a sentence. For instance, *human* is usually labeled both as an **adjective** (adj.) and as a **noun** (n.), with some indication that the latter use ("a human" rather than "a human being") is not generally accepted as appropriate to written English. *Annoy* is labeled a

transitive verb (v.t.); it is incomplete without an object. In other words, we usually annoy somebody or something; we don't just annoy. *Set* also is usually transitive ("*set* the bowl on the table"), but it is labeled **intransitive** (v.i.) when applied to one of the celestial bodies. In other words, the sun doesn't set anybody or anything; it just sets.

D 1e   Idiom

A good dictionary lists idiomatic phrases whose meanings may be more than the sum of their parts. A word often combines with other words in an expression that becomes the habitual way of conveying a certain idea. Such expressions are called **idioms.**

To write idiomatic English, you have to develop an ear for individual phrases and ways of saying things. For instance, we *do* a certain type of work, *hold* a job or position, *follow* a trade, *pursue* an occupation, and *engage in* a line of business. We *replace* an original *with* a copy, but we *substitute* a copy *for* the original. Here is an exceptionally full list of idiomatic phrases using the word *mind:*

bear in mind, to remember.
be in one's right mind, to be mentally well; be sane.
be of one mind, to have the same opinion; agree.
be of two minds, to be undecided or irresolute.
be out of one's mind, 1. to be mentally ill; be insane. 2. to be frantic (*with* worry, grief, etc.).
call to mind, 1. to remember. 2. to be a reminder of.
change one's mind, 1. to change one's opinion. 2. to change one's intention, purpose, or wish.
give a person a piece of one's mind, to tell a person plainly one's disapproval of him; rebuke; scold.
have a (good or great) mind to, to feel (strongly) inclined or disposed to.
have half a mind to, to be somewhat inclined or disposed to.
have in mind, 1. to remember. 2. to think of. 3. to intend; purpose.
keep in mind, to remember.
keep one's mind on, to pay attention to.
know one's mind, to know one's real thoughts, feelings, desires, or intentions.
make up one's mind, to form a definite opinion or decision; resolve.
meeting of minds, an agreement.
never mind, don't concern yourself; it doesn't matter.
on one's mind, 1. occupying one's thoughts. 2. worrying one.
pass out of mind, to be forgotten.
put in mind, to remind.
set one's mind on, to be determined on or determinedly desirous of.
speak one's mind, to say plainly what one thinks. ⁱ
take one's mind off, to stop one from thinking about; turn one's attention from.
to one's mind, in one's opinion.

From *Webster's New World Dictionary*

A special problem for inexperienced writers is the idiomatic use of **prepositions**. The following list reviews idiomatic uses of some common prepositions:

abide *by* (a decision)
abstain *from* (voting)
accuse *of* (a crime)
acquiesce *in* (an injustice)
adhere *to* (a promise)
admit *of* (conflicting interpretations)
agree *with* (a person), *to* (a proposal), *on* (a course of action)
alarmed *at* (the news)
apologize *for* (a mistake)
aspire *to* (distinction)
assent *to* (a proposal)
attend *to* (one's business)
avail oneself *of* (an opportunity)
capable *of* (an action)
charge *with* (an offense)
collide *with* (a car)
compatible *with* (recognized standards)
comply *with* (a request)
concur *with* (someone), *in* (an opinion)
confide *in* or *to* (someone)
conform *to* (specifications)
deficient *in* (strength)
delight *in* (mischief)
deprive *of* (a privilege)
derived *from* (a source)
die *of* or *from* (a disease)
disappointed *in* (someone's performance)
dissent *from* (a majority opinion)
dissuade *from* (doing something foolish)
divest *of* (responsibility)
find fault *with* (a course)

identical *with* (something looked for)
ignorant *of* (a fact)
inconsistent *with* (sound procedure)
independent *of* (outside help)
indifferent *to* (praise or blame)
infer *from* (evidence)
inferior *to* (a rival product)
insist *on* (accuracy)
interfere *with* (a performance), *in* (someone else's affairs)
jealous *of* (others)
long *for* (recognition)
object *to* (a proposal)
oblivious *of* (warnings)
part *with* (possessions)
partial *to* (flattery)
participate *in* (activities)
persevere *in* (a task)
pertain *to* (a subject)
preferable *to* (an alternative)
prevail *on* (someone to do something)
prevent someone *from* (an action)
refrain *from* (wrongdoing)
rejoice *at* (good news)
required *of* (all members)
resolve *on* (a course of action)
rich *in* (resources)
short *of* (cash)
secede *from* (the Union)
succeed *in* (an attempt)
superior *to* (an alternative)
threaten *with* (legal action)
wait *for* (developments), *on* (a guest)

NOTE: College dictionaries vary in their coverage of idioms. Only an unabridged dictionary giving one or more sample quotations for each possible use of a word can come close to being a complete guide to idiomatic usage.

Exercises

A. Compare *three* of the major college dictionaries by investigating the following:

1. Read the definitions of *dada, kitsch,* and *gobbledygook.* Are they clear and informative?

2. Study the order of meanings for *coy, nice, operate.* How does the order differ, and why?

3. Compare the treatment of synonyms (if any) for *dogmatic, prompt,* and *train* (v.).

4. What and where are you told about Dreyfus, Prometheus, Niels Bohr?

5. How does the dictionary deal with *Aryan, dago, nigger?*

B. Look up the following entries in your dictionary: *apothegm, denouement, farce, flying buttress, hauberk, limerick, machete, solecism, symbiosis, syncopation.* What special fields of interest do they represent? How clear and adequate are the definitions?

C. Explain to what extent the synonyms in each of the following groups overlap and how they differ: *agreement—contract— covenant; amateur—dilettante—tyro; apology—excuse—pretext; bearing—behavior—conduct; betray—divulge—reveal; common—ordinary—familiar; correct—discipline—punish; decline—reject—spurn; destiny—doom—lot; dogmatic—doctrinaire—arbitrary; enterprise—project—venture; fad—fashion—vogue; fantastic—imaginary—visionary; flippant—glib—impertinent; mumble—murmur—mutter.*

D. Explain the differences in connotation between the words in each of the following pairs: *clever—intelligent; famous—notorious; gaze—ogle; godsend—windfall; juvenile—youngster; lucre—wealth; obedient—obsequious; obstinate—persistent; petty—punctilious; populace—population; regret—remorse; revenge—retribution; revolt—revolution; slender—thin; teenager—adolescent.*

E. How does your dictionary distinguish among the changing meanings of each of the following words? Show how context determines your choice of the meaning appropriate in each phrase.

Bay leaves, at *bay, bayed* at the moon, *bay* window, bomb *bay,* a breeze from the *bay*

head of lettuce, *head* the procession, a *head* of steam, *heads* or tails, over the listeners' *heads,* went to his *head, heads* of government, *head* off complaints, not have a *head* for figures *let* blood, without *let* or hindrance, *let* go, *let* me see it, *let* us ignore him, rooms to *let*

car of recent *make, make* the beds, *make* money, *make* excuses, *makes* my blood boil, *make* a speech, *makes* easy reading, *made* him a sergeant

repair a car, *repaired* to the meeting, in good *repair, repair* the damage

straight to the point, *straight* alcohol, *straight* party line, the comedian's *straight* man, *straight* hair, thinking *straight*

a *tender* smile, *tender* an apology, legal *tender*

F. Each of the italicized words in the following expressions is a familiar word used in an unfamiliar sense. Find the meaning that fits the context.

To write an *abstract* of a speech; an *academic* painting; to write an *apostrophe* to the gods; an *arresting* performance; a monster of fearful *aspect;* to give someone a *civil* answer; an anti*clerical* political party; to give *countenance* to a crime; to wear a characteristic *habit;* to receive *intelligence;* to *justify* a line of type; to cultivate *polite* learning; to make a character stand out in full *relief;* to lie in *state;* to be *transported* with gratitude.

G. Check your answers to the following questions by consulting your dictionary: **1.** Is *incompetent* used as a noun? **2.** Which of the following words are used as verbs: *admonition, loan, lord, magistrate, minister, sacrilege, spirit, war?* **3.** Is "superior than" idiomatic English? **4.** Is *smooth* used as an adverb? **5.** Is *entertain* used as an intransitive verb? **6.** Is *very* used as an adjective? **7.** What idiomatic preposition goes with *glory* used as a verb? **8.** Do we always censure somebody or something, or can we just censure, period? **9.** How many different grammatical categories can *ill* belong to? **10.** Are "angry with," "angry at," and "angry about" interchangeable? **11.** Is *animate* used as an adjective? **12.** Is *predominate* used as an adjective?

H. Point out and correct unidiomatic use of prepositions:

1. To seek a good grade at someone else's expense would be a violation to our standards of conduct. **2.** During the past fifty years, deaths caused by highway accidents have been more numerous than those incurred from two world wars and the war in Korea. **3.** Plans for cost reduction have been put to action by different agencies of the federal government. **4.** Several families volunteered to take care for the children of flood victims. **5.** Only the prompt help of the neighbors prevented the fire of becoming a major disaster. **6.** During the first years of marriage we had to deprive ourselves from many things that other people take for granted. **7.** The arrival of the ship to its destination caused general rejoicing. **8.** Though I support Mr. Finchley's candidacy, I take exception with some of his statements. **9.** We

Americans do not hesitate in waving our flag if the occasion arises. **10.** The people of this country naturally shun at the thought of having any kind of censorship imposed upon their newspapers. **11.** As an instrument of the popular will, the senate suffers from defects inherent to its constitution. **12.** A businessman cannot succeed unless he takes heed to the preferences of his customers.

I. Study the general scheme, the introductory material, and several sample entries of *one* of the following specialized dictionaries. Report your findings.

> *Bartlett's Familiar Quotations;* Sir William A. Craigie and James R. Hulbert, *A Dictionary of American English on Historical Principles;* H. W. Horwill, *A Dictionary of Modern American Usage;* John S. Kenyon and Thomas A. Knott, *A Pronouncing Dictionary of American English;* Mitford M. Mathews, *A Dictionary of Americanisms;* Eric Partridge, *A Dictionary of Slang and Unconventional English;* Roget's *Thesaurus of English Words and Phrases.*

D 2   Word History

Knowledge of the history of a word helps a writer understand its uses, meanings, and associations.

After giving the spelling, pronunciation, and grammatical category of a word, college dictionaries often summarize its **etymology**; that is, they briefly trace its origin and history. The following sample entry relates the word *lock* to corresponding words in earlier English (ME. = Middle English; AS. = Anglo-Saxon or Old English), in other Germanic languages (G. = German; ON. = Old Norse or Early Scandinavian), and in the hypothetical common parent language of most European languages (IE. = Indo-European):

> **lock** (lok), *n.* [ME. *lokke;* AS. *loc,* a bolt, bar, enclosure, prison; akin to G. *loch,* a hole, ON. *lok,* a lid; prob. IE. base **leug-,* to bend, seen also in AS. *lucan,* to close (cf. LEEK)],

From *Webster's New World Dictionary*

In addition to tracing words to other languages, the etymologist is concerned with **semantic change** — that is, gradual changes in meaning. The most complete record of such changes is the unabridged *New English Dictionary on Historical Principles*, reissued in 1933 as the *Oxford English Dictionary* (OED). This monumental reference work gives the earliest date a word occurs and then provides quotations tracing its development down through the centuries.

The most extensive changes in vocabulary come about through contacts between different cultures. Armed conquest, colonial expansion, international trade, and cultural influences all make possible the absorption of words from other languages. Roughly three fourths of the words in your dictionary were absorbed into English from foreign sources. When the Anglo-Saxon tribes came to England from continental Europe during the period between 450 and 600 A.D., they spoke Germanic dialects, closely related in both grammar and vocabulary to the dialects from which modern Dutch and German are derived. The American tourist coming to Germany can still easily recognize the German equivalents of *arm, drink, father, fish, hand,* or *house.* However, the basic Germanic vocabulary of **Anglo-Saxon** or **Old English** was enriched and modified by an almost continuous absorption of words from other languages throughout early English history.

D 2a   Latin and Greek

The most persistent influences on the English vocabulary were Latin and Greek, the languages of classical antiquity. Latin had been the language of the Roman empire. It became the official language of the Roman Catholic Church, which established itself in England in the seventh century and remained the supreme spiritual authority until the sixteenth century. English early absorbed Latin words related to the Scriptures and to the doctrines and ritual of the church, such as *altar, candle, chalice, mass, palm, pope, shrine, relic,* and *rule.* Other early borrowings were related to church administration, to the everyday life of monks and clergymen, and to the exclusively church-controlled and church-conducted medieval system of education. Many have long since lost all suggestion of foreignness: *beet, cap, circle, cook, fever, lobster, mat, pear, school, silk, sock,* or *turn.*

Greek was the language of the literature, philosophy, and science of ancient Hellenic culture, flourishing both in Greece proper and in other parts of the Mediterranean world. Either in the original Greek or in Latin translation, this body of knowledge exercised a continuous influence on Christianity and Western civilization during the Middle Ages and Renaissance. Modern philosophical, scientific, and technological terminology draws heavily on Latin and Greek roots. More generally, the language of educated people is saturated with words that are in one way or another derived from one of the classical languages. Examples of words absorbed either directly from Greek or from Greek through Latin are *anonymous, atmosphere, catastrophe, chaos, climax, crisis, enthusiasm,* and *skeleton.* Examples of words absorbed from Latin are *contempt, gesture, history, incredible, index, individual, intellect, legal, mechanical, picture,* and *rational.*

(1) *Latin and Greek Roots.* Knowledge of a common Latin or Greek root often provides the key to a puzzling word. For instance, the Greek root *phys-* usually refers to the body or to material things, whereas the Greek root *psych-* usually refers to the mind or the soul. This distinction explains *physician* (heals the body) and *psychiatrist* (heals the mind), *physiology* (study of bodily functions) and *psychology* (study of mental functions), *physical* (characteristic of material reality) and *psychic* (going beyond material reality).

Here is a brief list of common Latin and Greek roots. Explain how each root is used in the sample words given for it:

auto-	*self*	autocratic, automatic, automobile, autonomy
capit-	*head*	capital, decapitate, per capita
carn-	*flesh*	carnal, carnivorous, incarnation, carnival
chron-	*time*	anachronistic, chronometer, synchronize
culp-	*fault*	culpable, culprit, exculpate
doc-	*teach*	docile, doctor, doctrine, indoctrinate
graph-	*write*	autograph, graphic, geography, orthography
hydr-	*water*	dehydrate, hydrant, hydraulic, hydrogen
jur-	*swear*	conjure, juror, perjury
man-	*hand*	manacle, manicure, manual, manufacture
phon-	*sound*	euphony, phonetics, phonograph, symphony
terr-	*land*	inter, terrestrial, subterranean
urb-	*city*	suburb, urban, urbane
verb-	*word*	proverb, verbal, verbiage, verbose
vit-	*life*	vitality, vitamin
vol-	*wish*	volition, voluntary, volunteer

(2) *Common Prefixes and Suffixes.* Especially useful is a knowledge of the most common Latin and Greek **prefixes** and **suffixes**— that is, syllables attached at the beginning or at the end of a word to modify its meaning. A common prefix like *sub-*, meaning "below" or "beneath," helps to explain not only *sub-standard* and *subconscious* but *submarine* (below the sea), *sub-lunar* (below the moon—that is, on earth; characteristic of existence on this earth), *subterranean* (beneath the surface, underground). The suffix *-cide* means "killer" or "killing" in *homicide* (of a human being), *suicide* (of oneself), *fratricide* (of a brother), *parricide* (of a parent), and *insecticide* (of insects).

Here is a brief list of Latin and Greek prefixes:

bene-	*good*	benediction, benefactor, benefit, benevolent
bi-	*two*	bicycle, bilateral, bisect
contra-	*against*	contraband, contradict, contravene
ex-	*out, out of*	exclude, exhale, expel
extra-	*outside*	extraordinary, extravagant, extrovert
omni-	*all*	omnipotent, omnipresent, omniscient
per-	*through*	percolate, perforate, permeate
pre-	*before*	preamble, precedent, prefix
poly-	*many*	polygamy, polysyllabic, polytheistic
re-	*back*	recall, recede, revoke, retract
tele-	*distant*	telegraph, telepathy, telephone, television
trans-	*across, beyond*	transatlantic, transmit, transaction, transcend

D 2b   French Borrowings

Over the centuries, thousands of words were absorbed into English from French. The historical event that most drastically influenced the development of the language was the conquest of England by the French-speaking Normans in the years following 1066. At the beginning of the so-called **Middle English** period, about 1150, the Norman conquerors owned most of the land and controlled the most important offices in state and church. The language of law, administration, and literature was French. When the native English of the conquered people gradually reestablished itself as the language of political and social life, thousands of French words were retained. Many of these words were associated with the political and military role of the aristocratic Norman overlords: *castle, court, glory, mansion, noble, prince, prison, privilege, servant, treason, treasure, war.* But hundreds of other words absorbed into Middle English were everyday words like *avoid, branch, chair, demand, desire, disease, envy, praise, table, uncle.*

NOTE: Many French words passed into English through the hands of English poets who found them in medieval French poetry and romance, both Norman and continental. Some of these words are still used mainly in imaginative literature and preserve a poetic and often old-fashioned flavor. Such words are *chevalier* for "knight," *damsel* for "girl," *fealty* for "loyalty," *paramour* for "sweetheart," *prowess* for "valor," *puissance* for "power" or "strength," *travail* for "toil."

D 2c   Recently Borrowed Words

A *number of foreign languages have influenced the vocabulary of special fields of interest.* Since the consolidation of **Modern English** (about 1500), numerous words have come into English from French, Italian, Spanish, and various other sources. The leadership of seventeenth- and eighteenth-century France in elegant living, artistic style, and military organization is reflected in words like *apartment, ballet, battalion, cadet, caress, corps, façade, infantry, negligee, patrol.* Italy, which saw the origin of modern opera and symphonic music, provided terms like *cantata, concert, falsetto, sonata, solo, soprano, violin.* From Spain, which pioneered in the discovery and exploitation of new continents, came words like *alligator, banana, cannibal, cocoa, mosquito, Negro, potato, tobacco, tomato,* some of them absorbed into Spanish from New World sources.

Modern English has a number of foreign words in different stages of assimilation. If they are still felt to be foreign rather than English, your dictionary puts a special symbol in front of them or labels them "French," "Italian," or whatever is appropriate. A writer may use an occasional foreign word because it sums up the particular flavor of a thing or of an idea more aptly than any possible native equivalent. For instance, the French word *esprit* describes a kind of irreverent and brilliant wit for which it is hard to find an English name. Do not use such foreign phrases merely in order to impress your reader.

Exercises

A. Find the original meaning of each of the following words: *Attenuate, circumlocution, cornucopia, egregious, metaphysics, philosophy, premise, protract, recalcitrant, translucent.* How does the original meaning help explain the current use of each word?

B. Investigate the history of the following words: *bedlam, bowdlerize, bowie knife, carnival, credit, curfew, dollar, emperor, fellow, gerrymander, glamour, gossip, hallmark, Halloween, jeep, kerchief, lynch, picayune, propaganda, thug.*

C. Select one of the following words: *boor, cattle, fee, husband, hussy, knave, lewd, meat, villain, virtue.* Report fully on the contrast in nature and extent of its treatment in your own dictionary and in the *Oxford English Dictionary.*

D. Explain the meaning of the common element in each of the following groups of words: *anarchy — monarchy — oligarchy; anthropology — misanthrope — philanthropy; antibiotic — biography — biology; audio-visual — audition — inaudible; biennial — centennial — perennial; centipede — century — percent; cosmic — cosmopolitan — microcosm; describe — prescribe — proscribe; effrontery — frontispiece — confrontation; eugenics — eulogy — euphonious; heterogeneous — homogeneous; insect — intersection — section; magnify — magnificent — magnitude; portable — portage — transport; precedent — procedure — secede.*

E. Indicate the basic meaning of each Latin and Greek prefix used in the following words: *anesthetic, ambivalent, antedate, antipathy, circumvent, concord, disunity, hypersensitive, international, introvert, malpractice, multimillionaire, neofascist, postgraduate, prelude, pseudo-scientific, retroactive, semitropical, synchronize, ultramodern, unilateral.*

F. Find out from which languages the following words were derived: *bandana, boomerang, brunette, caviar, chocolate, crescendo, cynic, focus, hurricane, Mumbo Jumbo, pretzel, pundit, skin, snoop, vaudeville.*

G. What are the meanings of the following expressions? How many of them does your dictionary consider foreign rather than English? *Ad hoc, aficionado, auto-da-fe, blitz, corpus delicti, coup de grâce, cum laude, de jure, enfant terrible, ersatz, eureka, fait accompli, hara-kiri, hoi polloi, laissez faire, non sequitur, pax Romana, quod erat demonstrandum, tour de force, Zeitgeist.*

D 3   Varieties of Usage

Some words are appropriate only to certain situations or limited to specific uses.

No matter what dictionary you buy, you should study the introductory notes and find out the significance of the various symbols and abbreviations used. The most important abbreviations are the **restrictive labels**. They indicate that a word is used only under certain circumstances and that it can be out of place when used without attention to its limitations. In the following dictionary entry, six of the nine principal meanings of *brass* are preceded by restrictive labels:

brass (bras, bräs), *n.* **1.** any of various metal alloys consisting mainly of copper and zinc. **2.** an article made of such an alloy. **3.** *Mach.* a partial lining of soft metal for a bearing. **4.** *Music.* **a.** an instrument of the trumpet or horn family. **b.** such instruments collectively. **5.** *Brit.* **a.** a memorial tablet or plaque incised with an effigy, coat of arms, or the like. **b.** *Slang.* money. **6.** *Furniture.* any piece of ornamental or functional hardware. **7.** *U.S. Slang.* **a.** high-ranking military officers. **b.** any very important officials. **8.** *Informal.* excessive assurance; impudence; effrontery. —*adj.* **9.** of or pertaining to brass. [ME *bras*, OE *bræs*; c. OFris *bres* copper. MLG *bras* metal] —**brass′ish,** *adj.*

— Subject Label

— Geographic Label

— Usage Label

From *Random House Dictionary*

Usage labels can help you develop your sense of what words are generally acceptable in written English. They provide a guide when roughly synonymous choices have different associations. One choice may suggest the nonstandard folk speech of factory and barracks ("nohow"); the other may suggest the standard English of school and office ("not at all"). One choice may suggest an informal variety of standard English ("gimmick"); the other may suggest a formal variety ("device"). College dictionaries differ sharply in their use of restrictive labels to indicate varieties of usage. Compare the practice followed in your own dictionary with the description of usage labels in the following section.

D 3a   Nonstandard Words

Some words suggest nonstandard speech rather than educated usage. Many words are appropriate to almost any occasion. A hand can be appropriately called a "hand" at any time and at any place. Other words are limited in their usefulness because of the associations they suggest. For instance, words like *anywheres* and *nohow* are either not listed in your dictionary at all or labeled illiterate, **nonstandard**, or vulgate. Like nonstandard grammatical patterns, they are often associated with low social standing or a lack of formal education. (See **G 1a**.)

D 3b   Informal Words

Some words suggest informal conversation rather than systematic exposition or argument. Some dictionaries label such words **colloquial**. The word does *not* mean "local" but "characteristic of informal speech." People use colloquial language when at ease and with their friends; as a result, it tends to sound relaxed and folksy. But the man who is most comfortable in a robe and slippers puts on a tie and a business suit when going to the office on Monday morning. Similarly, a writer has to be able to use formal language in formal situations. In particular, he has to guard against sudden shifts from the tone of the lecture hall to that of the snack bar around the corner.

Informal	Formal	Informal	Formal
boss	superior	kid	child
brainy	intelligent	mean	ill-natured
bug	germ	skimpy	meager
faze	disconcert	sloppy	untidy
flunk	fail	snoop	pry
folks	relatives	snooze	nap
hunch	premonition	splurge	spend lavishly
job	position	stump	baffle

Other familiar words are generally acceptable in one sense but colloquial in another. Colloquial are *alibi* in the sense of "excuse," *aggravate* in the sense of "annoy," *funny* in the sense of "strange," and *mad* in the sense of "angry."

Informal language uses qualifiers like *kind of* hard, *sort of* easy, *a lot, lots;* abbreviated forms like *ad, bike, exam, gym, phone.* It uses many **phrasal verbs**, verbs that combine a short basic verb with one or more prepositions: *check up on, chip in, come up with, cut out* (noise), *get across* (a point), *take in* (a show), *take up with* (a person). Informal English usually contains a liberal sprinkling of catch-all words like *nice, cute, awful, wonderful,* or *terrible.* It is fond of **figurative expressions** like *have a ball, polish the apple, shoot the breeze, hit the road.*

Used with discretion, colloquial expressions can set a casual, leisurely tone:

There was a broad streak of mischief in Mencken. He was forever *cooking up* imaginary organizations, having *fake* handbills printed, inventing exercises in pure nonsense. —Philip M. Wagner, "Mencken Remembered," *The American Scholar*

To reject the book because of the immaturity of the author and the *bugs* in the logic is to throw away a bottle of good wine because it contains bits of the cork. — E. B. White, "A Slight Sound at Evening," *Yale Review*

But more often, colloquialisms suggest a put-on folksiness, the public-relations heartiness of some advertisers and some political candidates (Uncle Sam from a billboard: "My folks mostly drive Ford V-8s"). Many college teachers require the student to keep expository writing free from a colloquial tinge.

D 3c   Slang

Slang is appropriate only in the most informal kinds of writing or when deliberately used for special effects. No one can fix the exact point at which informal language shades over into slang, but generally the latter is more drastic in its disregard for what makes language formal and dignified. Slang has typically adolescent qualities: a disregard for convention, a lack of restraint, a tendency to regard people and accepted social attitudes with condescension or contempt. Much slang is merely faddish: New slang expressions are born overnight, repeated over and over, and then forgotten. Different high schools, colleges, and professions develop their own special varieties of slang, which change from year to year. As a result, much slang is unintelligible to outsiders.

Slang often has a vigor missing in more pedestrian diction. The figurative expressions it substitutes for less imaginative formal terms are often apt: *blow-hard, gumshoe, highbrow, rubberneck, sawbones, whirlybird.* Often a striking slang expression has no very satisfactory formal equivalent: *eyewash, runaround, stuffed shirt.* Many slang terms appeal to the user's love of the grotesque: *beat one's brains out, blow one's top, chew the fat, fly off the handle, hit the ceiling, kick the bucket, lay an egg.*

Slang is the major resource of many a humorous writer:

> Despite that great wellspring of love and pity I have for the afflicted and the misbegotten, and those who have been *just plain took,* I find it hard to get worked up over the plight of those *gaffers* who play golf on the city's links. Little boys lurk in the brush, and when one of the superbly conditioned athletes knocks a *nifty* their way, they keep the ball. Then, if things haven't changed since my day, they sell the balls to other superbly conditioned athletes, who then *scream like banshees* when the golf-ball connoisseurs *steal 'em* again. Since grabbing the little thieves by the scruff of their necks and *beating the bejabbers out of them* would obviously be in violation of their civil rights, we must look elsewhere for a solution.

Unfortunately, the humor in slang tends to be crude. Calling a person "fatso" or "skinny" or "bonehead" may be funny, but it also suggests a lack of tact or respect. The extravagant and contemptuous elements in slang make many readers interpret all slang expressions as signs of bad taste and bad manners.

D 3d   Fancy Words

When writing formal English, avoid words that are pompous, affected, or stilted. Students whose writing has been criticized as slangy or colloquial sometimes have difficulty finding middle ground. Trying to avoid excessive informality, they may go to the opposite extreme.

Stilted: I sincerely believe that the government should *divulge* more on the subject of socialism and its *cohorts,* because its *impetus* has reached a frightening *momentum.*

Do not imitate writers who habitually prefer the fancy word to the plain word, the elegant flourish to the blunt phrase. Dictionaries do not usually distinguish between plain and fancy words. Some of the latter may carry the label *poetic* or *literary,* indicating that they are most appropriate in poetry, in fiction, in imaginative description.

Here is a brief list of words that can make your writing seem affected (see also D 6b):

Fancy	Plain	Fancy	Plain
adumbrate	hint	nuptials	wedding
ameliorate	improve	obsequies	funeral
asseverate	assert	pachyderm	elephant
astound	amaze	potentate	ruler
betrothal	engagement	presage	predict
commence	begin	pulchritude	beauty
concomitant	result	purchase	buy
demise	death	quaff	drink
diurnal	daily	residence	home
emolument	pay, reward	tome	volume
eschew	avoid	vernal	springlike
gelid	cold	vista	view

NOTE: Whether a word sounds natural or affected depends on its use. A word appropriate in a stylized social note may sound artificial in a personal letter. Contemporary expository prose, on the whole, avoids both "fine writing" and the strained joviality of a deliberately colloquial style in favor of simple, unpretentious language.

Exercises

A. Which of the following expressions would you expect to carry *restrictive labels*? Check your answers with the help of your dictionary. *Bookworm, Chinaman, go Dutch, grease monkey, guttersnipe, guzzle, hubbub, highfalutin, jalopy, mob, moniker, mooch, moonshiner, persnickety, rake-off, ritzy, schoolmarm, shyster, victuals, walkie-talkie, windbag, wallop, Yankee.*

B. Check the standing of the following *abbreviations*. Which does your dictionary list without a restrictive label? *Ad-lib, auto, bus* (for "omnibus"), *doc, econ, IQ, lab, math, photo, plane* (for "airplane"), *prof, snafu, TV, ump* (for "umpire"), *VIP.*

C. Arrange the expressions in each group in order *from the most formal to the most informal.* Be prepared to defend your decisions. (Your instructor may ask you to check your own judgments against those of your dictionary.)

1. live it up, live on little, live up to a promise

2. dress up for a party, dress down an offender, dress a wound

3. dream up a scheme, a cherished dream, dreamboat

4. tear up the bill, tear into someone, that tears it

5. hook up the microphone, got him off the hook, did it on his own hook

6. crack a book, his voice cracked, crack down on crime

7. have a go at it, go through with it, go for blondes

8. skip town, skip a grade, children skipping down the path

9. deal cards, make a deal, big deal!

10. sweat shirt, sweat out a decision, no sweat

D. Point out *colloquialisms and slang expressions* and comment on their appropriateness. If your instructor desires, rewrite the sentences, avoiding all expressions that are not appropriate to formal written English.

> **1**. Uncle Amos was a spendthrift in his youth, but he changed after he married a penny-wise wife.   **2**. My family was on the move all through my early childhood, but we finally located in the state of New York.   **3**. Psychologists have discovered that many young people get a kick out of cutting up in front of a group.   **4**. Our unlimited material resources will avail us nothing unless we keep alive the gumption that comes down to us from colonial farmers.   **5**. When the refugees were told that the train was going to leave in ten minutes, there was a mad rush to the station.   **6**. Parents only confuse a child by bawling him out every time he commits a minor mistake.   **7**. I prefer being blown to pieces by an atomic bomb to being brained with a club.   **8**. Sent to size up our new allies, he found most of them in good shape.   **9**. The concert was scheduled to start at eight o'clock, but unfortunately the soloist did not show up.   **10**. Guests who crash a party must not be surprised if the host gives them a cold shoulder.   **11**. In view of the late hour, we decided we better shove off and get some shuteye.   **12**. My education was rather lopsided; it never came to grips with the problems that really interested me.   **13**. It is too bad that we should run out of gas only a couple of miles from home.   **14**. When Lovelace fails to suggest a definite date for the wedding, Clarissa begins to suspect that he is only pulling her leg.   **15**. Modern medicine has found ways of licking many dread diseases.

E. Observe the language used by your fellow students, friends, or acquaintances to find *six current slang expressions* not listed in your dictionary. Define them, explain their use, and indicate what, if anything, they reveal about the speaker's attitude.

F. Study the writing of a *columnist* who makes frequent use of colloquialisms or of slang. Examine and describe his attitude toward his material and toward his readers.

G. Compare the use of usage labels for the following words in *three college dictionaries: batty, corny, fuddy-duddy, gimmick, gyp, shoo-in, snazzy, splendiferous, swap, yak.*

H. Study the treatment of usage in *three* of the following specialized dictionaries: H. W. Fowler, *A Dictionary of Modern English Usage* (or one of its modern adaptations); Bergen Evans and Cornelia Evans, *A Dictionary of Contemporary American Usage;* Margaret M. Bryant, ed., *Current American Usage;* Wilson Follett, *Modern American Usage;* Lester V. Berrey and Melvin Van Den Bark, *American Thesaurus of Slang;* H. Wentworth and S. B. Flexner, *Dictionary of American Slang.* For fruitful comparison, select several expressions treated in at least two of the books you have chosen.

D 4   Words in Limited Use

Some words have only regional currency; others are no longer in general use.

Dictionaries use restrictive labels to show that a word is not current throughout the English-speaking world, or not current at this time, or familiar mainly to specialists in a limited field.

D 4a   Regional Labels

Dictionaries use geographic labels to indicate words in use mainly in one region. During the centuries before travel, books, and finally radio and television exercised their standardizing influence, languages gradually developed regional varieties. These often differed greatly in pronunciation, grammar, and vocabulary. Sometimes, as in the case of German and Dutch, they grew far enough apart to become separate languages.

Here are the types of regional variation that you are likely to encounter:

(1) *Vocabulary differs somewhat from one English-speaking country to another.* Students of British English notice **Americanisms** brought into the language through American movies and television programs. American travelers in England notice the British uses of *tram, lorry, lift, torch, wireless, fortnight.* Here is a passage with many British terms:

A scale or two adhered to the *fishmonger's* marble slab; the *pastrycook's* glass shelves showed a range of interesting crumbs; the *fruiterer* filled a long-standing void with fans of cardboard bananas and a "Dig for Victory" placard; the *greengrocer's* crates had been emptied of all but earth by those who had somehow failed to dig hard enough. . . . In the *confectioner's* windows the ribbons bleached on dummy boxes of

chocolate among fly-blown cut-outs of pre-war blondes. *Newsagents* without newspapers gave out in angry red chalk that they had no matches either. — Elizabeth Bowen,
The Heat of the Day

(2) *Like most European languages, British English varies greatly
from area to area.* Such regional varieties within a country are called
dialects. Students of English literature usually encounter some dialect
writing. For instance, a poet to whom a pretty girl is a "bonny lass,"
a church a "kirk," and a landowner a "laird" is using one of the dialects of Scotland and Northern England rather than standard British
English.

(3) *American speech shows some regional differences.* These are
now being recorded in linguistic atlases. By and large, the constant
intermingling of settlers from many areas, and the rapid growth of
mass media of communication, have kept these American dialects
from drifting very far apart. Here are some of the words that your
dictionary is likely to mark as dialectal: *dogie, poke* (bag), *reckon*
(suppose), *tote* (carry), *you all.*

Dialect differences are exploited by comedians and comic-strip
writers for comic effects. Dramatists and novelists reproduce dialectal
differences to give a down-to-earth quality to the conversation of
their characters. You yourself may at times experiment with dialect
expressions when striving for local color or a quaint, folksy touch.

D 4b   Obsolete and Archaic

Dictionaries label words no longer in common use. Some words,
or meanings of words, have gone out of use altogether. They are
called **obsolete.** Examples of obsolete meanings are *coy* (quiet),
curious (careful), *nice* (foolish). Some words or meanings are no
longer in common use but still occur in special contexts. Such words
and meanings are called **archaic.** The King James version of the Bible
and the vocabulary of religious devotion preserve many archaisms
that were in common use in seventeenth-century England: *thou* and
thee, brethren, kine (cattle).

In the following dictionary entry, five of the numbered meanings
of *brave* are labeled obsolete:

> **brave** (brāv) *adj.* **brav·er, brav·est   1.** Having or showing
> courage; intrepid; courageous.   **2.** Making a fine display;
> elegant; showy.   **3.** *Obs.* Excellent.   **—** *v.* **braved, brav·ing**
> *v.t.*   **1.** To meet or face with courage and fortitude: to *brave*
> danger.   **2.** To defy; challenge: to *brave* the heavens.   **3.**
> *Obs.* To make splendid.   **—** *v.i.*   **4.** *Obs.* To boast.   **—** *n.*   **1.**
> A man of courage.   **2.** A North American Indian warrior.
> **3.** *Obs.* A bully; bravo.   **4.** *Obs.* A boast or defiance.

From *Standard College Dictionary*

Here are some archaisms familiar to readers of poetry and historical fiction:

anon	(at once)	*fere*	(companion)
brand	(sword)	*forsooth*	(truly)
childe	(aristocratic youth)	*methinks*	(it seems)
erst	(formerly)	*rood*	(cross)
fain	(glad or gladly)	*sprite*	(ghost)

NOTE: Some words have an old-fashioned flavor even though they may not be labeled archaic in your dictionary. *Albeit* (although), *lief* (gladly), and *threescore* (sixty) would sound quaint in a paper written by a college student.

D 4c   Neologisms

A writer should be cautious in using words that have recently come into the language. Lexicographers, who at one time resisted the introduction of new words, now compete in their coverage of **neologisms**, or newly coined expressions. Many new words serve a need and rapidly become generally accepted: *bookmobile, cybernetics, astronaut, supersonic, transistor.* But many other coined words make conservative readers squirm.

(1) Inexperienced writers sometimes coin words *inadvertently* by way of analogy: *vanishment* (analogous to "banishment"); *neglectfulness* (analogous to "bashfulness"). Much awkward, inexact prose suffers from improvisations like *cowardness* (cowardice) and *unpainful* (painless).

(2) Journalists and advertisers are constantly inventing terms designed to dazzle their customers. The most popular type is the combination of two familiar words, as in *beautility* (beautiful utility) or *modelovely* (lovely model). Some of these are entertaining, like *Time's phenomoppet* (phenomenal moppet), but many are neither humorous nor ingenious. Avoid copywriters' words like the following:

jumboize	paperamics	outdoorsman
moisturize	usership	

(3) Many new words are part of an impersonal *bureaucratic jargon* that lacks the life and color of real human language. Memos and reports often use words made up, by people with tin ears, on the model of *escapee, personalize, finalize, socio-economic.* (See D 6b.)

D 4d   Subject Labels

Dictionaries label technical terms that are not likely to be familiar to laymen. Labels like *Law, Naut.* (nautical), or *Mach.* (machinery) are called subject labels. The **technical terminology** or, on a less formal level, the **shoptalk** of a trade or profession makes possible precise and rapid communication among its members but requires careful definition or explanation in writing addressed to the general reader. The math student will have no difficulty with *set, natural number, integer, rational number,* and *number sentence.* But the layman would want them explained.

NOTE: Some words associated with a specific field have acquired unfavorable associations. *Contact* for "get in touch with," *deal* for "transaction," *feature* for "exhibit" or "offer for sale," and *proposition* for "proposal" are words used primarily by salesmen. Even when used in a noncommercial context, they may carry overtones of the hard sell. *Personnel, domicile,* and *dependents* are used primarily by public officials and administrators. When used in a nonofficial situation, such words suggest impersonality and red tape.

Exercises

A. Investigate the regional or dialect uses of the following words. Where necessary, consult an unabridged dictionary: *bannocks, bloke, bonnet, boot, cant (vb.), complected, coulee, cove, dogie, goober, petrol, power, pram, quid, rant, trolley, tube.*

B. E. B. White, in an article on Maine speech, discussed the following expressions among others: *tunk* a wedge, *soft* weather, *dozy* wood, people *from away,* a *snug* pasture, *gunkhole, nooning.* Write a paper in which you discuss a number of expressions that you associate with a specific region. For instance, investigate dialect features that set your own native speech apart from that of the region where you now live.

C. Which of the following words (or which of their uses) are archaic? Which are obsolete? *Bower, cark, costermonger, favor, gentle, goodman, hackney, perpend* (vb.), *thorpe, yestreen, ywis.*

D. Read a scene from a play by Shakespeare or by one of his contemporaries. Compile a list of ten words or meanings that have become obsolete, archaic, or old-fashioned. Check in an unabridged dictionary words not listed in your own.

E. Discuss the use of newly coined words in current advertising. Show which of these you think may eventually become standard English and explain why.

F. What special fields of interest do the following technical terms represent? Which of the terms would you expect the average high school graduate to know? *A priori, barbican, bend sinister, brochure, calorie, camshaft, crochet, de facto, denouement, epistemology, graupel, hole in one, lien, plinth, solstice, sonata, sprit, symbiosis, tachistoscope, thyroid, transubstantiation, umlaut, valence, venireman, ventricle.*

G. A student investigating Post Office shoptalk discussed the following terms: *swing room, star route, merry-go-round, Tour Three, fat stock, confetti, shedders, scheme man, nixie clerk.* Investigate and report on Post Office shoptalk in your area. Are any of the same terms in use? Are any of the terms recorded in general or specialized dictionaries? *Or* conduct a similar investigation of shoptalk in one of the following areas: railroading, trucking, flying.

D 5   Exactness

An effective writer uses the exact words needed to convey the intended meaning.

Effective writing is clear, exact, concise. The effective writer uses exactly the right words — and no more — for his intended purpose.

D 5a   Accurate Words

An effective writer employs accurate words and exact shades of meaning. Hastily written words often express the intended meaning almost but not quite. Thus, an editorial may start like this: "Only by widespread voting will the desires of the nation be executed on the administrative and legislative levels of our government." There are several inexact expressions here: Orders are "executed," but desires are "realized," "fulfilled," or "complied with." They would be fulfilled not *by* voting but perhaps as a result of it. The main divisions of the United States government are not really "levels" of which one could be more elevated than another, but collateral branches, each with more or less clearly defined and independent authority.

Similar instances of hit-or-miss diction are common in student papers that are merely a hasty first draft rather than a carefully revised final version:

Hasty: *The news* about widespread corruption was first *exposed* by the local press.

Revised: The news about widespread corruption first *appeared* in the local press. (Evildoers or shortcomings are "exposed," but news about evildoers is "printed," "presented," or "reported.")

Check your papers specifically for the following kinds of inaccurate diction:

(1) Watch out for words easily *confused* because closely related in sound or meaning.

The work was sheer *trudgery* (should be *drudgery*).
Similar choices *affront* every student (should be *confront*).
He grew up in a *staple* environment (should be *stable*).

(2) Watch out for *garbled idioms:*

| Garbled: | Unemployment *played* an important *factor.* |
| Should Be: | Unemployment *played* an important *role.* |

| Garbled: | Many young people have *lost their appeal* for fraternities. |
| Should Be: | Fraternities have *lost their appeal* for many people. |

(3) Watch out for words with the wrong *connotation:*

| Inexact: | Life in the suburbs *subjects* a family to the beauties of nature. |
| Revised: | Life in the suburbs *brings* a family *closer* to the beauties of nature. (The connotations of *subject* are unfavorable; it implies that we are exposed to something unwillingly.) |

D 5b   Redundancy

Avoid wordiness. As a rule, a finished paper is the better for some vigorous pruning. Try to substitute one word that gives your meaning exactly for two words that give it blurrily. The most easily spotted kind of wordiness is **redundancy**, or unnecessary duplication. The phrase *basic fundamentals* is redundant because *basis* and *foundation* mean nearly the same thing. *Important essentials* is redundant because something could not be essential and unimportant at the same time.

In the following sentences one or the other way of expressing the same idea should be omitted:

We left *in the morning* at about six o'clock *a.m.*
As a rule, the weather was *usually* warm.
There is more to it than *seems apparent.*
I was given the *choice* of *choosing* whether I wanted to go.
Physically, he has not grown much in *height.*
In my opinion, I think you are right.

Here are some sources of wordiness other than direct duplication:
(1) *All-purpose nouns* like *situation, angle, factor, aspect, line,* or *element* are often mere padding. (See also D 6b.)

Padded:	When I first came to Smith College, *there was a situation where* some students lived in better housing than others.
Concise:	When I first came to Smith College, some students lived in better housing than others.

Padded:	Another *aspect* that needs to be considered is the consumer relations *angle*.
Concise:	We should also consider consumer relations.

(2) *Roundabout transitions* sometimes take the place of economical transitional phrases like *for example, however,* and *therefore:*

Wordy:	*In considering this situation we must also take into account the fact that* other students do not feel this way.
Economical:	Others, *however*, do not feel this way.

Wordy:	*Taking these factors into consideration, we must conclude that* your request is unjustified.
Economical:	*Therefore*, your request seems to us unjustified.

(3) Introductory phrases like *the fact that* or *the question whether* can often be trimmed without loss. (See also S 3a on deadwood in sentences.)

Wordy:	*The question of whether* churches should unite agitates people of many denominations.
Economical:	*Whether* churches should unite agitates people of many denominations.

NOTE: Colloquial English uses many phrases that show a weakening of etymological meanings. *Continue* means "go on," *refer* means "point back," *eliminate* means "take out." *Continue on, refer back,* and *eliminate out* would be considered redundant in formal situations.

Exercises

A. Make sure you can distinguish between the confusing words in the following pairs: *antic — antique; biography — bibliography; clique — cliché; connive — conspire; difference — deference; ethical — ethnic; feudalism — fatalism; gentle — genteel; literal — literary — literate; manners — mannerisms; sensible — sensitive; specie — species; unfaithful — infidel; venal — venial.*

B. Write down a *more exact word* for the word italicized in each sentence.

1. The town's income *relies* heavily on the logging and fishing industries.

2. Civil disobedience *contorts* the issues because it keeps everyone from discussing the problem in a calm, adult manner.

3. A good listener can listen to his teachers and retain the knowledge they have *expelled.*

4. The most despised task *bestowed* upon the motorist is the changing of a flat tire.

5. The dog went bounding down the steps, emitting *whelps* at every leap.

6. Our next *fiascle* took place in Hollywood.

7. The March of Dimes was organized to help those *inflicted* with infantile paralysis.

8. The chairman *contributed* the low attendance to inadequate publicity.

9. The voters can hardly be *credible* enough to believe some of the things they are told.

10. Sick people no longer can pay for their hospital costs without a tremendous *drain* being put on their families.

C. Point out and correct examples of *inaccurate or unidiomatic diction.*
1. He felt that a hands-off policy was the best one for the government to play.   2. A teacher has to be able to handle emotionally disturbed children without bias or ill-favored feelings.   3. Few people accomplish the asset of ignoring gossip circulated about them by thoughtless persons.   4. The United States lost much of the prestige that other countries used to have for her.   5. The support we received from our parent organization has aided greatly to our success.   6. The situation has become drastic and requires immediate action.   7. Nations armed with nuclear weapons will be a constant fear to their less powerful neighbors.   8. In his speech, the mayor suggested several ways of helping the traffic problem.   9. The administration, in exposing the apathy of Congress, has done a great deed to the country.   10. If we accept your theory, our whole concept of democracy will have to make a drastic change.   11. If the new city hall is to serve the whole community, it should be centralized in the city.   12. In an emergency, some drivers become a panic and freeze to the wheel.   13. Most of our objections to the behavior of other people fall under the generalization of prejudice.   14. Competence alone should be the judge whether a teacher should be allowed to teach or not.   15. Pearl Buck explains how her early environment cultivated her toward a love of learning.

D. Point out and correct examples of *wordiness.*

1. Mormons fleeing persecution founded the beginning of our community.

2. In due time, a new fad will eventually replace this current craze.

3. Some of today's popular music seems to revert back to music popular thirty years ago.

4. The weatherman said that at times there would be occasional rain.

5. The reason that married students have high grades academically is that they have a definite goal in the future to come.

6. In the modern world of this day and age, economical operation has become an indispensable condition for business success.

7. Many steps toward equal opportunities were taken in the early days of our government's reign.

8. To be right at home in this modern age of today, one should choose a hobby like flying, which is right up to date with the times.

9. The majority of the time the literature of the nineteenth century was didactic in nature.

10. One important factor in the accident situation is the consumption of alcohol by the drinking driver.

E. Rewrite the following sentences to reduce padding. Try to convey the same idea, using *half as many words* as the original.

1. The act of effective teaching is an art that not many teachers are capable of doing.

2. Being a salesman, an individual has many responsibilities both to his employer as well as to his customers.

3. As a traveler who has made several trips to Europe of varying lengths of stay, I venture to say that I have reasonable background to discuss the merits of the various different types of transportation now available for travel to Europe.

4. The fact that the college forces one to pay for membership in a student organization seems to me a coercion of the student's funds.

D 6   Directness

A writer must know how to be blunt and direct.

At times, a writer will be deliberately indirect for tactical reasons. More common is the kind of careless indirectness that for no good reason slows down the reader.

D 6a   Euphemisms

Much roundabout diction results from the desire to be elegant. Refined or impressive names for unpleasant or prosaic things are known as **euphemisms**. The most familiar euphemisms are those for elementary facts of human existence.

(birth)	*blessed event, new arrival*
(pregnancy)	*to be expecting*
(spinsterhood)	*bachelor girl, career woman*
(age)	*senior citizens, the elderly*
(death)	*pass on, expire, the deceased, mortal remains*

Euphemisms are "beautiful words"—words more beautiful than what they stand for. Often they are required by politeness or tact. When referring to people you respect, you will prefer *stout* to *fat*, *intoxicated* to *drunk*, *indolent* to *lazy*, and *remains* to *corpse*. More often, however, euphemisms mislead, or even deliberately deceive. Waitresses become "hostesses," plumbers "sanitary engineers," file clerks "research consultants," undertakers "funeral directors," door-to-door salesmen "customer-contact personnel," and fortune tellers "clairvoyant readers." In much public-relations prose and political propaganda, euphemisms cover up facts that the reader is entitled to know: *straitened financial circumstances* for "bankruptcy"; *planned withdrawal* for "disorganized retreat"; *resettlement* for "forcible expatriation."

Many readers are annoyed by such evasive tactics; they will be grateful when you call a spade a spade.

Euphemism	Blunt
immoderate use of intoxicants	heavy drinking
lack of proper health habits	dirt
deteriorating residential section	slum

NOTE: The use of euphemisms to avoid the repetition of more unpretentious words is called **elegant variation**. A writer describing the habits of the swordfish will rightly feel that repeating the name of the fish in every second sentence would be monotonous. However, his writing will sound strained if he starts using circumlocutions like "scaled creature," "aquatic marauder," "denizen of the deep," and "knight of the brine."

D 6b   Jargon

Much inflated diction results from a writer's using two high-brow words where one lowbrow word would do. **Jargon** reflects the desire to make the trivial seem important. It cultivates an impressive pseudo-scientific air by using indirect, impersonal constructions; by blowing up simple ideas through abstract or roundabout diction; and by seeking out technical-sounding Latin and Greek terms.

Jargon:	Procedures were instituted with a view toward the implementation of the conclusions reached.
Plain English:	We started to put our ideas into practice.
Jargon:	Careful consideration of relevant data is imperative before the procedure most conducive toward a realization of the desired outcomes can be determined.
Plain English:	Look before you leap.

The jargon addict says "Reference was made" rather than "I mentioned"; "the hypothesis suggests itself" rather than "I think." He prefers *effectuate* to "bring about," *hypothesize* to "assume," *magnitude* to "size," *methodology* to "methods," *interrelationship* to "relation." He uses terms like *essential, primary,* and *individual* where no distinction between essential and nonessential, primary and secondary, or individual and society is implied or important. He discusses simple everyday happenings in terms of "factors," "phases," "aspects," "situations," "criteria," "data," "problems," "facets," "phenomena," "structures," "levels," and "strata."

Obviously, many scientific and scholarly subjects call for language that is technical, precise, impersonal. Jargon is the *unnecessary* use of technical language in order to borrow the prestige of science and scholarship. Jargon invites ridicule, since it suggests the pompousness of men overly impressed with their own importance.

Pompous:	A drastic reappraisal and reassessment of our present position on a number of issues, including the location of our offices, is being given meaningful consideration in order to maximize our opportunities and those of our clients in a National Capital filled with flux.
Plain Fact:	The company is moving its offices.

D 6c   Flowery Diction

Flowery and extravagant diction interferes with a writer's doing justice to his subject. Flowery diction results from an attempt to give a poetic varnish to prose. Some writers cannot resist the temptation to call a policeman a "minion of the law," an Irishman a "native of the Emerald Isle," a colonist who served in the War of Independence a "gallant warrior defending our infant republic."

Flowery:	The respite from study was devoted to a sojourn at the ancestral mansion.
Plain English:	I spent my vacation at the house of my grandparents.
Flowery:	The visitor proved a harbinger of glad tidings.
Plain English:	The visitor brought good news.

In the more showy kinds of journalism, the flowery phrase is supplemented by **hyperbole**, exaggeration for dramatic effect. "Crises" are constantly "racing toward a climax," "tragedies" are "stunning" peaceful communities, "daring" new detergents are overjoying housewives by bleaching clothes to a "dazzling" white. Basketball teams "clobber," "bludgeon," and "exterminate" each other; a 250-pound fullback "gambols," "capers," or "romps" to a touchdown; a boxer "slaughters" his opponent. A hyperbolical style sounds breathless or juvenile in serious discussion.

Exercises

A. Investigate the *current use of euphemisms* in one major area, such as education, medicine, or the funeral industry. Examine such euphemisms for intention, appropriateness, effect.

B. Translate the following specimens of jargon into *plain English.*

1. Innovations have to be judged as useful according to the possibility of their implementation.

2. To answer this question without clarification of my rationalizing would be senseless, since there are a great number of determinants that can be expressed pro and con.

3. Being in a profession marks a tangible asset usable as a means of support throughout life, including advancing years.

4. The individual's mental attitude is the factor that seems to make time spent in one geographical location more enjoyable than time spent in another.

5. Finding genuine leadership is a deciding factor in the possibility of the existence of good government.

6. As far as the status of women is concerned, I feel the strong tendency toward domestication in our society will never change, only modify.

The physical aspect plays an important part, it being the role of a woman to reproduce the offspring.

7. If an observation of the streets in various cities were to be made, it would reveal a considerable number of situations where traffic is delayed because of congested conditions.

8. Aid along the lines of scholastic achievement and integration into the social group is accorded the younger members of a fraternity by their older brothers.

9. The student commencing matriculation in the institution of his choice should not be subjugated to general education requirements above and beyond the prerequisites stipulated in his major field.

10. The existence or nonexistence of sufficient socio-economic incentives can be presumed to be a major factor in determining the availability of instructional personnel requisite to the successful functioning of the nation's educational establishment.

C. Point out specific features that make the following passage jargon. Rewrite the passage in a *less pompous, more natural* style.

We think of our audio-visual program as a method or medium, not as an end in itself. For example, a curriculum committee at its inception does not necessarily include a visual-aids representative. However, following the formulation of general philosophy and basic content, visual aids become an active and integral part of curriculum organization. The materials available then serve in many ways to orient and implement the program. The individual teacher is responsible for enriching the individual learning situation through the preplanned utilization of visual materials that vitalize interest. The principal must provide for physical and monetary aspects. But perhaps the greatest contributing factor to the success of the program is provision for continuous growth. Our concentration of effort is on individual evaluations of materials immediately following their use. This is further implemented by periodic evaluations by groups, on the vertical and horizontal grade-level basis.

D. What makes the language of the following *student-written paragraphs* pretentious? Rewrite one of the paragraphs in a more direct and natural style.

1. For some people the cartoons shown at the theaters are the high spot of the program. The majority of these people is the children. The slapstick comedy affords loads of laughs to the younger folks. However, the cartoons have more than a little effect on the older people too. Sometimes this effect is negative, and sometimes it is positive. The main criticism against the cartoons is that they are so completely abstract and ridiculous. For those people who enjoy the cartoons, the abstractness is the backbone of their favoritism.

2. The representation of the sub-teenagers at the scene of the accident was better than that of the teenagers. The sub-teeners, mostly girls, had a different attitude than did their elderly teenaged friends. One aspect of their different attitude centered on the concern for the people in the collision. The girls attempted to give any assistance that they could while the teenagers didn't even offer. The sub-teens' interest also revolved about the details of the incident although none of them kept quiet long enough to find out. Sprinkled among the outer edge of teenagers and the core of sub-teens stood the parents. Those garbed in aprons illustrated the time as being the dinner hour; those in short-sleeved shirts and pants characterized the "gardening in the summer-time."

E. Investigate the use of *jargon* in government publications or in professional publications in a major field of study. Use detailed examples, explaining what they show about the nature of jargon.

F. Study the language used by your favorite *sports writer, fashion analyst, or society editor.* Write a brief report, providing samples of characteristic diction.

D 7   Expressive Language

A writer who has something fresh to say should say it in fresh and expressive language.

Careful word choice can make the difference between colorless language and language that is fresh, graphic, and concrete.

D 7a   Specific Words

A good writer uses specific, informative words. Instead of a colorless general word like *building,* he will use a more expressive word like *barn, mansion, warehouse, bungalow, tenement, shack, workshop,* or *cabin. Tenement* carries more information than *building.* It also comes closer to concrete experience, making it possible for the reader to visualize an actual structure. When diction remains unnecessarily general, the reader is too far removed from what he can see, hear, and feel.

General: All the animals of the farm joined in singing "Beasts of England."

Specific: The whole farm *burst* out into "Beasts of England" in tremendous unison. The cows *lowed* it, the dogs *whined* it, the sheep *bleated* it, the horses *whinnied* it, the ducks *quacked* it.   (George Orwell)

A good writer is a patient observer of language and as a result has at his fingertips the right word for specific objects, shapes, sounds, textures, motions:

sand crabs *wriggling* and *scuttling* . . . heavy little creatures, shaped like *scarabs*, with grey-*mottled* shells and orange underparts . . . (John Steinbeck)

a big, squarish *frame house* that had once been white, decorated with *cupolas* and *spires* and *scrolled* balconies in the heavily lightsome style of the seventies . . . (William Faulkner)

(See also Chapter Two, pp. 76–77, on the use of specific and concrete language in descriptive writing.)

D 7b   Figurative Words

Figurative expressions make writing graphic and colorful by exploiting similarities between different things. A compressed but explicit comparison, introduced by *as* or *like*, is called a **simile**. An implied comparison that uses one thing as the equivalent of another is called a **metaphor**. Literally, *monkey* refers to a small, long-tailed animal. Metaphorically, it may mean a person who, like a monkey, is agile, mischievous, imitative, or playful.

Figurative language makes writing come to life. It provides one way of translating the abstract into the *concrete*:

There is always one moment in childhood *when the door opens* and lets the future in.   (Graham Greene)

Presenting us with images that we can visualize, figurative language brings into play not only our reason but also our *emotions*:

No book has ever revealed more starkly the senselessness of the disasters of war, nor shown up *with sharper X-ray vision, under the torn flesh of war*, the hidden, all-corrupting sickness of the vindictive world of peace-behind-the-lines.   (Kenneth Rexroth)

Observe the following cautions in your own use of figurative language:

(1) *Figurative expressions should be apt.* The implied analogy must fit:

Apt:	Putting the hubcap back on the rim is *like putting an undersized lid on an oversized jar.* (As one side of the hubcap is pounded into place, the opposite side pops out.)
Inept:	Lacking the ignition of advertising, our economic engine would run at a slower pace. (An engine without ignition would not run at a slower pace; it would just be dead.)

Inept: The reader's interest, *like so many feathers*, must be handled with extreme care. *Too rapid a wind of facts* will disperse his interest quite readily. (Facts seem too solid to be compared to a wind; facts might *crush* the reader but would hardly *blow away* his interest.)

(2) *Figurative expressions should be consistent.* When several figurative expressions appear closely together, they should blend into a harmonious whole rather than clash because of contradictory associations. Avoid the **mixed metaphor**:

Consistent: Fame cannot spread wide or endure long that is not *rooted* in nature, and *manured* by art.   (Samuel Johnson)

Mixed: America's colleges are the *key* to national survival, and the future of the country lies in their *hands*.
                (The second part of the statement is illogical, because keys do not have hands.)

Mixed: Enriched programs give the good student a chance to *dig* deeper into the large *sea* of knowledge.
                (Most people do their digging on solid ground rather than at sea.)

(3) *Figurative expressions should not call excessive attention to themselves.* Avoid metaphors that are strained enough to become distracting:

Extravagant: When the average overmothered college student is removed from parental control, the severance of the umbilical cord causes him to bleed to death, psychologically speaking.

(See also Chapter Two, pp. 78–79, on the use of figurative language in descriptive writing.)

D 7c   Fresh Words

Phrase ideas freshly in your own words; avoid too familiar ready-made phrases. Many phrases that may once have been striking have become trite through overuse. Such tired phrases are called **clichés**. They seduce the writer, because they spring to mind ready to use and thus help a paper write itself. But they make the yawning reader feel that nothing new is being said and that there is little point in paying attention.

Trite: He was always *wrapped up* in his own thoughts and feelings.
Fresh: Only the *cocoon* of his own thoughts and feelings existed for him.

Trite: The dean let us have it, *straight from the shoulder*.
Fresh: The dean spoke to us directly and urgently, *like a scout just returned from the enemy camp.*

Everyday language is full of ready-made phrases that invite unthinking repetition. To the cliché expert, ignorance is always "abysmal," fortitude "intestinal," and necessity "dire." Daylight is always "broad," silence "ominous," and old age "ripe." People make a "clean break" and engage in "honest toil" till the "bitter end." They make things "crystal clear"; they wait "with bated breath"; they work "by the sweat of their brow." Last but not least, sadder and wiser and a little the worse for wear, they retire to the sidelines to let a new generation make its appearance upon the busy stage of life.

Here are some of the clichés that at times spill over into student writing:

believe it or not	last but not least
better late than never	the last straw
beyond the shadow of a doubt	let's face it
bolt out of the blue	malice aforethought
burn the midnight oil	nature's glory
couldn't care less	off the beaten track
crying shame	pride and joy
dire straits	proud owner
easier said than done	rear its ugly head
the facts of life	rude awakening
few and far between	a shot in the arm
fine and dandy	sink or swim
the finer things	a snare and a delusion
first and foremost	sneaking suspicion
free and easy	something tells me
get in there and fight	straight and narrow
good time was had by all	strike while the iron is hot
green with envy	tender mercies
in one fell swoop	to all intents and purposes
in the last analysis	truer words were never spoken
it goes without saying	truth is stranger than fiction
it stands to reason	up in arms

Exercises

A. From your current reading, select five short sentences in which a writer uses words *more specific* than you might have expected. Here are two examples:

> The voyage of the best ship is a *zigzag* line of a hundred *tacks*. (Ralph Waldo Emerson)

> The sunlight *pressed* through the windows, *thieved* its way in, *flashed* its light over the furniture and the photographs. (Katherine Mansfield)

B. Point out all examples of figurative language in the following passages. What areas does each writer draw on for figurative analogies?

1. I remember glancing with sadness at the photographs of Newman, Oosterbaan and the other gridiron heroes and secretly wishing that the gladiatorial age had not so completely disappeared. Instead, my generation thirsted for another kind of action, and we took great pleasure in the sit-down strikes that burst loose in Flint and Detroit, and we gasped when Roosevelt went over the line with the TVA. — Arthur Miller, "University of Michigan," *Holiday*

2. Intelligence must necessarily be regarded as a central powerhouse that sends out current into any performance. The very nature of intelligence is adaptability, and it is this general quality which modern schools, modern tests, and modern life systematically neglect in favor of robot "aptitudes."

The excuse for doing so is slight but real. In the first place, an industrial world thinks it wants only a pinch of intelligence to season a great plateful of mechanical aptitudes. In the second place, though intelligence is and always will exist as a general power, it appears nowhere in full perfection. The man who can solve differential equations probably hits his thumb with the hammer at every stroke. Physical and emotional barriers keep intellect from shining like a bright light in all directions. Hence psychologists, noting the dark bands of interference, imagine separate entities which they name aptitudes. — Jacques Barzun, *Teacher in America*

3. Nabokov knows more about the maze of language than anyone since Joyce. His style is a magpie's trove of Russian, French, German, English, Middle English, and classical lexicography. He shuffles words with the strained nonchalance of a man doing precarious card tricks. — George Steiner, "Lament for a Language Lost," *The Reporter*

4. Many of them had part-time jobs in the automobile industry or its annexes. Even a Philosopher found it difficult to top the argument "I couldn't read the book this week, I have to *work*," with its implied reproach for a scholar's leisure. But alas, many of these stricken proletarians drove freshly-minted automobiles. They worked in order to keep up the payments, racing like laboratory mice around the cage of depreciation. — Herbert Gold, *The Age of Happy Problems*

C. Evaluate the use of figurative language in the following passages. Are the figurative expressions apt, consistent, unforced? Point out mixed or extravagant metaphors.

1. Most self-made successes kick down the ladder by which they themselves have risen.

2. Unnecessary precision is pedantic and fuzzy, like honing a razor to cut butter.   (Monroe C. Beardsley)

3. Each professor has four faces. The first face is that of the scholar; it was started with Socrates, sharpened by science, and honed on experience.

4. Descriptions of the average American which are based on statistical evidence tend to be portraits of a statistical meatball, with the lean and the fat all ground together to produce the average man.

5. The man who merely "plays back" what he has heard or read without any understanding of it is not truly educated.

6. Today our industrial giant, streamlined in accordance with the needs of the atomic age, stands on the threshold of a horizon of unlimited prosperity.

7. Powered by the germ cell of the Ruhr, the truncated Reich had surpassed the economic peak of 1936, Hitler's best year.   (William Manchester)

8. Selling an international language is like selling telephones. No one will buy either unless he thinks a lot of other people will do the same.

9. We should never tear a poem apart and wheel it gutless out of the classroom.

10. Scientific progress is a stream that owes its strength to many tributaries.

11. By taking the initiative in the current propaganda battle, the State Department has scored a bull's-eye of great magnitude.

12. This is one of those watershed moments in history, when the pendulum swing of public needs and public policies happens to coincide with a historical breaking point.   (Richard Nixon)

13. Africa is on the brink of television, and in one fantastic giant step the Dark Continent will be hurtled from the tom-tom to the television screen.

14. The Congressman insults his constituents' intelligence by dragging a red herring into the arena and by wrapping himself in the mantle of his war record to shield himself from honest criticism.

15. In this poem, the poet seems to be coming out of a dream world and stepping into the face of reality.

16. The administrators in Negro colleges are Joe Louises at a time when many of their students are Muhammad Alis.

17. No sooner does a teen-ager's car go off the road than he hits the front page of the newspaper.

18. A career is like a garden in that it, too, requires much plotting and planning, much preliminary spadework, the right seeds sown in the right soil, and a long period of careful cultivation.

19. Moral progress is at a low ebb and has reached the acme of stagnation. We have many outstanding religious and moral leaders, but their words of gold are falling on arid soil rather than on fertile ground.

20. Langland clung with tenacity to the complex theological explanation of the existing order that was thrown into his lap at the time of his birth into the Christian world. This theology rode on his shoulders and guided the thought and development of his life and art.

D. Rewrite the following sentences to *eliminate clichés*. Try to make your phrasing fresh enough to revive the reader's attention.

1. They will have to get his signature by hook or by crook.

2. After one more defeat, he will have to throw in the sponge.

3. The reporter swallowed their story hook, line, and sinker.

4. The typical organization man knows which side his bread is buttered on.

5. Party platforms never get down to brass tacks.

6. In trying to revitalize our neighborhoods, we too often throw out the baby with the bath water.

7. When we are asked to change administrations in the midst of a serious international crisis, we should remember that it is unwise to change horses in midstream.

8. The opposing candidate is a Johnny-come-lately who entered the campaign only at the urging of his influential backers.

E. Compile a list of ten clichés widely used in news reporting, campaign oratory, or advertising. What explains their popularity?

CHAPTER THIRTEEN

Sentence Style

An effective writer knows his tools. His most basic but also his most versatile tool is the sentence. Just as an effective writer must learn to exploit the rich resources of the English vocabulary, so he must learn to employ to advantage the rich structural resources of the English sentence. Notice how the basic idea in the following sentence may be stated in a variety of ways:

> The old man recited the verses with many a splendid gesture.
> With many a splendid gesture, the old man recited the verses.
> The verses were recited by an old man gesturing splendidly.
> A man—old, gesturing splendidly—was reciting verses.
> There was an old man reciting verses, gesturing splendidly.
> The man who recited the verses with many a splendid gesture was old.

When you work on sentence style, you focus on what makes sentences apt, varied, vigorous—a pleasure to read. As you work to improve your sentences, aim at the following results:

(1) *Make structural relationships reflect relationships between ideas.* Granted, there is seldom a one-to-one correlation between meaning and sentence structure, or a single "best" way to state a given idea. But notice how the more complex version of the following passage *does* bring out relations that the simpler version plays down:

Simple: The term *democracy* originated in ancient Greece. Different people have used it to describe quite different political systems. Usually the person who uses the word thinks it has only one meaning.

Complex: *Democracy*, a term that originated in ancient Greece, has been used to describe quite different political systems, though the person who uses it usually thinks it has only one meaning.

The second version *emphasizes* the fact that the word discussed has many different meanings. It works the remaining information into the same single sentence in a *subordinate* position, putting it "in its place."

(2) *Use structural resources to command and channel the reader's attention.* Focus interest on a key phrase by placing it conspicuously in its sentence. Or make the reader see the connection between closely related ideas or details by placing them in parallel grammatical position:

> Studies serve *for delight,*
>   *for ornament,* and
>   *for ability.*   (Sir Francis Bacon)

The only advice, indeed, that one person can give another about reading
is *to take no advice,*
 to follow your own instincts,
 to use your own reason,
 to come to your own conclusions.   (Virginia Woolf)

(3) *Use differences in structure to help set the tone or vary the mood.* Study the effects that differences in sentence style produce on the reader. Many modern readers are attuned to the terse, reportorial style that Ernest Hemingway frequently employs in his fiction. The short, "factual" statements seem to ward off all subjective comment, all intruding sentimentality:

Manuel lay back. They had something over his face. It was all familiar. He inhaled deeply. He felt very tired. He was very, very tired. They took the thing away from his face.

A quite different effect is aimed at in the leisurely, elaborate, reflective sentences often found in the fiction of Henry James. Everything seems ordered and under control; every little nuance is fully savored:

The gentleman, a man of fifty, very high and very straight, with a mustache slightly grizzled and a dark grey walking-coat admirably fitted . . . would have struck me as a celebrity if celebrities were often striking.

S 1   Sentence Building

A well-built sentence clearly signals important relationships.

Many simple sentences are built on the "Who does what?" model. When such a sentence moves with few or no modifiers from subject to verb and from there to one or more complements, we are likely to encounter few problems of clarity or proper perspective.

 My friend waited outside the restaurant.
 The relatives of the deceased *crowded the room.*
 The heavens declare the glory of God.

Our problem is to maintain the same clarity and directness when we build sentences designed to carry more, and more complicated, information.

S 1a Effective Predication

Give directness and vigor to a weak sentence by rewriting it on the "Who does what?" model. The subject and the predicate are *structurally* the mainstays of a sentence. Often the sentence gains in directness if at the same time the subject and the predicate carry a crucial part of the *meaning.* To give the reader a clear grasp of crucial relations, try to make the subject name the key agent. Then make the predicate state the key point.

Weak: *One crucial factor* in the current revolution in our social structure *is the relationship* between the white policeman and the black community.
(Subject and predicate carry little of the meaning; they are semantic blanks.)

Stronger: *The white policeman* standing on a Harlem street corner *finds himself at the very center* of the revolution now occurring in the world.
—James Baldwin, *Nobody Knows My Name*
(Sentence structure now makes the "crucial factor" also *grammatically* crucial—by making *policeman* the subject of the sentence.)

Watch out especially for sentences in which abstract nouns ending in *-ment, -ion, -ism,* and the like, serve as the subject of the sentence. Often these refer to actions, events, and activities that could be more vigorously expressed by a verb, with the agent clearly identified and serving as the subject.

Weak: Violent *arguments* frequently *took place.*
Revised: *We* often *argued* violently.

Weak: A certain *element* of confusion *was present.*
Revised: *The speaker confused us.*

Weak: A *criticism* which is prevalent against modern poetry *is* that *its appeal is* only to the super-sophisticated.
Revised: *Many critics charge* that *modern poetry appeals* only to the super-sophisticated.

Weak: *The solution* to the problem *was the result* of a careful examination of available records.
Revised: *We solved the problem* by carefully examining available records.

NOTE: You can often make the subject and predicate of a main clause carry your main point by eliminating tag statements like "The simple fact is that . . ." and "The question now confronting us is whether . . ."

Weak: *The question* now confronting us *is* whether we should yield to intimidation, and thus encourage other groups to resort to the same tactics.

Revised: *Should we yield* to intimidation, and thus encourage other groups to resort to the same tactics?

S 1b   Effective Coordination

Coordination is most appropriate when two ideas are about equally important. In sentences like the following, both clauses are about equally relevant to the general trend of the report, narrative, or argument:

We tried to locate the files, *but* we were unsuccessful.

We shall have to build several new classrooms, *for* we expect a large increase in the school-age population.

Our press is essentially provincial in this country, *and* except for a few syndicated columnists the reputation of our newspapermen is mainly local.

If you doubt the appropriateness of a coordinating connective like *and* or *but*, test the sentence by inserting a parenthetical "equally important":

Effective: Under one of the plans, a reservist spends only six months on active duty, *but* [equally important] he remains in the Ready Reserve for seven and one-half years.

In student writing, *excessive coordination* often results from the overuse of *and*. Note that it merely says "more of same," without indicating any specific relationship. It is appropriate when the clause that follows really gives us "more of same" by explaining or reinforcing the same point:

A tart temper never mellows with age, *and* a sharp tongue is the only edged tool that grows keener with constant use. — Washington Irving, "Rip Van Winkle"

And is also appropriate when events follow each other "as they happen," without emphasis on cause and effect or other logical relations:

There was a shock, *and* he felt himself go up in the air. He pushed on the sword as he went up and over, *and* it flew out of his hand. He hit the ground *and* the bull was on him. — Ernest Hemingway, "The Undefeated"

Avoid the use of *and* when it suggests a failure to examine the connection between ideas. The following sentence merely rambles on from one point to the next, without using connectives that would prepare the reader for what is coming:

Rambling: A member of the Reserve has to participate in weekly drills, *and* it may be called up in emergencies, which came as an unpleasant surprise to me, *and* you would do better to stay away from it.

S 1c   Effective Subordination

Subordination is most appropriate when details, reasons, or qualifications accompany a main point. Subordinating connectives *(when, while, since, because, if, though)* and relative pronouns *(who, which,* and *that)* can make the material they subordinate seem of secondary importance. It is true that in indirect quotations, for instance, the main idea quite appropriately appears in the grammatically subordinate part of the sentence: "He said *that he would be late.*" But subordinating connectives often seem particularly apt when the main clause states a major point, with the dependent clauses establishing relations in place, time, or logic:

The edge of the cape was wet with blood *where* it had swept along the bull's back *as* he went by. — Ernest Hemingway, "The Undefeated"

Remember the following points:

(1) Effective subordination *clarifies relationships in a sentence.* Merely placed next to each other, the following two statements may seem disjointed: "Kroger organized a counterfeiting ring. He had studied printing in Germany." When one is subordinated to the other, the connection between them becomes more obvious:

Effective: Kroger, *who had studied printing in Germany,* organized a counterfeiting ring.

Coordinated by *but,* the following two statements leave the relationship between fishing and strong wind vague: "We spent the days fishing, but sometimes there was a strong wind." The subordinating connective *unless* leaves no doubt about the relationship:

Effective: We spent the days fishing *unless there was a strong wind.*

(2) Unskillful subordination *blurs emphasis.* "*I was ten* when we moved to Alaska" focuses the reader's attention on you and your age.

"When I was ten, *we moved to Alaska*" focuses the reader's attention on Alaska. **Upside-down subordination** results when the wrong item seems to stand out. When tucked away in a subordinate part of a sentence, important information may catch the reader unaware and, as a result, have an ironic effect. *Avoid upside-down subordination when no irony is intended:*

Upside-Down:	The salary was considered good by local standards, *though* it was not enough to feed and clothe my family.
Improved:	*Though* considered good by local standards, my salary was not enough to feed and clothe my family.
Upside-Down:	He had a completely accident-free record up to the last day of his employment, *when* he stepped on a power line and almost lost his life.
Improved:	On the last day of his employment, *after* ten years without a single accident, he stepped on a power line and almost lost his life.

Dependent clauses are harder to focus on, to remember, and to quote than independent ones. Your reader may lose the trend of your argument if too many essential points appear in unobtrusive dependent clauses.

S 1d   Effective Modifiers

Part of the secret of effective prose is skillful use of modifying words and phrases where an inexperienced writer might use separate clauses. Observe the tightening of relationships and the gain in continuity in the following pairs:

Routine:	She had shiny eyes, an upturned nose, and a lively mouth, and her face never seemed to be at rest.
Effective:	Her face, *with its ever-shining eyes, its upturned nose, and mobile mouth,* was never in repose. — John Mason Brown, "Blithe Spirit," *Saturday Review*
Routine:	We caught two bass. We hauled them in briskly, as though they were mackerel. After we pulled them over the side of the boat, we stunned them with a blow on the back of the head.
Effective:	We caught two bass, *hauling them in briskly* as though they were mackerel, *pulling them over the side of the boat* in a businesslike manner without any landing net, and *stunning them with a blow on the back of the head.* — E. B. White, *One Man's Meat*

The following sentences, from a bull-fighting story by Ernest Hemingway, illustrate the variety in sentence rhythm made possible through the effective use of one or more modifiers *at different positions* in the sentence:

• breaking up subject and verb:

> The horse, *lifted and gored,* crashed over with the bull driving into him.
>
> Manuel, *lying on the ground,* kicked at the bull's muzzle with his slippered feet.
>
> Manuel, *facing the bull, having turned with him each charge,* offered the cape with his two hands.

• at the end of the sentence:

> Manuel walked towards him, *watching his feet.*
>
> The bull was hooking wildly, *jumping like a trout, all four feet off the ground.*

• at the beginning of the sentence:

> Now, *facing the bull,* he was conscious of many things at the same time.
>
> *Heads up, swinging with the music, their right arms swinging free,* they stepped out.
>
> *Arrogant, swinging,* they looked straight ahead as they marched.

• more than one position:

> The bull, *in full gallop,* pivoted and charged the cape, *his head down, his tail rising.*

Exercises

A. Rewrite the following sentences for *more effective predication.*

1. A conscientious teacher's satisfaction is incomplete unless he reaches a full realization of his goals.

2. As the result of unruly demonstrations, repeated interruptions of the committee's deliberations took place.

3. The conclusion is inevitable that considerable impairment of our country's military strength has come about.

4. A plan for safe driving is of no use if the cooperation of the individual driver is not present.

5. The accumulation of pressures to conform is so great that the student is in constant awareness of their presence.

6. The contribution of the alumni to the growth of the college will be in proportion to their information about its educational needs.

B. Write three pairs of related clauses. Then combine each pair in different ways, illustrating different possibilities of *coordination, subordination, or modification.*

EXAMPLE

The spring rains were heavy. The weeds grew at a furious rate.
The spring rains were heavy, *and* the weeds grew at a furious rate.
The weeds grew at a furious rate, *for* the spring rains were heavy.
Because the spring rains were heavy, the weeds grew at a furious rate.
The spring rains being heavy, the weeds grew at a furious rate.
The weeds, *with the spring rains heavy,* grew at a furious rate.

C. Rewrite the following passages, making effective use of *subordination or modifiers.*

1. The monkey family is large. It includes monkeys, baboons, lemurs, and apes. The animals in the monkey family are closely related to man. They are imitative. They can be trained to perform simple tasks. However, their intelligence is low.

2. My father came from a wealthy family, and my mother came from a very poor home, and it was strange that she held the purse strings in the family.

3. Many high school teachers follow a textbook word for word, and they go over each page until everyone understands it. In college, many teachers just tell the student to read the textbook, and then they start giving lectures on the material covered in the text, but they don't follow it word for word.

D. In the first three sentences, point out effective subordination. In the next three sentences, point out effective use of modifiers. Your instructor may ask you to use one or more sentences in each group as model sentences. For each such sentence, write a sentence of your own on a different topic but preserving as far as possible the grammatical structure of the original.

1. In Roman comedy the heroine, who is usually a slave or courtesan, turns out to be the daughter of somebody respectable, so that the hero can marry her without loss of face.   (Northrop Frye)

2. She stopped for a moment beside one of the prickly dark shrubs with which the city had beautified the Home, and then proceeded slowly toward the building, which was of whitewashed brick and reflected the winter sunlight like a block of ice.   (Eudora Welty)

3. The fame of each discovery rightly attaches to the mind that made the formula which contains all the details, and not to the manufacturers who now make their gain by it; although the mob uniformly cheers the publisher, and not the inventor.   (Emerson)

4. Curiosity, like all other desires, produces pain as well as pleasure. (Samuel Johnson)

5. All electric appliances, far from being labor-saving devices, are new forms of work, decentralized and made available to everybody.   (Marshall McLuhan)

6. The young moon recurved, and shining low in the west, was like a slender shaving thrown up from a bar of gold, and the Arabian Sea, smooth and cool to the eye like a sheet of ice, extended its perfect level to the perfect circle of a dark horizon.   (Joseph Conrad)

E. Choose one of the following as a model sentence. How closely can you reproduce the elaborate grammatical structure of the original?

1. The story had held us, round the fire, sufficiently breathless, but except the obvious remark that it was gruesome, as, on Christmas eve in an old house, a strange tale should essentially be, I remember no comment uttered till somebody happened to say that it was the only case he had met in which such a visitation had fallen on a child.   (Henry James)

2. I was born in a large Welsh town at the beginning of the Great War — an ugly, lovely town (or so it was and is to me) crawling, sprawling by a long and splendid curving shore where truant boys and sandfield boys and old men from nowhere beachcombed, idled and paddled, watched the dock-bound ships or the ships steaming away into wonder and India, magic and China, countries bright with oranges and loud with lions.   (Dylan Thomas)

S 2   Sentence Variety

An effective writer keeps his sentences from becoming plodding and monotonous.

An effective writer uses sentences of different length and structure for variety and emphasis.

S 2a   Sentence Length

Use short sentences for emphatic, memorable statement; use long sentences for detailed explanation and support. A short, incisive sentence is often appropriate for summing up a key idea or for giving pointed advice. The following sentences have a terse, aphoristic quality; they are quotable, emphatic, to the point:

Economy is the art of making the most of life.   (G. B. Shaw)
A man cannot speak but he judges himself.   (Emerson)

> As long as possible live free and uncommitted.   (Thoreau)
> Perversity is the muse of modern literature.   (Susan Sontag)

A complex, elaborate sentence is often appropriate for detailed explanation or argument. The following sentences from Thoreau's "Civil Disobedience" are carefully worked out, with all necessary ifs and buts fully stated:

> There will never be a really free and enlightened State until the State comes to recognize the individual as a higher and independent power, from which all its own power and authority are derived, and treats him accordingly.

> It is not a man's duty, as a matter of course, to devote himself to the eradication of any, even the most enormous wrong; he may still properly have other concerns to engage him; but it is his duty, at least, to wash his hands of it, and, if he gives it no thought longer, not to give it practically his support.

A *succession* of short sentences may accurately mirror random, idling thought. Though the impressions in the following passage are related, the short sentences give it an unevaluated, "documentary" quality:

> Manuel shook his head. He had nothing to do now until the next third. The gypsy was very good with the banderillos. The bull would come to him in the next third in good shape. He was a good bull. It had all been easy up to now. The final stuff with the sword was all he worried over. He did not really worry. He did not even think about it. — Ernest Hemingway, "The Undefeated"

In order to use short and long sentences to advantage, remember the following points:

(1) Excessive use of *short, isolated sentences* can make your writing sound immature. The more you develop your capacity for sustained thinking, the more you will get away from sentences like the following:

Choppy: Many teachers can give students information. Very few can inspire students to learn. Information is of little use to the student. Soon he will leave college. Then he will forget what he has memorized. He must be inspired to learn on his own.

Improved: Many teachers can give students information, but few can inspire them to learn. When a student leaves college, the information he has memorized will be of little use and will soon be forgotten. What he needs most is the ability to learn on his own.

(2) Your writing will gain in clarity and emphasis if you occasionally make your reader stop short at a *concise, memorable statement of an important point*. Notice the emphatic short sentences in the following passages:

With the great growth in leisure-time activities, millions of Americans are turning to water sports: fishing, swimming, water skiing, and skin diving. *Clean water exhilarates and relaxes.* — Vance Packard, "America the Beautiful — and Its Desecraters," *Atlantic*

Bennett was always facing the wonder of the actualities of living. It was wonderful to him that we live as we do, that time will pass and change us, that we will die and perhaps die painfully, that life is what it is. *He never decorates or embroiders. He is wholly materialistic. Common sense is the salt of his plate.* We are never swept away, but we are curiously won over, and we, too, are filled with wonder at the slow unspinning of life. — John Van Druten, "My Debt to Arnold Bennett," *Saturday Review*

(3) A short sentence can be especially effective if it sets off an important conclusion or a *key observation at the end of a passage composed of longer sentences:*

They have a constitutional right, of course, to tell us what we must do to be saved; as they have always done. Twenty years ago they were telling us the direct opposite of what they tell us now; but they were just as sure then as now that they had the sole and sufficient key to salvation, and that those who did not accept it were forever damned. *One becomes bored.* — Elmer Davis, "History in Doublethink," *Saturday Review*

S 2b   Varied Word Order

Variations from normal word order can keep sentences from being tiresomely alike. Though most of your sentences will follow the subject-verb sequence, there will usually be enough variety in the remaining sentence elements to prevent tiresome repetition. Monotony is most likely to result when a number of sentences start with the same subject, especially a pronoun like *I* or *he:*

Monotonous: A good example of a topic drawn from personal experience is a bus accident I once had. I wrote a paper about this experience of mine. I remembered the events which took place during the accident. I could describe them well. After all, I had experienced them. It was a shocking experience. I will never forget it. The facts stand out in my memory because it was so shocking.

(1) One way to break up a monotonous sequence is to *make a modifier that usually occurs later in the sentence precede the subject.* Like all stylistic effects, the **introductory modifier** can become an annoying mannerism if overused. Used sparingly, it becomes a reliable way of introducing variety into a group of plodding sentences:

Varied: He reversed the direction of the canoe. *After a few seconds* he stopped paddling. *Slowly* he made the canoe drift to the bank. *When within a yard of the shore*, he grabbed one of the overhanging branches.

Varied: The Trans World Terminal stems from the work of contemporary architects like Corbusier of France and Nervi of Italy, masters of the curve in concrete. *Like a true eagle*, this building is all curves and muscle, no right angles. *Built of reinforced concrete*, the whole structure swoops and turns and rises.—Ken Macrorie, "Arriving and Departing," *The Reporter*

(2) A less frequent variation from normal word order is to *make a verb precede its subject.* The subject-verb sequence is usually reversed only in questions, where all or part of the verb characteristically precedes the subject: *"Are* you ready?" *"Will* he *be* back?" "Why *did* your wife *leave* the car?" Writers aiming at poetic or dramatic effects occasionally use **inversion** even in ordinary declarative sentences:

Slowly *climbs* the summer moon.
Everywhere *was* silence.

S 2c   Emphatic Word Order

Variations from normal word order can direct attention to the word or phrase occurring in an unusual position.

(1) To gain emphasis, a writer may *shift a complement to a more emphatic initial position.* The **introductory complement** is normal in exclamations beginning with *what* or *how:* "*What stories* that man told!" "*What a liar* you are!" "*How true* that is!" In other sentences, the introductory complement is especially effective when it takes up something mentioned earlier:

Effective: The committee has asked me to resign. *That* I will never do.

Effective: Mr. Schlumpf fried two small pieces of fish. *One of these* he fed to his cat. *The other* he ate himself.

Effective: We really should not resent being called paupers. *Paupers* we are, and *paupers* we shall remain.

NOTE: Like other attention-getting devices, the introductory complement sometimes attracts attention to the speaker rather than to what he is saying. Sometimes the construction smacks of old-fashioned oratory:

More patient wife a husband never had.
Gone are the days of my youth.
Such deeds of glory we shall see no more.

(2) Often a sentence becomes clearer after you *shift the predicate of the main clause toward the end* and work some of the modifiers into the sentence earlier. Such treatment may strengthen a sentence

especially if a **final modifier** is a belated qualification or concession, unexpectedly weakening the main point:

Weak: We shall never dismiss a teacher because of the political beliefs of his associates without careful investigation. (*Without careful investigation* is a lame reversal of what starts out as a strong statement in support of teachers with controversial associations.)

Improved: We shall never, *without careful investigation,* dismiss a teacher because of the political beliefs of his associates.

Weak: Richard Wagner became one of the most successful composers of all time in spite of the jeers of his contemporaries. (This version may make your readers remember the jeers rather than the man's success.)

Improved: Richard Wagner, *though jeered at by his contemporaries,* became one of the most successful composers of all time.

S 2d Loose and Periodic

Experiment with shifts from the more common loose sentence to the more tightly structured periodic sentence. A loose sentence finishes one major statement relatively *early* but then leads on to further points or further detail. It is an expandable or cumulative sentence that looks as if it might have been built in stages, or as if it grew by addition. Can you see how the following sentences finish one major point and then "move on"?

Loose: *Comedy usually moves toward a happy ending,* and the normal response of the audience to a happy ending is "this should be," which sounds like a moral judgment. — Northrop Frye, *Anatomy of Criticism*

Loose: *The whistle of the locomotive penetrates my woods summer and winter,* sounding like the scream of a hawk sailing over some farmer's yard, informing me that many restless city merchants are arriving within the circle of the town, or adventurous country traders from the other side. — Thoreau, *Walden*

In a periodic sentence, an essential part of the main statement is *held in suspense* until the end, so that the sentence ends when the main statement ends. Everything else is worked into the sentence along the way, contributing its share to the main effect. As a result, the periodic sentence has an air of finality, of emphatic assertion. It makes the main idea stay with us.

Periodic: *Even Tom Jones,* though far more fully realized, *is still deliberately associated,* as his commonplace name indicates, *with the conventional and the typical.* — Northrop Frye, *Anatomy of Criticism*

Periodic: *Prayer* that craves a particular commodity, anything less than all good, *is vicious.* — Emerson, *Essays, First Series*

Exercises

A. Study the variations in sentence style in the following passages. Describe the functions performed or the effects produced by sentences of different *length*. Which passages make use of variations in *word order*?

1. Why conform to a group? Why throw away your birthright for a Greek pin or a peace button, for security and nonentity? This goes especially for the typical college student, who merely wants to do what "everyone else is doing." What everyone else is doing isn't best. It's merely common. One of the synonyms of "common" is "vulgar."

2. The dictionary can neither snicker nor fulminate. It records. It will offend many, no doubt, to find the expression *wise up*, meaning to inform or to become informed, listed in the Third International with no restricting label. To my aging ears it still sounds like slang. But the evidence — quotations from the *Kiplinger Washington Letter* and the *Wall Street Journal* — convinces me that it is I who am out of step, lagging behind.   (Bergen Evans)

3. The production of a work of art is not the result of a miracle. It requires preparation. The soil, be it ever so rich, must be fed. By taking thought, by deliberate effort, the artist must enlarge, deepen and diversify his personality. Then the soil must lie fallow. Like the bride of Christ, the artist waits for the illumination that shall bring forth a new spiritual life. He goes about his ordinary avocations with patience; the subconscious does its mysterious business; and then, suddenly springing, you might think from nowhere, the idea is produced.   (W. Somerset Maugham)

4. The wind roars up the avenue. Trees stoop and bend this way and that. Moonbeams splash and spill wildly in the rain. But the beam of the lamp falls straight from the window. The candle burns stiff and still.   (Virginia Woolf)

5. Morning is when I am awake and there is a dawn in me. Moral reform is the effort to throw off sleep. Why is it that men give so poor an account of their day if they have not been slumbering? They are not such poor calculators. If they had not been overcome with drowsiness they would have performed something. The millions are awake enough for physical labor; but only one in a million is awake enough for effec-

tive intellectual exertion, only one in a hundred millions to a poetic or divine life. To be awake is to be alive.   (Thoreau)

B. Which of the following sentences would you classify as loose, which as periodic?

1. Louise is the most lonely girl I have known, a beautiful little porcelain figurine placed into a world where porcelain figurines have gone out of style.

2. A thirty-hour ride in a troop train (model 1890) from Los Angeles had changed the dapper young man who had received personal greetings from the President of the United States into a sodden, wrinkled, tired, and bewildered draftee.

3. His friend Philinte, who is ready to lie quite cheerfully in order to enable other people to preserve their self-respect, is the more genuinely sincere of the two.   (Northrop Frye)

4. The book made me remember the things I wanted to forget, the things I had pushed to the back of my mind: the bombings in Germany when I was a child there, the dismembered bodies, the stench of human remains, the atrocities, and the fire and fury of war.

5. Bird-watchers were once figures of fun and they are still good for a laugh in *New Yorker* cartoons, but they are so numerous and often so highly placed that they might protest against "offensive stereotypes" as effectively as the other large minorities — racial, national, and religious — so vociferously do.   (Joseph Wood Krutch)

6. Far am I from denying in theory, full as far is my heart from withholding in practice (if I were of power to give or withhold) the *real* rights of man.   (Edmund Burke)

7. Liberals should not be ashamed to make positive claims about American society and politics, not only because they are true, but also because today's youth is being told so many other and contradictory things.

8. The nonchalance of boys who are sure of a dinner, and would disdain as much as a lord to do or say aught to conciliate one, is the healthy attitude of human nature.   (Emerson)

C. Select three sentences from your recent themes. For each, write down first the original version. Then add two or more revised versions, using *variations in word order* to make the sentence more emphatic or less routine.

EXAMPLE

We have always settled any disagreement over policy amiably by full and frank discussion.

By full and frank discussion, we have always settled any disagreement over policy amiably.

Any disagreement over policy we have always settled amiably by full and frank discussion.

S 3   Awkward Construction

A writer should avoid constructions that make for an indirect, awkward, wooden style.

Effective sentences may be long and complicated, as long as the words and structural relationships convey meaning clearly and directly. On the other hand, the grammatical equipment even in short sentences may become so heavy that it interferes with effective communication.

S 3a   Deadwood

Often a sentence proceeds more smoothly after it has been pruned of deadwood. Avoid unnecessary *there are*s and *who were*s:

Awkward: *There are* many farmers in the area *who* are planning to attend the meeting *which is* scheduled for next Friday.

Improved: Many farmers in the area plan to attend the meeting scheduled for next Friday.

Other sentences can be cleared of deadwood by effective use of pronouns:

Awkward: A child of pre-school age often shows a desire to read, but *the child's* parents often ignore this *desire.*

Improved: Often a child of pre-school age shows a desire to read—*which his* parents ignore.

Some connectives, prepositions, and pronouns are unnecessary or unnecessarily heavy:

Awkward: I wrote little, *because of the fact that* my childhood had been *an* uneventful *one.*

Improved: I wrote little, because my childhood had been uneventful.

S 3b   Awkward Passive

Unnecessary use of the passive makes sentences heavy or round-about. An active sentence is modeled on the "agent-action-target" relationship: "The woodsman *felled* the tree." A passive sentence reverses this perspective and looks at the action from the point of

view of the original object: "The tree *was felled* by the woodsman."
Students often overuse the passive under the mistaken impression
that it will make their sentences more formal, more scholarly. Practice translating such pseudo-formal passives back into the active
voice:

Pseudo-Formal: Although Bradley Hall *is* regularly *populated* by students, close
study of the building as a structure *is* seldom *undertaken.*

Direct: The students *passing* through Bradley Hall seldom *pause to study*
its structure.

Pseudo-Formal: My experiences at writing *were* greatly *increased* due to two large
essays due each week.

Direct: I *wrote* more than ever, *having to turn in* two long essays each week.

The reader is used to the who-does-what sequence; he can follow an account easily if he focuses first on the persons or forces at
work and then on the work they do. Unnecessary use of the passive
can make it hard for the reader to visualize actions or events. Since
the agent or performer is often *omitted* from a passive sentence, the
reader may find it hard to determine the person responsible for an
action or idea:

Evasive: A plan for popular election of Supreme Court justices *is* now *being
advanced.* (By whom? The passive spreads a protective cloak of
anonymity around the authors of the proposal.)

Evasive: The racial problem is clearly one that *could and should have been
solved* decades ago. (By whom?)

Some teachers and editors discourage *all* uses of the passive as
wordy and indirect. But not all passives are bad:
(1) The passive can pull the result, object, or goal of an action
into an *emphatic initial position.*

Unemphatic: *The common desire* for that which only a few can possess *causes*
much of the hostility that exists among men.

Emphatic: *The hostility* perpetually exercised between one man and another
is caused by the desire of many for that which only few can possess — Samuel Johnson, *The Rambler*

As a result, the passive is appropriate when the *recipient or target
of an action seems more important than the performer:*

The unpretentious monarchs of Scandinavia and the Low Countries are respectfully
accepted by their sober subjects. — Kingsley Martin, "Strange Interlude," *Atlantic*

(2) When no special emphasis is intended, the passive is most appropriate when the *originator or the performer of an action is unimportant, irrelevant,* or *hard to identify:*

Some of John's brain cells *were damaged* when he was a small child.
In World War II, millions of people *were driven* from their homes.

(On *shifts* to the passive, see G 12c.)

S 3c   Impersonal Constructions

Impersonal constructions are annoying when they obscure the identity of the forces at work. The impersonal *one,* the *it* without antecedent, and *there-is* or *there-are* sentences are most appropriate when the identity of persons or forces initiating an action is of secondary importance. We naturally say "it rains" or "it snows" when we are interested in the process and its results rather than in its causes. But guard against the unnecessary use of such constructions.

(1) The **impersonal *one*** is often a tiresome substitute for fuller identification of the persons concerned, especially if their identity is indirectly revealed by modifiers:

Tiresome:	*When teaching, one* should be patient.
Improved:	*Teachers* should be patient.

Tiresome:	*As a father, one* should not spoil his children.
Improved:	*Fathers* should not spoil their children.

Tiresome:	*If one is a citizen of a democracy, he* should exercise his voting rights.
Improved:	*A citizen of a democracy* should vote.

(2) In ***it-is*** and ***there-is*** sentences, the first two words are mere structural props, which can make the sentences sound lame and indecisive. Sometimes the subject of a sentence receives needed emphasis if it is introduced by *it is* or *there is* and has its predicate changed into a modifying clause:

Emphatic:	It is *his competence* that we question — not his honesty.

More often, however, the rearrangement of sentence elements made necessary by *it is* or *there is* causes awkwardness:

Awkward:	In 1958, *there was* a strike participated in by five thousand union members.
Improved:	In 1958, five thousand union members went on strike.

S 3d   Excessive Subordination

Excessive subordination causes various types of overburdened sentences.

(1) One common type *dovetails several dependent clauses into each other,* thus making a subordinating connective follow another subordinating connective or a relative pronoun. The resulting *that-if, if-because, which-when* **constructions** need not be awkward, but they almost always are when used by inexperienced writers:

Awkward: I think *that if* there were less emphasis on conformity in high school, college students would be better prepared for independent thinking.

Improved: In my opinion, college students would be better prepared for independent thinking *if* there were less emphasis on conformity in high school.

Awkward: I am against football scholarships *because if* football players are given preferential treatment, who will want to participate in other college sports?

Improved: I am against football scholarships. *If* football players are given preferential treatment, who will want to participate in other college sports?

(2) Another type of excessive subordination results in **"house-that-Jack-built" sentences.** Several dependent clauses of the same type follow each other, making the sentence trail off into *a confusing succession of modifiers:*

Awkward: When I was in Mexico City, I visited Jean, *who* was living with a Mexican girl *who* posed for the local artists, *who* are usually too poor to pay their rent, let alone the model's fee.

Improved: When I was in Mexico City, I visited Jean. She was living with a Mexican girl *who* posed for the local artists but seldom received any money for her work. Most Mexican artists are too poor to pay their rent, let alone the model's fee.

Sometimes too many dependent clauses of the same type delay the main clause:

Awkward: *When* a child is constantly watched *when* he is born and *while* he is a baby, the reason is that his mother wants to see whether he is developing as her books say he should.

Improved: Some mothers constantly watch young children to see whether they are developing as the books say they should.

(3) Unskillful subordination sometimes causes sentences with a teeter-totter effect. Such **seesaw sentences** start with a dependent clause, proceed to the main clause, and then add a *second dependent clause that in a confusing way qualifies the meaning of the first:*

Confusing: *Because many teen-agers marry hastily,* their marriages end in divorce, *because they are too immature to face adult responsibilities.*

Clearer: Many teen-agers are too immature to face adult responsibilities. They marry hastily, and often their marriages end in divorce.

S 3e   Awkward Modifiers

Awkwardness results when disproportionately heavy modifiers break up the pattern of a clause. Lengthy appositives, complicated verbal phrases, or clumsy dependent clauses sometimes separate elements that belong together:

Awkward: The pilot told his friends that he had flown Clinton Morris, *a resident of New York City sought by the government for income tax evasion,* out of the United States.

Awkward: The club treasurer, *being* the son of a father constantly *stressing* the importance of *maintaining* a proper sense of the value of money, refused to pay our expenses.

Awkward: In 1943, Independence Hall, *which had been the first building built on the campus and which had housed the administration of the college for many decades,* was torn down.

NOTE: The exact line between just enough and too much is hard to draw. Successful authors sometimes use sentences that would trip up a writer with a less sure touch:

The boys in his books got ahead by outwitting thieves and sharpers—yet he himself, a mild and generous little man who gave freely of his earnings to newsboys and bootblacks on the New York streets (the sort of boys who were his favorite heroes), was an easy mark for impostors.—Frederick Lewis Allen, "Horatio Alger, Jr.," *Saturday Review*

Exercises

A. Which of the following sentences seem clear and well built? Which seem awkward, overburdened, or confusing? If your instructor desires, revise the weak sentences.

1. Saturday mornings used to be my best time for studying, because I knew nothing was due the next morning (which was Sunday), until I started working.

2. From across the dinner-littered dining table, my father blinks myopically and asserts that current conflicts are no different from any other conflicts and that my dissent is no different from what his dissent used to be.

3. The magazine that is chosen by the reader is one that contains articles that the reader enjoys.

4. There are many ways in which a student who is interested in meeting a foreign student may come to know one.

5. A child's first impressions of people and places shape the course of his future life, frequently.

6. Knowing the right answers is sometimes less important than asking the right questions.

7. As we left the city, we approached a range of hills which seemed like giant waves which were about to break.

8. Having brothers and sisters to argue with and to adjust to was a useful experience because it helped me understand other people, because I don't always meet people sharing all my opinions.

9. John Milton was the first English writer who clearly and convincingly stated the idea that incompatibility is grounds for divorce, if I am not mistaken.

10. If someone is exercising his slightly off-key singing voice and a friend mockingly plugs his ears and winces in agony, the singer might well take the gesture as a personal insult if he didn't have a sense of humor.

11. As we were waiting for the doctor to see us, a boy with brown hair down to the small of his back played a flute, tears streaming down his face.

12. Various ways of living are being tested today and experimented with by youth whose dominant characteristic is the desire for flexibility.

B. For each of the following sentences, point out the perspective created or the special effect achieved by the use of the passive.

1. The scientific war against deliciousness has been stepped up enormously in the last decade.   (Philip Wylie)

2. When the portion of meat was brought down in its wooden tub at dinnertime, it was duly divided as fairly as possible into as many parts as there were mouths.

3. I was taken up a narrow staircase to the men's dormitory, in which were eight or ten beds and four miserable wash-hand stands.   (H. G. Wells)

S 4   Repetition

A writer must learn to make effective use of repetition and parallelism.

Unintentional, haphazard repetition can make a passage sound clumsy. Deliberate repetition, on the other hand, can emphasize important points and give continuity to a sentence or a paragraph.

S 4a   Awkward Repetition

Unintentional repetition of sounds, syllables, words, or phrases violates the requirements of **euphony**. A passage should sound pleasing, or at least inoffensive, when read aloud. Carelessly repeated sounds grate on the reader's ears.

Awkward:	Commercials seldom make for entertain*ing* and relax*ing* listen*ing*.
Improved:	Commercials seldom entertain and relax the listener.
Awkward:	Close examin*ation* of the results of the investig*ation* led to a re-organiz*ation* of the department.
Improved:	Close study of the results of the inquiry led to a reorganization of the department.
Awkward:	We listened to an account *of* the customs *of* the inhabitants *of* the village.
Improved:	We listened to an account of the villagers' customs.

Unintentional repetition is especially annoying when the similarity in sound covers up a *shift in meaning or relationship:*

My father lost his savings during the depression because he had *banked* on [better: "relied on"] the well-established reputation of our hometown *bank*.

S 4b   Emphatic Repetition

Intentional repetition makes for clarity and continuity. A writer may repeat important words and phrases for emphasis:

Emphatic: When I returned to State, *I studied* as I have never studied since. *I studied* before classes. *I studied* after classes. *I studied* till English, history, and zoology merged into one blurry mass of incoherent erudition.

Emphatic: In my mother's world, *no one ever* shrugged his shoulders; *no one* was *ever* bored and lazy; *no one* was *ever* cynical; *no one ever* laughed. — Alfred Kazin, "The Bitter 30's," *Atlantic*

Notice the cumulative effect of intentional repetition in the following passage from Stephen Crane's "The Open Boat":

In the meantime, the oiler *rowed,* and then the correspondent *rowed,* and then the oiler *rowed.* Grey-faced and bowed forward, they mechanically, turn by turn, plied the leaden oars.

S 4c   Parallel Structure

Effective use of parallel structure channels the reader's attention. Parallel structure pulls together related ideas through the repetition of characteristic grammatical patterns. The following passages make effective use of parallelism:

The way *to speak and write* what shall not go out of fashion,
                    is
        to speak and write sincerely.   (Emerson)

My lack *of excitement,*
        of curiosity,
        of surprise,
        of any sort of pronounced *interest,*
                began to arouse his distrust.   (Joseph Conrad)

The air *must be* pure
        if we are to breathe;
the soil *must be* arable
        if we are to eat;
the water *must be* clean
        if we are to drink.

Our houses *are* built *with* foreign taste;
our shelves *are* garnished *with* foreign ornaments;
        our opinions,
        our tastes,
        our faculties,
                lean and
                follow
                        the Past and
                        the Distant.   (Emerson)

In prose of exposition and argument, parallel structure is used for some of the following purposes:

(1) Parallel structure helps to *line up related ideas in a sentence;* it *draws together related ideas in a paragraph:*

When the world wars came, the people of the liberal democracies could not be aroused to the exertions and the sacrifices of the struggle until they *had been frightened by* the opening disasters, *had been incited to* passionate hatred, and *had become intoxicated with* unlimited hope.

The people wanted to be told that when this particular enemy had been forced to unconditional surrender, they would re-enter the golden age. *This* unique *war would end* all wars. *This* last *war would make* the world safe for democracy. *This crusade would make* the whole world a democracy. — Walter Lippmann, *The Public Philosophy*

(2) Often, parallel structure helps to *line up dissimilar ideas for comparison or contrast.*

His remarks provoked much comment, *self-righteous from his enemies, apologetic from his friends.*

Whereas *it is desirable that* the old *should treat with respect* the wishes of the young, *it is not desirable that* the young *should treat with respect* the wishes of the old.

The European democracies *chose to rely* on unarmed appeasement, and the American democracy *chose to rely on* unarmed isolation.

(3) Parallel structure enables a writer to *make a series of parallel sentences build up to a* climax. Notice how the author of the following passage starts with fairly innocuous generalities and leads up to a specific point dear to his heart:

The future *is not for* little men with little minds. It *is not for* men without vision who fear progress. It *is not for* timid men who early were frightened by the story of Frankenstein. And it *is not for* those arch reactionaries who seek to shatter big enterprise and to force American industry back into the puny production patterns of its nineteenth-century infancy.

(On *faulty* parallelism, see G 11.)

S 4d   Rhythm and Balance

Frequent use of parallel constructions makes for regularity and balance, especially when the parallel elements are of approximately equal length. Parallelism produces rhythmical patterns that are more distinctly felt than the highly variable rhythms of ordinary speech.

(1) A writer with an ear for rhythm makes use of the *variations* in sentence structure that prevent regularity from becoming predictable. In the following sentence the *which*-clause separating the subject and verb of the main clause makes for variety, while the prepositional phrases *(with remarkable vistas . . . , with weeping birches . . .)* make for balance:

Seattle, *which sits like Rome on seven hills,* was endowed by nature *with remarkable vistas* of water and mountains, *with weeping birches and monkey trees and dogwoods* big as maples. — Russell Lynes, "Seattle Will Never Be the Same," *Harper's*

Notice the role of variety and balance in the following passage:

India *is a poetic nation,* yet it *demands* new electrical plants. It *is a mystical nation,* yet it *wants* new roads. It *is* traditionally *a peaceful nation, yet it could,* if misled, *inflame* Asia. — James A. Michener, "Portraits for the Future," *Saturday Review*

There is just enough variation to keep the repetition of the pattern from becoming monotonous: "poetic — mystical — traditionally peaceful"; "demands — wants — could, if misled, inflame."

(2) The prose of a writer with a strong sense of rhythm often has a *musical quality.* Here is a passage whose rhythm is exceptionally stately and elaborate:

That Man is the product of causes which had no prevision of the end they were achieving; *that* his *origin,* his *growth,* his *hopes and fears,* his *loves and* his *beliefs,* are but the outcome of accidental collocations of atoms; *that* no *fire,* no *heroism,* no *intensity of thought and feeling,* can preserve an individual life beyond the grave; *that* all *the labours* of the ages, all *the devotion,* all *the inspiration,* all *the noonday brightness* of human genius, are destined to extinction in the vast death of the solar system, and *that* the whole temple of Man's achievement must inevitably be buried beneath the débris of a universe in ruins — all these things, if *not quite beyond dispute,* are *yet so nearly certain,* that no philosophy which rejects them can hope to stand. *Only within the scaffolding of* these truths, *only on the firm foundation of* unyielding despair, can the soul's habitation henceforth be safely built. — Bertrand Russell, *Mysticism and Logic*

The long series of noun clauses making up most of the first sentence, and the multiple subjects in most of them, are the most obvious instances of parallelism. Toward the end of the passage there are several pairs of neatly balanced phrases *(if not quite beyond dispute — yet so nearly certain; only within the scaffolding of these truths — only on the firm foundation of unyielding despair).*

NOTE: Like other stylistic devices, patterns that make for euphony and balance are most effective when the reader responds to them without becoming consciously aware of them. Today, workaday expository prose avoids elaborate parallelism and obtrusive rhythm. It uses stylistic resources *sparingly,* thus preserving the freshness and spontaneity that are lost when the use of recurrent devices becomes a habit.

Exercises

A. Examine the uses of *repetition and parallelism* in the following sentences. Your instructor may ask you to use one or more of these as model sentences. For each model sentence, write one of your own that as far as possible preserves the structure of the original.

1. Warren believed in applauding politely to reward effort, generously to reward competence, and frenetically to reward genius.

2. War, assuming that one does not love it for its own sake, or does not use it as a background for some isolated moral, or does not, worst of all, believe in its shabby rationale, can only produce one of two reactions: a tear, or a scream.

3. The businessman who writes a letter, the professor who fashions a lecture, the student who prepares a theme, needs style and covets style as much as the man who writes an editorial for the *Times.* (Charles W. Ferguson)

4. We are in such haste to be doing, to be writing, to be gathering gear, to make our voice audible a moment in the derisive silence of eternity, that we forget that one thing, of which these are but the parts — namely to live. (Robert Louis Stevenson)

5. The capital defect in the culture of These States is the lack of a civilized aristocracy, secure in its position, animated by an intelligent curiosity, skeptical of all facile generalizations, superior to the sentimentality of the mob, and delighting in the battle of ideas for its own sake. (H. L. Mencken)

6. It requires enormous intelligence, innate or acquired by cultivation, to discharge the full responsibilities of managing a household; doing its endlessly repetitive work without deadening the mind; bringing up children, restraining, encouraging and helping them; being a companion and helpmeet to one's husband, helpfully and intelligently

interested in his work; and being, at the same time, able to take on his duties and responsibilities if she must, as thousands of women have had to.   (Dorothy Thompson)

B. Examine the features that make for *rhythm and balance* in the following passages. Point out any other features that make for effective sentence style. Examine such features as sentence length, variety, emphasis. Point out any special or unusual effects.

1. We go to our libraries in order to read and take advantage of the experiences of others. I think we all realize that not every written word in a library is entirely true. Many different authors have here written what they think, what they have experienced, what they believe is true, and sometimes what they wish were true. Some are wrong, a few are right, and many are neither entirely wrong nor entirely right.

2. This is not a Utopian tract. Some of those who complain about the quality of our national life seem to be dreaming of a world in which everyone without exception has talent, taste, judgment and an unswerving allegiance to excellence. Such dreams are pleasant but unprofitable. The problem is to achieve some measure of excellence *in this society,* with all its beloved and exasperating clutter, with all its exciting and debilitating confusion of standards, with all the stubborn problems that won't be solved and the equally stubborn ones that might be. — John W. Gardner, *Excellence*

3. Another reason for Emerson's unpopularity is that he did not have a vision of evil. To count in criticism nowadays you must have a vision of evil. It seems that Herman Melville had a vision of evil in *Moby Dick,* that Nathaniel Hawthorne had a vision of evil in *The Scarlet Letter,* and that Henry James had a vision of evil in *The Turn of the Screw.* Precisely what the evil was in each case is in dispute, but it is there. Emerson had no vision of evil. His life was threatened by tuberculosis, he abandoned his pulpit, his first wife died young, his brothers were sick men, and his son perished —

> That hyacinthine boy, for whom
> Morn well might break and April bloom

he was ostracized by the conservative, he took the unpopular side in politics, he was accused of advocating atheism, he was said to be a radical, but he had no vision of evil. All he had was a vision of good. Good, he said, is something so tough, resilient, and timeless, it is indestructible. — Howard Mumford Jones, "The Iron String," *Harvard Alumni Bulletin*

4. We do not need to fear ideas, but the censorship of ideas. We do not need to fear criticism, but the silencing of criticism. We do not need to

fear excitement or agitation in the academic community, but timidity and apathy. We do not need to fear resistance to political leaders, but unquestioning acquiescence in whatever policies those leaders adopt. — Henry Steele Commager, "The Problem of Dissent," *Saturday Review*

5. Twenty-five years ago, when Calvin Coolidge and George V reigned over the English-speaking peoples, when H. L. Mencken was tearing the booboisie to shreds, when Lytton Strachey was demolishing one reputation after another, and when the monthly discovery of a radical new masterpiece by each of several book clubs still carried conviction, one department of literature was being thoroughly purged, revolution-ized, and set in its place. This was biography. It had been attacked by various columns of shock-troopers. Groups who had read "Eminent Victorians" with savage glee; groups who had gone like a cyclone through Freud (or a manual on Freud); groups intoxicated with the satiric mockery of Shaw and the mordant irony of Henry Adams; groups of second-sight psychologists who at a moment's notice could describe the ideas which surged through Cromwell's mind the night before Naseby, and report the precise words of an unrecorded conversation of Emerson and Thoreau — all these were lustily creating a "new biog-raphy." — Allan Nevins, "How Shall One Write of a Man's Life?" *New York Times Book Review*

CHAPTER FOURTEEN

Grammar

When a child begins to talk, he learns not only to name things but also to work the names of things into complicated patterns. Soon he is able to say "Suzie won't give me my ball back" or "Johnny says there isn't any Santa Claus." He has evidently mastered the major principles of **grammar**; that is, the *system by which words combine into larger units to convey ideas and information.* The study of grammar is conventionally divided into three major areas:

Phonology studies the sound system of a language. For instance, it would investigate the differences that set apart the words in a series like *bit, bet, bat, but, bought, boat, boot.*

Morphology studies the way the smallest meaningful units in a language combine into words. It would study the differences that set apart the words in series like *happy, happier, happiness* or *say, says, saying, said.*

Syntax studies the way words work together in sentences. The difference between "Call me John" and "Call me a cab" is a difference in syntax.

In recent years, there has been an extraordinary revival of interest in grammar as the result of much new research and vigorous controversy among grammarians. Current textbooks for school and college draw in varying degrees on the contributions of three major approaches:

(1) *Traditional school grammar* long dominated the teaching of grammar in the schools but today survives only in modified or modernized versions. It had originally been modeled on the teaching of *Latin* grammar and had carried over into the teaching of English grammar many Latin concepts and terms: *nominative* (subject form), *genitive* (possessive), *dative* (in Latin, the special form for *indirect* object), *accusative* (object form). Here are some features of traditional grammar:

- Traditional grammar approached grammatical study through a systematic survey of eight *parts of speech:* noun, pronoun, verb, adjective, adverb, conjunction, preposition, interjection.

- Traditional grammar relied to some extent on *meaning-based definitions*. The sentence was defined as a "complete thought." The noun was defined as the name of a person, idea, or thing; the verb was defined as expressing action or state of being.

(2) *Structural grammar* was an attempt to focus grammatical description directly on the specific features of English, and to make that description more rigorously "scientific" than is possible with meaning-based definitions. For instance, both in "she started *to walk*" and in "she went *for a walk*," the word *walk* refers to the action of walking. But *to walk* is a verb, *a walk* is a noun. The difference is not in the meaning but in the grammatical *signals*: *to* is the sign of the infinitive; *a* is an article signaling that a noun will shortly follow. Here are some features of school grammars indebted to "structural linguistics":

- Structural grammar stresses the concrete, observable features that make up the *signaling system* of the language. What turns a jumbled list of words (practice—type—Mary—afternoon) into a sentence like "Mary practices her typing in the afternoon"? One obvious signal is *word order*—the arrangement of words in the sentence. Another type of signal is the use of *in-*

flections — the *-s* of *practices*, the *-ing* of *typing*. A third type of signal is the use of *function words* — *in, the.*

• Structural grammars aim at developing the student's "sentence sense" by the study of the most common sentence patterns:

Subject — Verb	Dogs bark.
Subject — Verb — Object	Englishmen like tea.
Subject — Verb — Indirect Object — Object	Music gives men pleasure.
Subject — Verb — Object — Object Complement	Bert made Linda his wife.
Subject — Linking Verb — Noun	Hubert is a madman.
Subject — Linking Verb — Adjective	Hubert is mad.
Subject — Verb — Object — Adjective	Linda drove Hubert mad.

(3) *Transformational grammar* has developed rapidly during the last two decades and now dominates most scholarly research in the field. The transformational grammarian attempts to go beyond the "surface" features investigated by structural grammar. He tries to formulate the rules by which grammatical structures are generated. The basic procedure of transformational grammar is to identify first the **kernel sentences** from which more complex structures derive. These would be such simple statement patterns as "John eats," "Jean bakes a cake," "The cake is good." The grammar then provides the formula for each successive **transformation** by which we introduce into a simple sentence such elements as plural, past tense, interrogation, passive voice, and negation:

The cakes are good.
Jean baked a cake.
Did John eat?
The cake was baked by Jean.
Jean does not bake cakes.

Additional transformational formulas would guide us in adding to one simple statement ("Jean bakes a cake") material from another ("The cake is good"). By working into the first sentence additional material from such a *second* source sentence, we generate structures like the following:

Jean bakes a *good* cake.
Jean bakes a cake, *which John eats.*
John eats only *if Jean bakes a cake.*
The cake being good, John ate it.

The following chapter does not attempt to provide a complete grammar of the English sentence, nor does it attempt to settle matters now in dispute among grammarians. Its aim is to provide a *writer's grammar,* helping him to identify the forms and constructions that are appropriate for written English.

G 1   Grammar and Usage

The study of grammar can help a writer make appropriate use of the resources of the language.

The student in high school and college must learn to adapt the grammatical patterns he learned as a child to changing needs. The language that the educated adult uses in serious conversation and in writing differs to some extent from the language he uses when not on his best behavior. A student learns early that often he should say "is not" rather than "ain't," "can hardly wait" rather than "can't hardly wait," and "this kind of car" rather than "these kind of cars."

Differences such as these are called differences in **usage.** The study of usage investigates *choices among alternative words, word forms, and constructions.* An effective writer has learned to make the choices that will prove acceptable to his readers.

G 1a   Standard and Nonstandard

Serious writing employs the kind of English that enjoys social and cultural prestige. **Standard** usage is the language of education, journalism, and other white-collar occupations. You will use it in your written work except when you record or deliberately imitate **nonstandard** speech. Nonstandard speakers have usually had relatively little formal education. Their jobs often require little reading of instructions and little writing of reports. They may have few dealings with teachers, lawyers, newspapermen, and other presumably highly literate persons.

Here are some of the distinctive forms and constructions of nonstandard English:

Verb Forms: he *don't,* you *was,* I *says; knowed, growed;* I *seen* him

Pronoun Forms: *hisself, theirself; this here* book, *that there* car; *them* boys

Connectives: *without* you pay the rent; *on account of* he was sick; *being as* she couldn't come

Double Negatives: we *don't* have *no* time; a little rain *never* hurt *no* one

Here are some passages reproducing nonstandard speech:

Fella says to me, gov'ment fella, an' he says, she's gullied up on ya. Gov'ment fella. He says, if ya plowed 'cross the contour, she won't gully. Never did have no chance to try her. An' the new super' ain't plowin' 'cross the contour. Runnin' a furrow four miles long that ain't stoppin' or goin' aroun' Jesus Christ Hisself. — John Steinbeck, *The Grapes of Wrath*

We ain't got the dog yet. It won't take but one. But he ain't there. Maybe he ain't nowhere. The only other way will be for him to run by accident over somebody that had a gun and knowed how to shoot it. — William Faulkner, "The Bear"

While nonstandard English is the natural speech in many a home and on many a blue-collar job, standard English is essential to advancement in school and office. Many of the features of nonstandard speech are distinctive enough to stand out, and seem clearly out of place, in writing. Nevertheless, the exact point at which nonstandard shades over into standard is a matter of dispute. Expressions like *off of* and *irregardless,* widely considered nonstandard, are frequently heard in the speech of educated people, including college teachers of English. Scholars debate in learned journals whether the *ain't* in "Ain't I right?" and the *good* in "The motor runs good" are an accepted part of educated speech, at least in some parts of the country. In your *writing,* however, a simple principle applies: When in doubt, be safe. A reader who considers you half-educated because you use *irregardless* will seldom give you a chance to prove him wrong.

(See the Glossary of Usage for *as, being as, couple,* double comparative, double negative, *all the farther, hadn't ought to, learn, used to could, without.*)

G 1b Formal and Informal

Different kinds of standard English are appropriate to different occasions. Relatively **informal** usages are found primarily in casual conversation, but also in writing designed to sound chatty or familiar. Relatively **formal** usages are characteristic of the language of scholarly studies, books on serious subjects, articles in serious magazines. Though more characteristic of written than of spoken English, these usages are also found in formal lectures, speeches, and discussions.

Here are some grammatical features of informal English:[1]

Contractions:	*don't, doesn't, isn't, won't, can't; I'm, you've, they're*
Conversational Tags:	*well,* . . . ; *why,* . . . ; *now,* . . .
Pronoun Forms:	it's *me,* that's *him; who* did you invite
Pronoun Reference:	everybody took *theirs;* somebody left *their* gloves
Intensifiers:	*so* glad, *such* a surprise; *real* miserable, *awful* fast

[1] For a discussion of formal and informal diction, see D 3.

In *informal* English, sentences often preserve some of the loose, improvised quality of speech. A speaker may start one pattern and then shift to another in midsentence. He may rethink what he is saying while he is saying it. The result may be awkward backtracking or duplication. In *formal* English, grammatical relationships in a sentence are carefully and accurately worked out: predicates logically fit their subjects; modifiers are clearly related to what they modify.

In spite of the protests of conservative teachers and editors, serious written English has over the years moved steadily toward greater informality. Many accomplished writers no longer observe the traditional rulings on such matters as *shall* and *will* or the split infinitive. The advice given in this chapter is designed to help you write the kind of formal English that is appropriate to the discussion of serious issues, but that is not so punctiliously formal as to become stilted or affected.

(See the Glossary of Usage on *apt/liable, between/among, blame on, can* and *may, cannot help but, couple of, different than, due to, each other/one another, get hit, it's me, less/fewer, like I said, most everybody,* possessive with verbal noun, preposition at the end of a sentence, *providing, reason is because, shall/will,* split infinitive, *these kind* and *those kind, used to/didn't use to, where at, you* with indefinite reference.)

Exercises

A. How successful are the following attempts to reproduce in writing the characteristic forms and constructions of *nonstandard speech?* Which features of nonstandard usage do you recognize?

1. I be dog iffen there wadden more folks there. Coming by wagon and foot and car, they was. Brother Slynum, he was standing at the entrance in his preaching suit just a-waving and helloing to everybody. The women was in their print dresses and sunbonnets. The men folks, too, was in their Sunday-go-to-meeting clothes. That ere tent with the sign painted over the door, "Welcome! All Day Singing and Dinner on the Ground," it was sagging in the wind. Outen front was the tables where everybody was putting the victuals: salads, cakes, cornbread, preserves, puddins, and Lord knows what all. At the far end of the table over a stone-built stove they was frying the catfish.

It was a jump-rope day. The spring was all stretched out on the pastures beyond, pretty and a little shy maybe, like a lazy gal waiting for her feller. With buttercups for freckles. But that ere spring didn't have nothing on me, I had more freckles than ere was buttercups. Yep.

Mama said I swollered a dollar and it broke out in pennies. But she was just spoofing. I hadden never seen a dollar. — Clancy Carlile, "The Animal Fair," *New Campus Writing*

2. Well, anyway, they come over to help us celebrate the Golden Wedding and it was pretty crimpy weather and the furnace don't seem to heat up no more like it used to and Mother made the remark that she hoped this winter wouldn't be as cold as the last, referring to the winter previous. So Edie said if she was us, and nothing to keep us home, she certainly wouldn't spend no more winters up here and why didn't we just shut off the water and close up the house and go down to Tampa, Florida? You know we was there four winters ago and staid five weeks, but it cost us over three hundred and fifty dollars for hotel bill alone. So Mother said we wasn't going no place to be robbed. So my son-in-law spoke up and said that Tampa wasn't the only place in the South, and besides we didn't have to stop at no high price hotel but could rent us a couple rooms and board out somewheres, and he had heard that St. Petersburg, Florida, was *the* spot and if we said the word he would write down there and make inquiries. — Ring. W. Lardner, "The Golden Honeymoon," *How to Write Short Stories*

B. Study recent columns by a columnist using a deliberately informal or humorous style. Report on his use of distinctive grammatical features of *informal English*.

G 2 Grammatical Analysis

Grammar is the study of how words work together in a sentence.

Words convey only vague and tentative meanings as long as they are loosely strung together. G.I.s and tourists abroad can carry on a rudimentary conversation with foreigners after picking up a few isolated words. A foreign visitor to the United States can make some headway by taking individual words from a dictionary. But he will not be speaking English until he can work words into meaningful patterns like the following:

Actor	Action Verb	Target	
The agent	scrutinized	my passport.	

Sender	Action Verb	Address	Missive
The travel bureau	sent	me	a brochure.

Person	Linking Verb	Label	
Maurice	looked	disappointed.	

Actor	Action Verb	Target	Label
Maurice	called	the trip	a disaster.

G 2a   Grammatical Devices

English employs several kinds of grammatical devices to give precise meaning to a succession of words. In the typical written sentence, inflections, word order, and function words combine to help the reader select among the possible meanings of words and work those words into a meaningful sequence.

(1) **Inflections** are *changes in the form of a word that correspond to differences in grammatical relationships.* Inflections signal the differences in meaning between the sentences in each of the following pairs:

> Stop*s* annoy*ed* our passenger.
> Stop annoy*ing* our passenger.
>
> The physician studi*ed* burn*s.*
> The physician'*s* study burn*ed.*

The endings spelled *s, ed,* and *ing* are the inflections most frequently used in English.

NOTE: Some languages, such as Latin and German, rely heavily on inflections. Originally, English was close to German in number and importance of inflected forms. Through the centuries, however, English has shed many of these. Modern English relies primarily on other grammatical devices.

(2) A second major grammatical device is **word order**. In English, *different arrangements of words in a sentence produce different meanings.* Compare the sentences in the following pairs:

> *Gentlemen* prefer *blondes.*
> *Blondes* prefer *gentlemen.*
>
> A *tramp* called *the mayor a liar.*
> A *liar* called *the mayor a tramp.*
> *The mayor* called *a tramp a liar.*
>
> He ate *only* the steak.
> He ate the *only* steak.

(3) A third major grammatical device is the use of *words whose main function is to clarify relationships among other words.* Many modern grammarians group these words together as **function words**. Function words account for the differences in meaning in the following pairs:

> George set *a* poor example.
> George set *the* poor *an* example.

He left the lady his estate.
He left *with* the lady *for* his estate.

The nurse neglected the patient.
The nurse *was* neglected *by* the patient.

G 2b   Basic Sentence Elements

The most important of the basic grammatical categories are those required to make up the various typical sentence patterns. In analyzing sentences, grammarians assign words to basic categories, or **parts of speech**, according to the functions they perform. The same word may serve different functions, and belong to different grammatical categories, in different sentences. The word *light* performs a different function in each of the following:

Turn off the *light.*
Let's *light* a candle.
She had *light* hair.
The water was *light* blue.

(1) *The basic model of the English sentence consists of only two major elements.* A complete sentence normally has at least a **subject** and a **predicate**:

Subject	Predicate
The boy	reads.
A car	stopped.
Dogs	bark.

The most important part of the subject is usually a **noun**: *car, student, bulldog, college, education.* Characteristically, nouns name or classify things, places, people, animals, concepts. The housewife looking up entries in the Sears Roebuck catalog, the chemist giving names to new plastics, the businessman naming new products — all rely on the naming function of the noun.

Here are the most important formal and structural characteristics of nouns:

- They occur in typical noun positions: "*Dogs* bark," "I like *dogs,*" and "for my *dogs.*"

- Their appearance is often signaled by noun markers such as *a, an,* and *the* (**articles**); *this, these, that,* and *those* (**demonstrative pronouns**); or *my, our,* and *your* (**possessive pronouns**). Modern grammars group these noun markers together as **determiners**.

- They typically add the inflectional *-s* to refer to more than one (plural): *boys, dogs, cars, ideas, preparations.* But note irregular plurals like *children* and *oxen;* unmarked plurals like *deer, sheep, offspring;* and nouns normally occurring only in the singular: *chaos, courage, rice.*

- They often show noun-forming endings (**suffixes**) like *-acy, -age, -ance, -dom, -ness, -hood: literacy, bondage, importance, wisdom, happiness, brotherhood.*

The place of nouns may be taken by **noun equivalents** or noun substitutes, such as the **personal pronouns:**

He	reads.
It	stopped.
They	bark.

The predicate, the second major part of a simple sentence, normally makes some kind of assertion concerning the subject. (Sometimes the predicate asks a question about the subject.) The most important word, or group of words, in the predicate is the **verb:** *reads, stopped, has left, will return, is reprimanded, has been elected.* The verb signals the performance of an action, the occurrence of an event, or the presence of a condition. A noun may *name* an action: *theft, movement, investigation.* A verb refers to present, future, past, possible, or hypothetical performance: *steals, has moved, may investigate.*

Here are the most important formal and structural characteristics of verbs:

- They occur in typical verb positions: "Let's *eat*," "*Eat* your cereal," and "Big fishes *eat* little fishes."

- In the present tense, most verbs add the inflectional *-s* when *he, she,* or *it* could substitute for the subject (third person singular): "He eat*s*," "She write*s*," "It surprise*s* me." Many verbs have a separate inflected form for past tense: *eat—ate, sing—sang, ask—asked, investigate—investigated.*

- Typical verb-forming suffixes are *-ize* and *-en*: organi*ze*, redd*en*, sharp*en*.

- In verb forms consisting of several words, a limited number of **auxiliaries** occur. If there are several auxiliaries, they typically appear in the following order: first, a modal, if any — *will (would), shall (should), can (could), may (might);* second, a form of *have,* if any *(has, had);* third, a form of *be,* if only one such form occurs *(is, am, are, was, were, be, been);* fourth, *being,* if two forms of *be* are present. Here are some of the resulting combinations:

Modal	Have	Be	(Being)	Main Verb
can				happen
	has			arrived
could	have			called
		is		waiting
may		be		canceled
		is	being	checked
will	have	been		sold
		was	being	rebuilt
should	have	been		revised

(2) *In several typical sentence patterns, the predicate is completed by one or more complements.* **Complements** become essential parts of the basic structure. An action verb may carry its action across to its target (**direct object**). An action verb like *give, send,* or *write* may carry the pattern first to the destination (**indirect object**) and then proceed to the missive (direct object). A verb like *name, elect,* or *call* may carry the pattern first to a direct object and then pin a label on the direct object. (The second complement is then called an **object complement.**)

Subject	Action Verb	Complement	Complement
The student	reads	a book.	
My friend	sent	me	a letter.
Fred	called	his roommate	a liar.

In other sentences, the verb is a **linking verb,** which introduces a description of the subject. A linking verb pins a label on the subject.

Subject	Linking Verb	Complement
Schnoogle	is	a mailman.
He	may be	your brother.
The price	seemed	reasonable.
The food	tasted	good.

The description following the linking verb is often a noun (*mailman, brother*). It may also be an **adjective,** a word that can point out a quality of a noun (see G 2c).

(3) *Several simple transformations rearrange (and sometimes omit or expand) basic sentence elements.* Thus, the **passive** makes the

original *object* the subject of a new sentence. The original subject appears after *by* at the end of the pattern, or is omitted altogether. The verb is changed to its passive form, which uses the auxiliary *be* and the past participle (see G 4a). The resulting pattern reverses the more common actor-action sequence by making the receiver, the target, or the result of the action the subject of the sentence.[2]

Subject	Passive Verb	
The book	was read	(by the student).
A letter	has been sent	(by my friend).

A second transformation changes the verb to the form used in requests or commands (**imperative**) and omits the subject:

Verb	Complement
Shut	the door.
Be	a man.
Keep	quiet.

A third transformation introduces an initial *there* and postpones the subject:

	Verb	Subject
There	is	hope.
There	was	no time.
There	were	few survivors.

NOTE: In identifying basic sentence elements, you will have to distinguish between verbs and **verbals**. *Verbals are derived from verbs but do not by themselves function as predicates.* The most distinctive and the most important of the verbals are the *to* forms (**infinitives**) and the *-ing* forms (**gerunds** and **present participles**). Infinitives and gerunds often serve as subjects or as complements, taking the place of nouns:

Speeding	causes	accidents.
He	refused	*to pay.*
Teachers	discourage	*cheating.*

These verbals do have some important similarities to verbs. For instance, they are often followed by objects:

Studying *grammar*	inspires	me.
Fred	refused	to pay *his dues.*
Courtesy	forbids	calling *a policeman a cop.*

[2] On the overuse of the passive, see S 3b.

The -*ing* forms are called present participles when they function as adjectives (see G 2c).

G 2c   Modifiers

The typical sentence contains words, or groups of words, that develop, restrict, or otherwise modify the meaning of the basic sentence elements. Such **modifiers** can be roughly divided into two main groups: those that modify nouns or noun equivalents and those that modify other parts of a sentence or the sentence as a whole.

(1) All of the modifiers italicized in the following examples modify the noun *dog* and thus belong in the first group:

A *shaggy* dog barred my way.
A *big, yellow* dog was chewing the rug.
A dog *wearing a muzzle* emerged from the door.
A *police* dog tracked me down.
A dog *with droopy eyes* dozed in the sun.

Of these modifiers, the first three (*shaggy, big, yellow*) have the structural and formal characteristics of adjectives. An **adjective** can be identified as occurring in typical adjective positions: "a *reasonable* price," "The price is *reasonable*," "a very *reasonable* price." Most adjectives have distinctive forms for use in comparisons: *small — smaller — smallest; good — better — best; reasonable — more reasonable — most reasonable.* Typical suffixes serving to derive adjectives from other words are -*ic*, -*ish*, -*ive*, and -*ous*: bas*ic*, fool*ish*, expen*sive*, courage*ous*. In traditional grammar, however, any modifier that modifies a noun or noun equivalent is said to *function* as an adjective.

(2) The second group of modifiers is illustrated in the following sentences:

The bell rang *twice.*
Suddenly the bell rang.
The bell rang *loudly.*
The bell rang *at intervals.*

Twice, suddenly, and *loudly* belong to a class of words known as **adverbs.** Many of these show the distinctive -*ly* ending. *At intervals* is not formally an adverb, but in traditional grammar it is said to serve an adverbial function.

NOTE: Combinations introduced by *with, at, on,* and similar words may modify either nouns or other parts of a sentence.

The girl *from Chicago* disappeared.   (adjective function)
The girl disappeared *from Chicago.*   (adverbial function)

With, at, on, and *from* are **prepositions**. Their most characteristic function is to relate a noun or noun equivalent to the rest of the sentence. Other common prepositions are *about, by, during, in, of, through, to, under, until,* and *without.* A preposition plus the noun it introduces is called a **prepositional phrase**.

G 2d   Joining Clauses

When several subject-predicate groups combine, they need to be distinguished from the sentence as a whole. They are traditionally referred to as **clauses**. The following sentences illustrate different ways of joining one clause to another:

My brother proposed to Elvira;	*however,*	she dislikes him.
My brother proposed to Elvira,	*but*	she dislikes him.
My brother proposed to Elvira,	*though*	she dislikes him.
My brother proposed to Elvira,	*who*	dislikes him.

(1) Clauses are called **independent** when they are *self-sufficient enough to stand by themselves,* to be punctuated as complete sentences. They are still considered independent when they are joined to another independent clause by an adverbial connective or by a coordinating connective.[3] **Adverbial connectives** (often called conjunctive adverbs) are such words as *however, therefore, moreover, nevertheless, besides.* **Coordinating connectives** (often called coordinating conjunctions) are such words as *and, but,* and *for.* A grammatically complete sentence ordinarily contains at least one independent clause. A sentence combining two or more independent clauses is called a **compound sentence**.

(2) Clauses are called **dependent** when they are *subordinated to the clause to which they are joined* by a subordinating connective or by a relative pronoun. **Subordinating connectives** (often called subordinating conjunctions) are words like *if, when, because, though,* and *whereas.* **Relative pronouns** are *who, which,* and *that.* A sentence combining an independent clause with one or more dependent clauses is called a **complex sentence**.

Dependent clauses can be considered as modifiers. Those introduced by subordinating connectives usually, though not always, serve adverbial functions: "The bell rang *when I started to answer.*" Those introduced by relative pronouns usually serve adjective functions: "The bell *that had startled me* had ceased to ring."

(3) A special type of dependent clause, rather than being joined

---

[3] For a full discussion of connectives and their bearing on punctuation, see P 3–4.

to the main clause, *replaces one of its nouns.* Such a clause-within-a-clause is called a **noun clause**:

Noun: *The thief* returned my documents.
Noun Clause: *Whoever stole my wallet* returned my documents.

Noun: He was excited by *the news.*
Noun Clause: He was excited by *what he had heard.*

That, frequently used as a relative pronoun, is also used to introduce a noun clause:

Osbert denied *that he had forged the check.*
That Osbert forged the check has not been proved.

NOTE: Dependent clauses are often hard to recognize, because one or more elements of the clause may be missing. Especially in informal writing, *whom, which*, and *that* are often omitted. Supplying the missing element in such constructions often facilitates grammatical analysis:

The speaker [*whom*] *we had invited* failed to appear.
The support [*that*] *we received* was inadequate.

After a subordinating connective, the subject and all or part of the verb are often omitted, provided they can be inferred from the context. The resulting clause is sometimes called an **elliptical clause**:

When [*you are*] *in doubt,* consult your dictionary.
When [*he was*] *questioned,* the suspect readily admitted the theft.

Exercises

A. Take five groups of three or four words each (for example, *boy—follow—dog*). Arrange each group in five different patterns using the grammatical devices described in G 2a. Example: *The boy follows the dog. Dogs followed the boy. Follow the boy's dogs. Follow the dog, boys. Dog the following boys.*

B. Collect five groups of words that show the same root taking different suffixes for different parts of speech.

EXAMPLES

red   redness   reddish   redden
organ   organism   organic   organize

C. Choose three simple subject-predicate sentences that can be expanded and transformed so as to illustrate several of the sentence types described in G 2b.

EXAMPLE

John called.
John called me.
John called me rude.
I was called by John.
Call a taxi!

D. Compose ten simplified sentences illustrating the variations in sentence pattern described in G 2b.

E. From your current reading, select ten short sentences (one clause each) in which typical sentence patterns are complicated by modifiers. Underline all basic sentence elements: subjects, verbs, complements.

F. From your current reading, select ten sentences that illustrate different ways of joining clauses. Underline the basic elements of each clause.

G. Write three *pairs* that each consist of two simple source sentences. Then illustrate different ways of working the material in each pair into a more complicated sentence.

EXAMPLE

The guests had departed. Alvin tidied the room.
After the guests had departed, Alvin tidied the room.
Alvin tidied the room, for the guests had departed.
The guests had departed, so Alvin tidied the room.
The guests having departed, Alvin tidied the room.
Alvin tidied the room, the guests having departed.

H. In the following sentences, identify the basic elements in each clause. Describe the function and grammatical category of as many other elements as you can. Point out distinctive grammatical features.

1. The water in the bowl was purple, and the goldfish were gulping for air. 2. Throughout the length of the valley, the river's course widens and narrows by turns. 3. In recent years, sport parachuting has enjoyed a small boom. 4. The only means of access was to hack one's way through hundreds of miles of jungle. 5. He painted with the suppleness of an artist who wanted a deep union with nature. 6. Many customs were common to both sides of the Rio Grande when the river became a frontier. 7. Recipes for happiness cannot be exported without being modified. 8. Uncle Alfred complained that outboard motors had driven off the fish. 9. Avoiding traffic policemen

is easy if they ride in specially marked cars. **10.** Fritz annoyed the neighbors by blowing the bugle his father had brought back from France. **11.** What maintains one vice would bring up two children. (Benjamin Franklin) **12.** When lost in the woods, remember your Indian lore.

I. Analyze the following passage, using the terminology provided in G 2. Identify all basic sentence elements. Describe the function and grammatical category of as many other elements as you can. Point out unusual or difficult grammatical features.

The rain began with gusty showers, pauses and downpours; and then gradually it settled to a single tempo, small drops and a steady beat, rain that was gray to see through, rain that cut midday light to evening. And at first the dry earth sucked the moisture down and blackened. For two days the earth drank the rain, until the earth was full. Then puddles formed, and in the low places little lakes formed in the fields. The muddy lakes rose higher, and the steady rain whipped the shining water. At last the mountains were full, and the hillsides spilled into the streams, built them to freshets, and sent them roaring down the canyons into the valleys. The rain beat on steadily. And the streams and the little rivers edged up to the bank sides and worked at willows and tree roots, bent the willows deep in the current, cut out the roots of cottonwoods and brought down the trees. The muddy water whirled along the bank sides and crept up the banks until at last it spilled over, into the fields, into the orchards, into the cotton patches where the black stems stood. Level fields became lakes, broad and gray, and the rain whipped up the surfaces. Then the water poured over the highways, and cars moved slowly, cutting the water ahead, and leaving a boiling muddy wake behind. —John Steinbeck, *The Grapes of Wrath*

G 3   Agreement

The subject and its verb agree in number.

Most nouns and pronouns have one form for references to a single item (**singular**), another form for references to more than one (**plural**). Often, verbs also offer us two choices, one to be used when the subject is singular, the other when the subject is plural: *is/are, was/were, has/have, asks/ask*. When subject and verb are both either singular or plural, they are said to agree in **number**.

Singular	Plural
The boy *goes* home.	The boys *go* home.
Love *makes* fools.	Fools *make* love.
My girl friend *was* pleased.	My girl friends *were* pleased.

(See G 5e for agreement of a *pronoun* with its antecedent.)

G 3a   Irregular Plurals

Some nouns borrowed from other languages preserve irregular plurals. Although most English nouns use the familiar *s* plural (cars, buildings, trees, books, petitions), a number of words have difficult, irregular alternative forms.

(1) *Many Greek and Latin words require you to learn irregular plural forms:*

Singular	Plural	Singular	Plural
crisis	crises	criterion	criteria
thesis	theses	phenomenon	phenomena
analysis	analyses	medium	media
hypothesis	hypotheses	stimulus	stimuli

NOTE: "Data" are items of information, and "bacteria" *are* very small organisms that may cause disease. The singular forms of these two words (*datum* and *bacterium*) are rarely used, with the result that *data* now often occurs as a singular. A boy who graduates from college becomes an "alumn*us*," a girl an "alumn*a*." Several male graduates would call themselves "alumn*i*," several female graduates "alumn*ae*." (An "alumn*i* organization," on the other hand, may include *both* men and women.)

(2) *Many other Greek and Latin words are shedding their original plurals.* According to recent dictionaries and handbooks of usage, it is becoming both common and acceptable to say "ind*exes*" rather than "ind*ices*," "curricul*ums*" rather than "curricul*a*," and "formul*as*" rather than "formul*ae*." Even so, many scientists, physicians, and teachers who use Greek and Latin terminology as a matter of daily routine prefer the older forms.

G 3b   Confusing Singulars and Plurals

Check for agreement problems caused by expressions that are not clearly either singular or plural.

(1) *Each, neither, either, and everyone* (**indefinite pronouns**) may seem to refer to more than one person or thing, but they are treated as singulars in formal written English:

Each of the students *is* going to receive a diploma.
Either of the plans *sounds* all right.

A number of is treated as a plural if it means "several" or "many":

A number of people *were* standing in the hallway.

(2) Expressions indicating quantity may be treated as singulars even when they seem plural in form, provided the sentence is concerned with *the whole amount* rather than with the individual units:

In those days two dollars *was* much money.

It is the most imperative social truth of our age that about one-third of the world is rich and two-thirds of the world *is* poor. — C. P. Snow, "On Magnanimity," *Harper's*

(3) Words like *audience, committee, family, group, jury, police,* and *team* may be singular in one sentence and plural in another. We use these **collective nouns** as singulars when we are thinking of the group as a whole; we use them as plurals when we are thinking of the individual members of the group:

Singular: The family *is* a crucial social unit.

Plural: The family *were* seated around the dinner table.

(4) Words ending in *ics* look like plurals but are often singular. Singular are *aeronautics, mathematics, physics,* and similar words that identify a branch of knowledge or field of study:

Mathematics *is* an indispensable tool of modern science.

Athletics is used most often as a plural but may also occur as a singular: "Athletics *are* said [could be "*is* said"] to be good for a boy." Other words ending in *ics* are singular in some senses and plural in others. We say "Statistics *doesn't* appeal to me" when speaking of the *science* of statistics; we say "Statistics *don't* convince me" when speaking of statistical *data.*

NOTE: Consult a college dictionary when you are not sure whether a given form is to be treated as a singular or as a plural.

G 3c   Compound Subjects

Check for agreement problems in clauses that contain more than one subject. After such a **compound subject,** the verb may appear in the plural form even if each of the subjects is singular when taken by itself:

Tom and Sue *don't* smoke.
Hiking and canoeing *are* fun.

Whereas *and* actually adds one possible subject to another, *or* merely gives us a choice between two possible subjects, each of which may be just one single item. Thus, we say "Both his father and his mother *are* to blame" but "Either his father or his mother *is* to blame."

Note some special difficulties:

(1) *As well as, together with,* and *in addition to* often seem to add one subject to another. Strictly interpreted, however, they merely show that what is said about the subject applies *also* to other things or persons:

> Aunt Martha, together with her six children, *is* leaving town.

NOTE: Some writers use the plural form when the singular seems to fight with the overall meaning of such a sentence. However, you will be safer from criticism if you revise the sentence, using *and*:

> The president, as well as the deans and department heads, *was* sitting on the platform.
>
> The president, the deans, and the department heads *were* sitting on the platform.

(2) Sometimes even two nouns joined by *and* do not add up to a plural. They may be merely different parts of the *description of a single thing or person:*

> Pork and beans *is* not one of my favorite dishes.
> My closest friend and associate *was* a cocker spaniel.

(3) In some sentences, an *or,* an *either . . . or,* or a *neither . . . nor* gives the reader a *choice between a singular subject and a plural one.* Make the verb of such a sentence agree with the subject closer to it:

> Either laziness or excessive social obligations *have kept* him from his work.
>
> Either excessive social obligations or just plain laziness *has kept* him from his work.

Such a sentence often sounds more natural if the subjects can be changed so that they are *both* singular or *both* plural:

> Too much social life or just plain laziness *has kept* him from his work.

G 3d   Blind Agreement

Do not make the verb agree with a word that stands in front of it but is not its subject. The result would be **blind agreement**.

(1) Agreement errors are common when *a plural noun intervenes between a singular subject and its verb.* Beware of faulty agreement whenever the subject of a sentence is one thing singled out among several, one quality shared by several members of a group, or one action affecting different things or persons:

Only one of my friends *was* ready [not "*were* ready"] in time.

The usefulness of his remedies *has been* questioned [not "*have been* questioned"].

Understanding the opponent's motives *is* important [not "*are* important"].

(2) When for some reason *the subject follows the verb,* do not make the verb agree with a stray noun that stands in front of it:

Sleeping in the cradle *were* two rosy-cheeked infants.
(Who was sleeping? The infants *were* sleeping.)

In the very first chapter *occur* several incredible incidents.
(What occurs? Incidents *occur.*)

G 3e   Agreement After *There* and *It*

Check for agreement in sentences starting with "there is," "there are," "it is," and the like.

(1) *There* is neither a noun nor a pronoun and cannot be the subject of a sentence. After *there,* the verb agrees with the **postponed subject**—that is, with whatever is "there":

Singular: There *was* much *work* to be done.
Plural: There *were* scattered *rumblings* of dissent.

In formal usage, the plural verb is required even when followed by a compound subject of which each part is singular:

On the crown of the hill, there *are* a miniature plaza, miniature cathedral, and miniature governor's palace.—Arnold J. Toynbee, "The Mayan Mystery," *Atlantic*

(2) *It* is a pronoun and can occur as a subject. After *it,* the verb is *always* singular:

It's your last chance.
It *was* the Joneses.

G 3f   Agreement After *Who, Which,* and *That*

Check for agreement problems caused by relationships between several clauses. For instance, *who, which,* and *that* often serve as subjects in **adjective clauses** — that is, dependent clauses that modify a noun or pronoun. The verb following the *who, which,* or *that* agrees with the *word being modified:*

| Singular: | I hate a man who *stares* at me. |
| Plural: | I hate men who *stare* at me. |

NOTE: Formal English requires agreement in combinations like "one of those who know" and "one of those who believe." "Jean is *the only one* of those girls *who goes* to college for an education" means that one girl *goes* to college for an education but that the others don't. "Jean is one of *those girls who go* to college for an education" means that a number of girls *go* to college for an education and that Jean is one of them.

G 3g   Logical Agreement

Where meaning requires it, observe agreement in other sentence elements in addition to verbs. Often, you have to carry through agreement in number from the subject not only to the verb but also to the remainder of the sentence. (See G 5e for agreement of pronoun and antecedent.)

Illogical:	Average newspaper *readers* go through their whole *life* knowing a little about everything but nothing well.
Revised:	Average newspaper *readers* go through their whole *lives* knowing a little about everything but nothing well.
Illogical:	My more studious *friends* are wise like *an owl* and always look up to higher things.
Revised:	My more studious *friends* are wise like *owls* and always look up to higher things.

(See the Glossary of Usage on *these kind* and *those kind*.)

Exercises

A. In a college dictionary, look up the plural forms of the following nouns: *antenna, appendix, beau, bureau, cactus, cello, cherub, focus, hippopotamus, nucleus, oasis, stadium, stigma, vertebra, virus.* Check whether the following forms are singular or plural or both: *addenda, agenda, apparatus, candelabra, deer, dice, Saturnalia, series, species, strata.*

B. Select appropriate forms, paying special attention to *irregular plurals.*

1. Constant crises *(1)has/(2)have* undermined the confidence of the people in their government.   2. For many of us, prestige is one of the most important *(3)criterion/(4)criteria* of success.   3. Jean and Margaret were the only *(5)alumna/(6)alumnae/(7)alumni* present at the ceremony.   4. The college offers more than twenty *(8)curriculum/(9)curricula.*   5. The mass media of communication *(10)has/(11)have* rapidly increased their influence in recent decades.   6. The *(12)analysis/(13)analyses* of such material takes time.   7. The memoranda he sent out *(14)was/(15)were* often unintelligible.   8. These data *(16)invalidates/(17)invalidate* all previous *(18)hypothesis/(19)hypotheses* concerning the origin of life.

C. Check for *agreement problems* in the following sentences. Your instructor may ask you to revise all unsatisfactory sentences.

1. Her big mouth, bad temper, and insistence upon revealing the truth to everyone is canceled out by one charming quality.

2. The clear and bracing air, and the storms of autumn and winter, are irresistible attractions for those who love the sea.

3. Years ago there wasn't the same social and racial problems that young people face today.

4. Many girls give up their interest in education and art when they become a wife and mother.

5. The mechanical constituents and running order of a new car is no more absolutely reliable than that of a used car.

6. Learning tolerance and proper respect for people with other views are necessary to civilized living.

7. In a monopolistic society, the number of sellers is so small that each seller can influence the supply and thus the price of the commodity.

8. Jane's features and shape was far above average.

9. In former times there wasn't as many educational opportunities as there is today.

10. At one time I thought of college as a place where everyone studies hard and then relax during the week.

11. The political science courses one takes in college often shows that the nation's great men were men with human failings.

12. The significance of many of the words used by Shakespeare are hard to understand.

13. I am not one of those who believe in the indiscriminate use of force to restore "law and order."

14. A list of all the chores a housewife does in an average week show that she needs more energy than most men.

15. A person's outward appearance and bank account is much more important to a snob than what the person is really like.

16. Neither his promotion nor his inheritance quite explains his sudden affluence.

17. The deep thinkers among the students attempt to solve all the world's problems by the use of their powerful mind.

18. In college, a girl's ideals and outlook on life broadens.

19. My sister always was one of those who look for more in a boy than physical appearance.

20. There are many different ways of teaching American history.

D. Select *appropriate forms*, paying special attention to common sources of faulty agreement.

1. In many of my classes the attitude of the students *(1)was/(2)were* very poor. **2.** The benefits that the city has derived from its new industries *(3)is/(4)are* negligible. **3.** Cooking, as well as sewing or cleaning, *(5)has/(6)have* always bored me. **4.** I was raised in a home where smoking and excessive drinking *(7)was/(8)were* not permitted. **5.** Getting along with one's neighbors *(9)is/(10)are* not always easy. **6.** The qualities that a girl looks for in a future husband *(11)is/(12)are* determined in part by her family background. **7.** The World's Fair dazzled everyone who *(13)was/(14)were* there. **8.** The ability to talk about something other than money and children *(15)is/(16)are* important if a marriage is to last. **9.** Colleges have to make provision for students who are below average academically but who nevertheless *(17)wants/(18)want* a college education. **10.** Using words like *dichotomy* and *schizophrenia (19)is/(20)are* no sign of superior intelligence. **11.** She was one of those hostesses who *(21)makes/(22)make* no attempt to entertain the guests. **12.** His father felt that five dollars *(23)was/(24)were* more than sufficient as a monthly allowance. **13.** According to the judge, neither of the witnesses *(25)was/(26)were* guilty of perjury. **14.** We soon realized that our supply of food and fuel *(27)was/(28)were* dangerously low. **15.** Weapons like the bow and arrow, the spear, or the knife *(29)was/(30)were* among the first major inventions of man.

G 4   Difficult Verb Forms

Use verb forms appropriate to serious written English.

Verb forms like *knowed* and *growed* are among the most distinctive features of nonstandard English; differences like those between "If I *was*" and "If I *were*" help set apart informal from formal standard English. The most important verb forms are those traditionally grouped together to form the system of tenses. The **tenses** of a verb are the various *forms that indicate primarily, though not exclusively, different relationships of events in time:*

Active

		Progressive
Present	I ask	(I am asking)
Past	I asked	(I was asking)
Future	I shall (will) ask	(I shall be asking)
Perfect	I have asked	(I have been asking)
Past Perfect	I had asked	(I had been asking)
Future Perfect	I shall (will) have asked	(I shall have been asking)

Passive

Present	I am asked	(I am being asked)
Past	I was asked	(I was being asked)
Future	I shall (will) be asked	——
Perfect	I have been asked	——
Past Perfect	I had been asked	——
Future Perfect	I shall (will) have been asked	——

G 4a   Regular Verbs

Most English verbs, the regular verbs, have two basic forms (**principal parts**).

(1) The first form is the plain form of the verb (*consent, smoke, depart, investigate, organize*). Standing by itself, it can form the **present tense.** This "simple present" may indicate that something is actually happening now, but it often refers to something that is done regularly or habitually, or that will take place in the immediate future:

We *consent.*
I *smoke* a pack a day.
They *depart* tonight.

The plain form can combine with *will* or *shall* in the **future tense:**

He *will* talk to you later.[4]

The plain form plus -*ing* makes up the present participle, used in the various tenses of the **progressive construction.** The progressive con-

---

[4] See the Glossary of Usage for *shall — will, should — would.*

struction normally indicates that at a given time an action or event is in progress:

> We *are considering* your request.
> Her husband *was painting* the house.

(2) The second basic form of a verb can stand by itself as the **past tense**, which indicates that an action took place in the past and came to an end in the past. To form this "simple past," regular verbs add *-ed* or *-d* to the plain form:

> He *consented.*
> We *asked* him.
> They *investigated* him thoroughly.

Regular verbs make the *-ed* form do double duty as a verbal (past participle) combining with the various forms of *have* to make up the **perfect tenses**. The present perfect ("I *have considered* your request") describes something that may have happened in the fairly recent past and that has a bearing on the present. The past perfect ("I *had considered* his request very carefully") describes something that had already happened when *other* events in the past took place.[5]

G 4b   Irregular Verbs

Irregular verbs often have not two but three basic forms. The simple past is often different from the past participle: *run—ran—run; know—knew—known; go—went—gone.* Furthermore, the difference between the simple present and the simple past is not merely a matter of adding a characteristic ending. Instead, there are changes difficult to schematize: *run—ran; know—knew; go—went.*

(1) Pay special attention to verbs whose basic forms are *confusing in spelling or in sound.* Here is a brief list:

Present	Past	Perfect
begin	began	have begun
bend	bent	have bent
blow	blew	have blown
break	broke	have broken
bring	brought	have brought
burst	burst	have burst
choose	chose	have chosen
come	came	have come
deal	dealt	have dealt

[5] See G 12a for sequence of tenses and shifts in tense.

Present	Past	Perfect
dig	dug	have dug
do	did	have done
draw	drew	have drawn
drink	drank	have drunk
drive	drove	have driven
eat	ate	have eaten
fall	fell	have fallen
flee	fled	have fled
fly	flew	have flown
freeze	froze	have frozen
go	went	have gone
grow	grew	have grown
know	knew	have known
lead	led	have led
run	ran	have run
see	saw	have seen
send	sent	have sent
sing	sang	have sung
speak	spoke	have spoken
swim	swam	have swum
take	took	have taken
throw	threw	have thrown
wear	wore	have worn
write	wrote	have written

(2) Sometimes you have a *choice of two acceptable forms:*

They gracefully *dived* (or *dove*) into the pool.
She *dreamed* (or *dreamt*) of a sloe-eyed Arab prince.
He *lighted* (or *lit*) his cigarette.
Your prediction *has proved* (or *has proven*) wrong.
The ship *sank* (or *sunk*) within minutes.
Business *thrived* (or *throve*) as never before.
The sleepers *waked* (or *woke*) refreshed.

(3) In a few cases different forms for the same tense correspond to *differences in context or in meaning.* For instance, it is "The picture was *hung*" but "The prisoners were *hanged*"; "The sun *shone*" but "The boy *shined* my shoes."

NOTE: When in doubt about the basic forms of a verb, consult your dictionary. It lists the basic forms of all irregular verbs in the *choose — chose — chosen, run — ran — run* order.

G 4c   *Lie, Sit,* and *Rise*

Some verbs have doubles just different enough to be confusing.
(1) *Lie — lay — lain* indicates that somebody or something is situated somewhere. The same basic forms are used in the combination *lie down.*

On hot days the animals *lie* in the shade.
A letter *lay* on the floor.
He *should have lain down.*

Lay — laid — laid indicates that somebody is placing something somewhere. Use it when you can substitute *place* or *put.*

I wish I *could lay* my hands on him.
The weary travelers *laid down* their burdens.
You *should have laid aside* some money for emergencies.

(2) *Sit — sat — sat* indicates that someone is seated. *Sit down* follows the same scheme.

Though he told me that he seldom *sat* while at work, he *has sat* for an hour exactly where he *sat down* when he looked for a place to *sit.*

Set — set — set, one of the few verbs with only one basic form, belongs with *lay* as a possible substitute for *place* or *put.* You, yourself, *sit,* or *sit down;* you *set,* or *set down,* something else:

When you *have set* the alarm, *set* it down by the cot I *set* up.

(3) *Rise — rose — risen* means "get up" or "go up." *Raise — raised — raised* refers to lifting something or *making* it go up:

Since you *rose* this morning, the tax rate *has risen* ten cents.
Though he *is* always *raising* his prices, he *has* not *raised* the salaries of his employees.

G 4d   Subjunctive

One special set of verb forms is disappearing from informal speech and writing but is still often required in formal usage: "She would call us if she *were* [not "if she *was*"] ill." "We demand that he *answer* [not "that he *answers*"] the question." *Were* and *answer* here represent special forms that make no distinction between singular and plural. These **subjunctive** forms occur in clauses concerned with possibilities rather than with facts:

(1) After *if, as if,* and *as though,* use *were* instead of *was* if the possibility you have in mind is *contrary to fact or highly improbable:*

The bird looked as if it *were* a plane.
If I *were* you, I would try to improve my language habits.
He acts as if his name *were* John D. Rockefeller.

Use *is* or *was* if you are considering a genuine possibility:

> If your brother *was* ill, he should have notified you.
> It looks as if the plane *is* going to be late.

In borderline cases, make sure that the *if*-clause uses a verb form that corresponds to the point of view adopted in the main clause. Use the ordinary or factual form after *if* when the main clause uses a matter-of-fact form like *will*, *shall*, *can*, or *may*. Use the subjunctive form when the main clause uses a form suggesting improbability:

Factual: If she *is* wise, he *will* propose.
Subjunctive: If she *were* wise, he *would* propose.

NOTE: Do not use *would* in the *if*-clause as a kind of poor man's subjunctive: "If he *were* elected [not "*would be* elected"] he would eliminate corruption and graft."

(2) Use subjunctive forms in noun clauses *after verbs indicating that something is desirable or necessary* but has not yet come about. "I wish I *were* [not "I *was*"] a wise old man." Forms like *answer* instead of *answers*, *go* instead of *goes* or *went*, and *be* instead of *is* or *was* occur after verbs signaling a suggestion, a request, a command, or a resolution:

> His wife insists that he *spend* more time at home.
> We demand that he *repay* all his debts.
> I move that this question *be* referred to one of our innumerable committees.

(3) In some *set phrases* ("*be* that as it may") and *in writing that is distinctly formal or literary in tone*, the subjunctive expresses ordinary conditions or alternatives:

> He was determined to go on, *come* what might.
> The artist must have faith in the all-importance of art, and particularly in his own form of art, *be* it painting, sculpture, poetry, drama, fiction, or music.— Malcolm Cowley, "Artists, Conscience, and Censors," *Saturday Review*

Exercises

A. Select verb forms appropriate to formal written English.

1. If a teacher *(1)lays/(2)lies* a hand on an unruly student, he is likely to be sued by the student's parents. 2. In discussions touching on

religious issues, many perplexing questions can be *(3)raised/(4)risen.*
3. After the class *(5)sat/(6)set* down, Mrs. Warner wanted to know who
had *(7)wrote/(8)written* "The Student's Lament." **4.** The picture
showed two elderly gentlemen *(9)setting/(10)sitting* at a table and
playing chess. **5.** While the boys *(11)swam/(12)swum* in the clear,
cold water, I *(13)sat/(14)set* in the canoe watching them. **6.** While
(15)setting/(16)sitting up a new filing system, we must have *(17)mis-
laid/(18)mislain* your letter. **7.** The report has been *(19)laying/
(20)lying* on his desk all summer; at least I saw it *(21)lay/(22)lie* there
last week. **8.** When I *(23)saw/(24)seen* the deserted entrance, I
(25)knew/(26)knowed that the performance had already *(27)began/
(28)begun.* **9.** The Park Department finally *(29)sat up/(30)set up*
benches for visitors who might want to *(31)set down/(32)sit down.*
10. Satisfied with the conditions *(33)sat/(34)set* by the negotiators,
the rebels *(35)laid down/(36)lay down* their arms.

B. Select subjunctive forms where appropriate.

1. If there *(1)is/(2)was/(3)were* another war, untold millions would lose
their homes or their lives. **2.** I wish grammar *(4)was/(5)were* less
complicated than it is. **3.** Washington is often presented as if he
(6)is/(7)was/(8)were a godlike figure. **4.** It looks as if there *(9)is/
(10)were* just enough gasoline to get us back into town. **5.** The ordinance requires that subdivision signs *(11)are/(12)be* kept smaller than
the houses they advertise. **6.** If the vocationally minded student
(13)was/(14)were/(15)would be sent to a trade school, high schools
could put more emphasis on academic subjects than they do now. **7.** If
your record *(16)is/(17)were/(18)would be* as clean as you claim, the commission will gladly grant your request. **8.** Mariners used to drink rum
as if it *(19)is/(20)was/(21)were* water. **9.** No one suggested to Raymond that he *(22)read/(23)reads The Brothers Karamazov* rather than
Treasure Island. **10.** These practices would not be tolerated if the
founder *(24)is/(25)was/(26)were/(27)would be* still alive.

C. From the current issue of a magazine, select five sentences that illustrate
different uses of the subjunctive.

G 5   Reference of Pronouns

*To make a pronoun stand for the right noun, place the right
pronoun in the right position.*

When you use a pronoun like *he, it,* or *this,* it should be clear to
your reader who or what *he, it,* or *this* is. A pronoun has to refer clearly
to its **antecedent,** the thing or person for which the pronoun is a substitute.

G 5a   Ambiguous Reference

Do not let a pronoun point to more than one possible antecedent.
Look at the use of *she* and *her* in the following example: "Mary was
friendly to my sister because *she* wanted *her* to be *her* bridesmaid."
The reader here has no way of knowing which of the two girls was
getting married, and which was going to be a bridesmaid. The sentence is **ambiguous**; it confuses the reader because of an unintended
double meaning.

(1) If the substitute could refer to more than one antecedent,
you may have to repeat the noun itself: "When Tom was talking to
Jim's brother, *Jim's* girl friend smiled at *Jim's brother* from across the
street." Preferably, *shuffle the different parts of the sentence* until
the pronoun is preceded by only one possible antecedent:

Ambiguous:	After *Father* brought *Junior* back from the game, we took pictures of *him*.
Clear:	We took pictures of *Father* after *he* brought *Junior* back from the game.
Clear:	We took pictures of *Junior* after *Father* brought *him* back from the game.

(2) The pronouns that most often cause ambiguity have distinctive forms for singular and plural antecedents: the singular *he, she,*
or *it,* as against the plural *they.* If a *they* is preceded by two plural
nouns, you can sometimes avoid ambiguity by *making one of them
singular:*

Ambiguous:	*Students* like *science teachers* because *they* are realistic and practical.
Clear:	A *student* usually likes his *science teachers* because *they* are realistic and practical.
	(*They* can no longer be mistakenly referred to *students.*)

Similarly, one of two possible singular antecedents might be changed
into a plural:

A *writer* must necessarily talk to his *readers* [better than "to his *reader*"] in simple
language if *his* vocabulary is limited.
(The singular *reader* would leave it doubtful whose vocabulary is assumed to be limited.)

NOTE: The *farther removed* a pronoun is from its antecedent, the
greater the danger of ambiguous reference. Do not make a reader go
back through several sentences in a paragraph to check what *he,
this,* or *they* stands for.

G 5b   Reference to Modifiers

Make pronouns refer to one of the basic elements of a sentence rather than to a modifier. The following sentence would sound absurd: "During the summer, Grandfather worked on a river boat, but in the winter *it* usually froze over." The *it* seems to refer to the boat, but boats do not freeze over. Similarly absurd sentences may result when a pronoun is expected to refer to a **possessive**:

Ambiguous:	I reached for the *horse's* bridle, but *it* ran away. (The bridle seems to be running away.)
Clear:	The *horse* ran away after I reached for *its* bridle. (The possessive has been changed to a pronoun, and the noun put where it is needed to prevent confusion.)

NOTE: Reference to a possessive accounts for the awkwardness of sentences like the following: "In *John Steinbeck's* novel *The Grapes of Wrath,* he describes the plight of the marginal farmer." Better: "In *his* novel . . . *John Steinbeck* describes . . ."

G 5c   Vague *This* and *Which*

Avoid ambiguity caused by idea reference. Vague **idea reference** results when a *this* or *which* refers to the overall idea expressed in the preceding statement: "I knew that Bob was cheating, but the other students were not aware of *this.*" The *this* may refer either to Bob's *cheating* or to the writer's *knowing* it.

Ambiguous:	She spent her time getting special help for her English course, *which* her roommates considered unfair. (What did her roommates consider unfair—the English course, her getting special help, her spending her time this way?)

A vague *this* can be easily supplemented by a noun indicating the idea referred to: "this assumption," "this outrage." A vague *which* is more difficult to improve. Often you will find it easier to do without it:

Ambiguous:	I have received only one letter, *which* frightens me.
Clear:	Receiving only one letter frightened me.
Clear:	The letter (the only one I received) frightened me.

G 5d   Implied Antecedents

To make a sentence acceptable in formal English, eliminate indirect reference.

(1) In informal conversation, we often make a pronoun refer to an antecedent that we have not actually mentioned, though we *expect its identity to be understood.* We say, "In London, *they* have a great deal of fog" without explaining that the *they* means "Londoners" or "the people living in London." We say, "I like *Life* magazine, because *they* print many interesting articles." The implied antecedent of *they* is not the magazine itself but its editors or its publishers:

Revised:　　　　　　*Life* magazine prints many interesting articles.

(2) Avoid the orphaned *it* or *they,* which refers to an *implied idea* in a sentence like the following: "My mother was a teacher; therefore, I have also chosen *it* as my profession." The *it* stands not for "teacher" but for "teaching":

Revised:　　　　　My mother was a teacher; therefore, I have also chosen *teaching* as my profession.

Ambiguous:　　　The prisoner's hands were manacled to a chain around his waist, but *they* were removed at the courtroom door.
(What was removed? The prisoner's hands?)

Revised:　　　　　The prisoner's hands were manacled to a chain around his waist, but *the manacles* were removed at the courtroom door.

G 5e　Indefinite Antecedents

In formal usage, treat indefinite expressions that are singular in form as singular antecedents.

(1) Treat the **indefinite pronouns**—*everybody (everyone), somebody (someone), nobody (no one), anybody (anyone), one*— consistently as singular. Informal English typically uses a singular verb after these words but then often switches to a plural pronoun.

Formal:　　　　　Someone left *his* gloves [not *"their* gloves"].

Formal:　　　　　After hours everybody does as *he* pleases [not "as *they* please"].

Formal:　　　　　Nobody should meddle in affairs that are none of *his* business [not "none of *their* business"].

Formal:　　　　　One must honor *his* (or *one's*) obligations [not "*their* obligations"].

NOTE: *None* started as the equivalent of "no one," but today either singular or plural forms after it are acceptable:

None of the students *has his* books ready [or *"have their* books ready"].

(2) Consistently treat as singulars expressions like *a person, an individual, the typical student,* or *an average American.* These may seem to refer to more than one person but are singular in form.

Faulty:	*A person* can never be too careful about *their* use of language.
Revised:	*A person* can never be too careful about *his* use of language.
Faulty:	*A student* is here in college to study, but *they* are usually poorly prepared for this task.
Revised:	*A student* is here in college to study, but *he* is usually poorly prepared for this task.

NOTE: When we use *everybody, a person,* or *none,* we are often thinking of both men and women. However, "Everybody ate *his or her* lunch" would sound clumsy. *His* can do double duty in such cases.

Exercises

A. Check the following sentences for problems in *pronoun reference.* Your instructor may ask you to revise all unsatisfactory sentences.

1. Evelyn was the kind of neighbor who goes out of her way to help someone or make them feel good.

2. Every poet, novelist, and writer of nonfiction has tried their hand at writing a saga of the sea.

3. Most adults take notice of teen-agers only when they get into trouble, which is true of every generation.

4. Samuel Butler wrote *The Way of All Flesh,* which was published after his death.

5. Everyone at the convention was constantly being polled on subjects he knew little about.

6. The average individual respects the wishes of the group because they hate to be considered odd.

7. My father is extremely intelligent, though he does not always express it in a verbal form.

8. Each woman has their own reason for getting an education.

9. In true tragedy, the hero had to be from a noble family, which made his downfall all the more tragic.

10. The English taught in elementary school included a weekly spelling test, but they did little to teach me the correct use of spoken English.

11. No one is eager to examine his thinking for the hidden biases that determine his attitude toward other people.

12. Dave would go out of his way to help a person in the minority obtain their rights.

13. My writing skills are not as accomplished as I wish it were.

14. Newspapers give prominence to youths that participate in riots, which pins a bad label on all young people.

15. Somebody had left his collection of old books in the cottage, which was a perfect place to sit and read.

16. If some individual were to ask me what my philosophy of life is, they would get an involved answer.

17. Many people vaguely respect the arts, but for most of them it is not a source of increased awareness or self-realization.

18. One seldom has the satisfaction of converting his opponents to his own point of view.

19. The housewife of today is self-reliant in the managing of their household budget and the upbringing of their children.

20. Water spills from a pipe atop the rock formation; it resembles lava coming from an active volcano.

B. Of the numbered pronouns in each passage, identify the one that is *vague, ambiguous, or misleading.*

1. No one *(1)who* has ever been at a horse race can forget *(2)his* excitement at seeing *(3)them* come down the home stretch.   2. On the far side of the town, *(4)they* are clearing land for a housing project, *(5)which* is to be completed before next July.   3. When leading newspapers have *(6)their* top correspondents write stories accusing *(7)our* government of being corrupt, steps should be taken to correct *(8)this.*   4. We finally bought Uncle Peter a power lawnmower, but *(9)he* rarely cuts *(10)it* more than once every three or four weeks.   5. Gophers have been eating our geraniums. *(11)This* annoys my father, *(12)who* has been trying to get rid of *(13)them* for a long time.   6. A good secretary does not discuss business matters with *(14)her* friends unless *(15)they* are generally known or unless *(16)she* has the permission of *(17)her* employer.   7. While the little boy's father read *(18)his* newspaper, *(19)he* kept reaching for *(20)it* and crying "Daddy!"   8. The public often discovers that *(21)it* has been deprived of important information, *(22)which* goes counter to the traditional policy of *(23)our* government.   9. When Elizabeth came home, *(24)she* told *(25)her* grandmother that the cost of *(26)her* new permanent alone was enough to curl a woman's hair.   10. *(27)My* history instructor announced to the students in *(28)his* class that

(29)they would write a paper on the fall of Constantinople.   *(30)This* was a major catastrophe.

C. Select pronouns appropriate to formal written English.

1. Belonging to too many organizations keeps a person away from *(1)his/(2)his or her/(3)their* studies.   **2.** A child that has real problems is often too embarrassed to discuss them with *(4)his/(5)their* parents.   **3.** Teen-agers often adopt a new fad as a way of expressing *(6)his/(7)their* rebellion against authority.   **4.** A newspaper can never satisfy all *(8)its/(9)their* subscribers.   **5.** The American public enjoys Westerns because they give *(10)it/(11)them* a chance to escape from humdrum reality.   **6.** Participation in student government is good for the students because it develops an understanding of the institution of which *(12)he is/(13)they are* a part.   **7.** Sometimes it seems as if nowadays no one has the time to enjoy *(14)himself/(15)themselves*.   **8.** A number of my friends take more interest in playing golf in a gym class than *(16)he does/(17)they do* in solving mathematical problems.   **9.** Love stories are popular because love is something that everyone knows or will experience in *(18)his/(19)his or her/(20)their* lifetime.   **10.** Much confusion would have been avoided if each one of them had waited for *(21)his/(22)their* turn.

G 6   Pronoun Forms

Use pronoun forms in accordance with the conventions of formal written English.

Pronouns have alternative forms, used depending on the function of the pronoun in the sentence. *I* and *he* are **subject forms**, identifying the person that the predicate says something about. *Me* and *him* are **object forms**, identifying the object of a verb or preposition. Only half a dozen pronouns have a distinct object form: *I — me; we — us; he — him; she — her; they — them; who — whom*.

Subject	Object	Object of Preposition
I congratulated	*him.*	
He recommended	*me*	to *them.*
They prejudiced	*her*	against *me.*

These forms for subject and object, like the possessive of nouns, are isolated survivals of a once elaborate system of inflections indicating grammatical **case**.

A third possible form typically indicates that the object of an action is identical with the performer. *Himself, themselves, myself, ourselves*, and similar forms are **reflexive forms**:

He cut *himself.*
They asked *themselves* what had gone wrong.

They are also used as **intensives** reidentifying something for emphasis:

The dean told me so *himself.*
We should also weigh the testimony of the accused men *themselves.*

G 6a   Subject and Object Forms

Use the pronoun forms for subject and object as appropriate in written English. Formal use of these forms differs to some extent from what we commonly hear in informal and nonstandard speech.

(1) Choose the standard form when a pronoun is *one of several subjects or objects in a clause:*

My brother and *I* [not *"me* and my brother"] were reading comic books. (Who was reading? *I* was reading.)

She asked my brother and *me* [not "my brother and *I"*] to dry the dishes. (Whom did she ask? She asked *me.)*

(2) Since nouns have no distinct forms for subject and object, be careful with *pronoun-noun combinations* like *we Americans — us Americans* or *we girls — us girls:*

We boy scouts are always eager to help. (*We* are eager.)
He told *us boy scouts* to keep up the good work. (He told *us.)*

(3) Object forms are required *after prepositions* (with *her;* because of *him;* for *me).* Use the object form for a pronoun that is the second or third object in a prepositional phrase:

This kind of thing can happen to you and *me* — not "to you and *I."*
I knew there was something between you and *her* — not "between you and *she."*

(4) *As* and *than* are treated as connectives even when most of the clause they presumably introduce is missing. To decide whether they should be followed by the subject form or the object form, *reconstruct the missing clause:*

He is as tall as *I* (am).
I owe you as much as (I owe) *them.*
Her sister was smarter than *she* (was).
I like her better than (I like) *him.*

(5) In formal usage, subject forms are required *after linking*

verbs, which introduce not an object of an action but a description of the subject:

> The only ones not invited were *she* and a girl with measles.

The need for this use of the subject form seldom arises except after "it is," "it was," "it must be," and so on. (See the Glossary of Usage for *it's me*/*it is I*.)

NOTE: Formal English avoids the use of the reflexive pronoun as a substitute for the plain subject form or object form:

> My friend and *I* [not "and *myself*"] were the last ones to leave.
> I asked both his wife and *him* [not "and *himself*"] to come over after dinner.

G 6b   *Who* and *Whom*

Who and whom *are easily confused because their function in a sentence is not always obvious.* Futhermore, *who* is increasingly replacing *whom* in speech.

Spoken:	Tell me *who you are thinking of.*
Written:	It is good for the sanity of all of us to have *someone whom we continue to think of* as Mister even though we address him by his given name. — Philip M. Wagner, "Mencken Remembered," *The American Scholar*

An inappropriate *who* may sound too informal for its context; an inappropriate *whom* may sound ignorant and forced.

(1) When *who* or *whom* occurs *at the beginning of a question*, *who* asks a question about the subject. *He, she, we,* and *they* would be possible answers: *Who* did it? *He* did. *Whom* asks a question about an object. *Him, her, us,* and *them* would be possible answers: *Whom* did you meet? I met *him*. *Whom* also serves as the object of a preposition: To *whom* should I write? To *him*. The pronoun remains in the object form even if the preposition does not precede the pronoun but follows the verb: *Whom* are you looking *for?* I am looking for *him*.

In more complicated questions it may not be obvious whether a *who* inquires about a subject or about an object. However, the *he*-or-*him* test will always work:

> *Who* do you think will win? (I think *he* will win.)
> *Whom* did you expect to come? (I expected *him* to come.)

(2) *Who* and *whom* may *introduce dependent clauses.* They may introduce an indirect question or may link a modifier to the noun or pronoun being modified. In order to apply the *he*-or-*him* test to a dependent clause, separate it from the rest of the sentence:

Subject:	Ask her / *who* wrote the letter. (*He* wrote the letter.)
Subject:	We approached the man / *who* was waiting. (*He* was waiting.)
Subject:	Here is a nickel for / *whoever* gets there first. (*He* gets there first.)
Object:	*Whom* we should invite / is a difficult question. (We should invite *him*.)
Object:	She knew my brother, / *whom* I rarely see. (I rarely see *him*.)
Object:	He knew few people / on *whom* he could rely. (He could rely on *them*.)

NOTE: Often a parenthetic comment like *I think, he feels,* or *she thought* is inserted into the dependent clause. The "I think" does not affect the choice of *who* or *whom* if you could enclose it in parentheses without changing the meaning of the clause:

Subject:	He introduced us to Mrs. Sweets, /*who* (I think) is his mother-in-law.

G 6c   Who, Which, and That

Who and *whom* refer to persons ("the man *whom* I asked"). *Which* refers to ideas and things ("the car *which* I bought"). A *who, whom,* or *which* introducing a **restrictive modifier** may be replaced by *that* (but *need* not be):

The man *that* I asked liked the car *that* I bought.

A *whom* or a *which* that is the object in a restrictive modifier is often left out:

The man (*whom*) I asked liked the car (*which*) I bought.

NOTE: *Of which* and *in which* can easily make a sentence awkward. *Whose* is therefore widely used and accepted in reference to ideas and things: "the Shank-Painter Swamp, *whose* expressive name . . . gave it importance in our eyes" (Thoreau).

G 6d   Possessives with Verbal Nouns

Formal usage prefers a possessive pronoun before a verbal used as a verbal noun. A combination of a pronoun and a verbal with the *-ing* ending may express two different relationships. In the sentence "I saw *him returning* from the library," you actually saw *him*. In the sentence "I object to *his using* my toothbrush," you are not objecting to *him* but merely to one of *his* actions. In the first sentence, the object of the verb is *him*, while *returning* is a **present participle** modifying the object. In the second sentence, the object of the verb is *using*, while *his* is a **possessive pronoun** indicating *whose* action the speaker has in mind. The verbal here is a **gerund**, or **verbal noun**.

Use *my, our, his, their* instead of *me, us, him, them* when the object of a verb or of a preposition is not the person himself but one of his actions, traits, or experiences: [6]

> We investigated the chances of *his* being elected.
> There is no excuse for *their* not writing sooner.
> I do not like *your* associating with the neighborhood children.

Exercises

A. Which of the italicized pronoun forms are inappropriate to formal English? Why?

1. A teacher should not be condescending just because *he* knows more than *us* students.

2. Jack constantly enriched the conversation of my friends and *I* with brilliant comments.

3. People *who* are asked to "play *themselves*" in a movie often find that a good actor can portray their type more effectively than *them*.

4. My brother and *I* had no respect for the people with *whom* we worked, and soon we had no respect for *ourselves*.

5. I am tired of *his* spreading rumors about a rift between the board and *I*.

B. Select pronoun forms appropriate to formal written English.

1. When my mother punished my sister and *(1)I/(2)me/(3)myself*, she always seemed to suffer more than *(4)we/(5)us*.   2. I stopped at Jane's

---

[6] In formal usage, nouns observe a similar distinction, provided they have a distinctive possessive form. See Glossary of Usage under "possessives."

house because I had some letters for her mother and *(6)she/(7)her/ (8)herself.*   3. My parents did not mind *(9)me/(10)my* associating with artists as long as I did not imitate their habits.   4. Most of *(11)we girls/ (12)us girls* were looking for the tall, handsome athletic star with the winning personality.   5. I recognize the man's face; it was *(13)he/ (14)him* who started the riot.   6. My sister is much better than *(15)I/ (16)me/(17)myself* at learning foreign languages.   7. In discussing contemporary authors, the lecturer objected to *(18)their/(19)them* painting too gloomy a picture of the American scene.   8. Every year, my father takes my brother and *(20)I/(21)me* camping.   9. Between you and *(22)I/ (23)me,* I would rather have a husband in a Ford than a friend in a Jaguar.   10. Space navigators need to protect *(24)them/(25)themselves* against the powerful radiation of the sun to prevent *(26)their/(27)them* dying from acute sunburn.

C. Explain the choice of *who* or *whom* in the following sentences.

1. My closest friend is a Danish boy, whom I met when traveling in Europe.

2. People who cannot suffer can never grow up, can never discover who they are.   (James Baldwin)

3. The inhabitants of the coast, whom he called Ichthyophagi or Fish-eaters, not only ate fishes raw but gave them to their cattle.

4. Grandmother disapproved of John, who she felt lacked some of the qualities of a gentleman.

5. People whom I had not seen for months or whom I knew very slightly telephoned to advise me to get off the newly formed committee.

6. He was a man of singular patience and intelligence, who, when our queries struck him, rang as clear as a bell in response.   (Thoreau)

7. Every reader occasionally encounters a fictional character with whom he can immediately identify.

8. Giles would argue for hours with whoever was willing to listen to his tirades.

D. Select *whom* where required by formal usage.

1. No matter *(1)who/(2)whom* I meet, I always in the end have to listen to his problems.   2. I felt more at ease talking to boys *(3)who/ (4)whom* had definite ambitions in life than to those *(5)who/(6)whom* lived from football game to football game.   3. As a principal, he knew many parents *(7)who/(8)whom/(9)which* took only a casual interest in their children's education.   4. The man *(10)who/(11)whom* knocked at the door was not the one *(12)who/(13)whom* we expected.   5. After the abortive revolt, the prince surrounded himself with subordinates on *(14)who/(15)whom/(16)which* he could rely.   6. *(17)Who/(18)whom*

she corresponds with and *(19)who/(20)whom* is allowed to visit her are jealously guarded mysteries. **7.** *(21)Who/(22)whom* do you think was the girl with *(23)who/(24)whom* I saw him? **8.** I wonder *(25)who/(26) whom* you expect to believe these fantastic stories.

E. From a local newspaper, select ten sentences using *who* or *whom*. Which of them conform to the conventions of formal usage?

G 7   Forms of Modifiers

Distinguish between adjectives and adverbs.

Modifiers may be single words. Such single-word modifiers fall into two main categories. *Beautiful, strange,* and *happy* are **adjectives**. An adjective modifies a noun by identifying it as one of a kind or by pointing out one of its characteristics. *Beautifully, strangely,* and *happily* are **adverbs**. Characteristically an adverb comments on the manner or the circumstances of the action or condition indicated by the verb. (See G 2c.)

G 7a   Adverb Forms

Formal English requires a more frequent use of distinctive adverb forms than everyday conversation. Most adverbs are distinguished from the corresponding adjectives by the *-ly* ending: *bright — brightly, cheerful — cheerfully, considerable — considerably, frequent — frequently, happy — happily, rapid — rapidly, rare — rarely, single — singly*. However, some adverbs, such as *fast, much, thus,* and *well*, have no distinctive ending. Some words ending in *-ly* are not adverbs but adjectives: a *friendly* talk, a *lonely* life, a *leisurely* drive, a *manly* reply.

Use distinctive adverb forms in sentences like the following:

Adverb:	In my absence, the town had changed *considerably*.
Adverb:	A teacher must be firm if he wants to be taken *seriously*.

Note the following special problems:

(1) *Good* and *bad* used as adverbs are commonly heard in informal speech but are widely considered nonstandard. In formal English, "I don't hear so good" would be "I don't hear *well*." "I write pretty bad" would be "I write *badly*."

Objectionable:	This morning, the motor was running *good*.
Formal:	This morning, the motor was running *well*.

NOTE: The adverb *well*, however, may do double duty as an adjective, in the sense of "healthy," "not ill": "He looks *well*"; "I don't feel *well*."

(2) Formal usage prefers "talks *loudly*" to "talks loud," "go *slowly*" to "go slow," or "come *quickly*" to "come quick," though both the long form and the short form of these adverbs have long been standard English.

G 7b   Adjectives with Linking Verbs

Not every modifier appearing next to a verb is necessarily an adverb.

(1) Linking verbs link the subject to a description of it, which may be a noun but is often an adjective:

His habits are *expensive*.
Most of the bottles were *empty*.
The speaker seemed nervous.

A **predicate adjective**, even though it becomes part of the predicate, points back to the subject. Here are some other verbs that may function as linking verbs and may thus be followed by adjectives:

Genevieve *turned* pale.
The heat *grew* oppressive.
He *became* rich overnight.
Your fears *will prove* silly.
The accused *remained* silent.

Honeysuckle *smells* sweet.
The soup *tasted* flat.
His hands *felt* moist.
Sirens *sound* frightening.
Your friend *looks* ill.

NOTE: Some verbs may function either as ordinary verbs or as linking verbs. In "The waiter appeared hurriedly," *hurriedly* tells us how the man acted. In "The waiter appeared hurried," *hurried* describes the man himself. In "John slowly looked at me," *slowly* describes John's action. In "John looked slow," *slow* describes John.

(2) In some sentences, a verb and its object are followed by a description of the object. The description, called the **object complement**, may be either a noun ("He called me a *genius*") or an adjective ("He called me *lazy*"). Notice the difference between adjective and adverb in the following pairs:

He called the meeting *accidental*.
He called the meeting *accidentally*.

George called his girl friend *eager*.
George called his girl friend *eagerly*.

G 7c   Adverbs to Modify Modifiers

In formal usage, use the distinctive adverb form to modify either an adjective or another adverb. In "a *poorly* informed American," *poorly* is an adverb modifying the adjective *informed*. The man's supply of information is poor, though he himself may be wealthy.

Adverb + Adjective:	a surprising*ly* beautiful bird
	a hopeless*ly* retarded student
	an impressive*ly* versatile actor

Adverb + Adverb:	You sang admirab*ly* well.
	He answered surprising*ly* fast.
	She worked incredib*ly* hard.

Many everyday expressions use adjective forms instead of adverb forms as informal **intensifiers**: "He speaks *awful* fast." "Dean Howard is *real* popular." "I am *dreadful* sorry." In formal English, *omit* such intensifiers altogether or use a formal intensifier like *very*. Use *fairly* to replace the informal *pretty* in "pretty old."

Exercises

A. In simplified sample sentences, use each of the following words once as an adjective and once as an adverb: *better, early, fast, hard, just, only, well.*

B. Which of these sentences use adjectives and adverbs as required in formal written English? Your instructor may ask you to revise unsatisfactory sentences.

1. Because of my father's influence, I will do good in college and make the best of my opportunities for education.

2. During the time Judy spent in France, her French improved considerable.

3. No matter what dish Carolyn prepared, it tasted flat.

4. I read the questions as careful as the time allowed.

5. All the girls performed admirably, but Judy did exceptionally well.

6. I had to talk fast and furious before the householder could slam the door in my face.

7. An experienced cryptographer can decipher a simple code very easy.

8. My father didn't do very good in school because he had to work on my grandfather's farm.

9. On the night before our departure, everyone felt miserable.

10. Women of today want to be treated equal.

11. Falling from the slippery roof, he hurt himself badly.

12. As the questions continued, the lecturer sounded more and more impatient.

13. The characters in many current movies speak and act fairly realistic.

14. The interview with the star of the show proved real disappointing.

15. Most drivers drive too fast and careless most of the time.

16. The director stubbornly insisted on using a real lion.

17. A girl should not plan to become a secretary if she does not spell good.

18. He easily talked the man into giving us a real bargain.

19. The plans looked beautiful on paper, but progress has been awful slow.

20. The rescue party unaccountably lost its way.

G 8   Position of Modifiers

Place modifiers in such a way as to prevent misunderstanding or unintended double meanings.

A modifier may modify different things depending on where it occurs. A word like *only*, which serves both as an adjective and as an adverb, may appear almost anywhere in a sentence:

> *Only* I asked the girl for her name.
> I asked *only* the girl for her name.
> I asked the *only* girl for her name.
> I asked the girl for her name *only*.

In each of these sentences, *only* points clearly to what it modifies. But what is the meaning of the following sentence?

> I only asked the girl for her name.

In informal English, we often rely on the situation, or on intonation, to make the meaning clear:

> *I* only asked the girl for her name.
> I only asked the girl *for her name.*

In formal written English, we would have to recast the sentence to make the modifier point unambiguously in the right direction.

G 8a   Misplaced Modifiers

Place modifiers so that they point clearly to what they modify. Notice the changes in meaning that result from changes in the position of modifiers:

Adverb:	The car *almost* broke down on every trip we took. (It never quite did.) The car broke down on *almost* every trip we took. (It did frequently.)
Prepositional Phrase:	The man *with the ax* opened the door. The man opened the door *with the ax*.
Verbal:	Jerry married a wealthy wife *yearning for high social status*. *Yearning for high social status*, Jerry married a wealthy wife.

Misplaced modifiers seem to point to the wrong part of the sentence. Usually you can simply shift the modifier to a more appropriate position, though you may sometimes have to recast the sentence as a whole:

Misplaced:	He looked at the tree he had felled *with his hands in his pocket*. (It is hard to fell trees with one's hands in his pocket.)
Revised:	*With his hands in his pocket,* he looked at the tree he had felled.
Misplaced:	*Being made of stone,* the builder expected the house to stand for a century. (They called him Old Stoneface, no doubt.)
Revised:	Since *the house* was made of stone, the builder expected it to stand for a century.
Misplaced:	She was a well-proportioned woman dancing for an audience *trying to make a living*. (But there were no performances for idlers?)
Revised:	She was a well-proportioned woman *trying to make a living* by dancing for an audience.

Note the following special problems:
(1) A **squinting modifier** seems to point two ways at once:

Squinting:	I feel *subconsciously* Hamlet wanted to die. (Are you talking about *your* subconscious feelings — or Hamlet's?)
Revised:	I feel that Hamlet *subconsciously* wanted to die.

(2) The reader expects modifiers to point to major sentence elements rather than to possessives like *my* or *your*. *"At the age of ten,* my grandfather died" seems to mean that your grandfather died when he was ten years old. To improve such a sentence, you often need to *spell out the meaning intended by the modifier:*

> When I was ten, my grandfather died.

G 8b   Dangling Modifiers

Make sure that what a verbal (or verbal phrase) modifies actually appears in the sentence. A sentence containing a verbal or verbal phrase as a modifier can typically be analyzed as derived from two source sentences sharing *one major element:*

First Source:	*The bride* caught her rival's eye.
Second Source:	*The bride* was walking down the aisle.
Result:	*Walking down the aisle,* the bride caught her rival's eye.

When the two source sentences do *not* share a major element, the verbal may have nothing to hook onto in the combined sentence. It is then left dangling:

First Source:	The house was dark.
Second Source:	We were coming home late last night.
Dangling:	The house was dark, *coming home late last night.* (*Who* was coming home? Not the house.)

Some danglers merely throw the sentence off balance; others make it sound absurd. Revise by bringing back into the sentence what the verbal is supposed to modify.

| Dangling: | *To do well in college,* good grades are essential. |
| Revised: | To do well in college, *a student* needs good grades. |

| Dangling: | Often, *after convincing a girl to finish school,* she is married on the day of her graduation. |
| Revised: | Often, after *her friends* have convinced her to finish school, a girl is married on the day of her graduation. |

| Dangling: | *Walking down the aisle,* the wedding march began to play. |
| Revised: | While *the bride and groom* were walking down the aisle, the organist started to play the wedding march. |

NOTE: Some verbal phrases are not intended to modify any one part of the main sentence. These are called **absolute constructions**. The most common ones are the many generally acceptable expressions that *clarify the attitude or intention of the speaker:*

> *Generally speaking,* traffic is getting worse rather than better.
> He had numerous children — seven, *to be exact.*
> *Considering the location,* the house is not a bad bargain.

Formal English, more frequently than informal English, uses verbals that *carry their own subjects along with them:*

> *The air being warm,* we left our coats in the car.
> *Escape being impossible,* he prepared for the worst.
> *Most of his colleagues having left the room,* the senator decided to omit the last ten pages of his speech.

Exercises

A. Check the following sentences for *confusing or misleading modifiers.* Label each sentence S (satisfactory), DM (unsatisfactory because of a dangling modifier), or MM (unsatisfactory because of a misplaced modifier). If your instructor desires, rewrite unsatisfactory sentences.

1. It was very common for a family to commit their children to a prearranged marriage during the time of Shakespeare.

2. Being a normal, complex-ridden youth, I was bored by domestic chores and withdrew into a world of books.

3. The escaped lion was captured before anyone was clawed or injured by its keepers.

4. While walking on the hard concrete, the clicking or dragging of shoes is very evident to the ear.

5. Lacking a college education, the foreman constantly made comments about the importance of the working man and the knowledge to be gained from living.

6. Although we are the leading country in the world financially we lack something equally important.

7. These magazines clearly appeal to women readers with stories about torrid love affairs.

8. Sometimes a student studies only so that he can prove in class the professor is wrong just to be showing off.

9. Hope and doubt are the two main emotions one feels when answering the telephone.

10. The Nehru look being then in fashion, Fred walked around the campus clad like a diplomat from India.

11. Having grown up in a small mining town in West Virginia, most of her life was spent there cooking and cleaning.

12. The picture was described as the best ever painted by my art teacher.

13. By glancing over the magazine rack in any drugstore, many magazines can be classified as either men's magazines or women's magazines.

14. Such magazines as *Argosy, Adventure,* and *True* have on their covers brightly colored pictures of men fighting wars or hunting in wild country.

15. While taking a bath, a radio should never be left plugged into an outlet close to the tub.

B. Follow the same instructions as for A.

1. Stopped by a policeman in a 30-mile zone, George Van Meter was given a ticket for doing 42 mph on his bicycle. 2. While riding in pursuit of the bandits, the hero's horse was shot from under him. 3. Being a high school sophomore, Shakespeare meant very little to me. 4. Having lived in India for many years, he knew many of the country's problems from first-hand experience. 5. By assigning question-and-answer problems, students fail to develop the ability to think a problem through by themselves. 6. The weather being unusually mild, we decided to have supper on the terrace. 7. As a child, my mother used to tell me stories of handsome princes on white chargers and of lovely princesses asleep in charmed castles. 8. Its siren wailing frantically, the ambulance skidded into the stalled sedan. 9. Sharks are a danger when vacationing in tropical waters. 10. Considering his lack of training, his performance has been truly remarkable. 11. The author's critics conducted a running argument in a literary magazine, which lasted for several months. 12. Listening to a live concert, music has a spontaneous quality that no mechanical equipment can reproduce. 13. To speak a language well, one has to know the overtones as well as the dictionary meanings of words. 14. The searching party returned to the camp, all efforts to find the missing girl having been unsuccessful. 15. Sir Malcolm heard the news that an heir had been born with great pleasure.

G 9   Confused Sentences

Avoid garbled sentences resulting from hasty writing, inaccurate copying, or careless typing.

Even when the reader can make out the intended meaning, he will be annoyed at being temporarily tripped up by a defect that the writer should have caught in revision.

G 9a   Omission and Duplication

Check your sentences for carelessly omitted or duplicated elements. Make sure you have transcribed each sentence in full, without omitting minor sentence elements like *a, the, has, be,* or *am.* Make sure you have not awkwardly repeated minor elements, especially connectives like *that* or *when:*

> I think *that* because he is ill *(that)* he will not come.
> When school starts in the fall *(that is when)* most parents sigh with relief.

Many hastily written sentences lack some essential part:

Hasty: After my sister moved to Ohio, her little girl contracted polio, but did not cause paralysis.
           (It was not *the girl* that didn't cause paralysis, but the disease.)

Revised: After my sister moved to Ohio, her little girl contracted polio, but fortunately *the disease* did not cause paralysis.

G 9b   Mixed Construction

A writer should not confuse different ways of expressing the same idea. The experienced writer will try out various possible constructions and select the one that seems to fit best. The inexperienced writer may plunge ahead, confusing the various possibilities. The result is known as **mixed construction:**

Mixed: *Any pretty girl* he ran after her.
Consistent: *Whenever he saw a pretty girl,* he ran after her.
Consistent: Any pretty girl *caused him* to run after her.

Mixed: The department manager *rejected him to be* one of his assistants.
Consistent: The department manager *rejected his application.*
Consistent: The department manager *did not want him to be* one of his assistants.

To unscramble such sentences, you have to consider the alternatives and limit yourself to one of them. Thus, "In case of emergency should be reported to the head office" yields "*In case of emergency, report* to the head office" and "*Emergencies should be reported* to the head office."

Note some frequent causes of mixed construction:

(1) In informal English, an adverbial clause starting with *because* sometimes appears as the subject of a verb. Formal English requires a noun clause starting with *that*.

Mixed: *Because people enjoy watching a light comedy* does not mean that our society is in a state of decay.

Consistent: *That people enjoy watching a light comedy* does not mean that our society is in a state of decay.

(2) Confusion of *because* and *because of* is an especially frequent cause of mixed construction. *Because* introduces a clause: "The course was canceled *because not enough students registered.*" *Because of* introduces a prepositional phrase: "The course was canceled *because of insufficient enrollment.*" Disregard of this distinction produces sentences like this one: "The course was canceled *because of not enough students registered.*"

G 9c   Faulty Predication

The predicate of a sentence should not say something about the subject that does not logically apply to the subject. For instance, a writer may anticipate in the subject all or part of the assertion contained in the predicate. Suppose you say, "*The choice* of our new home *was selected* by my mother." What was actually selected? Not a choice, but a home.

Logical: The choice *was made* by my mother.
Logical: *The home* was selected by my mother.

The idea anticipated in the subject may only partly overlap with that expressed in the predicate: "*The price* of our new cabin *was* rather *expensive.*" (What was actually expensive? The cabin, not the price. A price can be high, and the expense can be great, but a price cannot be said to be expensive.)

Faulty: At the beginning of the year, *the participation* in club activities is always *overcrowded.*
(The meetings—not the participation—are overcrowded, though the fact that many people participate is the reason for the overcrowding.)

Logical: At the beginning of the year, *our club meetings* are always overcrowded.

G 9d   Faulty Equation

A linking verb should not equate two things that are not logically equal. In informal English, such equations are often loose and illogical. "His job *is* a mailman" is illogical because a mailman is a person, not a job. Formal English would require "*He* is a mailman" or "His job is *that of* a mailman."

To check for faulty equation in a more complicated sentence, reduce it to a simple Subject–Linking Verb–Complement pattern. Do you obtain a logical "A equals B" statement?

Faulty:	*A woman* going to college to increase her knowledge is as valid a reason as a man going to college to become a dentist or a lawyer. (A woman is a reason?)
Revised:	*A woman's* going to college . . . (Going to college is a reason.)
Revised:	*For a woman* to go to college . . . (To go to college is a reason.)

Note the following special problems:

(1) A common type of faulty equation makes a linking verb introduce an **adverbial clause.** Children, for instance, will say, "A zoo is *when you go to look at animals.*" "When you go to look at animals" is not logically a description of a zoo; normally it would indicate *when* an action takes place or a condition occurs.

Faulty:	Punishment is *when you are told to stand in the corner.*
Satisfactory:	When you are told to stand in the corner, you are being punished.
Satisfactory:	One form of punishment is to make the child stand in a corner.
Satisfactory:	Punishment is a means of keeping children out of mischief.

Sometimes, however, an *is-when* or an *is-where* sentence actually does describe a time or a place:

Satisfactory:	Tuesday *was when* I saw him last.
Satisfactory:	Poughkeepsie *is where* I was born.

(2) Linking verbs often cause faulty equation when they introduce **prepositional phrases** that would normally indicate the circumstances of an action. Use an infinitive (or similar noun equivalent) instead:

Our only hope *is to convince* your parents [not *"is by convincing* your parents"].

Their method of selection *was to question* the candidates carefully [not *"was by questioning* the candidates"].

G 9e   Faulty Appositives

Make sure that your appositives can be equated with the nouns they modify. An **appositive** is a noun placed next to another noun to explain or describe it: "John, *a sophomore,* came to see me." Here, John and the sophomore are identical. However, it does not make sense to say, "There was only *one telephone call, a friend* of yours." A friend can *make* a telephone call, but we would not say that he *is* one.

Faulty: We have only one *vacancy, a mathematics teacher.*
             (A teacher is not a vacancy, and a vacancy is not a teacher.)

Revised: We have only one *vacancy, a position* for a mathematics teacher.
             (What is actually vacant is a *position* for a teacher.)

Exercises

A. In the following sentences, point out all instances of hasty writing, mixed construction, faulty predication, and faulty apposition. Label each sentence S (satisfactory) or U (unsatisfactory). If your instructor desires, revise unsatisfactory sentences.

1. Scientists know how to distill drinking water from salt water, but the cost of such a project is too unprofitable.

2. One good example of romantic love triumphing against odds is when there is an interracial marriage.

3. *A Moon for the Misbegotten* is the story of Josie, a loud-mouthed country girl living on a Connecticut farm.

4. The differences in intellects of college students do not vary to the extremes that they do in high school students.

5. The nature of what is good and what is evil lies with the individual.

6. Don's sales technique was to flash a big smile and to call all customers by their first names.

7. Cornelia had always wanted to meet one of the artists of whom she had heard a great deal about.

8. I suddenly realized that we were no longer on level ground and that the road was tilting upward on great concrete stilts.

9. In my experience, the older a man is, the more chivalrous and the more gallantry he possesses.

10. Nowadays, the idea of love is begun at a very tender age.

11. Just because Lisa's father was a general is no reason for her to order everyone around.

12. Because little of the pledged money actually came in, the repertory company had to give up its noble experiment.

13. My father first met his business partner in the army, for whom he drove a jeep and was his immediate supervisor.

14. The romantic attitude toward Hamlet first appears in the writings of Schlegel and Coleridge and is called the "tragedy of reflection."

15. Joe had hardly batted the ball over the fence than we heard a splintering of glass and an anguished yell.

B. Follow the same instructions as for A.

1. In modern industrial society, the sponsorship of the fine arts is no longer supported by wealthy aristocratic patrons. 2. Amnesia is when a character in a second-rate novel temporarily loses his memory. 3. According to recent statistics, the divorce rate for couples from different racial backgrounds compared with couples of different religion had more success in marriage. 4. The purpose of the reception was to acquaint old-timers with some of the newcomers to the area. 5. A prizefighter is not the kind of profession that offers its devotees economic security. 6. Shirley's husband was unable to support her in the style to which she had become accustomed to. 7. At night, a thousand neon signs hide the shabbiness of the jerry-built stores and offices from the traveler's view. 8. Surrealism was a movement dedicated to artistic expression of the irrational and the subconscious. 9. It is very difficult for a teacher in the social sciences to avoid becoming personally involved than a teacher of chemistry or of physics. 10. I believe that if the government allowed everyone to do as he pleased that our country would not long survive. 11. A flash flood is when a river suddenly rises over its banks. 12. Sandra was offered her first acting role by the Civic Theater, an amateur group that picked up Broadway plays after everyone else was done with them. 13. Just because a person has a college degree does not mean that he is exceptionally intelligent. 14. Jargon is a kind of language composed mainly of words like *homologous, processual,* and *socializee.* 15. In case of new outbreaks of the disease should be reported to the health authorities immediately.

G 10   Incomplete Constructions

In formal English, spell out relationships merely implied in various informal constructions.

Formal written English requires accuracy in a number of relationships that, though common, are less central to the basic structure of a sentence than predication and apposition.

G 10a   Informal *So* and *Such*

Statements of degree need to be accurately worked out in formal English. *So* and *such* often indicate that something has reached a definite point, producing certain characteristic results:

> She was so frightened *that she was unable to speak.*
> There was such an uproar *that the chairman banged his gavel in vain.*

Informal English often omits the characteristic result. *So* and *such* then function as **intensifiers**: "I am *so* glad." "He is *such* a lovely boy." You can make such sentences generally acceptable in two different ways. You can substitute an intensifier like *very* or *extremely:* "I am *very* glad." You can add a clause giving the characteristic result: "He is such a lovely boy *that all the girls adore him.*"

G 10b   Incomplete Comparison

Formal English frowns on incomplete comparisons. Normally, *more, better,* and *whiter,* the **comparative forms,** establish a comparison between at least two elements:

> *Carpenters* make more money than *teachers.*
> *Half a loaf* is better than *a slice.*

Most, best, and *whitest,* the **superlative forms,** establish a comparison within a group of at least three elements: [7]

> The annual classic at Le Mans is the most dangerous *automobile race in Europe.*

Formal English gives a writer less leeway than informal English in letting the reader find out for himself *what is being compared with what.*

---

[7]See the Glossary of Usage for discussion of the double comparative and of the superlative in reference to two.

(1) Most obviously informal are incomplete comparisons resulting from the use of *more* and *the most* as intensifiers: "That girl has *more* luck" (than who or than what?). "I had *the most* wonderful experience" (of the day? of the year? of a lifetime?). "I saw *the most* exciting play" (the most exciting play of the season? the most exciting play ever produced?).

(2) To satisfy demanding readers, state explicitly what is being compared even when the *terms of a comparison can be inferred* from the context:

> After I took a course in Remedial Reading, I read twice as fast *(as I had before)*.
>
> When we saw the revised estimate, we realized we would have to spend more money *(than we had planned)*.

G 10c   Illogical Comparison

Avoid comparisons that are absurd or ambiguous.

(1) Some sentences compare things *that are not really comparable:* "The skin of her cheeks was as soft as a child." Actually, her skin was as soft as a *child's* (skin), or as soft as *that* of a child. Check for logical balance in sentences like the following:

Illogical:	*Her personality* was unlike *most other girls* I have known in the past.
Logical:	*Her personality* was unlike *that* of most other girls I have known.

Illogical:	*The teachings* of Horatio Alger reached a wider audience than Whitman.
Logical:	*The teachings* of Horatio Alger reached a wider audience *than those of* Whitman. — Saul Bellow, "The Writer as Moralist," *Atlantic*

(2) Some comparisons mention *three comparable items* without making it clear which two are being compared. "Tom liked Dick better than Harry" may mean two different things:

Clear:	Tom liked Dick better than Harry *did*.
Clear:	Tom liked Dick better than *he liked* Harry.

NOTE: Sometimes the absurdity of an illogical comparison is not immediately obvious: "Their fullback was heavier than *any man on their team*." Their fullback is part of their team, and he cannot be heavier than *any man* on the team, including himself. He can be heavier than *other* men on the team:

Logical:	Their fullback was heavier than *any other man* on their team.

G 10d   Contraction of Coordinate Elements

Telescoping of coordinate elements does not work in formal written English if the forms concerned are merely similar rather than identical. When several items of the same kind are coordinated by a connective like *and* or *but,* we often omit forms that would cause unnecessary duplication. But such omission may cause truncated sentences.

(1) If one of *several verbs* in a sentence appears in a shortened form, fill in the complete forms first and omit only identical items. In "It *can be done* and *will be done,*" the *be done* after *can* is identical with that after *will.* You can therefore omit it and say: "It *can* and *will be done.*" But formal writing would avoid "It *can* and *has been* done." The complete forms are *can be done* and *has been done. Been* would have to serve as a substitute for an omitted *be.*

Incomplete:	Some men never *have* and never *will master* the fundamentals of punctuation.
Complete:	Some men never *have mastered* and never *will master* the fundamentals of punctuation.
Incomplete:	The patient *was given* an injection and the instruments *made* ready.
Complete:	The patient *was given* an injection, and the instruments *were made* ready.

(2) A special kind of unsatisfactory telescoping occurs in *double-barreled comparisons* of the *as-good-if-not-better* type: "My theme is as good if not better than yours." The complete forms would be *as good as* and *better than,* and *than* cannot substitute for an omitted *as.* Formal English would require "My theme is as good *as,* if not better *than,* yours." Less awkward and equally acceptable is shifting the second part of the comparison to the end of the sentence:

My theme is as good as yours, *if not better.*

(3) When you coordinate *several prepositional phrases,* guard against omitting prepositions that are not identical but merely express a similar relationship:

Satisfactory:	I have great *admiration and respect* for him. (Taken up separately, the two prepositions would prove identical: "admiration *for* him" and "respect *for* him.")
Unsatisfactory:	I have great *respect and faith* in him. (Taken up separately, the two phrases would require different prepositions: "respect *for* him" and "faith *in* him.")

Notice the use of different prepositions in the following examples:

She was jealous *of* but fascinated *by* her rival.

His behavior during the trial adds *to* rather than detracts *from* my admiration for him.

Exercise

Check the following sentences for incomplete and ambiguous constructions. Point out unsatisfactory comparisons and unsatisfactory contraction. Label each sentence S (satisfactory) or U (unsatisfactory). If your instructor desires, revise unsatisfactory sentences.

1. Women on the whole understand children better than men.   2. Roger's stews and sauces were as good as the best restaurant in Paris, if not better.   3. The light at the intersection of Sixth and Grove will turn green exactly six seconds after the intersection of Wright and Grove.   4. In this district, teachers have always been and will always be hired on the basis of their professional competence alone.   5. In much of Europe, American films are more popular than any other country.   6. The discussion grew so heated that David decided to keep his views to himself.   7. The English spoken in the farm area where I grew up differs from that spoken on the East Coast or in the South.   8. Children seem to like the so-called "adult" Westerns as much as adults do.   9. Year after year, American colleges produce more physical education teachers than mathematics.   10. The Secretary of State usually attracts more criticism than any member of the President's cabinet.   11. Critics of our schools must realize that they can and are doing great harm by indiscriminate attacks.   12. Unlike a track coach, a history teacher seldom has a newspaper article written about him when his students do exceptional work.   13. Most young children learn a second language more readily than an older person does.   14. The impact of American books, magazines, and comics in Great Britain is much greater than British publications in the United States.   15. A good background in the liberal arts is excellent preparation for such practical professions as engineers and lawyers.   16. The United States has more television sets to the square mile than any other country in the world.   17. Mike never has and never will succeed in making his restaurant something more than a place to eat food.   18. Many of the legislators lacked the taste—and the capacity—for brilliant political debate.   19. Unlike America, traveling abroad is a rare luxury in many foreign countries.   20. Few of my friends were preoccupied or even interested in making a living.

G 11   Parallel Structure

Use parallel grammatical structure for elements serving the same function in a sentence.

Like a road full of unexpected twists and turns, sentences that lack parallel structure slow down and confuse the reader.

G 11a   Faulty Parallelism

Formal English requires consistency in the coordination of elements serving a similar function in a sentence. Sentence elements joined by *and, or,* and *but* have to be **parallel**; they have to fit into the same grammatical category. If you put an *and* after *body,* the reader expects another noun: "body and *chassis,*" "body and *soul.*" If you put an *and* after *swore,* he expects another verb: "swore and *affirmed,*" "swore and *raved.*" The same principle applies to other elements, including whole clauses:

Infinitives:	Two things that a successful advertisement must accomplish are *to be noticed* and *to be remembered.*
Participles:	I can still see my aunt *striding* into the corral, *cornering* a cow against a fencepost, *balancing* herself on a one-legged milking stool, and *butting* her head into the cow's belly.
Clauses:	The young people *who brood* in their rooms, *who forget* to come down to the dining hall, and *who burst out* in fits of irrationality are not worrying about who will win the great game. — Oscar Handlin, "Are the Colleges Killing Education?" *Atlantic*

You can often make elements parallel by *shifting one of them to a different grammatical category.* For instance, "*ignorant* and *a miser*" is off balance because it joins an adjective and a noun. You could change *ignorant* to a noun ("He was an *ignoramus* and a miser") or *miser* to an adjective ("He was ignorant and *miserly*"). But many ideas are not easily shifted from one grammatical category to another. You may have to consider several different ways of *shortening, expanding, or rewording a sentence*:

Faulty:	High school students want to be *popular* and *leaders.*
Parallel:	High school students want to *be* popular and *become* leaders.
Faulty:	My grandfather liked *the country* and *to walk* in the fields.
Parallel:	My grandfather liked *to live* in the country and *to walk* in the fields.

Faulty:	He told me *of his plans* and *that he was leaving.*
Parallel:	He *informed* me of his plans and *told* me that he was leaving.

Look especially for the following sources of faulty parallelism:
(1) Sentences sound awkward when a noun appears in coordination with an adjective as the modifier of *another noun:*

Faulty:	The schools must serve *personal and society* needs as they evolve.
Parallel:	The schools must serve *personal and social* needs as they evolve.

(2) Lack of parallelism is especially obvious after **correlatives**: *either . . . or, neither . . . nor, not only . . . but also, whether . . . or.*

Faulty:	I used to find him either *on the porch* or *dozing* in the living room.
Parallel:	I used to find him either *sitting* on the porch or *dozing* in the living room.

Faulty:	We wondered whether *to believe* him or *should we try* to verify his story.
Parallel:	We wondered whether we should *believe* him or *try* to verify his story.

G 11b   Faulty Series

Avoid faulty parallelism in a series of three or more elements.
Often a writer will lead his reader into what looks like a conventional series only to trip him up by making the last element snap out of the expected pattern:

Faulty:	He liked to *swim, relax,* and *everything peaceful.*
Parallel:	He liked *swimming, relaxation,* and peaceful *surroundings.*

Faulty:	Jim would always *open* doors, *walk* on the side toward the curb, and *helping* whenever needed.
Parallel:	Jim would always *open* doors, *walk* on the side toward the curb, and *help* whenever needed.

If the elements in a faulty series are not really parallel in *meaning,* the revision might break up the series altogether:

Faulty:	Her new friend was *polite, studious,* and *an only child.*
Parallel:	Her new friend was *a gentleman, a scholar,* and *an only child.*
Broken Up:	Her new friend, *an only child,* was a gentleman and a scholar.

Exercises

A. Check the following sentences for parallel structure. Label each sentence S (satisfactory), *FS* (unsatisfactory because of a faulty series), or *FP* (unsatisfactory because of other instances of faulty parallelism). If your instructor desires, rewrite unsatisfactory sentences.

1. Teen-agers assert their independence through the way they dress, comb their hair, and their tastes in music.

2. Parents can no longer rely on school and religious influences to set moral standards for their children.

3. O'Neill's last plays are alive with archetypal American experience and anguished family biography.

4. Students come to college to have fun, find a husband or wife, get away from home, and many other ridiculous reasons.

5. At the beginning, the story focuses on whether the old man will capture the large beautiful fish or will the fish elude him.

6. My work consists of planning the day's production, assigning the men to their jobs, and actual supervision of their work.

7. If the states are allowed to allot federal funds for education, and politics being what it is, the neediest school districts will not get much help.

8. My high school teachers never analyzed my essays from the structural and content point of view.

9. If we want mankind to survive, we had best produce men whose lungs thrive on poisoned air, whose bodies can tolerate polluted water, and whose minds resist the psychological effects of overcrowding.

10. Dr. Johnson was gruff, stern, and a man with many peculiarities.

11. Foreign exchange students often expect to see rugged, tanned cowboys roaming the prairies and pug-faced gangsters shooting people down in the streets.

12. My father thought that young girls should not go to dances, see young men only in the company of a chaperone, and many other old-fashioned prejudices.

13. In many gangster movies, the hero deceives the police, moves in the best society, and comes to a bad end only because his mother-in-law shoots him for having slapped her daughter.

14. To most readers, the word *home* suggests security and comfort as well as a place to live.

15. The success of a television program depends on how well the program has been advertised, the actors taking part, and is it comedy or serious drama.

B. Follow the same instructions as for **A**.

1. The editorial called the governor's speech vague, insincere, and repetitious.   **2**. He seemed like the type of person who would brag about his income and be extravagant with his money.   **3**. What the children lacked was the feeling of really belonging and that someone really cared.   **4**. Barbara was waiting for a talent scout to discover her and who would take her to Hollywood.   **5**. Newspapers do not always provide a reliable record of what ordinary people are thinking, saying, and doing.   **6**. A girl learns a lot about children when she cares for younger brothers and sisters or as a baby sitter during high school days.   **7**. This country needs a President skilled in diplomacy and who knows foreign countries well.   **8**. A physician has to be good not only at diagnosing diseases but also at understanding his patients.   **9**. Advertisers should admit that a deodorant cannot make a woman beautiful and that a healthy complexion alone cannot make a person happy.   **10**. A successful businessman usually has a pleasant personality, poise, and is a good speaker.   **11**. We should not judge a candidate's qualifications by whether he is a lawyer, farmer, or from some other occupation.   **12**. Maurice claimed to be Napoleon's great-grandson and that he was the rightful heir to the throne of France.   **13**. Apparently my friend's work consisted of sitting at a desk for eight hours a day and give orders.   **14**. Our Christmas dinner would consist of roast turkey with cranberry sauce, whipped potatoes, vegetables, and followed by mincemeat pie.   **15**. The mass media shy away from frank discussion of love but permitting the detailed treatment of crude violence.

C. Write or collect ten sentences illustrating parallel structure. Devote each sentence to a different type of word or construction.

G 12   Consistent Point of View

Do not confuse your readers by unmotivated shifts in tense, reference, or grammatical perspective.

The need for consistency makes a serious writer guard against confusing shifts in the perspective he adopts toward people and events.

G 12a   Shifts in Tense

Be consistent in your use of verb forms that indicate the relationship of events in time.

(1) Avoid the shift *from the past tense to the present tense* when something remembered becomes so real that it seems to be happening in front of you. Note the shift in time in the following sentences:

We *disembarked* at noon and fought our way through the jungle in the sultry afternoon heat. Suddenly, there *is* a tiger! I *aim* my rifle and *pull* the trigger! Nothing *happens* — the gun *wasn't* loaded. Luckily, one of my bearers *saved* me from the consequences of my carelessness.

If the writer wants the description to be especially vivid, he should tell *the whole story* as though it were happening now: "We *disembark* . . . *fight* our way . . . one of them *saves* me." Otherwise, he should describe everything in the past.

(2) Avoid shifts in perspective when two events happen *at different times or during different periods:* "When I *saw* the F on my report card, I *was* terribly disappointed, because I *studied* very hard." If studying hard was a matter of past history by the time the student received his grade, the **sequence of tenses** would be more accurate like this:

I was terribly disappointed, because I *had studied* very hard.

Formed with *have* or *has*, the **present perfect** indicates that something has happened prior to events taking place *now:* "He *has finished* his supper and *is getting* up." Formed with *had*, the **past perfect** indicates that something happened in the relatively distant past, prior to *other* events in the past: "He *had finished* his supper and *was getting* up." A confusing shift results when a writer disregards these relations:

Shift: Last March, the Secretary of the Air Force told the committee what *has happened* to air transport in this country.

Consistent: Last March, the Secretary of the Air Force told the committee what *had happened* to air transport in this country.
                (The secretary could not have told the committee what *has happened* since he testified and up to the present time.)

(3) *Avoid shifts resulting from failure to observe the distinction between direct and indirect quotation.* What the speaker felt or observed at the time he spoke would occur in the present tense in direct quotation: He said, "I *feel* fine." It would occur in the past tense in indirect quotation: He said that he *felt* fine. What the speaker felt *before* he spoke would occur in the past (or perhaps in the present perfect) when quoted directly: He said, "I *felt* fine." It would occur in

the past perfect when quoted indirectly: He said that he *had felt* fine.

Failure to adjust the tenses in indirect quotations can lead to sentences like the following:

> Her husband admitted that he *was* [should be *"had been"*] a confirmed bachelor.
>
> Mr. Chamberlain said that there *will be* [should be *"would be"*] peace in our time.

NOTE: When *a statement made in the past formulates a general truth* many writers find the present tense plausible:

Galileo said that the earth *moves* and that the sun *is* fixed; the Inquisition said that the earth *is* fixed and the sun *moves;* and Newtonian astronomers, adopting an absolute theory of space, said that both the sun and the earth *move.* — A. N. Whitehead, *Science and the Modern World*

(4) *Avoid inconsistent combinations between forms that indicate differences in attitude toward possible events* (called differences in **mood**). In the following sentences, note the differences between factual reference to a possibility and the **conditional**, which makes the same possibility seem less probable, or contrary to fact. (See also G 4c.)

Inconsistent:	If he *comes* to this country, the army *would* draft him.
Factual:	If he *comes* to this country, the army *will* draft him.
Conditional:	If he *came* to this country, the army *would* draft him.

G 12b   Shifts in Reference

Be consistent in the way you refer to yourself and others. The least ambiguous pronoun you can use to refer to yourself is of course *I, me,* or *my* (**first person singular**). When you do not want to focus attention on yourself, you may use *we, us,* or *our* instead (**first person plural**). This "editorial" we, however, sounds artificial in most student writing, especially in short themes.

Note the following special problems:

(1) When a writer wants to speak directly to his reader, he can call him *you* (**second person singular** and **plural**) and use *we* to refer both to the reader and himself:

> *You* will agree that *we* must do everything in our power.
>
> As *you* no doubt remember, *we* have witnessed several similar incidents during the past year.

But *you* also appears as an informal equivalent of *one* or *a person*, referring not so much to the reader as to people in general:

Formal: *One* cannot be too careful.

Informal: *You* can't be too careful.

Confusion results when a writer shifts to the indefinite, generalized *you* after he has already identified the person he has in mind in some other way: "I don't want to be a famous actress. *I* would rather lead my own life without people always knowing what *you* are doing." The easiest way to avoid this kind of shift is to use *you* only to mean "you, the reader."

(2) Similar in effect to shifts to *you* are shifts to the **imperative**, the request form of verbs: "*Come* in." "*Put* it down." "*Leave* him alone." Imperatives are most appropriate in directions and exhortations. They startle the reader when they suddenly break into ordinary expository prose:

Shift: High schools *should stop* educating all students at the same rate. *Give* aptitude tests for placement and then *separate* the students accordingly.

Consistent: High schools *should stop* educating all students at the same rate. They *should give* aptitude tests for placement and then *separate* the students accordingly.

G 12c   Shifts to the Passive

Avoid shifting to the passive when the person in question is still the active element in the sentence. Some sentences confuse the reader by shifting from an **active** construction ("*He built* the house") to a **passive** one ("*The house was built* by him"):[8]

Inconsistent: He *returned* to the office as soon as *his lunch had been eaten.* (This sounds as though his lunch might have been eaten by somebody else.)

Consistent: He *returned* to the office as soon as he *had eaten* his lunch.

Unsatisfactory shifts to the passive are especially frequent after an impersonal *one* or *you:*

Inconsistent: As *you scan* the area of your backyard, a small patch of uninhabited earth *is located.*

Consistent: As *you scan* your backyard, *you locate* a small patch of earth.

[8] For a fuller discussion of the passive see S 3b.

Exercises

A. Check the following passages for unnecessary or confusing shifts in perspective. Label each sentence S (satisfactory) or U (unsatisfactory). If your instructor desires, revise unsatisfactory sentences.

1. One of the most important things that I learned from my mother was how to appreciate your friends without being dependent on them.

2. When Marilyn walked down the hall, she often pretends not to notice a fellow student getting ready to greet her.

3. Now that I am in college I definitely found that I have to study in order to meet competition.

4. Suddenly the sky darkens, a breeze springs up, and a premonitory rumble rolls across the lake.

5. The boat moved quietly down the river, the girls sang, and mandolins were played by some of the older boys.

6. Our culture teaches the individual to maintain an even countenance at all times, especially when you are angry.

7. Men are not qualified to speak of good if evil has never been examined.

8. College should mean a place where one learns things to fit him for his chosen place in life.

9. If the club limited its membership, it would have to raise its dues.

10. If we believed nothing is sacred, our value system will be lost.

11. Millions of people every day rush off to jobs they detest.

12. To the early Christians, endurance meant seeing one's loved ones thrown to wild beasts without losing faith in your God.

13. You could not help finding Cheryl obnoxious, especially since one could never confront her successfully with a lie in which she had been caught.

14. A true gentleman behaves the way he does because courtesy has to him become second nature.

B. Follow the same instructions as for A.

1. If one insists on telling the truth at all times, he is not likely to be very popular. 2. After I finished my pie, a cup of coffee was ordered and a cigarette lighted to top off a perfect meal. 3. In the next scene, Antonio, who has just arrived in Venice, tells his friends that he is going to elope with the beautiful Elvira. 4. If a war comes, many small

nations would be at the mercy of those countries that have nuclear weapons.   **5.** Though Nietzsche is often mentioned, his books are infrequently read and seldom understood.   **6.** If you came early, you could join us for a walk along the shore.   **7.** Several witnesses testified that the crossing signal had failed to operate.   **8.** During the spring rains, the valley would have been flooded if it were not for the dams recently completed.   **9.** One doesn't gain anything by exercising to lose weight if afterward you are allowed to eat all you want.   **10.** The college catalog says that all students would take a year of science and a year of mathematics.   **11.** Often when you have an unemployed father there may be friction in the home and the child may feel unwanted.   **12.** Our newspapers should stop wasting their time on trivialities. Leave the love life of the stars to the fan magazines and put the news back on the front page.   **13.** If we refuse poorly qualified students admission to college, we would solve the problem of overcrowding.   **14.** Having a friend that really cares for you is one of the best things that one can get out of life.   **15.** As the lights go out and the curtain rises, the principal was revealed trying to abate the clouds of smoke pouring from the witches' cauldron.

CHAPTER FIFTEEN

Mechanics and Spelling

M 1   Manuscript Mechanics
    M 1a   Penmanship and Typing
    M 1b   Corrections
    M 1c   Titles of Themes
    M 1d   Spacing and Syllabication
    M 1e   Italics

M 2   Abbreviations and Numbers
    M 2a   Acceptable Abbreviations
    M 2b   Restricted Abbreviations
    M 2c   Numbers

SP 1   Spelling Habits

SP 2   Spelling Problems
    SP 2a   Spelling and Pronunciation
    SP 2b   Variant Forms
    SP 2c   Confusing Words

SP 3   Spelling Rules
    SP 3a   *I* Before *E*
    SP 3b   Doubled Consonant
    SP 3c   *Y* as a Vowel
    SP 3d   Final *E*

SP 4   Words Often Misspelled

SP 5   The Apostrophe
    SP 5a   Contractions
    SP 5b   Possessives
    SP 5c   Plurals of Letters and Symbols

SP 6   The Hyphen
    SP 6a   Compound Words
    SP 6b   Prefixes
    SP 6c   Group Modifiers

SP 7   Capitals
    SP 7a   Proper Names
    SP 7b   Titles of Publications

M 1   Manuscript Mechanics

Submit neat and competently prepared copy.

Whenever you hand in a theme or a report, the outward appearance of your manuscript is the first thing to strike your reader. A good first impression is likely to put him in a tolerant and receptive mood. A bad first impression is likely to linger even after he discovers compensating virtues in the text.

M 1a   Penmanship and Typing

All copy, whether handwritten or typed, should be neat and legible. To produce legible handwritten copy, use composition paper of standard size, preferably ruled in *wide lines,* and a reliable pen. You may find that you don't write fast enough, especially when you are asked to write in class. Don't try to develop speed by substituting a smudge for letters like *a, e,* or *i;* by running together combinations like *mm* or *mn;* or by substituting a vague scrawl for endings like *-ing* and *-tion.* Instead, practice speed writing while at the same time forcing yourself to make every *a* and *e* as distinct as your grade school penmanship book required. Dot all your *i*'s and cross all your *t*'s. Distinguish clearly between capitals and lower-case letters.

Prune your writing of flourishes; avoid excessive slanting or excessive crowding. Unconventional handwriting is much more likely to annoy than it is to impress the reader.

To prepare typewritten copy, use unlined paper of standard size. Onionskin paper or semitransparent sheets are for carbon copies; use solid, *nontransparent* paper of good quality for the copy you turn in. Change your typewriter ribbon at reasonable intervals.

Double-space all material except block quotations and footnotes. Leave two spaces after a period or other end punctuation; use two hyphens — with no space on either side — to make a dash. Proofread all typewritten copy carefully for typographical errors and for errors in transcription.

M 1b   Corrections

Last-minute corrections are permissible on the final copy, provided they are few in number, look neat, and conform to standard practice. (On papers written outside class, all major revisions are of course made on the rough draft.)

(1) Draw a line through words and phrases that you want to omit; *do not use parentheses or square brackets for this purpose.*

(2) To correct a word, draw a line through it and insert the cor-

rected word in the space immediately above; avoid crossing out or inserting individual letters.

(3) To add a missing word, insert a caret (∧) and write the word immediately above.

M 1c   Titles of Themes

Titles of themes follow the general rules for the capitalization of words in titles of publications (see SP 7b). Do *not* underline or put in quotation marks the title that you assign to one of your own themes. Use a question mark or an exclamation mark after it where appropriate, but do *not* use a period even if your title is a complete sentence:

Chivalry Is Dead
Is Chivalry Dead?
Chivalry Is Dead!

M 1d   Spacing and Syllabication

Observe conventional spacing and syllabication. Whether your papers are handwritten or typed, leave adequate margins. An inch and a half on the left and at the top, and an inch on the right and at the bottom are about standard. Indent the first lines of paragraphs, about an inch in longhand or five spaces in typed copy. To make a last-minute change in the paragraphing of a paper, insert the symbol ¶ to indicate an additional paragraph break. Insert *"no ¶"* in the margin to indicate that an existing paragraph break should be ignored.

On the whole, a somewhat uneven right margin is preferable to the practice of dividing words at the end of every second or third line. Dictionaries generally use centered dots to indicate where a word may conventionally be divided *(com·pli·ment).* A few generally observed practices are worth remembering:

(1) The setting off of single letters saves little or no space and tends to confuse the reader. Do not divide words like *about, alone,* and *enough* or like *many* and *via.* Similarly, do not set off the ending *-ed* in words like *complained* or *renewed.*

(2) Hyphenated words become confusing when divided at any other point than at the original hyphen. Do not break up the *American* in "un-American" or the *sister* in "sister-in-law."

(3) Do not divide the last word on a page.

M 1e   Italics

Italics (or slanted type) are indicated in the handwritten or typed manuscript by underlining.

(1) *Italics identify technical terms and words borrowed from foreign languages.* (See P 8e.)

(2) *Italics serve to emphasize or call special attention to part of a sentence:*

The judge told me to apologize *in person* to everyone who had sat down in the freshly painted pews.

The company is not liable for accidents caused by the negligence of employees or *by mechanical defects.*

Like other means of procuring emphasis, such italics lose their value if overused.

(3) *Italics set off the title of a publication from the text in which it is cited.* Italicize titles of periodicals and of works published as separate units. Use **quotation marks** to set off titles of articles, chapters, or poems that are merely a part of a complete publication:

Kipling's "Recessional" can be found in *A Treasury of Verse.*

"We Shall Overcome" has the ring of a gospel hymn rather than that of a *New Republic* editorial.

M 2   Abbreviations and Numbers

Avoid the overuse of abbreviations in ordinary expository prose.

Abbreviations save time and space. Here as in other matters, however, formal written English discourages excessive short cuts.

M 2a   Acceptable Abbreviations

Some abbreviations are generally appropriate in expository writing:

(1) Before or after names, the titles *Mr., Mrs., Dr., St. (Saint);* the abbreviations *Jr.* and *Sr.;* degrees like *M.D.* and *Ph.D.* (Mr. John J. Smith, Jr.; Dr. Alfred Joyce or Alfred Joyce, M.D.). Use *Prof.* only before the *full* name: Prof. James F. Jones.

(2) Before or after numerals, the abbreviations *No.,* A.D. and B.C., A.M. and P.M., and the symbol $ (in 1066 A.D.; at 5:30 A.M.; $275).

(3) Initials standing for the names of agencies, organizations, business firms, technical processes, chemical compounds, and the like, when the full name is awkward or unfamiliar: *AFL-CIO, FBI, PTA, TVA, UNESCO, DDT, FM radio.*

(4) Some common Latin abbreviations: *e.g.* (for example), *etc.* (and so on), *i.e.* (that is), *viz.* (namely). However, the modern tendency is to prefer the corresponding English expressions.

M 2b   Restricted Abbreviations

Some abbreviations are appropriate in addresses, newspaper reports, technical reports, and other special contexts. Most of these have to be written in full in ordinary expository prose:

(1) With a few exceptions, names of countries, states, streets, and the like, are spelled out in ordinary writing: *United States; Schenectady, New York; Union Street.* (Exceptions: *USSR; Washington, D.C.*)

(2) The ampersand ("&") and abbreviations like *Inc.* and *Bros.* occur in ordinary writing only in references to organizations that employ those abbreviations in their official titles: *Smith & Company, Inc.* Spell out % and ¢.

(3) In ordinary expository prose, *lb.* (pound), *oz.* (ounce), *ft.* (foot), and *in.* (inch) are usually spelled out. Some units of measurement are more unwieldy and are abbreviated, provided they are used with figures: *45 mph, 1500 rpm.*

NOTE: Check your dictionary whenever you are not sure of the use of capitals and periods with an abbreviation. Some dictionaries include common abbreviations in the main listing; others list them in a special appendix.

M 2c   Numbers

In ordinary expository prose, the use of figures is to some extent restricted. They are generally appropriate in references to the day of the month *(May 13)*, the year *(1917)*, street numbers *(1014 Union Avenue)*, and page numbers *(Chapter 7, page 18)*. For other uses of numbers, the following conventions are widely observed:

(1) Numbers from one to ten, and *round numbers* requiring no more than two words, are usually spelled out: *three dollars a seat, five hundred years later, ten thousand copies.*

(2) Figures are used for *exact sums, technical measurements, decimals, and percentages,* as well as for references to time using A.M. or P.M.: *$7.22; 500,673 inhabitants; 57 per cent; 2:30 P.M.*

(3) Figures are avoided at the beginning of a sentence: "Fifteen out of 28 replied . . ." or "When questioned, 15 out of 28 replied . . ." Except in special situations like this one, changes from figures to words (and vice versa) in a series of numbers are generally avoided.

(4) When spelled out, *compound numbers* from 21 to 99 are hyphenated: *twenty-five, one hundred and forty-six.*

Exercise

Rewrite the following passage, using abbreviations and numerals in accordance with standard practice:

> Mister Geo. Brown had resided at Eighteen N. Washington St. since Feb. nineteen-hundred and forty-four. Though he weighed only one hundred and twenty-six lbs. and measured little more than 5 ft., he was an ardent devotee of the rugged life. He did his exercises every a. m. and refused to send for the Dr. when he had a cold. 3 yrs. after he moved here from Chicago, Ill., the Boy Scouts of America made him an honorary member, & he soon became known in scout circles for the many $ he contributed to the Boy Scout movement. One Sat. afternoon B. forgot to spell out the amount on a check for one-hundred and twenty-five dollars intended for a bldg. drive and payable to the B. S. of A. The treasurer, Bernard Simpson of Arlington, Va., wrote in 2 additional figures, spelled out the changed amount, and left the U. S. after withdrawing B.'s life savings of twelve-thousand five-hundred and fifty dollars from the local bank. "Ah," said Geo. when he found 2$ and 36 cts. left in his account, "if I had only spelled out the No.'s and abbrev.!"

SP 1   Spelling Habits

Correct spelling is the result of good spelling habits, established by study and drill over the years.

The average high school graduate spells correctly most of the words he uses. According to recent studies, most of the trouble that college students have with spelling is caused by perhaps fewer than 250 words out of the 5,000 or 10,000 they are likely to use. The most common troublemakers are everyday words like *believe* or *definite*. The spelling of such a word may look right not because you have seen it in this particular word but because you have seen it in another word that is confusingly similar. Thus, you may spell the main syllable in *believe* like the main syllable in *receive*. You may spell the ending in *definite* like the ending in *ultimate*. To spell such a word correctly, you have to memorize it letter by letter, while at the same time seeing each letter as a part of the whole.

Merely looking up misspelled words has little long-range effect. The following procedure has a good chance of producing favorable results:

(1) *Find out which words you tend to misspell.* Make a list of all spelling errors pointed out to you in your themes, quizzes, and exams. Work your way through a list of common spelling demons (such as the one printed under SP 4) and copy out those that you have found troublesome in your own writing.

(2) *Put in twenty minutes three times a week over a fairly long period of time.* Unless you work on your spelling regularly, you will make little progress. You cannot unlearn in two or three hours the spelling habits that you developed over many years.

(3) *Work out a definite routine and stick to it.* At each sitting, take up a group of perhaps ten or twenty spelling words. If you are a "visualizer," place your spelling words before you in clear, legible handwriting. Try putting them on a set of small note cards that you can carry around with you. Run your eyes over each word until you can see both the individual letters and the whole word at the same time. Circle the letters that cause the most trouble. If you learn primarily by ear, read each word aloud. Then spell each letter individually: *Receive*—R-E-C-E-I-V-E. If you learn best when you can bring your nerves and muscles into play, try writing each word in large letters. Trace it over several times. Combine or alternate the three methods in the manner that seems to yield the best results.

(4) *Make use of memory devices like the following:*

MAC got ACquainted.
ALL RIGHT means ALL is RIGHT.
There's an INNING in begINNING.
Don't beLIEve LIEs.
There's a CRITIC in CRITICism.
There's IRON in the envIRONment.
Men who GOVERN are a GOVERNment.
PERhaps he will give a PERfect PERformance.
There's a COG in reCOGnition.
There's a VILLA in VILLAin.

(5) *Copy difficult new terms and names that you encounter in your reading for various courses.* Study and memorize them. If you are a science major, master words like *enzyme, anesthesia, protein,* or *arteriosclerosis.* If you are taking a literature course, focus on the exact spelling of names like *Oedipus, Xanthippe,* or *Omar Khayyam.*

SP 2   Spelling Problems

Learn to identify and master recurrent spelling problems.

Some words can be conveniently grouped together because they share common characteristics. Others are best studied together because they need to be carefully distinguished from each other.

SP 2a Spelling and Pronunciation

Some words become spelling problems because the gap between spelling and pronunciation is unusually wide:

(1) Some words are difficult to spell because of *silent consonants.* Be sure to insert the silent consonants in "condem*n*," "de*b*t," "dou*b*t," "*f*oreign," "mor*t*gage," and "sovereign."

(2) Frequent causes of confusion are *vowels occurring in unstressed positions. A, e,* and *i* become indistinguishable in the endings *-ate* and *-ite, -able* and *-ible, -ance* and *-ence, -ant* and *-ent.* You can sometimes learn to choose the right ending by associating the word with a closely related one: *definite* (finish, definition); *separate* (separation); *ultimate* (ultimatum); *indispensable* (dispensary). For many other words no such crutches are available. Watch out for the following:

a: acceptable, acceptance, advisable, attendance, attendant, brilliant, performance

e: consistent, excellence, excellent, existence, experience, independent, persistent, tendency

i: irresistible, plausible, possible, susceptible

(3) Some words are hard to spell because of *sounds not pronounced* in much nonstandard or informal speech:

accidentally, candidate, February, government, library, probably, quantity

(4) In unstressed positions, words like *have, can,* or *will* tend to appear in shortened forms. Do not substitute *of* for *have* in combinations like *could have been, might have been, should have seen.*

SP 2b Variant Forms

Some words are confusing because they appear in a variety of forms. Especially confusing are different spellings in variant forms of the *same root word:* "til*l*" but "unti*l*," "*four*" and "*four*teen" but "*for*ty," "*for*ward" but "*fore*most," "*nine*" and "*nine*ty" but "*nin*th."

(1) Watch out for spelling differences in pairs of words representing different parts of speech:

absorb—absorption, advise (v.)—advice (n.), conscience—conscientious, courteous—courtesy, curious—curiosity, dissent—dissension, generous—generosity, genius—ingenious, proceed—procedure, pronounce—pronunciation, renounce—renunciation

(2) Sometimes a confusing change in spelling accompanies a

change in the grammatical form of the same word. For instance, you "choose" and "lead" in the present, but you "chose" and "led" in the past. Some plural forms cause spelling difficulties: one *man* but several *men,* one *woman* but several *women.* Remember these especially:

Singular:	hero	Negro	potato	tomato	wife
Plural:	heroes	Negroes	potatoes	tomatoes	wives

Singular:	freshman	postman	life	veto	calf
Plural:	freshmen	postmen	lives	vetoes	calves

(3) Be sure to add the *-ed* for *past tense* or *past participle* in words like the following:

He used to come.
She was supposed to write.
They were prejudiced (biased).

NOTE: Your dictionary lists the correct spelling of plural forms that are difficult or unusual. Sometimes it lists two acceptable forms: *buffalos* or *buffaloes, scarfs* or *scarves.*

SP 2c   Confusing Words

Some words need attention because they sound similar but differ in spelling or in meaning. Here is partial list of these:

Accept:	to accept a bribe; to find something acceptable; to make an acceptance speech
Except:	everyone except Judy; to make an exception; to except (exempt, exclude) present company

Adopt:	to adopt a proposal (in its present form); the adoption racket
Adapt:	to adapt it to our needs (to make it more suitable); an adaptable worker; an adaptation from a novel

Capital:	unused capital; modern capitalism; the capital of France; capital letters
Capitol:	the cupola of the Capitol; remodeling the façade of the Capitol

Censor:	to censor a reporter's dispatch; to object to censorship
Censure:	to censure (blame, condemn) someone for his behavior; a vote of censure

Cite:	cited for bravery; to cite many different authorities; a citation for reckless driving

Site:	the site of the new high school (where it is *situated* or located)
Consul:	the American consul in Berlin; the French consulate in New York
Council:	the members of the city council; Councilor Brown
Counsel:	the counseling staff of the college; camp counselors
Desert:	he lost his way in the desert; he deserted his family; he got his just deserts
Dessert:	the dinner did not include a dessert
Effect:	to effect (produce, bring about) a change; immediate effects; an effective speech
Affect:	it affected (had an influence on) his grade; he spoke with an affected (artificial) British accent
Loose:	loose and fast; loosen your grip
Lose:	win or lose; a bad loser
Personal:	a personal appeal; speak to him personally
Personnel:	a personnel bureau; hire additional personnel
Presents:	visitors bearing presents
Presence:	your presence is requested; presence of mind
Principal:	his principal (main) argument; the principal of the school
Principle:	principles (rules, standards) of conduct; the principles of economics
Quiet:	be quiet; a quiet neighborhood
Quite:	quite so; not quite
Right:	right and wrong; right and left; all right
Rite:	savage rites (ceremonies); the rites of spring
-wright:	a playwright; a wheelwright (a man who wrought, or made, wheels and carriages)
Than:	bigger than life; more trouble than it is worth
Then:	now and then; until then
There:	here and there; there you are; no one was there
Their:	they lost their appetite; mental ills and their cure
To:	go to bed; cut to pieces; easy to do; hard to deny
Too:	too good to be true; bring your children, too
Two:	two and two makes four
Whether:	whether good or bad
Weather:	bad weather; to weather the storm

Exercises

A. In available dictionaries, check the status of simplified spellings like travel*e*d, thr*u*, anesthetic, th*o*, catalo*g*, or any others you have encountered.

B. Insert the missing letter in each of the following words: accept____nce, attend____nce, brilli____nt, consist____ncy, dcfin____te, excell____nt, exist____nce, experi____nce, independ____nt, indispens____ble, occurr____nce, irresist____ble, perform____nce, persist____nt, separ____te, tend____ncy.

C. Look up the plural of *cargo, Eskimo, hoof, mosquito, motto, piano, solo, soprano, wharf, zero.*

D. Select the appropriate word in each of the numbered pairs:

1. After Jean-Pierre *(1)accepted/(2)excepted* our invitation to spend a month in the nation's *(3)capital/(4)Capitol,* he applied to the American *(5)consul/(6)counsel* for a visa. 2. The *(7)presence/(8)presents* of federal troops prevented further *(9)incidence/(10)incidents.* 3. The city's employees presented the members of the city *(11)council/(12)counsel* with a declaration of *(13)rights/(14)rites* and *(15)principals/(16)principles.* 4. My moral *(17)principals/(18)principles* do not permit a *(19)personal/(20)personnel* appearance at a play depicting *(21)loose/(22)lose* behavior. 5. Though he can *(23)cite/(24)site* no precedent, the city *(25)council/(26)counsel* advises us to *(27)adapt/(28)adopt* a motion providing for the *(29)censoring/(30)censuring* of foreign films. 6. After our *(31)censor/(32)censure* of conditions at the plant, the owner *(33)affected/(34)effected* changes *(35)affecting/(36)effecting* most of his *(37)personal/(38)personnel.* 7. The teachers wanted to wait on the steps rather *(39)than/(40)then* enter the *(41)capital/(42)Capitol,* for all *(43)accept/(44)except* the *(45)principal/(46)principle* had already been *(47)their/(48)there.*

E. Explain the difference in meaning between the words in each of the following pairs: *aid – aide, causal – casual, complimentary – complementary, costume – custom, emigrant – immigrant, eminent – imminent, isle – aisle, key – quay, meet – mete, rational – rationale, stationary – stationery, straight – strait.*

SP 3   Spelling Rules

Spelling rules provide a key to a group of words that you would otherwise have to study individually.

The purpose of spelling rules is *not* to make English spelling appear more regular than it is but to help you memorize words that follow a common pattern.

SP 3a   *I* Before *E*

Identical sounds are often spelled differently in different words.
For instance, *ie* and *ei* often stand for the same sound. If you sort out
the words in question, you get the following:

ie: achieve, believe, chief, grief, niece, piece (of pie), relieve
cei: ceiling, conceited, conceive, perceive, receive, receipt

In the second group of words, the *ei* is regularly preceded by *c*. In
other words, it is *i* before *e* except after *c*. About half a dozen words
do not fit into this pattern:

ei: either, leisure, neither, seize, weird
cie: financier, species

SP 3b   Doubled Consonant

*In many words a single final consonant is doubled before an
ending* (or **suffix**) that begins with a vowel: *-ed, -er, -est, -ing.* Doubling
occurs under the following conditions:

(1) The vowel preceding the final consonant *must be a single
vowel.* It cannot be a "long" or double vowel (**diphthong**) indicated in
writing by combinations like *oa, ea, ee,* and *ou* or by a silent final *e*
(*kite,* h*ope,* h*ate*). Note the differences in pronunciation and in spelling in the following pairs:

bar – barred	bare – bared
bat – batted	boat – boating
hop – hopping	hope hoping
plan – planned	plane – planed
red – redder	read – reading
scrap – scrapped	scrape – scraped
slip – slipped	sleep – sleeping
stop – stopped	stoop – stooped

(2) In words of more than one syllable, the last syllable before
the suffix *must be the one stressed in pronunciation.* Sometimes a
shift in stress will be reflected in a difference in the spelling of different forms of the same word. Compare the following groups:

adMIT, adMITTed, adMITTance	EDit, EDited, EDiting
forGET, forGETTing, forGETTable	BENefit, BENefited
beGIN, beGINNing, beGINNer	HARDen, HARDened
overLAP, overLAPPing	deVELop, deVELoping
reGRET, reGRETTed, reGRETTable	proHIBit, proHIBited, proHIBitive
preFER, preFERRed, preFERRing	PREFerence, PREFerable
reFER, reFERRed, reFERRing	REFerence

NOTE: There is doubling after the single vowel *i* in *equip*—*equipped* (the *u* does not combine with *i* but is part of the consonant *qu*); there is no doubling of the final *x* in *mix*—*mixed* (*x* is really a double consonant: *ks*).

SP 3c   Y as a Vowel

Y is sometimes used *as a consonant* (*year*, *youth*), sometimes *as a vowel* (*my*, *dry*; *hurry*, *study*). As a single final vowel, it changes to *ie* before *s*, to *i* before all other endings except *-ing*.

ie: family — families, fly — flies, study — studies, try — tries, quantity — quantities

i: beauty — beautiful, bury — burial, busy — business, copy — copied, dry — drier, lively — livelihood, noisy — noisily

y: burying, copying, studying, trying, worrying

When it follows another vowel, *y* is usually preserved: *delays*, *joys*, *played*, *valleys*. A few common exceptions are *day* — *daily*, *gay* — *gaily*, *lay* — *laid*, *pay* — *paid*, *say* — *said*.

SP 3d   Final *E*

In some words a silent final vowel is omitted before an ending starting with a vowel.

(1) A silent *e* at the end of a word is dropped before an ending that begins with a vowel; it is preserved before an ending that begins with a consonant:

bore	boring	boredom
hate	hating	hateful
like	liking, likable	likely
love	loving, lovable	lovely

The following words do *not* fit into this pattern: *argue* — *argument*, *due* — *duly*, *dye* — *dyeing* (as against *die* — *dying*), *mile* — *mileage*, *true* — *truly*, *whole* — *wholly*.

(2) A final *e* may signal the difference in pronunciation between the final consonants in *rag* and *rage* or in *aspic* and *notice*. Such a final *e* is preserved not only before a consonant but also before *a* or *o*:

ge: advantage — advantageous, change — changeable, courage — courageous, outrage — outrageous

ce: notice — noticeable, peace — peaceable

Exercises

A. Insert *ei* or *ie:* ach___vement, bel___ver, dec___tful, f___ld, inconc___vable, misch___f, perc___ve, rec___ving, rel___f, s___ze, w___rd, y___ld.

B. Select the appropriate word in each of the numbered pairs: *(1)bared/ (2)barred* from office; his *(3)bating/(4)batting* average; *(5)caned/(6)canned* meat; *(7)biding/(8)bidding* their time; *(9)hoping/(10)hopping* for the best; *(11)pined/(12)pinned* to the mat; a *(13)well-planed/(14)well-planned* outing; *(15)robed/(16)robbed* in white; a boy *(17)spiting/(18)spitting* his parents; *(19)taped/(20)tapped* him on the shoulder.

C. Combine the following words with the suggested endings: accompany___ed, advantage___ous, argue___ing, benefit___ed, carry___s, come___ing, confide___ing, differ___ing, excite___able, friendly___ness, lively___hood, occur___ing, prefer___ed, remit___ance, sad___er, satisfy___ed, shine___ing, sole___ly, study___ing, tragedy___s, try___s, use___ing, valley___s, whole___ly, write___ing.

SP 4   Words Often Misspelled

Studies of the words most frequently misspelled in student writing have resulted in substantial agreement on words most likely to cause spelling difficulties.

In addition to words listed in SP 1-3, the following list will repay careful study:

absence	address	among	argue
abundance	adequate	amount	arguing
accessible	admit	analysis	argument
accidentally	adolescence	analyze	arising
acclaim	advantageous	annual	arrangement
accommodate	advertisement	anticipate	article
accompanied	afraid	anxiety	artistically
accomplish	against	apologize	ascend
accumulate	aggravate	apology	assent
accurately	aggressive	apparatus	athlete
accuses	alleviate	apparent	athletic
accustom	allotted	appearance	attendance
achievement	allowed	applies	audience
acknowledgment	all right	applying	authority
acquaintance	already	appreciate	balance
acquire	altar	approach	basically
acquitted	altogether	appropriate	basis
across	always	approximately	beauty
actuality	amateur	area	becoming

before
beginning
belief
believe
beneficial
benefited
boundaries
breath
brilliant
Britain
buses
business
calendar
candidate
career
careless
carrying
category
ceiling
cemetery
challenge
changeable
character
characteristic
chief
choose
chose
clothes
coarse
column
comfortable
comfortably
coming
commission
committed
committee
companies
competition
competitive
completely
comprehension
conceivable
conceive
concentrate
condemn
confident
confidential
conscience
conscientious
conscious
considerably

consistent
continually
continuous
control
controlled
convenience
convenient
coolly
courageous
course
courteous
criticism
criticize
cruelty
curiosity
curriculum
dealt
deceit
deceive
decision
definite
definitely
definition
dependent
describe
description
desirability
desirable
despair
desperate
destruction
devastate
develop
development
device
difference
different
difficult
dilemma
dining
disappear
disappearance
disappoint
disastrous
discipline
disease
disgusted
dissatisfaction
dissatisfied
doesn't
dominant

due
during
ecstasy
efficiency
efficient
eighth
eliminate
embarrass
embarrassment
eminent
emphasize
endeavor
enforce
enough
entertain
environment
equipped
erroneous
especially
etc.
exaggerate
excellent
exceptionally
exercise
exhaust
exhilarate
existence
experience
explanation
extraordinary
extremely
familiar
families
fascinate
finally
financial
financier
foreign
forward
friend
fulfill
fundamentally
further
gaiety
generally
genius
government
governor
grammar
guaranteed
guidance

happily
happiness
height
heroes
heroine
hindrance
hopeful
huge
humorous
hundred
hurriedly
hypocrisy
hypocrite
ignorant
imaginary
imagination
immediately
immensely
incidentally
indefinite
independent
indispensable
inevitable
influence
ingenious
intellectual
intelligence
interest
interpret
interrupt
involve
irrelevant
irresistible
itself
jealous
knowledge
laboratory
laid
leisure
likelihood
literature
livelihood
loneliness
losing
magnificence
maintain
maintenance
manageable
manufacturer
marriage
mathematics

meant	particularly	professor	sincerely
medieval	passed	prominent	sophomore
merely	past	propaganda	speech
mileage	peace	prophecy	sponsor
miniature	peculiar	psychology	strength
minute	perceive	pursue	stretch
mischievous	perform	quantity	strictly
muscle	performance	really	studying
mysterious	permanent	recommend	subtle
naïve	persistent	regard	succeed
necessarily	persuade	relief	successful
necessary	pertain	relieve	summarize
ninety	phase	religion	surprise
noticeable	phenomenon	repetition	temperament
obstacle	philosophy	representative	tendency
occasion	physical	resource	therefore
occasionally	piece	response	thorough
occurred	pleasant	rhythm	together
occurrence	possess	ridiculous	tragedy
omit	possession	roommate	transferred
operate	possible	safety	tries
opinion	practical	satisfactorily	undoubtedly
opponent	precede	schedule	unnecessary
opportunity	precede	seize	useful
optimism	prejudice	sense	using
original	prepare	separate	various
paid	prevalent	sergeant	vengeance
parallel	privilege	shining	villain
paralysis	probably	significance	weird
paralyze	procedure	similar	writing
	proceed		

SP 5   The Apostrophe

The **apostrophe** *has no exact equivalent in speech and is therefore easily omitted or misplaced.*

SP 5a   Contractions

Use the apostrophe in contractions to indicate that one or more letters have been omitted (I'll go now; I'm too tired; we're almost ready). It appears most frequently in contractions using a shortened form of *not: haven't, can't, wouldn't, won't, isn't.* Take care not to misspell *doesn't,* which is a shortened form of "*does* not."

A few contractions are easily confused with words of different spelling and different meaning. *It's,* meaning "it is," differs from *its,* meaning "of it" or "belonging to it." *Who's,* meaning "who is," differs from *whose,* which means "of whom" or "of which." *They're* means "they are" and differs from both *there* and *their:*

> It's time to give the cat *its* milk.
> Who's to say *whose* fault it is?
> If *their* lights are turned off, *they're* not *there.*

NOTE: Contractions are characteristic of informal conversation. Avoid them in formal reports, research papers, and letters of application. Some readers approve of contractions only in distinctly informal writing.

SP 5b   Possessives

Use the apostrophe for the possessive of nouns. A person closely associated with something named by another noun often appears in the **possessive,** usually produced by adding an apostrophe plus *s* to the plain form of a noun: *my sister's purse, Mr. Smith's garage, the student's notebook.* Often the possessive indicates where something belongs, or who owns an article. It also, however, indicates many other relationships: *the boy's friends, the firemen's ball, a man's world, the child's innocence, the children's capers, the general's dismissal.* Possessives occur in many familiar expressions: *an hour's drive, the day's news, a moment's notice, a dollar's worth, tonight's paper.*

Note the following variations:

(1) Sometimes the plain form of a noun already ends in *s.* The possessive is then formed by adding an apostrophe *only.* This applies especially to plural forms. Compare the following pairs:

> the Turk's wives (one Turk)   the Turks' wives (several Turks)
> a week's pay   two weeks' pay

Names of individuals do not always follow this rule. The writer may or may not add a second *s,* depending on whether he would expect an extra syllable in pronunciation: *Mr. Jones' car—Mr. Jones's car; Dolores' hair—Dolores's hair; Charles Dickens' first novel—Charles Dickens's first novel.*

(2) The apostrophe is *not* used in the *possessive forms of personal pronouns.* No apostrophe appears in *his, hers, its, ours, yours,* or *theirs.* It does appear, however, in the possessive forms of such indefinite pronouns as *one* (one's friends), *everyone* (to everyone's surprise), *someone* (at someone's suggestion; also, at someone else's house).

SP 5c   Plurals of Letters and Symbols

The apostrophe is often used to separate the plural s *from the name of a letter or a symbol or from a word named as a word* (two large 7's; if's and but's):

Those great big beautiful A's so avidly sought, those little miserly C's so often found, were meant for another time and another student body. — Oscar Handlin, "Are the Colleges Killing Education?" *Atlantic*

Exercise

Check for appropriate use of the apostrophe in choosing between the spellings in each of the following pairs.

1. When the mother and the father respect each *(1)other's/(2)others'* opinions, children learn to live harmoniously by following their *(3) elders/(4)elders'* example.   **2.** Since the *(5)chairmans/(6)chairman's* resignation, the *(7)members/(8)member's* have been speculating about *(9)whose/(10)who's* going to succeed him.   **3.** *(11)Mrs. Beattys/(12)Mrs. Beatty's* husband still sends her *(13)flowers/(14)flower's* on *(15)Valentines/(16)Valentine's* Day.   **4.** We were all overjoyed when my *(17) sister's/(18)sisters'* baby took *(19)its/(20)it's* first faltering steps.   **5.** A *(21)student's/(22)students'* lack of interest is not always the *(23)teachers/(24)teacher's* fault.   **6.** *(25)Its/(26)It's* the *(27)parents/(28)parents'* responsibility to provide for their *(29)children's/(30)childrens'* religious education.   **7.** *(31)Lets/(32)Let's* borrow *(33)someones/(34)someone's* car and go for an *(35)hour's/(36)hours'* drive.   **8.** *(37)Charles/(38) Charles's* father murmured audibly that the assembled *(39)relatives/ (40)relative's* had consumed at least ten *(41)dollars/(42)dollars'* worth of food.

SP 6   The Hyphen

Use of the **hyphen** *is the least uniform and the least stable feature of English spelling.* In doubtful cases, the most recent edition of a reputable dictionary is the best available guide.

SP 6a   Compound Words

Treatment varies for words habitually used together as a single expression. Some compound words are clearly distinguished from ordinary combinations by differences in both writing and pronunciation: *black bird* (black BIRD) but *blackbird* (BLACKbird), *dark room* (dark ROOM) but *darkroom* (DARKroom). Such unmistakable compounds are *bellboy, bridesmaid, headache, highway, newsstand, summertime,* and *stepmother.* In many similar compounds, however, the parts are conventionally kept separate: *bus boy, commander in chief, goose flesh, high school, labor union, second cousin.* Still other compound words conventionally require a hyphen: *able-bodied, bull's-eye, cave-in, great-grandfather, merry-go-round, mother-in-law.*

NOTE: Be sure to spell *today, tomorrow, nevertheless,* and *nowadays* as single words. Be sure *not* to spell as single words *all right, a lot* (a lot of time), *be able,* and *no one.*

SP 6b   Prefixes

Many hyphenated compounds consist of a prefix and the word it precedes.

(1) *All-, ex-* (in the sense of "former"), *quasi-, self-,* and sometimes *co-* require a hyphen: *all-knowing, ex-husband, quasi-judicial, self-contained, co-author.*

(2) All prefixes require a hyphen before words beginning with a capital letter: *all-American, anti-American, pro-American, un-American.*

(3) Often a hyphen prevents the meeting of two identical vowels: *anti-intellectual, semi-independent.*

NOTE: Sometimes a hyphen distinguishes an unfamiliar use of a prefix from a familiar one: *recover — re-cover* (make a new cover), *recreation — re-creation* (creating again or anew).

SP 6c   Group Modifiers

Several words may temporarily combine as a modifier preceding a noun. They are then usually joined to each other by hyphens: *a flying-saucer hat, a middle-of-the-road policy, a question-and-answer period, a step-by-step account, a devil-may-care attitude.* No hyphens are used when the same combinations serve some other function in a sentence: *tend toward the middle of the road; explain a process step by step.*

NOTE: No hyphen is used when a modifier preceding a noun is in turn modified by an adverb ending in *-ly: a fast-rising executive, a well-balanced account;* but *a rapidly growing city, a carefully documented study.*

Exercise

Insert hyphens or combine elements where appropriate.

1. The prospective son in law listened self consciously to Mother's praise of the bride to be.   2. Those who denounced the parking privileges for out of town students were obviously not from out of town. 3. Both pro British and anti British Arabs were united in their contempt for ex king Farouk.   4. The anti intellectual local news paper had called our candidate an absent minded ex professor and a tool of the labor unions; never the less he was elected.   5. Now a days few self respecting candidates conduct old fashioned campaigns taking them into out of the way places.   6. Mr. Andrews and his co author have written a well documented account of the un democratic procedures followed by quasi judicial agencies.

SP 7   Capitals

Although practice varies on minor points, certain conventions of capitalization are widely observed.

SP 7a   Proper Names

Proper names are always capitalized. Capitalize the names of persons, places, regions, historical periods, ships, days of the week, months (but not seasons), organizations, religions: *James, Brazil, the Middle Ages, S.S. Independence, Sunday, February, Buddhism.* Capitalize words derived from proper names: *English grammar, French pastry, German beer, Parisian fashions, Christian charity, Marxist ideas.*

Note the following difficulties:

(1) In some words the proper name involved has been lost sight of, and a lower-case letter is used: *guinea pig, india rubber, pasteurized milk.*

(2) The same word may serve as a general term but also as a proper name for one person, institution, or place:

democratic (many institutions)	Democratic (name of the party)
orthodox (many attitudes)	Orthodox (name of the church)
history (general subject)	History 31 (specific course)
west (general direction)	Middle West (specific area)
my mother (common relationship)	Mother (name of the person)

(3) The general term for a title, a family relationship, an institution, or a geographical feature is capitalized when it combines with a proper name: *Major Brown, Aunt Augusta, Sergeant Barnacle, Campbell High School, Indiana University, Tennessee Valley Authority, Medora Heights, Lake Erie.* Some titles refer to only one person and can take the place of the person's name: *the Pope, the Queen* (of England), *the President* (of the United States).

SP 7b   Titles of Publications

A capital letter marks the first and all major words in the title of a book, other publication, or work of art. The only words not counting as major are articles *(a, an,* and *the),* prepositions *(at, in, on, of, from, with),* and connectives *(and, but, if, when).* Prepositions and connectives are usually capitalized when they have five or more letters. Observe these conventions in writing the titles of a theme:

Life in a Dormitory
Get Rich Through Hypnosis
New Facts About the Common Cold
How to Become Extinct

The same conventions apply to titles of publications cited in a sentence:

Several generations of Americans read *Sink or Swim, Phil the Fiddler, Mark the Match Boy,* and *From Canal Boy to President,* records of achievement which rewarded personal goodness with happiness and goods. — Saul Bellow, "The Writer as Moralist," *Atlantic*

Exercise

Revise the following passage to make it conform to the conventions governing the use of capitals.

Boris was a young american pianist. His father came from a calvinistic new england family. His mother, who had been born in the caucasus, spoke french, german, and russian, as well as english and her native armenian. She had studied classical music in european cities like paris and vienna. Before he was ten, boris could play everything from viennese waltzes to presbyterian hymns. In high school he read books like *the life of beethoven, all about wagner,* and *brahms through the eyes of a friend.* At east bloomingdale city college, he took a course in music appreciation as well as a course entitled "the great composers." After he graduated, he spent the summer in california and the winter giving concerts in the middle west.

Fame came to boris in march one year when, armed with his bible, he set off for a contest in a country dominated by marxist ideology but susceptible to capitalist music. Even orthodox socialists cheered wildly when boris was awarded the first prize. Back home, the united states senate promptly commended boris's achievement as a national triumph and a vindication of democratic principles. Only one democratic and two republican senators abstained. The national broadcasting company paid the back rent on boris's piano after he performed in a sunday morning concert given by the new york philharmonic orchestra and broadcast from carnegie hall. In june, *lifemanship* magazine had an article on boris in its section entitled "speaking of pianists." The article said: "So catholic is the appeal of music that it reconciles, for a time, yankees and southerners, protestants and catholics, russians and americans."

CHAPTER SIXTEEN

Punctuation

P 1 End Punctuation
     P 1a Exclamations
     P 1b Questions
     P 1c Statements

P 2 Eliminating Fragments
     P 2a Breaks in Thought
     P 2b Explanation and Enumeration
     P 2c Permissible Nonsentences

P 3 Joining Independent Clauses
     P 3a Closely Related Sentences
     P 3b Adverbial Connectives
     P 3c Coordinating Connectives
     P 3d Comma Splice
     P 3e Fused Sentence

P 4 Adverbial Clauses
     P 4a Subordinating Connectives
     P 4b Restrictive and Nonrestrictive Adverbial Clauses
     P 4c Introductory Adverbial Clauses

P 5 Punctuating Modifiers
     P 5a Unnecessary Commas
     P 5b Restrictive and Nonrestrictive Modifiers
     P 5c Sentence Modifiers

P 6 Coordination
     P 6a Series
     P 6b Coordinate Adjectives
     P 6c Dates and Addresses
     P 6d Repetition and Contrast

P 7 Parenthetic Elements
     P 7a Dashes
     P 7b Parentheses
     P 7c Commas for Parenthetic Elements

P 8 Quotation
     P 8a Direct Quotation
     P 8b Terminal Marks in Quotations
     P 8c Insertions and Omissions
     P 8d Indirect Quotation
     P 8e Words Set Off from Context

When we speak, we do more than put the right words together in the right order. We pause at the right times, raise our voices for emphasis. To the structures and forms we study in the grammar of the written sentence, speech adds **intonation**: differences in timing, pitch, and stress that make our words mean what we want them to mean. Such differences are further supplemented by facial expressions and gestures: the knowing wink that indicates irony, the raised forefinger that signals emphasis. When writing, we use punctuation marks for similar purposes.

The English system of punctuation has relatively few ways of indicating differences in emotion or attitude. In speech, "George is an honor student" can express many different shades of meaning. When we try to reproduce these differences in writing, we are soon reduced to devices frowned upon by conservative readers:

George is an honor student!
George is an honor student?
George is an honor student (!).
George is an honor (?) student.
George is an "honor" student.

English punctuation is best equipped to signal differences in structure. Punctuation marks may separate groups of words from each other. They may establish different kinds of connection between them. For instance, punctuation may show two closely related groups of words to be a general statement followed by detailed explanation:

The room was full of noisy men: ranchers, merchants, and lawyers.

It may show them to be an important statement followed by incidental additional information:

Richard inherited his uncle's estate, which had been in the family since 1632.

The following chapter systematically surveys the relations within a sentence (and between sentences) that are conventionally signaled by punctuation. Typically, the question asked by a writer is not "What are some of the possible uses to which I may put the comma?" His question is "Does a sentence put together like this one need punctuation, and, if so, what kind?"

P 1   End Punctuation

Use end punctuation to put a stop to an utterance that is grammatically complete.

COMMA

before coordinating connectives	P 3c
with nonrestrictive adverbial clauses	P 4b
after introductory adverbial clauses	P 4c
with nonrestrictive modifiers (other than adverbial clauses)	P 5b–c
after introductory modifiers (other than adverbial clauses)	P 5c
with adverbial connectives	P 3b
with *especially, namely, for example*, etc.	P 2b
with *after all, of course*, and other sentence modifiers	P 5c
between items in a series	P 6a
in a series of parallel clauses	P 3d
between coordinate adjectives	P 6b
with dates and addresses, etc.	P 6c
with direct address and other parenthetic elements	P 7c
between repeated or contrasted elements	P 6d
with quotations	P 8a–b, d

SEMICOLON

between closely related sentences	P 3a
before adverbial connectives	P 3b
before coordinating connectives between clauses containing commas	P 3c
in a series with items containing commas	P 6a

COLON

to introduce a list or explanation	P 2b
to introduce a formal quotation	P 8a
between closely related sentences	P 3a

PERIOD

at end of sentence	P 1c, P 2
ellipsis	P 8c
with abbreviations	M 2

DASH

break in thought	P 2a, P 7a
before summary at end of sentence	P 7a

QUOTATION MARKS

with quotations	P 8a–d
quotation within quotation	P 8a
with terminal marks	P 8b
with slang or technical terms	P 8e
to set off titles	M 1e

EXCLAMATION MARK	P 1a
QUESTION MARK	P 1b
PARENTHESES	P 7b

Utterances terminated by end punctuation may have to become part of a coherent narrative or argument before their full *meaning* becomes clear. They do not need anything before them or after them to be complete as far as *grammatical structure* is concerned.

P 1a   Exclamations

Use the exclamation mark to give an utterance unusual emphasis. Such utterances range from a groan, curse, or shout to an order or a command. The **exclamation mark** can signal excitement, insistence, surprise, indignation, or fear:

Ouch!
Hurrah!
Silence! Get up! Close the book!
He loves me!
And this man wants to be President!

NOTE: Avoid using the exclamation mark as an easy way of making trivial things seem important. Avoid using more than one exclamation mark at a time.

P 1b   Questions

Use the question mark whenever an utterance is worded as a request for information. Whenever you raise your voice inquiringly at the end of something you say, you should terminate the written equivalent with a **question mark** (*He sent you a check?*). Not all questions, however, are marked by intonation.

Who are you?
What did he want?

Do not forget to use question marks at the end of questions that are long or involved:

How is the student who enters college as a freshman supposed to find his way through the maze of instructions and regulations printed in small print in the college catalog?

(1) Use question marks even after *rhetorical questions*. Rhetorical questions do not really ask for an answer but already indicate what the correct answer is supposed to be by the way they are worded.

Are you implying that our candidate is a liar?
Am I, life-long servant of this great republic, going to betray the trust placed in me by my constituents?

(2) You are free to omit the question mark after *requests phrased as questions* for the sake of politeness.

Will you please notify your clients of our decision?
Will you please notify your clients of our decision.

P 1c   Statements

Use the period at the end of a simple statement. In formal writing, the units separated by **periods** are grammatically self-contained; they are complete sentences. Guard against using a period to set off a unit that is not a complete sentence but merely a **sentence fragment** (see P 2). Guard against omitting the period between two complete sentences, thus producing a **fused sentence** (see P 3e).

Complete: He is gone. *He left for Alaska.*

Fragment: He left yesterday. *For Alaska*

Fused: You won't find him *he left for Alaska.*

P 2   Eliminating Fragments

Be sure to identify and eliminate from your writing all objectionable sentence fragments.

It used to be thought that sentence fragments result from a breakdown in grammar or in logic. Actually, most fragments merely transfer to the written page patterns that are acceptable in speech but *unconventional* in writing. Informal speech uses many fragmentary sentences whose meaning the listener can infer from gestures or from the context. When a fragmentary sentence occurs in writing, however, many teachers and editors take it as a sign of illiteracy. At best, they consider it too informal for ordinary expository prose.

The type of sentence fragment most common in student writing results when an afterthought is added to the main statement. After making a statement *(I left home)*, a writer may add an explanation without realizing that the addition is not a second complete sentence *(To go to college)*. He may make a statement *(These are my relatives)* and add a comment *(A fine group of people)*. He may make a statement *(I kept my eyes open for suspicious characters)* and add an example or illustration *(For example, policemen and store detectives)*. Each of these afterthoughts is a sentence fragment when separated from the main statement by a period.

Grammatically, such fragments are of several common types:

Appositives:	A great man. My history teacher. Carts loaded with fruit.
Adjectives, Adverbs:	Beautiful in the morning sun. Carelessly as usual.
Prepositional Phrases:	For the last time. With great trepidation. On behalf of the management.
Verbals, Verbal Phrases:	Leaving the car behind. Other things being equal.
Dependent Clauses:	Because I did not study. Though nobody replied. Which came far too late. (See P 4a.)

Many such fragments can be joined to the main statement either without any punctuation at all *(I left home to go to college)* or by a comma *(These are my relatives, a fine group of people)*. Whenever a fragment is pointed out to you, try first to connect it with the main idea in such a way that the sentence flows smoothly, without interruption:

Fragment:	Be sure to be there. *At seven o'clock.*
Revised:	Be sure to be there *at seven o'clock.*
Fragment:	He bought a used car. *In spite of my warnings.*
Revised:	He bought a used car *in spite of my warnings.*

If the fragment cannot become part of either the preceding or the following statement, you may have to develop the material it contains into a complete sentence:

Fragment:	He appealed to a higher court. *Being a futile effort.*
Revised:	He appealed to a higher court. *The effort was futile.*

P 2a   Breaks in Thought

At times, material added to the main statement is kept clearly separate as an afterthought. To indicate the break in thought, use a **dash** instead of a period:

These are my relatives—*a motley crew.*
He would close his eyes and talk into the dictaphone—*a strange way to write an English theme.*

Use dashes sparingly, since they can suggest the casual rambling of conversation or the jerky movement of an improvised speech. They are most effective when used only occasionally, to emphasize a break for ironic or dramatic effect. (See also P 7a.)

P 2b   Explanation and Enumeration

To establish a definite connection between an explanatory after-thought and the preceding statement, use a colon or a common transitional expression.

(1) The **colon** serves to introduce a *list or description* of something that has already been mentioned in a more general way:

> We have two excellent players this year: *Phil and Tom.*
> She served an old-fashioned breakfast: *fishballs, brown bread, and baked beans.*
> Your friend lacks an essential quality: *tact.*

NOTE: The colon, like the period, ordinarily has a complete statement *in front of it.* Do *not* use the colon to separate verb and complement ("The chest contained: . . ."; "The two best players were: . . .").

(2) Explanations or examples added to a complete statement are often introduced by expressions like *especially, such as, namely,* or *for example.* When they introduce material that is not a complete sentence, these expressions are usually preceded by a **comma**:

> He took several courses in the humanities, *such as French Literature and Elementary Logic.*
> Plato and Aristotle wrote in the same language, *namely Greek.*

In formal usage, another comma often keeps *namely, for example, for instance,* and *that is* separate from the explanations or examples they introduce:

> Professor Miller objected to my system of punctuating, for example, my use of dashes.

Do not use another comma if the introductory expression is *especially* or *such as.*

P 2c   Permissible Nonsentences

Permissible fragments are common in speech and are used in writing for special effects. Experienced writers use permissible fragments, better called **nonsentences**, for special purposes. The following examples illustrate the most common of these:

(1) *Common transitional expressions:*

> *So much for* past developments. *Now for* a look at our present problems.

(2) *Answers to questions,* suggesting the give-and-take of conversation or the rhetorical question-and-answer technique of the orator:

What did we gain? *Nothing.*

(3) *Descriptive passages,* especially when designed to give a static, pictorial effect:

We stood in the hot dry night air at one in the morning, waiting for a train at an Arizona station. *Nothing but the purple arc of sky and at the end of the platform the silhouette of a cottonwood tree lapped by a hot breeze. The stars big as sunflowers.* — Alistair Cooke, *One Man's America*

(4) In narrative, *passages suggesting random, disconnected thought:*

Fifty dollars to Dorothy's piano teacher. His sister. Another plain girl. She might as well learn how to play the piano. — Irwin Shaw, "Main Currents of American Thought"

There he is: the brother. *Image of him. Haunting face.* — James Joyce, *Ulysses*

(5) Transcripts of *conversation or dialogue:*

In one part of the picture you see five young men in white coats conferring around a microscope. The voice on the sound track rings out boldly, *"No geniuses here. Just a bunch of good Americans working together."* — William H. Whyte, Jr., "The New Illiteracy," *Saturday Review*

(6) Afterthoughts deliberately delayed for *ironic effect:*

Man is the only animal that blushes. *Or needs to.*   (Mark Twain)

Most teachers discourage their students from experimenting with such incomplete sentences until they have learned to use complete sentences effectively and confidently.

Exercises

A. In which of the following passages is the second unit a *sentence fragment?* In which is the second unit a complete sentence?

1. The ocean has always beckoned to man. Daring him to risk all to sail the seas.

2. What I mean by good music is not popular music but the more classi-

cal type. It is music that can be evaluated and criticized by experts.

3. The dictionary usually gives the etymology of a word. Its origin and later history.

4. We made our way to the train station in a blizzard. Only to find the ticket window closed.

5. My uncle gave me not only advice but also money. Without his help I could never have started college.

6. Writers in recent decades have done battle against the forces of censorship. Not just for their own benefit but for the benefit of all.

7. The population explosion has brought with it many major problems. One urgent problem is the education of the growing mass of children.

8. In "The Real Thing," a painter employs as his models a couple with true upper-class manners. Mr. Monarch being the picture of a true gentleman, and Mrs. Monarch that of a lady.

9. Bradley Hall is a large building. Not immense in height, but of considerable length and width.

10. The typical eighteen-year-old is really still a fledgling in the family nest. Untried in many of the everyday happenings of life.

B. Check the following passages for *conventional use of end punctuation.* Label each passage S (satisfactory), F (unsatisfactory because containing a fragment), or U (unsatisfactory for some other reason).

1. Fred was collecting pictures of architectural marvels, such as Gothic cathedrals and Aztec pyramids. 2. The next summer I tried a new sales technique. With good results. 3. You will not be able to reach them. They left no address. 4. I remember the festive spirit of the Christmas season in my home town. The many colorful lights along the city streets. 5. When will parents realize that their children's education is not someone else's responsibility but their own. 6. He left school after two years. To take over his father's business. 7. The airline refused to transport his pet: a tame puma. 8. Rapidly growing housing tracts have created many problems. The most serious one being inadequate school facilities. 9. Why should I spend my time making excuses for an incorrigible liar. 10. He remembered his first glimpse of the United States. The Manhattan skyline. 11. Many of my friends were studying a foreign language, especially Spanish or French. 12. The club invited a well-known guest lecturer. An anthropologist from Cornell. 13. The osprey dives into the water to seize its prey. Plunging down from heights of up to one hundred feet. 14. Please stop at the post office. We need some stamps. 15. The gallery was showing the work of several French painters, especially Degas and Monet.

C. From your current writing and reading, select ten sample sentences that illustrate the various conventions of punctuation discussed in the preceding section.

P 3   Joining Independent Clauses

Use a semicolon to join independent clauses unless they are linked by a coordinating connective.

The semicolon is the most typical punctuation between two statements that are still grammatically self-contained but that are closely enough related in meaning to combine in a single larger sentence. The semicolon then functions as a "semi-period," signaling a less definite break than the period but appearing in positions where a period would also be possible.

P 3a   Closely Related Sentences

A semicolon or colon may replace the period between two complete sentences.

(1) The **semicolon** joins *complete sentences that are closely related.* Often two statements go together as related pieces of information, develop the same mood or point of view, line up related ideas for contrast. When a semicolon replaces the period between two such statements, the first word of the second statement is *not* capitalized.

> Sunshine was everywhere; orchards were in bloom.
>
> Some librarians circulate books; others hoard them.
>
> The Queen is not allowed to wear a crown; nothing less than a halo will suffice. — Kingsley Martin, "Strange Interlude," *Atlantic*

(2) In informal writing, a **colon** often replaces the semicolon when the second statement gives the reader information or explanation that helps him understand the first one. Formal usage prefers the semicolon unless the *first statement clearly introduces the second.*

> One thing was certain: he would never race again.

P 3b   Adverbial Connectives

Adverbial connectives overlap with other groups of connectives in meaning but differ from them in typically requiring a semicolon. **Adverbial connectives** are *therefore, consequently, hence, accordingly, moreover, furthermore, besides, however, nevertheless, indeed,* and *in fact.* Since they show that two statements are closely related, these statements often are separated by a **semicolon** rather than by a period. A period, nevertheless, would still be possible and acceptable.

Business was improving; *therefore,* we changed our plans.
Business was improving. *Therefore,* we changed our plans.

The hall was nearly empty; *nevertheless,* the curtain rose on time.
The hall was nearly empty. *Nevertheless,* the curtain rose on time.

Notice the following points:

(1) The adverbial connective need not be placed at the point where the first statement ends and the second begins. The *semicolon appears at the point where the two statements join,* regardless of the position of the connective:

Attendance is compulsory; *therefore,* the students have no choice.
Attendance is compulsory; the students, *therefore,* have no choice.
Attendance is compulsory; the students have no choice, *therefore.*

The possibility of a shift in position is a test that you can employ to identify members of this group. They share their freedom of movement with adverbs (and are therefore called *"adverbial* connectives" or "connective *adverbs").*

(2) Adverbial connectives are often *set off from the rest of the second statement* by **commas,** as in the examples already given. You then have to make sure that there is a punctuation mark both before and after the connective:

The food, *however,* was impossible.

NOTE: Whether you should set off an adverbial connective depends partly on the level of formality of your writing. Informal and journalistic writing tend toward **open punctuation,** using fewer commas than formal writing does. Accordingly, the authors of popular books and magazine articles tend not to separate adverbial connectives from the rest of a clause.

P 3c   Coordinating Connectives

Coordinating connectives typically require a comma. And, but, for, or, nor, so, and *yet* establish a close relation between two clauses without making the one more important than the other. They are typically preceded by a **comma:**

The bell finally rang, *and* George rushed out of the room.
She saw me, *but* she did not recognize me.

We went inside, *for* it had started to rain.
You had better apologize, *or* she will not speak to you again.

Notice the reversal of subject and verb after *nor:*

We cannot through the courts force parents to be kind, *nor can we force* men to be wise by the pressure of committees. — Dan Lacy, "Obscenity and Censorship," *The Christian Century*

Do not use the comma with these connectives when they merely join two words or two phrases (came in *and* sat down, tired *but* happy, for cash *or* on credit) rather than two independent clauses.

Notice the following variations:

(1) *And, but,* and *or* are often used without a comma *when the clauses they join are short:*

The wind was blowing *and* the water was cold.

Yet and *so* are often used with a **semicolon**:

The critics praised Oliver's work; *yet* no one bought his paintings.

(2) Any coordinating connective may be used with a semicolon, especially if the connective joins *clauses that already contain commas* or that are unusually long:

Previously the river has always been accompanied by mountains near or far; *but* they lay generally parallel to its course. Now in the Big Bend the river encounters mountains in a new and extraordinary way; *for* they lie, chain after chain of them, directly across its way. — Paul Horgan, "Pages from a Rio Grande Notebook," *New York Times Book Review*

(3) Unlike adverbial connectives, coordinating connectives *are not set off from the rest of the clause* they introduce; there is no comma after *and, but,* or *yet* unless it is required by some other convention of punctuation. Like adverbial connectives, however, coordinating connectives leave the clauses they join self-sufficient or independent grammatically. Thus, the clauses they connect may still be kept separate from each other by a **period**:

I called your office twice. *But* nobody answered. *So* I left without you.

P 3d   Comma Splice

Do not use a comma alone to join two independent clauses. Next to the sentence fragment, the most noticeable departure from conventional punctuation is the **comma splice**, which runs on from one independent clause to the next with only a comma to keep them apart:

Comma Splice:	The doctor looked worn, he had stayed up all night.
Revised:	The doctor looked worn; he had stayed up all night.

One way of avoiding the comma splice is to insert a coordinating connective ("The doctor looked worn, *for* he had stayed up all night"). Note, however, that a sentence *remains* a comma splice even if there is an adverbial connective (which requires a semicolon instead of the comma):

Comma Splice:	French Canadians insist on preserving their language, therefore federal employees are being taught French.
Revised:	French Canadians insist on preserving their language; therefore, federal employees are being taught French.

Note the following exceptions to the traditional rule against the comma splice:

(1) Commas may appear between the independent clauses in a sentence composed of *three or more parallel clauses*. Note that the clauses in the following examples are closely related in meaning and similar in structure:

> Be brief, be blunt, be gone.
>
> Students in India demonstrate against the use of English, Vietnamese reformers protest against the use of French, young Israelis have no use for the languages once spoken by their parents.

(2) Some of the best modern writers use the comma between *two* clauses when the logical connection or similarity in structure is especially close. For instance, there may be a close *cause-and-effect* relationship, or a *carefully balanced contrast:*

> The fire was dead, the ship was gone.—William Golding, *Lord of the Flies*
>
> The grass is rich and matted, you cannot see the soil.—Alan Paton, *Cry, the Beloved Country*
>
> Rage cannot be hidden, it can only be dissembled.—James Baldwin, *Notes of a Native Son*
>
> Today Kleist gives pleasure, most of Goethe is a classroom bore.—Susan Sontag, *Against Interpretation*

Conservative teachers and editors consider this practice careless or, at best, informal. *Avoid it* in formal writing.

P 3e   Fused Sentence

Never merely juxtapose two independent clauses without any punctuation. And, but, and *or* sometimes appear between very *short* independent clauses without any punctuation (see P 3c). A **fused sentence** results when two such clauses are simply run together with any other type of connective, or with no connective at all:

Fused:	I am not sick or anything I just like to sit in a chair and think.
Revised:	I am not sick; I just like to sit in a chair and think.
Fused:	Today's young people do not readily affiliate with political factions instead they align themselves with causes.
Revised:	Today's young people do not readily affiliate with political factions; instead, they align themselves with causes.

Exercises

A. Check the following sentences for punctuation between independent clauses. Label each sentence *C* (conventional), *CS* (comma splice), or *FS* (fused sentence).

1. He ultimately followed Scully across the corridor, but he had the step of one hung in chains.

2. The most precious right of a free man is to choose for himself therefore no one should have the right to ban or censor books.

3. Today's demonstrators are not sensation seekers, they are using the only available means to call attention to their views.

4. He now seemed all eagerness, and his eyes glowed.

5. My father never answered my questions, he always countered with questions of his own.

6. Hitches for horses were in front; however, they had not been used for half a century.

7. The typical juvenile delinquent drives without a license it doesn't matter to him.

8. The two major types of characters in *Animal Farm* are the human oppressors and the rebellious animals.

9. He would promise to reform then a few days later he had forgotten everything.

10. John Montgomery was tall for his age; in fact, he measured almost six feet at the age of thirteen.

11. In today's society a person is no longer a human being, he is a social security number.

12. She was not merely sophisticated; she was sophistication itself.

13. I must give my friend credit, at least he has his pride.

14. Most of the people there were old-timers, there was seldom a young face in church.

15. To raise esteem we must benefit others; to procure love we must please them.

B. Check the following passages for conventional use of punctuation marks in joining clauses. Label each passage S (satisfactory), CS (unsatisfactory because of a comma splice), U (unsatisfactory for some other reason).

1. I asked my father for a car instead he gave me a bicycle. 2. I know the city very well; I used to live there, in fact. 3. In Europe family ties are close, the whole family does things together. 4. There is a growing audience for ballet, and the theater flourishes in half a dozen centers outside New York. 5. All the polls favored our candidate; the election, however, told a different story. 6. Previews consist of short selections from the movie being advertised, usually these are the most exciting or the most daring parts. 7. Children are like tape recorders; they repeat everything they hear. 8. We had planned to look for driftwood on the beach, but the rain kept us indoors. 9. The horses must have been frightened by the crowd, for they started rearing and tugging nervously at their bridles. 10. High costs make orchestra deficits perennial, yet almost everywhere performances are sold out. 11. I hurriedly went downstairs for breakfast was ready. 12. His landlady did not know his whereabouts, nor could she name his companions. 13. A teacher cannot do everything for his students they must meet him half way. 14. Classes are large, therefore few students have a chance to participate in discussion. 15. Our school annual was to give many students a chance to participate; the captain of the football team, consequently, became our sports editor.

C. Insert appropriate punctuation in the numbered spaces. *Use no capitals or periods not already supplied in the text.* Leave a blank space where no punctuation is required.

Elia Kazan is best known as a director of motion pictures____ (1) however____(2) he first worked in the theater____(3) and directed plays by Thornton Wilder____(4) and Arthur Miller. Kazan's life is an American success story____(5) of a familiar kind____(6) for he came to this country as the son of Greek immigrants____(7) at the age of five. He first lived in Manhattan____(8) later his parents moved to New Rochelle. Young Kazan long felt an outsider____(9) nevertheless____(10) he graduated with honors from Williams College____(11) and was soon highly praised as an actor. His numerous motion pictures have long since gained him lasting fame____(12) some critics____(13) indeed____ (14) consider him the most powerful and distinctive of Hollywood directors.

P 4   Adverbial Clauses

Distinguish between adverbial clauses set off by commas and those requiring no punctuation.

Adverbial connectives and coordinating connectives leave the clauses which they join independent. A third type of connective subordinates the second clause to the main clause of the sentence.

P 4a   Subordinating Connectives

Because of important differences in punctuation, distinguish subordinating connectives from other types of connectives. They normally introduce adverbial clauses, which tell us something about the circumstances of an action or event described in the main part of the sentence. *When, whenever, while, before, after, since, until, as long as,* and *where* introduce information about time and place. *Because, if, provided,* and *unless* introduce reasons or conditions.

(1) *A subordinating connective can turn a group of words into a sentence fragment* even though the group has both a subject and a predicate. An *if* or a *because* changes a self-sufficient, independent clause into a **dependent clause**, which normally cannot stand by itself. "If I were a boy" does not become a complete sentence until you answer the question "If you were a boy, then what?" Beware of dependent clauses added to a main statement as an afterthought:

Fragment: He failed the test. *Because he did not study.*

Revised: He failed the test *because he did not study*

(2) *Subordinating connectives introduce material that may precede rather than follow the main clause.* To identify a subordinating connective, try to reverse the order of the two statements which it joins:

Vote for me *if you trust me.*
If you trust me, vote for me.

I drove more slowly *after I noticed the police car.*
After I noticed the police car, I drove more slowly.

P 4b   Restrictive and Nonrestrictive Adverbial Clauses

Do not separate restrictive adverbial clauses from the rest of the sentence; set off nonrestrictive ones by a comma.

(1) Adverbial clauses usually *restrict or qualify in a significant way the meaning of the clause to which they are joined.* Suppose a father tells his son, "I'll raise your allowance *after I strike oil.*" Without the proviso about striking oil, the sentence would sound like an immediate promise of more money. With the proviso, it means that the son will get more money only by a very remote chance. When they *follow* the main clause, such **restrictive** clauses are not set off by punctuation:

> I consulted my notes *before I spoke.*
> Do not sign anything *until you hear from me.*
> We cannot keep you on the team *unless you improve.*

Occasionally, the *time, place, or condition for an action or event is already indicated in the main clause.* In that case, the dependent clause may merely *elaborate* on the information already given. Such dependent clauses are called **nonrestrictive** and are separated from the main clause by a **comma**:

> Bats were well developed *as far back as the Eocene, when man's ancestors were still in the trees.*
>
> He was born *in California, where one can pick oranges during the Christmas holidays.*

(2) *Though, although,* and *whereas* usually introduce nonrestrictive material and as a result require a **comma**. Rather than adding essential qualification, these words establish a *contrast between the statements they connect*:

> I like the work, *though the salary is low.*
> Her friend wore a sports shirt and slacks, *whereas the other men wore tuxedos.*

Combinations like *whether or not* and *no matter how* indicate that the main statement is true *regardless* of possibilities mentioned in the dependent clause:

> We are canceling the lease, *whether you like it or not.*
> She will never forgive you, *no matter what you do.*

(3) Some subordinating connectives introduce *either restrictive or nonrestrictive material, depending on the meaning of the sentence*

Notice the comma that signals the difference between the members of each of the following pairs:

Why are you going to town?
I am going to town *because I want to do some shopping.*
(The reason for your trip is the essential part of the sentence.)

What are you going to do?
I am going to town, because I want to do some shopping.
(The reason for your trip is added, nonrestrictive explanation.)

I am telling you this *so that* there will be no misunderstanding.
(*So that* reveals purpose or intention.)

The cafeteria was small, *so that* it was always overcrowded.
(*So that* introduces an unintended result.)

NOTE: Some connectives belong to different groups of connectives depending on their meaning in the sentence. *However* is normally an adverbial connective and requires a semicolon. It sometimes takes the place of the subordinating connective *no matter how* and requires a comma:

I cannot please him; *however, I am trying hard.*
I cannot please him, *however hard I try.*

Though, normally a subordinating connective, is often used in informal English as an adverbial connective placed in the middle or at the end of a clause:

I felt entitled to more freedom; *my parents, though, didn't agree with me.*

P 4c   Introductory Adverbial Clauses

Set off an adverbial clause that precedes rather than follows the main clause. After an introductory adverbial clause, a **comma** normally indicates where the main clause starts:

If you want to do well, you will have to work hard.
Whenever there is a heavy rain, the area is threatened by floods and slides.

Some writers consider this comma unnecessary, provided the sentence would be clear without punctuation:

As the cowboy drew his fur cap down over his ears his hands trembled. — Stephen Crane, "The Blue Hotel"

NOTE: Subordinating connectives are not the only way of relating a dependent clause to another clause. Two other types of dependent clauses are treated under P 5. (See P 5a for noun clauses, P 5b for adjective clauses.)

Exercises

A. Explain the use of punctuation marks in the following passage. Which adverbial clauses are *restrictive?* Which are *nonrestrictive?*

English and French were widely used in Africa until most African nations became independent. Now these countries are trying to assert their linguistic independence, although their people often speak several mutually incomprehensible native tongues. After the Belgians left the Congo, names like Leopoldville and Stanleyville disappeared. Swahili could become an official language in much of East Africa if linguistic minorities were willing to accept it. Similar developments accompanied the passing of colonialism in the Far East, where Batavia turned into Jakarta many years ago. A Malaysian city recently changed its name from Jesselton to Kinabalu, because Jesselton had been named for a British empire-builder.

B. Check the following passages for conventional use of punctuation marks with subordinating connectives. Label each passage S (satisfactory), F (unsatisfactory because of a sentence fragment), or U (unsatisfactory for some other reason).

1. Though his paintings were truly remarkable, few of them found buyers among museums or private collectors.   2. Cleaning pots and pans looks easy on television. Whereas at home it takes a lot of hard work.   3. Unless a man has an unusual fondness for teaching grade school children are best taught by women.   4. Most of the animals were extremely shy, so that photographing them required much patience.   5. After the camera had followed the hero to his destination in the West, it switched back to the freshly plowed fields of Iowa.   6. The city is desperately short of hospital space because, most people don't appreciate the need for adequate facilities.   7. Myrna has been afraid of heights since she was a small child.   8. Mountain climbing does not appeal to me; however exciting it may be to others.   9. Because many educated people in India know English, foreign visitors seldom learn Hindu.   10. If we didn't know the teacher usually supplied the answers in class.   11. In Mexico architecture seemed to flourish, whereas at home it had seemed a lost art.   12. The city relinquished one hundred acres of city-owned land so that the local baseball team could build a new stadium there.   13. Ralph was sus-

pended last year. After he put war paint on the bronze Indian decorating the principal's lawn.   **14.** Our house is a shambles, whenever my uncle's family pays us a visit.   **15.** Ask me when you need advice; ask your father when you need money.

C. Insert appropriate punctuation in the numbered spaces. *Use no capitals or periods not already supplied in the text.* Leave a blank space where no punctuation is required.

If my own experience is typical___(1) high school students are reluctant readers___(2) because books play only a very minor role in their environment. Few teachers make their students explore the school library___ (3) although it may contain everything from Chaucer to Sagan. The most popular students often read very little___(4) the newcomer___(5) therefore___(6) associates books with "longhairs" and intellectuals. When the student returns to his home___(7) the television set occupies the place of honor in the living room___(8) whereas___(9) the bookcase may stand as a dust catcher in a hidden corner.

D. From your current writing and reading, select ten sample sentences that illustrate the various conventions of punctuation discussed in P 3-4.

P 5   Punctuating Modifiers

Distinguish between modifiers set off by commas and those requiring no punctuation.

Often nouns and verbs are accompanied by further material that develops, embroiders, or modifies the meaning they convey. Such material is punctuated in accordance with its function and importance in the sentence.

P 5a   Unnecessary Commas

Unless extraneous material intervenes, do not use punctuation between basic elements of a sentence. Do not put a comma between a subject and its verb, between verb and complement, or between the two or three basic elements and the various phrases added to the sentence to describe circumstances, reasons, or conditions:

Andrew	studies	his textbooks	in bed.
Gaston	had been	a mess sergeant	during the war.
Jones	left	his wife	to shoot elephants.

The rule against punctuation breaking up the basic sentence pattern applies even when the place of the subject or complement is taken by a *clause within a clause*. Such clauses, which appear in positions frequently occupied by nouns, are called **noun clauses**. They become *part* of another clause and should not be confused with clauses which are *joined* to another clause:

Noun (subject):	*The writer* knew your name.
Noun Clause:	*Whoever wrote it* knew your name.

Noun (object):	John announced *his plans*.
Noun Clause:	John announced *that he would retire*.

Noun (description):	Your net gain is *a small sum*.
Noun Clause:	Your net gain is *what little remains after taxes*.

Be careful not to put a comma before or after a noun clause, especially one introduced by *that:*

We knew *that he is unreliable.*
That he failed to answer your letter is a bad sign.

P 5b   Restrictive and Nonrestrictive Modifiers

Do not separate restrictive modifiers from what they modify; set off nonrestrictive modifiers by commas. This convention applies especially to modifiers inserted after a noun (or noun equivalent) to clarify or develop its meaning. Such modifiers become an essential part of the main statement if *used for the purpose of identification*. In that case, they are **restrictive**; they restrict or narrow down a general term like *student* to help the reader single out one particular student, or type of student. Restrictive modifiers are *not* set off:

(*Which* student studied the book?)
The student *wearing the red hunting cap* studied the book.

(*Which* man took the money?)
The man *dressed in the pink shirt* took it.

(*What kind* of course appeals to you?)
Courses *which require hard work* appeal to me.

Often information accompanying a noun is not necessary for the purpose of identification. It merely gives your reader *further information* about something on which he has already focused; it is **nonrestrictive**. Nonrestrictive material is set off from the rest of the sentence by a **comma,** or by a comma both before and after it if it occurs in the middle of the sentence:

The student studied his book.
(*What else* about him?)
　　The student, *a freshman,* studied his book.
　　The student, *looking weary,* studied his book.
　　The student, *who had little time,* studied his book.

I talked to my lawyer.
(*What else* about him?)
　　I talked to my lawyer, *a well-known Boston attorney.*
　　I talked to my lawyer, *who is a very impatient man.*

The commas used to set off nonrestrictive modifiers often make the difference between a very cautious and a very sweeping statement. "Americans *who do not speak French* need not apply" narrows down the scope of the statement to certain Americans, those that do not speak French. "Americans, *who do not speak French,* need not apply" is aimed at *all* Americans and at the same time makes a sweeping claim about their linguistic abilities. The commas used to signal the difference in meaning correspond to a break signaled in speech by a characteristic change in the tone of voice. You can train your ear to catch the distinction by going over the sample sentences already given and reading them out loud.

Note the following points:

(1) **Dashes** occasionally set off a nonrestrictive *modifier that contains internal punctuation* and that would not be clearly marked without them:

His lawyer — *a gruff, stubborn, impatient man* — stalked out of the hall.

(2) A *proper name* is usually adequate identification; a modifier following the name usually becomes nonrestrictive and is set off by commas. Several such modifiers may succeed each other:

Mr. Smith, *my history teacher,* dismissed his class early.

In 1942, he joined the Actors' Theater, *a repertory company with strong political views.*

David Daiches, *English-born but Scottish-educated, formerly a professor at Chicago and Cornell, now at the University of Sussex,* chaired the meeting with the skill and courage of a lion-tamer. — Ralph W. Condee, "Bedlam at Edinburgh," *The Reporter*

But occasionally a *restrictive* modifier is needed to help the reader distinguish between several people of the same name:

I find it hard to distinguish between Holmes *the author* and Holmes *the Supreme Court justice.*

NOTE: When your reader already knows whom you have in mind, even a proper name may be additional, nonrestrictive information:

His oldest sister, *Martha,* has always helped him when he was in trouble.

(3) **Adjective clauses** modify a noun (or noun equivalent) and usually begin with *who, which,* or *that.* Clauses beginning with *when, where,* and *why* are also adjective clauses if they are used to modify a noun. Adjective clauses, like other modifiers, may be *either restrictive or nonrestrictive:*

Restrictive: According to my sister Irene, all boys *who carry briefcases* are "brains."

Nonrestrictive: Grade school teachers, *who have become more militant over the years,* are no longer satisfied with genteel poverty.

But note that two types of adjective clauses are *always* restrictive: those beginning with *that,* and those from which the pronoun or connective has been omitted:

The book *that you sent me* was exciting reading.
Most of the things [*that*] *I like to eat* are fattening.
She wrote a long passionate letter to the man [*whom*] *she loves.*

P 5c   Sentence Modifiers

Many sentence modifiers are set off by commas. Modifiers may modify sentence elements other than nouns. They may also modify the sentence as a whole rather than any part of it.[1]

(1) *Verbals and verbal phrases modifying a verb* may be either restrictive or nonrestrictive. Notice the **comma** indicating the difference:

Restrictive: He always came into the office *carrying a shirt box full of letters under his arm.*

Nonrestrictive: Deadline newspaper writing is rapid because it cheats, *depending heavily on clichés and stock phrases.*

Always set off *verbal phrases modifying the sentence as a whole:*

To tell you the truth, I don't even recall his name.

The business outlook being rosy, he invested his savings in highly speculative stocks.

Our new manager has done rather well, *considering his lack of experience.*

[1]Adverbial clauses, which can be classified as sentence modifiers, are treated under P 4.

(2) If a *sentence is introduced by a long or substantial modifying phrase*, a **comma** usually indicates where the main sentence starts:

After an unusually solemn Sunday dinner, Father called me into his study.

Like all newspapermen of good faith, Mencken had long fumed at the low estate of the journalistic rank and file. — Philip M. Wagner, "Mencken Remembered," *The American Scholar*

Set off *introductory verbals and verbal phrases* even when they are short:

Smiling, she dropped the match into the gas tank.
To start the motor, turn the ignition key.

The comma after an introductory modifier can be an important clue to the meaning of a sentence. Omitting the comma may cause serious misreading. Compare the following two sentences:

When hunting, lions stay away from wooded areas.
When hunting lions, stay away from wooded areas.

(3) Expressions like *after all, of course, unfortunately, on the whole, as a rule,* and *certainly* often do not modify the subject or the predicate of a sentence but establish a connection between one sentence and another. Depending on the amount of emphasis you would give such a modifier when reading, you can make it stand out from the rest of the sentence by a **comma**:

After all, we are in business primarily for profit.
On the other hand, the records may never be found.
You will submit the usual reports, *of course.*

Sentence modifiers that are set off require *two* commas if they do not come first or last in the sentence:

We do not, *as a rule,* solicit applications.
A great many things, *to be sure,* could be said for him.

Exercises

A. Explain the use (or lack) of punctuation in the following sentences. Point out *restrictive and nonrestrictive* modifiers.

1. A person who leases a car still has to pay for repairs and maintenance.

2. During Joe's practice rides, the few children who do remain outside huddle behind the nearest tree or bush.

3. Thoreau was well aware that no one can alert his neighbors who is not wide awake himself.   (E. B. White)

4. On the main island of Britain, the Welsh, whose own Gaelic tongue is radically different from English, are now mostly bilingual.

5. Those who guide our worries on large issues regularly ask us to ponder man's losing competition with the machine.   (John Kenneth Galbraith)

6. Few people in the West study Mandarin, the traditional literary and official language of China.

7. The Latin of the Roman Empire, once established as a world language, continued in that role through the Middle Ages.

8. I am not the only one who has worked fifty hours a week and every instant ached to be elsewhere.

9. During sessions of the United Nations, the Soviet representatives have almost always used Russian in their addresses, letting the chips fall where they may.

10. Americans, who had long been isolationists in matters of language as well as politics, became acutely language-conscious during World War II.

B. Check the following passages for conventional punctuation of modifiers. Label each passage S (satisfactory), F (unsatisfactory because of a sentence fragment), or U (unsatisfactory for some other reason).

1. With only a cautious enthusiasm, newspapers are giving a little extra Sunday space to culture.   2. Despite the opposition of a crooked sheriff, the hero, a handsome screen cowboy on a $5,000 horse, succeeded in straightening things out.   3. The proctor — a waspish, restless man — kept his eye on the whispering students.   4. Everyone, who is physically able, should have some exercise each day.   5. The kind of history that we were taught dealt mainly with the pageantry of princes and with the intrigues of empire.   6. Queen Victoria, brought from retirement by the skill of Disraeli, became the adored symbol of domestic virtue and imperial greatness.   7. Having swallowed enough water to last me all summer I decided to leave water skiing to those who had an aptitude for it.   8. My father who taught both in high school and in college gave me many helpful pointers on how to budget my time.   9. Major medical news — the discovery of a new surgical technique, the development of a cure for heart disease — is sometimes buried on the back pages.   10. Work after school can cut severely into study time, forcing the student to study late at night.   11. All kinds of opinion-makers —

people who would never dream of insulting a Negro, Jew, Catholic, or
Paiute Indian — delight in slipping their daily needle of sarcasm into the
politician.   **12.** Usually a selfish person is a spoiled person. One who
must have his way or else.   **13.** A good example of our neglect of public health problems, is the lack of hospital space for the mentally ill.
14. With print orders now running fourteen million monthly, the
Reader's Digest faces no serious competition in its field. **15.** Pontius
Pilate, Procurator of Palestine, the highest judge and top administrator
of the country, had few of the marks of greatness.

C. Insert appropriate punctuation in the numbered spaces. *Use no capitals or
periods not already supplied in the text.* Leave a blank space where no punctuation is required.

1.   Good television plays____(1) which are not very numerous____(2)
do not have a predictable ending. The viewer cannot tell____(3) what
will happen____(4) until the play is over. *Arts Theater*____(5) discon-
tinued last June____(6) was a good example of a type of program____(7)
appealing to the viewer's intelligence and curiosity. The play____(8)
I remember best____(9) dealt with a punch-drunk prizefighter____(10)
who fell in love with an attractive and well-educated girl. Until the very
end of the play____(11) I did not know____(12) whether the fighter
would win the girl.

2.   My father____(1) the oldest child in a family with seven chil-
dren____(2) grew up on a farm____(3) first cultivated by my grandpar-
ents____(4) Swedish immigrants in Minnesota. My grandfather having
died in an accident____(5) my father helped out at the local post of-
fice____(6) to help support his mother____(7) and the younger children.
Being an unusually earnest young man____(8) he studied for an
exam____(9) that would enable him____(10) to become an inspector.
Having passed it with excellent grades____(11) he went to work investigating the activities of swindlers____(12) who used the mails to
defraud the public.

D. From your current writing and reading, select ten sample sentences that
illustrate the various conventions of punctuation discussed in P 5.

P 6   Coordination

*Use the comma (and some other marks) as appropriate when
several elements of the same kind appear together.*

P 6a   Series

*Use commas to separate three or more items of the same kind ap-
pearing in a series.* The most common pattern separates the elements

from each other by **commas**, with the last comma followed by a connective tying the whole group together:

> *Phil, Jim,* and *Harry* came to see me.

> After dinner, we *talked, laughed,* and *sang.*

> *The new students enter* after a rigid selective process, *they present* few disciplinary problems, and *they arrive* after good and uniform preparation. — Oscar Handlin, "Are the Colleges Killing Education?" *Atlantic*

This basic *A, B, and C* pattern can be expanded to accommodate any number of elements:

> The boys had spread out around them the homely tools of mischief — *the long wires, nails, hammers, pliers, string, flashlights, paraffin* saved from the tops of their mothers' jelly jars, *knives* for cutting a clothesline or carving out insults to the grown-up world, and *tin cans* filled with rocks for making a farewell noise after the damage was done. — Lois Phillips Hudson, "The Buggy on the Roof," *Atlantic*

Notice the following variations:

(1) Occasionally, you will want to arrange in a series *groups of words that already contain commas.* To prevent misreading, use **semicolons** instead of additional commas to indicate the major breaks:

> Three persons were mentioned in her will: *John, her brother; Martin, her nephew;* and *Helen, her faithful nurse.*

(2) The *last comma* in a series is often left out, even in formal writing. (Most teachers, however, insist on its use.)

> Then amid the silence, he *took* off his hat, *laid* it on the table and *stood* up. — James Joyce, "Ivy Day in the Committee Room"

(3) For variety or special effect, a writer may use *commas only,* leaving out the connective:

> The idea was to pool all the needs of all those who had in one way or another been bested by their environment — *the crippled, the sick, the hungry, the ragged.* — John Lear, "The Business of Giving," *Saturday Review*

P 6b   Coordinate Adjectives

Separate coordinate adjectives by a comma corresponding to a characteristic break in speech. Two adjectives describing different qualities of the same noun may be coordinated by a **comma** rather than by *and.* They are then called coordinate adjectives:

a *black* and *shaggy* dog	a *black, shaggy* dog
a *starved* and *exhausted* stranger	a *starved, exhausted* stranger
a *grand* and *awe-inspiring* sunset	a *grand, awe-inspiring* sunset

Not every sequence of adjectives falls into this pattern. Often an adjective combines with a noun to indicate a type of person or object (a *public* servant, a *short* story, a *black* market). An adjective preceding such a combination modifies the combination *as a whole* and should not be separated from it by a comma. Use the comma only if you could use *and* instead.

a *secretive* public servant (not "secretive *and* public")
a *long* short story (not "long *and* short")
a *lively* black market (not "lively *and* black")

NOTE: One method of distinguishing between the two kinds of adjective is to read the sentence out loud. This method will help when the difference in meaning is not obvious (a *tired, weary old man* but *an old, tired, weary man; chattering, giggling little girls* but *tiny, anemic, undernourished children*).

P 6c   Dates and Addresses

Use commas with dates, addresses, page references, and similar information consisting of three or four parts. The different items are kept separate from each other by a **comma**; the last item is followed by a comma unless it is at the same time the last word of the sentence:

The date was *Tuesday, December 16, 1952.*
Please send my mail to *483 Tulane Street, Jackson, Oklahoma,* starting the first of the month.
The quotation is from *Chapter V, page 43, line 7,* of the second volume.

Commas are also used to keep separate the different parts of *measurements* employing more than one unit of measurement. Here the last item is usually *not* separated from the rest of the sentence:

The boy is now *five feet, seven inches* tall.
Nine pounds, three ounces is an unusual weight for this kind of fish.

P 6d   Repetition and Contrast

Use commas between expressions that are identical or give two different versions of the same meaning. Use the **comma** after a word

or phrase to be repeated or to be followed by a definition or explanatory paraphrase:

> *Produce, produce!* This is a law among artists, or rather it is their inner com-
> pulsion. — Malcolm Cowley, "Artists, Conscience, and Censors," *Saturday Review*
>
> I am asking *whether you recall his exact language, whether you remember ex-*
> *actly what he said.*

Commas also separate words or groups of words that establish
a *contrast:*

> *His wife, not his brother,* needs the money more.
> *The days were warm, the nights cool.*

Exercises

A. Explain the use of punctuation in the following passages, paying special
attention to coordinate or closely related elements.

1. The floor of the room was gritty with cigarette butts, superfluous
correspondence, crushed coffee cartons, and honest gray dirt.

2. Shortly after seven o'clock, a taxi disgorges a bearded, bearlike man,
who shambles slowly toward the brownstone.

3. Ralph ran stumbling along the rocks, saved himself on the edge of
the pink cliff, and screamed at the ship.   (William Golding)

4. After a while the bagelman arrives with a large box full of breakfast:
coffee, steaming hot; a triple order of bacon; two fried eggs; and bagels,
split and buttered.

5. In the simplified, censored biographies I read as a child, courteous,
considerate heroes displayed magnanimity in victory and dignity in
defeat.

6. Great writers can be temporarily put off by illness, by disappointment, or by some difficulty inherent in the process of composition, one
of those snags, those pitfalls that lie in wait on every page.

7. One corner of the room is fitted with three worn turntables, a huge
electric clock, and a cantilevered microphone that hangs over a console
of switches, buttons, and dials.

8. Lee was known as a strategist, not as a tactician.

B. Check the following passages for conventional punctuation of coordinate or closely related elements. Label each passage S (satisfactory) or U (unsatisfactory).

1. Congress has the right to approve presidential appointments, to override presidential vetoes, and to impeach the President. 2. The old, the infirm and the widowed, are the most frequent victims of the confidence man's schemes. 3. While living there, I knew I was sharing a room with a friend, not just a roommate. 4. To my weary, apprehensive parents, November 12, 1951, was a momentous day. 5. More people than ever are painting pictures going to museums and listening to classical music. 6. The new hospital was faced partly with aluminum sun-breakers, partly with ceramic tile. 7. The alderman complained that the Henry E. Lee Memorial Library was a gigantic, white elephant. 8. Our editorial and executive offices are located in the Newsweek Building, Broadway and 42nd Street, New York 36, New York. 9. The ores of the Comstock Lode not the natural beauty of the sierras had brought my family to Nevada. 10. The miles upon miles of small houses are new, spick-and-span, and highly sanitary, but they are also indistinguishable from those in Kankakee, Illinois; Lincoln, Nebraska; or Oakland, California.

C. In the following passages, insert appropriate punctuation in the numbered spaces. *Use no capitals or periods not already supplied in the text.* Leave a blank space where no punctuation is required.

1. In recent months___(1) senators___(2) ex-athletes___(3) and the clergy have added their voices to a mounting chorus of indignation. They agree with the many American___(4) physical___(5) education teachers___(6) who condemn Americans as flabby___(7) lazy___(8) and generally unfit. These people seem to fear___(9) that the Russians___(10) a race of tawny___(11) muscle-bound gymnasts___(12) will one day descend upon our shores and thresh each of us individually. My own fear is that the slender___(13) bony look in fashion among Americans today may be a handicap in the battle for the minds of men. How can the hungry___(14) human beings of other countries believe that a nation of gaunt___(15) emaciated people is as well off as it pretends to be?

2. The purpose of a quick___(1) warm___(2) synthesis between research___(3) thinking___(4) and writing is to attain the three prime qualities of historical composition___(5) clarity___(6) vigor___(7) and objectivity. You must think about your facts___(8) analyze your material___(9) and decide exactly what you mean. Most of the facts___(10) that you excavate from the archives___(11) are dumb things___(12) it is for you to make them speak by proper selection___(13) arrangement___(14) and emphasis.

D. From your current writing and reading, select ten sample sentences that illustrate the various conventions of punctuation discussed in P 6.

P 7 Parenthetic Elements

Use dashes, parentheses, or commas to set off parenthetic elements.

To some extent, conventions of punctuation follow the rhythms of speech. This is true of conventional ways of setting off parenthetic elements, which *interrupt* a sentence without becoming grammatically a part of it.

P 7a Dashes

Use the dash — sparingly — to signal a sharp break in a sentence. A speaker may stop in the middle of a sentence to supply some preliminary detail or additional clarification. In writing, such material is set off from the rest of a sentence by **dashes**. Dashes tend to emphasize or dramatize the material they set off. (See also P 2a.)

Use dashes sparingly for the following situations:

(1) A *complete sentence is inserted into another sentence*, without a connective or relative pronoun to join them:

Lady Macbeth — *has this been noted?* — takes very little stock in the witches. — Mary McCarthy, "General Macbeth," *Harper's*

(2) A *list enumerating details or examples* interrupts rather than follows a clause:

Women tolerate qualities in a lover — *moodiness, selfishness, unreliability, brutality* — that they would never countenance in a husband. — Susan Sontag, *Against Interpretation*

(3) After a list, a sentence starts anew with a summarizing *all, these,* or *those:*

The visual essay, the rhythmic album, the invitation to drop in on a casual conversation — these are the idiosyncratic traits by which television, as television, has come to be recognized. — Walter Kerr, "What Good Is Television?" *Horizon*

(4) A word or phrase is made to stand out for emphasis or for a *climactic effect:*

After twenty-three years, he was leaving Newston jail — *a free man.*

P 7b   Parentheses

Use parentheses to enclose inserted material that supplies relatively unimportant data (or mere asides). **Parentheses** play down the importance of what they enclose; they are most appropriate for things mentioned in passing:

Fatal accidents *(we had three of them last year in a town of 5,000 people)* can often be traced to excessive speed.

Kazan directed the rest of his considerable steam into studying English *(he graduated with honors),* waiting on tables, and joining as many extracurricular campus clubs as he could. — Thomas B. Morgan, "Elia Kazan's Great Expectations," *Harper's*

Parentheses are commonly used to enclose dates, addresses, page references, chemical formulas, and similar information if it might be of interest to some readers but is not an essential part of the text. Here are some typical examples: *(p. 34)   (first published in 1910) (now called Market Street).*

NOTE: When inserted into another sentence, a sentence in parentheses, like a sentence set off by dashes, usually begins with a lower-case letter and has no end punctuation. When a sentence in parentheses begins *after* end punctuation, end punctuation is required inside the final parenthesis:

Select your purchases with care. *(No refunds are permitted.)*

P 7c   Commas for Parenthetic Elements

Use commas for parenthetic elements that blend into a sentence with only a slight break. Take note especially of the following possibilities:

(1) Use commas when you interrupt a statement to *address the reader* or to *comment* on the source, validity, or plausibility of what you are saying:

Marriage, *dear boy,* is a serious business.
Politicians, *you will agree,* were never popular in this part of the country.
Our candidate, *it seems,* is not very well known.

(2) Commas set off the *introductory greetings and exclamations,* as well as the introductory *yes* and *no,* which frequently precede a statement in conversation and in informal writing:

Why, I don't even know that man.
Yes, you can now buy Pinko napkins in different colors.
Well, you can't have everything.

(3) Commas set off the *"echo questions"* often added to a statement to elicit agreement or confirmation:

You are my friend, *aren't you?*
So he says he is sick, *does he?*

(4) Slight breaks similar to those caused by parenthetic elements are sometimes caused by *sentence elements that have changed their usual position in the sentence:*

Laws, *to be cheerfully obeyed,* must be both just and practicable.
Philip, *for no apparent reason at all,* got up and left the room.
Marriage, *unless it is to be a failure,* must be completely voluntary.

(5) Commas may take the place of dashes to set off a word for emphasis. They suggest a *thoughtful pause* rather than a dramatic break:

We should act, *and suffer,* in accordance with our principles.
People cannot, *or will not,* put down the facts.

Exercises

A. Explain punctuation in the following passages, paying special attention to *parenthetic elements.*

1. Fashions (especially adolescent fashions) do not as a rule outlast their generation.

2. The good grey people of Washington — the civil servants — are not renowned for the courage of their convictions.   (David Sanford)

3. Many people would agree, offhand, that every creature lives its life and then dies. This might, indeed, be called a truism. But, like some other truisms, it is not true. The lowest forms of life, such as the amoebae, normally (that is, barring accidents) do not die. (Susanne K. Langer)

4. The underdeveloped countries have about 69 per cent of the earth's adults — and 80 per cent of the world's children.   (Kingsley Davis)

5. Your true artist, let us note, always does finish. Sometimes he rages, like Wagner. Sometimes he finishes in serenity, and writes at the bottom of his music paper, like Palestrina and Bach, the words *Soli Dei Gloria.* But he finishes.   (Catherine Drinker Bowen)

6. Nowhere in the world has the old cliché of European romanticism —

the assassin mind versus the spontaneous heart—had such a long career as in America.   (Susan Sontag)

B. Check the following passages for conventional punctuation of parenthetic elements. Label each passage *S* (satisfactory) or *U* (unsatisfactory).

1. Photography, you will agree, is not yet generally accepted as an art form.   2. For years, English Methodists have debated the merits of reunion with the Anglican Church (2,922,000 members).   3. Many fine programs though presented mainly for entertainment, supplement what the child learns in school.   4. Painter Du Bois—his work is represented in Manhattan's Metropolitan Museum of Art—resisted the modern trend toward abstraction.   5. The lone rider, the barroom fight, and the gingham-clad heroine—these are the indispensable ingredients of the third-rate cowboy movie.   6. At one time President Wilson was a university president wasn't he?   7. A dozen last-inning victories (six of them since July 4) have given hometown fans something to cheer about.   8. He reports that political independents—his term is the mugwumps—have ejected the old-line party hacks from the city government.   9. Why if I were you Alice I would see a lawyer first thing tomorrow morning.   10. Peter Minuit I am sure you remember bought Manhattan Island from the Indians for a handful of trinkets. 11. The government, many businessmen feel, should insure foreign investments against expropriation.   12. A trip abroad, to be truly enjoyable, should be carefully planned.

C. From your current writing and reading, select ten sample sentences that illustrate the various conventions of punctuation discussed in P 7.

P 8   Quotation

Know how to punctuate different kinds of quoted material.

Often, you will need to indicate that you are reproducing information or ideas derived from a specific source, that you are quoting something first said or observed by someone else.

P 8a   Direct Quotation

In repeating someone's exact words, distinguish them clearly from your own text. Such direct quotations are enclosed in **quotation marks**. They are usually separated by a **comma** from the credit tag (the statement identifying the source):

She said, "Leave me alone."
"I don't care," he said.

Often the *credit tag interrupts the quotation* instead of introducing or concluding it. You then need **commas** both before and after the credit tag if it splits one complete sentence:

> "All men," Aristotle wrote, "naturally desire knowledge."

You need a comma before and a **period** after the credit tag if it comes between two complete sentences:

> "All men are curious," Aristotle wrote. "They naturally desire knowledge."

The following variations are important:

(1) No comma is required with extremely *short quotations* or with *quotations worked into the pattern of a sentence* that is not a mere credit tag:

> Your saying "I am sorry" was not enough to soothe his wounded pride.

> The clatter of dishes and tableware, mingled with lusty shouts of "Seconds here!" and "Please pass the butter!", will resound across the country. — John Crawford, "A Plea for Physical Fatness," *Atlantic*

No comma is required when the credit tag follows a question or an exclamation:

> "Is everybody all right?" he shouted at the top of his voice.

(2) *Long or formal quotations* are often introduced by a **colon** instead of a comma. Whether you use a comma or a colon, capitalize the first word of the quotation if it was capitalized in the original source (or if it would have been capitalized if written down):

> Saarinen's definition of architecture's purposes describes his work: "To shelter and enhance man's life on earth and to fulfill his belief in the nobility of his existence."

(3) *Long quotations* (more than ten typed lines) should be set off from the rest of a paper *not* by quotation marks but by indention and single-spacing. The same applies to quotations consisting of more than a full line of poetry. (See Chapter 9 and the sample paper that follows it for examples of such **block quotations**.)

(4) Indicate when the person you are quoting is quoting someone else. In a quotation marked by the conventional set of double quotation marks, **single quotation marks** signal a *quotation within a quotation:*

He said, "Our Congressman's constant cry of 'Cut that budget!' deceives no one."

In the words of Chester Bowles, "In our national efforts to prove that we are 'realists' who do not 'go off half-cocked,' we have developed an appalling gap between the moral beliefs to which we subscribe and our day-to-day performance."

P 8b   Terminal Marks in Quotations

Observe conventional sequence when quotation marks coincide with other marks of punctuation.

(1) Commas conventionally precede the final quotation mark, whereas semicolons and colons conventionally follow it:

As he said, "Don't worry about me," the ship pulled away from the quay.
You said, "I don't need your sympathy"; therefore, I didn't offer any.

(2) End punctuation usually precedes the final quotation marks, as in all the examples given so far. Sometimes, however, you will have to use a question mark or an exclamation mark after the quotation has formally ended. This means that the quotation itself is not a question or an exclamation. Rather, you are asking a question or exclaiming about the quotation.

Who said, "We are strangers here; the world is from of old"?
Don't ever tell a girl, "There'll never be another woman like my mother"!

NOTE: *A terminal mark is not duplicated at the end of a quotation*, even when logic might seem to require its repetition. For instance, use only one question mark even when you are asking a question about a question:

Were you the student who asked, "Could we hold the class on the lawn?"

P 8c   Insertions and Omissions

In direct quotation, any changes you make in the original text should be clearly indicated to your reader.

(1) If for any reason you insert *explanations or comments of your own*, set them off from the quoted material by **square brackets**:

As Dr. Habenichts observes, "Again and again, they [the Indians] saw themselves deprived of lands of whose possession they had been assured with solemn oaths."

The note read: "Left Camp B Wednesday, April 3 [actually April 4]. Are trying to reach Camp C before we run out of supplies."

A comment sometimes inserted in a quotation is *sic,* the Latin word for "thus," which indicates that a passage that seems questionable or contains errors was transcribed exactly the way it occurred in the original source.

> The police records contained this short entry: "The accomplices of the suspect is [*sic*] unknown."

(2) When you *omit unnecessary or irrelevant material* from a quotation, indicate the omission by three spaced periods (called an **ellipsis**). If the omission occurs after a period in the original text, retain the sentence period and then insert the ellipsis.

> The report concluded on an optimistic note: "All three of the patients . . . are making remarkable progress toward recovery."

> "To be a bird is to be alive more intensely than any other living creature, man included. . . . They live in a world that is always present, mostly full of joy." So wrote N. J. Berrill, Professor of Zoology at McGill University.—Joseph Wood Krutch, "If You Don't Mind My Saying So," *The American Scholar*

To indicate extensive omissions (a line or more of poetry, a paragraph or more of prose), you may use a single typed line of spaced periods.

NOTE: An ellipsis can *distort* a quotation by omitting important details or qualifications. A testimonial reading "This might have been a good book if it had been more carefully planned" should not be shortened to read ". . . a good book."

P 8d   Indirect Quotation

In indirect quotations, reproduce someone else's ideas or thoughts but translate them into your own words. Indirectly quoted statements often take the form of noun clauses introduced by *that;* indirectly quoted questions take the form of noun clauses introduced by words like *whether, why, how,* and *which.* Such clauses are *not* separated from the statement indicating the source by a comma or colon. They are *not* enclosed in quotation marks:

> Aristotle stated *that all men naturally desire knowledge.*
> General Grant replied *that he doubted the wisdom of such a move.*
> The artist asked me *which of the drawings I liked best.*

Note two exceptions:

(1) The following passage shows ways of *working the source statement into the indirect quotation as parenthetic material,* requiring **commas**:

As Gandhi remarked, the first consequence of nonviolent action is to harden the heart of those who are being assaulted by charity. But, *he continued,* all the while they are being driven to a frenzy of rage, they are haunted by the terrible knowledge of how wrong they are. — Michael Harrington, "Whence Comes Their Passion," *The Reporter*

(2) Even in an indirect quotation, you may reproduce some words or phrases exactly as they were used by the person you quote. To indicate that you are *preserving part of the original wording,* enclose such directly quoted words and phrases — but not any other part of the quotation — in **quotation marks**:

> The author felt that students could not be "tricked or coerced into thinking."

> The government radio referred to the accused men as "bandits" and "murderers" and promised that justice would be upheld "regardless of the cost."

P 8e   Words Set Off from Context

Use quotation marks to indicate words and phrases that are not part of the vocabulary you would normally employ. Use them for expressions that are not your own, even though you may not be quoting them from any specific source.

(1) **Quotation marks** may identify words that you employ for *local color or comical effect.* They enable you to show irony by holding an expression, as it were, at arm's length:

At the school I attended, a girl who did not go on "dates" or take an interest in "fellows" was not accepted as a normal human being.

It would seem that every modern child's pleasure must have its "constructive aspects." — Lois Phillips Hudson, "The Buggy on the Roof," *Atlantic*

Avoid using such quotation marks by way of apology for undesirable or inappropriate expressions.

(2) Quotation marks may call attention to familiar words used in *unfamiliar* ways:

Partisan Review thrived on its mutual interests in radicalism in politics and experimentalism in literature, each helping to "generalize" the other's concerns. — Theodore Solotaroff, "Radicals and Writing," *The New Republic*

(3) Either quotation marks or italicized print (underlining in a typed manuscript) identifies *technical terms* presumably new to the reader or *words discussed as words,* as in a discussion of grammar or meaning:

She wore a "Mother Hubbard," a loose, full gown long since out of fashion.

In logic, the term *inference* refers to a conclusion or deduction arrived at by reasoning.

The word *mob* was attacked as slang by some eighteenth-century writers.

(4) **Italics** rather than quotation marks identify *words that have been borrowed from foreign languages* and have not become part of the general vocabulary of English:

Logrolling and back scratching are his exercises; *Quid pro quo* and *Cui bono?* are his mottoes. —William Lee Miller, "Confessions of a Conferencegoer," *The Reporter*

Many legal and scientific terms borrowed from Latin belong in this category:

A writ of *certiorari* is issued by a superior court to obtain judicial records from an inferior court or quasi-judicial agency.

The sperm whale, *Physeter macrocephalus,* is valuable for its oil and spermaceti.

Exercises

A. Explain the use of punctuation in the following passages. Pay special attention to *quoted material.*

1. Young Southerners often admire the somewhat anarchic qualities Latin Americans refer to as *machismo.*

2. The *Michigan Daily* called him "a planner, an innovator, a persuader, a sympathizer . . . who is willing to align himself on the side of the students interested in getting an education here."

3. "I weep for you," the walrus said; "I deeply sympathize."

4. Shepley, Bulfinch, Richardson & Abbott were retained to design a "championship amphitheater."

5. In the *Random House Dictionary*, the reader can find such concoctions as *Franglais* and *Guesstimate.*

6. "The *Random House Dictionary*," I learn from a press release, "demanded seven years of editorial research and about $3,000,000 to produce."

7. Punctuation was unknown to the ancients. Latin teachers used to give their students a sentence that can mean: "My mother, O pig, is

wicked." It can also mean: "Priestess, my sow is ugly"; or, "Come on, goddess, a boar is eating the apples."

8. How many students will understand what Marlowe meant by "the topless towers of Ilium"?

B. Check the following passages for conventional punctuation of quotations. Label each passage *S* (satisfactory) or *U* (unsatisfactory).

1. "Everything has already been said," wrote André Gide, "but since nobody ever listens we always have to start all over again."

2. "I am Grace Anders," she said, "do you mind if I come in?"

3. "Terrible!" the director shouted. "Let's take that passage again, starting from 'O, that this too too solid flesh would melt . . .'"

4. Newspaper veterans turned the phrases "culture beat" and "culture editor" over in their mouths with the gusto of a man biting into an unripe olive.

5. The lady from Buffalo kept asking the guide "what he meant by primitive?"

6. Wild applause and shouts of "Encore!" greeted us when the curtain parted.

7. Instead of congratulating me, John said, "Beauty contests—what a farce!"

8. According to one irate bystander, the murderer deserved no more sympathy than a "rabid dog."

9. "I'm all right," said my uncle, "just watch what you are doing the next time."

10. The speaker charged "that the television audience resembled the ancient Romans, who liked to see gladiators do battle to the death."

11. The speaker quoted Jefferson as saying that "our new circumstances" require "new words, new phrases, and the transfer of old words to new objects."

12. The constant war cry of my high school English teachers was give an example!

C. In the following passage, insert appropriate punctuation in the numbered spaces. Underline lower-case letters that should be replaced with capitals (english). Leave a blank space where no punctuation is required.

The article points out____(1) that many commercials are directed at the younger and more impressionable among television fans____(2) for instance____(3) a commercial might go like this____(4) Harry the Bat eats Bang Cereal every morning to grow big and strong____(5) so why don't you kiddies have your mom buy some today____(6) Mom is then plagued by the____(7) kiddies____(8) until she buys the cereal____(9) wasn't it Edgar Guest who said____(10) none but the hard of heart can resist the pleading look of a child____(11) this technique takes unfair advantage of the parents____(12) for____(13) as a friend of mine recently put it____(14) children are often even more gullible than adults____(15)

D. From your current writing and reading, select ten sample sentences that illustrate the various conventions of punctuation discussed in the preceding section.

E. (**Review of punctuation**) Explain the use of punctuation marks in each of the following passages. Point out sentences that you would have punctuated differently and explain why. Explain effects achieved by unconventional punctuation.

1. In recent years it has been possible to make motionpicture films of events on the surface of the sun, and by speeding them up several hundred times to project on the screen the life story of cataclysmic solar events which may occupy hours of time and quadrillions of cubic miles of space. Some of these films are awe-inspiring: they show immense fountains of flame spurting to heights of a hundred thousand miles from the sun's edge; bridges of fire, which could span a dozen earths, forming and crumbling; exact replicas of A-bomb bursts — but a thousand times as large — shooting up into space. — Arthur C. Clarke, "The Secret of the Sun," *Holiday*

2. Many of the greatest classics were written, assuredly, without children in mind, and were taken over by children who cheerfully disregarded what they could not understand and cherished what they could. Thus Defoe, old and cantankerous, did not mean to write for children, but they adopted Robinson Crusoe and own him still; soon Crusoe spread all over the globe; he was celebrated in every language; he suffered one metamorphosis after another, most famously in "Swiss Family Robinson," but in dozens of others as well. After two hundred years he is read avidly by children in Montana and Tasmania and Norway, and very little by their parents. Nor did the harsh and embittered Jonathan Swift mean to write for the young, but he could not help himself either, it seems. The children took over Gulliver and went with him on his travels, they made him into a fairy-story character. — Henry Steele Commager, "When Majors Wrote for Minors," *Saturday Review*

3. Men are brought to these conferences, regularly, in a sort of balanced ticket: one Jew, one Catholic, one Protestant; one labor leader to every businessman; one Republican to every Democrat; very carefully, a Negro and a woman; an economist with the Economist's View, a psychoanalyst with the Psychoanalytical View, a philosopher with the

Standpoint of Philosophy. In my earliest conferencegoing days I myself was a College Student, attending as representative decoration
conferences composed mainly of older people. Invariably there would
come a golden moment when — since I then had sense enough to keep
my mouth shut and would not have spoken — the chairman would
pounce: "But let us hear from the Student Mind"; or "And how does
this sound to Young People?" — William Lee Miller, "Confessions of a
Conferencegoer," *The Reporter*

CHAPTER SEVENTEEN

Glossary of Usage

NOTE: The following glossary reviews the status of words, word forms, and constructions that are frequently criticized as careless, illogical, excessively informal, or otherwise restricted in appropriateness and effectiveness. The glossary is limited to information that goes beyond the scope of the ordinary dictionary entry or that tends to be lost in the wealth of other information a dictionary provides.[1]

a, an.   The *a* should appear only before words that begin with a consonant when pronounced: *a desk, a chair, a house, a year, a* C, *a university.* The *an* should appear before words that begin with a vowel when pronounced (though, in writing, the first letter may be a consonant): *an eye, an essay question, an honest man, an* A, *an* M, *an uninformed reader.* In the latter position, *a* is nonstandard.

above, above-mentioned, aforementioned, aforesaid.   Avoid the use of *above, above-mentioned, aforementioned,* and the like, to refer to something previously mentioned. These phrases suggest the wooden, bureaucratic style of some business letters, many government publications, and most legal documents. Use a less mechanical, less obtrusive expression like *this point, this fact, these considerations.* If a *this* would not be clear, restate or summarize the point to which you wish to refer.

allusion, illusion.   An "allusion" is a hint or indirect reference (to call an athlete a "Goliath" is to use a Biblical allusion). An "illusion" is a deceptive sense impression or a mistaken belief. When an illusion is serious and persistent enough, it may become a "delusion."

amount, number.   *Amount* is sometimes used loosely instead of *number* in reference to things counted individually and as separate units.

> Satisfactory: A large number [not *amount*] of people were waiting.
> Satisfactory: The *number* [not *amount*] of unsold cars on dealers' lots was growing steadily.

***and* and *but* at the beginning of a sentence.**   When *and* and *but* are used at the beginning of a sentence, or at the beginning of a paragraph, they have the effect of partly canceling out the pause signaled by the period or by the paragraph break. They can therefore suggest

---

[1] For confusing words often included in a Glossary of Usage, see SP 2c; for a list of idiomatic prepositions, see D 1e.

a sudden or an important afterthought. But many modern writers start sentences with *and* or *but* merely to avoid heavier, more formal connectives like *moreover, furthermore, however,* and *nevertheless.*

and/or.   *And/or* is an awkward combination sometimes necessary in commercial or official documents. Its use in ordinary expository prose is an annoying mannerism.

angle, approach, slant.   *Angle, approach,* and *slant* are currently overused as synonyms for "attitude," "point of view," "position," or "procedure."

apt, liable, prone.   In informal speech and writing, *apt, liable,* and *prone* all appear in the sense of "likely." In formal usage, *apt* suggests that something is likely because of someone's aptitude ("He is apt to become a successful artist"); *liable* suggests that what is likely is burdensome or undesirable ("He is liable to break his leg"); *prone* suggests that something is almost inevitable because of strong habit or predisposition ("He is prone to suspect others").

as.   *As* as a substitute for *that* or *whether* ("I don't know *as* I can come") or as a substitute for *who* ("Those *as* knew her avoided her") is nonstandard. As a substitute for *because* or *while, as* is often criticized as ambiguous, unemphatic, or overused:

> *As* [better: "because"] we had no money, we gave him a check.

attenuate, extenuate.   Both *attenuate* and *extenuate* basically mean "to thin out." *Extenuate* is the legal term: "Extenuating circumstances" make a crime seem less serious or contemptible than it originally appeared.

attribute, contribute.   *Contribute* means "to give one's share" or "to have a share" in something; *attribute* means "to trace or ascribe something to a cause or source" ("He *attributed* the crossing of the letters in the mail to the intervention of a supernatural power").

being as, being that.   As substitutes for *because* or *since, being as* and *being that* ("*being that* I was ill") are nonstandard.

between, among.   *Between* is historically related to *twain,* which in turn is a variant of *two.* As a result, grammarians have often restricted *between* to references to two of a kind (distinguish *between* right and wrong) and required *among* in references to more than two (distinguish *among* different shades of color). *Between* is also appropriate when more than two things can be considered in pairs of two:

> He had sand *between* his toes.
> Bilateral trade agreements exist *between* many European countries.

Indiscriminate substitution of *between* for *among* invites avoidable criticism.

blame for, blame on.   There are two idiomatic uses of the word *blame:* "He blamed the passenger *for* the accident" and "He blamed the accident *on* the passenger." The first of these is preferred in formal English.

calculate, reckon, expect, guess.   In formal written English, *calculate* and *reckon* usually imply computing or systematic reasoning; *expect* implies expectation or anticipation; *guess* implies conjecture. In the sense of "think," "suppose," or "consider," these verbs are colloquial or dialectal.

can and **may.**   Formal English uses *can* in the sense of "be able to" or "be capable of," *may* to indicate permission. The use of *can* to indicate permission, increasingly common in speech and writing, is generally considered informal:

> Formal: You *may* (have my permission to) take as much as you *can* (are able to) eat.
> Informal: *Can* I speak to you for a minute?

cannot help but.   Although occasionally found in writing, *cannot help but* is widely criticized as an illogical or confused variant of *cannot help:*

> Satisfactory: I *cannot help* wishing that I had never met you.
> Satisfactory: I *cannot but* wish that I had never met you.

childish, childlike.   "Childish gesture" and "childlike gesture" both remind us of children; but the former suggests silliness or immaturity, the latter endearing innocence.

compare with, compare to.   We compare two cities *with* each other to see what they have in common, but we compare a city *to* an anthill to show what a city is like.

continual, continuous.   To be "continuous," something must extend without interruption in space or in time. People may keep up a "continual" conversation, interrupted because they have to pause for breath.

couple of.   In formal writing, *couple* refers to two of a kind, a pair. Used in the sense of "several" or "a few," it is colloquial. Used before a plural noun without a connecting *of*, it is nonstandard.

Colloquial: We had to wait *a couple of* minutes.
Nonstandard: We had only *a couple* dollars left.

credible, credulous, creditable.   Stories may be credible or incredible; the people who read them may be credulous or incredulous. An act that does someone credit is a creditable act.

cute, great, lovely, wonderful, swell.   Words like *cute, great, lovely,* and *wonderful* so often express thoughtless or insincere praise that their use in formal writing can suggest immaturity. *Cute* is colloquial. *Swell* is slang.

different than.   *Different from* is characteristic of formal written English. Nevertheless, *different than*, widely used in speech, is becoming acceptable in writing ("Life in cadet school for Major Major was no *different than* life had been for him all along." — Joseph Heller, *Catch-22*). Recent writers on usage point out that *different than* is the more economical way of introducing a clause:

Economical: We tried a different method *than* we had used last year.
Less Economical: We tried a different method *from the one* we had used last year.

disinterested, uninterested.   In formal writing, *disinterested* usually means "unswayed by personal, selfish interest" or "impartial." The word is used especially to indicate the absence of financial interest or personal ambition ("We were sure he would be a *disinterested* judge"). *Disinterested* used in the sense of "uninterested" or "indifferent" is objectionable to many readers.

***do* form for emphasis.**   Verb forms with *do, does,* or *did* can serve as emphatic variants of the simple present and the simple past: "She may not wear the latest fashions, but she *does* know how to cook." In student writing, the emphatic *do* is sometimes overused:

Overdone: I really *did appreciate* the teacher's help an awful lot.
Better: I *appreciated* the teacher's help.

double comparative, double superlative.   Short adjectives usually form the comparative by adding the suffix *er (cheaper)*, the superlative by adding the suffix *est (cheapest)*. Long adjectives, and adverbs ending in *ly*, usually employ the intensifiers *more* and *most* instead *(more expensive, most expensive; more carefully, most carefully)*. Forms using both the suffix and the intensifier are nonstandard *(more cheaper, most cheapest)*.

double negative.   Double and triple negatives — the use of additional negative words to reinforce a negation already expressed — are nonstandard: "I *didn't* do *nothing*." "*Nobody* comes to see me *no more*."

***due to* as a preposition.**   *Due to* is generally accepted as an adjective: "His absence was *due to* ill health." "His absence, *due to* ill health, upset our schedule." As a preposition meaning "because of," *due to* is often criticized:

> Objectionable: He canceled his lecture *due to* ill health.
> Safe: He canceled his lecture *because of* ill health.

each other, one another.   Conservative writers distinguish between *each other* (referring to two persons or things) and *one another* (referring to more than two).

enthuse.   *Enthuse* is a "back formation" from the noun *enthusiasm* and is used in colloquial English as a convenient shortcut for "become enthusiastic" and "move to enthusiasm." Similar back formations, like *reminisce* from *reminiscence*, have become generally acceptable. *Enthuse* still has a long way to go.

etc.   *Etc.*, the Latin abbreviation for "and so on" or "and the like," often serves as a vague substitute for additional details, examples, or illustrations. Furthermore, *ect.* is a common misspelling; "and etc." and "such as . . . etc." are redundant and unnecessarily reveal the writer's ignorance of Latin.

farther, further; all the farther.   A traditional rule required *farther* in references to space and distance ("We traveled *farther* than we had expected"), *further* in references to degree and quantity ("We discussed it *further* at our next meeting") and in the sense of "additional" ("without *further* delay"). *Further* is now widely accepted as appropriate in all three senses.

All the farther in the sense of "as far as" ("This is *all the farther* we go") is variously classified as colloquial, nonstandard, or dialectal.

fortuitous, fortunate.   "Fortuitous" changes are accidental, unplanned developments that are not always fortunate.

full, fulsome.   *Fulsome*, except when used by people who are confused by its similarity with *full*, means "offensive," or "disgusting." "Fulsome praise" is offensively exaggerated or insincere.

gentleman, lady, female.   In nineteenth-century, and especially British, use, *gentleman* and *lady* identified people whose manners and social rank set them apart from the uneducated. Now both terms are usually used as polite equivalents of the blunter *man* and *woman*. Since they suggest refinement, they may sound pretentious when used in unrefined situations. *Female* is biological and impersonal; it is often condescending.

get, got, gotten.   The verb *get* is used in many idiomatic expressions. Some of these are colloquial:

> *have got* (for "own," "possess," "have available")
> I *have got* ten dollars; she *has got* blue eyes; you *have got* ten minutes.
>
> *have got to* (for "have to," "must," "be obliged")
> I *have got to* leave now; we *have got to* think of our customers.
>
> *get to* (for "succeed")
> I finally *got to* see him.
>
> *get* (for "understand")
> *Get* it?
>
> *get* (for "arrest," "hit," "kill")
> The police finally *got* him.
>
> *get* (for "puzzle," "irritate," "annoy")
> What really *gets* me is that he never announces his tests.

Some grammarians commend the use of *get* in sentences like "He *got hit* by a truck" as an emphatic and unambiguous alternative to the ordinary passive, formed with *be, am, was, were* ("He *was hit* by a truck"). This use of *got* is still widely considered informal.

In American English, *have gotten* is an acceptable alternative to *have got*, except when the latter means *have* or *have to*.

hadn't ought to.   In formal English, *ought*, unlike some other auxiliaries, has no form for the past tense. *Hadn't ought* is informal; *had ought* nonstandard.

Informal:	You *hadn't ought* to ask him.
Formal:	You *ought not to have* asked him.

hopefully.   When used instead of expressions like "I hope" or "let us hope," *hopefully* is considered illogical by conservative readers.

Informal: *Hopefully*, the forms will be ready by Monday.
Formal: *I hope* the forms will be ready by Monday.

human, humane.   Not every human being is "humane"—that is, kind, compassionate, sensitive, or refined.

if, whether.   Conservative readers object to *if* when used to express doubt or uncertainty after such verbs as *ask, don't know, wonder, doubt*. The more formal connective is *whether*: "I doubt *whether* his support would do much good."

in, into.   Formal writing often requires *into* rather than *in* to indicate direction: "He came *into* [not *in*] the room."

in terms of.   A vague all-purpose connective frequent in jargon: "What have you seen lately *in terms of* new plays?"

Jargon: *Virtue* originally meant "manliness" *in terms of* [better: "in the sense of"] warlike prowess or fortitude.

infer, imply.   In formal usage, *imply* means to "indicate or suggest a certain conclusion"; *infer* means "to draw a conclusion on the basis of what has been indicated or suggested." A statement can have various implications, which may lead to inferences on the part of the reader.

irregardless.   Used instead of *regardless, irregardless* is often heard in educated speech but is widely considered nonstandard.

it's me, it is I.   Traditional grammarians required *it is I* on the grounds that the linking verb *is* equates the pronoun *I* with the subject *it* and thus makes necessary the use of the subject form. Modern grammarians accept *it is me* on the grounds that usual English word order (he hit *me*; she asked *me*) makes the object form natural. *It's me* is now freely used in informal speech; other pronouns *(us, him, her)* are still occasionally criticized as uneducated usage.

Informal: I thought it was *him*. It could have been *us*.

judicial, judicious.   A "judicial" decision is a decision reached by a judge or by a court. A "judicious" decision shows sound judgment. Not every judicial decision is judicious.

later, latter. "Although both Alfred and Francis were supposed to arrive at eight, the former came earlier, the *latter later.*"

learn, teach. In standard English, the teacher *teaches* (rather than *learns)* the learner; the learner is *taught* (rather than *learned)* by the teacher.

leave, let. In formal usage, *leave* does not mean "allow" or "permit"; you do not "leave" somebody do something. Nor does *leave* take the place of *let* in suggestions like "Let us call a meeting."

less, fewer. *Less* is often used interchangeably with *fewer* before plural nouns. This use of *less* was once widely condemned. The safe practice is to use *less* in references to extent, amount, degree *(less* friction, *less* money, *less* heat) but not in references to number *(fewer* people, *fewer* homes, *fewer* requirements).

like **as a connective.** In informal speech, *like* is widely used as a connective replacing *as* or *as if* at the beginning of a clause:

Informal:	Do *like* I tell you.
Formal:	Do *as* I tell you.
Informal:	The patient felt *like* he had slept for days.
Formal:	The patient felt *as if* [or *as though*] he had slept for days.

Note that *like* is acceptable in formal usage as a preposition: "The girl looked *like* her mother."

luxuriant, luxurious. A "luxurious" house may be surrounded by "luxuriant" — that is, profusely growing — vegetation.

moral, morale. We talk about the "moral" of a story but about the "morale" of troops. People with good morale are not necessarily very moral, and vice versa.

most, almost. *Most* is informal when used in the sense of "almost" or "nearly": "*Most* everybody was there." "Mrs. Jones considers herself an authority on *most* any subject."

on account of. Nonstandard as a substitute for *because.*

Nonstandard:	Once she is married, a teacher is likely to stop teaching *on account of* [should be "because"] she will have to take care of her own children.

plan on.   In formal usage, substitute *plan to*.

> Informal: My father had always *planned on* him taking over the farm.
> Formal: My father had always *planned to* have him take over the farm.

possessives with verbal nouns.   A traditional rule requires that a verbal noun (gerund) be preceded by a possessive in sentences like the following:

> Formal: He mentioned *John's winning* a scholarship.
> Formal: I am looking forward to *your mother's staying* with us.

This rule is widely observed in formal writing. In informal speech and writing, the plain form is more common:

> Informal: Imagine *John winning* a scholarship!

practicable, practical.   A "practicable" plan seems capable of being put into practice. A "practical" plan, when put into practice, is workable or effective. Unlike things, people can be practical but not practicable.

preposition at the end of a sentence.   Teachers no longer tell students not to end a sentence with a preposition. The preposition that ends a sentence is idiomatic, natural English, though more frequent in informal than in formal use.

> Idiomatic: I don't remember what we talked *about*.
> Idiomatic: She found her mother-in-law hard to live *with*.
> Idiomatic: You know very well what I hired you *for*.

Note, however, that placing a comparatively unimportant word at the end of a sentence can make a sentence sound unemphatic:

> Emphatic: Let us not betray the ideals *for* which these men died.
> Emphatic: Do not ask *for* whom the bell tolls.

prepositions often criticized.   *Inside of* (for *inside*), *outside of* (for *outside*), and *at about* (for *about*) are redundant.
      Back of for *behind* (*back of* the house), *inside of* for *within* (*inside of* three hours), *off of* for *off* (get *off of* the table), *outside of* for *besides* or *except* (no one *outside of* my friends), and *over with* for *over* (it's *over with*) are colloquial.
      As to, as regards, and *in regard to* are generally acceptable, but they can seem heavy-handed and bureaucratic when used as indiscriminate substitutes for briefer or more precise prepositions.

> Awkward: I questioned him as to the nature of his injury.
> Preferable: I questioned him *about* his injury.

As to whether, *in terms of*, and *on the basis of* flourish in all varieties of jargon.

Per (a dollar *per* day), *as per* (*as per* your request), and *plus* (quality *plus* service) are common in business and newspaper English but inappropriate in a noncommercial context.

provided, provided that, providing. *Provided*, *provided that*, and *providing* are interchangeable in a sentence like "He will withdraw his complaint, *provided* you apologize." However, only *provided* has consistently escaped criticism and is therefore the safest form to use.

reason is because, reason why. In informal speech, *the reason . . . is because* often takes the place of the more formal *the reason . . . is that*. The former construction is often criticized as redundant, since *because* repeats the idea of cause already expressed in the word *reason*. Either construction can make a sentence unnecessarily awkward.

Informal:	*The reason* that the majority rules *is because* it is strongest.
Formal:	*The reason* that the majority rules *is that* it is strongest.
Less Awkward:	The majority rules *because* it is strongest.

Reason why, though equally open to the charge of redundancy, is less widely criticized.

respectfully, respectively. *Respectfully* means "full of respect"; *respectively* means "with respect or reference to each of several things in the order in which they were mentioned" ("*Un* and *deux* mean one and two respectively").

shall, will. In current American usage, *will* usually indicates simply that something is going to happen:

I *will* ask him tomorrow.
You *will* find it on your desk.
Mr. Smith *will* inform you of our plans.

The more emphatic *shall* often indicates that something is going to happen as the result of strong determination, definite obligation, or authoritative command:

I *shall* return.
We *shall* do our best.
Wages of common laborers *shall* not exceed twenty dollars a day.

Shall is also common in questions that invite the listener's approval or consent:

Shall I wait for you?
Shall we dance?

Formal English used to reverse the relationship between *will* and *shall* in the first person; that is, after *I* and *we* but not after *you*, *he*, or *they*. "I *shall* see him tomorrow" then expressed simple, unemphatic future; "I *will* not yield" expressed determination. Questions used the form expected in the answer: "*Shall* you see him tomorrow?" Current handbooks of grammar no longer require the observance of this convention.

should, would.   In many uses, *should* and *would* are parallel to *shall* and *will*. "I *would* help you if I could" is parallel to "I *will* help you"; the formal alternative, "I *should* help you if I could," is parallel to "I *shall* help you." However, both *should* and *would* are also used with distinctive meanings of their own. *Should* may express obligation ("I *should* study more"), probability ("I *should* be able to finish it tonight"), or a hypothetical condition ("If he *should* resist, call me for help"). *Would* may express customary action ("He *would* listen patiently to my excuses").

split infinitives.   Occasionally a modifier breaks up an infinitive; that is, a verbal formed with *to* (*to come, to promise, to have written*). The resulting split infinitive has long been idiomatic English and occurs in the work of distinguished writers. The traditional rule against it is now all but obsolete. Note, however, that a split infinitive can be awkward, especially if the modifier intervening after *to* consists of more than one word:

> Awkward: He ordered us *to* with all possible speed *return* to our stations.
> Better: He ordered us *to return* to our stations with all possible speed.

The words that most frequently split infinitives are overused intensifiers like *actually, definitely, literally, really,* and *virtually.* Omitting these altogether often improves the sentence:

> We expect the public *to* [literally] *overwhelm* us with orders.
> Education may be able *to* [virtually] *eliminate* race prejudice.

superlative in reference to two.   In informal speech and writing, the superlative rather than the comparative frequently occurs in comparisons between only two things. This use of the superlative is widely considered illogical and generally labeled inappropriate to formal usage.

> Informal: Which of the two candidates is the *best* speaker?
> Formal: Which of the two candidates is the *better* speaker?

take and, try and, up and.   *Take and* (in "I'd *take and* prune those roses") and *up and* (in "He *up and* died") are dialectal. *Try and* for *try to* ("I'd *try and* change his mind") is colloquial.

these kind.   Agreement requires "*this kind* of car" or "*these kinds* of fish." "*These kind* of cars" and "*those kind* of cars" are informal.

titles: *Dr.*, *Prof.*, *Reverend*.   In references to holders of academic degrees or titles, *Dr. Smith* and *Professor Brown* are courteous and correct. *Professor* is sometimes abbreviated when it precedes the full name: *Prof. Paul F. Brown.* In references to a clergyman, *Reverend* is usually preceded by *the* and followed by the first name, by initials, or by *Mr.* (*the Reverend William Carper; the Reverend W. F. Carper; the Reverend Mr. Carper*).

too.   The use of *too* in expressions like "He isn't *too* well off" is often condemned as vague or overused.

type, type of, -type.   The practice of omitting the *of* in expressions like "this *type* of plane" is colloquial. *Type* is increasingly used as a suffix to turn nouns into adjectives: "an escape-type novel," "a drama-type program." Such combinations strike many readers as barbarisms, foreign to idiomatic, natural English. Often they are used to turn simple ideas into fuzzy, wordy phrases: "A subsidy-type payment" says no more than "subsidy."

unique, perfect, equal.   It is often argued that one thing cannot be *more unique, more perfect,* or *more equal* than another; either it is unique or it isn't. Formal English therefore often substitutes *more nearly unique, more nearly perfect, more nearly equal.*

up.   *Up* is often criticized as redundant in expressions like *finish up, heat up, hurry up, rise up,* or *sober up.* In other expressions it modifies meaning or adds emphasis: *buy up, clean up, dress up, speak up, use up.* Most of these combinations have a colloquial flavor. *Beat up* is slang.

used to, didn't use to, used to could.   *Used to* in questions or negative statements with *did* is informal and only occasionally seen in print ("the strident . . . anti-police slogans which *didn't use to* be part of the hippie mode"—*National Review*).

| Informal: | She *didn't use to* smoke. |
| Formal: | She *used not to* smoke. |

Used to could is nonstandard for *used to be able.*

***very* and *much*.**   Formal usage prefers *much* or *greatly* to *very* before a verbal like *surprised* or *embarrassed* (past participle) if the verbal idea is still strong; that is, if the verbal has not yet become an ordinary adjective with little suggestion of action or process:

Sometimes Criticized	Safe
very surprised	*much* surprised
very embarrassed	*greatly* embarrassed
very astonished	*very much* astonished

***where*, *where at*, *where to*.**   In formal English, *where* takes the place of *where to* ("*Where* was it sent?") and *where at* ("*Where* is he?"). Both *where to* and *where at* are generally condemned as redundant.

Where used instead of *that* ("I read in the paper *where* a boy was killed") is colloquial.

-*wise*.   The practice of converting a noun into an adverb by tacking on -*wise* is characteristic of business or advertising jargon. Use *grammatically* for *grammar-wise*, *linguistically* for *language-wise*.

***without*.**   *Without* is nonstandard when used as a connective introducing a clause.

| Nonstandard: | The landlord won't let me stay *without* I pay the rent. |
| Standard: | The landlord won't let me stay *unless* I pay the rent. |

***you* with indefinite reference.**   Formal writing generally restricts *you* to the meaning of "you, the reader." Much informal writing uses *you* with indefinite reference to refer to people in general; formal writing would substitute *one:*

| Informal: | In ancient Rome, *you* had to be a patrician to be able to vote. |
| Formal: | In ancient Rome, *one* had to be a patrician to be able to vote. |

CHAPTER EIGHTEEN

Grammatical Terms

NOTE: Use the index to locate fuller discussion of many of the grammatical terms listed in this glossary.

Absolute Construction. A word or phrase that is grammatically independent of the rest of the sentence. Typically, a verbal or verbal phrase: *"The guests having departed,* Arvin locked the door."

Active. See VOICE.

Adjective. A class of words that can point out a quality of a noun (or noun equivalent). They occur characteristically as modifiers of nouns ("the *happy* child") and as predicate adjectives ("The child was *happy*"). They normally have distinctive forms for use in comparisons (*happier, happiest; more reasonable, most reasonable*).

Adjective Clause. A dependent clause serving an adjective function: "The man *who had startled us* apologized."

Adverb. A class of words used to modify verbs, adjectives, other adverbs, or a sentence as a whole:

> He ran *quickly.*
> He was *strangely* silent.
> He sang *moderately* well.
> *Surprisingly,* he did not answer.

Many adverbs show the distinctive *-ly* ending.

Adverbial Clause. A dependent clause serving an adverbial function: "We left *after the rain had stopped." "When the bell had ceased to ring,* I opened the door."

Agreement. Correspondence, mainly in number, between grammatically related elements. Use of matching forms of a subject and its verb (the *dog barks* — the *dogs bark*); choice of a pronoun matching its antecedent ("*Each* member must be aware of *his* responsibility").

Antecedent. The noun (or equivalent) for which a pronoun substitutes: "*Aunt Hertha* fell sick soon after *she* arrived."

Appositive. A noun (or equivalent) placed as a modifier next to — usually after — another noun: "Mr. Brown, *the registrar,* proved most helpful."

Articles. *A* and *an* (the **indefinite** articles) and *the* (the **definite** article), used as noun markers: *a* book, *an* honest man, *the* door.

Auxiliaries. "Helping" verbs used in forming complete verbs: *be* (*am, are, was,* etc.), *have, shall (should), will (would), can (could), may (might), must, ought.*

Case. Inflected forms of nouns and pronouns, signaling certain grammatical relationships within a sentence: the **possessive** of nouns (*George's* friend), the **subject forms** and **object forms** of pronouns (*I — me, he — him,* etc.).

Clause. A subject-predicate unit that may combine with other such units in a sentence. **Independent** clauses are grammatically self-contained and can be punctuated as complete sentences:

> I think; therefore, I am.
> I think. Therefore, I am.

Dependent clauses are grammatically subordinate to an independent clause (main clause):

> Arvin had a dog, *which barked all night.*
> *After the rain stopped,* we went home.

See also ADJECTIVE CLAUSE, ADVERBIAL CLAUSE, NOUN CLAUSE.

Collective Noun. A group noun that is singular in form but may require a plural verb:

> Singular: The *jury votes* tomorrow. (thought of as a unit)
> Plural: The *jury are* out to lunch. (thought of as individuals)

Comparative. The form of adjectives and adverbs that is used to indicate higher degree: "Blood is *thicker* than water."

Complement. A sentence element completing the predication of the verb. The complements of action verbs are called **objects**:

> Arvin called *the sheriff* (**direct** object).
> She wrote *my father* (**indirect** object) a *letter* (**direct** object).

The complement of a linking verb is a noun or adjective describing the subject (**subjective complement**):

> Her father was a *businessman* (**predicate noun**).
> The girl looked *pale* (**predicate adjective**).

After some verbs, an object is followed by a description of the object (**objective complement**):

> The editorial called the project a *failure.*
> Arvin labeled the charges *ridiculous.*

Conjunction.   See CONNECTIVES.

Conjunctive Adverb.   See CONNECTIVES.

Connectives.   Words connecting sentence elements or clauses: **coordinating connectives** (*and, but, for, or, nor*); **subordinating connectives** (*if, when, because, though, whereas*); **adverbial connectives** (*however, therefore, consequently*).

Coordinate Adjectives.   Two or more adjectives describing different qualities of the same noun, with a comma taking the place of *and*: "a *noisy, unruly* crowd."

Correlatives.   Pairs of connectives coordinating sentence elements or clauses: *either . . . or, neither . . . nor, not only . . . but also, whether . . . or.*

Determiners.   Noun markers including **articles** (*a, an, the*), **demonstrative pronouns** (*this, these; that, those*), and **possessive pronouns** (*my, your, his, her, its, our, their*).

Elliptical Constructions.   Constructions in which missing elements can be supplied to facilitate grammatical analysis:

> The paintings [*that*] he collected filled a large room.
> When [*she was*] interviewed, the actress denied rumors of an impending engagement.

Expletives.   The *it* and *there* used as mere introductory words in *it-is, there-is, there-are* sentences.

Finite Verb.   A term used to distinguish a complete verb from a verbal, which cannot by itself function as a predicate.

Function Words.   Words whose major function is to establish grammatical relationships within a sentence: articles, connectives, prepositions.

Gender.   The quality of nouns and pronouns that determines choice between *he, she,* or *it;* between *actor* and *actress, alumnus* and *alumna, fiancé* and *fiancée.*

Gerund.   See VERBAL.

Idiom.   An expression that does not conform to general grammatical patterns but is established by usage as the habitual way of conveying a given meaning: *bear in mind, have a mind to, keep in mind.*

Infinitive.   See VERBAL.

Inflection.   Changes in the form of words to reflect changes in grammatical relationships: the plural *-s* of nouns; the *-s, -ed,* or *-ing* of verbs; the *-er* or *-est* of adjectives.

Intensifier.   Words that modify adjectives or adverbs and express degree; also called **intensive adverbs**: *very* hot, *quite* calm, *rather* young.

Interjection.   A grammatically independent element used to express attitude or emotion: *ah, oh, ouch,* etc.

Kernel Sentences.   The minimum sentences from which more complicated structures are derived in transformational grammar. They are the **source sentences** from which actual sentences are generated by successive transformations.

Linking Verb.   See VERB.

Modifier.   A word, phrase, or clause that develops or restricts the meaning of another sentence element or the sentence as a whole (see ADJECTIVE, ADVERB). **Restrictive** modifiers contribute to identification and need no punctuation; **nonrestrictive** modifiers provide additional information not essential to identification and are set off, normally by commas:

> **Restrictive:**   The man *who returned my wallet* was a complete stranger.
> **Nonrestrictive:**   Mr. Norton, *who found my wallet,* is an old friend.

Mood.   The classification of verb forms as **indicative** (plain or factual: "I am ready"); **imperative** (request or command: "Be quiet"); and **subjunctive** (hypothetical or contrary to fact: "I wish he were here!").

Noun.   A class of words that name or classify people, animals, things, ideas. They occur typically as subjects of clauses or as objects of verbs and prepositions. Their appearance is often signaled by noun markers like the **articles** *(a, an, the)*. Many nouns add *-s* to the plain form to form the plural: *dogs, cars, houses, colleges.*

Noun Clause.   A dependent clause taking the place of a noun: *"That he was late* does not surprise me."

Noun Equivalent.   A sentence element (pronoun, infinitive, gerund, noun clause) that is grammatically equivalent to a noun.

Number.   Choice of appropriate forms to express **singular** (one of a kind) or **plural** (more than one).

Object.   See COMPLEMENT.

Object Form.   See CASE.

Participle.   See VERBAL.

Passive.   See VOICE.

Past.   See TENSE.

Perfect.   See TENSE.

Person.   Choice of appropriate forms to express the person speaking (**first person:** *I know, we know*); the person spoken to (**second person:** *you know*); or the person spoken about (**third person:** *he knows, they know*).

Phrase.   A group of related words, typically a preposition or a verbal accompanied by its object or other related material.

| Prepositional Phrase: | Irene sat *at the window.* |
| Verbal Phrase: | Father gave up *smoking cigars.* |

Predicate.   The second basic element of the typical written sentence, making an assertion about the subject. The predicate consists of a complete (finite) verb and its possible complements and modifiers.

Preposition.   A class of words that relate a noun (or equivalent) to the rest of the sentence: "Arvin left *after* dark."

Present.   See TENSE.

Principal Parts.   The basic forms of a verb: simple present (*know*), simple past (*knew*), past participle (*known*).

Progressive Construction.   Verb form expressing action in progress: "Fred *was lighting* a cigarette."

Pronoun. A class of words taking the place of nouns; classified as **personal** (*I, you, he*), **possessive** (*my, your, his*), **reflexive** or **intensive** (*myself, yourself, himself*), **demonstrative** (*this, that*), **relative** (*who, which, that*), **interrogative** (*who, which, what*), and **indefinite** (*one, anyone, everyone*). See also CASE.

Relative Clause. A dependent clause related to the main clause by a relative pronoun: "The article *that I mentioned* begins on page 5."

Restrictive. See MODIFIER.

Sentence. A grammatically complete and self-contained unit of thought or expression, set off from other such units by end punctuation. The typical written sentence contains at least a subject and a predicate ("Birds sing"). The most common exception is the subjectless request or command, in which the subject is said to be understood ("Show him in").

Sentences combining two or more independent clauses are called **compound**. Sentences combining an independent and one or more dependent clauses are called **complex**. A combination of the two types is called **compound-complex**.

Compound:	He hummed, and she sang.
Complex:	He hummed when she sang.
Compound-Complex:	When they heard the news, he hummed and she sang.

Source Sentence. See KERNEL SENTENCE.

Subject. The first basic element of the typical written sentence, about which the predicate makes an assertion.

Subject Form. See CASE.

Subjunctive. See MOOD.

Superlative. The form of adjectives and adverbs used to express highest degree: "Fred is the *fastest* runner on the team."

Tense. The system of verb forms expressing primarily different relationships in time:

Present:	I know	Perfect:	I have known
Past:	I knew	Past Perfect:	I had known
Future:	I will (shall) know	Future Perfect:	I will (shall) have known

Transformation. One of the successive steps by which more complicated structures are produced from simple ones in a transformational grammar. The reshuffling, addition, or deletion of grammatical elements needed, for instance, to turn present into past tense, active into passive voice, or an affirmative into a negative statement. See also KERNEL SENTENCE.

Transitive. See VERB.

Verb. A class of words that signal the performance of an action, the occurrence of an event, or the presence of a condition. Verbs appear in typical verb positions: "Let's *leave*." "The boys *left* the scene." They typically take an *-s* in the third person singular of the present tense (*asks, leaves, condones*). They use characteristic **auxiliaries** in forms consisting of more than one word (*have left, was asked, will be leaving*). **Action verbs** are modified by adverbs; **linking verbs** are followed by adjectives:

Action Verb	He *responded* quickly.
Linking Verb	His response *seemed* quick.

Regular verbs use the same form for the simple past and the past participle:

Regular:	I *laughed*	I have *laughed*
Irregular:	I *knew*	I have *known*

Transitive verbs normally require an object:

Transitive:	He *raises* chickens.
Intransitive:	He *rises* early.

See also TENSE, MOOD, VOICE.

Verbal. A form that is derived from a verb but does not by itself function as a predicate: **infinitive** (*to* form), **present participle** (*-ing* form used as an adjective), **gerund** (*-ing* form used as a verbal noun), **past participle** (*-ed* form in regular verbs, irregular in others). Verbals appear as noun equivalents, modifiers, and *parts* of verbs.

Infinitive:	He liked *to dream.*
Present Participle:	Her *dreaming* look entranced him.
Gerund:	*Dreaming* got him nowhere.
Past Participle:	He had *dreamed* of childhood days.

Voice. The verb form that shows whether the subject is acting (**active**) or acted upon (**passive**):

Active:	Eileen *feeds* the children.
Passive:	The children *are fed* by Eileen.

CHAPTER NINETEEN

Practical Prose Forms

X 1   Summaries

X 2   Letters
      X 2a   Format and Style
      X 2b   The Request
      X 2c   The Letter of Application
      X 2d   The Follow-Up Letter
      X 2e   The Letter of Refusal

X 3   The Essay Examination

X 1   Summaries

By writing summaries, train yourself to grasp the structure of written material and to concentrate on essentials.

Practice in writing summaries will benefit you in important ways as a student and as a writer:

- It will give you practice in *close, attentive reading.* It will train you to do justice to what you read. Too many readers read *into* a piece of writing what they want to hear, or what they expect to hear. Too many writers are ineffectual because they have not learned to listen first, to think second, and to formulate their own reactions third and last.

- It will strengthen your sense of *structure* in writing. It will make you pay close attention to how a writer organizes his material, how he develops a point, how he moves from one point to another.

- It will develop your sense of what is *important* in a piece of writing. It will make you distinguish between a key point, the material backing it up, and mere asides.

In writing a summary, concentrate on three closely related tasks:

(1) *Make sure you grasp the main trend of thought.* Above all, you need to see clearly the *organization* of what you are asked to summarize. Identify key sentences: the thesis that sums up the major point of an essay (or section of an essay); the topic sentence that is developed in the rest of a paragraph. Formulate in your own words major points that seem to be *implied* but not spelled out in a single sentence. Distinguish between the major steps in an argument and merely incidental comment.

(2) *Reduce explanation and illustration to the essential minimum.* Omit passages that are mere paraphrase, restating a point for clarity or emphasis. Drastically condense lengthy explanations. Preserve only the most important details, examples, statistics. Reduce or omit anecdotes, facetious asides, and the like.

(3) *Use the most economical wording possible.* Where the original uses a whole clause, try to sum up the same idea in a phrase. Where it uses a phrase, try to use a single word. Where several near-synonyms restate the same idea, choose the one that best gives the central common meaning. Cut out all grammatical deadwood.

Unless the original version is already severely condensed, a summary of about one third or one fourth the original length can usually preserve the essential points. The shorter the summary, however, the greater the danger of oversimplification or outright misrepresentation. Be careful to preserve essential conditions and distinctions: *if-* and *unless-*clauses; differences between *is, will,* and *might;* words like *only, almost,* and *on the whole.* Preserve the relative emphasis of the original, giving more prominence to a point treated at great length than to one mentioned in passing.

Study the following passage. The running commentary suggests points you would have to note in writing an adequate summary.

We might characterize popular art first, as is most often done, with respect to its *form.* Popular art is said to be simple and unsophisticated, aesthetically deficient because of its artlessness. It lacks quality because it makes no qualifications to its flat statement. Everything is straightforward, with no place for complications. And it is standardized as well as simplified: one product is much like another. It is lifeless, Bergson would say, because it is only a succession of mechanical repetitions, while what is vital in art is endlessly variable. But it is just the deadly routine that is so popular. Confronted with that, we know just where we are, know what we are being offered, and what is expected of us in return. It is less unsettling to deal with machines than with people, who have lives of their own to lead. For we can then respond with mechanical routines ourselves, and what could be simpler and more reliably satisfying? — Abraham Kaplan, "The Aesthetics of the Popular Arts," *Journal of Aesthetics and Art Criticism*

(1) *Key idea:* Emphasis will be on *form* rather than content of popular arts.

(2) *Essential qualification:* "Most often done" and "is said to be" show this view to be widely held, but not necessarily fully shared by *author.*

(3) *Synonyms:* "Simple," "uncomplicated," "artless," "flat," "straightforward" all reinforce same major point.

(4) *Added step:* Popular art is "standardized" as well as "simplified."

(5) *Another added step:* It is "mechanical" rather than "variable."

(6) *Major transition:* The "mechanical" element in the popular arts is what makes them popular.

(7) *Explanation:* Why is "deadly routine" easy to live with?

Here is the summary you might write after close study of the passage:

Summary: According to a widely held view, popular art is simple and uncomplicated in form, and therefore "artless." It is standardized, and it lacks life because of mechanical repetition. But it is just the mechanical quality that is popular, because it is simple to react to what we know, but unsettling to deal with something that has a life of its own.

(See also the section on summarizing quoted material in Chapter 9, "The Research Paper.")

Exercises

A. Study the differences between the full text and the summary in each of the following pairs. Would you have noted the same major points and essential qualifications?

> **Original:** The invention of the process of printing from movable type, which occurred in Germany about the middle of the fifteenth century, was destined to exercise a far-reaching influence on all the vernacular languages of Europe. Introduced into England about 1476 by William Caxton, who had learned the art on the continent, printing made such rapid progress that a scant century later it was observed that manuscript books were seldom to be met with and almost never used. Some idea of the rapidity with which the new process swept forward may be had from the fact that in Europe the number of books printed before the year 1500 reaches the surprising figure of 35,000. The majority of these, it is true, were in Latin, whereas it is in the modern languages that the effect of the printing press was chiefly to be felt. But in England over 20,000 titles in English had appeared by 1640, ranging all the way from mere pamphlets to massive folios. The result was to bring books, which had formerly been the expensive luxury of the few, within the reach of all. More important, however, was the fact, so obvious today, that it was possible to reproduce a book in a thousand copies or a hundred thousand, every one exactly like the other. A powerful force thus existed for promoting a standard uniform language, and the means were now available for spreading that language throughout the territory in which it was understood. — Albert C. Baugh, *A History of the English Language*

> **Summary:** Printing from movable type, invented in Germany about 1450 and brought to England about 1476, had a far-reaching influence on all European languages. Within a hundred years, manuscript books had become rare. Though at first most printed books were in Latin, over 20,000 titles in English had appeared by 1640. Books were now within the reach of everyone and could exert a powerful standardizing influence upon language.

> **Original:** The tendency to erect "systems" — which are then marketed as a whole — affects particularly the less mature sciences of medicine and psychology. In these subjects we have had a succession of intellectual edifices originally made available only in their entirety. It is as if one cannot rent a room or even a suite in a new building, but must lease

the whole or not enter. Starting with a substantial contribution to medicine the authors of such systems expand their theories to include ambitious explanations of matters far beyond the original validated observations. And after the first pioneer, later and usually lesser contributors to the system add further accretions of mingled fact and theory. Consequently systems of this kind—like homeopathy, phrenology, psychoanalysis, and conditioned reflexology (the last dominant for years in Russia)—eventually contain almost inextricable mixtures of sense and nonsense. They capture fervid adherents, and it may take a generation or several for those who preserve some objectivity to succeed in salvaging the best in them while discarding the dross.—Dr. Ian Stevenson, "Scientists with Half-Closed Minds," *Harper's*

Summary: Medicine and psychology have produced a number of intellectual systems that one is asked to accept as a whole or not at all. The ambitious authors and adherents of such systems go beyond original valid findings to produce a mixture of truth and error that attracts enthusiastic supporters. Objective observers may not succeed in separating the valuable from the worthless till much later.

B. Select a passage of about 250 words from a history or science textbook. Prepare a summary running to about a third of the original length. Provide a copy of the original.

X 2   Letters

Make the appearance and style of your business letters suggest the qualities prized by business people: competence and efficiency.

Correspondence creates special problems of manuscript form. In writing or answering a formal invitation, you will do well to follow forms suggested in a book of etiquette. In writing a personal letter, you may allow yourself considerable freedom, as long as you keep your handwriting legible and use presentable stationery. Between these extremes of formality and informality is the kind of letter that you may have to write to a teacher, to a college official, or to a future employer. In applying for a scholarship or for a job, you will do well to follow a conventional letter form.

X 2a   Format and Style

Make sure your business letters are neat and consistent in format, clear and courteous in style. The specimen letter on page 647 illustrates a format widely used in business correspondence. You may use it as a model for spacing, indention, and punctuation.

CALIFORNIA STATE COLLEGE, [Letterhead]

809 East Victoria Street   •   Dominguez Hills, California 90247

[Heading] ──────→   June 14, 19___

Institute for Better Business Writing, Inc.
1000 University Way
Los Angeles, California   90025   ←── [Inside Address]

Gentlemen: ←── [Salutation]

I was happy to receive your request for information
regarding business letter formats.

The format of this letter is the one most frequently
used in business. It's called the block format.
With the exception of the heading and the signature
block, all its elements begin at the left hand margin,
even the first word of each paragraph. The body of
the letter is single-spaced, with double spacing
between paragraphs.

[Body]

Secretaries generally like the block format better
than the older indented formats. It has a clean and
precise appearance, and is quicker to type -- no
fiddling around with indentations.

There are other formats in use, but the block format
seems to have the widest appeal. You won't go wrong
adopting it for all your official correspondence.

[Signature Block
    complimentary close
    signature
    signature identification]

Sincerely yours,

Walter Wells

Walter Wells
Department of English

WW:mea   ←── [IEC Block
cc: Dean Howard Brody   initials (of author and typist)
                                enclosures (if any)
                                carbon copies]

Notice the following possible variations:

(1) When you are not using the letterhead of a firm or institution, type in *your address* above the date, as follows:

138 South Third Street
San Jose, California 95126
January 12, 1968

Mr. Ralph J. Clark, Jr.
Personnel Manager
San Rafael Independent-Journal
185 Washington Street
San Rafael, California

Dear Mr. Clark:

(2) A *married woman* should put *(Mrs.)* in front of her typed name.

Try to write clearly and naturally; do not adopt a special business jargon when you write a business letter. Avoid especially the following: a *stodgy*, old-fashioned businessese ("wish to advise that," "beg to acknowledge," "am in receipt of," "pursuant to," "the aforementioned"); a *breezy* "shirtsleeve" English ("give it the old college try," "fight tooth and nail," "give them a run for their money").

X 2b   The Request

State inquiries and requests clearly and positively, and aim them at the intended reader. Many of the business letters you write will ask someone else to *do* something for you: to provide information, to perform a service, to correct a mistake. Make such letters clear, businesslike, and persuasive.

(1) Make sure you state your request clearly and directly *early* in the letter. The basic question in your reader's mind is "What do you want?"

(2) If you are making *several* requests in the same letter, or if several points need attention, make sure *each* stands out clearly. Consider numbering them for emphasis. Too often, only the first major point gets attention; other matters, buried later in a letter, are forgotten.

(3) Whenever possible, relate your request directly to the *interests and responsibilities* of the person you are writing to. Avoid a "To-Whom-It-May-Concern" effect; avoid using form letters if at all possible.

(4) Even when you have a legitimate complaint, remain *courteous*. Emphasize the mutual satisfaction to be derived from a mistake corrected, rather than the mutual frustration occasioned when an error is first made.

The following sample letters attempt to put these principles into practice:[1]

LETTER 1

Dear Mr. Bliss:

Largely because of the success of The Muse, your new
campus literary magazine, we at Colfax College feel
the time is right for a similar publication on this
campus. Your help on a few important questions would
get us moving in the right direction.

We would like to know

  1. How you went about soliciting manuscripts
  for your first edition.
  2. How you decided upon the proportions of
  space to devote to fiction, poetry, criticism,
  reviews, and advertising.
  3. Whether you use university or commercial
  printing facilities.
  4. What mailing list you used to solicit
  charter subscriptions.
  5. Why you decided to price The Muse at $1.25.

Our enthusiasm runs high over the possibility of a
literary review at Colfax. Target date for the first
issue is October 1 of this year. We've got the administration's green light and the faculty is solidly
behind us. With your aid, we can be that much closer
to realizing our goal--a first-rate campus publication
capable of standing beside the best from the larger
schools, The Muse most certainly among them.

                    Sincerely,

                    Jeffrey Cantwell

                    Jeffrey Cantwell
                    Student Body Vice-President

[1]Most of the sample letters in this section are adapted from Walter Wells, *Communications in Business* (Belmont, California: Wadsworth Publishing Company, 1968).

LETTER 2

Gentlemen:

I was surprised to receive your recent request for
more transcripts to complete my application to the
Graduate School. I will, of course, have them sent
if absolutely necessary, but I do feel that your
request penalizes me.

Upon coming to State as a transfer undergraduate in
1965, I paid two dollars, for transcripts in duplicate, to each of the three institutions I had previously attended. At that time, you informed me
that all my papers were in order, and you admitted
me. Now you request the very same transcripts in
support of my graduate application.

Would it not be possible for you to refer to the
transcripts already in your possession? Or if copies
must be sent to the graduate advisor, could you not
duplicate my transcripts and send me the bill? In
either case, you would save me the time of recon-
tacting each institution, and perhaps preclude a
delay in their responding.

I hope this request is in no way unjustified. It
should be more expedient for both of us as you process
my application.

Sincerely yours,

Kenneth Darwin

Kenneth Darwin

X 2c   The Letter of Application

*Make your letter of application suggest competence, confidence,
and a genuine interest in the position for which you apply.* Employers
look for employees who will prove an asset to their organization and
who are at the same time good to work with and good to know. They
shy away from applicants who seem to promise problems, trouble,
complexes, or an overinflated ego. Remember the following advice:

(1) If possible, be *specific* about the position for which you apply.
Introduce the letter by mentioning the advertisement or the person

that informed you of the vacancy (but do not mention leads that smack of the "grapevine").

(2) Stress *previous training* and practical experience that you can show to be relevant to the job. Give a factual tone to the account of your qualifications, while at the same time presenting them to advantage.

(3) Give your letter *character*. Establish your identity. Many job applications look very much the same, and the anonymous, average applicant has little chance to be remembered—and to be preferred. If you have strong positive convictions about the work of the organization to which you apply, state them in a paragraph or two. If you have some serious thoughts about the role of business in a free society, hazard them.

(4) If you list *references*, obtain prior permission from those whose names you use. Common sense suggests that you quietly drop from your list the name of any teacher or former employer who shows little enthusiasm when you tell him about your plans.

(5) If the account of your qualifications is extensive, put it on a separate "data sheet," or *résumé*.

Study the following sample letters:

LETTER 3

Dear Mr. Clark:

In answer to your advertisement, I wish to apply for a post as a general reporter. My credentials are that I am a journalism major, and I have had some practical experience of working for a newspaper.

On February 1, I shall graduate from San Jose State College. While getting a degree, I have taken a broad range of courses, representing all areas of editing and reporting. Also, I have been a general reporter for the Spartan Daily for two years and a feature editor for one year. Last summer I worked for thirteen weeks on the Santa Clara Journal, as an "intern" sponsored by the Journalism Department of my college. I did general reporting and some photography.

The following gentlemen have agreed to supply references:

> Dr. John Williams
> Department of Journalism
> San Jose State College
> San Jose, California
>
> Mr. Thomas Bigelow
> General Manager
> Santa Clara Journal
> Santa Clara, California
>
> Mr. Richard H. James
> Editor
> Los Angeles Examiner
> Los Angeles, California

I am prepared to be interviewed when you find it convenient.

> Yours truly,
>
> Gerald P. Johnson
>
> Gerald P. Johnson

LETTER 4

Mr. Daniel Levin, Attorney at Law
Peale, Corman, Bishop, Levin & Dilworthy
80 Lomita Canyon Boulevard, Suite 7630
Beverly Hills, California   92025

Dear Mr. Levin:

Edith Winters informs me of an opening in your secretarial staff, a position for which I should very much
like to become a candidate.

I understand that you need a legal secretary with a
rapid stenographic skill and the ability to handle a
large volume of correspondence. Along with my degree
in legal stenography from Foothill Junior College, I
have four years of secretarial experience in retail
dry goods and in insurance. My shorthand speed is
145 words per minute. On my present job, I handle
between forty and sixty letters every day. Both at
Foothill and on the job, I have had training sufficient to prepare me to handle routine letters without
supervision.

My present job at Southwestern Life & Indemnity has
been quite satisfactory, but, having taken my degree
recently, I seek the further challenges and rewards
of a top-flight legal firm. Miss Winters' enthusiasm
for her work assures me that I would like the job. I
hope the enclosed résumé will help interest the firm in
me.

I can be in Los Angeles for an interview any afternoon
convenient for you. May I look forward to speaking
with you about the position you have available?

                    Yours sincerely,

                    Laura Edmondson
                    Laura Edmondson

SAMPLE RÉSUMÉ

<u>ADAM PIERCE</u>

Demmler Hall   Age: 23
Valhalla University   Ht: 6-1 Wt: 170
Kent, Ohio   26780   Single
613 KE 8 7600   Willing to relocate

Education

> B.S. in Industrial Engineering, Valhalla University,
> June 1969; top 10% of class, with special course
> work in statistics, motivational psychology,
> business law, and communications.
>
> Won U.S. Paint Company Scholarship 1968
> Member of Industrial Relations Club
> Elected Secretary of the Student Council
> On Dean's Honor Roll since 1966

> Also attended Colfax College, Colfax, Indiana, 1964-65

Experience

> Staff Supervisor, Cleveland Boys' Club Camp, Kiowa, Ohio,
> summer 1968; responsible for housing, activities
> scheduling and occasional discipline of fourteen
> counselors and 110 campers.

> Camp Counselor, Cleveland Boys' Club Camp, Kiowa, Ohio,
> summers of 1966 and 1967.

Personal Interests

> Politics, world affairs, camping, chess, junior chamber
> of commerce member, and volunteer hospital worker.

Military Service

> Served six months' active duty, U.S. Army, Fort Dix,
> New Jersey, Oct. 1965 to April 1966. Presently
> on reserve duty, attending one weekend meeting
> per month.

References

> Will gladly be provided upon request.

X 2d   The Follow-Up Letter

Keep interest alive, or reinforce a good first impression, by a timely follow-up letter. Though many businessmen pride themselves on being hard-headed calculators, in practice business is often 51 per cent human relations. The follow-up letter serves important human needs: it shows positive interest and thus *reassures* the recipient; it serves as a *reminder,* keeping alive an impression that is beginning to pale as other business calls for attention.

Study the following sample letter, written by an applicant *after* a job interview:

LETTER 5

Dear Mr. Goodfellow:

Just a note of thanks for the many courtesies shown me during my interview on Monday. Seeing National Motors from the inside has, as I said then, made the Executive Training Program all the more attractive to me.

Incidentally, I located a copy of Michaelson's <u>The Corporate Tempo</u> and found his chapter on training programs as fascinating and as eye-opening as you did.

Needless to say, I am looking forward to hearing from you. After Monday's meeting, I am confident I can bring to the program the energy and ability for success at National Motors.

Sincerely,

Adam Pierce

Adam Pierce

X 2e   The Letter of Refusal

Write letters of refusal that create good will rather than antagonism. There are many ways of saying no. The basic difference is between "No, thank you" and "No—and good riddance." A refusal that at the same time shows an appreciation of the interest expressed generates good will and at the same time leaves the door open for future contacts.

Study the following sample letter:

LETTER 6

Dear Mr. Tibbins:

I want to thank you for your letter of July 20 and for
your generous offer of the post as market-research analyst at Continental.

With more qualms than I thought myself capable of, I
have decided to forsake that offer and accept one made
me by the Grollier Food Company of San Francisco. While
the salary they offer is slightly less than Continental's,
their market-research department is small, making possible,
I feel, more rapid advancement. The decision was made
quite difficult by the obvious attractiveness of your
offer, not to mention the congeniality of your staff.
Only time will prove if it's a wise one.

Once again, let me express my genuine thanks for all the
consideration you and the Continental staff have given my
candidacy.

Very sincerely yours,

Michael Henriques

Michael Henriques

Exercises

A. In an effective business letter, as in all effective persuasion, the writer
shows his ability to imagine himself in the place of the reader. Compare and
contrast the letters in each of the following pairs. Which letter in each pair
is the more successful in this respect?

1. (a)
Enclosed is our draft in the amount of $31.90, which is
the amount over your deductible for which Smith Motors,
the garage of your choice, agreed to repair your automobile. You will also find enclosed a copy of the estimate on the basis of which they agreed to repair.

(b)

I'm happy to send you our draft for $31.90. It represents
the repair cost for your car in excess of the deductible
amount in your policy. The enclosed repair estimate was,
as you requested, made by Smith Motors in Dalhart.

Smith will, I'm sure, get your car back into fine running
order. I know you will be glad to be back on the road
again.

2. (a)

Just what kind of outfit are you people running? We
place a simple order, delivery takes forever, and when
it finally gets here, half the pieces are broken. To
top it all off, in the same day's mail we get your bill.
Some joke!

We feel we can do without this kind of rotten service.
There's no time left for us to place an order with a
decent company (although we'd like to), so get on the
ball and send us a replacement order right away.

(b)

On January 10, we placed an order with you for 500 pieces
of glassware in various patterns. Yesterday the order
arrived with only 234 pieces in salable condition. All
the rest were chipped or broken.

You can understand our disappointment, I am sure. Customers have been requesting your glasses, and we have
been promising them a prompt supply. Now some of them
will probably go elsewhere--their faith in us destroyed,
and our potential profit lost--unless you take immediate
action.

We ask that you send us an immediate duplicate order, and
allow us to adjust our payment to cover only the salable
glassware. We are confident that you will be able to get
this shipment to us as soon as possible.

B. Find a project or recent development that merits publicity or support. Write a letter about it to the editors of a newspaper or magazine, to a legislator, or to a responsible official. Observe conventional letter form.

C. Write a letter of inquiry or request in connection with some project in which you are currently interested. Observe conventional letter form.

D. Write a letter of application for a position in which you have at one time or another taken an interest. State the qualifications that you might have by the time you are ready to apply for the position in earnest.

E. Write a follow-up letter or a letter of refusal in connection with some business contact that you can imagine yourself being engaged in after your graduation from college. Observe conventional letter form.

X 3   The Essay Examination

Learn to write a structured essay examination that makes the best possible use of what you know.

For many students, the most direct test of their writing ability is the essay examination. To improve your own performance on such examinations, remember the following points:

(1) Study not for total recall but for a *writing* test. In studying the material, identify the key terms that might provide the focal point for a paragraph or short essay: *alienation, irony, agrarianism*. Fix firmly in your mind the three or four points you would cover if asked to trace the major step in an argument, or the key stages in a process. Then, for each key term or major point, try to retain *supporting detail* that would help you define or illustrate it. Do not merely memorize material; ask yourself practice questions that make you *select and arrange* materials in different ways to prove a point, to trace a comparison.

(2) Memorize *verbatim* at least some key phrases, definitions, or short passages. These will give an authoritative, authentic air to your writing. Nothing more reliably identifies the student who aims at better than *C* than the sentence that follows a pattern like this:

The term ＿＿＿＿＿＿＿＿, which Frederick Marcus defines as "＿＿＿＿＿＿＿＿," has developed two important new applications: . . .

Michael Henchard, whom Thomas Hardy describes as "＿＿＿＿＿＿＿＿," was aware of his own capacity for impulsive action. . . .

(3) Determine exactly what the *instructions* ask you to do. Do not simply get a general notion of what the question is "about."

Assume the question in a history course is "What do you consider the most important difference between the fall of Greece and the fall of Rome?" Do not simply put down everything you can remember about the fall of Greece and the fall of Rome. Focus on the key word in the instructions: *difference*. What *is* the difference? How can you line up material that will bring out this difference as clearly and convincingly as possible? Look also for specific writing instructions: Are you being asked to *summarize*, to *define*, to *compare*, to *evaluate*—or merely, more vaguely, to *discuss*?

(4) No matter what the pressure of time, take time to *structure* your answer. Come straight to the point. Especially in a one-paragraph answer, make your very first sentence sum up your key point, or your answer to the question being asked. Then use the rest of a paragraph to explain, support, or argue your point. Select what is clearly relevant; try to avoid a mere rambling effect. Whenever you can, work from a brief *outline* jotted down on scratch paper before you begin to write.

In addition to these basic points, here are a few practical hints:

• Bring an extra pen.

• Budget your time, especially if there are several questions. If you gain five points by treating one question at great length, and then lose twenty-five points by slighting the next two questions, you are twenty points behind.

• Get a general picture of the examination before you start writing. If there are several questions or topics, work first on those that you feel best qualified to take up.

• Relax. You will need a cool head to read the instructions without missing an important point.

Study the following essay exam, rated as above average by the teacher. The comments that follow it point out some features likely to have made a favorable impression on the reader.

Exam Question: A common type of character in much contemporary literature is the individual who is trapped by a trick of fate, by his environment, or by his own nature. Choose such a character from a short story you have recently read. Define the trap in which he is caught. Describe the way in which he struggles, if he does, to free himself.

Answer: Miss Brill finds herself trapped by her spinsterhood and the advancement of age. She is old, as the story tells us; she's as old as her out-of-date fox fur. She is alone, with no friends, relatives, or close neighbors. This is her trap. Like a bird that will create its own prison in its own territory, Miss Brill makes hers. She does not socialize, nor does she try to make something useful out of her life but rather preys like a parasite on other people's more interesting, colorful lives. In her own way Miss Brill struggles to escape her prison. She daydreams. The world that she lives in is a fantasy world where all people are friendly and related. She "belongs" in this world whereas in the other world, the real world, she actually belongs to no one.

Quite successfully Miss Brill loses the real world for a time, but she cannot escape the real world entirely. The real world sticks its head in, in the form of a boy who says "Ah, go on with you now." So she goes home, more aware than ever of her prison's boundaries and helpless (by her own nature) to do anything else. She can only fly on home to the security and solitude of her cold dark nest.

Note the following points about this answer:

(1) It responds directly to the *key term or key idea* in the assignment. The assignment asks about a character who is *trapped*. Note how this word and its synonyms keep echoing *throughout* the student's answer: "trapped," "prison," "boundaries."

(2) The first sentence serves as a *topic sentence* for the answer as a whole. It gives the brief, clear definition of the "trap" that the question asks for.

(3) The point about the character's trying to escape through daydreaming responds to the *second* part of the question. But note that this point is worked *organically* into the first paragraph. The student has *planned* his answer; there are no afterthoughts, no "Oh-I-forgot" effect.

Exercises

A. Study the following assignment for an essay examination and the two answers that follow it. One of the answers was rated good, the other poor. Which is which? Defend your choice in detail.

Assignment: The following lines by Walt Whitman bear a close relationship to several ideas contained in essays you have read in this course. Explore, in an essay of 300 words, the connections you discern.

When I heard the learn'd astronomer,
When the proofs, the figures, were ranged in columns
    before me,
When I was shown the charts and diagrams, to add,
    divide, and measure them,

> When I sitting heard the astronomer where he lectured
>   with much applause in the lecture-room,
> How soon unaccountable I became tired and sick,
> Till rising and gliding out I wander'd off by myself,
> In the mystical moist night-air, and from time to time,
> Look'd up in perfect silence at the stars.

Answer 1. Several points in Walt Whitman's lines are important in exploring the connections between his ideas and the ideas pertaining to humanism in the essays we have read. First, we get the image of a man of letters attending a lecture of a man of science. Secondly, the lecture material consists of certainties—proofs and figures, charts, diagrams. Finally, we get a feeling of complete isolation and peacefulness as Whitman stands outside in the night air.

In C. P. Snow's essay on "The Two Cultures," the author states that our intellectual society is divided into two sections—scientific and literary. Each section believes the other is unaware of man's condition in life and shows no regard for its fellow men. Each section believes it has the "right" answer for society. Each section is so intense in its feelings that no communication is possible between the two sections. C. P. Snow says that we must "rethink education" to achieve a broad outlook on life in contrast to the narrow outlook that is the result of specialization and technicalities in science and in literary studies. This is the thought that I get when Whitman attends the astronomer's lecture.

The lecture material contains figures, charts, diagrams to prove the astronomer's theories. I believe Whitman is putting across the same point as Saisselin in his essay on "Humanism, or the Eulogy of Error." Saisselin claims that there are no proofs or certainties for the humanist. Man is a single entity; he lives alone and dies alone. This is man's fate. Man must recognize his isolation and his potential for error. Man must be flexible, but the astronomer suggests rigidity. Furthermore, man must not confine himself to one area in life but must be aware of the whole world about him. When Whitman steps outside into the night air and gazes at the stars, he feels the vastness of the universe. The astronomer looks at the universe to collect proofs and figures for his small world of lecture and research. He does not comprehend man's fate.

Answer 2. In the lines by Walt Whitman I am given the general impression that this person cannot comprehend the meaning of the lecture, the figures, or the charts and diagrams. It seems as though he is not scientifically inclined in his thinking and cannot grasp even a thread of the knowledge the lecturer is trying to communicate to him.

In his discussion of "The Two Cultures," C. P. Snow points out some of the reasons for the division between the literary and scientific scholars. One of these reasons is a lack of communication. The literary scholars feel that they are an elite intellectual group and that they should not talk to such illiterates as scientists. The scientists, on the other hand, have a much more exacting knowledge and think they are doing more for the world than reading or writing books.

Remy Saisselin said that humanism can't be defined. It is lived. I think this is true, and it shows in Walt Whitman's poem. The lines don't say anything about wanting to learn a little about philosophy or art or literature. Walt Whitman just wanted to look around. He had no real reason. He didn't want to become educated for a reward. He merely wanted to explore and become educated in something besides strict science for his own satisfaction and enjoyment.

Students today are made to specialize, and this cuts down on a general well-rounded education. If one lives in a small world of one type of life day after day, he cannot fully enjoy life. Diversity makes for more enjoyment. By learning a little in both science and the arts, a person becomes more happy with himself and those around him.

B. Do you have a copy of an essay examination you have written recently? Select one or more passages totaling 250–300 words. Rewrite the material in accordance with the suggestions in this section. If you can, submit the original assignment, the original answer, and the improved version.

INDEX

HANDBOOK KEY